REVIEW OF
RESEARCH IN
EDUCATION

Review of Research in Education is published annually on behalf of the American Educational Research Association, 1430 K St., NW, Suite 1200, Washington, DC 20005, by SAGE Publishing, 2455 Teller Road, Thousand Oaks, CA 91320. Send address changes to AERA Membership Department, 1430 K St., NW, Suite 1200, Washington, DC 20005.

Member Information: American Educational Research Association (AERA) member inquiries, member renewal requests, changes of address, and membership subscription inquiries should be addressed to the AERA Membership Department, 1430 K St., NW, Suite 1200, Washington, DC 20005; fax 202-238-3250; e-mail: members@aera.net. AERA annual membership dues are $180 (Regular Members), $180 (Affiliate Members), $140 (International Affiliates), and $55 (Graduate Students and Student Affiliates). **Claims:** Claims for undelivered copies must be made no later than six months following month of publication. Beyond six months and at the request of the American Educational Research Association, the publisher will supply missing copies when losses have been sustained in transit and when the reserve stock permits.

Subscription Information: All non-member subscription inquiries, orders, back-issue requests, claims, and renewals should be addressed to SAGE Publishing, 2455 Teller Road, Thousand Oaks, CA 91320; telephone (800) 818-SAGE (7243) and (805) 499-0721; fax: (805) 375-1700; e-mail: journals@sagepub.com; website: http://journals.sagepub.com. **Subscription Price:** Institutions: $356; Individuals: $68. For all customers outside the Americas, please visit http://www.sagepub.co.uk/customercare.nav for information. **Claims:** Claims for undelivered copies must be made no later than six months following month of publication. The publisher will supply missing copies when losses have been sustained in transit and when the reserve stock will permit.

Copyright Permission: To request permission for republishing, reproducing, or distributing material from this journal, please visit the desired article on the SAGE Journals website (journals.sagepub.com) and click "Permissions." For additional information, please see www.sagepub.com/journalspermissions.nav.

Advertising and Reprints: Current advertising rates and specifications may be obtained by contacting the advertising coordinator in the Thousand Oaks office at (805) 410-7763 or by sending an e-mail to advertising@sagepub.com. To order reprints, please e-mail reprint@sagepub.com. Acceptance of advertising in this journal in no way implies endorsement of the advertised product or service by SAGE or the journal's affiliated society(ies). No endorsement is intended or implied. SAGE reserves the right to reject any advertising it deems as inappropriate for this journal.

Change of Address: Six weeks' advance notice must be given when notifying of change of address. Please send old address label along with the new address to ensure proper identification. Please specify name of journal.

International Standard Serial Number ISSN 0091-732X
International Standard Book Number ISBN 978-1-5063-8999-8 (Vol. 41, 2017, paper)
Manufactured in the United States of America. First printing, March 2017.

Printed on acid-free paper

REVIEW OF RESEARCH IN EDUCATION

Disrupting Inequality Through Education Research

Volume 41, 2017

Maisha T. Winn, Editor
University of California, Davis

Mariana Souto-Manning, Editor
Teachers College, Columbia University

AMERICAN EDUCATIONAL RESEARCH ASSOCIATION
FOUNDED 1916

Review of Research in Education

Disrupting Inequality Through Education Research

Volume 41

EDITORS

MAISHA T. WINN
University of California, Davis

MARIANA SOUTO-MANNING
Teachers College, Columbia University

AMERICAN EDUCATIONAL RESEARCH ASSOCIATION

Tel: 202-238-3200 Fax: 202-238-3250
http://www.aera.net/pubs

FELICE J. LEVINE
Executive Director

JOHN NEIKIRK
Director of Publications

MARTHA YAGER
Managing Editor

JESSICA SIBOLD
Publications Associate

Contents

Cover image © Exarte Design

Introduction

Foundational Understandings as "Show Ways" for Interrupting Injustice and Fostering Justice in and Through Education Research

MARIANA SOUTO-MANNING
Teachers College, Columbia University

MAISHA T. WINN
University of California, Davis

In her American Educational Research Association Social Justice Lecture titled "Just Justice," Gloria Ladson-Billings (2015) invited education researchers to move away from the label "social justice," which has become a "buzzword" and/or an afterthought in many contexts, and toward *justice* in and through education research. Inspired by Ladson-Billings (2015), our call, which resulted in this volume on "Disrupting Inequality Through Education Research," engaged with Dowd and Bensimon's (2015) theories of justice: justice as equity, justice as care, and justice as transformation.

As we sought to envision and promote equity through education research, we called for researchers to take on issues of justice centrally, to care for and about those being studied (learning from and with them in respectful ways), and to transform the current landscape of educational and societal injustices and inequities. That is, we sought to "move from justice as theory to justice as praxis" in education research (Ladson-Billings, 2015). Wrestling with in/justice in education research necessitates moving away from empty and shallow discourses of social justice (merely talking about it and/or pretending to engage in the work) or using the term *social justice* as a way of dismissing the justice work that needs to be done. Thus, moving away from what Paulo Freire (1970) called verbalism (talk without action), we solicited chapters that theoretically, methodologically, and pedagogically engaged in critical reviews of research with the aim of rethinking, confronting, and interrupting injustice and inequity.

Review of Research in Education
March 2017, Vol. 41, pp. ix–xix
DOI: 10.3102/0091732X17703981
© 2017 AERA. http://rrc.aera.net

The chapters in this volume of *Review of Research in Education* offer powerful ways to disrupt inequities in education research and practice. Together, they engage with a set of important foundational issues, which must be undertaken if we are to disrupt inequities and injustices in and through education research. While we know that these are not all-inclusive, we see them as foundational to the development of a collective research agenda, which fosters equity and justice. The foundational understandings identified and explained in this introduction emanate from the reviews of research, which make up this volume. Instead of simply listing chapter abstracts (which are also included in this volume), we offer principles, which together have the potential to help us interrupt inequities in education research, according to the chapters that make up this volume. We hope that after you carefully consider the collective principles undergirding the chapters in this volume of *RRE*, you will delve into reading about how they come to life in a variety of settings, informing im/possible frameworks and methodologies grounded in justice as equity, care, and transformation (Dowd & Bensimon, 2015).

FOUNDATIONAL PRINCIPLES: "SHOW WAYS" FOR FRAMEWORKS THAT FOSTER JUSTICE THROUGH EDUCATION RESEARCH

In her picture book *Show Way*, award-winning author Jacqueline Woodson (2005) shares how patchwork quilts brought together pieces that seemingly did not fit together to document histories and even serve as "show ways" to freedom for enslaved Africans. In her book, quilts are framed as ways of communicating important information pertaining to navigating a pathway to freedom and justice. While we understand that Jacqueline Woodson's book is a realistic fiction story, we use "show ways" as a metaphor as we quilt together four foundational principles that serve as "show ways" for education research that seeks to foster justice. We know that there are other foundational understandings for justice-focused research, yet, here we aim to get this "show way" to justice in and through education research started. We hope that you will continue adding your own patches, forging your own paths, and critically reflecting on your own story of engaging in research that disrupts educational inequity and injustice. In such a spirit, we offer the following foundational principles as "show ways" for developing frameworks and research that interrupt injustice and foster justice through education research.

1. Suspending judgment and learning from the resourcefulness and brilliance of communities and individuals minoritized by societal norms;
2. (Re)Valuating the lives and experiences of people of color;
3. Reconsidering whose bodies are at the center of research and rethinking the spaces where research takes place; and
4. Centrally acknowledging issues of access and power and/in identities and languages.

As we consider these principles, we invite you to bring them to life and reinvent them as you forge your own particular "show way" to disrupting injustice through education research—just as the authors of the chapters included in this volume have done.

1. Suspending Judgment and Learning From the Resourcefulness and Brilliance of Communities and Individuals Minoritized by Societal Norms

The first patch for our "show way" quilt of foundational principles involves rethinking concepts of deprivation, risks, and code words, such as "urban" or "inner city," often equated with students of color (Brown, 2017; Watson, 2014). This means acknowledging, troubling, and interrupting the role of ethnocentrism and White supremacy in education inequalities—in and through research. It necessitates recognizing the brilliance and resourcefulness of members of historically marginalized communities. It requires rejecting racist, colonialist, and assimilationist assumptions, which often keep harmful power hierarchies in place. It involves blurring boundaries, learning from and with minoritized[1] communities (McCarty, 2002) instead of teaching them or sponsoring the idea that they are somehow inferior or deficient.

In this volume, a number of chapters offer situated representations of how this foundational principle can paradigmatically (re)frame research in more equitable and just ways. Michelle Salazar Pérez and Cinthya M. Saavedra (Chapter 1) invite us to (re)center early childhood education, moving away from Eurocentric norms and concepts that have historically oppressed and disempowered children of color. Kris D. Gutiérrez and the UC Berkeley Connected Learning Network (Chapter 2) offer ways in which education research can learn from the ingenuity of people in their everyday practices and conversations. Catherine Kramarczuk Voulgarides, Edward Fergus, and Kathleen A. King Thorius (Chapter 3) tackle disproportionality in special education, examining why it persists and questioning why a legally sound civil rights law like IDEA (the Individuals With Disabilities Education Act) has been unable to abate disproportionality over nearly 40 years.

Carol D. Lee (Chapter 4) invites us to trouble prevalent deficit assumptions and pay close attention to research on how people learn and on learning across settings as windows of opportunity to unveil the brilliance of people of color and to address inequity in educational processes and outcomes. Anna Stetsenko (Chapter 5) urges us to put the radical notion of equality in the service of disrupting inequality in education, anchored in the recognition of the infinity of human potential. Nicole Mirra and Antero Garcia (Chapter 6) challenge dominant narratives about the civic disengagement of youth from marginalized communities by reconceptualizing what counts as civic participation in public life and how youth are positioned as civic agents, examining ideologies that undergird traditional forms of civic education, and considering how digital media has fundamentally transformed the public sphere and expanded opportunities for youth civic expression and action. Beatrice S. Fennimore

(Chapter 7) challenges the traditional concept of parent involvement (as parents serving the school agenda), unpacking it in powerful ways and reframing it in light of the power of parents and families in nondominant communities: redefining according to their actions, (re)framing them capably.

Stetsenko (Chapter 5) knowledgeably reminds us: "The core argument is that all persons have *infinite potential*—incalculable in advance, unlimited, and not predefined in terms of any putatively inborn 'endowments.' This potential is realized in the course of *activity-dependent generation* of open-ended, dynamic, and situated developmental processes that are critically reliant upon sociocultural supports, tools, mediations, and access to requisite resources, especially through education" (p. 112). We view this as a charge to explore and disentangle often-conflicting meanings of equality and its promises. Her review reminds us,

Researchers continue to equivocate between commitment to the idea that *all* humans are equal in their core capacities versus the tendency to attribute developmental outcomes to differences in "natural" inborn talents and endowments. (p. 112)

Taking heed of her call—and the work of many others included in this volume—we urge education researchers to learn from the brilliance of minoritized communities and individuals.

2. (Re)Valuating the Lives and Experiences of People of Color

The second foundational principle we identify is that of (re)valuating the lives and experiences of people of color. Historically, in the United States, the lives of people of color have been positioned as property (Ladson-Billings & Tate, 1995). For example, according to the Naturalization Act, "free White persons" could become American citizens. Only White people had rights. Legally, only White males were fully human. We see evidence of that in other lawful acts, such as the Native American boarding schools, the Chinese Exclusion Act (1882–1943), and *Plessy v. Ferguson* (1896). Such mindsets and beliefs frame education research in harmful and damaging ways, by positioning people of color incapably and inhumanely. Instead of documenting brilliance and expertise in communities of color (Delpit, 2012), researchers engage in privileging White cultural practices ethnocentrically.

Individuals and communities of color have been and continue to be objectified (positioned as objects) in education research studies. At times, this is seen as superior to participatory approaches whereby researchers learn alongside minoritized communities. There is even an assumption (which must be troubled and rejected) that research designed, implemented, and written up by Black and Brown people is not of "high quality" (Tobin & Steinberg, 2015). The chapters in this volume invite us to ask: According to whose notion of quality? According to whose paradigms, interests, and practices? Thus, this volume of *RRE* urges all researchers in the field to ask these questions as well, learning from and with researchers of color instead of scaling and rating their epistemologies and methodologies ethnocentrically.

The chapters in this volume urge the education research community to move beyond discomfort and carefully consider the ways in which the dehumanization of Black and Brown bodies happens every day in the name of and through education research. They invite us to recognize the centrality of White privilege and supremacy frameworks by learning from McIntosh (1988), who stated,

As a white person, I realized I had been taught about racism as something that puts others at a disadvantage, but had been taught not to see one of its corollary aspects, white privilege, which puts me at an advantage.

A number of chapters in this volume critically review education research and propose that if education researchers are to challenge and dismantle racism and other isms through education research, we must interrupt the pervasiveness and reject the desirability of Whiteness. We must reclaim the humanity of minoritized communities by humanizing and decolonizing research (Paris & Winn, 2013).

Chapters featured in this volume take up this issue centrally. Rita Kohli, Marcos Pizarro, and Arturo Nevárez (Chapter 8) challenge racism-neutral and racism-evasive approaches to studying racial disparities by making visible normalized facets of racism in K–12 schools. Nicole M. Joseph, Meseret Hailu, and Denise Boston (Chapter 9) explore how Black women and girls (like other women and girls of color in the U.S. education system) negotiate and integrate multiple marginalized identities in mathematics, using critical race theory and Black feminism as interpretive frames to explore factors that contribute to Black women's and girls' persistence in the mathematics pipeline and the role these factors play in shaping their academic outcomes. Maisie L. Gholson and Charles E. Wilkes (Chapter 10) argue that the identities of Black children as doers and knowers of mathematics in research are often confused (or mistaken) with stereotypical images of various social identities, as well as wrongly confiscated (or mis-taken), in order to perpetuate persistent narratives of inferiority, criminality, and general ineducability of these children. Anne Gregory, Russell J. Skiba, and Kavitha Mediratta (Chapter 11) unveil race and gender disparities in school discipline and offer a research-based framework for increasing equity in school discipline, grounded in epistemologies and theories that honor the brilliance and resources of minoritized populations. Vaughn W. M. Watson and Michelle G. Knight-Manuel (Chapter 12) challenge ethnocentrism by disrupting three areas of inequalities affecting educational experiences of immigrant youth: (a) homogenizing notions of a monolithic West Africa and immigrant youth's West African countries, (b) deficit understandings of identities and the heterogeneity of Black immigrant youth from West African countries living in the United States, and (c) singular views of youth's civic engagement.

3. Reconsidering Whose Bodies Are at the Center of Research and Rethinking the Spaces Where Research Takes Place

The third foundational principle we identified pertains to the places and spaces where research takes place—as well as on whose knowledges research is centered. It is a foundational principle because all too often education research is anchored or grounded in Whiteness as the norm. In this volume, many chapters reconsider whose bodies are at the center of research. For example, Limarys Caraballo, Brian D. Lozenski, Jamila J. Lyiscott, and Ernest Morrell (Chapter 13) urge us to recognize how academic and professional research-based knowledges have long been valued over the organic intellectualism of those who are most affected by educational and social inequities. After all, becoming more aware of which spaces are sanctioned as sites for learning and expanding our understandings of whose voices count, whose spaces are included and excluded, is a necessity if we are to engage in education research that disrupts inequities, especially within a context in which traditional curriculum and teaching in formal spaces often exclude, silence, and invisiblize the practices of so many. To do so, chapters in this volume propose that we must re-spatialize not only physical sites of research but relational sites as well. Below, we briefly expand on these premises, seeking to illustrate the richness and depth of the chapters that compose this volume and collectively take up the charge of (re)centering research pedagogically and methodologically.

Historically, research has been conducted on minoritized populations, resulting in damaging perspectives that continue to perpetuate the status quo of inequalities. Here, we propose that such relationships must be re-spacialized, so as to disrupt the single story of historically minoritized populations in research. To be sure, the problem with single stories is not that they are untrue but that they are one incomplete perspective of a much more complex picture (Adichie, 2009).

This foundational principle calls for moving from doing *research on* to doing *research with*, questioning whose knowledges count and whose perspectives are included and excluded. This requires that researchers redefine their own roles, learning from and with communities. We argue for a restorative and transformative research agenda that acknowledges mass incarceration and the criminalization of Indigenous, Black, Latinx, immigrant, Muslim, and LGBTQIA (lesbian, gay, bisexual, transsexual, queer, intersex, asexual) children, youth, and their families (Winn, 2016). This foundational principle raises the need to consider moral and theoretical issues, such as addressing the question, "Critical for whom?" when conducting research from a critical perspective (Souto-Manning, 2013b).

The chapters in this volume invite education researchers to consider re-centering knowledges, theories, and paradigms on the lives, experiences, and perspectives of minoritized individuals and communities. As readers of these critical reviews, we are invited to rethink our roles as researchers. We are invited to pledge allegiance to disrupting inequalities in education research in the kinds of questions we ask, the methodologies we espouse, and the theories we choose. We are invited to not only become competent in culturally-grounded ways of doing research but also develop critical consciousness through and in research.

For example, Caraballo et al. (Chapter 13) posit that unlike positivist and post-positivist epistemological traditions and research methods that rely on the objectivity and expertise of university-sanctioned researchers (Isenhart & Jurow, 2011; Noffke, 1997), participatory action research (PAR) projects are collective investigations that rely on local knowledge, combined with the desire to take individual and/or collective action (Fine et al., 2004; McIntyre, 2000). PAR with youth (YPAR) engages in rigorous research inquiries and represents a radical effort in education research to take inquiry-based knowledge production out of the sole hands of academic institutions and include the youth who directly experience the educational contexts that scholars endeavor to understand. In Chapter 13, they outline the foundations of YPAR and examine the distinct epistemological, methodological, and pedagogical contributions of an interdisciplinary corpus of YPAR studies and scholarship.

Amy Stornaiuolo and Ebony Elizabeth Thomas (Chapter 14) propose that youth digital activism can serve as a key space and mechanism to disrupt inequity, and urge education researchers to pay close attention to these youth activist practices, particularly by youth from marginalized communities or identities, in order to provide important counternarratives to characterizations of youth as disaffected or "at risk." They frame youth digital activism as a form of restorying, in which young people's counternarratives work as a central mechanism for disrupting normative and deficitizing frameworks.

Bic Ngo, Cynthia Lewis, and Betsy Maloney Leaf (Chapter 15) review the literature on community-based arts programs serving minoritized youth to identify the conditions, spaces, and practices for fostering sociopolitical consciousness. They engage with the notion that "education is simultaneously an act of knowing, a political act, and an artistic event" (Freire, 1985, p. 17) and propose that community-based arts programs have the capacity to promote teaching and learning practices that engage youth in the use of academic skills to pursue inquiry, cultural critique, and social action. Those are spaces where learning takes place; this learning is no less than so-called academic learning, housed within the walls of classrooms and schools.

Bianca J. Baldridge, Nathan Beck, Juan Carlos Medina, and Marlo A. Reeves (Chapter 16) urge us to re-spatialize research in community-based educational spaces (e.g., after-school programs and community-based youth organizations), which have a long history of interrupting patterns of educational inequity and continue to do so under the current educational policy climate. Through a review of seminal education research on community-based spaces, they unveil the ways diverse out-of-school spaces inform the educational experiences, political identity development, and organizing and activist lives of minoritized youth.

4. Centrally Acknowledging Issues of Access and Power and/in Identities and Languages

Collectively, the chapters in this volume unveil a number of ways in which power has been deployed to dehumanize and deny access to minoritized communities. Across chapters, this power is portrayed in ways that are instrumental (via laws and official mandates) and emotional (via feelings of inferiority: Carter & Goodwin, 1994; Valdés, 1996; and double consciousness: Du Bois, 1903). By engaging in education research that disrupts inequity, the chapters in this volume of *Review of Research in Education* centrally acknowledge issues of access and power and/in identities and languages. They illustrate how—historically and con-temporarily—issues of access and power, as they relate to identities and languages, are foundational.

The chapters in this volume critically review research, showing how it has histori-cally used power and coercion to harm populations and individuals of color. Through reviews of a variety of issues in education, they make visible how research malpractice continues to be inflicted onto communities of color by researchers who pose as sav-iors and do *research on* these populations, as if they were objects, as if they were nobody (Hill, 2016). To refute such malpractice, which continues to inflict harm on communities of color, chapter authors invite education researchers to rethink and reinvent our relationships with the communities we study, centrally acknowledging issues of responsibility and answerability, revisioning our roles from experts to learn-ers, and moving from learning about to learning from and learning with. They urge us to value the voices, perspectives, and practices of minoritized communities, issuing a number of cautionary notes about the education of minoritized students (McCarty, 2002; Valdés, 1997).

Claudia G. Cervantes-Soon, Lisa Dorner, Deborah Palmer, Dan Heiman, Rebecca Schwerdtfeger, and Jinmyung Choi (Chapter 17) take up this issue by reviewing criti-cal areas of research on issues of equity and equality in a highly proclaimed and expo-nentially growing model of bilingual education: two-way immersion. They offer evidence that two-way immersion programs are not living up to their ideal of provid-ing equal access to educational opportunity for transnational emergent bilingual stu-dents. Seeking to disrupt inequalities for English language learners, Oscar Jiménez-Castellanos and Eugene García (Chapter 18) merge intersectionality and policy analysis to develop an analytical tool to understand and interrupt the educa-tional inequities encountered by low-income, Latino Spanish-speaking multilingual students in Arizona's K–12 public schools. Both of these chapters unveil how educa-tional success ideologies are often fashioned and defined according to raciolinguistics, even in dual-language programs, affecting educational and social realms. They call for both a theoretical and a practical way to understand the construction of linguistic and social competence as perceived by bilingual and multilingual students of color in American schools, learning from and with their communicative practices (Souto-Manning, 2013a).

Expanding on the language of power (or on the language practices of those who have power—Delpit, 1988), the chapters in this volume take up the inextricable links between racial and linguistic profiling (Baugh, 2003). They recognize that such pro-filing not only happens in research but is instantiated in classrooms and educational spaces each and every day. Ayanna F. Brown, David Bloome, Jerome E. Morris, Stephanie Power-Carter, and Arlette I. Willis (Chapter 19) examine classroom con-versations about race with a theoretical framing oriented to understanding how such conversations may disrupt social and educational inequalities, offering a social, his-torical, and political discussion that contextualizes how classroom conversations, and their omission, are part of a larger dialogue within the broader society. In inviting education researchers to learn from the diverse and sophisticated communicative repertoires of youth, Danny C. Martinez, P. Zitlali Morales, and Ursula S. Aldana (Chapter 20) explain,

> Youth enter schools and bring with them a range of linguistic resources that could be used in the service of learning. For many youth, however, their linguistic resources or their ways of communicating in their homes and communities do not align with the ways of communicating privileged in schools. This is particularly true for minoritized and racialized children and youth of color whose linguistic flexibility often indexes for educators a host of deficit categorizations. (p. 478)

Critically considering the intersection of language, culture, and care, Christina Passos DeNicolo, Min Yu, Christopher B. Crowley, and Susan L. Gabel (Chapter 21) invite education researchers to (re)consider belonging in light of a context that devalues and dehumanizes the practices of immigrant children, denying them access to education success, proposing that we seek to foster *cariño conscientizado* (critically conscious and authentic care).

In light of the critical reviews authored by the scholars who collectively populate this volume of *Review of Research in Education*, we call for rethinking the ethical and professional norms of education research if we are to fulfill the promise of transforming inequity and injustice in and through education research. The scholars whose work is included in this volume help us envision what this call means and the multiple ways it can come to life. After all, we have the responsibility of "putting the radical notion of equality in the service of disrupting inequality" (Stetsenko, 2017, p. 112).

FROM "SHOW WAY" TO PATH TRAVELED: REVIEW OF EDUCATION RESEARCH ACROSS FIELDS

This volume seeks to provide reviews of research in education that go beyond identifying and stating problems. It names urgent issues that must be problematized if we are to disrupt inequity through and in education research. It proposes that disrupting inequalities—in preschools/schools and in society—is a moral imperative for education research. With this urgency in mind, and with a commitment to sharing multiple ways traveled by multiple disciplines, populations, and theoretical constructs, we have assembled a range of scholars who offer new ways of disrupting inequity and injustice through education research using various methods—YPAR, design experiments, discourse analysis—across a range of disciplines—math education, literacy, science education—and for a range of learners, including students with multiple racial identities, abilities, linguistic repertoires, age groups, gender, and many more. We hope that as you turn the pages of this volume, you will be as thrilled as we were to learn from the many paths traveled along "show ways" to justice and freedom in and through education research.

ACKNOWLEDGMENT

We wish to acknowledge our project assistant, Malaika Baxa, for her time and commitment to this volume.

NOTE

¹Inspired by McCarty (2002), we

use the term "minoritized" rather than "minority." As a characterization of people, "minority" is stigmatizing and often numerically inaccurate . . . "Minoritized" more accurately conveys the power relations and processes by which certain groups are socially, economically, and politically marginalized within the larger society. (p. xv)

REFERENCES

Adichie, C. (2009). *The danger of a single story*. Retrieved from http://www.ted.com/talks/cchimamanda_adichie_the_danger_of_a_single_story.html

Baugh, J. (2003). Linguistic profiling. In S. Makoni, G. Smitherman, A.F. Ball, & A.K. Spears (Eds.), *Black linguistics: Language, society, and politics in Africa and the Americas* (pp. 155–168). New York, NY: Routledge.

Brown, K. (2017). *After the "at risk" label: Reorienting educational policy and practice*. New York, NY: Teachers College Press.

Carter, R. T., & Goodwin, A. L. (1994). Racial identity and education. *Review of Research in Education, 20*, 291–336.

Delpit, L. (1988). The silenced dialogue: Power and pedagogy in educating other people's children. *Harvard Educational Review, 58*, 280–98.

Delpit, L. (2012). *"Multiplication is for white people": Raising the expectations for other people's children*. New York, NY: The New Press.

Dowd, A., & Bensimon, E. (2015). *Engaging the "race question": Accountability and equity in U.S. higher education*. New York, NY: Teachers College Press.

Du Bois, W. E. B. (1903). *The souls of Black folk*. New York, NY: Bantam Classic.

Fine, M., Roberts, R. A., Torre, M. E., Bloom, J., Burns, A., Chajet, L., . . . Payne, Y. (2004). *Echoes of Brown: Youth documenting and performing the legacy of Brown v. Board of Education*. New York, NY: Teachers College Press.

Freire, P. (1970). *Pedagogy of the oppressed*. New York, NY: Continuum.

Freire, P. (1985). Reading the world and reading the word: An interview with Paulo Freire. *Language Arts, 62*, 15–21.

Hill, M. L. (2016). *Nobody: Casualties of America's war on the vulnerable, from Ferguson to Flint and beyond*. New York, NY: Atria Books.

Isenhart, M., & Jurow, A. S. (2011). Teaching qualitative research. In N. K. Denzin, & Y. K. Lincoln (Eds.), *The Sage handbook of qualitative research* (pp. 699–714). Thousand Oaks, CA: Sage.

Ladson-Billings, G. (2015). *Just justice* [American Educational Research Association Social Justice in Education Award Lecture video]. Retrieved from https://www.youtube.com/watch?v=ofB_t1oTYhI

Ladson-Billings, G., & Tate, W. (1995). Toward a critical race theory of education. *Teachers College Record, 97*, 47–68.

McCarty, T. (2002). *A place to be Navajo: Rough Rock and the struggle for self-determination in Indigenous schooling*. New York, NY: Routledge.

McIntosh, P. (1988). *White privilege and male privilege: A personal account of coming to see.* Wellesley MA: Wellesley College Center for Research on Women. Retrieved from http://www.collegeart.org/pdf/diversity/white-privilege-and-male-privilege.pdf

McIntyre, A. (2000). Constructing meaning about violence, school, and community: Participatory action research with urban youth. *The Urban Review, 32,* 123–154.

Noffke, S. E. (1997). Professional, personal, and political dimensions of action research. *Review of Research in Education, 22,* 305–343.

Paris, D., & Winn, M. (Eds.). (2013). *Humanizing research: Decolonizing qualitative inquiry with youth and communities.* Thousand Oaks, CA: Sage.

Plessy v. Ferguson, 163 U.S. 537 (1896).

Souto-Manning, M. (2013a). Competence as linguistic alignment: Linguistic diversities, affinity groups, and the politics of educational success. *Linguistics and Education, 24,* 305–315.

Souto-Manning, M. (2013b). Critical for whom? Theoretical and methodological dilemmas in critical approaches to language research. In D. Paris, & M. Winn (Eds.), *Humanizing research: Decolonizing qualitative inquiry with youth and communities* (pp. 201–222). Thousand Oaks, CA: Sage.

Tobin, K., & Steinberg, S.R. (Eds.). (2015). *Doing educational research* (2nd ed.). Rotterdam, Netherlands: Sense.

Valdés, G. (1996). *Con respeto: Bridging the distances between culturally diverse families and schools: An ethnographic portrait.* New York, NY: Teachers College Press.

Valdés, G. (1997). Dual-language immersion programs: A cautionary note concerning the education of language-minority students. *Harvard Educational Review, 67,* 391–429.

Watson, D. (2014). What do you mean when you say urban? Speaking honestly about race and students. In W. Au (Ed.), *Rethinking multicultural education: Teaching for racial and cultural justice* (2nd ed., pp. 77–79). Milwaukee, WI: Rethinking Schools.

Winn, M. T. (2016). *Transforming justice. Transforming teacher education.* Ann Arbor: University of Michigan, Teaching Works.

Woodson, J. (2005). *Show way.* New York, NY: G. P. Putnam's Sons.

Chapter 1

A Call for Onto-Epistemological Diversity in Early Childhood Education and Care: Centering Global South Conceptualizations of Childhood/s

MICHELLE SALAZAR PÉREZ
New Mexico State University

CINTHYA M. SAAVEDRA
The University of Texas Rio Grande Valley

In this chapter, we call for onto-epistemological diversity in the field of early childhood education and care (ECEC). Specifically, we discuss the need to center the brilliance of children and communities of color, which we argue, can be facilitated by foregrounding global south perspectives, such as Black and Chicana feminisms. Mainstream perspectives in ECEC, however, have been dominantly constructed from global north perspectives, producing a normalized White, male, middle-class, heterosexual version of childhood, where minoritized children are viewed as deficit. Although there have been important challenges to the discourse of a normalized, deficit child, we argue much of this work has remained grounded in global north positionings, which separate theory from the lived realities of children of color. As such, we introduce Black and Chicana feminisms as global south visions to transform approaches to research and pedagogy in ECEC and, in turn, disrupt inequities.

The brilliance of children of color is rarely positioned as a starting point for discussion in early childhood studies.[1] Even when research and pedagogy involve working with historically marginalized youth, it seems the conversation typically begins with matters of intervention. A prime example is the Head Start program, created to stop the "cycle of poverty" through deficit assumptions about economically underresourced

Review of Research in Education
March 2017, Vol. 41, pp. 1–29
DOI: 10.3102/0091732X16688621
© 2017 AERA. http://rre.aera.net

children and families without recognition of larger systemic injustices that produce poverty (Ellsworth & Ames, 1998). What if we, instead, centered the extraordinary and necessary contributions of marginalized children to society? What possibilities to disrupt and transform inequities in early childhood and beyond can occur?

The Global South/North

To make sense of the profound inequities that exist for children at promise (Swadener & Lubeck, 1995) in the United States and globally, we situate our current social and political context within the global south/north divide. Global north onto-epistemologies are ways of knowing grounded in Eurocentric modernity (Grosfoguel, 2008) that influence the world over through cultural and intellectual colonization. Global south onto-epistemologies decolonize and disrupt global north dominance by centering the lived ways of knowing and being of minoritized peoples. Examples of global south, theories in the flesh (Moraga & Anzaldúa, 1983) include Chicana feminism (Anzaldúa, 1987; Saldivar-Hull, 2000), Black feminism (Collins, 2008; hooks, 2000), and Indigenous knowledges (Meyer, 2008), to name only a few. Global south onto-epistemologies have great promise to transform early childhood education and care (ECEC), and therefore, we situate our discussion in these positionings.

We note that while using the dichotomous nomenclature of the global south/north, we problematize geographic and political boundaries of "south" and "north" to describe the complex and dynamic social, gendered, and economic inequities that persist within many local spaces—even within the global south—and that persist on a worldwide scale (Arrighi, 2001). E. Pérez (1999) reminds us that when colonialism becomes enmeshed with once indigenous ways of being, it can produce a mestiza consciousness (Anzaldúa, 1987) and, at times, a sustained colonial consciousness of global south peoples. These contradictions and complexities must be accounted for when examining the historical construction of childhoods and early childhood as a field, along with acknowledgement and problematization of the very privileged position Cinthya and I assume as academics living in and drawing from the colonized land of the United States.

Global South Perspectives in Early Childhood

In ECEC, global south onto-epistemologies assume that we must definitively "go beyond the view of culture as a 'problem'" (González, 2005, p. 40). When early childhood is theorized from a global south perspective, multilingual children are lauded for the complex ways in which they are able to navigate monolingual, "standard" English-centric educational spaces and for the powerful contributions they make to their communities and families as cultural brokers (Saavedra, 2011a). As Delpit and Dowdy (2002) contend, it is not "children's language that causes educational problems, but the educational bureaucracy's response to the language" (p. xxi).

Global south onto-epistemologies give promise for research and pedagogy informed by marginalized ways of knowing that deviate from postpositivist worldviews. For early childhood, centering global south standpoints means no longer relying on observational tools to classify and measure children against universal (e.g., colonizing, racist, sexist, heteronormative, ableist) standards. Multilingual children of color are inherently and continuously affirmed for their situated knowledge. Afrocentric and indigenous approaches to curriculum and pedagogy are an expectation of programs serving children of color (Delpit, 2006; Delpit & White-Bradley, 2003; Lomawaima & McCarty, 2002; Rau & Ritchie, 2011; Skerrett, 2015). Moreover, the early childhood workforce diversifies, with teachers having critical, global south orientations and coming from the communities they serve. To enable these imperative shifts and bring about equity in ECEC, we make an urgent call for recentering global south perspectives.

Onto-Epistemologies

Because onto-epistemologies are inherent to our discussion on equity in ECEC, we provide the definitions that have guided our thinking. *Epistemology* refers to what can be known, and the relationship between the knower and the known (Guba & Lincoln, 2005; Lincoln & Guba, 1985). Ladson-Billings (2000) cautions, however, that "epistemology is more than a 'way of knowing'" (p. 257); rather it encompasses a "system of knowing" that has historically privileged Euro-American perspectives as if they are "the only legitimate way to view the world" (p. 258). This epistemological dominance has had devastating consequences for marginalized children both in their educational experiences and everyday encounters with the world (Cannella & Viruru, 2004; L. T. Smith, 1999). In a call to acknowledge, recenter, and make visible marginalized epistemologies, such as those that stem from Chicana feminism, Delgado Bernal (1998) posits that "employing a Chicana feminist epistemology in educational research thus becomes a means to resist epistemological racism (Schuerich & Young, 1997) and to recover untold stories" (p. 556). For early childhood, the use of marginalized epistemologies prompts us to question which knowledge systems have historically (and dominantly) informed the field and inspires us to rethink our approaches to research and praxis.

A term closely related to epistemology is *ontology*, which refers to beliefs about reality, existence, and notions of truth and being (Guba & Lincoln, 2005; Lincoln & Guba, 1985; St. Pierre, 2016). One's ontology informs assumptions about her or his paradigmatic positioning—for example, if a researcher is positivist, she believes there is one reality that can be found, while a researcher who is postmodernist challenges the notion of reality, truth, and universals (Guba & Lincoln, 2005; Lincoln & Guba, 1985). Many argue that ontology and epistemology are inextricably linked (Kincheloe & McLaren, 2005; Lincoln & Guba, 1989; S. Smith, 1996). Dixon and Jones (1998) explain, "Any ontology is itself grounded in an epistemology about how we know 'what the world is like'" (p. 250). As such, in this text, we have chosen to merge the terms as *onto-epistemology* to emphasize their symbiotic relationship. We note that we do not intend for our use of onto-epistemology to draw from Barad's (2007) ideas on quantized diffraction.

METHOD FOR REVIEWING THE EARLY CHILDHOOD
SCHOLARSHIP: A GLOBAL SOUTH APPROACH

As authors of this call for onto-epistemological diversity in ECEC, we have petitioned for some time to recenter global south perspectives, mainly through the use of Chicana and Black feminisms (Demas & Saavedra, 2004; M. S. Pérez 2014, 2017; M. S. Pérez, Medellin, & Rideaux, 2016; M. S. Pérez, Ruiz Guerrero, & Mora, 2016; M. S. Pérez & Saavedra, 2014; M. S. Pérez & Williams, 2014; Saavedra, 2011a, 2011b; Saavedra & Nymark, 2008; Saavedra & M. S. Pérez, 2012). In our efforts to reframe the field through global south perspectives, we have brought attention to and critiqued the lack of people of color, and in particular, women of color, who have theoretically informed both critical and mainstream scholarship (M. S. Pérez & Saavedra, 2015), with the latter having much less representation. Problematizing the absence of onto-epistemological diversity in ECEC has therefore informed our process to reviewing the literature.

We begin with a discussion on scholarship that foregrounds the brilliance of children of color. By valuing and building on their rich cultural experiences and knowledges, both pedagogy and research in ECEC can be transformed (Souto-Manning, 2013). Next, we review mainstream early childhood scholarship grounded in global north onto-epistemologies that have dominated, regulated, and managed the field. We then discuss the critically oriented research that has made important challenges to dominant constructions of early childhood, while problematizing how it often remains situated in global north perspectives. Last, we examine Black and Chicana feminist, global south literature that alerts us to the need for onto-epistemological diversity, inspiring new imaginaries and possibilities for equity in ECEC.

Our approach to reviewing scholarship provides possibilities not only to diversify perspectives on children and communities of color but also to disrupt deficit assumptions embedded in much of the literature in the field. Ultimately, it is our hope that centering global south onto-epistemologies can provide a refreshed and empowered view of children of color, giving promise for greater equity.

THE BRILLIANCE OF CHILDREN OF COLOR

Scholars have examined and offered tangible examples of the brilliance and success of minoritized children in the public school system and early years contexts. The works of Carter and Kumasi (2011), Delpit (2006, 2012), Ladson-Billings (1994), González, Moll, and Amanti (2005), Gutierrez, Bien, Selland, and Pierce (2011), and Orellana (2001) discuss approaches and methodologies that demonstrates how, when we center children's cultures and epistemologies, and ways with words (Brice-Heath, 1983), education becomes meaningful—but more important, they demonstrate that there is no achievement or developmental gap between White children and what has been constructed as the Other (Delpit, 2012). In fact, even research grounded in developmental psychology shows that children of color have demonstrated their success in developmental markers (Delpit, 2012). Thus, in early childhood, the supposed "gap" is nonexistent. Yet the focus on early literacy and readiness skills, for example, seems to project a different image of minoritized children, one where they are positioned as 'less than' beginning as early as birth (Delpit, 2012) and in some instances prenatally (Kaomea, 2005). These colonizing and deficit worldviews completely ignore the social and political context in which the notion of a gap has been constructed. That is, the gap exists only when education is seen and enacted from three perspectives: one rooted in colonization—the epistemological global north belief in the inherent (genetic) deficiency and inferiority of people of color from the global south (Gould, 1981; L. T. Smith, 1999) or who have global south positionings within the global north (Trinidad Galván, 2014), the superiority and standardization of global north knowledge, and finally, the corporatization of education through sweeping reforms, neoliberal public policy, and accountability systems (M. S. Pérez & Cannella, 2011; Ross & Gibson, 2007). For years, multicultural educators (Banks & Banks, 2004; Grant & Sleeter, 1990; Nieto, 1996; Spring, 2010) have problematized the separation of sociocultural, historical, and political factors from meaningful education (McCarty, 2002; Souto-Manning, 2013). Indeed, educational transformations are possible and real when we use a "comprehensive perspective" (Nieto, 2010, p. 34) to educate children. That is, we must address the sociohistorical and political context of education and care when considering the education of young children.

With the growing number of White teachers in the field and the rising number of children of color who speak a Native language other than English (Boser, 2014), it is imperative that we seriously address the notion of an achievement "gap" in early childhood teaching and research. In both, we must center the imaginative and intellectual world of minoritized children and communities (Delpit, 2012). We can no longer afford to allow global north research and perspectives to be the only decree on what is good, what works pedagogically, and what counts in education (Marx & Saavedra, 2014). As such, we propose to center scholarship that empowers educators to use different theoretical, onto-epistemological, and philosophical approaches. Research much start with the premise that all children are brilliant and have skills and knowledges worthy of incorporating, if not centering, in early childhood.

SITUATING MINORITIZED CHILDHOODS: A HISTORY OF GLOBAL NORTH PERSPECTIVES IN EARLY EDUCATION AND CARE

Like other facets of social life in the United States and globally, early childhood is dominated by onto-epistemologies from the global north (Fleer, Hedegaard, & Tudge, 2008; Nsamenang, 1999). Historically, White, mainly European, men (e.g., Piaget, Vygotsky, Rousseau, etc.) have informed how children have been constructed, governing how we engage with young children pedagogically and approach our work with families and communities. Especially concerning is how global north perspectives have privileged—and measured children with marginalized positionalities against—White, middle-/upper-class culture, while functioning as an apparatus to advance capitalist agendas (Burman, 2008).

Global north influences on early childhood can be traced through centuries of ways in which "childhood" has been discursively constructed (Burman, 1994, 2008). Since Western enlightenment, children have been categorized, individualized, othered, viewed as separate from/less than adults, and stripped of interconnections to the land/earth. As a result, children have had to navigate and create spaces of resistance within social and institutional power hierarchies. These hierarchies have been produced and maintained by adults, who continue to subject young children to "scientific" observation, constant surveillance, and intervention at every stage of their "development" (Cannella, 1997). Even more susceptible to adult interventions are children of color and those who speak a language or embody a gender identity different from the constructed standard (e.g., middle class, White, monolingual, heterosexual, able-bodied, etc.). The image of a normalized child has been legitimized and is becoming more widespread through global north onto-epistemologies, permeating every aspect of ECEC.

In the United States and more increasingly as a worldwide phenomenon, global north perspectives have produced vast inequities for those with Othered positionalities through (1) overreliance on developmental psychology and developmentally appropriate practice (DAP; Copple & Bredekamp, 2009), (2) narrowly defined and regulatory "quality" measures (M. S. Pérez & Cahill, 2015), and (3) implementation of postpositivist, culturally biased instructional and observational instruments (Dahlberg, Moss, & Pence, 2007; Lopez, 1997). To understand why such inequities exist among childhoods, and to find ways in which to challenge and transform these circumstances, we trace and examine the scholarship that has informed the field historically.

Developmentally Appropriate Practice

Although heavily contested (Bloch, 1992; Burman, 1994; Cannella, 1997), the National Association for the Education of Young Children's DAP (Bredekamp, 1987; Bredekamp & Copple, 1997) remains a pillar of ECEC. The articulation of DAP has had major implications for what counts as "appropriate" in early years settings and in turn driven accreditation standards, public policy, and dominant approaches to childhood research (Dickinson, 2002). With its far-reaching influence, DAP has informed early learning guidelines and outcomes developed by states across the United States, which are tied to teacher performance, child assessment, curriculum, and the structure of classroom environments. As such, in any particular program, there lies concern for whether the teacher is implementing DAP, if the children are engaging in and reaching markers of DAP, and if the curriculum and environment are conducive to/facilitating DAP. This pervasiveness becomes problematic when a one-size-fits-all mentality, grounded in the image of the White, monolingual, male, heterosexual child, not only disaffirms diversity but also stigmatizes children of color through discourses of underdevelopment and underachievement.

Quality

Intimately tied to DAP are notions of quality in early education and care. While one cannot disavow the importance of providing safe, caring, and nourishing spaces and experiences for young children (as we should for all in our communities), quality in early childhood has been produced through a developmental framework that attempts to standardize childhoods across contexts (Dahlberg et al., 2007). As a term borrowed from the private sector, quality is measured by efficient production outcomes (e.g., producing the ideal White child) and framed by notions of consumerism (e.g., ECEC as a product for the consumption of parents and society). Quality, like DAP, is ubiquitous in the field and defined through "measurable" teacher practices, program curriculum, child outcomes, and school readiness. For children who are socially marginalized, the propagation of quality in early childhood means yet another criterion used to measure the Other against and the production of intervention programs such as Head Start to ensure children's readiness for Kindergarten (Graue, 1993; Iorio, Parnell, & Borch, 2015). As Graue (2006) argues:

> Interventions that provide quality learning contexts include publically funded preschool programs for children seen to be at risk (like Head Start), parent education programs, and health resources. Targeting resources to particular subgroups is a response to scarce resources *but also belies a deep distrust in the ability of certain families to support their children* [emphasis added]. It also allows us to ignore the basic inequities that produce the differences in contexts for White middle class children and children living in poverty. (p. 49)

Graue's (2006) assessment of "quality"-based interventions illustrates what some might argue are misguided efforts to care for our most underresourced children and families through deficit approaches that stigmatize people living in poverty and ignore systemic issues that perpetuate inequities.

Measuring Quality

Prominent assessment tools that purport to measure quality are the Early Childhood Environmental Rating Scale–Revised (Harms, Clifford, & Cryer, 2004) and the Infant and Toddler Environmental Rating Scale–Revised (Harms, Clifford, & Cryer, 2006). These tools are said to assess the quality of early childhood environments for the "use of space, materials, and experiences" (Red Leaf Press, n.d., p. 1). In problematizing rating instruments, Dahlberg et al. (2007) posit,

> The concept of quality is primarily about defining, through the specification of criteria, a generalizable standard against which a product can be judged with certainty . . . intended to enable us to know whether or not something—be it a manufactured or service product—achieves the standard. (p. 93)

In relation to early childhood, instruments like the Early Childhood Environmental Rating Scale–Revised and Infant and Toddler Environmental Rating Scale–Revised, by means of a gendered, postpositivist scientific gaze, are said to measure whether a teacher, the classroom environment, and children's engagement within that environment meet a universalized standard. Especially problematic is that these tools are being increasingly used as a global standard of quality in ECEC. We can find many more examples of assessment instruments in K–3 educational contexts like DIBELS and the IOWA Test of Basic Skills. We must question, however, against what standards we are measuring children of color, who, in particular, are most likely to be excessively tested and constructed as needing to be "fixed"—to become the White, middle-class, monolingual child. As Delpit (2012) reminds us, "African American children do not come into this world as a deficit" (p. 5).

Quality Rating and Improvement Systems

In the United States, quality in ECEC has gained additional momentum in recent years through infusion of federal dollars that, if sought by individual states, require the design and implementation of Quality Rating and Improvement Systems (QRISs). Through QRISs, child cares and preschools become part of a tiered or star rating system that judges programs based on children's adherence to early learning guidelines and teacher/program evaluation by the state. While QRISs are often presented as voluntary, many programs are obliged to participate because they are linked to accreditation and funding streams.

As an example QRIS, New Mexico's FOCUS has enforced yet another required assessment. In programs like Head Start, which serve low-income, mainly bilingual children of color in New Mexico, FOCUS has become an assessment tool teachers are required to implement in addition to other assessment programs like Teaching Strategies Gold, mandated by state and/or federal agencies. On numerous occasions across programs in the state, we have witnessed teachers' stress and anxieties about implementing FOCUS. They cite that rather than being present with children during pedagogical engagements and having time to build meaningful relationships with families, they are spending valuable time documenting outcomes and filling out forms.

Mainstays of early childhood, such as DAP, quality, assessment tools, and QRISs, contribute to the labeling, tracking, and inequities imposed on children of color and those with marginalized identities not only in the United States but also on a global scale. Early childhood has become a mechanism to "fix" children and families, and to "close the gap" between the ideal child and children who embody racialized/ Othered identities. Critical perspectives on early childhood have challenged and rethought developmental viewpoints (Bloch, 2013). Examples of early childhood critical scholarship (which we expand on in the following section) include work that has theorized power hierarchies and made challenges to truth and universal claims embedded in developmental perspectives. While these have been important acts of resistance to the struggle for equity and social justice in early childhood, we find that critically oriented scholars continue to dominantly draw and theorize from global north positionings.

Global North Disruptions From Global North Perspectives

As an attempt to open new spaces for theory and praxis within ECEC, critically oriented scholars have engaged with theoretical perspectives that are outside the developmental psychology that has unquestionably influenced and perhaps dogmatically constructed the field (Burman, 1994, 2008; Cannella, 1997; Lubeck, 1996; Walkerdine, 1993). By doing so, critical scholars are finding different language, discourses and philosophical suppositions that create or break open spaces for rethinking and reconceptualtizing early childhood. Drawing from global north perspectives in sociology, and poststructuralist, feminist, and posthumanist theories, many critical scholars have offered new ways to think about working with young children in ways developmental psychology has not allowed (Blaise, 2005; Blaise, Banerjee, Pacini-Ketchabaw, & Taylor, 2013; Cannella, 1997; Dahlberg et al., 2007; James & Prout, 1990; Jenks, 2005; MacNaughton, 2005; Olsson, 2009; Taylor, 2013).

Inherent in critically oriented scholarship is the recognition that what is seen or observed is heavily influenced by the theories that frame not only the concept of childhood but also the way particular knowledge production is valued over others. From critical perspectives, childhoods have been reimagined through theoretical discussions on the linguistic and deconstructive turn (Derrida, 1976, 1981; Foucault 1972, 1977, 1978; Rorty, 1967), rhizomatic lines of flights (Deleuze & Guattari, 1987), and, most recently, posthumanist studies and new materialism (Barad, 2003, 2007; Haraway, 1991, 2004; Latour, 2004). As such, critical voices from the global north are de/re/constructing the concept of childhood and consequently ECEC. This scholarship is indeed pointing to deep philosophical, ontological, and epistemological elements that contribute to inequities in early childhood. However, theorizing remains situated in global north positionings.

Sociopolitical and Historical Constructions of the Child

Reexaminations of origins are powerful ways to deconstruct and reconstruct images of childhood (Cannella, 1997). What we know today about childhood is influenced not merely by a pure search for objective knowledge but perhaps, more centrally, also by discourses and fictions established in society through dominant his/ stories told. Understanding childhood as a separate and distinct stage in life, for instance, has not been a natural, inevitable evolution of society's treatment of younger human beings. Consequently, many have problematized the origins and allegiance to developmental psychology and DAP in ECEC (Burman, 2008; Cannella, 1997; Lubeck, 1996; Walkerdine, 1984, 1993).

Burman (2008) states that the rise of developmental psychology occurred within a time of social unrest, in which there was great concern for how "urbanization brought about rapid industrialization [and] produced the appalling conditions of the Victorian slums" (p. 18). This concern coalesced with growing interests in fields like statistics and sociology, whose purpose was to study and regulate populations. Important in this brief historical account is that the most influential field for early childhood, developmental psychology, was in fact a tool designed to examine human deficiencies and pathologies (poverty, bad habits, etc.) and how to "fix" them. This is no different than most contemporary educational reforms like NCLB or RTTT-ELC that have constructed an achievement gap, rooted in a view of the individual, without regard to inequitable structural conditions produced in our society and the racist and colonizing instruments used to measure a supposed gap. Soto (1997) and Bloch (1991, 1992) have critiqued how a vast majority of the scholarship in the field of early childhood has been created through and relied solely on the science and post-positivist empiricism prevalent in modernist understandings of the world. Historically, the pursuit of modernity was to establish universal claims through order and purity (Burman, 2008). Within early childhood, developmental psychology has been used to frame empirical research in early years contexts, like nurseries, to produce universal norms and the hierarchical ordering of childhoods (Rose, 1990). The scientific gaze, then, was turned onto the child in order to monitor her or his every move, attitude, and demeanor (Walkerdine, 1993).

In 1960s and 1970s Europe, young children were being measured at every turn. No longer was it necessary to know if a child could learn certain concepts, she/he had to be constantly measured. Perhaps it could be argued that testing and measuring allow a society to "know" and "understand" children. However, fields cannot be separated from their sociohistorical and political roots, and as such, critical early childhood scholars have posited that developmental psychology has not been an innocent nor neutral force. In fact, to be viewed as a legitimate field and to gain status, developmental psychology has attempted to emulate the science of western medicine. We can find contemporary evidence of these constructions in the 2010 National Council for Accreditation of Teacher Education report that uses medically situated terminology to make recommendations for teacher education by suggesting an "Rx for Transformation" (p. 16). Other examples include technologies such as IQ testing, which creates social hierarchies that privilege White, middle-class children as intellectually superior (Bowles & Gintis, 2002). Clearly the inheritance of "scientific legitimation upon practices of social regulation, social division and (supposed) reform" (Burman, 2008, p. 21) has not served all children, much less children of color (Cannella, 1997; Soto, 1997). The opposite has occurred, with an ever-widening "achievement gap," where the pathology lies within the mental realm of children of color and their communities (Goodwin, Cheruvu, & Genishi, 2007). The contemporary notion of an achievement gap, then, can be viewed as socially, politically, and even medically constructed.

What we can learn from critical scholarship is that ECEC is (and works for) certain children, namely, those coming from cultures with privilege like European and Anglo-American White, male, middle classes. The discourses of DAP, quality, and observational instruments are extensions of historical constructions of childhood that have led to the design of research and pedagogy from very narrow perspectives (Cannella, 1997; Lubeck, 1996). It is no great mystery, then, why White middle- to upper-class children perform "better" on developmental rating scales and in schools; they are positioned on the high end of the achievement gap. It is not that children from this group are inherently smarter; rather they are advantaged because the very construction of early childhood is patterned, normed, and created for them.

(RE)CENTERING GLOBAL SOUTH PERSPECTIVES IN EARLY CHILDHOOD EDUCATION AND CARE

[epistemological] diversity involves the recognition that the theories produced in the global North are best equipped to account for the social, political, and cultural realities of the global North and that in order adequately to account for the realities of the global South other theories must be developed and anchored in other epistemologies—the epistemologies of the South. (de Sousa Santos, 2012, p. 45)

As we have illustrated, there has been a marked persistence of global north onto-epistemologies in early childhood studies, whether in what is considered "traditional" early childhood or in critical scholarship. When contemplating a more equitable field, where our thoughts and actions begin with visions of children of color as extraordinary, we argue that early childhood research and pedagogy must be derived from global south onto-epistemologies. Chicana feminism (Anzaldúa, 1987) and Black feminist thought (Collins, 2008) are two examples of global south worldviews that can move early childhood in a more equitable and socially just direction.

Black and Chicana Feminisms as Essential to Early Childhood Education and Care

For some time, we, as Latina scholars (and Others, including our White allies), have pushed for the centralization of marginalized onto-epistemologies in both traditional and critical ECEC scholarship (Bloch & Swadener, 2009; Habashi, 2005; Pacini-Ketchabaw, 2007; M. S. Pérez, 2017; Ritchie & Rau, 2013; Saavedra, 2011a, 2011b; Soto, 2001; Souto-Manning, 2013; Viruru, 2001). The absence of theories in the flesh (a Chicana feminism concept centering on lived/corporeal experiences as theory; Moraga, 1983) is disconcerting, not only because it excludes the presence of women and people of color from the conversation but also because it has dire consequences for how we construct and view historically marginalized children and what is prioritized (or in some cases, completely ignored) in research and pedagogy. We continue to head down a dangerous path, however, with significant scholarship showing no concern for critical identity politics, or even just as troubling, that we have somehow moved beyond the need to make central the lived realities of so many in oppressive conditions the world over (M. S. Pérez & Saavedra, 2015). In traditional early childhood, this plays out in the reification of deficit perspectives through developmental and quality narratives and is propagated by public policy and the early childhood industrial complex. For scholars theorizing critically, it seems as if there is a constant need to engage in what is viewed as innovative contemplations, such as decentering the human (Braidotti, 2013)—scholarship that is not only usurped from indigenous worldviews, at times without acknowledgement but that we find also often ignores and/or continues to disregard the ways in which young children of color and their communities are constructed and minoritized. This moment in all aspects of the field, we believe, is a consequence of the persistent reliance on global north positionings.

As such, we posit that theories in the flesh (Moraga & Anzaldúa, 1983) can influence how we engage with children of color in both research and practice. Moraga (1983) conceptualizes theory in the flesh as "the physical realities of our lives—our skin color, the land or concrete we grew up on, our sexual longings—all fuse[d] to create a politic born out of necessity" (p. 23). The necessity is "naming ourselves and telling our stories in our own words" (p. 23). It is undeniable that marginalized embodied experiences are important not only to emphasize inequities but also to give birth to new theories–ways of understanding the world around us. Therefore, as we envision the future of ECEC, we hope for a space that honors the legacies and contemporary knowledges that women of color and indigenous peoples have bestowed on us—and how these global south perspectives are essential (and will continue to be essential as long as injustice exists) to any research or pedagogical project, especially ones that entail working with and advocating for minoritized youth and communities.

As theories in the flesh, both Black and Chicana feminisms are derived from the everyday embodied experiences of people of color. At the same time, both are unique. As such, in the forthcoming, we share a brief account of how Black and Chicana feminisms, as global south onto-epistemologies, can individually and collectively transform ECEC.

Black Feminisms

Black feminisms are diverse and span across a number of fields, including sociology, women's studies, and education (Collins, 2008; Dillard, 2006; Evans-Winters & Love, 2015a; hooks, 2000). Through multiple and varied articulations, such as endarkened feminism (Dillard, 2012), womanism (Maparpan, 2012), and Black feminist thought (Collins, 2005, 2006, 2008, 2011), the Subaltern voices of women of color have theorized their lived experiences of oppression and empowerment (Guy-Sheftall, 1995; hooks, 2000, 2006, 2010). Theory as lived (and the lived as theory) makes Black feminisms distinctive from most global north positionings, which often separate embodied knowing from theorizing. Black feminist onto-epistemologies, instead, are communicated through spoken, corporeal, and written word in the forms of storytelling, poetry, song, and art, to provide her-sotrical accounts of the lived realities of Black women's subjugation, resistance, and self/collective empowerment and liberation (Lorde, 1984; Morrison, 1994; Walker 1983; Washington, 1975). An example is Audre Lorde's (1984) approach to collective resistance through poetry. She explains:

As we come more into touch with our own ancient, non-european consciousness of living as a situation to be experienced and interacted with, we learn more and more to cherish our feelings, and to respect those hidden sources of power from where true knowledge and, therefore, lasting action comes. (p. 37)

Lorde (1984) goes on to explain how poetry can allow us to tap into embodied knowledge, inspiring resistance and action that stems from a place beyond the use of the master's tools.

Another central aspect of Black feminisms is intersectionality (Crenshaw, 1991). Intersectionalities make up the myriad identities that one embodies (through constructions of gender, sexuality, race, language, and ability, to name a few), and influence the ways in which one is socially positioned in a given context. For a girl in early childhood, when her identity as a "young" "child" intersects with her class, race, sexuality, and language, the multiple circumstances she encounters can *both* privilege *and* oppress her. The notion of intersectionalities has been further theorized in what Collins (2008) refers to as matrices of domination. As a mainstay of Black feminist thought, matrices of domination function as domains of power that materialize as structural, disciplinary, hegemonic, and interpersonal oppressions (for an in-depth explanation of domains of power, see Collins, 2008, 2009; M. S. Pérez & Williams, 2014). Other important aspects of Black feminisms are transnationalism, spirituality, the notion of individual struggle/empowerment as connected to the collective, working toward social justice across cultural groups (especially ones that experience similar oppressive circumstances), and activism as imperative to social transformation (Dillard, 2006; hooks 2006, 2010; Collins, 2008). It is clear that Black feminisms, as a form of global south thinking, can help shift our historical and contemporary reliance on global north perspectives in early childhood, while at the same time creating a more equitable and just world.

Chicana Feminism

Drawing from the works of Anzaldúa (1987, 1990, 2002), Moraga (1983, 1993), and Moraga and Anzaldúa (1983), Chicana feminist scholars have made important and critical contributions to the field of education (Calderón, Delgado Bernal, Huber, Malagón, & Vélz, 2012; Delgado Bernal, 1998; Delgado Bernal, Elenes, Godinez, & Villenas 2006; Saavedra & Nymark, 2008). The conceptual frameworks in this scholarship stem from centering the marginalized ways of knowing and living of Chicana/o and Latina/o communities. Villenas, Godinez, Delgado Bernal, and Elenes (2006) "challenge the starting points and theoretical lenses against which Chicana/Latina lives and ways of knowing are measured" (p. 4). By centering lived experiences, Chicana feminist educational scholars complicate the boundaries of theories, methodologies, and pedagogies (Calderón, 2014; Cervantes-Soon, 2014; Elenes, 2013; Franquiz, Avila, & Ayala, 2013; Prieto, 2013; Saavedra, 2011b).

Chicana feminism opens spaces of possibilities within ECEC. Concepts like cultural intuition (Delgado Bernal, 1998), embodied experiences (Cruz, 2001; Trujillo,

1998), and borderlands (Anzaldúa, 1987; Elenes, 1997) become centralized and necessary to "see" minoritized children in their brilliance. As Villenas et al. (2006) assert, researchers and teachers can understand the "sensibilities that children and youth bring to school from their mothers and other family members" (p. 5). Furthermore, Delgado Bernal's (1998) concept of cultural intuition is one way Chicana feminists have drawn from their lived experiences, community knowledge, and genealogies to inform their work. Instead of dissecting them/selves from who they are, their multiple selves are collectively made central to research and praxis (Calderón et al., 2012; Soto, 2009).

Embodied experiences also play a crucial role in the education of Brown bodies. Cruz (2001) explores the ways that Brown bodies are disciplined and fragmented in school settings but offers hope when she states that rethinking the Brown body as a site of knowledge production "begins the validation of the narratives of survival, transformation, and emancipation of our respective communities, reclaiming histories and identities" (p. 668). Furthermore, Chicana feminists' use of the literal and metaphorical concept of the borderlands (Anzaldúa, 1987; Elenes, 1997; Saavedra & Nymark, 2008) gives way to hybrid identities and knowing. The notion of borderlands is another powerful illumination of how people who embody multiple minoritized cultures and speak several languages navigate dominant discourses and find third spaces of resistance and transformation (Anzaldúa, 2002; E. Pérez, 1999).

Using Black and Chicana Feminisms to Honor Lived Experiences, Challenge Deficit Constructions of Childhood/s, and Transform Teacher Education

As illustrated in our brief theoretical discussion, both Black and Chicana feminisms offer important resistance to hegemonic worldviews and imaginaries for sites of empowerment. In similar but unique ways, identity and the body are theorized as connected to cultural epistemologies, and used not only to challenge power hierarchies but also to connect our-selves to a larger collective spirit and action toward social justice. When theories in the flesh like Black and Chicana feminisms are centralized in early education and care, the following occurs:

- Lived experiences of children of color, who are most prominent in the world, are legitimized.
- We begin to question our own onto-epistemologies as scholars, teachers, and teacher educators that often prohibit us from recognizing and taking seriously marginality and oppressive, deficit constructions of the Other.
- Teacher education and the workforce are transformed.

Most important, as these points of equity come to fruition, viewing minoritized children as brilliant becomes foundational to the field.

In the forthcoming, we provide illustrations of global south imaginaries in ECEC. While some of the examples we share are from scholars who are not explicitly using

Black or Chicana feminisms, we find that their messages speak directly to the aims/intentions of these theories. Additionally, while some, but not all, examples address an early childhood context, we believe that it speaks to the need for us to borrow more often from the important sociopolitical scholarship in other fields, including elementary, secondary, and higher education, to find ways they can be useful for challenging inequities in early childhood.

Lived Experiences Matter

When we use global south onto-epistemologies in early childhood, lived experiences of children of color, who are most prominent in the world, are legitimized. In engaging with emergent bilingual children, for example, research and teaching become grounded in the understanding that linguistically minoritized children bring important skills and knowledges to education and care contexts. Emergent bilingual children readily draw from their cultural intuition (Delgado Bernal, 1998) and funds of knowledge (González et al., 2005) to make sense of their daily lives not only at home and in their communities but also in schools (Riojas-Cortez, 2001). The effort then lies with researchers and educators to recognize and affirm young children's intuitive ways of knowing and being.

Orellana's (2001) study with Mexican and Central American children highlights the importance of honoring bilingual youth's everyday worlds. Orellana's thesis is to move away from seeing children as merely in preparation to becoming adults. Latina/o children are much more than this. They are cultural and linguistic brokers, helpers, and volunteers and are important contributing members of their communities and families. When the curriculum centers these experiences, children are able to use their cultural intuition and funds of knowledge to make deeper and more meaningful connections to school knowledge, thereby fostering an opportunity for them to participate in early education and care environments on their own terms with their own cultural understandings. As an example of this, rethinking the concept of language and literacy through a Chicana/Latina feminist lens, Saavedra (2011b) has centered the Latin American literary genre of testimonio (Beverly, 2005; Elenes, 2000; The Latina Feminist Group, 2001) as a tool for young children in the borderlands to draw from and center their lived experiences as part of the language arts curriculum.

Testimonio is a type of personal narrative that connects to a larger collective experience of oppressed communities (Blackmer Reyes & Curry Rodriguez, 2012; Delgado Bernal, Burciaga, & Flores Carmona, 2012). Sharing testimonios becomes important as it captures the realities of emergent and immigrant children living in geopolitical, epistemological, and cultural borderlands (Anzaldúa, 1987). Through testimonio, the hybridity of knowledge becomes an important tool for learning processes, living, and navigating between worlds. Centering a child's stories is a way to validate embodied experiences as essential to learning. As a result, children do not have to hide their expertise, skills, and knoweldges and, in fact, become organic intellectuals where they are encouraged to theorize their lived ways of knowing. Using testimonios, then, is a way to not only honor their stories but also, equally important, to allow teachers and researchers to learn from their wisdom.

Norton's (2008) work surrounding the intersections of race, spirituality, gender, and song in early childhood, and the knowledge produced from such lived experiences, is another articulation of what many Black feminists describe as embodied ways of knowing (hooks, 2000; Maparyan, 2012). Song historically, has been regarded in some Black communities as "sacred and serves as a manifestation of spirituality to alter mental, physical, emotional, and physical states of people's beings and to struggle against oppressive structures (Cone, 1997; George, 1988)" (Norton, 2008, p. 343). As such, Norton (2008) points to the significance of seeing music and song not merely as a part of early years' curriculum but rather as part of the spiritual identities and practices of many communities of color.

To capture this embodied way of knowing in young children, in her participatory research, Norton (2008) engages in the school and home environments of Kevin, a working-class, male, Black, and self-identified spiritual first grader. When she joins Kevin at church, Norton finds that he is accustomed to expressing his spirituality through song and dance. However, when he goes to school, Kevin struggles with policies that limit movement. Furthermore, he encounters oppressive stereotypes of Black males as "unruly" or "unable to control themselves" (Norton, 2008, p. 351; Phillips, 1994). Norton (2008) posits, "Situating Kevin's body movements as spiritual practices challenges inequitable constructions of Kevin's intersecting identities as male child, Black child, and/or Black male child" (p. 351). In problematizing child development discourses that sustain younger children as unable to self-regulate and therefore, prohibit body movements, Norton further explains that "children are sustained as unknowing, untamed beings in need of developing self-control (Burman, 1994). In turn, body movements of children such as Kevin are read as out of control rather than as manifestations of spiritual control and knowing" (p. 351).

Instead of evaluating Kevin as behind on developmental markers of self-regulation, or reprimanding him for not assimilating to the ideal of a "properly" developing White child, Kevin's teacher, who connects to Kevin's struggle as a Black spiritual man, encourages Kevin to move when he needs to (whether in his seat or around the classroom), listen to music with headphones, or sing softly to himself. In this way, the teacher is fostering and honoring Kevin's lived, embodied experiences in a school setting, as a Black, young, spiritual, male being.

In using global south onto-epistemologies in early education and care, connections can be made between the everyday experiences of children of color and the theories and methods we use to engage with them as teachers and researchers. If we view children of color through a completely detached, global north lens, we reify disconnections between their lived experiences and our scholarship and teaching. The purpose for research and pedagogy, then, shifts as our encounters with children of color are informed by global south positionings, which honor situated and embodied knowledges.

Challenging Hegemonic Understandings of Marginalized Childhoods

In our previous examples of global south scholarship, we see how Black and Chicana feminisms assist in recognizing how lived experiences and cultural knowledge influences our thinking and approaches to research and pedagogy. For far too long, young children of color have been viewed as needing to be "fixed" so they can be productive in society as well as to assimilate to the values, attitudes, and ways of being of the dominant culture (Spring, 2010). These deep-seated beliefs about children of color and/or working-class people only serves to perpetuate the idea that White Euro-American middle-upper class families are superior. Global south onto-epistemologies can change not only the current conversation that focuses on deficit conceptualizations of children of color but also the discourses that go unquestioned and keep us from seeing their potentials, brilliance, and capabilities (Delpit, 2006). Diversifying our onto-epistemological positionings in early childhood research and pedagogy by taking seriously and legitimizing the important contributions of global south scholars, like Chicana and Black feminists, challenges and shifts hegemonic worldviews.

Redeaux (2011) and Montaño and Quintanar-Sarellana (2011) are examples of scholars engaging in such work. Redeaux expresses, "I am a Black youth. I teach Black youth. I am attentive to the way these youths are described, portrayed, perceived. Because I teach "these children." And I am one of "these children" (p. 177). Drawing from her lived experiences as a woman of color, Redeaux has problematized the "culture of poverty" espoused by programs like Ruby Payne's "framework for understanding poverty." Used for teacher's professional development in birth through Grade 12 education, Payne has built a multimillion-dollar empire on discussing class in a way that she believes transcends intersectional identity markers. However, the methods and scenarios Payne teaches from blame the individual and ignore how White supremacy, heteronormativity, and structural and institutional patriarchy (e.g., matrices of domination) perpetuate poverty conditions. There is no acknowledgement of children's intersectional and varied lived realities and the role that ethnicity, race, language, and Othered social positionings play in one's experience with class oppression—instead Payne lumps all into one "culture of poverty." In subtle and at times obvious ways, harmful stereotypes are propagated in the vignettes used by Ruby Payne to engage in discussions with teachers about class, where too often, "the White mother is a victim of circumstance . . . [and] the Black mother is the victim of her own bad choices and behavior" (Redeaux, 2011, p. 186).

Similarly, Montaño and Quintanar-Sarellana (2011) find that Ruby Payne ignores struggles of immigrant children in oppressive school contexts, viewing their poverty conditions "as merely a consequence of language deficiencies that need to be remediated" (p. 199). They explain:

The cultural and linguistic knowledge of the immigrant student and his/her ability to negotiate the unfriendly terrain of schooling and society are completely ignored . . . Payne's failure to acknowledge the complexities of language learning also allows teachers to easily chalk up the social discourse of Chicana/o-Latina/o and African American students as an inferior language form. (p. 199)

Providing an alternative to Ruby Payne, Montaño and Quintanar-Sarellana (2011) suggest that schools use valuable resources (e.g., time and scarce funds) to support teachers in making stronger relationships with families and "tap the cultural and linguistic knowledge of the students, infuse this knowledge into the curriculum and ultimately facilitate the process where students resist the policies and practices that reproduce the social inequality and perpetuate class differences" (p. 202).

Deficit-based programs like Ruby Payne's are a prime example of what happens when we continue to use global north perspectives in early childhood. Unfortunately, some educators, especially those who have not had the opportunity to critically challenge global north viewpoints on poverty and education, view Ruby Payne as a resource to support "poor" children and families. A global north onto-epistemology supports such programs and misguides teacher's equity advocacy when it constructs poverty within a vacuum. When a teacher/scholar activist, such as Redeaux (2011), however, uses her global south positioning to culturally and intuitively connect to her students' experiences and livelihoods (Delgado Bernal, 1998), the construction of the deficit Other no longer persists; instead, her students are regarded as brilliant and their identities seen as attributes and essential to learning, curriculum, school culture, and larger society.

Transforming Teacher Education and the Workforce

A critical worldview requires teachers to develop an understanding between ideology, culture, hegemony, and power and to become transformative educators committed to radically changing the "traditional" curriculum, to transform society. (Montaño & Quintanar-Sarellana, 2011, p. 210)

Black and Chicana feminisms inspire us to question and deviate from the commonsense knowledge (Kumashiro, 2009) that children's underdevelopment and underachievement are rooted in—individual psychology and/or the biology of minoritized children. At the same time, looking at the sociohistorical context that drives the political and economic divisions between White people and people of color also serves a way to interrogate "failure" within a larger context. Even though these deficit discourses have been extensively challenged (Delpit, 2006; Ladson-Billings, 1994; Swadener & Lubeck, 1995), we have yet to experience a radical shift in early childhood, whether in teacher education, public policy, or research. Specific to teacher education, we find instead that in most programs, global south worldviews continue to only be addressed in one multicultural education class or perhaps in a graduate feminist or critically oriented research course. If we are to move the field in new and equitable directions, we believe early childhood teachers and teacher educators must be at the forefront of the movement.

Examples of scholars who have engaged in transformative early childhood teacher education from global south positionings include Souto-Manning (2010), M. S.

Pérez, Ruiz Guerrero, and Mora (2016), and Reza-López, Huerta Charles, and Reyes (2014), among many others (Delpit & Dowdy, 2002; Genishi & Goodwin, 2007; Saavedra, 2011b; Soto, 2009). Souto-Manning (2010) has employed Freirean cultural circles with teachers in order to "move away from the model of education that is based on transmission of knowledge to students' brains like money into banks" (p. 11). Instead, both she and the teachers she works with become critical ethnographers and learners of their students, tapping into and engaging in conversations surrounding race, class, gender, language, and sexuality oppressions, based on the valuable cultural knowledges and experiences that educators and children bring with them to school. Souto-Manning (2010) explains that "in this process, authority is dialectically negotiated as teachers assume the role of facilitators and focus on problem posing as they seek to engage in critical education (Kincheloe & Steinberg, 1998)" (p. 14). Through dialogic, transformative teacher education, approaches like cultural circles can "build and change the world" (p. 31).

M. S. Pérez, Ruiz Guerrero, and Mora (2016) have taken a similar action oriented approach to teacher education through the use of Black feminist thought (Collins, 2008) in combination with photovoice. Photovoice (Wang & Burris, 1997) is a Freirean, feminist, participatory research and pedagogical tool where participants use photography to capture images that illustrate oppressive social conditions. Connecting course content on issues like colonization, racism, sexism, heteronormativity, and language oppression, early childhood undergraduate students, who are predominately women of color, engaged in Black feminist photovoice to explore their own intersectional identities and uncover power hierarchies embedded in early education and care and larger society. Black feminist photovoice prompted pre/in-service teachers' critical understandings and discussion of oppressions that marginalized children and families face systemically and in their everyday worldly encounters. Students then collectively generated possibilities for engaging in transformative action that supports families and communities and works toward challenging inequities.

For Reza-López et al. (2014), transforming the early childhood workforce, and in particular, educators of children in the U.S./Mexico borderlands, requires a different theoretical framework by using multiple concepts like Anzaldúa's (2002) conocimiento and nepantla, Freire's (1978) conscientization, and Bakhtin's (1981) dialogism and ideological becoming. Important is how the authors use Anzaldúa's work as an epistemological, cultural, and geopolitical perspective that centers on borderland communities. Anzaldúa has theorized nepantla as an in-between space where the straddling of epistemologies, cultures, and languages occurs. Conocimiento is the process of understanding life through a series of recursive stages that allow for individual spiritual growth that transforms into social action or what Anzaldúa (2002) calls spiritual activism. Reza-Lopez et al. (2014) recognize that nepantla and conocimiento allow educators "to understand the space that positions . . . bilingual students . . . as individuals with potential and not as *at risk* or *in limbo*" (p. 110). The authors argue that in order for teachers to connect with minoritized children's ambiguities, angsts, and daily navigations, in-between spaces like nepantla must be acknowledged. However, the authors posit that this cannot occur if teachers are unable to recognize and draw from their own nepantla. Reza et al. then envision a nepantlera pedagogy where in-/preservice teachers "recognize themselves as both social subjects and cultural workers committed to social sensibility and compassion, recognizing that all students have the potential to learn" (pp. 117-118). This requires "respect for Latino students and their families' cultural and linguistics background" and for teachers to "embrace the commitment of social activism to transform any oppressive and discriminatory social practices" (pp. 117-118).

In these examples of transformative teacher education, we find that Chicana, Black feminist, and Other global south perspectives inspire new imaginaries that can challenge our global north approaches to early childhood teacher education. With the rising number of White teachers entering the field, teacher educators must be equipped with theories of the flesh to connect pedagogical engagements with the lived realities of marginalized families and communities. Furthermore, Valenzuela (2016) reminds us that being a teacher of color and/or multilingual does not in itself make a global south–oriented teacher. Through feminist, global south rethinkings of teacher education, however, "critical educators realize that changes in inequitable conditions will only happen through political action, not through the reinforcement of deficit views. Children are not changed to fit into society, but society changes to meet the realities of the student" (Montaño & Quintanar-Sarellana, 2011, p. 210). As scholar activists, we must then continue to forge spaces in teacher education for centering global south onto-epistemologies. Shifting from global north to global south perspectives can transform the early childhood workforce and, in turn, provide more meaningful, nondeficit, dialogic, and decolonial spaces for children of color.

IMAGINING NEW GLOBAL SOUTH DIRECTIONS IN EARLY CHILDHOOD EDUCATION AND CARE: QUESTIONS AND PROVOCATIONS

As early childhood educators, feminists of color, and scholar activists, we make an urgent call for recentering global south perspectives in ECEC. Our advocacy for onto-epistemological diversity stems from a deep place of love and concern for marginalized youth and families. In our discussions with early childhood educators and scholars across the United States and the globe, we find that many times, even our White, global north colleagues (whether taking a critical or traditional approach to early childhood) have similar concerns about the deficit positioning of marginalized communities. What, then, must we do to move forward as advocates for a more socially just and equitable early childhood? We believe, without question, that centering global south perspectives is a necessary place to begin. When we do so, injustices are unveiled and challenged, and the brilliance of children of color is the starting point for all discussions, whether surrounding research, pedagogy, teacher education, or public policy. It is this focus on children of color's brilliance where the real transformation lies. In centering global south onto-epistemologies, we will no longer persist in using scales to construct and measure developmental and achievement gaps. More scholars and educators of color will feel as if they are a welcomed part of the conversation, and profitability will no longer determine the value of a child's livelihood. Furthermore, all children's identities will be "seen" and treated with love and respect. When our worldviews shift from deficit to recognizing children of color's brilliance, so can our engagements with early childhood research and pedagogy.

When we ask ourselves what contributions we will make to a global south recentering in early childhood, we think about continuing to read, learn from, and engage with women of color scholars, like Patricia Hill Collins and Gloria Anzaldúa, and the many her/historical figures who have come before them to teach us valuable lessons about collective struggle, perseverance, and transformation (Evans-Winters & Love, 2015b). We think about working across our many constructed boundaries in order to challenge our engagements in oppositional politics and whose or what agenda they really serve (Keating, 2013). We think about our connections with our communities and Other communities of color (children, teachers, and elders alike), and how to learn from them, strengthen our bonds and collaborative efforts, and advocate *with* them. And finally, we think of how we will move forward in our scholarship and teaching, always questioning its purpose and ways that it can enhance efforts to bring about equity and social justice in ECEC. In some ways, this transformation in worldviews seems simple, yet we believe it is revolutionary. For the readers of our urgent call, we must turn the question to you and ask, "What role will you play in the global south revolution?"

NOTE

[1]Although "early childhood" can take on many meanings, for the purposes of this chapter, we define it as birth to age 8.

REFERENCES

Anzaldúa, G. E. (1987). *Borderlands/la frontera*. San Francisco, CA: Aunt Lute Books.

Anzaldúa, G. E. (1990). Introduction. In G. E. Anzaldúa (Ed.), *Making face, making soul/ haciendo caras: Creative and critical perspectives by women of color* (pp. xv–xxviii). San Francisco: Aunt Lute Books.

Anzaldúa, G. E. (2002). Now let us shift . . . the path of conocimiento . . . inner work, public acts. In G. Anzaldúa, & A. Keating (Eds.), *This bridge we call home: Radical visions for transformation* (pp. 540–578). New York, NY: Routledge.

Arrighi, G. (2001). Global capitalism and the persistence of the north-south divide. *Science & Society, 65*, 469–476.

Bakhtin, M. M. (1981). *The dialogic imagination: Four essays* (M. Holquist, Ed.). Austin: University of Texas Press.

Banks, J., & Banks, C. A. M. (Eds.). (2004) *Multicultural education: Issues and perspectives* (5th ed.). Hoboken, NJ: John Wiley.

Barad, K. (2003). Posthumanist performativity: Toward an understanding of how matter comes to matter. *SIGNS: Journal of Women in Culture and Society, 28*, 801–831.

Barad, K. (2007). *Meeting the universe halfway: Quantum physics and the entanglement of matter and meaning*. Durham, NC: Duke University Press.

Beverly, J. (2005). Testimonio, subalternity, and narrative authority. In N. K. Denzin, & Y. S Lincoln (Eds.), *Handbook of qualitative research* (3rd ed., pp. 547–556). Thousand Oaks, CA: SAGE.

Blaise, M. (2005). *Playing it straight: Uncovering gender discourses in the early childhood classroom.* New York, NY: Routledge.

Blaise, M., Banerjee, B., Pacini-Ketchabaw, V., & Taylor, A. (2013). Special issue: Researching the naturecultures of postcolonial childhoods. *Global Studies of Childhood, 3,* 350–441.

Bloch, M. N. (1991). Critical science and the history of child development's influence on early education research. *Early Education and Development, 2*(2), 95–97.

Bloch, M. N. (1992). Critical perspectives on the historical relationship between child development and early childhood education research. In S. Kessler, & E. B. Swadener (Eds.), *Reconceptualizing the early childhood curriculum: Beginning the dialogue* (pp. 3–20). New York, NY: Teachers College Press.

Bloch, M. N. (2013). Reconceptualizing theory/policy/curriculum/pedagogy in early childhood (care and) education: Reconceptualizing early childhood education (RECE) 1991-2012. *International Journal of Equity and Innovation in Early Childhood, 11*(1), 65–85.

Bloch, M. N., & Swadener, B. B. (2009). "Education for all": Social inclusions and exclusions: Introduction and critical reflections. *International Critical Childhood Policy Studies.* Retrieved from http://journals.sfu.ca/iccps/index.php/childhoods/article/view/6/10

Boser, U. (2014, May 4). *Teacher diversity revisited: A new state by state analysis. Report for the Center for American Progress.* Retrieved from https://www.americanprogress.org/issues/race/report/2014/05/04/88962/teacher-diversity-revisited/

Bowles, S., & Gintis, H. (2002). Schooling in capitalist America revisited. *Sociology of Education, 75*(1), 1–18.

Braidotti, R. (2013). *The posthuman.* Cambridge, England: Polity Press.

Bredekamp, S. (1987). *Developmentally appropriate practices in early childhood education.* Washington, DC: National Association for the Education of Young Children.

Bredekamp, S., & Copple, C. (1997). *Developmentally appropriate practice in early childhood programs.* Washington, DC: National Association for the Education of Young Children.

Brice-Heath, S. (1983). *Ways with words: Language, life and work in communities and classrooms.* New York, NY: Cambridge University Press.

Burman, E. (1994). *Deconstructing developmental psychology.* London, England: Routledge.

Burman, E. (2008). *Deconstructing developmental psychology* (2nd ed.). London, England: Routledge.

Calderón, D. (2014). Anticolonial methodologies in education: Embodying land and indigeneity in Chicana feminisms. *Journal of Latino/Latin American Studies, 6*(2), 81–96.

Calderón, D., Delgado Bernal, D., Huber, L., Malagón, M. C., & Vélez, V. N. (2012). A Chicana feminist epistemology revisited: Cultivating ideas a generation later. *Harvard Educational Review, 88,* 513–539. doi:10.17763/haer.82.4.l518621577461p68

Cannella, G. S. (1997). *Deconstructing early childhood education: Social justice and revolution.* New York, NY: Peter Lang.

Cannella, G. S., & Viruru, R. (2004). *Childhood and postcolonization: Power, education, and contemporary practice.* New York, NY: Routledge.

Carter, S., & Kumasi, K. D. (2011). Double reading: Young Black scholars responding to whiteness in a community literacy program. In V. Kinloch (Ed.). *Urban literacies: Critical perspectives on language, learning and community* (pp. 72–90). New York, NY: Teachers College Press.

Cervantes-Soon, C. (2014). The U.S.-Mexico border-crossing Chicana researcher: Theory in the flesh and the politics of identity in critical ethnography. *Journal of Latino/Latin American Studies, 6*(2), 97–112.

Collins, P. H. (2005). *Black sexual politics: African Americans, gender, and the new racism.* New York, NY: Routledge.

Collins, P. H. (2006). *From Black power to hip hop: Racism, nationalism, and feminism.* Philadelphia, PA: Temple University Press.

Collins, P. H. (2008). *Black feminist thought: Knowledge, consciousness, and the politics of empowerment* (3rd ed.). New York, NY: Routledge.

Collins, P. H. (2009). *Another kind of public education: Race, schools, the media, and democratic possibilities.* Boston, MA: Beacon Press.

Collins, P. H. (2011). Toward a new vision: Race, class, and gender as categories of analysis and connection. In T. E. Ore (Ed.), *The social construction of difference and inequality: Race, class, gender, and sexuality* (5th ed., pp. 760–774). New York, NY: McGraw-Hill.

Copple, C., & Bredekamp, S. (2009). *Developmentally appropriate practice in early childhood programs serving children from birth through age 8* (3rd ed.). Washington, DC: National Association for the Education of Young Children.

Crenshaw, K. W. (1991). Mapping the margins: Intersectionality, identity politics, and violence against women of color. *Stanford Law Review, 43,* 1241–1299.

Cruz, C. (2001). Towards an epistemology of the brown body. *International Journal of Qualitative Studies in Education, 14,* 657–669.

Dahlberg, G., Moss, P., & Pence, A. (2007). *Beyond quality in early childhood education and care: Postmodern perspectives* (2nd ed.). London, England: Falmer Press.

Deleuze, G., & Guattari, F. (1987). *A thousand plateaus: Capitalism and schizophrenia* (B. Massumi, Trans.). Minneapolis: University of Minnesota Press.

Delgado Bernal, D. (1998). Using a Chicana feminist epistemology in educational research. *Harvard Educational Review, 68,* 555–582. doi:http://dx.doi.org/10.17763/haer.68.4.5wv1034973g22q48

Delgado Bernal, D., Burciaga, R., & Flores Carmona, J. (Eds.). (2012). Chicana/Latina testimonios: Mapping the methodological, pedagogical and political. *Equity & Excellence in Education, 45,* 363–372. doi:10.1080/10665684.2012.698149

Delgado Bernal, D., Elenes, C. A., Godinez, F. E., & Villenas, S. (Eds.). (2006). *Chicana/Latina education in everyday life: Feminist perspectives on pedagogy and epistemology.* Albany: SUNY Press.

Delpit, L. (2006). *Other's people children: Cultural conflict in the classroom* (2nd ed.). New York, NY: New Press.

Delpit, L. (2012). *"Multiplication is for white people:" Raising expectations for other people's children.* New York, NY: New Press.

Delpit, L., & Dowdy, J. (Eds.). (2002). *The skin that we speak: Thoughts on language and culture in the classroom.* New York, NY: New Press.

Delpit, L., & White-Bradley, P. (2003) Educating or imprisoning the spirit: Lessons from ancient Egypt. *Theory Into Practice, 42,* 283–288. doi:10.1207/s15430421tip4204_4

Demas, E., & Saavedra, C. M. (2004). Reconceptualizing language advocacy: Weaving a postmodern mestizaje image of language. In K. Mutua, & B. Swadener's (Eds.), *Decolonizing research in cross-cultural contexts: Critical personal narratives* (pp. 215–234). New York: SUNY Press.

Derrida, J. (1976). *Of grammatology* (G. C. Spivak, Trans.). Baltimore, MD: Johns Hopkins University Press.

Derrida, J. (1981). *Dissemination* (B. Johnson, Trans.). Chicago, IL: University of Chicago Press.

de Sousa Santos, B. (2012). Public sphere and epistemologies of the south. *Africa Development, 37*(1), 43–67.

Dickinson, D. K. (2002). Shifting images of developmentally appropriate practice as seen through different lenses. *Educational Researcher, 31*(1), 26–32.

Dillard, C. B. (2006). *On spiritual strivings: Transforming an African American woman's academic life.* Albany: SUNY Press.

Dillard, C. B. (2012). *Learning to (re)member the things we've learned to forget: Endarkened feminisms, spirituality, & the sacred nature of research & teaching.* New York, NY: Peter Lang.

Dixon, D., & Jones, J. P., III. (1998). My dinner with Derrida, or spatial analysis and post-structuralism do lunch. *Environmental and Planning A, 36,* 247–260.

Elenes, C. A. (1997). Reclaiming the borderlands: Chicana/o identity, difference, and critical pedagogy. *Educational Theory, 47,* 359–375.

Elenes, C. A. (2000). Chicana feminist narrative and the politics of the self. *Frontiers, 11*(3), 105–123.

Elenes, C. A. (2013). Nepantla, spiritual activism, new tribalism: Chicana feminist transformative pedagogies and social justice. *Journal of Latino/Latin American Studies, 5,* 132–141.

Ellsworth, J., & Ames, L. J. (Eds.). (1998). Critical perspectives on project Head Start: Revisioning the hope and challenge. Albany: SUNY Press.

Evans-Winters, V. E., & Love, B. L. (Eds.). (2015a). *Black feminism in education: Black women speak back, up and out.* New York, NY: Peter Lang.

Evans-Winters, V. E., & Love, B. L. (2015b). Why we matter: An interview with Dr. Cynthia Dillard (Nana Mansa II of Mpeasem, Ghana, West Africa). In V. E. Evans-Winters, & B. L. Love (Eds.), *Black feminism in education: Black women speak back, up and out* (pp. 201–209). New York, NY: Peter Lang.

Fleer, M., Hedegaard, M., & Tudge, J. (2008). Constructing childhood: Global-local policies and practices. In M. Fleer, M. Hedegaard, & J. Tudge (Eds.), *Childhood studies and the impact of globalization: Policies and practices at global and local levels* (pp. 1–20). New York, NY: Taylor & Francis.

Foucault, M. (1972). *The archeology of knowledge* (A. M. S. Smith, Trans.). New York, NY: Pantheon.

Foucault, M. (1977). *Discipline and punish: The birth of the prison.* New York, NY: Pantheon.

Foucault, M. (1978). *The history of sexuality* (Vols. 1–3). New York, NY: Pantheon.

Franquiz, M., Avila, A., & Ayala, B. (2013). Engaging bilingual students in sustained literature study central Texas. *Journal of Latino/Latin American Studies, 5,* 142–155.

Freire, P. (1978). Conscientization for liberation: Notions on the word conscientization. In C. A. Torres (Ed.), *The educational praxis of Paulo Freire* (pp. 107–120). Mexico City, Mexico: Ediciones Gernika.

Genishi, C., & Goodwin, A. L. (Eds.). (2007). *Diversities in early childhood education: Rethinking and doing.* New York, NY: Teachers College Press.

González, N. (2005). Beyond culture: The hybridity of funds of knowledge. In N. González, L. C. Moll, & C. C. Amanti (Eds.), *Funds of knowledge: Theorizing practices in households, communities, and classrooms* (pp. 29–46). New York, NY: Routledge.

González, N., Moll, L. C., & Amanti, C. (Eds.). (2005). *Funds of knowledge: Theorizing practices in households, communities, and classrooms.* New York, NY: Routledge.

Goodwin, A. L., Cheruvu, R., & Genishi, C. (2007). Responding to multiple diversities in early childhood education: How far have we come? In C. Genishi, & A. L. Goodwin (Eds.), *Diversities in early childhood education: Rethinking and doing* (pp. 3–11). New York, NY: Teachers College Press.

Gould, S. (1981). *The mismeasure of man.* New York, NY: W. W. Norton.

Grant, C. A., & Sleeter, C. E. (1990). *After the school bell rings* (2nd ed.). Philadelphia, PA: Falmer.

Graue, M. E. (1993). *Ready for what? Constructing meanings of readiness for kindergarten.* Albany: SUNY Press.

Graue, M. E. (2006). The answer is readiness—Now what is the question? *Early Education and Development, 17*(1), 43–54.

Grosfoguel, R. (2008). Transmodernity, border thinking, and global coloniality: Decolonizing political economy and postcolonial studies. *Eurozine*. Retrieved from http://www.eurozine.com/articles/2008-07-04-grosfoguel-pt.html

Guba, E. G., & Lincoln, Y. S. (2005). Paradigmatic controversies, contradictions, and emerging confluences. In N. Denzin, & Y. S. Lincoln (Eds.), *The SAGE handbook of qualitative research* (3rd ed., pp. 191–215). Thousand Oaks, CA: SAGE.

Gutierrez, K., Bien, A. C., Selland, M. K., & Pierce, D. M. (2011). Polylingual and polycultural learning ecologies: Mediating emergent academic literacies for dual language learners. *Journal of Early Childhood Literacy, 11*, 232–261. doi:10.1177/1468798411399273

Guy-Sheftall, B. (Ed.). (1995). *Words of fire: An anthology of African American feminist thought*. New York, NY: New Press.

Habashi, J. (2005). Creating indigenous discourse: History, power and imperialism in academia. *Qualitative Inquiry, 11*, 711–788.

Haraway, D. (1991). *Simians, cyborgs and women: The reinvention of nature*. New York, NY: Routledge.

Haraway, D. J. (2004). Otherworldly conversations; terran topics; local terms. In *The Haraway reader* (pp. 125–150). New York, NY: Routledge.

Harms, T., Clifford, R. M., & Cryer, D. (2004). *Early Childhood Environment Rating Scale–Revised edition*. New York, NY: Teachers College Press.

Harms, T., Clifford, R. M., & Cryer, D. (2006). *Infant/Toddler Environment Rating Scale–Revised Edition*. New York, NY: Teachers College Press.

hooks, b. (2000). *Feminist theory: From margin to center* (2nd ed.). Cambridge, MA: South End Press.

hooks, b. (2006). *Homegrown: Engaged cultural criticism*. Cambridge, MA: South End Press.

hooks, b. (2010). *Teaching critical thinking: Practical wisdom*. New York, NY: Taylor & Francis.

Iorio, J., Parnell, W., & Borch, K. (Eds.). (2015). *Rethinking readiness in early childhood education: Implications for policy and practice*. New York, NY: Palgrave.

James, A., & Prout, A. (Eds.). (1990). *Constructing and reconstructing childhood: Contemporary issues in the sociological study of childhood*. London, England: Routledge

Jenks, C. (Ed.). (2005). *Childhood* (2nd ed.). London, England: Routledge.

Kaomea, J. (2005). Reflections of an "always already" failing Native Hawaiian mother: Deconstructing colonial discourses on indigenous childbearing and early childhood education. *Hulili: Multidisciplinary Research on Hawaiian Well-Being, 2*(1), 67–85.

Keating, A. (2013). *Transformation now! Toward a post-oppositional politics of change*. Urbana: University of Illinois Press.

Kincheloe, J. L., & McLaren, P. (2005). Rethinking critical theory and qualitative research. In N. Denzin, & Y. S. Lincoln (Eds.), *The SAGE handbook of qualitative research* (3rd ed., pp. 303–342). Thousand Oaks, CA: SAGE.

Kumashiro, K. K. (2009). *Against common sense: Teaching and learning toward social justice* (2nd ed.). New York, NY: Routledge.

Ladson-Billings, G. (1994). *The dreamkeepers: Successful teachers of African American children*. San Francisco, CA: Jossey-Bass.

Ladson-Billings, G. (2000). Racialized discourses and ethnic epistemologies. In N. Denzin, & Y. S. Lincoln (Eds.), *The SAGE handbook of qualitative research* (2nd ed., pp. 257–277). Thousand Oaks, CA: SAGE.

The Latina Feminist Group. (2001). *Telling to live: Latina feminist testimonio*. Durham, NC: Duke University Press.

Latour, B. (2004). *The politics of nature: How to bring the sciences into democracy* (C. Porter, Trans.). Cambridge, MA: Harvard University Press.

Lincoln, Y. S., & Guba, E. G. (1985). *Naturalistic inquiry.* Newbury Park, CA: SAGE.

Lomawaima, K. T., & McCarty, T. L. (2002). *To remain an Indian: Lessons in democracy from a century of Native American education.* New York, NY: Teachers College Press.

Lorde, A. (1984). *Sister outsider: Essays and speeches by Audre Lorde.* Berkeley, CA: Crossing Press.

Lopez, R. (1997). The practical impact of current research and issues in intelligence test interpretation and use for multicultural populations. *School Psychology Review, 26,* 249–254.

Lubeck, S. (1996). Deconstructing "child development knowledge" and "teacher preparation." *Early Childhood Quarterly, 11,* 146–167.

MacNaughton, G. (2005). *Doing Foucault in early childhood studies: Applying post-structural ideas.* New York, NY: Routledge.

Maparyan, L. (2012). *The womanist idea.* New York, NY: Routledge.

Marx, S., & Saavedra, C. M. (2014). Understanding the epistemological divide in ESL education: What we learned from a failed university-school district collaboration. *Urban Education, 49,* 418–439.

McCarty, T. L. (2002). *A place to be Navajo-Rough Rock and the struggle for self determination in Indigenous schooling.* Mahwah, NJ: Lawrence Erlbaum, 2002.

Meyer, M. A. (2008). Indigenous and authentic: Hawaiian epistemology and the triangulation of meaning. In N. K. Denzin, Y. S. Lincoln, & L. T. Smith (Eds.), *Handbook of critical and indigenous methodologies* (pp. 217–232). Thousand Oaks, CA: SAGE.

Montaño, T., & Quintanar-Sarellana, R. (2011). Undoing Ruby Payne and other deficit views of English language learners. In R. Ahlquist, P. C. Gorski, & T. Montaño (Eds.), *Assault on kids: How hyper-accountability, corporatization, deficit ideologies, and Ruby Payne are destroying our schools* (pp. 199–213). New York, NY: Peter Lang.

Moraga, C. (1983). *Loving in the war years.* Boston, MA: South End Press.

Moraga, C. (1983). Theories in the flesh. In C. Moraga, & G. Anzaldúa (Eds.), *This bridge called my back: Writings by radical women of color* (p. 23). Watertown, MA: Persephone Press.

Moraga, C. (1993). *The last generation: Prose and poetry.* Boston, MA: South End Press.

Moraga, C., & Anzaldúa, G. (1983). *This bridge called my back: Writings by radical women of color.* Watertown, MA: Persephone Press.

Morrison, T. (1994). *The bluest eye.* New York, NY: Plume.

National Council for Accreditation of Teacher Education. (2010). *Transforming teacher education through clinical practice: A national strategy to prepare effective teachers.* Washington DC: Author.

Nsamenang, B. (1999). Eurocentric image of childhood in the context of world's cultures. Essay review of *Images of Childhood* edited by Philip. C. Hwang, Michael Lamb, & Irving E. Sigel. Mahwah, NJ: Lawrence Erlbaum. *Human Development, 42,* 159–168.

Nieto, S. (1996). *Affirming diversity: The sociopolitical context of multicultural education* (2nd ed.). White Plains, NJ: Longman.

Nieto, S. (2010). *The light in their eyes: Creating multicultural learning communities* (10th Anniversary ed.). New York, NY: Teachers College Press.

Norton, N. E. L. (2008). Singing in the spirit: Spiritual practices inside public school classrooms. *Education and Urban Society, 40,* 342–360.

Olsson, L. M. (2009). *Movement and experimentation in young children's learning: Deleuze and Guattari in early childhood education.* New York, NY: Routledge

Orellana, M. F. (2001). The work kids do: Mexican and Central American immigrant children's contributions to households and schools in California. *Harvard Educational Review, 71,* 366–389.

Pacini-Ketchabaw, V. (2007). Racialized migrant women's narratives on child care: An antiracist, transnational feminist analysis. *International Journal of Equity and Innovation in Early Childhood Education, 5*(1), 69–88.

Pérez, E. (1999). *The decolonial imaginary: Writing Chicanas into history*. Bloomington: Indiana University Press.

Pérez, M. S. (2014). Complicating "victim" narratives: Childhood agency within violent circumstances. *Global Studies of Childhood, 4,* 126–134.

Pérez, M. S. (2017). Black feminist thought in early childhood studies: (Re)centering marginalized feminist perspectives. In K. Smith, K. Alexander, & S. Campbell (Eds.), *Feminism in early childhood* (pp. 49–62). New York, NY: Springer.

Pérez, M. S., & Cahill, B. (2015). "Readiness" as central to the (re)production of quality discourses in the United States: An early childhood public policy analysis. In G. S. Cannella, M. S. Pérez, & I. F. Lee (Eds.), *Critical examinations of quality in childhood education and care: Regulation, disqualification, and erasure* (pp. 8–25). New York, NY: Peter Lang.

Pérez, M. S., & Cannella, G. S. (2011). Disaster capitalism as neoliberal instrument for the construction of early childhood education/care policy: Charter schools in post-Katrina New Orleans. *International Critical Childhood Policy Studies Journal, 4*(1), 47–68.

Pérez, M. S., Medellin, K., & Rideaux, K. (2016). Repositioning childhood experiences within adult contexts: A Black feminist analysis of childhood/s regulation in early childhood care and education. *Global Studies of Childhood, 6*(1), 67–79.

Pérez, M. S., Ruiz Guerrero, M. G., & Mora, E. (2016). Black feminist photovoice: Fostering critical awareness of diverse families and communities in early childhood teacher education. *Journal of Early Childhood Teacher Education, 37*(1), 41–60.

Pérez, M. S., & Saavedra, C. M. (2014). Black and Chicana feminisms: Journeys towards spirituality and reconnection. In M. Bloch, B. B. Swadender, & G. S. Cannella (Eds.), *Reconceptualizing early childhood care and education: Critical questions, new imaginaries and social activism* (pp. 157–166). New York, NY: Peter Lang.

Pérez, M. S., & Saavedra, C. M. (2015, October). *Black and Chicana feminisms: (Re)centering marginalized perspectives in early childhood education and care.* Paper presented at the 23rd Reconceptualizing Early Childhood Education conference, Dublin, Ireland.

Pérez, M. S., & Williams, E. (2014). Black feminist activism: Theory as generating collective resistance. *Multicultural Perspectives, 16,* 125–132.

Phillips, C. (1994). The movement of African-American children through sociocultural contexts. In B. L. Mallory, & R. S. New (Eds.), *Diversity and developmentally appropriate practices: Challenges for early childhood education* (pp. 137–153). New York, NY: Teachers College Press.

Prieto, L. (2013). Maestras constructing mestizaje consciousness through agency within bilingual education. *Journal of Latino/Latin American Studies, 5,* 167–180.

Rau, C., & Ritchie, J. (2011). Ahakoa he iti: Early childhood pedagogies affirming of Māori children's rights to their culture. *Early Education and Development, 22,* 795–817.

Redeaux, M. (2011). A framework for maintaining white privilege: A critique of Ruby Payne. In R. Ahlquist, P. C. Gorski, & T. Montaño (Eds.), *Assault on kids: How hyper-accountability, corporatization, deficit ideologies, and Ruby Payne are destroying our schools* (pp. 177–198). New York, NY: Peter Lang.

Red Leaf Press. (n.d.). *Early childhood environment rating scale revised edition, description.* Retrieved from http://www.redleafpress.org/Early-Childhood-Environment-Rating-Scale-Revised-Edition-P88.aspx?gclid=CIzA0O7NncwCFQKTaQodQYEETQ

Reyes, K. B., & Curry Rodriguez, J. E. (2012). Testimonio: Origins, terms and resources. *Equity & Excellence in Education, 45,* 525–538.

Reza-López, E., Huerta Charles, L., & Reyes, L. V. (2014). Nepantlera pedagogy: An axiological posture for preparing critically conscious teachers in the borderlands. *Journal of Latinos and Education, 13,* 107–119. doi:10.1080/15348431.2013.821062

Riojas-Cortez, M. (2001). Pre-schoolers' funds of knowledge displayed through sociodramatic play episodes in a bilingual classroom. *Early Childhood Education Journal, 29,* 35–40.

Ritchie, J., & Rau, C. (2013). Renarrativizing Indigenous rights-based provision within "mainstream" early childhood services. In B. B. Swadener, L. Lundy, J. Habashi, & N. Blanchet-Cohen (Eds.), *Children's rights and education: International perspectives* (pp. 133–149). New York, NY: Peter Lang.

Rorty, R. (Ed.). (1967). *The linguistic turn: Recent essays in philosophical method.* Chicago, IL: University of Chicago Press.

Rose, N. (1990). *Governing the soul: The shaping of the private self.* London, England: Routledge.

Ross, E. W., & Gibson, R. (Eds.). (2007). *Neoliberalism and education reform.* Cresskill, NJ: Hampton Press.

Saavedra, C. M. (2011a). De-academizing early childhood research: Wanderings from a Chicana/Latina feminist researcher. *Journal of Latinos and Education, 10,* 286–298. doi:1 0.1080/15348431.2011.605678).

Saavedra, C. M. (2011b). Language and literacies in the borderlands: Acting upon the world through testimonios. *Language Arts, 88,* 261–269.

Saavedra, C. M., & Nymark, E. D. (2008). Borderland-mestizaje feminism: The new tribalism. In N. K. Denzin, Y. S. Lincoln, & L. Tuhiwai-Smith's (Eds.), *Handbook of critical and indigenous methodologies* (pp. 255–276). Thousand Oaks, CA: SAGE.

Saavedra, C. M., & Pérez, M. S. (2012). Chicana and Black feminisms: Testimonios of theory, identity and multiculturalism. *Equity & Excellence in Education, 45*(3), 1–14.

Saldivar-Hull, S. (2000). *Feminism on the border: Chicana gender politics and literature.* Berkeley: University of California Press.

Skerrett, M. (2015). The determinants of "quality" in Aotearoa/New Zealand: Māori perspectives. In G. S. Cannella, M. S. Pérez, & I. Lee (Eds.), *Critical examinations of quality in early education and care: Regulation, disqualification, and erasure* (pp. 59–82). New York, NY: Peter Lang.

Smith, L. T. (1999). *Decolonizing methodologies: Research and indigenous peoples.* London, England: Zed Books.

Smith, S. (1996). Positivism and beyond. In S. Smith, K. Booth, & M. Zalewski (Eds.), *International theory: Positivism and beyond* (pp. 11–44). Cambridge, MA: Cambridge University Press.

Soto, L. D (1997). Constructivist Theory in the Age of Newt Gingrich: The post-formal concern with power. *Journal of Early Childhood Teacher Education, 18*(2), 43–57.

Soto, L. D. (2001). *Making a difference in the lives of bilingual/bicultural children.* New York, NY: Peter Lang.

Soto, L. D. (2009). Toward a "critical emancipatory mezcla praxis": Xicana participatory action research in teacher education. In S. Mitakidou, E. Tressou, B. Swadener, & C. Grant (Eds.), *Beyond pedagogies of exclusion in diverse childhood contexts: Transnational challenges* (pp. 167–176). New York, NY: Palgrave Macmillan.

Souto-Manning, M. (2010). *Freire, teaching, and learning: Culture circles across contexts.* New York, NY: Peter Lang.

Souto-Manning, M. (2013). *Multicultural teaching in the early childhood classroom: Approaches, strategies, and tools preschool-2nd grade.* New York, NY: Teachers College Press.

Spring, J. (2010). *Deculturalization and the struggle for equality: A brief history of the education of dominated cultures in the United States.* New York, NY: McGraw-Hill.

St. Pierre, E. A. (2016). The empirical and the new empiricisms. *Cultural Studies ↔ Critical Methodologies, 16,* 111–124.

Swadener, B. B., & Lubeck, S. (Eds.). (1995). *Children and families "at promise": Deconstructing the discourse of risk.* Albany: SUNY Press.

Taylor, A. (2013). *Reconfiguring the natures of childhood.* London, England: Routledge.

Trinidad Galván, R. (2014). Chicana/Latin America feminist epistemologies of the global south (within and outside the north): Decolonizing el concocimeiento and creating global alliances. *Journal of Latino/Latin American Studies, 6,* 135–140.

Trujillo, C. (Ed.). (1998). *Living Chicana theory*. Berkeley, CA: Third Woman Press.

Valenzuela, A. (Ed.). (2016). *Growing critically conscious teachers: A social justice curriculum for educators of Latino/a youth*. New York, NY: Teachers College Press.

Villenas, S., Godinez, F. E., Delgado Bernal, D., & Elenes, C. A. (2006). Chicanas/Latinas building bridges: An Introduction. In D. Delgado Bernal, C. A. Elenes, F. E. Godinez, & S. Villenas (Eds.), *Chicana/Latina education in everyday life: Feminist perspectives on pedagogy and epistemology* (pp. 1–9). Albany: SUNY Press.

Viruru, R. (2001). *Early childhood education: Postcolonial perspectives from India*. San Francisco, CA: SAGE.

Walker, A. (1983). *In search of our mother's gardens*. New York, NY: Harcourt Brace Jovanovich.

Walkerdine, V. (1984). Developmental psychology and the child-centered pedagogy. In J. Henriques, W. Holloway, C. Urwin, C. Venn, & V. Walkerdine (Eds.), *Changing the subject: Psychology, social regulation and subjectivity* (pp. 153–202). London, England: Methuen.

Walkerdine, V. (1993). Beyond developmentalism? *Theory & Psychology, 3*, 451–469.

Wang, C. C., & Burris, M. A. (1997). Photovoice: Concept, methodology, and use for participatory needs assessment. *Health Education & Behavior, 24*, 369–387.

Washington, M. H. (Ed.). (1975). *Black-eyed Susans: Classic stories by and about Black women*. Garden City, NY: Anchor.

Chapter 2

Replacing Representation With Imagination: Finding Ingenuity in Everyday Practices

Kris D. Gutiérrez
Krista Cortes
Arturo Cortez
University of California, Berkeley

Daniela DiGiacomo
University of California, Riverside

Jennifer Higgs
Patrick Johnson
José Ramón Lizárraga
University of California, Berkeley

Elizabeth Mendoza
University of California, Santa Cruz

Joanne Tien
University of California, Berkeley

Sepehr Vakil
University of Texas at Austin

This chapter is a call for consequential education research that has transformative potential: intellectually, educationally, and socially. It is about learning to see differently. It is an argument about seeing our work with youth and communities in ways that can help education researchers see ingenuity instead of ineptness and inability, to see resilience instead of deficit, and to imagine futures with youth from nondominant communities instead of imposing failure. We use the notion of "learning to see" both metaphorically and as a theoretical lens and methodological guide to illustrate how rigorous and consequential education research can help us imagine and design new forms of learning and schooling. We argue that rupturing educational inequality also involves new forms of inquiry that help reconceptualize what it means to work with nondominant communities.

Review of Research in Education
March 2017, Vol. 41, pp. 30–60
DOI: 10.3102/0091732X16687523

The kind of "seeing" on which we focus is undergirded by a historical epistemology (Wartofsky, 1979) that counters ahistorical and universalist notions of epistemology, the study of the nature of knowledge itself. As Wartofsky argues, how we observe, discern, or perceive has a history (p. 189). And if objects of perception are transformed by human thought and action, then perceptions are cultural historical artifacts. From this perspective, are not nondominant communities, their learning, and their worth the objectification of a mode of perception (Gutiérrez, 2016)? These are questions with which we grapple in our work as methodologists, learning scientists, and critical scholars.

As we have written elsewhere (Gutiérrez, 2016), our work is organized around proleptic and future-oriented arrangements for learning and the social world that involve more robust ways of seeing individuals, communities, and their practices. Toward this end, this review and discussion of relevant literature, including our own work, is designed to move beyond traditional questions of representation in education research toward those grounded in imagination, as Wartofsky (1979) directs us. For us, representation is deeply intertwined with how we theorize our work with communities, our knowledge of the history of their practices (including both those stable and divergent), the constructs that orient our work, and our relationship in and to the communities in which we work. However, representation also involves how we perceive the possibilities of youth and communities, an aspect that is not often addressed in traditional research. In this chapter, we call attention to the importance of employing a historicized and future-oriented ecological approach, while remaining embedded and contextualized in participants' meaningful everyday life activity to capture the fullness of people's activities, as well as their potential (Engeström, 2008). Learning to see the past and future in the present, as Cole and Distributive Literacy Consortium (2006) has reminded us, is key to co-imagining new social futures for people, their communities, and schools and to seeing ingenuity in the everyday practices of nondominant communities.

There is a long history of research that has served to pathologize nondominant communities, and much has been written in that regard. Instead of revisiting that work, we begin by contextualizing our argument in scholarship that makes visible that history of research, proffering critiques of the narrow and static frames that produce flat renderings of communities. Research that diminishes differences that matter in nondominant communities involves more than methodological sloppiness. Failure to capture the regularity and variance in communities, the nuanced textures of community members' lives, and the ingenuity that is inherent in human activity contributes to flawed research, poor educational and social policies and practices, and persistent racialized perceptions of communities and their practices. Flattened representations of communities lead us away from seeing the complexity and diversity in human activity (Gutiérrez & Arzubiaga, 2012). And in doing so, such work propels research that is incomplete and inaccurate and serves to stigmatize rather than expand our understanding of human learning activity.

We begin by highlighting the work of scholars from nondominant communities who have pushed back on the ways cultural communities have been studied and represented, and the conclusions drawn based on those analyses. We then present a discussion of design-based research (DBR) approaches that conceptualize and engage communities as partners in addressing important problems of practice. We elaborate one particular approach to DBR, social design–based experiments (SDBEs), and address several of its key dimensions: a historicized ecological approach and a focus on people's everyday practices as a productive unit of analysis for understanding human activity and the learning therein. In the final section, we draw on our current research with a cohort of families to discuss the ingenuity in youth and families' everyday and new media practices. In particular, we focus on one kind of ingenuity, what we identify as a kind of boundary crossing, to illustrate how families innovate and leverage familial and other everyday knowledge to imagine and enact new practices. We use this work as an example of how we might reconceive our perceptions of people-in-practice, that is, the way we see and work with nondominant communities. In general, the challenge we raise here is how to do empirical work that captures the full range of a community's activities toward deeper analyses of the community's ecology, the available resources and constraints of the ecology, and the influences on everyday practices. The task becomes more complex but necessary when we account for race and ethnicity and racialized practices, and when we attempt to account for local, distal, and historical influences that mediate people's activity (Gutiérrez & Arzubiaga, 2012).

REFRAMING THE PAST FOR THE FUTURE: RESEARCH ON NONDOMINANT COMMUNITIES

In this section, we focus on how past and contemporary theorizations of and approaches to studying nondominant communities often render individuals and communities as the problem— deficient or dysfunctional—rather than addressing the relevant pressing social or educational problems. Even when it is not the intent, our analytical frames and constructs employed lie at the intersection of our methods, theoretical perspectives, our commonsense assumptions, practices, and the position of power and privilege we hold vis-à-vis the communities we study and teach (Gutiérrez, 2006). In order to call attention to this power differential and begin to counter a deficit perspective, we prefer the term *nondominant* to others such as minority, marginal, at-risk, or disadvantaged, for example (Gutiérrez, Morales, & Martinez, 2009).

We have argued that theorizing and studying communities—especially those different from our own—require us to examine the ideological positions at work in the constructs and methods we employ. We have highlighted the importance of attending, in particular, to the history of constructs we use in our research, their use, as well as the frameworks and fields in which they operate—with attention to what has been naturalized and what has been ignored. For example, there is a need to examine what has been normalized in commonplace education terms such as "disadvantaged, at risk, underclass, community, diversity, urban, rural, immigrant, refugee, migrant, English Learners, and code-switching" (Gutiérrez, 2006, p. 227). The analytical directive here is to ask, What has already been taken for granted or assumed in these concepts and their use? What are the material effects of the resulting analyses on nondominant communities and the kinds of policies and practice we recommend? These are not simply ideological questions; they are central to the conduct of rigorous, useful, and consequential research.

Nondominant communities have grown skeptical of research purported to be about or in service to them, as researchers are often complicit in framing these students in damaging ways (Gutiérrez & Arzubiaga, 2012; Tuck, 2009). Traditionally, researchers have entered communities bringing with them unacknowledged power and privileges that narrowly shape how these communities are seen (Gutiérrez, 2006). Deficit-centered research is rooted in maintaining unequal relationships between participants and investigators. Specifically, those conducting the research reify and shape a narrative of nondominant communities that centralizes damage, pain, depletion, and loss (Tuck, 2009). The resulting research often lays claim to people's existing knowledge while diminishing the value and agency of these very people in the process; ultimately, such research offers little benefit for the participants and instead allows those who are already privileged to profit (Smith, 1999).

We address in this article several ways research can undo its purpose and highlight scholarship that offers new research sensibilities. We argue the importance of examining the role that our theories and methods play in circumscribing and narrowing what can be known. Theoretical constructs rooted in deficiency can overdetermine the orientation a researcher may take toward a community and its inhabitants. Consider, for example, historian Robin Kelley's (2004) critique of the concept of the "ghetto" and the work it does to one's perception of and position toward research in African American communities. Kelley contends that social scientists constructed the idea of the ghetto in their quest to define an authentic Black culture—a perception that framed their expectation to see only destitute Black men, gangstas and thugs, and young women with children out of wedlock (p. 122). These tropes mirror rather than challenge those reproduced in popular culture and media; the resulting research furthers the deficit narrative. Kelley contrasts social scientists' reliance on stereotypical characters by referencing the "everyday people" who inhabited his diverse West Harlem neighborhood as a youth:

Of course, there were other characters, like the men and women who went to work every day in foundries, hospitals, nursing homes, private homes, police stations, sanitation departments, banks, garment factories, assembly plants, pawn shops, construction sites, loading docks, storefront churches, telephone companies, grocery and department stores, public transit, restaurants, welfare offices, recreation centers; or the street vendors, the cab drivers, the bus drivers, the ice cream truck drivers, the seamstresses, the numerologists and fortune tellers, the folks who protected or cleaned downtown buildings all night long. (p. 122)

The specificity and variance captured in Kelley's (2004) description illustrates the merit of the mundane, the richness in the regular.

On the other hand, the persistent assumption of a homogenous African American neighborhood, as found in the "ghetto," is often extrapolated to construct a quintessential image of the Black neighborhood. As sociologist Mario Small (2008) observes,

Ethnographers . . . describ[ing] conditions in a given poor Black neighborhood—say a drug transaction on a desolate Detroit street corner—[. . .] rely on the reader's tacit agreement that the patterns described therein manifest themselves similarly in poor Black neighborhoods in Philadelphia, Cincinnati, Los Angeles, and other cities. (p. 390)

Research can feed this recurring imagery in popular culture by painting the ghetto as desolate without recognizing the range of inhabitation that occurs in these areas (Small, 2008). Such analyses support other broad-brush explanations for social problems. For example, in challenging the assumption that Black people remain in ghettos because they are unable to move elsewhere, Small (2008) offers, "Residential segregation results from a complex combination of institutional and interpersonal, economic and cultural, majority-driven and minority-driven factors" (p. 395). He calls for complexity that better reflects the reality of human activity, and challenges models that do not "see" the agency of either the poor or African Americans (p. 395). In fact, he argues, these models "obscure more than they illuminate" (p. 395). Conquergood (2002) discusses research conducted in this way as "epistemic violence" that forecloses the "finely nuanced meaning that is embodied, tacit, intoned, gestured, improvised, co-experienced, [and] covert" in the practices of nondominant communities (p. 146). Rather than recognizing the plethora of cultural resources that exist in communities, research has tended to focus on what is lacking.

As illustrated above, this review is concerned, in part, with how reductive conceptions of culture and traditional forms of research portray practices in which young people and their families participate—particularly those of migrant, immigrant, and diasporic communities—as being deficient or aberrant from dominant cultural practices. It is also concerned with how static notions of culture and cultural communities advance assumptions of homogeneity about nondominant communities that influences the research produced. Even when following canonical methods that conceptualize culture-as-text and fieldwork-as-reading (Geertz, 1973), we are led to believe that meaning resides in what we see if only we look hard enough. Understanding ethnography as "trying to read [. . .] a manuscript" (Geertz, 1973, p. 10) privileges ways of knowing and doing that uphold the values of the researcher, while silencing those being researched by positioning the researcher as the only possible knower of reality. As John Jackson (2013) notes, in pretending to see everything, we see less than we could (p. 14).

In his book, *Thin Description: Ethnography and the Hebrew Israelites of Jerusalem,* Jackson (2013) argues that the notion of "thin description is a response to a kind of overconfidence in anthropology, an arrogance borne of the powers that 'thick description' . . . is believed to grant adherents" (p. 13). Jackson's critique is not so much an argument about how Geertz (1973) and others privileged "symbolic interpretation to cross-cultural understanding and analysis" (p. 13); rather, the central issue is that the currency of thick description should be reconsidered. Jackson elaborates,

And these days, even shorn of its strictest Geertzian moorings, "thick description" is used like a mystic metaphor or methodological talisman that denotes an attempt at—an ambition for—rich, rigorous, and even *full* social knowing. . . . The popular imagery anthropologists use to mark this thicked knowledge is revealing, discussions of anthropologists morphing into "flies on the wall" or "seeing through other people's [blinking and winking and fake-winking] eyes"—or even (at the frowned-upon extreme) simply "going native." These aspirations and characterizations signal some of the hubris at the center of the anthropological project, a hubris that has always probably imagined ethnographic thickness to be far thicker than it actually is. (p. 14)

Learning how to see complexity and resilience in people's practices requires us to care for multiplicity and variance in our work. It also involves learning *where* to see. Scholars employing cultural-historical approaches to human development with interpretive and multisited ethnography argue the need for tools that better capture youths' learning within and across multiple contexts. A multisited ethnographic sensibility opens up the space for a more expansive approach to learning—one that focuses on the learning that takes hold as people move within and across practices (Gutiérrez, 2008; Vossoughi & Gutiérrez, 2014). Furthermore, when the analytical lens shifts from youths' perceived deficiencies to the ways their repertoires of practice are developed, extended, and leveraged across time and space, it becomes easier to see and "to better account for their history of involvement in a range of practices and to attend to what is learned in the boundary and border crossings, across hybrid spaces and activity system" (Vossoughi & Gutiérrez, 2014, p. 604). Drawing in part from Marcus (1995), as we elaborate later, this approach argues for a "multisited ethnographic sensibility" that understands learning as "movement" within and across activity systems—a view that recognizes that people participate and are part of multiple activity systems and that learning and human activity should be studied accordingly (Vossoughi & Gutiérrez, 2014, p. 607).

When we ground research in dominant epistemologies that are based on Western ways of seeing (Bang, Medin, Washinawatok, & Chapman, 2010), practices that are commonplace in nondominant communities become ". . . masked, camouflaged, indirect, embedded or hidden in context" (Conquergood, 2002, p. 146). Tacit forms of expression, what de Certeau calls (2000) "the elocutionary experience of a fugitive communication," require the researcher to take up new ways of seeing that open up space for the indirectness, the mundane, of the everyday (p. 133).

One example of this kind of research in education comes from the tradition of participatory design where researchers work "side by side" (Erickson, 2006) with research participants to tackle practical and theoretical problems of mutual concern (e.g., Cammarota & Fine, 2008, Gutiérrez & Vossoughi, 2010; Paris & Winn, 2013). Participatory approaches to education research highlight the intensely relational nature of conducting research with and alongside historically marginalized communities, relations that are always mediated by dynamics of race and power (Vakil, de Royston, Nasir, & Kirshner, 2016; Vossoughi, Hooper, & Escudé, 2016). Naming the often asymmetrical relationship itself can provide for richer analysis and understanding what it means to design for equity. DiGiacomo and Gutiérrez (2015) illustrate how particular social organizations of materials, peoples, and spaces afford different outcomes for community members. Specifically, the authors advance the concept of "relational equity" (p. 142) to describe the more symmetrical relationships central to robust and equitable learning. Here, "relational equity" is both tool and object of design. These perspectives highlight that there is real (ideological *and* practical) work involved in eschewing deficit perspectives, and learning to see communities differently. Designing research studies and analytical constructs to more deeply understand and appreciate the ingenuity of diverse communities cannot be divorced from the sociocultural processes of developing trust and solidarity with communities in which the research is being conducted.

Taken together, this interdisciplinary body of scholarship repositions and remediates the researcher's perception to make possible new ways of working in and with cultural communities. It opens up spaces for new relationships with communities and new designs that orient our work.

DESIGN-BASED RESEARCH/SOCIAL DESIGN–BASED EXPERIMENTS

In the past several decades, researchers have taken up the challenge of viewing research as a means to address a range of educational problems in ways that are more useful, collaborative, and socially relevant. This focus has been particularly evident in various forms of DBR. From more classical forms of design research (Cobb, Confrey, diSessa, Lehrer, & Schauble, 2003), to design-based intervention research (Penuel, Fishman, Cheng, & Sabelli, 2011), formative experiments (Engeström, 2011), SDBEs (Gutiérrez, 2008, 2016), to participatory design research (Bang & Vossoughi, 2016; Vakil et al., 2016), research is being reconceived in ways that decenters the researchers, and reframes the aims, goals, and outcomes of research. In particular, this body of work foregrounds important principles about knowledge production and tries to advance a new generation of methods with new sensibilities. In this section, we discuss work that addresses the tension between researchers and participants in ways that trouble, realign, and leverage participants' subject positions, and, more broadly, positions new kinds of work as rigorous, thoughtful, and consequential.

There is a rich history of contribution to our understanding of the transformative potential of people in communities that are vulnerable, yet replete with possibility (Gutiérrez, Engeström, & Sannino, 2016). And new forms of research are responding to the need to expand the ways social science research is conceptualized. Gutiérrez and Penuel (2014) argue that making "relevance to practice a key criterion of rigor" (p.19) supports a more equitable and consequential way of doing research. Bringing together contemporary equity-minded research on learning with DBR, they offer methodological strategies to address inequities in social science research:

Studying the "social life of interventions" moves us away from imagining interventions as fixed packages of strategies with readily measurable outcomes and toward more open-ended social or socially embedded experiments that involve ongoing mutual engagement. (p. 20)

By shifting normative and often deficit-reifying standards of what the "outcome" of research should be, Gutiérrez and Penuel (2014) suggest the aim of interventionist research as facilitating "participants in activity to deal with the historically accumulated tensions and contradictions of the systems within which they work in order to transform the activity of teaching and learning" (p. 22). Their work illustrates the contemporary sentiment emerging in design-based education research. Though this approach to research is still evolving, we find it important to provide a brief history of DBR and then highlight new approaches to design research that foreground equity and transformative kinds of learning.

Design-Based Research

Design-based research is interventionist research that evolved from a commitment to studying learning environments or learning ecologies, rather than isolated individual learners (Engeström, 2011). Broadly speaking, design-based researchers aim to design, carry out, and study an educational intervention in the real world—an intervention that is informed by prior research and that will help develop a local theory of learning as well as the means to support that learning (Collins, Joseph, & Bielaczyc, 2004). DBR is premised on five tenets: (1) generation of theories about learning processes and means to support those processes, (2) highly interventionist, (3) prospective and reflective, (4) highly iterative, and (5) use of humble theories that do real work (Cobb, Confrey, et al., 2003). Working within and across settings ranging from a technology-supported intervention in a classroom, to a district-level restructuring experiment, DBR takes as its unit of analysis elements of a learning ecology such as the kinds of discourse, norms of participation, and/or tools and related material means (Cobb, Confrey, et al., 2003). The researcher(s) in DBR is expected to let prior research guide current design and carry out investigations on the enactment of a particular local theory of learning.

Design-based research has contributed in significant ways to how people learn within and across complex learning ecologies (see Cobb, McClain, Gravemeijer, 2003; Jurow et al., 2008; Lehrer, Strom, & Confrey, 2002). From the evolution of strategies such as "reciprocal teaching" and "fostering a community of learners" to the design of "intentional learning environments" (Brown & Campione, 1990; Brown & Palincsar, 1989; Scardamalia & Bereiter, 1994), DBR has demonstrated its central commitment to iteration, collaboration, and utility for practical problem solving (Penuel et al., 2011), which has the potential to improve education research, as well as learning for diverse stakeholders and populations.

While DBR is best characterized as a research approach that can entail multiple methodologies, DBR researchers share a methodological and theoretical orientation to learning as situated within complex social ecologies (Lave, 1996; Vygotsky, 2004). Despite this common orientation to studying learning in context, and because of the wide-ranging methodological possibilities inherent to DBR research, Engeström (2011) has noted that the unit of analysis has often remained vague. As a result, it has been critiqued as having a weak "argumentative grammar" (Shavelson, Phillips, Towne, & Feuer, 2003) and lack of a strong conceptual structure and/or methodology (Kelly, 2004).

While the epistemic underpinnings of DBR have led to important theoretical and methodological consequences, more attention to how equity, diversity, and the role of participants are affected by this approach to education research is warranted. We draw here on Engeström's (2011) elaborated discussion of some of the limitations of DBR research that are instructive, while noting that later iterations of DBR have certainly been informed by first generation DBR. Engeström directs attention to the potential problematic in DBR with issues of who, what, and through what means knowledge and intended change are constructed and implemented, and raises the key question of "Who does the design, and why?" Because design-based researchers remain primarily responsible for the design, enactment, and analysis of the learning, their ontological and epistemological values and theories necessarily inform both the process and "end point" for the design experiment (Engeström, 2011). Accordingly, alongside the oft–well-intentioned and evidence-based research that informs the development of the theory guiding the intervention, there is potential for a misalignment with the ontological and epistemological values that imbue the context of the experiment itself. Said differently, because DBR is still primarily carried out from a "top-down," researcher-driven perspective, it carries with it the possibility of reifying normative and deficit-oriented conceptualizations of nondominant community practices and ways of being, as co-participation and co-design are not part of its conceptualization. As such, the transformative ability of DBR to respond robustly to issues of equity in education research and design is constrained, as well as the agency of the students and other stakeholders involved in the experiment. And despite commitment to iteration, there is a linearity to DBR that can obscure the reality that interventions are "contested terrains, full of resistance" (Engeström, 2011, p. 3).

Social Design–Based Experiments

While sharing features with more traditional forms of DBR, SDBEs depart from DBR in a number of ways, especially with regard to the roles of participants and researcher and the object of activity. Grounded in cultural historical activity theory (Cole, 1996; Cole & Levitin, 2000; Cole & Wertsch, 1997) and, in part, by the epistemological underpinnings of "formative experiments" (Cole & Engeström, 2007; Engeström, 2011; Engeström & Sannino, 2010), SDBEs evolved in response to a need for DBR to attend to issues of equity and diversity in ways that reflected the multiplicity of epistemologies that constitute a given learning ecology. While we will not elaborate SDBEs more fully in this chapter, briefly stated, the design principles foregrounded in this approach help construct an argumentative grammar built on hope and possibility. Specifically, its design principles of re-mediation, historicity, equity, resilience, transformability, and sustainability (Gutiérrez, 2016) help constitute an equity-oriented social change agenda that advances an emerging argumentative grammar that differs from others used to organize design research. What researchers do foregrounds the values and commitments of SDBEs, specifying how these commitments are operationalized in social design–based research, including how these commitments enter into everyday inquiry processes and the evaluation of the designed outcomes (American Educational Research Association, 2006; Gutiérrez & Jurow, 2014; Sandoval, 2014).

SDBEs are fundamentally about a re-mediation of the functional system (Cole & Griffin, 1986; Gutiérrez, 2005, 2008; Gutiérrez, Morales, & Martinez, 2009; Gutiérrez & Vossoughi, 2010), that is, a disruption in ways that participants in activity systems coordinate meaning with their environment. The concept of re-mediation versus remediation is more than just a play on words; it is significant to understanding transformation as the object of SDBEs (Cole & Griffin, 1983). The notion of re-mediation focuses attention to the social organization of a learning environment in ways that promote both individual and collective transformation (Cole & Griffin, 1983; Gutiérrez, Hunter, & Arzubiaga, 2009). Briefly, re-mediation involves the reorganization of systems and environments with a "conscious and strategic use of a range of theoretical and material tools" that promote learning and harness a student's repertoire of practice to create an environment where everyone can be "smart" (Gutiérrez et al., 2009, p. 12). Learning, within this perspective, is located both in the individual and the activity system itself: that is, it involves individual and collective transformation. In line with the principles of a design intervention known as a "change laboratory" (Engeström, 2011), SDBEs are oriented toward *expansive forms of learning*. Engeström and Sannino (2010) define expansive learning as "learning in which the learners are involved in constructing and implementing a radically new, wider, and more complex object and concept for their activity" (p. 2). With the development of a "mirror"[1] designed to support reflection in practice, participants are agentic in reflecting on, critically examining, and transforming their own activity in ways that lead to new concept formation, or expansive learning (Engeström & Sannino, 2010). This approach reflects an important contribution, as it puts the "primacy on communities as learners, on transformation and creation of culture, on horizontal movement and hybridization, and on the formation of theoretical concepts" (Engeström & Sannino, 2010, p. 2; Gutiérrez, 2014).

The SDBE sees design as a vehicle for equitable change and transformative learning (Gutiérrez, 2005, 2008; Gutiérrez et al., 2009). With their commitment to organizing learning in the present for the future, SDBEs embody a "productive tension between present and possible social realities" (Gutiérrez & Vossoughi, 2010, p. 111) in that they understand tensions as impetus for change, thus promoting a futuristic orientation. Social design–based researchers attend not only to the current practices of a given learning environment but also to the complex and contradictory connections that a particular community has with a particular set of local and historical practices (Gutiérrez & Rogoff, 2003). In line with a cultural historical approach, SDBEs' commitment to epistemological plurality expects disruptions and contradictions within, between, and among competing activity systems of an ecology (Engeström, 2011; Gutiérrez, 2005). These tensions and contradictions are made visible and become the object of study, design, and re-mediation. Importantly, its exploration of diversity and plurality works to account for the "repertoires of practice" people develop, bring, and leverage in learning environments (Gutiérrez & Rogoff, 2003), with a concomitant focus on identity development and the relationship between the individual and the collective.

By attempting to make visible the often seemingly neutral local practices that constitute learning environments, SDBEs add value to the critical reflection and development of both theory and local practice. For example, the cognitive ethnography written by aspiring teachers in one of the authors'[2] Fifth Dimension afterschool clubs (discussed in depth below) serves as a principal tool for mediating novice teachers' critical reflections on the often underexamined theories of learning, culture, and teaching; this is consequential insofar as teachers hold and instantiate commonsense (and often reductive) understandings of these concepts in their work with youth from nondominant communities (Mendoza, 2014; Mendoza, Paguyo, & Gutiérrez, 2015). This reflective tool is central to supporting teachers' movement from unexamined to examined assumptions about teaching and learning, and the role of culture in those processes. In this way, it is as much about teacher learning as it is student learning. Importantly, the cognitive ethnography serves to make visible and transform deficit approaches that can define power-laden spaces such as schools. SDBEs are necessarily organized in ways that facilitate the creation of learning environments built on the idea that diversity is a resource and the playful imagination a robust zone of learning, as the following examples of designed ecologies will help illustrate.

At *El Pueblo Mágico* after-school club, an SDBE modeled after its Los Angeles predecessor *Las Redes* (also considered a Fifth Dimension site; see Cole, 1996; Cole & Distributive Literacy Consortium, 2006; Vásquez, 2013), the aim is to engender transformative learning for both undergraduate preservice teachers and elementary-age youth from nondominant communities. The *El Pueblo* social design–based team works to create a playful environment that stretches the current developmental level of the children by purposefully designing activities around the co-construction of the zone of proximal development (Vygotsky, 1978). These activities, often supported through new media and digital technologies, are embedded within a hybrid environment in which multiple languages, epistemologies, and intergenerational relationships are privileged and leveraged toward engagement in joint activity.

Social design–based experiments like *El Pueblo* are designed to support and build on what the researchers know about the local community and the history of schooling and its role in the community, as well as on the "repertoires of practice" (Gutiérrez & Rogoff, 2003) children bring and can leverage in such innovative spaces. Pushing against traditional forms of afterschool educational programming and remedial approaches to learning often associated with schools in nondominant communities, designed activities offer students various entry points into higher order problem solving with technology-mediated tools, and various forms of assistance readily available, such as support from peers or more experienced others (Stone & Gutiérrez, 2007). Children from nondominant communities are not always given opportunities to partake in high-status educational programming (Ford Foundation, 2013; Nasir, 2012). SDBEs like *El Pueblo* are purposeful in attending to the ways historical and contemporary deficit beliefs and practices shape learning activity and the participants within. These designed environments build on what is known about how children learn best—that is, in contexts where children and adults co-construct knowledge through joint mediated activity (Cole, 1996; Gutiérrez, Morales, & Martinez, 2009; Gutiérrez & Vossoughi, 2010; Vygotsky, 1978), mistakes are acceptable, and children feel a sense of social belonging and safety (Nasir, 2008, 2012).

Fundamentally, SDBEs seek to create and study change. As educational and social interventions, they design for new learning, as well as *un*learning stereotypic or deficit perceptions of learners and their communities. Gutiérrez (2016) elaborates,

As educational experiments, like other design experiments, social design[–based] experiments are grounded in empirically-derived hypotheses about learning and human development but are iterated, implemented, and continuously reflected on, refined and repaired over the course of the experiment; in other words, these are theoretical and experientially informed models of the future that are designed, studied, and revised in the present. (p. 192)

We lift up the examples of *El Pueblo* and *Las Redes*, as they illustrate the importance of partnering and co-designing with deep understanding of communities, their practices, and their histories—that is, designing with robust notions of culture and cultural communities with which designers can better capture the fullness, variance, and complexity of communities and their members. Of consequence, SDBEs' future orientation stands in contrast with approaches that see failure instead of resilience, see despair where there is possibility, and see powerlessness where there is agency and people are historical actors.

A HISTORICIZED ECOLOGICAL APPROACH TO MORE EQUITABLE AND RIGOROUS RESEARCH

Design-based approaches to research such as SDBEs invite ecological approaches that direct us to examine and consider proximal and distal influences on human activity. Motivated by a commitment to transforming the educational and social circumstance of youth from nondominant communities, SDBEs centralize the development of learning ecologies that are foremost equitable, resilient, robust, and sustainable. Scholars have long critiqued traditional laboratory-based experiments, which produce results that are not relevant beyond the lab (Barker, 1968; Gibson 1966; Neisser, 1976). In contrast, we use ecological approaches, which are based on the idea that human development takes place through processes of progressively more complex reciprocal interaction between the human organism and the people, objects, and symbols in its environment (Bronfenbrenner, 1994). Moreover, the form, power, content, and direction of these interactions—or "proximal processes"—vary as a function of the developing person, the environment, and the nature of the developmental outcomes under consideration (Bronfenbrenner, 1994, p. 38). An ecological understanding of human development suggests that because the process and product of making human beings varies by place and time, the fact that there are ecologies yet untried indicates that there is also potential for human natures not yet seen (Bronfenbrenner, 1994).

In foregrounding the affordances of an ecological approach, Cole, Hood, and McDermott (1982) have argued that experiments must account for context and a deep understanding that context must inform how behavior is conceptualized. We are aware that the term *context* has been used in differing ways. One understanding interprets context as nested levels (Bronfenbrenner, 1994) surrounding the individual. Although powerful in turning the reader's attention to proximal surroundings, this interpretation fails to account for the interconnectedness of space and time and the mutual constitution of human activity. Moreover, such an understanding of context also lends itself to the interpretation of context as static. In contrast, Vygotsky limited the concept of *context* to descriptions of written and spoken word; context beyond language he framed as *situation* or *ecology*. Thus, a Vygotskian perspective leads us to an understanding of ecology as interwoven and "actively achieved" (Cole, 1996, p. 134), "like tangled roots" (Packer, 2010, p. 24), rather than concentric circles (Gutiérrez, 2016). It is important to understand human behavior in the contexts of our full ecologies, because activity systems all exist interdependently as ever-changing, fluid practices, which are grounded in a larger history (Cole, 1996; Lee, 2010).

In taking an ecological approach, we also center the importance of "seeing" historically across multiple time scales. In cultural historical activity theory, time scales emphasize the way that multiple domains of history, including the history of our species (phylogenies), the history of the cultural group into which we are born (cultural-history), the history of an individual human being (ontogeny), and the moment-to-moment interactions of the present (micro genesis) all influence the construction and interpretation of the current situation (Cole, 1998). Thus, each moment is interwoven with not only the surroundings in the present day but also the historical legacy of each time scale that manifests through artifacts, including language (Cole, 1998). Historicity is thus fundamental for developing a full understanding of the structural conditions that mediate people's lives, as well as how people come to see who they are and who they can become (Gutiérrez, 2016). In centering historicity, we are better able to understand the tensions, constraints, and possibilities of activity systems (Engeström, 1999) and focus on the history of people's participation in practices to understand what gives meaning to their lives (Gutiérrez, 2016).

Moreover, a historical view enables us to "see" differently and thus create resilient learning ecologies by attending to the history of the ecology, its participants, its resources, its level of diversity and identifying potential threats to the ecology's resources, health, and resilience (Gutiérrez, 2016; Gutiérrez & Jurow, 2016). Resilient ecologies refer to a community's ability to cope with, shape, and adapt to social, political, and environmental changes (Adger, 2000; Brand & Jax, 2007; Folke, 2003, 2006; Gutiérrez, 2016) and are diverse, transformable, and sustainable (Walker & Salt, 2006). Most research on resiliency focuses on an individual's ability to transcend difficult circumstances (e.g., Garmezy, 1991; Rutter, 1987, 1990; Werner, 1990, 1993). However, in discussing *resilience*, we are concerned with not only individuals but also the larger sociocultural and activity systems in which they are embedded. This is especially important in designing learning ecologies for students from nondominant communities. Rather than viewing a student as deficient in a particular skill set, we aim to understand the student's history of involvement in that practice. By paying attention to the student's ecological history, and developing a broader picture of the tools, support systems, and constraints available to the student, we are better able to design new tools and arrangements for proleptic learning, for learning in the present for the future. In contrast to deficit perspectives of nondominant communities, we argue that the development of sustainable and resilient learning ecologies allows for an approach to learning and design that recognizes students' full humanity (Gutiérrez, 2016).

An ecological approach is also concerned with what people learn in their participation in everyday practices. de Certeau's (1984) study of the ways by which people individualize mass culture to make it their own has served to reorient our understanding of the everyday. In *The Practice of Everyday Life*, de Certeau argues that cultural consumption of rituals and representations produced by the dominant social order is in actuality also a production. Ordinary people *make* the rituals, representations, and laws imposed on them into something different from what the dominant social order intended. This act of enunciation—or reappropriation—is thus also an act of subversion. Drawing on Foucault's work, de Certeau notes that if power currently operates through "miniscule" technical procedures, the infinitesimal transformations ordinary people make of and within the dominant cultural economy are in fact political acts. In other words, there is a political dimension to everyday practices. For de Certeau, these procedures of the everyday—the reappropriation *made* by consumers—can serve as a therapeutic for the fragmentation of today's social fabric.

This concept of everyday practices as political resonates strongly with our work on "learning as movement." As argued in previous work, learning as movement describes the ways by which historical actors deploy repertoires of practice across time, space, and activity to experience possible futures (Gutiérrez, 2008). In other words, in entering a practice, all learners also reinvent that practice, opening up new possibilities for and understandings of the self (Vossoughi & Gutiérrez, 2014). In lieu of "vertical" trajectories of learning, which assume that there is a linear trajectory from novice to expert, we focus on what scholars have called "horizontal," or everyday, forms of learning (Tuomi-Gröhn, Engeström, & Young, 2003). Such a perspective centers the learning that emerges as people, tools, practices, and interests move across settings, social contexts, or activity systems. In attending to horizontal forms of learning, we highlight how practices are transformed and hybridized, rather than merely reproduced or applied. This in turn sheds light on the ways by which expertise is in reality a distributed phenomenon. An understanding of learning as movement also attends to the ways that tools enable or constrain learning across practices, and illuminates the ways in which tools and practices get reorganized as people move within and across ecologies (Gutiérrez, 2008; Vossoughi & Gutiérrez, 2014).

In our work with nondominant youth and their families, we have documented learning as movement and transformation across the contexts of the school, home, and community, and we use this work as arguments for highlighting the importance of focusing on everyday practices and routines across ecologies to understand human activity (Weisner, 1998). We use mixed methods but privilege multisited ethnography (Marcus, 1995) to develop a historicized understanding of students' learning ecologies. A multisited ethnographic sensibility enables us to honor the ways by which people are simultaneously part of multiple activity systems, and methodologically acknowledge that it is within multiple activity systems that cross place, space, and time that people develop repertoires of practice (Vossoughi & Gutiérrez, 2014). In his early work, Marcus (1995) defined multisited ethnography:

[moving] out from the single sites and local situations of conventional ethnographic research designs to examine the circulation of cultural meanings, objects, and identities in diffuse time-space. This mode defines for itself an object of study that cannot be accounted for ethnographically by remaining focused on a single site of intensive investigation. It develops instead a strategy or design of research that acknowledges macrotheoretical concepts and narratives of the world system but does not rely on them for the contextual architecture framing a set of subjects. This mobile ethnography takes unexpected trajectories in tracing a cultural formation across and within multiple sites of activity that destabilize the distinction, for example, between lifeworld and system by which much ethnography has been conceived. (p. 96)

In being mobile, multisited ethnography creates space for an ethnography of movement and change (Vossoughi & Gutiérrez, 2014) and shifts the methodological gaze away from students' perceived deficiencies toward the ways youth practices are developed across time and space, in sites of boundary crossing and hybridity. Multisited ethnography is also appropriate for our research and move toward re-mediation (Gutiérrez et al., 2009), which aims not to "fix" people and their communities but to re-organize, or transform, systems of activity so that participants can become designers of their own futures. In documenting student practices across space, time, and activity systems, we are able to design for learning ecologies that allow for students to become "historical actors," subjects who are able to see historically so that they can transform their own sociohistorical circumstances and futures as learners and agents of social change (Espinoza, 2004; Gutiérrez, 2008). In understanding the present as a product of history and as the starting point for the future, each actor, or more specifically each interaction, has the potential to create change and to redefine practices and boundaries. It is in this view of the present that we invite a reimagination of ingenuity as part of everyday practices.

LEVERAGING EVERYDAY EXPERTISE

We use our study, "Leveraging Horizontal Expertise: The New Media Practices of Latino and Working Class Families," as a case for examining the importance of studying people's everyday activity. In this SDBE, the "where" and the "how" of seeing youth, families, and their practices differently can be illustrated. Specifically, our analysis of a rich corpus of data on families' everyday lives, including their new media practices, has engaged "new ways of seeing." Building, in part, on our previous University of California, Los Angeles (UCLA), study on the middle-class lives of working families in Los Angeles (Gutiérrez, Izquierdo, & Kremer-Sadlik, 2010; Ochs & Kremer-Sadlik, 2013), the present study was interested in the learning that occurs in people's movement across everyday practices (i.e., learning as movement) and the resulting "repertoires of practices" that are constructed and leveraged across time and space.

This was a multisited ethnography in which we observed 60 to 75 youth from our STEM-oriented afterschool club, *El Pueblo Mágico*, and a subset of 14 of these youth and their families. As part of the study design, we worked with these families to jointly document families' everyday practices and their uses of new media across a range of settings and activities. For 3 years, we spent a minimum of 8 hours in the homes of 14 families from low-income communities—the majority of whom were a heterogeneous group of Latino families—and collected an extensive data set that included home videos taken by researchers, youth, and other family members, family-generated videos, new media surveys, artifacts, and interviews. We especially learned about families while interacting with them and while documenting and understanding family and individual's daily routines and their beliefs and practices around health, new media, social networks, education, and energy use. The field notes written by undergraduates working and learning with children in *El Pueblo Mágico* and artifacts produced by the children and their adult amig@s in joint activity were important to understanding children's movement across settings.

Our work in leveraging horizontal or everyday expertise examined how tools and practices traveled, got taken up, or were reorganized and reinvented in that movement across people's ecologies. In particular, we examined the new media and everyday practices of families, and in the course of doing so, we began to document the novel, interesting, and creative ways families took up new media tools toward new ends. But there was more than their ingenuity with new media practices; we also documented the range of inventive ways they lived socially. Ingenuity became an important empirical and theoretical focus. As we will elaborate below, we conceptualize ingenuity from a generative frame that takes into account ecological factors and strategies for negotiating the complex and dynamic movement of working-class families. From this view, human ingenuity is constituted by the complex, dynamic, everyday practices in which families engage routinely and over time. Informed by Vygotsky's (1978) notion of the playful imagination that is fundamental in a range of ways to ingenuity, thus far we have identified the following kinds of everyday ingenuity in family practices: playfulness, resourcefulness, making, tinkering, fixing, and new forms of boundary crossing.

INGENUITY

We situate our notion of ingenuity in everyday creative responses to constraints and (un)intentional moves to blur boundaries. Being attuned to the ways in which people interact, create, and are influenced by their surroundings is an essential part of reframing the everyday as a wellspring of ingenuity. Through careful observation of the mundane, the problem solving, creativity, and resilience that often drive routine practices undiscerned come to light. The prevalent perception of ingenuity is that it is a "skill or cleverness that allows someone to solve problems" ("Ingenuity," n.d.). This approach centers ingenuity as an individual achievement, and one that is often extraordinary. Such a conceptualization is problematic in that it advances assumptions that ingenuity is a property of the exceptional mind rather than an everyday phenomenon distributed across people, environments, and materials (e.g., Gutiérrez, 2008; McDermott & Raley, 2011; Pea, 1993). Moving beyond narrow understandings of ingenuity as individualistic and rare requires new ways of looking for and at performances of skill, inventiveness, and resourcefulness as people encounter and respond creatively to constraints in their everyday environments. Looking anew does not come easily; it calls for willingness and training to frame and reframe how we view ingenuity (McDermott & Raley, 2011; Mendoza, 2014). However, with eyes wide open, we can see that ingenuity is much more than an individual, exceptional attribute; it is embedded in people's interactions with and across their everyday resources. Focusing on the everyday as a natural—and often overlooked—site/sight[3] for ingenuity can help us question categories that may otherwise go unchallenged, and identify solutions that can address the institutional constraints in which people are placed.

New understandings of ingenuity require replacing entrenched assumptions about where we see ingenuity and how we recognize it. In other words, locating ingenuity in the everyday is both an empirical and a theoretical undertaking. Scholars such as McDermott and Raley (2011) have pointed to school environments as prime examples of prosaic places where ingenuity is abundant but often missed due to narrow scope of vision. In their study of a reading lesson in a kindergarten classroom, these authors demonstrate how one of the Spanish language–dominant student's (Alexis's) achievement of reading was actually the result of "arranging bodies, materials, and talk to keep people in their respective positions" (p. 382) rather than successful, solitary decoding of text. In broadening their vision to include the other kindergarteners who helped Alexis "read" through their interrupting, pointing, and whispering, McDermott and Raley illustrate the distributed nature of performances of competence that are often seen as individualistic. By looking closely and differently at a string of seemingly unremarkable classroom interactions, they highlight how knowledgeable, imaginative, and resourceful children are in school, a fact often lost in standardized "intelligence measures." Ingenuity, they argue, is not a characteristic of the exceptional mind but rather the agentive repurposing and reorganizing of "materials and persons and moments at hand . . . into something interesting, fun, or new" (p. 387).

Drawing on McDermott and Raley (2011), Gutiérrez and Barton (2015) argue that all human activity is always socially organized, including in classrooms. In their discussion of how the social positioning of the classroom is a collective social accomplishment, Gutiérrez and Barton advance a discussion of how the social order of classrooms implicates which students get positioned as successful while others less so, and whose ingenuity gets valued in science classrooms. The authors provide a vignette to illustrate this point.

Akira is the top student in her science class. Not only is she the best reader in the class, she is familiar with and can detail her understandings and arguments with care and precision. While there is no doubt that Akira is an accomplished student with her own history of engagement in a range of practices, how we understand and the assumptions we hold about her status in the social order of the classroom is often misunderstood as a sole accomplishment. However, if we were to document carefully and observe how the social life of the classroom gets constituted, we could unpack how learning and its social situation get organized in ways that make Akira the "best" student in the class. We would ask ourselves: What work gets done for this to happen? What gets organized and reorganized in the classroom? And in what ways does this positioning of youth influence how science learning is accomplished? (p. 574)

The social organization and making of the "best" student has important implications for whose knowledge and practices are taken up. It is in the acknowledgement and leveraging of youths' repertoires of practice, the knowledge and expertise developed across everyday practices and settings of the ecology, that the buds and kernels of ingenuity, the roots and possibilities of youths' playful imagination, resourcefulness, and inquisitiveness are revealed. The social order of classrooms and attendant practices we describe have particular significance for how deficit frames, social relations, and opportunity spaces are created and maintained for youth from nondominant communities.

In the same vein, Gutiérrez (2008) shows us that ingenuity is also revealed as people develop and leverage expansive repertoires of practice across multiple settings and communities. With a team of colleagues, her long-term design and study of the Migrant Student Leadership Institute (MSLI) at UCLA, a residential summer program for high school students from migrant farmworker backgrounds, has emphasized the development of powerful literacies as both everyday and institutional literacies are reframed in the students' movement across settings. The MSLI learning ecology was intentionally designed to counter English-only, one-size-fits-all policies and practices and reveal "how people are made smart by use of artifacts and participation in particular social groups and settings" (Gutiérrez, 2008, p. 150). The program supported students in developing sociocritical literacy (Gutiérrez, 2002) and "[reconceiving] who they are and what they might be able to accomplish academically and beyond" (Gutiérrez, 2008, p. 148). In creating learning opportunities mediated by a wide range of tools in natural daily activity (e.g., during walks on the UCLA campus, in residential life, at mealtimes) and in formal instructional activity, the program made space for students to reframe themselves as historical actors in "the world as it is and the world as it could be" (p. 160). Helping youths see their past, present, and future differently is a major design objective of the MSLI program, as is "retraining" the vision of educators and researchers so that they can see the transformative potential of leveraging horizontal and vertical forms of learning. Learning and creativity were everywhere, from the spaces where *teatro del oprimido* (theatre of the oppressed) took life to the writing of students' *testimonios* about what it meant to be a migrant farmworker in the United States. As we have written previously (Espinoza, 2009; Gutiérrez, 2008; Vossoughi & Gutiérrez, 2014), space, place, and time were transformed and reimagined by instructors and students as they engaged in collective forms of learning and imagining referred to as "social dreaming"—the collective imagining of a more just educational and social world.

Studies such as these illustrate empirically where we might look for ingenuity in our day-to-day surroundings. Where we look, however, cannot be separated from the theories that inform how we look for ingenuity. Situated views of learning and development guide our analyses of ingenuity as a distributed phenomenon in our families' everyday practices. Approaching ingenuity as an everyday, distributed phenomenon, it is not difficult to see across our varied and rich family data how resourceful, clever, resilient, and inventive the participating family members were as they reconfigured and reimagined their available resources to address constraints in their surroundings. Attending to how families in our study transgressed the rules and constraints in their routines has helped us recognize "ingenuity in everyday moments." We exemplify this theoretical point in one salient example of the everyday ingenuity observed in our participating families; we describe here how one of the mothers, Katie, transformed commonplace resources and constraints into opportunities within the daily routine to support her children's learning.

A divorced parent to three young children (Jake, 11; Mary, 8; and Andrew, 2), Katie had made the decision to undertake a twice-daily commute between the house she had shared with her ex-husband in one town and the children's school and daycare in another small town in order to provide her children with stable routines. With her ex-husband working away from home during the week, Katie and her children braved long morning and evening commutes between the two cities. A self-employed massage therapist who worked from home and also traveled to clients, Katie shared that her various daily responsibilities necessitated precise coordination of family routines. Although commuting commanded time that could be used for work, Katie highly valued her children's academic improvement and the support programs available at their current school, including our after-school program in which her children were enrolled. As a result, Katie chose to manage the constraints she faced rather than relocate her children.

As part of joint study of families' everyday practices, Katie created the "morning routine" videos that all of our participating families recorded. One video captured the hour before they all left together for school, day care, and work and the other captured the family's 17-mile commute from their home to where the children went to school in a nearby town. Alternating her video camera to capture the scenic drive, the cars in front of her, and, briefly, her sleeping children, Katie narrated the drive, describing this daily commute as "annoying" due to the steady single line of traffic that defined their commute. The long but necessary commute was understandably trying to Katie, a busy single parent. However, it is in this seemingly mundane routine that we can see ingenuity and, thus, Katie's creative response to the particular constraints posed by this commute. Despite the tediousness of the drive, she saw it as a time they could use productively as a family. She explained that she and the children often used the drive back home to do homework, practice reading, and "problem solve out loud." For example, after having her two school-age children read assignments aloud, she would help them think through the answers. Katie also explained that due to the stretches of idling in slow traffic, her children could get some writing done as well without worrying about shaky printing. Math problems could also be completed in the car so that the answers were ready to be checked by Katie once the family reached home. Near the end of the video, Katie referred to this commute as "good time" because she and the children "[tried] to be productive." In reorganizing time, space, children, and materials, Katie restructured a mundane commute and repurposed it to promote family interaction and her children's academic achievement through literacy learning, math talk, and problem-solving. As in the case of young Alexis described by McDermott and Raley (2011) earlier, we argue that Katie demonstrated ingenuity through this organization of everyday learning in a way that mattered most for her family.

A Theoretical Note: We insert a theoretical note here to further ground our notion of ingenuity as a rich site of learning. In particular, we draw on the work of Russian psychologist Lev Vygotsky (1978), as a Vygotskian approach to learning and development requires critical attention to more than just the individual learner; it also involves attention to the social context of development in which the learner is developing, whether in informal or formal learning spaces. We briefly review some key and relevant principles to illustrate how this view of learning orients researchers to the affordances of understanding people's learning in everyday activity, including play and the playful imagination as rich zones of learning and development (Vygotsky, 1987).

We believe Vygotsky's views of play and cognition are worth revisiting as they provide a context for understanding why play is a natural site for seeing everyday ingenuity. In his writings on play and child development, Vygotsky (1967) distinguished play—specifically, pretend play—as a dynamic social activity that requires and leads to complex symbolic constructions, emotional impulse control, and experimentation with behavioral rules. Vygotsky attributed the appearance of play to the child's interest in attaining personal desires. As these desires are largely unattainable in reality, the child creates an imaginary situation to realize them. According to Vygotsky, "[A]ction in the imaginative sphere, in an imaginary situation, the creation of voluntary intentions, and the formation of real-life plans and volitional motives–all appear in play and make it the highest level of preschool development" (p. 16). It is within this first kind of early childhood play that "a child's greatest achievements are possible" (Vygotsky, 1987, p. 100). Although the concept of the ZPD (zone of proximal development) has often been taken to literally refer to a child being assisted by a single more knowledgeable other, Vygotsky's view of play expands the idea to include assistance provided by a group (e.g., of peers, as we saw in the analysis of Alexis and her classmates; McDermott & Raley, 2011).

In particular, Vygotsky's (1978) notion of the playful imagination offers us a generative lens for understanding the ingenuity of families in their everyday lives. He notes that all play creates an imaginary situation and all imaginary situations contain rules that are reflective of societal norms. It is through play that the child is able to gradually learn to transcend her reality. As Vygotsky notes,

Play is a transitional stage . . . At that critical moment when a stick—i.e., an object—becomes a pivot for severing the meaning of horse from a real horse, one of the basic psychological structures determining the child's relationship to reality is radically altered. (p. 12)

By engaging her playful imagination, a child moves from being constrained by her situation to thinking beyond constraints. She can recreate and, in doing so, even transgress, her surroundings in this creative space. As Cole and Griffin (1986) have noted, play is not just the domain of children; it is a leading activity that spans the lifetime. In this view of constraints and playful imagination, we ground our analysis and understanding of ingenuity as altering and bending rules and blurring boundaries to achieve goals through playfulness, resourcefulness, making, tinkering, fixing, creativity and boundary crossing.

BOUNDARY CROSSING AND *LINE-STEPPING* AS INGENUITY

In this article, we have expounded on the importance of examining learning as work that is done across both vertical and horizontal dimensions of development (Cole & Gajdamashko, 2009). We see boundary crossing as part of the domain of ingenuity, as boundary crossing especially attends to horizontal dimensions of learning, bringing to the fore the everyday ingenuity in movements through and across domains of practice. We build on expansive notions of learning to argue that boundary crossing requires re-mediation of reductive constructions of nondominant communities. Moreover, we contend, as have others (cf. Bang & Vossoughi, 2016; Engeström & Sannino, 2010; Jurow & Shea, 2015; Vossoughi & Gutiérrez, 2014), that researchers often fail to capture ingenious practices that occur in the horizontal movement of knowledge and the boundary crossing that is part of such practices. In our present study, we have gained a better understanding of how families take up the tools and resources available to them by tracing their movement and the boundary crossing that are part of their everyday practices. We argue that boundary and border crossing, as critical dimensions of ingenuity, offer theoretical and practical means for us to see differently. Of special interest to us are the observations of youth engaging in boundary crossing acts that are ingenious and rebellious, a point we will discuss shortly.

As discussed earlier, methodological focus on everyday practices is important to seeing novelty, creativity, and ingenuity in people's activity. There is particular analytical affordance in understanding the practices that thrive on the boundary and the hybridity and counterscripts that help characterize agency, transformation, and openings for those navigating cultural, affective and cognitive borderlands (cf. Anzaldúa, 1999; Gutiérrez, Rymes, & Larson, 1995). As conditions for ingenuity, boundaries and borders are not strictly instruments for exclusion that restrict the flow of people and ideas; rather as Conquergood (2002) contends, boundaries are more akin to membranes than walls. Approaching boundaries as fluid and dynamic can help researchers notice how boundaries and borders are often altered by the very people they are designed to exclude (De Genova, Mezzadra, & Pickles, 2014; Hand, Penuel, & Gutiérrez, 2012).

In this section, we begin by examining the analytical purchase of boundary crossing in our exploration of ingenuity with nondominant communities, recognizing that much has been written about boundary crossing in education research (Akkerman & Bakker, 2011; Akkerman & Bruining, 2016; Garraway, 2010). We continue our review and offer theorizations of boundary crossing that are particularly expansive for understanding people's agency and everyday forms of resistance (Pacheco, 2012).

Akkerman and Bakker (2011) describe a boundary as "a sociocultural difference leading to discontinuity in action or interaction" (p. 133). As such, boundaries and borders can be both material and ideal, ideology playing a role in the formation of both. In education research, material boundaries are those that physically exist between school, after-school activities, home, and community (Barron, Gomez, Pinkard, & Martin, 2014; Soep & Chavez, 2010; Willis, 1977). Ideal boundaries can encompass the explicit and implicit norms that learners are expected to conform to as they move across various contexts (Givens, Nasir, ross, & de Royston, 2016; Love, 2012; Nasir, ross, de Royston, Givens, & Bryant, 2013; Vaught, 2004). However, crossing boundaries amplifies tensions between the activity systems and the individuals moving across them. These material and ideational manifestations of borders attune us to the ways ingenuity can be sparked through negotiating discontinuity and encountering the unfamiliar (Suchman, 1994).

In our own study of everyday working-class family life, we perceive youths' ingenious, subversive, and rebellious acts of boundary crossing as attempts to present more authentic, often liminal, selves. At times, these transgressions can seem fleeting and even inconsequential; yet a momentary *queering* of time and space can expand our field of vision to the transformative potential in testing and pushing established norms, acknowledging and contesting boundary lines. To better understand the experiences of those occupying liminal spaces, we turn to queer theorizations of boundary crossing as a robust and refined lens for queering the familiar and seeing the ambiguity and playfulness of movement across material and ideational domains (Halberstam, 2005; E. P. Johnson, 2003; J. M. Johnson & Nunez, 2015; Royster, 2012). These are scholars who have radically pushed disciplinary and epistemological boundaries, challenging researchers to look at the communities we study in more dynamic ways. We draw on the work of queer scholars of color, in particular, to gain insight into the pliable nature of boundaries and in the process see where boundaries blur, blend, and at times rupture, bleeding across ecologies.

The works of Gloria Anzaldúa (1999) and José Esteban Muñoz (1999) have been especially instrumental in expanding our field of vision. Their scholarly contributions re-mediated old ways of seeing, offering us new lenses and alternative spaces for making sense of the lives of nondominant communities. Muñoz advances the concept of disidentification as a means for crossing and contesting the borders and boundaries set forth by coloniality's normalizing White and heteronormative impulse. As Bhabha (1990), Soja (1996), and Gutiérrez (2008) have posited, this is achieved not by identifying with or rejecting prevailing ideologies but by operating within a third space where the disidentificatory subject "tactically and simultaneously works on, with, and against a cultural form" (Muñoz, 1999, p. 12). Muñoz's notion of disidentification provides a generative frame for looking at the ideational resources required of nondominant learners who sit at the intersection of multiple borders. Ideational resources refer to an individual's perception of self (Norris, 2014) and "place in a practice in the world, as well as ideas about what is valued and what is good" (Nasir, 2012, p. 110). For Nasir (2012), ideational resources, including how an individual negotiates them in schooling practices, influence the formation of racialized and academic identities. These resources not only are key to racialized identities but also have affordances for the construction of gendered identities, identities also mediated by the materials within schooling contexts, as well as notions of self and relationships with others. Here, the transformative potential of boundary crossing practices begins to emerge.

In *Borderlands: La Frontera*, Anzaldúa (1999) describes the transformative potential of "crossing borders" as a queer Chicana. As an act of rebellion, boundary crossing was a reaction to cultural forces that expected her to conform to normative conceptions of being a woman and of being a Mexican, specifically. Anzaldúa's quest for enacting a hybrid identity required transgressing the borders erected around gender, sexuality, and language, leaving her in 'the borderlands' (p. 37). Anzaldúa's experience presents us with a way to look at boundary crossing as transformative, rectifying the dissonance between an authentic self and the norms perpetuated through oppressive structures. The agency and rebellion modeled by Muñoz (1999) and Anzaldúa (1999) lend us new orientations for seeing what Pacheco (2012) has referred to as enactments of "everyday resistance" (p. 121) by youth in nondominant communities, while also illustrating the political impetus behind attempted and successful boundary crossings.

In our research, we have witnessed agentive, rebellious, and political attempts at boundary crossing by nondominant youth. This focus on the everyday practices of youth has allowed us to see the gradual progression—characterized by the queering of norms—toward the crossing of boundary lines, a progression that we have theorized as *line-stepping*. The concept of line-stepping opens up a new way of seeing ingenious boundary crossing in action, that playful resistance that occurs at the time that the boundary *line* is acknowledged and engaged. Line-stepping necessarily involves a playful imagination and can bring new degrees of freedom, but as with any playful and/or transgressive act, including acts of resistance, line-stepping is not free of rules or of potential consequence.

Our use of the term *line-stepping* derives from comedian Dave Chappelle's hit television series, *Chappelle's Show*. In a recurring segment titled "Charlie Murphy's True Hollywood Stories," cast regular Charlie Murphy recounts his memorable encounters with A-list celebrities. In the first installment, Murphy reenacts his experiences with funk music superstar Rick James (played by Chappelle in the skit). Murphy describes the volatile nature of their relationship, which often resulted in physical altercations between the two men because, as Murphy puts it, James "step[ped] across the line, habitually" (Brennan, 2004; Chappelle & Brennan, 2004). Chappelle's portrayal of James as a "habitual line-stepper" is productive for marking the outer edges of transgressing boundaries. However, the privilege associated with

James's age, gender, class, and sexuality enables his reckless disregard for societal norms. Without such entitlements, most youth are required to tread familial and societal boundaries with a much lighter touch than the musician. Thus, our conceptualization of line-stepping pivots from Murphy's in that it describes a form of transgression that is processual, more methodical, and often executed with deftness and some sense of consequence and caution.

Line-stepping is an instantiation of boundary crossing where an individual deliberately and consciously pushes against society's ideological constraints. Rather than seeing boundaries as static, we recognize their dynamism. By subtly identifying and testing a line, the line-stepper learns how and where lines are permeable and the available latitude in their enforcement. At times, youth will encroach the lines without going over them; at other times, they will cross the lines, attempting to ascertain the severity of the consequences of their boundary crossing. In our study, we saw youth engage forms of line-stepping as they challenged established gender norms around video game playing or acted in ways to counter deficit school labels through their online identities.

Through analysis of youths' routine activity, we found line stepping to be a collective and distributed activity, where youth employed the assistance of those in their home to push boundaries in ways they found meaningful (McDermott & Raley, 2011). It is important to note that this defiance or testing of the rules is not the result of ignorance. Rather, intimate awareness of the lines is a prerequisite for their skillful manipulation. Hearkening back to Vygotsky's (1978) notion of play, we also understand young people's line-stepping as a form of transcending reality through the engagement of the playful imagination. What is implicit in our conception is the acknowledgement that lines can and often do change. We propose such line-stepping as something that youth, in particular, engage in, as they playfully (and sometimes more seriously) negotiate with the bounding rules and norms of the multiple activity systems in which they participate. By seeing young people as "habitual line-steppers," we view their actions as agentic and deliberate and recognize how they can move the lines that are used to demarcate "appropriate" behavior. In looking anew at the everyday, the seemingly mundane and subtle, we are able to see the creative ways youth engage in redefining themselves and the worlds in which they live. The analytical concept of line-stepping offers a way to more fully conceptualize youths' deployment of their repertoires in sense-making activity, and to more accurately capture how youth negotiate the demands of family, school, and social life.

CONCLUSION

Education research has had a complex history and role in the schooling of youth from nondominant communities. In line with the call of this special issue, we have addressed how particular analytical frames and methodological approaches have had deleterious effects on the social and educational opportunities, trajectories, and social futures of these youth. We hoped to advance a conversation about what it means to conduct consequential, robust, and respectful research in partnership *with* nondominant communities. Specifically, we advanced an argument about rethinking education research in ways that could help researchers see ingenuity and new forms of agency in youth and communities that have heretofore been perceived through a reductive and racialized lens. Toward this end, we marshaled scholarship that provided insight, frames, and tools for learning to see and engage our work differently, to see the link between how we theorize and study nondominant communities.

Drawing from our current study Leveraging Horizontal Expertise: Understanding the New Media Practices of Families,[4] we also discussed SDBEs, a form of design-based inquiry that is organized around a new social imagination about how to do consequential research with nondominant communities. Notably, the historical and ecological concerns central to this methodology privilege a focus on the everyday and on the learning that takes hold as youth move within and across activity systems, that is, their repertoires of practice. Its critical cultural historical theoretical approach offers new analytical tools to help social scientists see ingenuity and possibility instead of deficit. In particular, a focus on boundary crossing and line-stepping as forms of ingenuity offer new ways of "seeing" youths' learning-in-activity more expansively.

NOTES

The Berkeley MacArthur Connected Learning Research Network authors are listed alphabetically. The conceptualization and writing of this article were equally distributed across all authors and should be understood accordingly.

[1]The mirror is a tool "used to stimulate involvement, analysis and collaborative design efforts among the participants" (Engeström, 2011, p. 14). For more on the "'mirror" in SDBE, see also Mendoza (2014).

[2]Gutiérrez served as principal designer and director of two designed after school environments in Los Angeles, California, and Boulder, Colorado.

[3]Parham (2009) finds Nora's (1989) theorization of *les lieux de mémoire*—sites of memory—useful for examining the relationship between memory and haunting in Black life. She notes,

Site/sight: where we put it, how we see it (or the myriad ways we see without seeing—hauntings, specters, and uncanny repetitions); site/cite: where we find it (the dig site, the grave, the Middle Passage), how we express it, or how loss informs or structures experience—citationality. (p. 10)

P. Johnson (2014) draws on Parham's work in his analysis of haunting and the Black athletic body in ESPN's *30 for 30* documentaries.

[4]This study is funded by the MacArthur Foundation Connected Learning Research Network, PI, Mimi Ito, University of California, Irvine; co-PI, Kris D. Gutiérrez, University of California, Berkeley.

REFERENCES

Adger, W. N. (2000). Social and ecological resilience: Are they related? *Progress in Human Geography, 24*, 347–364.

Akkerman, S. F., & Bakker, A. (2011). Boundary crossing and boundary objects. *Review of Educational Research, 81*, 132–169.

Akkerman, S., & Bruining, T. (2016). Multilevel boundary crossing in a professional development school partnership. *Journal of the Learning Sciences, 25,* 240–284.

American Educational Research Association. (2006). Standards for reporting on empirical social science research in AERA publications. *Educational Researcher, 35*(6), 33–40.

Anzaldúa, G. (1999). *Borderlands: La frontera.* San Francisco, CA: Aunt Lute Books.

Bang, M., Medin, D., Washinawatok, K., & Chapman, S. (2010). Innovations in culturally-based science education through partnerships and community. In M. Khine, & I. Saleh (Eds.), *New science of learning: Cognition, computers and collaboration in education* (pp. 569–592). New York, NY: Springer.

Bang, M., & Vossoughi, S. (2016). Participatory design research and educational justice: Studying learning and relations within social change making. *Cognition and Instruction, 34,* 173–193.

Barker, R. G. (1968). *Ecological psychology.* Stanford, CA: Stanford University Press.

Barron, B., Gomez, K., Pinkard, N., & Martin, C. K. (2014). *The Digital Youth Network: Cultivating digital media citizenship in urban communities.* Cambridge: MIT Press.

Bhabha, H. (1990). The third space: Interview with Homi Bhabha. In J. Rutherford (Ed.), *Identity, community, culture, and difference* (pp. 207–221). London, England: Lawrence & Wishart.

Brand, F. S., & Jax, K. (2007). Focusing the meaning(s) of resilience: Resilience as a descriptive concept and a boundary object. *Ecology and Society, 12*(1), 23. Retrieved from http://www.ecologyandsociety.org/vol12/iss1/art23/

Brennan, N. (2004, February 11). *Chappelle's show* [Television series]. New York, NY: Comedy Central.

Bronfenbrenner, U. (1994). Ecological models of human development. In M. Gauvain, & M. Cole (Eds.), *Readings on the development of children* (2nd ed., pp. 37–43). New York, NY: Freeman.

Brown, A. L., & Campione, J.C. (1990). Communities of learning and thinking, or a context by any other name. *Human Development, 21,* 108–125.

Brown, A. L., & Palincsar, A. S. (1989). Guided, cooperative learning and individual knowledge acquisition. In L. Resnick (Ed.), *Knowing, learning, and instruction: Essays in honor of Robert Glaser* (pp. 393–451). New York, NY: Routledge.

Cammarota, J., & Fine, M. (2008). Youth participatory action research. In *Revolutionizing education: Youth participatory action research in motion* (pp. 1–12). New York, NY: Routledge.

Chappelle, D. (Writer), & Brennan, N. (Writer & Director). (2004). 204 [Television series episode]. In D. Chappelle, N. Brennan, & M. Armour (Producers), *Chappelle's show* [Television series]. New York, NY: Comedy Central.

Cobb, P., Confrey, J., diSessa, A., Lehrer, R., & Schauble, L. (2003). Design experiments in educational research. *Educational Researcher, 32*(1), 9–13.

Cobb, P., McClain, K., & Gravemeijer, K. (2003). Learning about statistical covariation. *Cognition and Instruction, 21*(1), 1–78.

Cole, M. (1996). *Cultural psychology: A once and future discipline.* Cambridge, MA: Harvard University Press.

Cole, M. (1998). Can cultural psychology help us think about diversity? *Mind, Culture, and Activity, 5,* 291–304.

Cole, M., & Distributive Literacy Consortium. (2006). *The fifth dimension: An after-school program built on diversity.* New York, NY: Russell Sage Foundation.

Cole, M., & Engeström, Y. (2007). Cultural-historical approaches to designing for development. In J. Valsiner, & A. Rosa (Eds.), *The Cambridge handbook of sociocultural psychology* (pp. 484–507). New York, NY: Cambridge University Press.

Cole, M., & Gajdamashko, N. (2009). The concept of development in cultural-historical activity theory: Vertical and horizontal. In A. Sannino, H. Daniels, & K. D. Gutiérrez

(Eds.), *Learning and expanding with activity theory* (pp. 129–143). New York, NY: Cambridge University Press.

Cole, M., & Griffin, P. (1983). A socio-historical approach to re-mediation. *Quarterly Newsletter of the Laboratory of Comparative Human Cognition, 5*(4), 69-74.

Cole, M., & Griffin, P. (1986). A sociohistorical approach to remediation. In S. de Castell, A. Luke, & K. Egan (Eds.), *Literacy, society, and schooling: A reader* (pp. 110–131). Cambridge, England: Cambridge University Press.

Cole, M., Hood, L., & McDermott, R.P. (1982). Ecological niche picking. In U. Neisser (Ed.), *Memory observed: Remembering in natural contexts* (pp. 366–373). San Francisco, CA: W. H. Freeman.

Cole, M., & Levitin, K. (2000). A cultural-historical view of human nature. In N. Roughley (Ed.), *Being humans: Anthropological universality and particularity in transdisciplinary perspectives* (pp. 64–80). New York, NY: Walter de Gruyter.

Cole, M., & Wertsch, J.V. (1997). Beyond the individual-social antimony in discussions of Piaget and Vygotsky. *Human Development, 39*, 250–256.

Collins, A., Joseph, D., & Bielaczyc, K. (2004). Design research: Theoretical and methodological issues. *Journal of the Learning Sciences, 13*(1), 15–42.

Conquergood, D. (2002). Performance studies: Interventions and radical research. *The Drama Review, 46*, 145–156.

de Certeau, M. (1984). *The practice of everyday life* (S. Rendall, Trans.). Berkeley: University of California Press.

de Certeau, M. (2000). Ethno-graphy, speech, or the space of the other: Jean de Léry. In Ward Graham (Ed.), *The Certeau reader* (pp. 129–150). Oxford, England: Blackwell.

De Genova, N., Mezzadra, S., & Pickles, J. (Eds.). (2015). New keywords: Migration and borders. *Cultural Studies, 29*(1), 55–87.

DiGiacomo, D. K., & Gutiérrez, K. D. (2015). Relational equity as a design tool within making and tinkering activities. *Mind, Culture, and Activity, 23*, 141–153.

Engeström, Y. (1999). *Learning by expanding: Ten years after. Introduction to the German edition of learning by expanding* (F. Seeger, Trans.). Marburg, Germany: BdWi-Verlag.

Engeström, Y. (2008). *From teams to knots: Activity-theoretical studies of collaboration and learning at work*. Cambridge, England: Cambridge University Press.

Engeström, Y. (2011). From design experiments to formative interventions. *Theory & Psychology, 21*, 598–628.

Engeström, Y., & Sannino, A. (2010). Studies of expansive learning: Foundations, findings and future challenges. *Educational Research Review, 5*(1), 1–24.

Erickson, F. (2006). Studying side by side: Collaborative action ethnography in educational research. In G. Spindler, & L. Hammond (Eds.), *Innovations in educational ethnography: Theory, methods and results* (pp. 235–257). Mahwah, NJ: Lawrence Erlbaum.

Espinoza, M. (2004). *UCLA statewide Migrant Student Institute curriculum*. Los Angeles: University of California, Los Angeles.

Espinoza, M. (2009). A case study of educational sanctuary in one migrant classroom. *Pedagogies, 4*(1), 44–62.

Folke, C. (2003). Social-ecological resilience and behavioural responses. *Individual and Structural Determinants of Environmental Practice, 1*, 226–242.

Folke, C. (2006). Resilience: The emergence of a perspective for social-ecological systems analyses. *Global Environmental Change, 16*, 253–267.

Ford Foundation. (2013). *More and better learning time*. Retrieved from http://www.fordfoundation.org/issues/educational-opportunity-and-scholarship/more- and-better-learning-time

Garmezy, N. (1991). Resilience in children's adaptation to negative life events and stressed environments. *Pediatric Annals, 20*, 459–466.

Garraway, J. (2010). Knowledge boundaries and boundary-crossing in the design of work-response university curricula. *Teaching in Higher Education, 15*, 211–222.

Geertz, C. (1973). *The interpretation of cultures.* New York, NY: Basic Books.

Gibson, J. J. (1966). *The senses considered as perceptual systems.* Boston, MA: Houghton Mifflin.

Givens, J. R., Nasir, N., ross, k., & De Royston, M. (2016). Modeling manhood: Reimagining Black male identities in school. *Anthropology & Education Quarterly, 47,* 167–185.

Gutiérrez, K. D. (2002, November). *Rethinking critical literacy in hard times: Critical literacy as transformative social practice.* Paper presented at the annual meeting of the National Council of Teachers of English, Atlanta, GA.

Gutiérrez, K. D. (2005, April). *Intersubjectivity and grammar in the third space* (Scribner Award lecture). Lecture presented at the annual meeting of the American Educational Research Association, Montreal, Quebec, Canada.

Gutiérrez, K. D. (2006). White innocence: A framework and methodology for rethinking educational discourse and inquiry. *International Journal of Learning, 12,* 223–230.

Gutiérrez, K. D. (2008). Developing a sociocritical literacy in the third space. *Reading Research Quarterly, 43,* 148–164.

Gutiérrez, K. D. (2014). Integrative research review: Syncretic approaches to literacy learning. Leveraging horizontal knowledge and expertise. In P. Dunston, L. Gambrell, K. Headley, S. Fullerton, & P. Stecker (Eds.), *63rd Literacy Research Association Yearbook* (pp. 48–61). Alamonte Springs, FL: Literacy Research Association.

Gutiérrez, K. D. (2016). Designing resilient ecologies: Social design experiments and a new social imagination. *Educational Researcher, 45,* 187–196.

Gutiérrez, K. D., & Arzubiaga, A. E. (2012). An ecological and activity theoretic approach to studying diasporic and nondominant communities. In W. Tate (Ed.), *Research on schools, neighborhoods, and communities: Toward civic responsibility* (pp. 203–216). Plymouth, England: Rowman & Littlefield.

Gutiérrez, K. D., & Barton, C. A. (2015). The possibilities and limits of the structure-agency dialectic in advancing science for all. *Journal of Research in Science Teaching, 52,* 574–583.

Gutiérrez, K. D., Engeström, Y., & Sannino, A. (2016). Expanding educational research and interventionist methodologies. *Cognition and Instruction, 34,* 275–284.

Gutiérrez, K. D., Hunter, J. D., & Arzubiaga, A. (2009). Re-mediating the university: Learning through sociocritical literacies. *Pedagogies, 4*(1), 1–23.

Gutiérrez, K. D., Izquierdo, C., & Kremer-Sadlik, T. (2010). Middle class working families' beliefs and engagement in children's extra-curricular activities: The social organization of children's futures. *International Journal of Learning, 17,* 633–656.

Gutiérrez, K. D., & Jurow, A. S. (2014, June). *Designing for possible futures: The potential of social design experiments.* Paper presented in "Toward an argumentative grammar for socio-cultural/cultural-historical activity approaches to design research," symposium at the 11th International Conference of the Learning Sciences, Boulder, CO.

Gutiérrez, K. D., & Jurow, S. (2016). Social design experiments: Toward equity by design. *Journal of Learning Sciences, 25,* 565–598.

Gutiérrez, K. D., Morales, P. Z., & Martinez, D. C. (2009). Re-mediating literacy: Culture, difference, and learning for students from nondominant communities. *Review of Research in Education, 33*(1), 212–245.

Gutiérrez, K. D., & Penuel, B. (2014). Relevance to practice as a criterion for rigor. *Educational Research, 43*(1), 19–23.

Gutiérrez, K. D., & Rogoff, B. (2003). Cultural ways of learning: Individual traits or repertoires of practice. *Educational Researcher, 32*(5), 19–25.

Gutiérrez, K., Rymes, B., & Larson, J. (1995). Script, counterscript, and underlife in the classroom: James Brown versus *Brown v. Board of Education. Harvard Educational Review, 65,* 445–472.

Gutiérrez, K. D., & Vossoughi, S. (2010). Lifting off the ground to return anew: Mediated praxis, transformative learning, and social design experiments. *Journal of Teacher Education, 61*(1–2), 100–117.

Halberstam, J. (2005). *In a queer time and place: Transgender bodies, subcultural lives.* New York: New York University Press.

Hand, V., Penuel, W., & Gutiérrez, K. (2012). (Re)Framing educational possibility: Attending to power and equity in shaping access to and within learning opportunities. *Human Development, 55*, 250–268.

Ingenuity. (n.d.). In *Merriam-Webster Online.* Retrieved from http://www.merriam-webster.com/dictionary/ingenuity

Jackson, J. L., Jr. (2013). *Thin description: Ethnography and the African Hebrew Israelites of Jerusalem.* Cambridge, MA: Harvard University Press.

Johnson, E. P. (2003). *Appropriating Blackness: Performance and the politics of authenticity.* Durham, NC: Duke University Press.

Johnson, J. M., & Nunez, K. (2015). Alter egos and infinite literacies, Part III: How to build a real gyrl in 3 easy steps. *The Black Scholar, 45*(4), 47–61.

Johnson, P. (2014). *Seeing ghost stories in ESPN's 30 for 30 documentaries.* Paper presented at the 99th annual convention of the Association for the Study of African American Life and History, Memphis, TN.

Jurow, A. S., Hall, R., & Ma, J. Y. (2008). Expanding the disciplinary expertise of a middle school mathematics classroom: Re-contextualizing student models in conversations with visiting specialists. *Journal of the Learning Sciences, 17*, 338–380.

Jurow, A. S., & Shea, M. (2015). Learning in equity-oriented scale-making projects. *Journal of the Learning Sciences, 24*, 286–307.

Kelley, R. D. G. (2004). Looking for the real nigga: Social scientists construct the ghetto. In M. Forman, & M. A. Neal (Eds.), *That's the joint: The hip-hop studies reader* (pp. 119–136). New York, NY: Routledge.

Kelly, A. (2004). Design research in education: Yes, but is it methodological? *Journal of the Learning Sciences, 13*(1), 115–128.

Lave, J. (1996). Teaching, as learning, in practice. *Mind, Culture, and Activity, 3*, 149–164.

Lee, C. (2010). Soaring above the clouds, delving the ocean's depths: Understanding the ecologies of human learning and the challenge for education science. *Educational Researcher, 39*, 643–655.

Lehrer, R, Strom, D., & Confrey, J. (2002). Grounding metaphors and inscriptional resonance: Children's emerging understanding of mathematical similarity. *Cognition and Instruction, 20*, 359–398

Love, B. L. (2012). *Hip hop's li'l sistas speak: Negotiating hip hop identities and politics in the new South.* New York, NY: Peter Lang.

Marcus, G. E. (1995). Ethnography in/of the world system: The emergence of multi-sited ethnography. *Annual Review of Anthropology, 24*, 95–117.

McDermott, R., & Raley, J. (2011). Looking closely: Toward a natural history of human ingenuity. In E. Margolis, & L. Pauwels (Eds.), *Handbook of visual research methods* (pp. 372–391). Thousand Oaks, CA: Sage.

Mendoza, E. (2014). *Disrupting common sense notions through transformative education: Understanding purposeful organization and movement toward mediated praxis* (Doctoral dissertation). Retrieved from ProQuest Dissertations & Theses database. (UMI No. 3635879)

Mendoza, E., Paguyo, C. H., & Gutiérrez, K. D. (2015). Understanding the intersection of race and dis/ability through common sense notions of learning and culture. In D. J. Connor, B. A. Ferri, & S. A. Annamma (Eds.), *DisCrit: Critical conversations across race, class, & dis/ability* (pp. 71–86). New York, NY: Teachers College Press.

Munoz, J. E. (1999). *Disidentifications: Queers of color and the performance of politics.* Minneapolis: University of Minnesota Press.

Nasir, N. S. (2008). Everyday pedagogy: Lessons from basketball, track, and dominoes. *Phi Delta Kappan, March*, 529–532.

Nasir, N. S. (2012). *Racialized identities: Race and achievement among African American youth.* Stanford, CA: Stanford University Press.

Nasir, N. S., ross, k. m., de Royston, M., Givens, J., & Bryant, J. N. (2013). Dirt on my record: Rethinking disciplinary practices in an all-black all-male alternative class. *Harvard Educational Review, 83*, 489–512.

Neisser, U. (1976). *Cognition and reality: Principles and implications of cognitive psychology.* San Francisco, CA: W. H. Freeman.

Nora, P. (1989). Between memory and history: Les lieux de mémoire. *Representations, 26*, 7–24.

Norris, A. (2014). Make-her-spaces as hybrid places: Designing and resisting self constructions in urban classrooms. *Equity & Excellence in Education, 47*(1), 63–77.

Ochs, E., & Kremer-Sadlik, T. (2013). *Fast forward family: Home, work, and relationships in middle class America.* Berkeley: University of California Press.

Pacheco, M. (2012). Learning in/through everyday resistance: A cultural-historical perspective on community resources and curriculum. *Educational Researcher, 41*, 121–132.

Packer, M. (2010). Educational research as a reflexive science of constitution. *NSSE Yearbook, 109*(1), 17–33.

Parham, M. (2009). *Haunting and displacement in African American literature and culture.* New York, NY: Routledge.

Paris, D., & Winn, M. T. (2013). *Humanizing research: Decolonizing qualitative inquiry with youth and communities.* Los Angeles, CA: Sage.

Pea, R. D. (1993). Practices of distributed intelligence and designs for education. In G. Salomon (Ed.), *Distributed cognitions: Psychological and educational considerations* (pp. 47–87). Cambridge, England: Cambridge University Press.

Penuel, W. R., Fishman, B. J., Cheng, B. H., & Sabelli, N. (2011). Organizing research and development at the intersection of learning, implementation, and design. *Educational Researcher, 40*, 331–337.

Royster, F. T. (2012). *Sounding like a no-no: Queer sounds and eccentric acts in the post-soul era.* Ann Arbor: University of Michigan Press.

Rutter, M. (1987). Psychosocial resilience and protective mechanisms. *American Journal of Orthopsychiatry, 57*, 316–331.

Rutter, M. (1990). Psychosocial resilience and protective mechanisms. In J. Rolf, A. S. Masten, D. Cicchetti, K. Nuechterlein, & S. Weintraub (Eds.), *Risk and protective factors in the development of psychopathology* (pp. 181–215). New York, NY: Cambridge University Press.

Sandoval, W. (2014). Conjecture mapping: An approach to systematic educational design research. *Journal of the Learning Sciences, 23*(1), 18–36.

Scardamalia, M., & Bereiter, C. (1994). Computer support for knowledge building communities. *Journal of the Learning Sciences, 3*, 265–283.

Shavelson, R. J., Phillips, D. C., Towne, L., & Feuer, M. J. (2003). On the science of education design studies. *Educational Researcher, 32*(1), 25–28.

Small, M. L. (2008). Four reasons to abandon the idea of "the ghetto." *City & Community, 7*, 389–398.

Smith, L. T. (1999). *Decolonizing methodologies: Research and indigenous peoples.* New York, NY: Zed Books.

Soep, E., & Chavez, V. (2010). *Drop that knowledge: Youth Radio stories.* Berkeley: University of California Press.

Soja, E. W. (1996). *Thirdspace: Journeys to Los Angeles and other real-and-imagined places.* Cambridge, England: Blackwell.

Stone, L. D., & Gutiérrez, K. D. (2007). Problem articulation and the processes of assistance: An activity theoretic view of mediation in game play. *International Journal of Educational Research, 46*(1), 43–56.

Suchman, L. (1994). Working relations of technology production and use. *Computer Supported Cooperative Work, 2,* 21–39.

Tuck, E. (2009). Suspending damage: A letter to communities. *Harvard Educational Review, 79*), 409–428.

Tuomi-Gröhn, T., Engeström, Y., & Young, M. (2003). From transfer to boundary-crossing between school and work as a tool for developing vocational education: An introduction. In T. Tuomi-Gröhn, & Y. Engeström (Eds.), *Between school and work: New perspectives on transfer and boundary-crossing* (pp. 1–15). Amsterdam, Netherlands: Pergamon.

Vakil, S., de Royston, M., Nasir, N. S., & Kirshner, B. (2016). Rethinking race and power in design-based research: Reflections from the field. *Cognition and Instruction, 34,* 194–209.

Vásquez, O. A. (2013). *La clase mágica: Imagining optimal possibilities in a community of learners.* New York, NY: Routledge.

Vaught, S. (2004). The talented tenth: Gay Black boys and the racial politics of Southern schooling. *Journal of Gay & Lesbian Issues in Education, 2*(2), 5–26.

Vossoughi, S., & Gutiérrez, K. (2014). Studying movement, hybridity, and change: Toward a multi-sited sensibility for research on learning across contexts and borders. *National Society for the Study of Education, 113,* 603–632.

Vossoughi, S., Hooper, P., & Escudé, M. (2016). Making through the lens of culture and power: Toward transformative visions for educational equity. *Harvard Educational Review, 86,* 206–232.

Vygotsky, L. S. (1967). Play and its role in the mental development of the child. *Soviet Psychology, 5,* 6–18.

Vygotsky, L. S. (1978). *Mind in society.* Cambridge, MA: Harvard University Press.

Vygotsky, L. S. (1987). *The collected works of L. S. Vygotsky: Vol. 1. Problems of general psychology, including the volume thinking and speech* (R. W. Rieber & A. S. Carton, Eds.; N. Minnick, Trans). New York, NY: Plenum Press.

Vygotsky, L. S. (2004). Imagination and creativity in childhood. *Journal of Russian and East European Psychology, 42,* 7–97.

Walker, B., & Salt, D. (2006). *Resilience thinking: Sustaining ecosystems and people in a changing world.* Washington, DC: Island Press.

Wartofsky, M. W. (1979). Perception, representation, and the forms of action: Towards an historical epistemology. In R. S. Coher, & M. W. Wartofsky (Eds.), *A portrait of twenty-five years* (pp. 215–237). Dordrecht, Netherlands: Springer.

Weisner, T. S. (1998). Human development, child well-being, and the cultural project of development. *New Directions for Child and Adolescent Development, 1998*(80), 69–85.

Werner, E. E. (1990). Protective factors and individual resilience. In S. J. Measles, & J. P. Shonkoff (Eds.), *Handbook of early intervention: Theory, practice and analysis* (pp. 97–116). Cambridge, England: Cambridge University Press.

Werner, E. E. (1993). Risk, resilience, and recovery: Perspectives from the Kauai Longitudinal Study. *Development and Psychopathology, 5,* 503–515.

Willis, P. (1977). *Learning to labor: How working-class kids get working-class jobs.* London, England: Saxon House.

Chapter 3

Pursuing Equity: Disproportionality in Special Education and the Reframing of Technical Solutions to Address Systemic Inequities

CATHERINE KRAMARCZUK VOULGARIDES
EDWARD FERGUS
New York University

KATHLEEN A. KING THORIUS
Indiana University School of Education, Indiana University-Purdue University, Indianapolis

In the review, we examine what is known about disproportionality with the intention of informing the direction of policy and practice remedies. We outline the definition, contours, and characteristics of disproportionality and examine some of the prevailing explanations as to why the issue persists. We then pivot the review to consider how policy, through the Individuals with Disabilities Education Act (IDEA), has sought to address disproportionality in special education and disciplining of students with disabilities. We question why a legally sound civil rights law like IDEA has been unable to abate disproportionality for nearly 40 years. We then turn our attention to review interventions embedded in IDEA that have been recommended to address disproportionality and question why they have not improved outcomes for "nondominant" students in special education. We conclude with some recommendations for disrupting disproportionality.

The United States is experiencing large demographic shifts. In the span of three decades, between 1980 and 2008, the U.S. White population has declined from 80% to 66%; the Black population has remained steady around 12%; and the Hispanic population has more than doubled from 6% to 15% (Aud, Fox, & Kewal Ramani, 2010). While the country's racial demographics continue to shift and diversify, education research has repeatedly documented achievement differences associated with race (Jencks & Phillips, 1998), wealth and income levels (Duncan & Murnane, 2011), linguistic and ethnic differences (Fry, 2008), gender (DiPrete &

Review of Research in Education
March 2017, Vol. 41, pp. 61–87
DOI: 10.3102/0091732X16686947
© 2017 AERA. http://rre.aera.net

Buchmann, 2013), and lack of educational opportunity associated with the increasing segregation of students of color in America's schools (Orfield, Ee, Frankenberg, & Siegel-Hawley, 2016). Race, gender, language status, and other social markers of difference consistently stratify students and directly influence academic success and attainment (Alexander, Entwisle, & Olson, 2014; Gamoran 1986; Hallinan, Bottoms, Pallas, & Palla, 2003; Lucas, 1999; Oakes, 1985; Rosenbaum, 1980). Thus, as the nation diversifies, education research continues to show *who* a student is matters more for their educational attainment more so than *how* a student performs in school.

One of the most perplexing "durable inequalities" (Tilly, 1998) related to social markers of difference in American society is racial disproportionality in special education. The issue has been documented for over 40 years (see Donovan & Cross, 2002; Dunn, 1968; Heller, Holtzman, & Messick, 1982) in education research despite advances in policy and practice. Disproportionality is defined by a group's over- or underrepresentation in an educational category, program, or service in comparison with the group's proportion in the overall population (Donovan & Cross, 2002).

METHOD

In the review, we examine what is known about disproportionality with the intention of informing the direction of policy and practice remedies. We outline the definition, contours, and characteristics of disproportionality and examine some of the prevailing explanations as to why the issue persists. We then pivot the review to consider how policy, through the Individuals with Disabilities Education Act (IDEA), has sought to address disproportionality in special education and disciplining of students with disabilities. We question why a legally sound civil rights law like IDEA has been unable to abate disproportionality for nearly 40 years. We then turn our attention to review interventions embedded in IDEA that have been recommended to address disproportionality and question why they have not improved outcomes for "nondominant"[1] students in special education. We conclude with some recommendations for disrupting disproportionality.

We relied on descriptive, explanatory, and theoretical studies on disproportionality to construct the review. The majority of the articles included in the review provide some critical recognition or discussion of race, equity, and/or inequity in special education. We identified mixed-method, quantitative, and qualitative studies that are empirically based (including experimental and quasi-experimental) on the topic. We searched for empirical studies on disproportionality with a priority on the past 15 years (2000–2015). Some empirical studies were included outside of the 15-year time frame because of their seminal contributions to knowledge on racial disproportionality in special education. In addition, theoretical literature was included in the review that challenges common understandings of race as a social construct, disproportionality, and the efficacy of current remedies to address disproportionality. Literature was excluded from the review if it did not explicitly focus on race and/or disproportionality in special education.

Terms used to identify studies in the review were drawn from prominent research on the topic and available on electronic databases (e.g., EBSCO, Wilson Web Social Sciences Full Text, ERIC, Google Scholar, PsycInfo, ProQuest, JSTOR) as well as nonmainstream sources (e.g., newspapers, magazines, dissertations, conference papers, and technical reports). Several keywords such as "disproportionality," "under-representation," "overrepresentation," "Individuals with Disabilities Education Act," "race," "discipline," "classification," "placement," and "special education" were used in various combinations until similar studies were consistently identified. The synthesis process involved reading and summarizing findings of each study including research design, analytic foci, numbers and populations of participants, and main findings. The following criteria were generally applied to studies included in the review: studies pertaining to disproportionate discipline and special education placement and classification of historically underrepresented racial and ethnic groups; studies published between 2000 and 2015; and studies within United States K–12 schooling environments.

TRENDS IN DISPROPORTIONALITY: OVER- AND UNDERREPRESENTATION

Nondominant students are overrepresented in the high-incidence (subjective) disability categories (Donovan & Cross, 2002; U.S. Department of Education, 2009) and/or are disproportionately subject to exclusionary disciplinary practices (Losen, 2014).[2] The high-incidence disability categories include emotional and behavioral disorders, learning disabilities (LD), intellectual disability, and speech and language impairments. The students most affected by disproportionality tend to be low-income, Black, and American Indian youth with disabilities (Coutinho & Oswald, 2000; Fierros & Conroy, 2002; Losen & Orfield, 2002; Oswald, Coutinho, & Best, 2002; Parrish, 2002; Skiba et al., 2011; U.S. Department of Education, 2009; Waitoller, Artiles, & Cheney, 2010; Zhang, Katsiyannis, Ju, & Roberts, 2014). In contrast, English language learners (ELLs) tend to become overrepresented later in the schooling process and in districts that serve large populations of ELLs (Artiles, Rueda, Salazar, & Higareda, 2005; Samson & Lesaux, 2009; Sullivan, 2011).

Research on disproportionate suspensions identifies patterns in which nondominant students (i.e., Black, Hispanic, and American Indian) are not only identified with a high-incidence disability (e.g., emotional disturbance, LD, speech and language impairments, other health impairment) but also suspended more severely for the same infraction as their White counterparts, are suspended more repeatedly, and most devastatingly, these patterns heighten the likelihood for youth to engage with the criminal justice system (Fabelo et al., 2012; Kim, Hewitt, & Losen, 2010). Black students are referred at higher rate for special education services stemming from behavioral issues (Planty et al., 2009). Research has also shown that Black males are the most likely to be disciplined or suspended for subjective reasons, as compared with their White peers, and to receive harsher and longer duration in punishments

(Achilles, McLaughlin, & Croninger, 2007; Bradshaw, Mitchell, O'Brennan, & Leaf, 2010; Cartledge & Lo, 2006; Mendez & Knoff, 2003; Rausch & Skiba, 2004; Skiba, Michael, Nardo, & Peterson, 2002; Vincent & Tobin, 2010). Office disciplinary referrals also indicate disproportionality, with Black students being two to four times more likely than White students to be referred (Skiba et al., 2011).

In addition, underrepresentation is equally as important, but less explored in disproportionality research. For example, Yoon and Gentry (2009) found, using Office of Civil Rights data, that at both the national and state levels, White and Asian American students are consistently overrepresented in gifted programs. On the other hand, American Indian, Alaskan Native, Hispanic, and Black students are underrepresented in gifted programs (Ford, 1998; Harris & Ford, 1999; Worrell, 2003, 2009). Although there is intra group variability within each racial category, the aggregate trends surrounding both over- and underrepresentation have been relatively consistent over time.

SOURCES OF DISPROPORTIONALITY

Disproportionality has multiple causes that extend beyond the special education system. The explanatory research on disproportionality in special education and suspension provide at least two terrains of inquiry—practice-based and sociodemographic "causal" factors—each raising questions on the role of bias specifically related to race.

Practice-Based Factors Explaining Disproportionality

The disproportionality research on practice-based factors maintains two theoretical arguments: (a) a cultural mismatch between middle class, White teachers and school administrators with low-income and/or racial and ethnic minority student populations and (b) gaps in the development and implementation of interventions and other referral systems, which cause disproportionate outcomes.

The cultural mismatch argument situates the notion of Whiteness and/or colorblindness as a default frame utilized in assessment, intervention, cognitive, behavior problem identification, and so on (Annamma, Connor, & Ferri, 2013; Artiles, 2009; Connor, Ferri, & Annamma, 2015). For instance, Miner and Clark-Stewart (2008) identified White teachers labeled externalizing behaviors as increasing among Black children as their age increases; meanwhile, these teachers identified non-Black children's externalizing behaviors as decreasing. Similarly, Skiba, Michael, and Nardo (2000) documented Black children receiving behavioral referrals more frequently for less subjective categories. Other studies found similar patterns, such as Neal, McGray, Webb-Johnson and Bridgest (2003) identified White teachers perceive Black children's walking and talking mannerisms as more fearful and related to lower achievement; and Skiba et al. (2006) also found White teachers were aware of not being prepared to deal with specific behavioral issues among racial and ethnic minority students and perceive special education as an appropriate placement.

Within the cultural mismatch research, various studies also explore how to iden-tify interventions that improve cultural matching. For instance, Simmons-Reed and Cartledge (2014) argue for the development of culturally responsive interventions for Black males given the manner in which zero-tolerance policies target this population. Other researchers (e.g., Raines, Dever, Kamphaus, & Roach, 2012) argue for improved early identification metrics that minimize the propensity of racial and eth-nic minority students to be situated as severely deficient; and others argue for address-ing the mismatch in the core instructional program with more culturally responsive instruction (Griner & Stewart, 2013; Shealey, McHatton, & Wilson, 2011) or assess-ing schools' culturally responsive capacity (Fiedler et al., 2008).

The cultural mismatch argument also engages with the role of practitioner beliefs. Prior research on teacher beliefs highlights significant patterns between how beliefs intersect with race constructs and cognitive abilities. Ford, Scott, Moore, and Amos (2013) identify how teacher beliefs about cognitive ability relate to the identification of Black students in gifted programs. And yet other research suggests expectations about a group may have more impact on achievement than individual-level expecta-tions because the group norm perception operates as a gauge for understanding indi-vidual student interactions (Agirdag, Van Houtte, & Van Avermaet, 2012; Van Houtte, 2011).

Beliefs alone do not result in disparate outcomes though. Discriminatory behav-iors help mediate how beliefs effect overrepresentation, referral to special education, and/or discipline. Eccles, Wong, and Peck (2006) in a study of 11th-grade Black students identified how daily encounters of racial discrimination effect academic motivation and engagement. Gregory and Thompson (2010) in a study of 35 under-performing Black students identified variability in teacher perceptions of these stu-dents, and students who perceived teacher practice as unfair, were more likely to receive office disciplinary referrals. Thus, there is growing empirical evidence that teacher beliefs and expectations of students, based on race, relate to disproportionate outcomes.

Disproportionality has also been attributed to gaps in district- and/or school-level educational practices and policies that are "feeding the problem." This line of research demonstrates an adequacy and inadequacy argument regarding how practice can affect disproportionality rates. For instance, Kurth, Morningstar, and Kozleski (2014) explored national data on least restrictive environment and identified the increasing pattern of special education segregation among some subjective categories. Other studies focused on multiple dimensions of school-level practice such as limited inter-ventions, procedures, and teams for implementing these interventions (Gravois & Rosenfield, 2006); differential implementation of referral processes (Harry & Klingner, 2006, 2014); inappropriate approaches to behavior management (Milner, 2006; Skiba, Peterson, & Williams, 1997; Weinstein, Curran, & Tomlinson-Clarke, 2003); inadequate framing of zero tolerance and other behavior management policies (Noguera, 2003; Skiba et al., 2002); and problematic beliefs about poverty, race, and learning in framing of solutions to address disproportionality (Ahram, Fergus, & Noguera, 2011; Skiba et al., 2006).

Sociodemographic Factors Explaining Disproportionality

The explanatory research on disproportionality in special education and suspension also explores the relative impact of sociodemographic factors on disproportionate outcomes. This research uses variables such as race, free/reduced-price lunch (FRPL) status, family structure, and so on, as either deficits of individual students or as factors related to structural disparities. There are several perspectives taken in this line of research.

The first line of research situates the variables as predictive and/or contributing to patterns of disproportionality. This approach inadvertently promulgates that these sociodemographic variables demonstrate compromised human development, in particular FRPL status (O'Connor & Fernandez, 2006). Studies such as Morgan Farkas, Hillemeier, and Maczuga (2012) and Morgan et al. (2015) promote the conclusions from the National Research Council (2002) report in which FRPL status is argued to minimize cognitive and behavioral development and in turn is a sufficient rationale for their inferential analyses A subsequent step in such sociodemographic analyses is the treatment of race and FRPL as confounding variables, and by default conceptually arguing that race and FRPL both compromise human development. These conclusions are drawn despite decades of research that provides qualitative, quantitative, and mixed-method studies that explore the complexity of practice-based conditions as setting the stage for disproportionate outcomes. Thus, unintentionally, this line of explanatory research fails to situate the presence of institutionalized practice of racism and in turn uses a conceptual research frame that "blames the victim" for not being successful despite racism.

The second line of research on sociodemographic factors maintains a conceptual focus on the presence and intensity of disproportionality in special education and suspension. The focus is centered on the manner in which racial/ethnic minority and FRPL-eligible students are distributed in certain schools or experience special education or suspension. For example, Oswald et al. (2002) suggest disproportionality occurs because students have "differential susceptibility," or exposure to community, health, economic, school, and environmental resources which can lead to variation in identification of student disability. The sociodemographic studies tend to have varying and sometimes contradictory findings. However, they do establish that a school district's sociodemographics are strongly associated with the proportion of students identified for special education (Losen & Orfield, 2002). This relationship, however, depends on the disability category, on the methods used to measure disproportionality and the type of data collected.

In relationship to discipline, Beck and Muschkin (2012) identify student-level demographic factors (i.e., gender, race, parent educational level, eligibility for FRPL) as explanatory variables of disciplinary infractions. Additionally, they cite academic differences comprise the largest racial difference contributing to behavioral infractions. Sullivan, Klingbeil, and Van Norman (2013) also identify a similar pattern between student-level demographic factors and discipline infractions. Moreover, Bryan, Day-Vines, Griffin, and Moore-Thomas (2012) identify students' race, gender, and teachers' postsecondary expectations as predictors of behavioral referrals, specifically race is treated as predictive of the distribution of teacher referral. More recently, Martinez, McMahon, and Treger (2016) identified in an individual- and school-level data set with 1,400 students moderation effects of student–teacher ratio and racial/ethnic student concentration as contributing to the rates of office discipline referrals. Also, Skiba et al. (2014), in a multilevel model, identify the varying influence of infraction type, individual, and school-level characteristics on out-of-school suspensions. The most salient findings include schools with higher proportions of Black students contribute to out-of-school suspensions; and systemic school-level variables are more important in determining Black overrepresentation in suspension. And in an attempt to understand whether disproportionate office discipline referrals are explained by school effects and/or student behaviors, Rocque (2010) conducted a nested analysis in which office discipline referrals are overrepresented by Black students; however, the inability of school effect variables to explain the pattern raised some significant questions.

In sum, these various lines of research provide a textured documentation of possibly flawed school practices and processes. But, more important, these studies point to the manner in which racism and/or other forms of bias are present in the schooling process. Despite the range of practice-based areas raised by this research, the research on practice-based remedies focuses on singular elements of practice shifting overall disproportionality rates. Simultaneously, the research on sociodemographic variables, which tends to use large-scale inferential analyses, conceptually situates these variables as representations of compromised human development or structural racism. Both topics, practice-based and sociodemographic factors, demonstrate complexities in the sources of disproportionality and a substantive representation of these studies suggest nuanced patterns of racism and other forms of bias.

EXISTING REMEDIES TO DEFINE, TRACK, MEASURE, AND ADDRESS DISPROPORTIONALITY THROUGH THE INDIVIDUALS WITH DISABILITIES EDUCATION ACT

IDEA is a civil rights law based on the 14th Amendment, which ensures equal treatment of all U.S. citizens by providing equal educational opportunity to students with disabilities through a free and appropriate public education. The law was created to address and redress historical inequities associated with the education of students with disabilities in American schools and has governed how students with disabilities should be educated for nearly four decades (Minow, 2010). It was not until the 1997 reauthorization of IDEA that disproportionality was mentioned in the law despite the fact that research identified disproportionality in special education in the 1960s (e.g., Dunn,

1968). The 1997 amendment of IDEA [20 U.S.C. §1418(c), 1998] established a specific policy approach for identifying disproportionality in special education. The language included attention to data collection surrounding disproportionality:

Each State that receives assistance under this part, and the Secretary of the Interior, shall provide for the collection and examination of data to determine if significant disproportionality based on race is occurring in the State with respect to—(A) the identification of children as children with disabilities, including the identification of children as children with disabilities in accordance with a particular impairment described in section 602(3); and (B) the placement in particular educational settings of such children.

However, as various researchers argue (Albrecht, Losen, Chung, & Middelberg, 2012; Hehir, 2002), the regulations and guidance did not provide sufficient direction for what it meant to collect such information. Additionally, in a policy review memo, Markowitz (2002) identified 29 states, which developed criteria for collecting and identifying districts with disproportionality in special education. Among the 29 states, 26 utilized one criteria and 3 others focused on multiple criteria; the most common criteria included a discrepancy point or a significance test. Given the variation in data collection points, Office of Special Education Programs (OSEP; 2007) provided further guidance in the March 1999 Federal Register (Vol. 64, No. 48) and asked in addition to collecting data on disproportionality patterns, states were required to review policies, practices, and procedures associated with IDEA implementation.

The reauthorization of IDEA in 2004 [20 U.S.C. §1412(a)(22, 24)] further altered the educational policy approach for addressing disproportionality because the 1997 regulations provided very little change in reducing patterns of disproportionality (Albrecht et al., 2012; Hehir, 2002). The 2004 guidance added attention to least restrictive environment and discipline. The 2004 IDEA statute also included recognition that Black students continue to be overrepresented in special education in specific settings. OSEP recognized disproportionality was ever-present which led the reauthorization to include (a) guidance for states to monitor disproportionality, (b) to describe the formula used for identifying disproportionate districts, (c) to require districts found with "significant disproportionality" to set aside up to 15% of IDEA funds for coordinated early intervening services,[3] and (d) require the school district to publicly report on the revision of policies, practices, and procedures.

There are two significant provisions related to the guidance and monitoring of disproportionality. The first involves the identification of disproportionality via performance indicators. States have to monitor special education outcomes through 20 quantifiable and qualitative indicators [20 U.S.C. 1416(a)(3)], known as State Performance Plan indicators. Three State Performance Plan indicators are focused on disproportionality.

- Indicator 9 refers to the disproportionate representation of racial and ethnic groups in *special education and related services* that is the result of *inappropriate identification*.

- Indicator 10 refers to disproportionate representation of racial and ethnic groups in *specific disability categories* that is the result of *inappropriate identification*.
- Indicator 4 has two components.
  - 4A refers to significant discrepancies in the rates of long-term suspensions of students with disabilities compared to districts in a state.
  - 4B refers to significant discrepancies in the rates of long-term suspensions of students with disabilities, based on race and ethnicity, compared with districts in a state *due to inappropriate policies, procedures, or practices*.

The second provision in IDEA 2004 provides for the identification of districts with "significant disproportionality," though there is no clear definition of what "significant disproportionality" is. Significant disproportionality is identified around (a) overrepresentation in special education and a specific disability (b) overrepresentation in special education placement, and (c) the duration, intensity, and type of suspensions in special education (IDEA Data Center, 2014). Additionally "significant disproportionality" does not require a finding of inappropriate policies, practices, and procedures; however, it does require a review of, and if appropriate, revision of policies, practices, and procedures related to IDEA. The citation also triggers an automatic allocation of up to 15% of Part B funds to remedy disproportionality and public reporting on any revisions of policies, practices, or procedures.

Measuring Disproportionality and Assuring Compliance With IDEA

OSEP requires states to set a numerical threshold to identify significant disproportionality in school districts. The process of identifying significant disproportionality is fraught with inconsistencies because each state has its own threshold and way for identifying disproportionality. In addition, there are a variety of measures a state can use to identify disproportionality. The three most common are composition index, risk index, and risk ratio (Boneshefski & Runge, 2014; Donovan & Cross, 2002). The risk ratio is the most commonly used measure.

The risk ratio identifies a specific racial group's risk of a particular outcome compared with that of all other students. It does this by comparing the risk of one racial group on a particular outcome to the risk of all other racial groups for the same outcome. Disproportionality is indicated through this measure when a particular group's risk is higher than 1. Thus, a risk ratio of 1 implies equal risk for a particular outcome and a risk ratio below 1 indicates underrepresentation. There is little consistency across states over who should be the comparison group when using risk ratios. The U.S. Department of Education urges comparison against all other groups, while some scholars recommend using White students as the referent because they are the presumed norm.

In addition, as previously mentioned, OSEP's monitoring of disproportionality is related to compliance with IDEA. If a citation is issued through numerical detection of disproportionate outcomes in special education, OSEP requires local education agencies (LEAs) to examine their policies, practices, and procedures that are influenced by IDEA for compliance. A citation for placement and classification of students with disabilities requires examination into the *process* of special education referral and placement. However, when there is disproportionality in disciplinary outcomes, there are several procedural protections for students with disabilities. These include functional behavior assessments (FBAs), behavioral intervention plans (BIPs), manifestation determination meetings (MDs), and the provision of interim academic educational services.[4]

Despite the plethora of procedural protections in IDEA, nondominant students are still disproportionality excluded from schooling. Losen, Hodson, Ee, and Martinez (2015) argue that if schools were adequately meeting the legal requirements of IDEA and effectively serving students under IDEA, then nondominant students would not be disproportionality excluded. However, this is not the case. Hyman, Rivkin, and Rosenbaum (2011) also question why Black and Hispanic students are disproportionality suspended despite extensive procedural provisions in IDEA. As with detection of disproportionality, each state has its own time frame and process outlined for assuring compliance with IDEA. Thus some states may require extensive compliance monitoring, while others require very little of LEAs (Albrecht et al., 2012; Artiles, 2011).

Issues With Current Monitoring Structures

Overall, the development of disproportionality legislative policy and guidance provides increased opportunity for targeted data collection, identification of policies, practices and procedures related to disproportionality, and the reallocation of funds to remedy issues of inappropriate identification. However, the improvements between the 1997 and 2004 reauthorizations of IDEA have been fraught with complications. These include confusion regarding the interpretation of disproportionality and significant disproportionality, the allowance of states to provide definitions of disproportionality, and the latitude allowed for states to identify a threshold and develop a formula for identifying disproportionality. Recent reports and research (Albrecht et al., 2012; U.S. Government Accountability Office [GAO], 2013) argue state-level latitude has resulted in significant variations across states as to what constitutes disproportionality and conceptually challenges the notion of what is disproportionality. For example, the U.S. GAO (2013) reports Maryland, Iowa, and Louisiana identify districts as disproportionate based on a relative risk ratio numerical threshold of 2.0 or more, while South Carolina, California, Mississippi, and Connecticut use a 4.0 or more threshold.

Further evidence from the U.S. GAO in 2013 highlights the concern as to whether policy provisions are adding to the disparate outcome because of the absence of clarity in the policy, processes, and formula. The evidence on disproportionality suggests that despite extensive federal legal protections for students with disabilities, gross inequities and violations of educational rights persist—indicating current efforts to address disproportionality through policy mechanisms are relatively ineffective (Albrecht et al., 2012; Cavendish, Artiles, & Harry, 2015; Skiba, 2013).

THE PARADOX OF IDEA

There is a perplexing paradox deeply embedded in the intersections between disproportionality and IDEA legislation. Artiles (2011) states, an interesting paradox

arises with the racialization of disabilities [because the] civil rights response for one group of individuals (i.e., learners with disabilities) has become a potential source of inequities for another group (i.e. racial minority students), despite their shared histories of struggle for equity. (p. 431)

The paradox essentially highlights a tension between technical understandings and application of IDEA and the sociocultural contexts within which policy is appropriated to practice. Cavendish et al. (2015) state the policies designed to address disproportionality "are not inherently discriminatory, but the impacts of the policy(s) on educational equity are hidden until we examine the consequences behind these engagements" (p. 3). Thus, the paradox calls for a deeper understanding into why technical solutions cannot address disproportionate outcomes.

The Limits of Technical Approaches for Understanding Disproportionality

Disproportionality is often framed as a technical issue that can be "fixed," through interventions or programs. However, Artiles, Kozleski, Trent, Osher, and Ortiz (2010) highlight how problematic this view is and state "the reluctance to frame disproportionality as a problem stresses technical arguments that ignore the role of historical, contextual, and structural forces" (p. 281). The technical view of special education and IDEA is based on the idea that disability, and deficits, reside within individuals and can be fixed by individual remedies. Thus, the "structural underpinnings" of disproportionality are ignored when a technical approach is relied on (Artiles, 2011). Simply mandating "equal access" through IDEA is not enough to effectively address the historical, political, and economic power differentials associated with race in America (Cavendish et al., 2015).

Leonardo and Broderick (2011) suggest the very definitions associated with disproportionality are problematic. They state,

By conceptualizing the problem [disproportionality] as one of overrepresentation, there is risk of tacit reification and legitimation of the naturalness and neutrality of the bureaucratic system of special education as a whole, and, by extension, of the deficit driven and psychological understandings of "ability" and "disability" within which it is grounded. (p. 2208)

In a similar fashion, Artiles (2013) critiques the impact of individualized definitions of disability in federal law. He states that disability categories such as LD, when they are defined without consideration of culture and context "naturalizes the racialization of disabilities, marshaling evidence that conceivably legitimizes racial disproportionality"

(p. 338). This suggests that when labels, and remedies for addressing students embodying these labels, do not recognize the importance of context, students become deficitized. They are the issue, the source of disproportionality, and are thus justifiably classified, placed, or excluded from the education process.

In addition, when solutions for addressing inequities are applied in a technical manner, the impetus of the legislation, or the social justice project, becomes lost. McCall and Skrtic (2010) argue that the social agenda behind special education has been "depoliticized" through the bureaucracy of the system. They state,

> Those whose needs had been politicized were recast as individual clients rather than participants in a political movement, thus re-positioning them as individual victims and passive recipients of predefined services rather than political agents involved in interpreting their needs and shaping their life conditions, thereby stripping them of their human dignity. (p. 12)

Under current legislative efforts, the focus on individual needs decenters the systemic nature of disproportionality.

Ideological Underpinnings: Examining Race- and Context-Neutral Assumptions in Disproportionality Policy

Behind technical approaches to addressing disproportionality lies a colorblind ideology, which fails to explicitly recognize how Whiteness is often viewed as race neutral. This taken-for-granted ideological assumption has consequences for groups that do not fit into the implicit cultural norms associated with Whiteness. Saito's (2009) study on urban public policies identifies the pernicious effects of unrecognized colorblindness embedded in public policies. He states,

> People working to enact and support race-neutral public policies may ignore the ways in which race is already present in the ideologies and practices of the larger society that shape the formation and implementation of policies. As a result, policies that appear race neutral may in fact be structured in ways that have racialized outcomes. This occurs because the policies do nothing to counter the ways in which race is already present, and thus the policies serve to reinforce racialized practices. (p. 4)

Saito emphasizes that polices which appear to be racially neutral become racialized when the effects of the policy differentially affects racial groups. The same reasoning can be applied to IDEA.

On the surface, IDEA is a race-neutral policy. Although recognition of disproportionality through IDEA highlights a race-based outcome the remedies, procedural protections, and interventions embedded in IDEA do not explicitly attend to racial, ethnic, and cultural differences. Thus the race-neutral approach embedded in IDEA contributes to an understanding of disability that is separate from race and therefore racialized outcomes are located within an individual rather than in systems of oppression. This individual-centered and race-neutral approach limits the ability of research-based interventions to eliminate disproportionate outcomes in special education.

EXAMINING DISPROPORTIONALITY REMEDIES: INDIVIDUAL SOLUTIONS FOR A SYSTEMIC ISSUE

The next section is dedicated to understanding current interventions recommended in IDEA, legitimated in research and practice, as effective means for meeting the educational needs of students with disabilities and hence, for addressing disproportionality. However, as Sullivan, Artiles, and Hernandez-Saca (2015) state, special education interventions "may have been misconceived in foci" because they are "too molecular to affect the other interconnected and distal forces that drive disproportionality" (p. 131). Thus, although each intervention described below is research based, they do not collectively improve outcomes for *all* students.

Multitiered Systems of Support (MTSS) and Response to Intervention (RtI)

Response to Intervention emerged within the special education research community in the early 2000s in response to a commission by the U.S. Congress of a set of papers and related research conference to discuss U.S. special education (Finn, Rotherham, & Hokanson, 2001). The papers and conference centered on examining weaknesses in the traditional approach of determining a significant discrepancy between students' academic achievement and intellectual ability, as measured by standardized achievement and intelligence test batteries, typically administered outside students' classrooms by schools' psychologists and special education teachers, as the basis for determining special education eligibility under the federal category of specific learning disability (SLD; Lyon et al., 2001), such approaches as "wait-to-fail" models whereby students who were struggling did not receive formalized supports until such a discrepancy could be evidenced (Bradley, Danielson, & Hallahan, 2002). Soon thereafter, RtI was included in IDEA 2004 as an option, state education agencies (SEAs) could allow LEAs (i.e., school districts) to utilize in special education eligibility determination processes, particularly related to SLD (Vaughn & Fuchs, 2003). Since, RtI frameworks have been well-documented in multidisciplinary education research, and have been the subject of scrutiny with regard for their adequacy in addressing issues of inequity in general and special education, including disproportionate representation of racial, ethnic, and linguistic nondominant students (e.g., Artiles, Bal, & Thorius, 2010; Thorius & Maxcy, 2015).

Although there is considerable variability in how RtI frameworks have been operationalized, key premises on which all frameworks are grounded include attention to prevention of school failure, reliance on curriculum-based measurements of students' progress to determine the need for alteration of instruction or application of some form of academic or social intervention, and focus on early application of such intervention (Thorius & Maxcy, 2015). Several variations exist across the application of RtI frameworks; the first is in the number of framework "tiers." This variation is reflected in a recent vernacular shift to the term MTSS (Jimerson, Burns, & VanDerHeyden, 2016) as both a synonym for RtI, and inclusive of students' social and emotional functioning, intervention, and special education determination typically under the category of Emotional Disturbance addressed by Positive Behavior

Interventions and Supports (PBIS; described in the subsequent section) in addition to traditional RtI frameworks' focus on literacy (Vaughn & Fuchs, 2003). Second, RtI frameworks vary in relation to whether instruction and interventions are standardized in selection and application with students across similar performance profiles (i.e., standard-protocol models), or selected by educators as they interpret a student's individual performance (i.e., problem-solving models). Within the first tier across all RtI framework variations, students are to experience evidence-based general education instruction and have their progress monitored by educators for expected rates of improvement in relation to peers. Also common across all iterations of RtI is a reliance on instruction and intervention tested in experimental research, as well as reliance on monitoring students' progress using curriculum-based measures (Fuchs, Fuchs, & Stecker, 2010). Finally, across RtI frameworks, the intensity of interventions and supports increases as the number of students expected to require such supports as a result of failure to respond to less intensive evidence-based instruction and intervention within earlier tiers intensive tier of intervention decreases; students who reach the top, typically the third, tier (Fuchs, Fuchs, & Compton, 2013), are considered for special education eligibility on the basis of failure to respond adequately to all previous interventions and on the assumption that poor instruction as the reason for failure has been ruled out (Fuchs, 2002, as cited in Artiles, 2015). Several researchers and policymakers have expressed hope in the potential for RtI to address the disproportionate representation for nondominant racial, ethnic, and linguistic students in special education on the basis of redistribution of quality opportunities to learn earlier and more intensively on the basis of assessed student need (e.g., Artiles et al., 2010), yet also cautioned that such approaches must account for multilayered and nuanced understandings of culture which shape how RtI is conceptualized and enacted locally (Artiles, 2015; Thorius & Maxcy, 2015).

Recently, Artiles (2015) illustrated how RtI is imbued with a five-dimensional framework of culture shaping how students' cultures "IN the classroom" is or is not considered within RtI research, or when considered, done so without attention to students' "identity kaleidoscopes," (p. 14), echoing in part Thorius and Sullivan's (2013) review of existing research on RtI applications with ELLs, which found little attention to the quality of universal instruction in RtI's first tier. Moreover, concerns with the impact of RtI on special education disproportionality continue to mount; in 2010, McKinney, Bartholomew, and Gray found patterns of nondominant racial and linguistic student overrepresentation in RtI's second and third tiers and Bouman found that African American student SLD disproportionality in California actually increased over a 5-year period of RtI implementation despite overall reduction in SLD eligibility across all racial groups combined. More recently, Thorius, Maxcy, Macey, and Cox (2014) illustrated how urban elementary school educators enacted RtI in competition with other policy and political factors, and informed by normative and deficit assumptions about racially nondominant students and families, contributing to a local "zone of mediation" (Welner, 2001), where nondominant students were often considered for special education eligibility without or with limited interventions.

Taken together, we hope to have illustrated the need for RtI research that provides "insight into the apparent immutability of certain equity concerns such as the disproportionate representation of students of color in special education, along with contextual considerations for those who develop policy and introduce it into local sites" (Thorius & Maxcy, 2015, p. 7). With regard for the latter, contextual considerations for RtI (i.e., MTSS) policy development and introduction into local settings, we conclude that attention to strong "implementation" fidelity of RtI emphasized in the bulk of existing research with regard to instruction (e.g., VanDerHeyden, Witt, Gilbertson, 2007), progress monitoring (e.g., Busch & Reschly, 2007), interventions (e.g., Koutsoftas, Harmon, & Gray, 2009), and special education eligibility determination (e.g., Shinn, 2007) is not enough to examine why and how RtI enacted in everyday practice may or may not lead to the reduction of special education disproportionality for nondominant students. We contend that inquiry into the complexity of local factors shaping interpretation, implementation, and negation of RtI policy is of equal importance.

Discipline and Positive Behavioral Intervention Systems

There are two sections of federal policy that focus on discipline disparities—IDEA 2004 and Every Student Succeeds Act (ESSA) 2015. The former outlines a focus on the rates of suspension occurring among students with disabilities already discussed. The reauthorization of the Elementary Secondary Education Act (2015)—now described as the Every Student Succeeds Act (ESSA S. 1177)—also establishes a federal perspective and approach on discipline. The main approach of ESSA on school discipline is to reduce the overuse of exclusionary practices that remove students from the classroom.

These policy provisions provide some important movement forward in addressing discipline disparities. For instance, SEAs will now be required to collect data from school districts on different forms of exclusionary discipline practices; SEAs will receive funds to support activities and programs on behavioral interventions; and LEAs will identify schools with high rates of discipline disaggregated by subgroups. In the aggregate, these policy provisions require identification of a discipline problem, collection of data on the problem, and behavioral interventions to address the problem. Though ESSA does not explicitly highlight disproportionate discipline outcomes, the guidance package provided by the U.S. Department of Education/Department of Justice (2014) articulates the conceptual connection between disparate outcomes and some of the ESSA policy provisions. The guidance frames for LEAs that the racial disparities demonstrated in the Civil Rights Data Collection, collected by Office for Civil Rights, are not occurring by chance and as such LEAs need to be aware of their statutory obligations to ensure administration of discipline without discrimination on the basis of race, gender, color, or national origin. In order to prevent discrimination, the guidance argues LEAs need to understand "fair and equitable discipline policies" are components of a school environment that ensures all students learn and grow; "Equipping school officials with an array of tools to support positive student behavior—thereby providing a range of options to prevent and address misconduct—will both promote safety and avoid the use of discipline policies that are discriminatory or inappropriate" (U.S. Department of Education/Department of Justice, 2014, p. 6).

Overall, the combination of IDEA 2004, ESSA 2015, and the U.S. Department of Education/Department of Justice guidance package "make room for schools" to consider additional remedies for handling student behavior differently such as considering social and emotional learning approaches. For example, the compendium directory in the guidance package for LEAs provides resources that cite trainings and interventions focused on social and emotional learning. Over the past 10 years, remedies such as PBIS have become prominent strategies for addressing disparate outcomes. However the research is mixed in understanding whether PBIS is structured to address disparate outcomes.

Influenced by public health models designed to change behaviors, PBIS uses a multitiered systems approach to proactively and positively address discipline in schools (Mrazek & Haggerty, 1994; Walker et al., 1996). PBIS is generally composed of three tiers that provide a continuum of behavioral interventions. Similar to RtI, the PBIS model has a universal, or primary tier to support all learners, a secondary tier which focuses on targeted groups of students, and a third tier which provides the most intense behavioral supports and interventions (see Sugai & Horner, 2002, for a thorough description).

The development of PBIS appears to hold a great deal of promise for identifying and changing micro-level teacher behaviors and school structures that may decrease the effectiveness of school discipline and classroom management. PBIS (see, e.g., Horner, Sugai, Todd, & Lewis-Palmer, 2005) uses the examination of local disciplinary data by school personnel as a springboard for reengineering disciplinary behaviors and structures in those schools. The federally sponsored National Technical Assistance Center on PBIS reports that, as of 2016, over 21,000 schools in 47 states (including Washington, D.C.) are implementing PBIS as it is defined by that Center.

Rates of problem behaviors appear to decrease with PBIS by increasing systematic and consistent use of active supervision, positive feedback, and social skills instruction (Colvin, Sugai, Good, & Lee, 1997; Heck, Collins, & Peterson, 2001; Kartub, Taylor-Greene, March, & Horner, 2000; Leedy, Bates, & Safran, 2004; Lewis, Colvin, & Sugai, 2000; Lewis, Sugai, & Colvin, 1998; Nelson, Colvin, & Smith, 1996; Putnam, Handler, Ramirez-Platt, & Luiselli, 2003). Positive behavioral interventions, based on FBAs, have demonstrated a positive impact on the functioning of students with serious problem behaviors (Fairbanks, Sugai, Guardino, & Lathrop, 2007; Ingram, Lewis-Palmer, & Sugai, 2005; Newcomer & Lewis, 2004). In general, there appears to be a high probability that, when implemented with fidelity, PBIS can contribute to reductions in school suspension and expulsion and other positive educational outcomes.

Despite its general promise as a method of making school discipline more efficient and less exclusionary, there is little to no evidence concerning how or indeed whether PBIS could be used to address issues of culture and disproportionality. Outside of theoretical reviews, concerning what such a system might look like (see, e.g., Kozleski, Sobel, & Taylor, 2003; Utley, Kozleski, Smith, & Draper, 2002), the sole empirical investigation of a culturally responsive model of PBIS is Jones, Caravaca, Cizek, Horner, and Vincent (2010), who adapted schoolwide PBIS for an elementary school–serving Navajo students. Although the preliminary results of incorporating Dine language, culture, and history into one school's PBIS implementation suggested a substantial decrease in the overall rate of office discipline referrals, it is clearly impossible to offer practical guidance to the field from a single case study.

Although it might be presumed that an intervention that reduced suspension/ expulsion rates in general might also reduce disproportionality in discipline, emerging data seem to contradict this assumption. Skiba et al. (2008) explored patterns of office disciplinary referrals in a nationally representative sample of 436 elementary and middle schools that had been implementing schoolwide PBIS for at least 1 year. Aggregated results appeared to show that schools that have been implementing PBIS tend in general to use an efficient, graduated system of discipline (e.g., minor infractions receive less severe punishments and more severe consequences are reserved for more serious infractions). A dramatically different pattern was exhibited, however, when the data were disaggregated. Across the national sample, African American and Latino students were up to five times more likely than White students to receive suspension and expulsion for minor infractions. Such data make a strong case that explicit adaptations will be required to ensure that all interventions, including PBIS, are culturally responsive.

The difficulty that educators, especially White educators, have in openly talking about race and racism has been extensively documented (Haberman, 1991; Henze, Lucas, & Scott, 1998; King, 1991; Pollock, 2004; Skiba, Poloni-Staudinger, Simmons, Feggins-Azziz, & Chung, 2005). The typical understanding of racism, that one is either seen as "racist" or "nonracist" (Trepagnier, 2006), provides a strong motivation to avoid the topic, since any indication of a lack of cultural responsiveness induces a fear that one could be seen as "racist" (Pollock, 2004). Together these data make a compelling case that, although PBIS has proven to be a generally promising intervention for creating changes in school discipline and behavior management, PBIS implementation by itself in no way guarantees changes in ubiquitous racial and ethnic disparities in school discipline practices. Indeed, if interventions addressing disciplinary and management practices are framed within traditional institutional structures and perspectives that have historically advantaged students from the majority culture, it is possible they will be effective only with White students. This could *increase* the racial/ethnic disciplinary gap, even while appearing to reduce overall rates of referral, suspension, and expulsion.

RECONCEPTUALIZING EDUCATIONAL EQUITY REMEDIES TO ADDRESS DISPROPORTIONALITY

Currently, the field of special education is focused on interventions and remedies that are individualized, discreet, and proven effective through rigorous randomized control experiments. For example, Trainor and Bal (2014), in their review of intervention research on transitions for students with disabilities, found there are very few studies that consider culture and context when an "effective" intervention is validated. This is highly problematic because IDEA legislation has an explicit "peer review" requirement that encourages states and districts, educational leaders, and practitioners to rely on rigorous peer-reviewed research to improve outcomes for students with disabilities.

A more nuanced approach is needed that allows for systemic factors (Kozleski & Smith, 2009), and culture (Artiles, 2015) and context (Thorius & Maxcy, 2015) to be included in efforts to improve outcomes for students with disabilities. To address deep-seated and systemic special education inequities like disproportionality, researchers and practitioners should actively engage with the implications of culture, context, and difference on practice (Sullivan & Artiles, 2011). Work done by principal investigators and staff of the National Center on Culturally Responsive Educational Systems—a U.S. Office for Special Education Programs funded technical assistance and dissemination center charged with eliminating special education disproportionality—take this perspective. For example, Kozleski and Zion created a systemic assessment of policies and practices related to special education disproportionality to be utilized by multiple stakeholder teams at the district level (Kozleski & Zion, 2006a, 2006b).

More recently, a new generation of scholars, many of whom studied under National Center on Culturally Responsive Educational Systems' principal investigators have continued and extended this earlier work. For example, Thorius and Tan (2015) described how under the auspices of a regional equity assistance center, they and other center staff worked with a state department of education to apply and refine the use of Zion and Kozleksi's earlier work, including how such application shapes the identification of local priorities and professional learning with regard for eliminating special education disproportionality. In addition, Bal has led a group of colleagues (e.g., Bal, Kozleski, Schrader, Rodriguez & Pelton, 2014; Bal, Thorius, & Kozleski, 2012) in the application of formative intervention (Engeström, 2011) and more broadly, cultural historical activity theory (Foot, 2001; Gutierrez, 2008; Gutierrez & Larson, 2007) in the creation of, *learning laboratory methodology* within local enactments of PBIS to generate points of praxis for practitioners to facilitate systems change and address disproportionality in discipline. Efforts like these must continue in order to disrupt disproportionate outcomes. In conclusion, it is important that future work on disproportionality ceases to simply describe the issue or debate whether or not it exists. Rather, the research should dynamically frame the issue of disproportionality because it is a complex educational issue that cannot be solved with individualized remedies devoid of consideration of context and culture.

ACKNOWLEDGMENTS

The first author would like to acknowledge the support of the William T. Grant Foundation Grant Number 184607. The funding agency's endorsement of the ideas expressed in this article should not be inferred. The first author would also like to personally acknowledge the research grant team members that contributed to the thinking of the piece: Alfredo Artiles, Adai Tefera, Sarah Diaz, Lisa Jackson, and Alexandra Aylward. The third author is grateful for the support of the Great Lakes Equity Center, under the Office of Elementary and Secondary Education's Grant S004D110021. The funding agency's endorsement of the ideas expressed in this article should not be inferred.

NOTES

[1]We use the term "nondominant" to collectively refer to groups most affected by disproportionality. We model this choice from Artiles (2015), where he states, "Following Gutierrez (2008), I use the term 'nondominant' to emphasize the oppressive role of power and power relations in the lives of these individuals. Note, however, that this term does not imply that non-dominant students are passively subjected to oppression; indeed, agency and active participation play key roles in the lives of these individuals" (p. 18).

[2]Some scholars have questioned whether overrepresentation exists by employing sophisticated quantitative research methods. For example, Morgan et al. (2015) used individual-level data, multilevel modeling that goes beyond the bivariate analyses of past studies, and the authors include more covariates. Their findings suggest students of color are underrepresented in special education.

[3]Coordinated early intervening service funds can be used for professional development activities that are focused on scientifically based academic and behavioral interventions and for educational and behavioral supports. However, despite the availability of these funds, very few states actually use them and tracking their usage has been inconsistent (Burdette & Sopko, 2010).

[4]Each procedural protection is individualized and designed to assure that a student with a disability is protected from being unfairly disciplined. The FBA and BIP are preventative measures tailored to individual student needs. An FBA is designed to provide insight into why a student behaves in a certain way and leads to a solution for that behavior through the development of a BIP. A BIP tries to proactively divert and change unproductive behaviors (Moreno & Bullock, 2011). In addition, students with disabilities are protected from being excluded from the school setting for more than 10 days when suspended through an MD meeting. An MD is convened with several school staff in order to determine whether a student's behavior is a manifestation of a student's disability. If the student's behavior is related to their disability, they cannot be suspended. If they have inflicted serious bodily harm, the student can be placed in an interim alternative education setting for up to 45 school days (Ryan, Katsiyannis, Peterson, & Chmelar, 2007) and still have access to the general education curriculum, the capacity to meet their Individualized Education Program goals, and receive an FBA or BIP as needed (Katsiyannis, Losinski, & Prince, 2012).

REFERENCES

Achilles, G. M., McLaughlin, M. J., & Croninger, R. G. (2007). Sociocultural correlates of disciplinary exclusion among students with emotional, behavioral, and learning disabilities in the SEELS national dataset. *Journal of Emotional and Behavioral Disorders, 15*, 33–45.

Agirdag, O., Van Houtte, M., & Van Avermaet, P. (2012). Ethnic school segregation and self-esteem: The role of teacher-pupil relationships. *Urban Education, 47*, 1135–1159.

Ahram, R., Fergus, E., & Noguera, P. (2011). Addressing racial/ethnic disproportionality in special education: Case studies of suburban school districts. *Teachers College Record, 113*, 2233–2266.

Albrecht, S. F., Skiba, R. J., Losen, D. J., Chung, C. G., & Middelberg, L. (2012). Federal policy on disproportionality in special education: Is it moving us forward? *Journal of Disability Policy Studies, 23*, 14–25.

Alexander, K., Entwisle, D., & Olson, L. (2014). *The long shadow: Family background, disadvantaged urban youth, and the transition to adulthood.* New York, NY: Russell Sage Foundation.

Annamma, S., Connor, D., & Ferri, B. (2013). Dis/ability critical race studies (DisCrit): Theorizing at the intersections of race and dis/ability. *Race Ethnicity and Education, 16,* 1–31.

Artiles, A. J. (2009). Re-framing disproportionality research: Outline of a cultural-historical paradigm. *Multiple Voices for Ethnically Diverse Exceptional Learners, 11*(2), 24–37.

Artiles, A. J. (2011). Toward an interdisciplinary understanding of educational equity and difference: The case of the racialization of ability. *Educational Researcher, 40,* 431–445.

Artiles, A. J. (2013). Untangling the racialization of disabilities. *Du Bois Review, 10,* 329–347.

Artiles, A. J. (2015). Beyond responsiveness to identity badges: Future research on culture in disability and implications for Response to Intervention. *Educational Review, 67,* 1–22.

Artiles, A. J., Bal, A., & Thorius, K. A. K. (2010). Back to the future: A critique of response to intervention's social justice views. *Theory Into Practice, 49,* 250–257.

Artiles, A. J., Kozleski, E. B., Trent, S. C., Osher, D., & Ortiz, A. (2010). Justifying and explaining disproportionality, 1968–2008: A critique of underlying views of culture. *Exceptional Children, 76,* 279–299.

Artiles, A. J., Rueda, R., Salazar, J. J., & Higareda, I. (2005). Within-group diversity in minority disproportionate representation: English language learners in urban school districts. *Exceptional Children, 71,* 283–300.

Aud, S., Fox, M. A., & Kewal Ramani, A. (2010). *Status and trends in the education of racial and ethnic minorities.* Retrieved from http://nces.ed.gov/pubs2010/2010015.pdf

Bal, A., Kozleski, E. B., Schrader, E. M., Rodriguez, E. M., & Pelton, S. (2014). Systemic transformation from the ground–up using learning lab to design culturally responsive schoolwide positive behavioral supports. *Remedial and Special Education, 35,* 327–339.

Bal, A., Thorius, K. A. K., & Kozleski, E. B. (2012). *Culturally responsive positive behavior interventions and supports* (What Matters Brief Series). Tempe, AZ: Equity Alliance at ASU.

Beck, A., & Muschkin, C. (2012). The enduring impact of race: Understanding disparities in student disciplinary infractions and achievement. *Sociological Perspectives, 55,* 637–662.

Boneshefski, M. J., & Runge, T. J. (2014). Addressing disproportionate discipline practices within a school-wide positive behavioral interventions and supports framework: A practical guide for calculating and using disproportionality rates. *Journal of Positive Behavior Interventions, 16,* 149–158.

Bouman, S. (2010). *Response-to-intervention in California public schools: Has it helped address disproportional placement rates for students with learning disabilities?* (Unpublished doctoral dissertation). Retrieved from ProQuest Dissertations and Theses database. (UMI No. 2076080451)

Bradshaw, C. P., Mitchell, M. M., O'Brennan, L. M., & Leaf, P. J. (2010). Multilevel exploration of factors contributing to the overrepresentation of black students in office disciplinary referrals. *Journal of Educational Psychology, 102,* 508–520.

Bradley, R., Danielson, L., & Hallahan, D. P. (Eds.). (2002). *Identification of learning disabilities: Research to practice.* London, England: Routledge.

Bryan, J., Day-Vines, N. L., Griffin, D., & Moore-Thomas, C. (2012). The disproportionality dilemma: Patterns of teacher referrals to school counselors for disruptive behavior. *Journal of Counseling & Development, 90,* 177–190.

Burdette, P., & Sopko, K. M. (2010). *Coordinated early intervening services: Programs in local education agencies that are required to reserve IDEA funds.* Retrieved from http://nasdse.org/DesktopModules/DNNspot-Store/ProductFiles/75_e4e7064f-c4a4-4d89-8f79-94e895ec42a9.pdf

Busch, T. W., & Reschly, A. L. (2007). Progress monitoring in reading using curriculum-based measurement in a response-to-intervention model. *Assessment for Effective Intervention, 32,* 223–230. doi:10.1177/15345084070320040401

Cartledge, G., & Lo, Y. (2006). *Teaching urban learners: Culturally responsive strategies for developing academic and behavioral competence.* Champaign, IL: Research Press.

Cavendish, W., Artiles, A., & Harry, B. (2015). Tracking inequality 60 years after Brown: Does policy legitimize racialization of disability? *Multiple Voices for Ethnically Diverse Exceptional Learners, 14*(2), 1–11.

Colvin, G., Sugai, G., Good, R. H., III, & Lee, Y. Y. (1997). Using active supervision and precorrection to improve transition behaviors in an elementary school. *School Psychology Quarterly, 12,* 344–363.

Connor, D. J., Ferri, B. A., & Annamma, S. A. (Eds.). (2015). *DisCrit—Disability studies and critical race theory in education.* New York, NY: Teachers College Press.

Coutinho, M. J., & Oswald, D. P. (2000). Disproportionate representation in special education: A synthesis and recommendations. *Journal of Child and Family Studies, 9,* 135–156.

DiPrete, T. A., & Buchmann, C. (2013). *The rise of women.* New York, NY: Russell Sage Foundation.

Donovan, M. S., & Cross, C. T. (Eds.). (2002). *Minority students in special and gifted education/Committee on minority representation in special education.* Washington, DC: National Academies Press.

Duncan, G. J., & Murnane, R. J. (Eds.). (2011). *Whither opportunity? Rising inequality, schools, and children's life chances.* New York, NY: Russell Sage Foundation.

Dunn, L. M. (1968). Special education for the mildly mentally retarded: Is much of it justifiable? *Exceptional Children, 35,* 5–22.

Eccles, J. S., Wong, C. A., & Peck, S. C. (2006). Ethnicity as a social context for the development of African-American adolescents. *Journal of School Psychology, 44,* 407–426.

Engeström, Y. (2011). From design experiments to formative interventions. *Theory & Psychology, 21,* 598–628.

Fabelo, T., Thompson, M., Plotkin, M., Carmichael, D., Marchbanks, M., & Booth, E. (2012). *Breaking school rules: A statewide study of how school discipline relates to students' success and juvenile justice involvement.* Washington, DC: Council of State Governments Justice Center.

Fairbanks, S., Sugai, G., Guardino, D., & Lathrop, M. (2007). Response to intervention: Examining classroom behavior support in second grade. *Exceptional Children, 73,* 288–310.

Fiedler, C. R., Chiang, B., Van Haren, B., Jorgensen, J., Halberg, S., & Boreson, L. (2008). Culturally responsive practices in schools: A checklist to address disproportionality in special education. *Teaching Exceptional Children, 40*(5), 52–59.

Fierros, E. G., & Conroy, J. W. (2002). Double jeopardy: An exploration of restrictiveness and race in special education. In D. Losen & G. Orfield (Eds.), *Racial inequity in special education* (pp. 39–70). Cambridge, MA: Harvard Education Press.

Finn, C. E., Jr., Rotherham, A. J., & Hokanson, C. R., Jr. (Eds.). (2001). *Rethinking special education for a new century.* Washington, DC: Thomas B. Fordham Institute.

Foot, K. (2001). Cultural-historical activity theory as practical theory: Illuminating the development of a conflict monitoring network. *Communication Theory, 11*(1), 56–83.

Ford, D. Y. (1998). The underrepresentation of minority students in gifted education problems and promises in recruitment and retention. *Journal of Special Education, 32*(1), 4–14.

Ford, D. Y., Scott, M. T., Moore, J. L., & Amos, S. O. (2013). Gifted education and culturally different students examining prejudice and discrimination via microaggressions. *Gifted Child Today, 36,* 205–208.

Fry, R. (2008). *The role of schools in the English language learner achievement gap.* Retrieved from http://www.pewhispanic.org/2008/06/26/the-role-of-schools-in-the-english-language-learner-achievement-gap/

Fuchs, L. S., Fuchs, D., & Compton, D. L. (2013). Intervention effects for students with comorbid forms of learning disability: Understanding the needs of nonresponders. *Journal of Learning Disabilities, 46,* 534–548.

Fuchs, D., Fuchs, L. S., & Stecker, P. M. (2010). The "blurring" of special education in a new continuum of general education placements and services. *Exceptional Children, 76,* 301–323.

Gamoran, A. (1986). Instructional and institutional effects of ability grouping. *Sociology of Education, 59,* 185–198.

Gravois, T. A., & Rosenfield. S. A. (2006). Impact of instructional consultation teams on the disproportionate referral and placement of minority students in special education. *Remedial and Special Education, 27*(1), 42–52.

Gregory, A., & Thompson, A. R. (2010). African American high school students and variability in behavior across classrooms. *Journal of Community Psychology, 38,* 386–402.

Griner, A. C., & Stewart, M. L. (2013). Addressing the achievement gap and disproportionality through the use of culturally responsive teaching practices. *Urban Education, 48,* 585–621.

Gutierrez, K. (2008). Developing a sociocritical literacy in the third space. *Reading Research Quarterly, 43,* 148–164.

Gutierrez, K., & Larson, J. (2007). Discussing expanded spaces for learning. *Language Arts, 85*(1), 69–77.

Haberman, M. (1991). Can cultural awareness be taught in teacher education programs? *Teaching Education, 4*(1), 25–32.

Hallinan, M. T., Bottoms, E., Pallas, A. M., & Palla, A. M. (2003). Ability grouping and student learning. *Brookings Papers on Education Policy, (6),* 95–140.

Harris, J. J., III, & Ford, D. Y. (1999). Hope deferred again: Minority students underrepresented in gifted programs. *Education and Urban Society, 31,* 225–237.

Harry, B., & Klingner, J. (2006). *Why are so many minority students in special education?* New York, NY: Teachers College Press.

Harry, B., & Klingner, J. (2014). *Why are so many minority students in special education?* New York, NY: Teachers College Press.

Heck, A., Collins, J., & Peterson, L. (2001) Decreasing children's risk taking on the playground. *Journal of Applied Behavior Analysis, 34,* 349–352.

Hehir, T. (2002). IDEA and disproportionality: Federal enforcement, effective advocacy, and strategies for change. In D. J. Losen & G. Orfield (Eds.), *Racial inequity in special education* (pp. 219–238). Cambridge, MA: Harvard Education Press.

Heller, K. A., Holtzman, W. H., & Messick, S. (1982). *Placing children in special education: A strategy for equity.* Washington, DC: National Academies Press.

Henze, R., Lucas, T., & Scott, B. (1998). Dancing with the monster: Teachers discuss racism, power, and white privilege in education. *Urban Review, 30,* 187–210.

Horner, R. H., Sugai, G., Todd, A. W., & Lewis-Palmer, T. (2005). School-wide positive behavior support. In L. Bambara & L. Kern (Eds.), *Individualized supports for students with problem behaviors: Designing positive behavior plans* (pp. 359–390). New York, NY: Guilford Press.

Hyman, E., Rivkin, D. H., & Rosenbaum, S. (2011). How IDEA fails families without means: Causes and corrections from the frontlines of special education lawyering. *Journal of Gender, Social Policy & the Law, 20,* 107–162.

IDEA Data Center. (2014). *Methods for assessing racial/ethnic disproportionality in special education: A technical assistance guide.* Retrieved from https://ideadata.org/resource-library/methods-for-assessing-racialethnic-disproportionality-in-special-education—a-technical-assistance-guide-revised.html

Ingram, K., Lewis-Palmer, T., & Sugai, G. (2005). Function-based intervention planning comparing the effectiveness of FBA function-based and non-function-based intervention plans. *Journal of Positive Behavior Interventions, 7,* 224–236.

Jencks, C., & Phillips, M. (Eds.). (1998). *The Black-White test score gap.* Washington, DC: Brookings Institution Press.

Jimerson, S. R., Burns, M. K., & VanDerHeyden, A. M. (Eds.). (2016). *Handbook of response to intervention: The science and practice of multi-tiered systems of support* (2nd ed.). New York, NY: Springer Science.

Jones, C., Caravaca, L., Cizek, S., Horner, R., & Vincent, C. (2010). Culturally responsive schoolwide positive behavior support: A case study in one school with a high proportion of Native American students. *Multiple Voices for Ethnically Diverse Exceptional Learners, 9*(1), 108–119.

Kartub, D. T., Taylor-Greene, S., March, R. E., & Horner, R. H. (2000). Reducing Hallway noise: A systems approach. *Journal of Positive Behavior Interventions, 2,* 179–182.

Katsiyannis, A., Losinski, M., & Prince, A. M. (2012). Litigation and students with disabilities: A persistent concern. *NASSP Bulletin, 96,* 23–43.

Kim, C. Y., Hewitt, D. T., & Losen, D. J. (2010). *The school-to-prison pipeline: Structuring legal reform.* New York: New York University Press.

King, J. E. (1991). Dysconscious racism: Ideology, identity, and the miseducation of teachers. *Journal of Negro Education, 60,* 133–146.

Koutsoftas, A. D., Harmon, M. T., & Gray, S. (2009). The effect of tier 2 intervention for phonemic awareness in a response-to-intervention model in low-income preschool classrooms. *Language, Speech, and Hearing Services in Schools, 40,* 116–130. doi:10.1044/0161-1461(2008/07-0101)

Kozleski, E., Sobel, D., & Taylor, S. (2003). Embracing and building culturally responsive practices. *Multiple Voices for Ethnically Diverse Exceptional Learners, 6*(1), 73–87.

Kozleski, E. B., & Smith, A. (2009). The complexities of systems change in creating equity for students with disabilities in urban schools. *Urban Education, 44,* 427–451. doi:10.1177/0042085909337595

Kozleski, E. B., & Zion, S. (2006a). *Preventing disproportionality by strengthening district policies and procedures: An assessment and strategic planning process.* Denver, CO: National Center for Culturally Responsive Educational Systems.

Kozleski, E. B., & Zion, S. (2006b). *Technical assistance and professional development planning guide.* Denver, CO: National Center for Culturally Responsive Educational Systems.

Kurth, J. A., Morningstar, M. E., & Kozleski, E. B. (2014). The persistence of highly restrictive special education placements for students with low-incidence disabilities. *Research and Practice for Persons with Severe Disabilities, 39,* 227–239.

Leedy, A., Bates, P., & Safran, S. P. (2004). Bridging the research-to-practice gap: Improving hallway behavior using positive behavior supports. *Behavioral Disorders, 29,* 130–139.

Leonardo, Z., & Broderick, A. (2011). Smartness as property: A critical exploration of intersections between whiteness and disability studies. *Teachers College Record, 113,* 2206–2232.

Lewis, T. J., Colvin, G., & Sugai, G. (2000). The effects of precorrection and active supervision on the recess behavior of elementary school students. *Education and Treatment of Children, 23,* 109–121.

Lewis, T. J., Sugai, G., & Colvin, G. (1998). Reducing problem behavior through a schoolwide system of effective behavior support: Investigation of a school-wide social skills training program and contextual interventions. *School Psychology Review, 27,* 446–460.

Losen, D., Hodson, C., Ee, J., & Martinez, T. (2015). Disturbing inequities: Exploring the relationship between racial disparities in special education identification and discipline. *Journal of Applied Research on Children: Informing Policy for Children at Risk, 5*(2), 15.

Losen, D. J. (Ed.). (2014). *Closing the school discipline gap: Equitable remedies for excessive exclusion.* New York, NY: Teachers College Press.

Losen, D. J., & Orfield, G. (Eds.). (2002). *Racial inequality in special education.* Cambridge, MA: Harvard University Press.

Lucas, S. R. (1999). *Tracking inequality: Stratification and mobility in American high schools* (Sociology of Education Series). New York, NY: Teachers College Press.

Lyon, G. R., Fletcher, J. M., Shaywitz, S. E., Shaywitz, B. A., Torgesen, J. K., Wood, F. B., . . . Olson, R. (2001). Rethinking learning disabilities. In: C. E. Finn Jr., A. J. Rotherham, & C. R. Hokanson Jr. (Eds.), *Rethinking special education for a new century* (pp. 259–287). Washington, DC: Thomas B. Fordham Institute.

Markowitz, J. (2002, February). *State criteria for determining disproportionality. Quick Turn Around (QTA)*. Retrieved from https://archive.org/details/ERIC_ED462810

Martinez, A. A., McMahon, S. D., & Treger, S. (2016). Individual- and school-level predictors of student office disciplinary referrals. *Journal of Emotional and Behavioral Disorders, 24*(1), 30–41.

McCall, Z., & Skrtic, T. (2010). Intersectional needs politics: A policy frame for the wicked problem of disproportionality. *Multiple Voices for Ethnically Diverse Exceptional Learners, 11*(2), 3–23.

McKinney, E., Bartholomew, C., & Gray, L. (2010). RTI and SWPBIS: Confronting the problem of disproportionality. *NASP Communique, 38*(6), 1–5.

Mendez, L. M. R., & Knoff, H. M. (2003). Who gets suspended from school and why: A demographic analysis of schools and disciplinary infractions in a large school district. *Education and Treatment of Children, 26*, 30–51.

Milner, H. R. (2006). Classroom management in urban classrooms. In C. M. Evertson & C. S. Weinstein (Eds.), *The handbook of classroom management: Research, practice, and contemporary issues* (pp. 491–522). Mahwah, NJ: Lawrence Erlbaum.

Miner, J. L., & Clarke-Stewart, K. A. (2008). Trajectories of externalizing behavior from age 2 to age 9: Relations with gender, temperament, ethnicity, parenting and rater. *Developmental Psychology, 44*, 771–786.

Minow, M. (2010). *In Brown's wake: Legacies of America's educational landmark*. New York, NY: Oxford University Press.

Moreno, G., & Bullock, L. M. (2011). Principles of positive behavior supports: Using the FBA as a problem-solving approach to address challenging behaviors beyond special populations. *Emotional & Behavioral Difficulties, 16*, 117–127.

Morgan, P. L., Farkas, G., Hillemeier, M. M., & Maczuga, S. (2012). Are minority children disproportionately represented in early intervention and early childhood special education? *Educational Researcher, 41*, 339–351.

Morgan, P. L., Farkas, G., Hillemeier, M. M., Mattison, R., Maczuga, S., Li, H., & Cook, M. (2015). Minorities are disproportionately underrepresented in special education longitudinal evidence across five disability conditions. *Educational Researcher, 44*, 278–292.

Mrazek, P. J., & Haggerty R. J. (Eds.). (1994). *Reducing risks for mental disorders: Frontiers for preventive intervention research*. Washington, DC: National Academies Press.

National Research Council. (2002). *Minority students in special and gifted education*. Retrieved from https://www.nap.edu/read/10128/chapter/1#ii

Neal, L. I., McGray, A. D., Webb-Johnson, G., & Bridgest, S. T. (2003). The effects of African American movement styles on teachers' perceptions and reactions. *Journal of Special Education, 37*(1), 49–57.

Nelson, J. R., Colvin, G., & Smith, D. J. (1996, Summer/Fall). The effects of setting clear standards on students' social behavior in common areas of the school. *Journal of At-Risk Issues, 3*, 10–18.

Newcomer, L. L., & Lewis, T. J. (2004). Functional behavioral assessment an investigation of assessment reliability and effectiveness of function-based interventions. *Journal of Emotional and Behavioral Disorders, 12*, 168–181.

Noguera, P. A. (2003). Schools, prisons, and social implications of punishment: Rethinking disciplinary practices. *Theory Into Practice, 42*, 341–350.

Oakes, J. (1985). *Keeping track: How schools structure inequality*. New Haven, CT: Yale University Press.

O'Connor, C., & Fernandez, S. D. (2006). Race, class, and disproportionality: Reevaluating the relationship between poverty and special education placement. *Educational Researcher, 35*(6), 6–11.

Office of Special Education Programs. (2007). *Memorandum: Disproportionality of racial and ethnic groups in special education*. Washington, DC: U.S. Department of Education.

Orfield, G., Ee, J., Frankenberg, E., & Siegel-Hawley, J. (2016). *Brown at 62: School segregation by race, poverty and state.* Retrieved from https://civilrightsproject.ucla.edu/research/k-12-education/integration-and-diversity/brown-at-62-school-segregation-by-race-poverty-and-state/Brown-at-62-final-corrected-2.pdf

Oswald, D. P., Coutinho, M. J., & Best, A. M. (2002). Community and school predictors of overrepresentation of minority children in special education. In D. J. Losen & G. Orfield (Eds.), *Racial inequity in special education* (pp. 1–13). Cambridge, MA: Harvard Education Press.

Parrish, T. (2002). Racial disparities in the identification, funding, and provision of special education. In D. J. Losen & G. Orfield (Eds.), *Racial inequity in special education* (pp. 15–38). Cambridge, MA: Harvard Education Press.

Planty, M., Hussar, W., Snyder, T., Kena, G., KewalRamani, A., Kemp, J., . . . Dinkes, R. (2009). *The condition of education 2009* (NCES 2009-081). Washington, DC: National Center for Education Statistics, Institute of Education Sciences, U.S. Department of Education

Pollock, M. (2004). *Colormute: Race talk dilemmas in an American school.* Princeton, NJ: Princeton University Press.

Putnam, R. F., Handler, M. W., Ramirez-Platt, C., & Luiselli, J. K. (2003). Improving student bus riding behavior through a whole-school intervention. *Journal of Applied Behavior Analysis, 36,* 583–589.

Raines, T. C., Dever, B. V., Kamphaus, R. W., & Roach, A. T. (2012). Universal screening for behavioral and emotional risk: A promising method for reducing disproportionate placement in special education. *Journal of Negro Education, 81,* 283–296.

Rausch, M. K., & Skiba, R. (2004). *Disproportionality in school discipline among minority students in Indiana: Description and analysis. Children Left Behind Policy Briefs. Supplementary Analysis 2-A.* Bloomington: Center for Evaluation and Education Policy, Indiana University.

Rocque, M. (2010). Office discipline and student behavior: Does race matter? *American Journal of Education, 116,* 557–581.

Rosenbaum, J. E. (1980). Track misperceptions and frustrated college plans: An analysis of the effects of tracks and track perceptions in the National Longitudinal Survey. *Sociology of Education, 53,* 74–88.

Ryan, J. B., Katsiyannis, A., Peterson, R., & Chmelar, R. (2007). IDEA 2004 and disciplining students with disabilities. *NASSP Bulletin, 91,* 130–140.

Saito, L. T. (2009). *The politics of exclusion: The failure of race-neutral policies in urban America.* Stanford, CA: Stanford University Press.

Samson, J. F., & Lesaux, N. K. (2009). Language minority learners in special education: Rates and predictors of identification for services. *Journal of Learning Disabilities, 42,* 148–162.

Shealey, M. W., McHatton, P. A., & Wilson, V. (2011). Moving beyond disproportionality: The role of culturally responsive teaching in special education. *Teaching Education, 22,* 377–396.

Shinn, M. R. (2007). Identifying students at risk, monitoring performance, and determining eligibility within response to intervention. *School Psychology Review, 36,* 601–661.

Simmons-Reed, E. A., & Cartledge, G. (2014). School discipline disproportionality: Culturally competent interventions for African American males. *Interdisciplinary Journal of Teaching and Learning, 4,* 95–109.

Skiba, R. (2013). CCBD'S Position summary on federal policy on disproportionality in special education. *Behavioral Disorders, 38,* 108–120.

Skiba, R., Simmons, A., Ritter, S., Kohler, K., Henderson, M., & Wu, T. (2006). The context of minority disproportionality: Practitioner perspectives on special education referral. *Teachers College Record, 108,* 1424–1459.

Skiba, R. J., Chung, C. G., Trachok, M., Baker, T. L., Sheya, A., & Hughes, R. L. (2014). Parsing disciplinary disproportionality contributions of infraction, student, and school characteristics to out-of-school suspension and expulsion. *American Educational Research Journal*, *51*, 640–670.

Skiba, R. J., Horner, R. H., Chung, C. G., Rausch, M. K., May, S. L., & Tobin, T. (2011). Race is not neutral: A national investigation of African American and Latino disproportionality in school discipline. *School Psychology Review*, *40*, 85–107.

Skiba, R. J., Michael, R. S., & Nardo, A. C. (2000). *The color of discipline: Sources of racial and gender disproportionality in school punishment*. Retrieved from http://indiana.edu/~equity/docs/ColorofDiscipline2002.pdf

Skiba, R. J., Michael, R. S., Nardo, A. C., & Peterson, R. L. (2002). The color of discipline: Sources of racial and gender disproportionality in school punishment. *Urban Review*, *34*, 317–342.

Skiba, R. J., Peterson, R. L., & Williams, T. (1997). Office referrals and suspension: Disciplinary intervention in middle schools. *Education and Treatment of Children*, *20*, 295–315.

Skiba, R. J., Poloni-Staudinger, L., Simmons, A. B., Feggins-Azziz, R., & Chung, C. (2005). Unproven links: Can poverty explain ethnic disproportionality in special education? *Journal of Special Education*, *39*, 130–144.

Skiba, R. J., Simmons, A. B., Ritter, S., Gibb, A. C., Rausch, M. K., Cuadrado, J., & Choong-Geun, C. (2008). Achieving equity in special education: History, status, and current challenges. *Exceptional Children*, *74*, 264–288.

Sugai, G., & Horner, R. (2002). The evolution of discipline practices: School-wide positive behavior supports. *Child & Family Behavior Therapy*, *24*, 23–50.

Sullivan, A. L. (2011). Disproportionality in special education identification and placement of English language learners. *Exceptional Children*, *77*, 317–334.

Sullivan, A. L., & Artiles, A. J. (2011). Theorizing racial inequity in special education: Applying structural inequity theory to disproportionality. *Urban Education*, *46*, 1526–1552. doi:10.1177/0042085911416014

Sullivan, A. L., Artiles, A. J., & Hernandez-Saca, D. I. (2015). Addressing special education inequity through systemic change: Contributions of ecologically based organizational consultation. *Journal of Educational and Psychological Consultation*, *25*, 129–147.

Sullivan, A. L., Klingbeil, D. A., & Van Norman, E. R. (2013). Beyond behavior: Multilevel analysis of the influence of sociodemographics and school characteristics on students' risk of suspension. *School Psychology Review*, *42*, 99–114.

Thorius, K. A. K., & Maxcy, B. D. (2015). Critical practice analysis of special education policy: An RTI example. *Remedial and Special Education*, *36*, 116–124. doi:10.1177/0741932514550812

Thorius, K. A. K., Maxcy, B. D., Macey, E., & Cox, A. (2014). A critical practice analysis of response to intervention appropriation in an urban school. *Remedial and Special Education*, *35*, 287–299. doi:10.1177/0741932514522100

Thorius, K. A. K., & Sullivan, A. L. (2013). Interrogating instruction and intervention in RTI research with students identified as English language learners. *Reading & Writing Quarterly: Overcoming Learning Difficulties*, *29*(1), 64–88. doi:10.1080/10573569.2013.741953

Thorius, K. A. K., & Tan, P. (2015). Expanding analysis of educational debt: Considering intersections of race and ability. In D. Connor, B. Ferri, & S. A. Annamma (Eds.), *DisCrit: Critical conversations across race, class, & dis/ability* (pp. 87–97). New York, NY: Teachers College Press.

Tilly, C. (1998). *Durable inequality*. Berkeley: University of California Press.

Trainor, A. A., & Bal, A. (2014). Development and preliminary analysis of a rubric for culturally responsive research. *Journal of Special Education*, *47*, 203–216.

Trepagnier, B. (2006). *Silent racism: How well-meaning white people perpetuate the racial divide*. Boulder, CO: Paradigm.

Turnbull, H. R., III, Wilcox, B. L., Turnbull, A. P., & Sailor, W. (2001). IDEA, positive behavioral supports, and school safety. *Journal of Law & Education, 30,* 445–504.

U.S. Department of Education. (2009). *Children with disabilities receiving special education under Part B of the Individuals with Disabilities Education Act* (Office of Special Education Programs, Data Analysis Systems, OMB No. 1820-0043). Washington, DC: Author.

U.S. Department of Education/Department of Justice. (2014). *U.S. Departments of Education and Justice release school discipline guidance package to enhance school climate and improve school discipline policies/practices.* Washington, DC: Author. Retrieved from http://www. ed.gov/news/press-releases/us-departments-education-and-justice-release-school-discipline-guidance-package-

U.S. Government Accountability Office. (2013). *Individuals with Disabilities Education Act: Standards needed to improve identification of racial and ethnic overrepresentation in special education.* Retrieved from http://www.gao.gov/products/GAO-13-137

Utley, C. A., Kozleski, E., Smith, A., & Draper, I. L. (2002). Positive behavior support a proactive strategy for minimizing behavior problems in urban multicultural youth. *Journal of Positive Behavior Interventions, 4,* 196–207.

Van Houtte, M. (2011). So where's the teacher in school effects research? The impact of teacher's beliefs, culture, and behavior on equity and excellence in education. In K. van den Branden, P. Van Avermaet, & M. Van Houtte (Eds.), *Equity and excellence in education: Towards maximal learning opportunities for all students* (pp. 75–95). New York, NY: Routledge.

VanDerHeyden, A. M., Witt, J. C., & Gilbertson, D. (2007). A multi-year evaluation of the effects of a response to intervention (RTI) model on identification of children for special education. *Journal of School Psychology, 45,* 225–256.

Vaughn, S., & Fuchs, L. S. (2003). Redefining learning disabilities as inadequate response to instruction: The promise and potential problems. *Learning Disabilities Research & Practice, 18,* 137–146. doi:10.1111/1540-5826.00070

Vincent, C. G., & Tobin, T. J. (2010). The relationship between implementation of schoolwide positive behavior support (SWPBS) and disciplinary exclusion of students from various ethnic backgrounds with and without disabilities. *Journal of Emotional and Behavioral Disorders, 19,* 217–232.

Waitoller, F. R., Artiles, A. J., & Cheney, D. A. (2010). The miner's canary: A review of overrepresentation research and explanations. *Journal of Special Education, 44*(1), 29–49.

Walker, H. M., Horner, R. H., Sugai, G., Bullis, M., Sprague, J. R., Bricker, D., & Kaufman, M. J. (1996). Integrated approaches to preventing antisocial behavior patterns among school age children and youth. *Journal of Emotional and Behavioral Disorder, 4,* 194–209.

Weinstein, C., Curran, M., & Tomlinson-Clarke, S. (2003). Culturally responsive classroom management: Awareness into action. *Theory Into Practice, 42,* 269–276.

Welner, K. G. (2001). *Legal rights, local wrongs: When community control collides with educational equity.* Albany: State University of New York Press.

Worrell, F. C. (2003). Why are there so few African Americans in gifted programs? In C. C. Yeakey & R. D. Henderson (Eds.), *Surmounting the odds: Education, opportunity, and society in the new millennium* (pp. 423–454). Greenwich, CT: Information Age.

Worrell, F. C. (2009). What does gifted mean? Personal and social identity perspectives on giftedness in adolescence. In F. D. Horowitz, R. F. Subotnik, & D. J. Matthews (Eds.), *The development of giftedness and talent across the lifespan* (pp. 131–152). Washington, DC: American Psychological Association. doi:10.1037/11867-008

Yoon, S. Y., & Gentry, M. (2009). Racial and ethnic representation in gifted programs: Current status of and implications for gifted Asian American students. *Gifted Child Quarterly, 53,* 121–136.

Zhang, D., Katsiyannis, A., Ju, S., & Roberts, E. (2014). Minority representation in special education: 5-Year trends. *Journal of Child and Family Studies, 23,* 118–127.

Chapter 4

Integrating Research on How People Learn and Learning Across Settings as a Window of Opportunity to Address Inequality in Educational Processes and Outcomes

CAROL D. LEE
Northwestern University

This chapter addresses how fundamental principles regarding how people learn in the last decade open up possibilities for conceptualizing a broad ecological culturally rooted framework for the design of robust learning environments in a variety of settings, especially schools. These cross-disciplinary principles emerging from across relevant disciplines run against the persistent metanarratives warranting inequitable educational and life course outcomes for youth in minoritized nondominant communities and those living in persistent poverty in deficit claims. This chapter synthesizes research findings from across cognition, human development, the neurosciences, and learning in academic disciplines to document emerging consensus around generative principles that can inform the design of robust learning environments.

Inequality in educational outcomes associated with race, ethnicity, and class have been a persistent challenge in the United States (National Center for Education Statistics, 2013). It is evident that such inequalities are outgrowths of many contributing factors: structurally the ways that resources are inequitably allocated for

- Schools—funding levels, teacher quality, curriculum quality, access to early child-hood education (Darling-Hammond, 2004, 2010)
- Neighborhood resources with regard to housing, transportation options (Tate, 2008)
- Health care

The structural factors are historical and can be understood as embodiments of ideological belief systems with regard to race, ethnicity, and class (Mills, 1997).

Review of Research in Education
March 2017, Vol. 41, pp. 88–111
DOI: 10.3102/0091732X16689046
© 2017 AERA. http://rre.aera.net

We do not need to infer such ideological beliefs as they have been directly articulated in official documents and pronouncements (see Lee, 2009, for a review). Whether from the founding of the United States when Blacks were calculated as three fifths of a human being to the Dred Scott Supreme Court decision of 1857, which stated Blacks were "beings of an inferior order, and altogether unfit to associate with the White race, either in social or political relations, and so far inferior that they had no rights which the White man was bound to respect" or the presumed scientific basis of the eugenics movement of the early part of the 20th century (note that the founders of the American Psychological Association were eugenicists; Gould, 1981). These assumptions of inherent deficits attributed to particular communities of people have been transformed in many ways in both practice and the academy. These deficit assumptions have moved from arguments of biological determinism to arguments of environmental deficits—deficits in language (Bereiter & Engelmann, 1966), in family socialization practices (Coleman, 1988), and most recently in psychological attributes associated with emotional self-regulation and executive self-control (Heckman, 2012). Mills (1997) argues that the persistence of these belief systems is rooted in what he calls "the racial contract," an ideology that structures hierarchies across human communities, with those designated as "White" at the top of the hierarchy. However, it is interesting to note, in the United States, that who gets to be White and non-White has shifted historically, but where Blacks remain at the bottom (Ignatiev, 1996; Williamson, Rhodes, & Dunson, 2007).

In the period post *Brown v. Board of Education* and the passage of civil rights legislation since 1965, such warrants are more likely to be couched in indirection. We know how such ideological beliefs have been warranted by biological, psychological, and social sciences (e.g., various fields of psychology, measurement, assessment theory, sociology, linguistics; Gould, 1981; Hernstein & Murray, 1994; Hilliard, 1996; Lee, 2009). Such deficit warranting across these fields has been documented in detail. Of concern here is a focus on the emerging opportunities that recent findings about how people learn and develop over time and across space open up opportunities to move beyond metanarratives about deficit (Lee, 2008, 2010). I am not arguing that the availability of such knowledge will lead to changes in policies that structure opportunities, but rather that fields that seek to understand the complexities of human learning and development can open up new conceptual space. Specifically, I will focus on emergent findings from studies of cognition, human development, ecological systems theory, dynamic systems, and the neurosciences. The synthesis for each field will be brief and in no way intended to be exhaustive. For each field, I will highlight the conundrums inherent in how fundamental propositions have been taken up in terms of implications for education. I will then synthesize patterns that emerge across these fields and discuss the implications of these patterns for the design of robust learning environments, and how attention to these big ideas relate to our expanded conceptions of what students need to learn and be able to do in academic disciplines in middle and high school.

OPPORTUNITIES FROM THEORY

Cognition

How People Learn (HPL) (Bransford, Brown, & Cocking, 1999) represented a synthesis of core constructs around human learning through 1999. HPL is currently being updated and we expect greater attention to findings from the neurosciences. The Research Advisory Council of the National Academy of Education has made recommendations about new findings that should be incorporated in syntheses around understandings of how people learn. This brief synthesis will include both findings from HPL and recommendations from the National Academy.

For decades, cognition has been viewed as individual brain functioning. Through evolution, the human brain operates efficiently by structuring knowledge as patterns or structures inferred from experience in the world as schema held in long-term memory (Quartz & Sejnowski, 2002; Rumelhart, 1980). Such schema then serve as frameworks through which we make sense of new experiences (Anderson, 1984). New learning may involve top-down processes of schema activation (e.g., using our prior knowledge to expand our current understandings) or bottom-up processes of restructuring existing schema or building new knowledge structures (Rumelhart, 1980). In both cases, prior knowledge is a powerful resource for new learning. Young children from birth make observations of the natural and social world and infer patterns (Carey, 1985; DiSessa, 1982; Mintzes, 1984). For example, young children come to recognize that if you hold an object and let it go, the object will fall. Research on what are called naïve theories document the ways that children construct explanatory models of physical processes, of number, classifications of living forms (e.g., animals with four legs even when they do not recognize the difference between a dog and a cat; distinctions between what animate creatures can do vs. inanimate objects; of human intentionality; Baillargeon, 1995; Carey & Gelman, 1991; Massey & Gelman, 1988; Starkey & Gelman, 1982). One of the challenges of formal learning, particularly in mathematics and the sciences, is wrestling with tensions between informal naïve understandings inferred from experience in the natural and social world from formal operations in disciplines that may be counterintuitive (Clement, 1982; DiSessa, 1982). This challenge is sometimes conceptualized as conceptual change where the question is what features of learning environments are most robust at helping learners reorganize existing schema (DiSessa & Sherin, 1998; Schwartz, Varma, & Martin, 2008). The broad takeaway is that learners must explicitly examine the tensions or oppositions between one's current state of understanding of say, a model or process, and the targeted formal understanding. These fundamentally cognitive foci on schema activation and transformations, the role of prior knowledge, and the demands of conceptual change have been taken up in deficit explanations for the persistent gap in academic achievement with the idea that the range of prior knowledge that youth from particular backgrounds bring to learning in school somehow is not a resource for new learning, in fact a detractor (Brottman, 1968; Jensen, 1969; Orr, 1987; see Box 1).

BOX 1

"In an attempt to discover the underlying cause or causes of the poor reading performance of black inner-city children, several explanations have been suggested. Some have argued that these children show a cultural, cognitive, and/or linguistic deficit resulting from either genetic pathology (Jensen, 1969) or from an impoverished environment (Bereiter & Engelmann, 1966; Bernstein, 1961; Blank & Solomon, 1968; Clark & Richards, 1966; Deutsch, Brown, Deutsch, Goldstein, John, Katz, Levinson, Peisach, & Witeman, 1967). Regardless of the etiology, many educators and psychologists have held that many black children come to school with a deficient language system that militates against making progress in academic subjects, especially reading. Intensive language remediation is therefore considered a prerequisite to the task of learning to read. Language programs such as DISTAR (Engelmann & Osborn, 1970) reflect this perspective."

Reported in Harber and Bryen (1976). Black English and the task of reading. *Review of Educational Research, 46,* 387–405.

Another dimension of cognition that is receiving increased attention is the role of epistemology as a category of knowledge that is important in how people conceptualize tasks to be learned (DiSessa, 1993; F. E. Hart, 2001; Hofer, 2000; Lee, Goldman, Levine, & Magliano, 2016). Traditional studies of schema including the role of prior knowledge have attended to the structure of concepts. Epistemology, on the other hand, addresses questions around the criteria we use in determining whether something is indeed knowable and what criteria are invoked to assess the truth value of knowledge claims, how do we justify claims, and what counts as evidence. Hofer and Pintrich (1997) focused on two important dimensions of people's epistemological beliefs: simplicity versus complexity and certainty versus uncertainty. It is interesting to consider how these personal orientations may play out in everyday contexts, for example, as citizens evaluate public policy positions with regard to issues like climate change, immigration, addressing poverty (Gutmann, 1993; Suad Nasir & Kirshner, 2003). It is equally interesting to consider what may be epistemological orientations or dispositions reflected in claims made within the research community—now and historically—and within communities of educational practice (e.g., publications and pronouncements made by educational consultants, educational publications meant for a practice audience) with regard to these two dimensions. I would argue the field—both in research and practice—have tended to assert deficit claims about learning trajectories for particular populations in ways that reflect a disposition toward simplicity and certainty. One goal of this chapter is to suggest that inferences across disciplines now strongly suggest the phenomena in question are more likely to be complex and our claims likely need to be tentative and contextual (see Box 2).

Chinn, Buckland, and Samarapungavan (2011) have expanded studies of the role of epistemology in learning to zero in on what they call epistemic cognition. They argue for five dimensions of epistemic cognition:

BOX 2

"Poverty holds a seemingly unbreakable grip on families, neighborhoods, cities, and entire countries. It stretches from one generation to the next, trapping individuals in a socioeconomic pit that is nearly impossible to ascend. Part of the fuel for poverty's unending cycle is its suppressing effects on individuals' cognitive development, executive functioning, and attention, as four scientists demonstrated during the inaugural International Convention of Psychological Science, held March 12–14 in Amsterdam, the Netherlands."

Retrieved from http://www.psychologicalscience.org/index.php/publications/observer/2015/september-15/how-poverty-affects-the-brain-and-behavior.html

(a) Epistemic aims and epistemic value; (b) the structure of knowledge and other epistemic achievements; (c) the sources and justification of knowledge and other epistemic achievements, and the related epistemic stances; (d) epistemic virtues and vices; and (e) reliable and unreliable processes for achieving epistemic aims. We further argue for a fine-grained, context-specific analysis of cognitions within the five components. (p. 141)

The relevance of these five dimensions will become clearer when I discuss the implications of more recent findings across the multiple domains addressed in this chapter as they provide resources for thinking about the demands of learning in particular academic content areas. These dimensions of how youth perceive what it means to validly know something is in no way limited to academics. And as a consequence, the opportunities for recruiting such epistemological knowledge and dispositions as resources for navigating new spaces for learning, particularly in formal contexts, is an important opportunity window that I argue is not sufficiently explored to address the persistent gaps in academic and life course outcomes associated with race, ethnicity, class, and gender.

Many empirical studies have validated the proposition that epistemological knowledge and dispositions contribute to robust learning around conceptual understanding, text comprehension, analyses of complex issues, among others (Conley, Pintrich, Vekiri, & Harrison, 2004; Hofer, 2004; Kardash & Scholes, 1996; Mason & Boscolo, 2004; Sinatra, Southerland, McConaughy, & Demastes, 2003).

Thus, from a cognitive perspective, the structure of conceptual and categorical knowledge (existing schema, relations across schema, their relations with new targets of learning) as well as dispositions toward what counts as knowledge and what counts as reliable justifications for claims and whether one views such knowledge as simple or complex, as subject to certainty or uncertainty, all matter for what and how people learn. And as a consequence, these need to be considerations in how we conceptualize addressing the challenges in gaps in opportunity to learn, particularly in the context of schooling.

Becoming more prominent in studies of cognition is attention that goes beyond internal cognitive structures to include the role of affect. In prior purely cognitive studies, affect was not considered as a factor in cognitive processing. There are at least two perspectives from which affect and cognition are considered. One is the question of whether affect or emotions themselves are cognitive (Ortony, 1979). The other examines how affective states influence cognition (Dalgleish & Powers, 1999; Zajonc & Marcus, 1984). Clore and Ortony (2000) argue human emotions entail four components: "a cognitive component, a motivational-behavioral component, a somatic component, and a subjective-experiential component" (p. 24). They define the cognitive component as "the representation of the emotional meaning or personal significance of some emotionally relevant aspect(s) of the person's perceived world . . . [that] may be conscious or nonconscious" (p. 24). The motivational–behavioral component involves the disposition to act on the emotional valence we attribute to experience. The somatic component involves the physiological changes that unfold in our bodies (e.g., chemical release of cortisol, adrenaline, and norepinephrine) that are embodied across multiple systems in our bodies (e.g., cardiovascular, nervous, endocrine). And the subjective–experiential component is the holistic way in which we feel and experience the affect. According to Damasio, "The full range of the phenomenon of emotion, in its most traditional sense, . . . includes 1) evaluation, 2) dispositions to respond, and 3) feelings" (p. 20).

Damasio explains the physiological processes embodied in the experience of emotion as such experiences are processed through multiple regions of the brain as well as other body systems:

The body state changes specific to emotions are enacted by neural signals (e.g. autonomic, musculoskeletal) and chemical signals (e.g. endocrine). The brain state changes are enacted by neural signals toward neurotransmitter and neuromodulator nuclei in the thalamus, the brain stem, and the basal forebrain, as well as toward some sectors of the basal ganglia (such as the ventral striatum), which in turn send signals to a variety of neural sites, e.g. cerebral cortex. Direct chemical signaling from the body proper also affects the operation of brain networks. The changes in cognitive mode I mentioned above are the result of these brain state changes. (p. 21)

My point here is not to delve into the details of how we process emotions but to argue the breadth of evidence that emotional states, excited by perceptions that learners bring are essential to human learning and development. As a consequence, the design of robust learning environments (whether in families, in schools, in informal community-based settings) ignore the perceptions and as a consequence, the emotional experience of learners at their peril. Attention in recent years to socioemotional learning in schools is certainly influenced by our understandings about the centrality of emotions (Farrington et al., 2012). However, both the emerging work in socioemotional learning in schools as well as discussions of implications for the neurobiology of emotions typically do not consider how perceptions of experience are deeply influenced by perceptions with regard to race, ethnicity, class, gender, and other categorical variations in human experience such as conceptions of disability (Sellers, Caldwell, Schmeelk-Cone, & Zimmerman, 2003; Sellers, Copeland-Linder, Martin, & Lewis, 2006; Spencer, 1985; Steele, Spencer, & Aronson, 2002).

Human Development

One of my overall concerns in this review is to point out the ways that these disciplines so central to understanding how humans learn and develop typically do not talk with one another. Each focuses on a slice or silo of human functioning. Among the arguments I am proposing in this review are the opportunities that developing conceptual frameworks that encompass big ideas from across relevant disciplines may make possible for us to interrogate more deeply and in more complex ways the phenomenon that are human communities.

My personal focus on human development grows from the opportunity I had for 10 years to coteach a seminar with colleagues from Northwestern University's Human Development and Social Policy Program. That seminar sought to help PhD students explore intersections between the Learning Sciences focus on cognition and the foci in Human Development on identity, motivation, development over the life course, risk, and resiliency as these are socialized in contexts. I have constrained my focus in human development to issues around the role of identity in the context of child and adolescent development, and how issues of motivation are interconnected with identity in the context of life course development. In particular, I am focusing on these issues from a risk–resiliency framework; that is, understanding how life course outcomes are an outgrowth of relationships between the nature of risks faced and supports available (Spencer, 2006). Because this review aims to articulate big ideas in and across relevant disciplines that can help us think in conceptually rich ways about what is entailed in expanding opportunity to learn, particularly in the context of schooling, this human development discussion is framed around understanding what we know about how identity development, at particular life course transition points, intersects with motivation to offer sources of risk and/or sources of support that can influence resilience in the face of difficult life circumstances associated with the experiences of race, ethnicity, class, and gender.

I want to start by framing human development as the unfolding of dynamic relationships among characteristics of the individual as these interact with—shape and are shaped by—features of the social spaces in which the individual operates (e.g., nuclear family, extended family, social networks of peers and adults, socially organized settings outside the home such as church, school, community settings, etc.). Characteristics of the individual include attributes that themselves are an outgrowth of biological factors and the organization of social spaces in which the individual routinely participates (McAdams & Pals, 2006). In terms of the focus of this review around issues of educational equity, some may be concerned about invoking biological factors considering the history of how biological explanations have historically been used in psychology and by extension in popular metanarratives to categorize particular groups of humans as lacking, as less than (e.g., the eugenics movement, assumptions around the construct of IQ; Gould, 1981). However, one of the main goals of this review is to invoke more recent findings around the complex and dynamic relations between the biological and social worlds of human development to make exactly the opposite argument (Wilson, 1998): namely, the human species survives over ecological time precisely because of its variation, and as a consequence, a core scientific enterprise is to understand the functionality of that variation and use such understandings for conceptualizing resources rather than deficits. This proposition, for example, is evident in more recent developments in the deaf community of not viewing deafness as a disability, but simply as a difference that offers other affordances for navigating the social world. This framing of development as the outgrowth of dynamic relations among the biological and the social, between the individual and others—other people, across multiple settings, across people, and artifacts that may be physical and/or ideational (e.g., conceptual systems about number and space)—is a core and central tenet through which the fields of human development, cognition, and the neurosciences now understand how people learn and navigate across time and space. This relational framing is central to conceptualizing what promotes resilience in the face of risks; that is, resilience is an outgrowth of ecological relations and not simply features or characteristics of individuals. Articulating the new focus as developmental science, Damon and Lerner (2008) offer the following as the key contemporary themes (p. 12):

1. Focus on developmental systems theories
2. Role of context in human development
3. Individual differences—diversity
4. Importance of a multidisciplinary approach
5. Study of biological development and of developmental neuroscience
6. Diverse methodologies
7. Application of developmental science
8. Promotion of positive child and adolescent development

Another important grounding has to do with how we understand culture (Cole, 1996; Rogoff, 2003). Conceptions of culture are important here because this intertwining of the biological and the social itself entails participation in cultural practices (Lee, 2010). One illustration may be informative from work in the area of epigenesis (Cloud, 2010; Russo, Martienssen, & Riggs, 1996)—the study of how gene expression can change as a function of environmental stimuli.[1] Researchers have documented transformation of genetic markers of irritability in a liter of mice based on shifts in their experiences in the social world (Francis, Diorio, Liu, & Meaney, 1999; Szyf, Weaver, & Meaney, 2007). With a rat mother who was not nurturing, the mice exhibited erratic behavior under conditions of stress. When transferred to a rat mother who was nurturing—licking them for comfort when they were under stress—the mice not only ceased to exhibit the erratic behavior under conditions of stress (e.g., the expression of a genetic marker), but the moderation of the gene expression passed on to the next generation. The idea here is that the genetic marker is not deterministic, but rather its expression can be modulated by experience. We must be cautious not to read these findings to reinforce claims that particular experiences, particularly associated with poverty, are somehow inherently deficit. Rather, I read these findings as evidence of human adaptability and variation within human cultural communities.

In this framing, cultural experiences entail shared cultural practices (e.g., here mice living in a nurturing environment where positive stimulation is the norm of practice), norms, and belief systems. In human cultural communities, these shared practices, norms, and belief systems are often sustained across generations. Such cultural communities can range from micro-level practices in family socialization practices or practices in youth video clubs to more macro-level practices shared within religious communities, nation states, ethnic enclaves within and across nations (e.g., shared diaspora cultural practices). This conception of membership in cultural communities is important because it makes clear that people never belong to single cultural communities (Gutierrez & Rogoff, 2003). In addition, it is important to understand that cultural communities are complex, being both homogenous and heterogeneous, being both stable and changing. While this is a complex construct to think about, we can easily understand these dimensions in terms of membership in our families. There are practices that we experience in our family life growing up that we know are not the same across all families. Some of those practices are ones that we know our parents experienced in their childhood, but we can see how they may have been adapted from our grandparents' generation to our parent's generation. At the same time, we know that there are certain things that the members of our immediate family share, but also know that each member of the family is also distinct, different. Thus in family life, we can see stability and change, homogeneity and heterogeneity all operating simultaneously. This idea then that people participate in multiple cultural communities, each of which has these complex dimensions suggests that studying and examining the influences of culture on learning and development needs to push beyond the boundaries typically invoked in research on learning and development. Currently and historically, such research has tended to either sample particular populations as the norm for comparisons around normative expectations (e.g., White middle-class samples; Graham, 1992) or to sample within social categories (e.g., race, ethnicity, class) as though these categories are homogenous and somehow deterministic (Orellana & Bowman, 2003). Such research also has tended to study learning and development in one setting (e.g., school, in family life, in informal settings) without considering people's navigation across settings.

Such navigations clearly provide the contexts that influence development. We need then to understand the demands for participation within particular settings, such as schools, examine whether the presumed normative demands for participation are actually necessary for developing competence, and examine the resources that such navigations make available, with the likelihood that such resources likely entail both affordances and constraints. I offer these considerations in light of the ways in which so much research addressing opportunity to learn for particular populations often propose deterministic explanations (e.g., what poverty does to the brain, limits of language resources among children growing up in poverty, lack of executive control among youth living in poverty—where poverty has become the synonym for race). The takeaway is human adaptability.

In this multidimensional framing, from a developmental science perspective, identity is not singular. We have identities in terms of personality, as members of families, as members of other kinds of communities of practice (e.g., basketball player, rapper, video gamer), in terms of gender and sexual orientation, and so on. And identity is contextual. That means that particular features of how we self-identify and what values we place on such self-identifications may shift over time—for example, from childhood to adolescence to adulthood to elderhood—and in different contexts one aspect of our identity repertoires may surface as more salient. This contextualization of identity repertoires is not merely an attribute of the individual, but rather an outgrowth of intersections between the ways that social/cultural settings are organized—who is there, what are the tasks to be accomplished, what is available to accomplish the tasks—and particular attributes of the person. And these relationships are bidirectional.

Research on racial identity has documented the multiple ways that people of African descent—at least in the context of the United States—may view race as salient or not, may view race as personally meaningful or not, may have different conceptions of how others view race (Cross, 1991; Sellers, Smith, Shelton, Rowley, & Chavous, 1998). Other researchers have conceptualized racial identity from a developmental perspective, arguing that people of African descent in the United States may go through ideological stages, depending on experience (Cross, 1979). An array of instruments have been constructed and validated to measure these dimensions of racial identity and used in correlational and longitudinal studies to examine how different kinds of racial identity may be connected to particular life course outcomes—for example, grades, college attendance, healthy psychological development, resilience (Bowman & Howard, 1985; Chavous et al., 2003; Mandara, 2006; O'Connor, 1999; Perry, 1993; Spencer, Noll, Stoltzfus, & Harpalani, 2001).

A related body of research has examined ethnic identity. I argue that understanding intersections between race and ethnicity is important. Race is a political construct that creates particular challenges because of the pervasiveness of racism as an ideology. Race is defined on the basis of questionable physiognomy. The skin color spectrum represented among people of African descent (e.g., Black people) is diverse. However, I argue that people of African descent in the United States and diaspora must also be understood in terms of ethnicity, recognizing the many cultural practices and belief systems that have been sustained from their African roots (Asante, 1990; Asante & Asante, 1990; DuBois, 1996). Ethnic identity research has also addressed the complex and diverse ways in which such identities develop—exploration and consolidation, differences in salience, multiethnic identities (Phinney, 1990; Portes, 1995). Studies have also documented relationships between positive ethnic identity and a number of outcomes from self-esteem, lack of substance abuse, academic self-efficacy, and grades (Phinney, Cantu, & Kurtz, 1997).

One important takeaway from the research on racial and ethnic identity is that wrestling with positioning with regard to race and ethnicity constitute developmental tasks across the life course, but especially during adolescence. This is, in part, because it becomes integrated into the normative challenges of adolescence—beginning consolidation of self-construals connected to the health of the ego (Erikson, 1959; Marcia, Waterman, Matteson, Archer, & Orlofsky, 2012). Adolescence is a key transition point in the life course. It is complicated by enhanced social cognition (Flavell & Miller, 1998; e.g., nuances in the ability to read the internal states of others, including the salience of social comparisons), the emergence of sexual arousal, the importance of peer relationships, the anticipation of future adult roles and responsibilities, all heightened by immense physiological changes occurring, much of which are embodied in development as a sexual being. These normative challenges of adolescence are now complicated by identity wrestling with regard to ethnicity and race in societies such as the United States where there are ubiquitous structures that heighten the salience of racial and ethnic identity (Spencer, 2006). They are further complicated by the nature of the academic and social demands of high school—where subject matters tend to become further removed from the everyday, where youth must learn to navigate multiple adults who play consequential roles in how and whether they experience success, and where they already bring well established perceptions about schooling from 8 years of elementary education.

Issues of identity and motivation then come into play in terms of the perceptions people bring to settings and the ways that settings are organized to also influence perceptions. For example, if I come into a setting with certain preconceived stereotypes about what participation will be like, what it will require in relation to my own ego-related needs, it is possible that what people do, say, how they act, what is available in the setting may stimulate me to rethink my stereotypes, and change my perceptions. Eccles, Wigfield, and Schiefele (1998) offer a multidimensional framework for academic motivation that is fundamentally ecological in its scope. It includes the cultural milieu with regard to cultural stereotypes about people (e.g., girls are not good at math) as well as subject matter (e.g., math is about right answers); the beliefs and behaviors of those seeking to socialize the child (e.g., teachers, parents), the aptitudes of the child and his or her previous experiences with schooling; the child's perceptions of those seeking to socialize him or her and the stereotypes in the air to use Steele's (2004) term with regard to categories of people (likely those that can be attributed to the child) and the academic tasks; to what the child attributes his or her perceptions (e.g., ability, effort, in my control, not in my control); the array of relevant schemata the child brings to the enterprise, expectations for success, and perceptions of the tasks to be mastered; the child's affective memories around similar experiences, and what they call the subject task value in terms of interests, utility and what costs the child must weigh in putting forth effort. They articulate these factors as situated inside a set of dynamic relationships that together influence what they call achievement-related choices. The framework has been subject to empirical measures. Important caveats that Eccles introduces that are relevant to the focus of this review include how ego-related choices may differ by cultural communities and within cultural communities by gender. For example, research has documented broad cultural orientations distinguishing historical cultural communities that favor interdependence over independence, emphasizing collectivism and family obligation (Markus & Kitayama, 1991). In such societies, for example, stereotypes will differ, causal attributions for choices will likely differ, and the influences on subject task value will differ (Stigler & Baranes, 1989). The Eccles framework is further bolstered by longstanding research around the importance of a sense of self-efficacy (Pintrich & Schrauben, 1992; Zimmerman, Bandura, & Martinez-Pons, 1992); and also Oyserman and colleagues' work (Oyserman, Bybee, & Terry, 2006; Oyserman & Destin, 2010) on the role of perceptions of future selves (who and what can I become) in influencing effort toward a goal and persistence in such efforts in the face of challenge, or what they now refer to as identity-based motivation.

Thus, relevant perceptions include the following:

- What am I being asked to do?
- Am I capable of tackling these tasks?
- Is this task meaningful to me?
- What supports are available to me to wrestle with this task?
- Do I feel safe in attempting to wrestle with this task?
- How do I weigh any risks or competing goals?

This framing of motivation in terms of what is entailed in decisions by learners to put forth effort to learn, particularly in the contexts of schooling, integrates in many ways what has been articulated in cognitive studies with regard to knowledge structures (now to include knowledge of cultural worlds and knowledge of self), the role of emotions and the salience of perceptions (Erickson et al., 2007).

There are a number of salient issues in regard to what these propositions mean for how we understand the challenges entailed in inequities in opportunity to learn and educational outcomes associated with race, ethnicity, class and gender. I will illustrate issues in terms of race, in part because race and ethnicity are so intertwined in the social and ideological spaces within the United States. As discussed earlier, particularly at the critical transitions of adolescence, one aspect of identity that must be wrestled with is how youth come to understand the meaning of race in terms of navigating the world beyond their immediate families. Margaret Beale Spencer examined and replicated the famous doll experiment conducted by Kenneth and Mamie Clark, evidence from which was used in the 1954 *Brown v. Board of Education* Supreme Court Case. The Clarks argued that Black children choosing the white doll as beautiful was evidence of the detrimental effects of segregation on the sense of self-worth of Black children. Drawing on well-established research regarding the egocentrism of very young children (Piaget, 1926), Spencer argued that the choice by young children of the white doll was simply evidence of their recognition that negative stereotypes around Black physiognomy was "in the air," but because of their essential egocentrism did not make such negative attributions to themselves. When Spencer then repeated the experiment with older children, she found them clearly emotionally burdened in making the decision because at this point in terms of their more advanced social cognition, they realized the negative attributions could now be applied to them (Spencer, 2008). On the other hand, Spencer also repeated the same experiment with young children enrolled in an African-centered preschool, where issues of positive Black identity were centrally socialized, these young children eagerly pointed to the black doll as beautiful, as the smart doll. This replication demonstrates the role of socialization around the meaning and salience of race matters. These implications are also reinforced by the extensive body of research on positive racial socialization (referenced earlier) as a resource for resilience in the face of challenge.

Returning to Spencer's phenomenological variant of ecological systems theory model, the research indicates that Black, Brown, and youth living in persistent intergenerational poverty must learn to engage the normative challenges of development at particular points in the life course (early childhood, middle childhood, adolescence, young adulthood)—learning language, learning to manage one's body, learning to read the internal states of others, regulating emotions, setting goals, interpreting ego-related needs, establishing and maintaining attachments, constructing knowledge that allows one to engage in meaningful new tasks—as well as the complications and ego-related challenges that emerge in the risks that racism, gender bias, ethnocentrism, and homophobia structurally pose. These structural risks include exposure to violence, facing a culture of low expectations in schools, living in food deserts, lack of green space, inadequate housing, insufficient community based spaces for youth development, inadequate health care. These are structural risks because they do not emerge randomly but systematically, structured into public policies and institutional configurations. And they are particularly pernicious psychologically as embodied in metanarratives of deficit, of being less than, and as a consequence pose significant threats to the ego. We know from decades of research on identity that the ego drives self-concept, drives engagement, as ego defines what we think we need to be centered, to be whole (Maslow, 1943).

These propositions, empirically supported, from the field of human development suggest that efforts to transform schools into places where Black, Brown, and youth living in persistent intergenerational poverty thrive must explicitly address the ways that racism, ethnocentrism, gender bias, homophobia, and stereotypes around the experience of poverty are enacted in the lives of young people and in the practices and organization of schooling. Schools must develop tools that allow teachers and administrators to understand how perceptions of ability and of resources for coping are enacted even in the ways that curriculum content and instruction are structured. Such orientations can help us move away from the tendency to "blame the victim" rather than to examine the ways that ecologies of learning can address the fundamental human development needs that all youth face.

The Neurosciences

I want to close this review of findings from disciplines in the social and biological sciences that can expand how we conceptualize the challenges and opportunities of

addressing the persistent achievement gap associated with race, ethnicity, and class with a brief review of big findings from the neurosciences. Just as early work in cognition focused on individual mental functioning, so early work in neuroscience focused on cognitive activity within the individual brain. In more recent years, however, the field has expanded into a number of specializations—cultural neuroscience, social neuroscience, developmental neuroscience, among others. It is not the intent of this review to provide a detailed synthesis of research in these subdisciplines (Cacioppo & Berntson, 2004; Chiao, Cheon, Pornpattananangkul, Mrazek, & Blizinsky, 2013; Han et al., 2013; Organization for Economic Co-operation and Development, 2007). However, my goal is to extrapolate big ideas emerging that converge with findings in cognition and human development that open up broader conceptions of human learning and development. These central propositions include (a) dynamic relations between biological and cultural resources, (b) the inherent plasticity of human development, (c) the centrality of culture in human development, (d) how human learning and development unfold within and across ecological spaces and time, and (e) the ways that human thinking and development are connected to contexts.

These particular subfields of cultural, social, and developmental neuroscience converge around the framing of human development unfolding within and across ecological spaces, and not merely as deterministic biologically driven trajectories. Cultural and social neurosciences in particular stress the fundamental interdependence of the biologic and the cultural. Chiao and Ambady (2007) define cultural neuroscience as "a theoretical and empirical approach to investigate and characterize the mechanisms by which [the] hypothesized bidirectional, mutual constitution of culture, brain, and genes occurs" (p. 238). Han et al. (2013) go on to say,

CN research does not study culture as a set of biologically determined predispositions/constraints that can be used to rigidly categorize collections of people. Instead, the CN approach emphasizes the flexibility of the human brain that enables humans to adapt to sociocultural environments. (p. 351)

This is important considering the history of attributing particular cultural practices as determining and fixed. An important emerging consensus argues for the inherent neoplasticity of the brain. In addition to empirical studies (Starlinger & Niemeyer, 1981), we know from everyday experience the ways that blind persons develop enhanced auditory acuity. Cultural neuroscience works from propositions shared in fields of cultural psychology and anthropology that culture consists of shared belief systems embedded in routine cultural practices. Sampling from cross-cultural studies examining how neural processing of culturally congruent and culturally incongruent stimuli differ have shown that categorizing people by pan ethnic identities (e.g., Chinese Americans and Chinese from the Mainland) does not account for differences in processing, suggesting rather it is the actual participation in routine practices over time that counts (Han et al., 2013).

IMPLICATIONS FOR RECONCEPTUALIZING HOW WE STUDY AND DESIGN FOR DIVERSITY

I want now to contrast these empirically supported propositions running across studies of cognition, of human development, and of neural processing through the various new fields in the neurosciences with the implied propositions currently dominant around how to address the persistent achievement and opportunity gap associated with race, ethnicity, and class. I in no way intend to impute the good intentions of any of the people involved in the examples I share. The examples are only intended to be illustrative. Rather, I suggest we may be at a kind of Kuhnian revolution transition point (Kuhn, 1970) where tensions between older and new sets of propositions are emerging.

Originally in 2000, the National Research Council authorized a study of policies with regard to early childhood development and poverty titled *From Neurons to Neighborhoods: The Science of Early Childhood Development* (Shonkoff & Phillips, 2000). More recently, in 2012, the National Research Council published an updated report on a commemorative workshop held in 2011 (Institute of Medicine and National Research Council, 2012). It is important to note that both the earlier and the more recent workshop actually sought to integrate findings from cognition, human development, and the neurosciences. Several propositions put forward I think are worthy of interrogating. In the updated report, summarizing a presentation by Bruce McEwen of Rockefeller University, the following assertion is made: "Low socioeconomic status is associated with poor language skills, poor executive function, and other effects on learning ability" (Institute of Medicine and National Research Council, 2012, p. 16). In the updated workshop summary, McEwen makes a compelling case for the relevance of understanding neurological and other physiological processes entailed in the experience of stress. Even though in the workshop summary he references brain plasticity, sources of resilience in the face of stress are discussed in general, but not in relation to resources internal to populations living in poverty. He makes an important contribution in stating that "policies and health interventions need to work in tandem" (p. 17) and cites examples of effective early childhood collaborations such as the Perry Preschool Project and the Abecedarian Project. The report goes on to summarize Deborah Stipek's of Stanford University workshop presentation on learning and focused on challenges associated with verbal skills, social skills, mathematical skills, and executive control functions. These have become the most widely cited areas of deficit functioning among children living in poverty and are routinely argued to predict low functioning in schools. I want to reexamine these arguments from the perspectives I have been articulating as a cultural and ecological framework on human learning and development, and to consider some of the methodological and conceptual conundrums entailed in current metanarratives on opportunity to learn exemplified in some aspects of the *Neurons to Neighborhoods* reports.

First, while I applaud the focus on the need for ecological supports—such as partnerships between schools and health initiatives—the problem space is more complex.

The array of initiatives proposed and cited are fundamentally programs intended to fix poor children and their families. They presume these children embody deficits that good school programs—in this case early childhood programs—can fix. The measures typically used in studies of language competencies and executive control, for example, themselves only capture a slice of what such competencies entail. Many of the warrants for language deficits come from the B. Hart and Risley (1995) study of 42 families from middle-income and low-income communities. B. Hart and Risley (1995) argued that middle-class children come to school knowing 30 million more words than poor children and as a consequence are ill prepared to learn to read. In a similar vein, decades earlier some had argued that children who spoke African American English did not possess a full linguistic repertoire and therefore had difficulties with reading (Baratz, 1969; Bereiter & Engelmann, 1966). The sociolinguistic community (Smitherman, 1999, 2003), anchored initially by Labov's (1972) response, argued quite the contrary. Many studies of language competence use the Peabody Vocabulary test without acknowledging its possible middle-class biases (Stockman, 2000). Although Washington and Craig (1999) have argued for the validity of the Peabody Vocabulary Test III with African American children, Peña (2000) has argued for the use of more ecologically valid methods for eliciting the range of semantic knowledge that children from culturally and linguistically diverse have. Just in terms of learning to read, there are an array of linguistic competencies that contribute to comprehension beyond vocabulary (which is unquestionably important), including metalinguistic knowledge of indirection, of figuration, of point of view; for comprehending narratives, repertoires for inferring the internal states of psychologically complex characters (Champion, Seymour, & Camarata, 1995; Gee, 1989).

With regard to social functioning and executive control, studies on children and youth living in poverty typically assume that these competencies are independent of context. While using existing measures, it is likely that many of the bankers whose decision making led to the most recent economic depression would have scored well on measures of executive control, and it is likely there are many areas of their lives where they do/did exert self-control, it is clear professionally they did not. We all know cases of children who will push the boundaries with their parents but will exert self-control with their grandparents; or adolescents who will exert self-control in one teacher's class and act out in another. This construct of self-control, conceptually related to my earlier discussion of motivation, is multidimensional—including perceptions of ability, utility, relevance, weighing against competing aims, perceptions of what is available to help one navigate. The focus and structure of most programs aimed at helping poor children and adolescents develop self-control or some generic sense of executive control do not design for these multiple dimensions, and especially how these dimensions are affected by the experience of race and the experience of poverty. Just as the conceptualizations of racial identity take into account the range of differences in how racialized persons view the meaning, value and salience of race, so too the experience of poverty is not homogeneous. And certainly if we take an international perspective, there are many countries where the absolute measure of poverty is moderated by the ubiquitous availability of social supports provided by governments. In the United States, we have many traditional ways of measuring class status—income, mother's education, neighborhood residence. However, these markers do not account for variation based, for example, on the availability of social networks—extended family members as caretakers, church communities, peer extended social networks, and so on.

The issue raised by Stipek around mathematical skills provides an opportunity to interrogate the question from within the knowledge base regarding the content area. Stipek notes evidence that math skills at kindergarten are better predictors of math and reading skills at the third grade. One of the reasons Stipek may see longer term effects of early skills in mathematics than measured skills in language is that in terms of teaching and learning, the domain of mathematics articulates what children need to know and be able to do in ways that in terms of disciplinary knowledge are more well specified. In addition, mathematics standards, educators in mathematics education, and those studying the cognitive dimensions of mathematical understanding stress the importance of diversity in approaches to representing mathematical problems and the fruitfulness of pursuing multiple solution paths, and the importance of the ability to warrant one's claims based on the science of the mathematics (Schoenfeld, 1985). In teaching reading comprehension, we typically ask students to produce outcomes of comprehension without specifying pathways, including multiple pathways for addressing problems of comprehension. In the field, when we do talk about strategies, they are often broad abstractions like—ask questions, reread, read ahead, make predictions, and monitor when you do not understand. These metacognitive moves are certainly important, but once you get stuck, if you do not have a much more fined-tuned repertoire of kinds of knowledge on which you can draw, knowing you are stuck is not much help. National Assessment of Educational Progress data trends over the past four decades show a trajectory of growth in mathematics across grades, while trends in reading not only remain relatively flat, they also worsen as youth proceed across the grades (Lee, 2014; National Center for Education Statistics, 2013). If indeed we have challenges in terms of our conceptualization of the demands of using language skills to learn to read, and we see patterns of lack of growth across grades and historical time, it may be that the problem lies not so much with what children living in poverty bring or do not bring, but more so with what the relevant fields—for example, research in reading comprehension, teacher training, organizational learning in schools, tools used for assessment and what we assess—make available.

And my argument is that how we as research communities focusing on education and the enhancement of life course outcomes, especially for those who face some of the greatest challenges due to racism, poverty, gender bias, homophobia, and so on, conceptualize the problem space we seek to understand matters: Do we think the problem space can be understood by single silos of inquiry; Do we believe in the fundamental proposition with regard to human plasticity, indeed across the life course, and take the challenge as not one constrained within the individual but rather a challenge to how we conceptualize the nature of risks and the diversity in the range of repertoires that may be available to wrestle with the problem(s); Do we believe that institutionalized metanarratives matter for the perceptions that all players bring to the inquiry and teaching enterprise; Do we believe that diversity is actually a real strength of humanity and not merely a politically correct aphorism, and as a consequence, how do we imagine recruiting diversity as a resource. Recruiting diversity as a resource means rethinking the range of prior knowledge, dispositions, epistemologies that may be relevant to our targets of learning, since from long-term studies of cognition, we know that prior knowledge matters, but we also know that people are constantly inferring from experience to construct mental representations that when meaningful will most likely be stored in long-term memory. If we accept that identity is multidimensional, influenced by context, shifts in some ways across ontogenetic time, and whether focused on independence or interdependence is always driven by the need for ego fulfillment, might not understanding identity unfolding within and across contexts be useful for thinking about how schooling might recruit different dimensions of identity as resources for learning.

I argue that these fundamental propositions undergird all of human functioning, that these intersections between the biological and the social or cultural are driven as essential propellants of human functioning derived from our evolutionary history as a species. Perceptions matter. Feelings or emotions matter. Attachments matter. Mental representations of phenomenon in the world matter. Beliefs in self-efficacy and effort matter. These fundamental underpinnings of human learning and development are ubiquitous to the species. Designed environments—such as schools—will be most robust and generative when they take these fundamental underpinnings of human learning and development as starting points.

In the end, my recommendations for schooling will not differ much from those who argue from multiculturalism, sociocultural theory, particular political or ideological positions. I agree with warrants from all these frames. I simply want to argue that science—the biological, psychological and social sciences—also are now converging on big propositions supported by empirical studies that diversity, human plasticity, the centrality of culture, understanding the diverse pathways through which humans at each stage of the life course learn to navigate—sometimes in ways that are resilient and sometimes in ways that are maladaptive—are central foundations for human learning and development. And understanding that within all communities, we will find people who succumb to risks and others who are resilient in face of those risks. We need to better understand those sources of resiliency within and across communities and to accept—as my friend Margaret Beale Spencer always asserts—to be human is to be at risk.

NOTE

[1]"At its most basic, epigenetics is the study of changes in gene activity that do not involve alterations to the genetic code but still get passed down to at least one successive generation. These patterns of gene expression are governed by the cellular material—the epigenome—that sits on top of the genome, just outside it (hence the prefix *epi-*, which means above). It is these epigenetic 'marks' that tell your genes to switch on or off, to speak loudly or whisper. It is through epigenetic marks that environmental factors like diet, stress and prenatal nutrition can make an imprint on genes that is passed from one generation to the next" (Cloud, 2010).

REFERENCES

Anderson, R. (1984). Reflections on the acquisition of knowledge. *Educational Researcher, 13*(9), 5–10.

Asante, M. K. (1990). The African essence in African-American language. In M. K. Asante & K. Welsh-Asante (Eds.), *African culture: The rhythms of unity* (pp. 233–252). Trenton, NJ: Africa World Press.

Asante, M. K., & Asante, K. W. (1990). *African culture: The rhythms of unity.* Trenton, NJ: Africa World Press.

Baillargeon, R. (1995). Physical reasoning in infancy. In M. S. Gazzaniga (Ed.), *The cognitive neurosciences* (pp. 181–204). Cambridge: MIT Press.

Baratz, J. C. (1969). Linguistic and cultural factors in teaching reading to ghetto children. *Elementary English, 46,* 199–203.

Bereiter, C., & Engelmann, S. (1966). *Teaching disadvantaged children in pre-school.* Englewood Cliffs, NJ: Prentice Hall.

Bowman, P., & Howard, C. (1985). Race related socialization, motivation and academic achievement: A study of black youths in three generation families. *Journal of American Academy of Child Psychiatry, 24,* 134–141.

Bransford, J., Brown, A., & Cocking, R. (1999). *How people learn: Brain, mind, experience and school.* Washington, DC: National Academies Press.

Brottman, M. A. (1968). *Language remediation for the disadvantaged preschool child.* Chicago, IL: University of Chicago.

Cacioppo, J. T., & Berntson, G. (2004). *Social neuroscience: Key readings.* London, England: Psychology Press.

Carey, S. (1985). *Conceptual change in childhood.* Cambridge, MA: Bradford Books.

Carey, S., & Gelman, R. (1991). *The epigenesis of mind.* Hillsdale, NJ: Psychology Press.

Champion, T., Seymour, H., & Camarata, S. (1995). Narrative discourse among African American children. *Journal of Narrative and Life History, 5,* 333–352.

Chavous, T. M., Bernat, D. H., Schmeelk-Cone, K., Caldwell, C. H., Kohn-Wood, L., & Zimmerman, M. A. (2003). Racial identity and academic attainment among African American adolescents. *Child Development, 74,* 1076–1090.

Chiao, J. Y., & Ambady, N. (2007). Cultural neuroscience: Parsing universality and diversity across levels of analysis. In S. Kitayama & D. Cohen (Eds.), *Handbook of cultural psychology* (pp. 237–254). New York, NY: Guilford.

Chiao, J. Y., Cheon, B., Pornpattananangkul, N., Mrazek, A., & Blizinsky, K. (2013). Cultural neuroscience. *Advances in Culture & Psychology, 4*(1). doi:10.1093/acprof: osobl/9780199336715.003.0001

Chinn, C. A., Buckland, L. A., & Samarapungavan, A. L. A. (2011). Expanding the dimensions of epistemic cognition: Arguments from philosophy and psychology. *Educational Psychologist, 46,* 141–167.

Clement, J. (1982). Student preconceptions of introductory mechanics. *American Journal of Physics, 50,* 66–71.

Clore, G. L., & Ortony, A. (2000). Cognition in emotion: Always, sometimes, or never? In L. Nadel, R. Lane, & G. L. Ahern (Eds.), *The cognitive neuroscience of emotion* (pp. 24–61). New York, NY: Oxford University Press.

Cloud, J. (2010, January 6). Why your DNA isn't your destiny. *Time.* Retrieved from http://content.time.com/time/subscriber/article/0,33009,1952313-2,00.html

Cole, M. (1996). *Cultural psychology, a once and future discipline.* Cambridge, MA: Belknap Press of Harvard University Press.

Coleman, J. (1988). Social capital in the creation of human capital. *American Journal of Sociology, 94*(Suppl.), S95-S120.

Conley, A. M., Pintrich, P. R., Vekiri, I., & Harrison, D. (2004). Changes in epistemological beliefs in elementary science students. *Contemporary Educational Psychology, 29,* 186–204.

Cross, W. (1979). Empirical analysis of the negro-to-black conversion experience. In A. W. Boykin, A. J. Anderson, & J. Yates (Eds.), *Research directions of black psychologists* (pp. 107–130). New York, NY: Russell Sage Foundation.

Cross, W. (1991). *Shades of black: Diversity in African American identity.* Philadelphia, PA: Temple University Press.

Dalgleish, T., & Powers, M. (Eds.). (1999). *Handbook of cognition and emotion.* Sussex, England: Wiley.

Damasio, A. (1995). Toward a neurobiology of emotion and feeling: Operational concepts and hypotheses. *Neuroscientist, 1,* 19–25.

Damon, W., & Lerner, R. M. (2008). The scientific study of child and adolescent development: Important issues in the field today. In W. Damon & R. M. Lerner (Eds.), *Child and adolescent development an advanced course* (pp. 3–13). Hoboken, NJ: Wiley.

Darling-Hammond, L. (2004). The color line in American education: Race, resources, and student achievement. *Du Bois Review, 1,* 213–246.

Darling-Hammond, L. (2010). *The flat world and education: How America's commitment to equity will determine our future.* New York, NY: Teachers College Press.

DiSessa, A. A. (1982). Unlearning Aristotelian physics: A study of knowledge-base learning. *Cognitive Science, 6,* 37–75.

DiSessa, A. A. (1993). Toward an epistemology of physics. *Cognition and Instruction, 10,* 105–225.

DiSessa, A. A., & Sherin, B. L. (1998). What changes in conceptual change? *International Journal of Science Education, 20,* 1155–1191.

DuBois, W. E. B. (1996). The concept of race. In M. K. Asante & A. S. Abarry (Eds.), *African intellectual heritage: A book of sources* (pp. 409–417). Philadelphia, PA: Temple University Press.

Eccles, J., Wigfield, A., & Schiefele, U. (1998). Motivation to succeed. In W. Damon & N. Eisenberg (Eds.), *Handbook of child psychology* (Vol. 3, 5th ed.). New York, NY: Wiley.

Erikson, E. H. (1959). *Identity and the life cycle: Selected papers.* New York, NY: International Universities Press.

Erickson, F., Cook-Sather, A., Espinoza, M., Jurow, S., Shultz, J. J., & Spencer, J. (2007). Students' experience of school curriculum: The everyday circumstances of granting and withholding assent to learn. In M. Connelly, M. F. He, & J. Phillion (Eds.), *The Sage handbook of curriculum and instruction* (pp. 198–218). Thousand Oaks, CA: Sage.

Farrington, C. A., Roderick, M., Allensworth, E., Nagaoka, J., Keyes, T. S., Johnson, D. W., & Beechum, N. O. (2012). *Teaching adolescents to become learners. The role of noncognitive factors in shaping school performance: A critical literature review.* Retrieved from https://consortium.uchicago.edu/sites/default/files/publications/Noncognitive%20Report.pdf

Flavell, J. H., & Miller, P. H. (1998). Social cognition. In D. Kuhn & R. Siegler (Eds.), *Handbook of child psychology* (Vol. 2, 5th ed., pp. 851–898). New York, NY: Wiley.

Francis, D., Diorio, J., Liu, D., & Meaney, M. J. (1999). Nongenomic transmission across generations of maternal behavior and stress responses in the rat. *Science, 286,* 1155–1158.

Gee, J. P. (1989). The narrativization of experience in the oral style. *Journal of Education, 171*(1), 75–96.

Gould, S. J. (1981). *The mismeasure of man.* New York, NY: Norton.

Graham, S. (1992). "Most of the subjects were white and middle class": Trends in published research on African Americans in selected APA journals, 1970–1989. *American Psychologist, 47,* 629–639.

Gutierrez, K., & Rogoff, B. (2003). Cultural ways of learning: Individual traits or repertoires of practice. *Educational Researcher, 32*(5), 19–25.

Gutmann, A. (1993). Democracy & democratic education. *Studies in Philosophy and Education, 12*(1), 1–9.

Han, S., Northoff, G., Vogeley, K., Wexler, B. E., Kitayama, S., & Varnum, M. E. (2013). A cultural neuroscience approach to the biosocial nature of the human brain. *Annual Review of Psychology, 64*, 335–359.

Harber, J. R., & Bryen, D. N. (1976). Black English and the task of reading. *Review of Educational Research, 46*, 387–405.

Hart, B., & Risley, R. T. (1995). *Meaningful differences in the everyday experience of young American children.* Baltimore, MD: Paul H. Brookes.

Hart, F. E. (2001). The epistemology of cognitive literary studies. *Philosophy and Literature, 25*, 314–334.

Heckman, J. J. (2012). An effective strategy for promoting social mobility. *Boston Review, 103*, 10155–10162.

Hernstein, R., & Murray, C. (1994). *The bell curve: Intelligence and class structure in American life.* New York, NY: Free Press.

Hilliard, A. G. (1996). Either a paradigm shift or no mental measurement: The non-science and nonsense of the bell curve. *Cultural Diversity and Mental Health Journal, 2*(1), 1–20.

Hofer, B. (2000). Dimensionality and disciplinary differences in personal epistemology. *Contemporary Educational Psychology, 25*, 378–405.

Hofer, B. (2004). Exploring the dimensions of personal epistemology in differing classroom contexts: Student interpretations during the first year of college. *Contemporary Educational Psychology, 29*, 129–163.

Hofer, B., & Pintrich, P. (1997). The development of epistemological theories: Beliefs about knowledge and knowing and their relation to learning. *Review of Educational Research, 67*, 88–140.

Ignatiev, N. (1996). *How the Irish became White.* New York, NY: Routledge.

Institute of Medicine and National Research Council. (2012). *From neurons to neighborhoods: An update: Workshop summary.* Washington, DC: National Academies Press.

Jensen, A. (1969). How much can we boost IQ and scholastic achievement. *Harvard Educational Review, 39*, 1–123.

Kardash, C. M., & Scholes, R. J. (1996). Effects of preexisiting beliefs, epistemological beliefs, and need for cognition on interpretation of controversial issues. *Journal of Educational Psychology, 88*, 260–271.

Kuhn, T. S. (1970). *The structure of scientific revolutions.* Chicago, IL: University of Chicago Press.

Labov, W. (1972). *Language in the inner city: Studies in the black English vernacular.* Philadelphia: University of Pennsylvania Press.

Lee, C. D. (2008). The centrality of culture to the scientific study of learning and development: How an ecological framework in educational research facilitates civic responsibility. *Educational Researcher, 37*, 267–279.

Lee, C. D. (2009). Historical evolution of risk and equity: Interdisciplinary issues and critiques *Review of Research in Education, 33*, 63–100.

Lee, C. D. (2010). Soaring above the clouds, delving the ocean's depths: Understanding the ecologies of human learning and the challenge for education science. *Educational Researcher, 39*, 643–655.

Lee, C. D. (2014). Reading gaps and complications of scientific studies of learning. In S. Harper (Ed.), *The elusive quest for civil rights in education: Evidence-based perspectives from leading scholars on the 50th anniversary of the Civil Rights Act.* Philadelphia: Center for the Study of Race and Equity in Education, University of Pennsylvania.

Lee, C. D., Goldman, S. R., Levine, S., & Magliano, J. P. (2016). Epistemic cognition in literary reasoning. In J. Green, W. Sandoval, & I. Bråten (Eds.), *Handbook of epistemic cognition* (pp. 165–183). New York, NY: Taylor & Francis.

Mandara, J. (2006). The impact of family functioning on African American males' academic achievement: A review and clarification of the empirical literature. *Teachers College Record, 108*, 206–223.

Marcia, J. E., Waterman, A. S., Matteson, D. R., Archer, S. L., & Orlofsky, J. L. (2012). *Ego identity: A handbook for psychosocial research.* Berlin, Germany: Springer Science + Business Media.

Markus, H., & Kitayama, S. (1991). Culture and the self: Implications for cognition, emotion, and motivation. *Psychological Review, 98,* 224–253.

Maslow, A. H. (1943). A theory of human motivation. *Psychological Review, 50,* 370–396.

Mason, L., & Boscolo, P. (2004). Role of epistemological understanding and interest in interpreting a controversy and in topic-specific belief change. *Contemporary Educational Psychology, 29,* 103–128.

Massey, C. M., & Gelman, R. (1988). Preschoolers decide whether pictured unfamiliar objects can move themselves. *Developmental Psychology, 24,* 307–317.

McAdams, D. P., & Pals, J. L. (2006). A new big five: Fundamental principles for an integrative science of personality. *American Psychologist, 61,* 204–217.

Mills, C. W. (1997). *The racial contract.* Ithaca, NY: Cornell University Press.

Mintzes, J. J. (1984). Naive theories in biology: Children's concepts of the human body. *School Science and Mathematics, 84,* 548–555.

National Center for Education Statistics. (2013). *The nation's report card: Trends in academic progress* (NCES 2013 456). Washington, DC: Author.

O'Connor, C. (1999). Race, class, and gender in America: Narratives of opportunity among low-income African American youths. *Sociology of Education, 72,* 137–157.

Orellana, M., & Bowman, P. (2003). Cultural diversity: Research on learning and development: Conceptual, methodological and strategic considerations. *Educational Researcher, 32*(5), 26–32.

Organization for Economic Co-operation and Development. (2007). *Understanding the brain: The birth of a learning science.* Paris, France: Author.

Orr, E. W. (1987). *Twice as less: Black English and the performance of Black students in mathematics and science.* New York, NY: Norton.

Ortony, A. (1979). *The cognitive structure of emotions.* New York, NY: Cambridge University Press.

Oyserman, D., Bybee, D., & Terry, K. (2006). Possible selves and academic outcomes: How and when possible selves impel action. *Journal of Personality and Social Psychology, 91,* 188–204.

Oyserman, D., & Destin, M. (2010). Identity-based motivation: Implications for intervention. *The Counseling Psychologist, 38,* 1001–1043.

Peña, E. D. (2000). Assessment of semantic knowledge: Use of feedback and clinical interviewing. *Seminars in Speech and Language, 22*(1), 51–62.

Perry, T. (1993). *Toward a theory of African American school achievement.* Retrieved from http://eric.ed.gov/?id=ED366418

Phinney, J. S. (1990). Ethnic identity in adolescents and adults: Review of research. *Psychological Bulletin, 108,* 499–514.

Phinney, J. S., Cantu, C. L., & Kurtz, D. A. (1997). Ethnic and American identity as predictors of self-esteem among African American, Latino, and White adolescents. *Journal of Youth and Adolescence, 26,* 165–185.

Piaget, J. (1926). *The language and thought of the child.* New York, NY: Harcourt Brace.

Pintrich, P. R., & Schrauben, B. (1992). Students' motivational beliefs and their cognitive engagement in classroom academic tasks. In D. Schunk & J. Meece (Eds.), *Student perceptions in the classroom: Causes and consequences* (pp. 149–183). Hillsdale, NJ: Erlbaum.

Portes, A. (1995). Segmented assimilation among new immigrant youth: A conceptual framework. In R. G. Rumbaur & W. A. Cornelius (Eds.), *California's immigrant children* (pp. 71–76). San Diego, CA: Center for U.S.-Mexican Studies.

Quartz, S. R., & Sejnowski, T. J. (2002). *Liars, lovers, and heroes: What the new brain science reveals about how we become who we are.* New York, NY: William Morrow.

Rogoff, B. (2003). *The cultural nature of human development*. New York, NY: Oxford University Press.

Rumelhart, D. (1980). Schemata: The building blocks of cognition. In R. Spiro, B. Bruce, & W. Brewer (Eds.), *Theoretical issues in reading comprehension: Perspectives from cognitive psychology, linguistics, artificial intelligence and education* (pp. 33–58). Hillsdale, NJ: Erlbaum.

Russo, E. A., Martienssen, R. A., & Riggs, A. D. (Eds.). (1996). *Epigenetic mechanisms of gene regulation*. Plainview, NY: Cold Spring Harbor Laboratory Press.

Schoenfeld, A. H. (1985). *Mathematical problem solving*. Orlando, FL: Academic Press.

Schwartz, D. L., Varma, S., & Martin, L. (2008). Dynamic transfer and innovation. In S. Vosniadou (Ed.), *International handbook of research on conceptual change* (pp. 479–506). New York, NY: Routledge.

Sellers, R. M., Caldwell, C. H., Schmeelk-Cone, K. H., & Zimmerman, M. A. (2003). Racial identity, racial discrimination, perceived stress, and psychological distress among African American young adults. *Journal of Health and Social Behavior, 44*, 302–317.

Sellers, R. M., Copeland-Linder, N., Martin, P. P., & Lewis, R. H. (2006). Racial identity matters: The relationship between racial discrimination and psychological functioning in African American adolescents. *Journal of Research on Adolescence, 16*, 187–216.

Sellers, R. M., Smith, M. A., Shelton, J. N., Rowley, S. A., & Chavous, T. M. (1998). Multidimensional model of racial identity: A reconceptualization of African American racial identity. *Personality and Social Psychology Review, 2*(1), 18–39.

Shonkoff, J. P., & Phillips, D. A. (Eds.). (2000). *From neurons to neighborhoods: The science of early childhood development*. Washington, DC: National Academies Press.

Sinatra, G. M., Southerland, S. A., McConaughy, F., & Demastes, J. W. (2003). Intentions and beliefs in students' understanding and acceptance of biological evolution. *Journal of Research in Science Teaching, 40*, 510–528.

Smitherman, G. (1999). CCCC's role in the struggle for language rights. *College Composition and Communication, 50*, 349–376.

Smitherman, G. (2003). The historical struggle for language rights in CCCC. In G. Smitherman & V. Villanueva (Eds.), *Language diversity in the classroom: From intention to practice* (pp. 7–39). Carbondale, IL: Southern University Press.

Spencer, M. B. (1985). Cultural cognition and social cognition as identity factors in black children's personal-social growth. In M. Spencer, G. K. Brookins, & W. Allen (Eds.), *Beginnings: The social and affective development of black children* (pp. 59–72). Hillsdale, NJ: Erlbaum.

Spencer, M. B. (2006). Phenomenology and ecological systems theory: Development of diverse groups. In W. Damon & R. M. Lerner (Eds.), *Handbook of child psychology* (Vol. 1, 6th ed., pp. 829–893). New York, NY: Wiley.

Spencer, M. B. (2008). Lessons learned and opportunities ignored since Brown v. Board of education: Youth development and the myth of a color-blind society. *Educational Researcher, 37*, 253–266.

Spencer, M. B., Noll, E., Stoltzfus, J., & Harpalani, V. (2001). Identity and school adjustment: Revisiting the "acting white" assumption. *Educational Psychologist, 36*(1), 21–30.

Starkey, P., & Gelman, R. (1982). The development of addition and subtraction abilities prior to formal schooling. In T. Carpenter, J. M. Moser, & T. Romberg (Eds.), *Addition and subtraction: A developmental perspective* (pp. 99–116). Hillsdale, NJ: Erlbaum.

Starlinger, I., & Niemeyer, W. (1981). Do the blind hear better? Investigations on auditory processing in congenital or early acquired blindness I. Peripheral functions. *Audiology, 20*, 503–509.

Steele, C. M. (2004). A threat in the air: How stereotypes shape intellectual identity and performance. In J. Banks & C. Banks (Eds.), *Handbook of research on multicultural education* (2nd ed., pp. 682–698). San Francisco, CA: Jossey-Bass.

Steele, C. M., Spencer, S. J., & Aronson, J. (2002). Contending with group image: The psychology of stereotype and social identity threat. *Advances in Experimental Social Psychology, 34*, 379–440.

Stigler, J., & Baranes, R. (1989). Culture and mathematics learning. In E. Z. Rothkopf (Ed.), *Review of research in education* (Vol. 15, pp. 253–307). Washington, DC: American Educational Research Association.

Stockman, I. J. (2000). The new Peabody Picture Vocabulary Test-III: An illusion of unbiased assessment? *Language, Speech, and Hearing Services in Schools, 31*, 340–353.

Suad Nasir, N. I., & Kirshner, B. (2003). The cultural construction of moral and civic identities. *Applied Developmental Science, 7*, 138–147.

Szyf, M., Weaver, I., & Meaney, M. (2007). Maternal care, the epigenome and phenotypic differences in behavior. *Reproductive Toxicology, 24*(1), 9–19.

Tate, W. (2008). "Geography of opportunity": Poverty, place, and educational outcomes. *Educational Researcher, 37*, 397–411.

Washington, J. A., & Craig, H. K. (1999). Performances of at-risk, African American preschoolers on the Peabody Picture Vocabulary Test-III. *Language, Speech, and Hearing Services in Schools, 30*(1), 75–82.

Williamson, J. A., Rhodes, L., & Dunson, M. (2007). A selected history of social justice in education. *Review of Research in Education, 31*, 195–224.

Wilson, E. O. (1998). *Consilience: The unity of knowledge.* New York, NY: Knopf.

Zajonc, R. B., & Marcus, H. (1984). Affect and cognition. In C. E. Izard, J. Kagan, & R. B. Zajonc (Eds.), *Emotions, cognition and behavior* (pp. 73–102). Cambridge, England: Cambridge University Press.

Zimmerman, B. J., Bandura, A., & Martinez-Pons, M. (1992). Self-motivation for academic attainment: The role of self-efficacy beliefs and personal goal setting. *American Educational Research Journal, 29*, 663–676.

Chapter 5

Putting the Radical Notion of Equality in the Service of Disrupting Inequality in Education: Research Findings and Conceptual Advances on the Infinity of Human Potential

Anna Stetsenko

The Graduate Center of the City University of New York

Research on disrupting inequality in education can benefit from situating it within the debates on varying and often conflicting meanings of equality and its perils and promises. Especially in the wake of achievement testing and resurgent biological determinism, researchers continue to equivocate between commitment to the idea that all *humans are equal in their core capacities versus the tendency to attribute developmental outcomes to differences in "natural" inborn talents and endowments. This chapter examines contemporary research and theorizing to address the tenet of fundamental equality to counter biological determinism laden with mythic racial, gender, and other types of unproven assumptions and biases. Drawing on a wide range of emerging positions and evidence across neurosciences, epigenetics, developmental systems perspective, and cultural-historical framework, the core argument is that all persons have* infinite potential*—incalculable in advance, unlimited, and not predefined in terms of any putatively inborn "endowments." This potential is realized in the course of* activity-dependent generation *of open-ended, dynamic, and situated developmental processes that are critically reliant upon sociocultural supports, tools, mediations, and access to requisite resources, especially through education. An educational policy along these lines would be centrally premised on the imperative to remedy the effects of discrimination and marginalization.*

Justice—this is undeniable—is impossible (perhaps justice is the "impossible") and therefore it is necessary to make justice possible in countless ways.

—Jacques Derrida, quoted in Lawlor (2014)

Review of Research in Education
March 2017, Vol. 41, pp. 112–135
DOI: 10.3102/0091732X16687524

In 1967, Martin Luther King, Jr. delivered the Invited Distinguished Address at American Psychological Association's Annual Convention. In it, he passionately called on social scientists to "tell it like it is" and to rise to the challenge of changing society "poisoned to its soul by racism." In further referencing words "that all men are created equal," he described these words as truth "lifted to cosmic proportions" (see King, 1968). This call and these words went against discourses, practices, and ideologies, still dominant today, that rationalize inequities of social order, including in education, by appealing to innate, unequal, and largely unalterable individual traits, predispositions, and capacities.

The concept of equality has been employed in education in many ways with apparently infinite quandaries brought up by the question of how to address and conceptualize, let alone achieve equality. Equality is multifaceted, includes multiple overlapping dimensions, and is open to varying interpretations. The complex history of equality as a political ideal and a dimension of social practices infused with struggles for power and access to resources (Anderson, 2007), the ties between educational equality and justice, its implications for protection from discrimination, the relationship between equality and egalitarianism—all of these topics continue to be discussed by philosophers, scholars, policymakers, and educators. Notions that figure prominently in discussions of equality—such as difference, opportunity, privilege, worth, multiculturalism, citizenship, and human rights—add further layers of complexity to these discussions.

The principle of equality cannot be easily reduced to some straightforward formula. For example, stated as an apparently simple idea that learners should receive an *equally good education*, this principle brings up concerns of whether fairness and respect for diversity are addressed so that the equalization of differences within the present status quo is avoided. It has been noted that any vision of equality defined in merely one dimension might inadvertently create inequalities in other dimensions (e.g., Sen, 1999), and therefore extreme care is necessary in addressing this topic, including avoiding uncomplicated views on parity of opportunities and outcomes. The notion of equality in education is embedded in no less than the perennial problems of how to define the aims of a just society, the mission of education in achieving such aims, and the contingency of these projects on understandings of human development and diversity. It is a social, political, ethical, and economic question at once, and it cannot be addressed outside considerations about the current dynamics, developments, and contradictions in society.

The notion of equality has been somewhat sidestepped in recent educational scholarship. According to Oakes (2005),

Educational equality is an idea that has fallen from favor. In the eighties we have decided that excellence is what we want and that somehow excellence and equality are incompatible. . . . We got bogged down in conceptualizing what educational equality really meant. (p. xv)

In surveying the topic of equality in education, Nash (2004, p. 375) observed that "the very word 'equality' has been all but expunged from contemporary educational policy (with its lexicon of 'excellence', 'choice', 'standards', and 'efficiency')." This view is echoed by Orfield (2014, p. 274), who states that "our central approach in recent years . . . has been to quietly accept segregation and inequality and to try to figure out some things to ameliorate it—money, tests, sanctions, and charters." He continues to say that this is happening "without [us] really admitting to ourselves that we are now several decades into a process of dismantling civil rights, even as the country changes and the need becomes much more urgent" (Orfield, 2014, p. 274). The ramifications of these gaps in addressing inequality have been drastic (see Kucsera & Orfield, 2014), including that "our children are being reared in contexts that may lead them to believe that social inequality and social divisions are the natural order of things" (Carter & Reardon, 2014).

Many critical and sociocultural scholars who passionately pursue agendas of social justice in education and beyond recently do not favor the discourse of equality as they justly insist on putting a premium on difference and diversity. For example, as Chávez, Nair, and Conrad (2015, p. 275) note in reflecting on what they see as a conundrum of equality, "No matter how it is framed, it is bound to not only exclude people but actively create strategies with which to exclude specific groups of people." Scholars working in Critical Race Theory have been explicit on this topic, stating that "'color-blind, or 'formal,' conceptions of equality, expressed in rules that insist only on treatment that is the same across the board, can thus remedy only the most blatant forms of discrimination" (Delgado & Stefancic, 2012, p. 8). This work has drawn attention to associations between certain connotations of equality, on one hand, and colorblind racism and denial of White privilege, on the other. In many cases, "an ideological assertion of the fundamental equality of all racial groups—not only in terms of rights, but also in terms of experiences . . . asserts that race-based programs and policies only serve to further solidify racial divisions" (McDermott & Samson, 2005, p. 248; see also Doane & Bonilla-Silva, 2003).

Summarizing these and similar trends, Nash (2004) states that

"critical" sociology of education has abandoned equality of educational opportunity as an imperfect objective, recognising it as one fully compatible with the competitive ideology of liberalism and, in as much as it is not even realised, one that serves principally to sustain the myth of equality in an unequal society. (p. 361)

Indeed, as Sefa Dei, Mazzuca, McIssac, and Zine (1997, p. 124) have argued, traditional approaches that frame equality based in meritocratic principles "cannot be applied in a society where racial disparities exist, as they are in effect corrupted by social and cultural biases." Engaging with issues of equality appears to be fraught with contradictions. Darling-Hammond (2007a) aptly observes that

while we bemoan the dramatically unequal educational outcomes announced each year in reports focused on the achievement gap, as a nation we often behave as though we were unaware of—or insensitive to— the equally substantial inequalities in access to educational opportunity . . . (p. 318)

A similar paradox is recorded by Orfield (2014, p. 274), who writes that "although it is very clear that educational success is related to family resources, peers, and teacher experience and skills, and all of those are related to race, those issues have been largely ignored."

However, there is a risk in dismissing the discourses and the matters of equality including through associating them with meritocratic conceptions only. Ideals of equality have stood for social justice, fairness, and antiracism in moral, political, and economic terms, especially since the Civil Rights movement. These ideals and ideas might turn out to be useful especially in the present climate of growing racial and class-based disparities, divisions, and inequalities. Indeed, issues of segregation and inequality are now more prominently back on the cultural and policy agendas after a protracted period of neglect. This dynamic is reflected in major policy documents such as the *World Economic Forum Report* aptly titled "Why inequality is 2015's most worrying trend" (Mohammed, 2014). As stated in the recent symposium at the American Educational Research Association meeting (Eaton & Black 2016), "After decades of near silence, high-impact media reports have shone new light on racial segregation in schools and neighborhoods as a driver of inequality and social division." In the changing political and socioeconomical situation, it is important to revive discussions on what equality is, what it stands for now and could stand for in the future.

Moreover, a renewed focus on the topic of equality is warranted because rather than ameliorating background inequalities, the U.S. educational system may be exacerbating them in reversing previous gains through policies that disenfranchise populations of color and the poor (Darling-Hammond, 2007a; Orfield, 2014). There is a pressing need for the new, concerted efforts at disrupting inequality including through novel and bold approaches to conceptualizing equality. As Gary Orfield (2014) has powerfully argued,

We need *a new civil rights agenda*. . . . Our challenge now is to create a vision appropriate to our society in this century. This is the work of this generation, and it will involve creating new understandings of the forces that create and sustain unequal opportunity and expanding the definition of basic rights so that it works in transformed context. (p. 276; italics added)

The purpose of this chapter is to join in with the efforts currently underway to renew the hard work involved in the ongoing struggles for radical democracy including efforts to understand how ideals of equality might be implicated in disrupting inequalities in public debates, policies, research, and practices in education. This social justice work can only be done in combination with a recognition and respect for difference and plurality and an acknowledgment of systemic inequalities, power differentials, and persistent effects of structural discrimination. Such an approach would avoid connecting equality with traditional universal discourses that homogenize differences and hide inequality by taking the current status of groups and individuals as a measure of where they somehow should be. Instead, the topic of equality has to be placed alongside discourses of social justice, struggles against discrimination, and respect for diversity.

One of the layers of this work, as suggested in this chapter, is to contest the still prevalent and deeply entrenched, biologically reductionist beliefs in presumably fixed and rigidly defined ("hardwired") "natural endowments." These "natural endowments" are understood to be somehow conferred on people from birth and to have the power to unidirectionally shape and limit prospects for performance, achievement, and even future roles and status in society. These beliefs have historically emerged from and continue to support discriminatory and racialized practices, discourses, and policies and thus, represent a serious obstacle to disrupting inequality across all of these layers. As will be discussed in the next section, even though the attribution of differential capabilities, achievement potentials, and natural talents across social groups has been thoroughly discredited, and attempts to find a gene or a set of biological markers implicated in developmental outcomes have failed, appeals to natural endowments and differential talents as explanations of inequality continue to persist. These biologically reductionist views continue to make "nature herself" a de facto accomplice in the crime of political inequality (see Gould, 1996). Increasingly influential, they have been in part spurred by progress in genetic and brain research which is often applied uncritically to interpret human behavior and social inequalities (examples to be reviewed in the next sections). This trend, at least in part akin to a resurgence of eugenics according to some estimates, needs to be resolutely contested and disrupted as part of the struggle for equality and social justice. Doing so is one of the ways to support the work of those scholars in education who advocate broad causes of equality and social justice yet often lack expertise in human development (including biology, genetics, neurophysiology, and neuropsychology; see Lickliter & Honeycutt, 2003a) to resolutely break with the biological reductionism that stands in the way of radically disrupting inequalities.

The main message to be developed in this chapter is that given the recent progress in developmental sciences amounting to no less than *a conceptual revolution* (e.g., Lickliter & Honeycutt, 2003a) that has "swept away old ways of thinking" (Thelen, 1995, p. 80), there is a need and a possibility for a renewed emphasis on equality as a fundamental feature of human development. The advances across a number of disciplines applicable to the problematic of equality (surveyed in the next sections) have to do with a growing acknowledgment that human development is not rigidly constrained from the outset by any biologically determined factors. Instead, development is a transactional, nonlinear, historical, contingent, and dynamic process in which patterns and phenomena (including any and all capabilities and "talents") are *dynamically generated rather than evolved according to some inherited programs or blueprints*. In this process, there are no programs or instructions determining development and no "biological givens" (such as genes or brain structures) that could unfold or mature, on their own and outside of the context and the process of development, to produce developmental outcomes. This position implicates understanding human capabilities to be the emergent results of an open-ended, nonlinear, contingent, and de facto limitless (i.e., unidentifiable in advance) *process of development* rather than these capabilities being contained in any biological "givens" existing prior to development.

In drawing on this conceptual revolution and expanding its achievements to the topic of equality, the implication can be drawn that all students have unlimited potential (in the sense that it is not inherently limited from the outset and cannot be calculated or defined in advance) to learn with *no rigidly preimposed "natural" constraints or ceiling*. Therefore, although each student is individually unique and her or his development requires varied interactive supports and mediations, including access to requisite educational resources and tools, *students are equal precisely in the incalculable and immeasurable infinity of their potential*.

TRADITIONAL APPROACHES: THE PERSISTENT DANGERS OF BIOLOGICAL DETERMINISM

Many researchers in education have been critical about biologically reductionist explanations of development and achievement outcomes, especially those with racist implications (e.g., as in the infamous book by Herrnstein & Murray, 1994; for a critique, see e.g., Darling-Hammond, 2007b). For example, a strong contribution to this critique has been made by scholars in the fields of disability and special education advancing egalitarian, inclusive, and social justice–based approaches (e.g., Gabel & Danforth, 2008; Smagorinsky, 2016). In dispelling these views, many critical and sociocultural scholars in education and beyond accept what has been termed "an interactionist view" (see details in the next section)—namely, that it is both biology and culture (nature and nurture) that play a role in development and learning. Yet believing that a wide consensus has been reached on this topic is at best premature because this interactionist view in fact hides many nuances and conundrums, including a residual reliance on taken-for-granted assumptions about fixed and inert biological bases for academic achievement, intelligence, talent, potential for learning, and other capabilities relevant to schooling. These assumptions have played a major role in psychology and continue to thrive despite their troubled history, the myriad of conceptual, methodological, and analytical conundrums they entail and their sociopolitical, legal, ethical, and policy implications. For example, as Lynch and Lodge (2002) observe,

Even a cursory analysis of psychological research on education indicates that what constitutes 'ability' is a hotly contested subject. . . . While the IQ-generated view of ability [with biologically-based assumptions prominent in such a view] has been largely discredited by developmental psychologists, . . . the concept of fixed and immutable intelligence has a strong hold in public consciousness, including that of teachers. (p. 64)

The power of biologically reductionist concepts is evident in the pervasiveness of so-called "ability" groupings and tracking in schools based in presumably inborn and immutable talents and achievement potentials (see Oakes, 2005). It is directly present in that "recurring explanations of educational inequality among pundits, policy makes, and everyday people typically blame children and their families for lack of effort, poor child rearing, a 'culture of poverty,' or inadequate genes" (Darling-Hammond, 2007a, p. 320).

The biologically based explanations have become prevalent in recent decades when neuroscience has experienced rapid growth, especially since the 1990s (designated as "The Decade of the Brain") and the arrival of neuroimaging techniques (e.g., Varma,

McCandliss, & Schwartz, 2008; Willingham & Dunn, 2003). Practically during the same period of time, progress in mapping the human genome has reawakened interest in using genetic technology to examine differences in complex outcomes such as health and intelligence across demographic groups and populations (Anderson & Nickerson, 2005). The mapping of the human genome, including efforts to define human genetic diversity, has even reawakened the debates of whether genetics can be used to define race (Collins, 2004). These parallel developments have led to increased financial support and prioritized funding for brain and genome research, propelling efforts to explore genes, neurons, and brain regions as often the ultimate and the only level to explain human development and learning. As many scholars have observed,

There is a growing trend among behavioral scientists (particularly psychologists) to view more and more of human behavior as in large measure attributable to our genes. In the old debate of "nature versus nurture," nature now seems to have regained the ascendancy. (Charney, 2008, p. 299)

These effects extend far beyond the confines of science so that "there is growing consensus in popular culture that by understanding genes [or brain] . . . it is possible to understand all of life, including human nature" (Lickliter & Honeycutt, 2003a, p. 819).

However, given the recency of advances in both human genome research and neuroscience, which are actually both still in their infancy (or in adolescence, according to Miller, 2008), much remains to be figured out in terms of how to interpret findings from these fields while unpacking the many philosophical, theoretical, ethical, and conceptual conundrums they entail and are based in. Often there is a tendency to jump to unwarranted conclusions (Reardon, 2015) and sensationalist reporting. The public is often presented with the neuroimaging findings without explanations of the limitations, contingencies, and complexities of research behind these findings, which leads to misinterpretations (see Racine, Bar-Ilan, & Illes, 2005). What remains invisible, for example, is the growing concern among neuroscientists themselves that this field needs to confront many problems, including its core methodological limitations, in order to increase its scientific rigor (Miller, 2008). For example, Shifferman (2015) surveys a vast body of literature suggesting that much research is still needed on both a consensual framework for studying cognition and on a unified theory of how the brain works.

Misinterpretations include notions such as that students are hardwired for achievement, that they have genes for certain types of performance (e.g., in mathematics), and certain levels of intelligence and talent that are somehow biologically and genetically determined from birth. The underlying belief is that quantities definable as "intelligence" or "talent" exist and that they can be reliably measured such as with "IQ tests." As Cooper (2005) observes, this erroneous assumption is combined with beliefs that molecular genetics can (or will) make it possible to define the architecture of complex traits in terms of "genes for X or Y" (including "genes for intelligence") and that significant variation in polymorphisms in those genes overlap with the traditional demographic categories. This assumption is sometimes further combined with equally erroneous beliefs that human population can be divided into demographic groups known as "races" as discrete categories on the basis of genetically determined traits, even though this position that has been repeatedly debunked (e.g., Graves, 2001).

Similar beliefs that the brain research can explain all of life including learning potential and achievement also prevail and extend beyond common culture into education research and public policies due to their strong intuitive appeal (see McCabe & Castel, 2008; Weisberg, Keil, Goodstein, Rawson, & Gray, 2008). It is quite telling that the term "neuromythologies" has been coined to describe "a misunderstanding, a misreading, and in some cases a deliberate warping of the scientifically established facts to make a relevant case for education or for other purposes" (Organization for Economic Cooperation and Development, 2002, p. 71; see also Fischer, Goswami, & Geake, 2010). Common neuromythologies include sweeping statements such as about "10% brain usage," "left- and right-brained thinking," and "female versus male brains."

The biologically determinist beliefs fly in the face of a lack of evidence for neuronal or genetic bases for any complex behaviors and psychological processes. For example, MacLeod (2010) sums up evidence about how not even elementary processes such as color perception are presently understood in their neural foundations. Remarkably, even the perception of a continuous vertical line is a mystery that neurology has not yet solved (see Mausfeld, 2012). Furthermore, no gene has yet been conclusively linked to intelligence or any other complex ability, and no findings of this sort are even on the horizon. At the present time, very little is known even about the genetic component of diseases of complex causation and the genetic variants that predispose persons to common chronic diseases, *let alone* complex behaviors, mental processes, and psychological traits (e.g., Kaufman & Cooper, 2001).

Importantly, intelligence and other constructs such as talent do not stand for discrete entities and at best refer to multiple types of cognitive functioning that are manifested differently depending on a myriad of circumstances (for a recent discussion, see Howe, 2015). Drawing on Anastasi (1984), Howe reminds that there is no effective way to isolate developed cognitive capacities from access to opportunities and other factors influencing human development, and no educational test can measure natural or innate talent. The conclusions reached by Gould (1996, p. 60)—"that determinist arguments for ranking people according to a single scale of intelligence, no matter now numerically sophisticated, have recorded little more than social prejudice"—still stands out in force.

Relevant in this context is also that the widely reported estimates of heritability of intelligence and other complex social behaviors drawn from behavioral genetics often obscure the degree to which these estimates may encompass environmental mediation (e.g., Stenberg, 2013). The field of behavior genetics that produces heritability estimates based in adoption design is fraught with conceptual and methodological flaws in its core procedures (e.g., Burt & Simons, 2015; Charney, 2012; Joseph, 2010; Richardson & Norgate, 2005). Moreover, although the term "heritability" evokes a connection through transmission of genes between parent and offspring, its technical meaning involves no reference to measurable genetic factors (Taylor, 2007) and "the only practical application of a heritability coefficient is to predict the results of a program of selective breeding" (Wahlsten, quoted in Joseph, 2010, p. 558).

In this light, the persistent attempts to find a neuronal or genetic foundation of intelligence and talent and especially to link them and other complex processes to race are not only not feasible (Sternberg, Grigorenko, & Kidd, 2005) but based on such a mix of untested and improbable assumptions that they should be considered misguided and misleading at best. Most critically, such research dismisses the role of institutionalized racism and other forms of discrimination in shaping the structural constraints affecting development (Cooper, 2005). The same argument can be made about brain research into presumed gender-related differentials in achievement, intelligence, talent, and other capacities.

Many scholars including neuroscientists and genetics researchers have sounded alarm about overinterpreting and exaggerating implications of brain and genetic research for education research, policies, and practices (for an overview, see Shifferman, 2015; Varma et al., 2008). A number of leading scholars who signed the *Santiago Declaration* (Hirsh-Pasek et al., 2007) have cautioned against careless claims both within scholarly debates and in the political discourses echoed in the public media coupled with irrational exuberance regarding immediate relevance of neuroscience to education. As Lee (2010) observes, "One worrisome development is the current tendency to use studies of brain imaging and structural functioning to cast children and adolescents from low-income backgrounds as having deficits" (p. 646).

Yet despite all cautionary comments and warnings, the consolidation of the biologically determinist views continues in "a growing trend among behavioral scientists . . . to view more and more of human behavior as in large measure attributable to our genes" (Charney, 2008, p. 299) or to brain processes. This trend recently amounts to a powerful new "grand synthesis" (Stetsenko, 2008) implemented and often imposed across a wide spectrum of social practices, policies, and discourses including in education. This dominant research orientation has been characterized as the "resurgence of extremist biological determinism laden with mythic gender [and other types of] assumptions" (Morawski, 2005, p. 411). Such an unequivocally condemnatory assessment is justified in view of a long and troublesome history of biologically based research, especially on genetically based racial and ethnic group differences (Guthrie, 1998; Tobach & Rosoff, 1994; Winston, 2004; see also Anderson & Nickerson, 2005) that continues under old and new guises till today. As Winston (2004) writes,

Even after a century of severe criticism, discussions of the size of Black versus White brains still appear in psychology journals, race is still treated as a set of distinct biological categories, and racial comparisons of intelligence test scores are still presented as meaningful scientific questions. (p. 3)

According to Allen (2001), we are presently facing no less than a return of eugenics as a means of social control. The term "eugenics" was introduced in the 19th century by Francis Galton to describe a program of selective breeding which, in his view, was "supported" by "experiments" on testing for a racial hierarchy of human capacities (Winston, 2004). Galton sought to demonstrate that Africans were of "lower intelligence" than European Whites. Both in the United States and Europe, eugenics thrived on the fears fueled by racist associations, dramatically influencing discriminatory policies on education, immigration, and mental health (Tucker, 1994). Alarmingly in the extreme, some of the recent developments in research on biological bases of human development bear similarity to what was happening in the 1920s and against the same background of deep economic crisis, bitter anti-immigration sentiment, and social upheaval (Allen, 2001). Other authors echo this assessment in exposing the rise of eugenics across history, again in evidence today, reflecting the power of persistent genetic essentialist biases in sciences and societies (Dar-Nimrod & Heine, 2011). For example, as Smedley and Smedley (2005) state,

Recent advances in the sequencing of the human genome and in an understanding of biological correlates of behavior have fueled *racialized science*, despite evidence that racial groups are not genetically discrete, reliably measured, or scientifically meaningful. (p. 16, italics added)

Appeals to unalterable biological underpinnings of human attributes have grave social consequences and negative policy implications for how people are treated and how social resources are distributed. As aptly summarized by Haslam (2011), the common thread of both neurological and genetic essentialisms is the tendency to deepen social divisions and promote forms of social segregation, "making differences appear large, unbridgeable, inevitable, unchangeable, and ordained by nature" (p. 819). Essentialist thinking attaches, he argues, to the same social distinctions that are the focus of the most troubling forms of prejudice and discrimination along the dimensions of race, gender, sexuality, and what is defined as mental disorder or disability. The most pernicious applications include the rationalization of unequal treatment of different groups and segregation of minorities.

There is a need to be extremely vigilant about assumptions concerning the role of biological dimensions in human development, such as genetics and neuronal processes, that might lead to conclusions that some humans or even ethnic groups are somehow superior to others in skills, talents, intellectual capacities, or moral worth. Extreme caution is necessary because, as Cooper (2005) sums up is stark and uncompromising terms,

For the last four centuries Western science has been obsessed with the need to justify White privilege and in so doing has provided crucial support for racist ideas in society at large. To use the rhetoric of science to sell the idea that historical inequity should be embraced as biological inevitability is an insult to those who value a common humanity. (p. 75)

MOVING BEYOND THE "INTERACTIONIST CONSENSUS": IMPLICATIONS FOR DISRUPTING INEQUALITIES IN EDUCATION

The serious flaws and risks associated with biologically based explanations of developmental outcomes bear direct implications for research on and theorizing of equality with the goal of disrupting inequalities in education. Speculations about biological and largely innate (inherited) bases of human development and differential capacities are almost always recruited to provide a justification for social and educational inequalities within the status quo, including existing privileges for certain groups according to race, class, and sex. Biological idioms have been recruited to reify social constructs of race, gender, and class as immutable natural phenomena, and to warrant the acceptance of disparities including in education on these bases as if they were somehow natural (e.g., Eisenberg, 1995; Hruby, 2012). Such approaches consistently stifle diversity in disadvantaging poor and minority students (e.g., Darling-Hammond, 2007a) and legitimizing their purported "deficiency" (e.g., Ladson-Billings, 2006).

To continue with appeals to differentials according to "human nature" as somehow a rationale for inequality is unsustainable and unethical. Even Charles Darwin—under the limits of his era and his elitist social status—was prescient enough to make a conjecture that "if the misery of the poor be caused not by the laws of nature, but by our institutions, great is our sin" (quoted in Gould, 1996, p. 19). Early in the 20th century, Walter Whitman challenged what he described as "aristocratic tradition which tends to rationalize inequities of our social order by appealing to innate and unalterable psychological strata" (cited in Danforth, 2008, p. 47). Today, on the grounds of new advances in developmental sciences, to be reviewed in this section, it is well past time to unequivocally acknowledge, in the face of the obvious, that indeed poverty and inequality are not the results of nature and, even more importantly, that our sins as society are indeed truly great.

The recent advances in biological and developmental sciences, including psychology, can be recruited to resolutely dispel the harmful stereotypes, mythologies, and misguided generalizations about genetic and brain determinism in application to the problematics of disrupting inequality in education. Although not much research has yet endeavored to connect these advances to matters of equality in education, the time is ripe for such efforts. Recent attempts, albeit from differing positions, include works by Howe (2010, 2015) and by Ceci and his colleagues (e.g., Ceci & Papierno, 2005; Ceci & Williams, 2010). Both lines of works recruit recent advances in developmental sciences to explore and interrogate conceptions of equality in education especially in their connection to the concept of talent. In the second line of these works, however, the assumption about "natural talents" is not challenged even though the authors admit that their "evidence of innate talent is purely theoretical" (Papierno, Ceci, Makel, & Williams, 2005). The works by Howe are more radical in that they do challenge the dogma of natural talents specifically in the context of discussing equality in education.

As Howe (2015) demonstrates, the dominant conceptions of educational equality continue to rely on individual "natural" talents as if these talents were well defined, could be taken for granted and even measured or otherwise used in predicting and explaining educational outcomes. Furthermore, the meritocratic conceptions presuppose that "natural talent" can be isolated from structural factors related to ethnicity, gender, and social class along the lines of existing privileges. The idea of natural talents is fundamental to the meritocratic conceptions because differences in natural talents are believed to explain and justify inequalities, although no support for defining natural talents exists or is even on the horizon. Howe (2015) has challenged appeals to natural talent to explain differential performance in relying on suggestions and evidence that "nurture does much, much more to explain differences in performance than nature does, including in cases of individuals whose performance is so extraordinary that intuition strongly supports recourse to natural talent as the explanation" (p. 185). Quite boldly, he argued that "as such, natural talent is a myth working hand in glove with an *ideology* in Mills's sense of a 'set of group ideas that reflect, and contribute to perpetuating, illicit group privilege'" (p. 183).

Howe (2015) does not aim to establish the *strong* claim that natural talents do not exist. Instead his claim is that

to the extent that natural talents exist, they can manifest themselves only under conditions favorable to their development. Thus, to the extent that they do exist, over time they become thoroughly melded with nurture—which, we now know, begins in the womb. (p. 186)

His related conjecture is that the distribution of measured levels of natural talents so overlaps with the distribution of measured levels of performance that "no credible inference can be made in individual cases from a given level of natural talent to a corresponding level of performance" (p. 186).

In sharing the main thrust of Howe's arguments, there are ways to further expand critique of the myths about "natural talents" based in works in biological and developmental sciences that are moving, in truly radical ways, beyond many traditional assumptions in opening new horizons in research and theorizing about human development. In particular, one line of recent research shows that contrary to the long-standing stereotypes, brain structures are neither rigidly preformed ("wired"), nor unidirectionally driven by maturation. Instead, brain structures and patterns of neural activation are *constructed within development dynamics and in relation to individual experiences and learning* (e.g., Gottlieb, 2003). In a related vein, many researchers recently caution that the brain is not a separate organ but is part and parcel in activities of organisms as a whole (e.g., Fox, Levitt, & Nelson, 2010; Nelson & Luciana, 2001). Neural plasticity, in particular, is used to refer to processes that involve major connectional changes of the nervous system in response to experience (e.g., Huttenlocher, 2002; Kolb & Gibb, 2011; Li, 2009, 2013). The dominant view throughout the 20th century (with few exceptions such as Luria's works) was that the adult human brain is organized in fixed and immutable function-specific neural circuits. The discovery of the profound plasticity of the brain in the late 1990s has overturned this canon (cf. Li, 2009; Rees, 2010; Stetsenko, 2003).

This work highlights the property of neural circuits to potentially acquire nearly any function depending on the vicissitudes of individual ontogenetic development. This approach is further aligned with the notions of neuroconstructivism or "interactive brain specialization" that highlight activity-dependent nature of brain development (Johnson, Grossmann, & Cohen-Kadosh, 2009). Thus, neuroscience is moving in the direction of revealing how pliable something as presumably genetic as intelligence can be (e.g., Hruby, 2012). Findings pertaining to brain plasticity (likely linked to an evolved *under*-specialization of brain circuits in humans at birth; see Moss, 2006) suggest that there are no predetermined ties of these circuits to specific sensory or motor functions. As a result, the brain is able to acquire a wide range of noninnate skills, including those linked to the use of cultural tools such as language while interacting with and learning from others (see works that use the *Tools of the Mind* approach by Bodrova & Leong, 2007; e.g., Diamond, Barnett, Thomas, & Munro, 2007). Importantly, these processes occur long past the supposedly critical first years of life. The idea of brain plasticity and the premise that the growth of neural connections across the life span is highly contingent on individual experiences, cultural mediation, social exchanges, and teaching–learning was the singularly most important hallmark of Luria's (1973) approach. In summary, current evidence indicates that, in response to different types and aspects of experiences (e.g., activity, learning, or task demands), the brain develops and exhibits multiple forms of plasticity, allowing for it to adapt to various forms of experiential tunings (see Li, 2013).

These significant shifts in neuroscience parallel developments in genetics that are now also moving past the impasses of biological reductionism. As recently expressed by Charney (2012), for example,

[T]he science of genetics is undergoing *a paradigm shift*. Recent discoveries . . . are challenging a series of dogmas concerning the nature of the genome and the relationship between genotype and phenotype. According to three widely held dogmas, DNA is the unchanging template of heredity, is identical in all the cells and tissues of the body, and is the sole agent of inheritance. (p. 331; italics added)

In dispelling these long-standing stereotypes, Charney (2012) draws on a vast literature to show how

[r]ather than being an unchanging template, DNA appears subject to a good deal of environmentally induced change. Instead of identical DNA in all the cells of the body, somatic mosaicism appears to be the normal human condition. And DNA can no longer be considered the sole agent of inheritance. (p. 311)

These and similar discoveries in molecular biology and its branch known as epigenetics have spurred much research and theoretical developments, influential especially since the 1990s, including evolutionary developmental biology (known as "evo-devo") and development systems perspective (known as DSP; see, e.g., Lerner, 2006). The latter perspective (of more relevance for the present discussions), furthermore, is composed of various strands of approaches often described as the developmental systems theory and dynamic systems theory (for recent overviews, see Lickliter & Honeycutt, 2015; Witherington, 2007). Some differences among them notwithstanding, all of these approaches are united in emphasizing the complex systemic relations among multiple levels (both internal and external to the organism) that give rise to behavioral and biological traits (Gottlieb, 2003; Oyama, 2000). That is, the core idea shared by the various forms of DSP is that all biological and behavioral traits emerge from the interactions of a large number of factors that together constitute a developmental system and cannot be regarded in isolation (Oyama, Griffiths,

& Gray, 2001). Thus, a wide range of epigenetic processes (i.e., those above the level of genes) contribute to individual development and therefore, no prediction of outcomes is possible before the actual development of the organism runs its course. This approach is focused on *process* and *developmental* character of the links among genes, behavior, and the multiple levels of the extra-organism context, the social and physical ecology of development (e.g., Keller, 2010).

The special privileges assigned to genetic factors as if genes could mechanically encode programs or instructions that predetermine (from the start of life on) the development of traits and behaviors are thus rejected. Instead, the conjecture is that all levels of developmental system reciprocally influence each other and there is a multidirectional and probabilistic causation that is top-down as well as bottom up (e.g., Robert, 2004). As Lickliter and Honeycutt (2013, p. 186) summarize, "Combinations of genetic, hormonal, neural, physiological, behavioral, and social mechanisms act synergistically as a system from which behaviors emerge and are maintained within and across generations." A number of frameworks such as bioecological model (Bronfenbrenner & Ceci, 1994), developmental contextualism (Lerner, 2006), developmental psychobiological systems view (Gottlieb, 2003), relational metatheoretical framework (Overton, 2006), and models based in multiplier effect (Dickens & Flynn, 2001) offer similar or complementary views.

Many of these findings are often interpreted in the sense that it is *both* biology and culture (nature and nurture) that shape the course of development and its outcomes. However, these broad statements, recently disseminated and praised as the resolution on the topic, still often hide many important distinctions and conceptual specifications that are in fact far from resolved. There are many nuances that have to be carefully disentangled in these approaches in order to avoid the paradox of "consensus" that hides actual tensions and contradictions. In particular, despite the proffered "interactionist consensus" stating that genes and environments interact in the generation of individual traits, reciprocal influences of sociocultural contexts on neurobiological mechanisms are rarely considered (Li, 2009). Moreover, it is not uncommon that alongside statements about gene–environment interactions, debates continue as to the relative power of each of these entities to contribute to developmental outcomes, often falling back into what has been termed "genomania" (Robert, 2004, p. xiii; see also Oyama, 2000).

One of the core conundrums appears to be that nature and nurture continue to be viewed as independent, if even not mutually exclusive, processes and resources of variation and influence on development. That is, "interaction itself is generally conceptualized as two split-off pure entities that function *independently* in cooperative and/or competitive ways" (Overton, 2006, p. 33). As Overton (2006) further states, relying on works by Anastasi and Lehrman, "despite overt conciliatory declarations to the contrary, the classical *which one* and *how much* questions . . . continue as leading divisive frames of inquiry" (p. 33). The consensus that "nature and culture interact" does not do enough to override traditional ways of thinking. As Oyama (2000) commented, it is extremely hard to relinquish a way of thinking about the role of genes and environment in ontogeny that ensures that we will continue to find ways to carve up the living world into innate and acquired portions, no matter how vociferously we declare the distinction to be obsolete." (p. 21)

In this light, it is important to continue exploring the radical implications from the DSP and related frameworks including those that question the binary itself between nature and culture, genes and environment, and external and internal processes. One of such implications is a shift away from additive notions of "gene-plus" environmental models that portray development as an unleashing of endowments that are erroneously supposed to be "always already there in the genome" (Robert, 2004, p. 397) to be merely triggered by environment. The works on epigenetic developmental dynamics pioneered by Oyama et al. (2001) emphasize how developmental processes and outcomes are *emergent* within developmental processes rather than transmitted in advance of development. They call these the "cycles of contingency," because the ensemble literally creates itself through reiterative activity. What is at stake is a "constructive interactionsim" (Oyama, 2000) that renders impossible any prespecification of traits, characteristics, or behaviors, including psychological processes in even their "skeletal forms." In this emphasis, genes are placed within a coacting, dynamic system of relations among the multiple levels of organization that comprise the ecology of human development (see Lerner, 2006).

One of the stunning conclusions is that "whatever developmental potential there is resides not in genes or in other developmental resources but rather emerges from their synergistic interaction" (Robert, 2004, p. 397) so that genes do not preexist developmental process and are instead themselves generated by it (p. 74). An eloquent formulation of this position is that "one way of beginning to think about epigenetics is to realize that the genome, as much as the organism, is a process rather than a static thing" (Dupré, 2012, p. 3). A remarkable implication from this position is that any behavior or psychological process is "fully a product of biology *and* culture" (Lickliter & Honeycutt, 2003b, p. 469) and what counts as "biological" falls entirely within the domain of what counts as "cultural" and vice versa (see Ingold, 2011). This was (almost verbatim) the position spelled out by Vygotsky (1993; for a discussion, see Stetsenko, 2009).

In this light, the gene-centric and nativist explanations currently serve to hinder understanding of developmental outcomes including school-related achievements. As Lickliter and Honeycutt (2013) argue in uncompromising terms,

To describe a behavior pattern as innate (or genetically determined) is in fact a statement of ignorance about how that trait actually develops. (p. 185)
    Attempts to identify traits that are innate versus acquired are both meaningless and invalid. A belief in innate traits reflects a commitment to preformationism and ultimately, mysticism. (p. 186)

Another remarkable implication currently on the cutting edge of developmental systems perspective is that development is not only nonlinear, transactional, and probabilistic but also, and importantly, a *self-organizing process contingent on experiential history and activities of the individuals themselves.* The focus on activity- and experience-dependent character of development is compatible with holistic, ecological frameworks that identify development with the pathways of individuals active engagement in the world (e.g., Ingold, 2008, 2011; Thelen, 2000, 2005). This focus is also in sync with an acknowledgment that because organisms are not passive, the context in which they act has the features it does in part precisely because of these very organisms' behaviors (e.g., Lewontin, 1995). That is, both individual and environmental characteristics continuously emerge in the life course, while *codefining and generating* each other in the very process of developmental transactions, rather than them existing independently. This approach builds on important insights from earlier works by Ethel Tobach, Theodor Schneirla and Daniel Lehrman according to whom, "the interaction out of which the organism develops in *not* one, as is so often said, between heredity and environment. It is between *organism* and environment!" (Lehrman, 1953, p. 345; emphasis in the original). Esther Thelen (2005) has championed this line of research in developmental psychology suggesting that "development is . . . the product of the child's everyday and *continual efforts to make things happen in the world*" (p. 263; italics added), rather than a process that is predetermined and preprogrammed by any initial conditions "set in place" at the start of development.

This line of work can be strengthened by integrating conceptual breakthroughs made in the 20th century by John Dewey, Jean Piaget, and Lev Vygotsky, among others, in developing a relational and activity-based approach. Dubbed "the second psychology," this broad framework was focused on *people in relation to their world* in distinction from the "first psychology" concerned with isolated individuals (Cahan & White, 1992). The core of this approach (still to be fully integrated into the DSP, see Stetsenko, 2016) is that human beings are understood to be carrying out, right from birth, the ongoing process of relational activities inextricably connecting them with their environment and other people. It is these activities that constitute the irreducible reality of development that supersedes the dualisms of outside and inside influences (Vygotsky, 1997). This relational approach can be interpreted in the sense that not only do genetic and environmental factors (nature and nurture) interact or mesh with each other in contributing to development, but that people themselves play an active role in organizing and orchestrating their own engagements (activities) with the world in thus critically contributing to and *generating* their own development.

The focus on human beings coactively constructing their own development in interacting with the world including other people was especially prominent in cultural–historical activity theory by Vygotsky (e.g., 1997) and his followers. In integrating this perspective and insights from the DSP, development can be understood as an emerging activity that undergoes constant changes during the life course and gives rise to psychological processes and complex traits (for details, see Stetsenko & Arievitch, 2010). Moreover and quite critically, this is not a solo activity by an isolated organism. Instead, this activity itself is embedded within larger activity systems (i.e., social practices) and critically reliant on interactions with others, mediation by cultural tools, and access to social resources (cf. Gutiérrez & Rogoff, 2003). The difference between this position and the additive approaches is tacit but significant because the former moves beyond the concept of development as being an additive, hybrid product with a focus on a confluence of factors understood as extraneous to activities, whereby genetic and environmental influences are thought to interact or even mesh together yet are taken to be independent of activities by human beings themselves (see Stetsenko, 2009, 2016).

As an illustration (in expanding on Lickliter & Honeycutt, 2013), explanations of any normative or nonnormative behavior, from alcohol abuse to exceptional abilities (e.g., "talent" in mathematics) can never be reduced to genetics or the brain processes. Instead, these explanations must draw on the whole developmental system including its resources internal and external to the organism that contribute to the emergence of these behaviors and traits. This system includes experiential history of each individual (starting with the prenatal or early postnatal nutrition, exposure to harmful substances, etc.), family histories and practices, and the contextualized and situated activities each human being is included in from the start of life—in the full complexity of their structural organization, relational composition, social norms, cultural affordances, tools, and so on. Importantly (in expanding on the emphasis on resources as such, which is still central in the DSP), this understanding includes analysis into how developmental resources *are made use of and enacted by persons themselves* in the dynamics of activities they carry out. Attention to how the resources are made use of entails analysis into processes such as meaning making and motivational reasons for engaging or abstaining from particular pursuits (see Leontiev, 1979), with amount of practice the person engages in often serving as the strongest predictor for exceptional abilities (Ericsson, 2014).

The emphasis on joint determination by multiple causes, contextual sensitivity, and contingency, and on *development as activity-dependent, emergent co-construction of developmental outcomes by human beings coacting with others* (in relying on available cultural resources) undermines any claims that inborn talents, cognitive modules, or even skeletal innate mechanisms preexist individual development and lie dormant awaiting activation under certain conditions. It also provides a complex and contingent model for understanding nature and nurture as one process—that of literally *"natureculture"* composed of collective social practices that are contextually embedded, culturally mediated, interactively accomplished, and continuously extending through history. Therefore,

Development . . . does not just happen to people—it is a collaborative and creative accomplishment, a process that comes down to work and effort within and through collective social practices and their affordances and mediations, as well as obstacles and contradictions, as these are created by people collaborating [co-acting] in together agentively enacting these very practices. (Stetsenko, 2016, p. 257)

How society provides conditions for or, alternatively, deprives individuals of access to participating in social practices and their resources necessary for their development is therefore of critical significance.

From this point of view, all human beings have *infinite potential* that is not predefined and, therefore, incalculable and unidentifiable in terms of any preconceived (hardwired) inborn "endowments." Moreover, this potential is only realized in the course of development which does not happen in a vacuum but instead, is *critically reliant* upon sociocultural supports, tools, and mediations. This conjecture implies that the requisite cultural mediations and supports (broadly understood to include educational opportunities, incentives, cultural tools, spaces, and other resources), tailored to the needs of each individual, must be made accessible and available to all individuals and communities—including through teaching–learning tailored to their needs and requirements. An educational policy along these lines would be centrally premised on the need and the imperative to remedy effects of discrimination and marginalization especially for students from historically underrepresented groups and to eliminate structural social injustices that lead to such effects.

The premise of fundamental equality does not negate that each person is, at the same time, individually unique. That is, the notion of equality does not imply that we are born as "blank slates," which is a straw person position that distorts relational and dynamic approaches. Instead, what is implied is that whatever is present at the start of life is present in the form of a dynamic, developmental potential—a process that will undergo continuous transformations with no predetermined outcomes since these outcomes emerge from development itself (including through extended brain–body–behavior networks; see Byrge, Sporns, & Smith, 2014), realized in and through ongoing, interactive, situated, and open-ended activities and interactions. This potential, therefore, needs to be actualized by individuals themselves, as a unique "achievement" (with no connotations of either finality or predetermined norms) of togetherness, while being supported with access to requisite conditions, tools, and interactive resources. Although individual differences exist and are especially pronounced by the time children get to school, these differences result from complex activities within the environment and are thus contingent on what the environment has or has not offered by way of cultural mediation and support. Because development and learning are thoroughly contingent on activities mediated by social interactions and supports provided by society, no biological endowment (natural predispositions) can be evoked to account for, let alone justify, failure or success in development and learning by either groups or individuals. How these notions of individual uniqueness, fundamental equality, and social justice—that is not color-blind and does not ignore structural inequalities and their histories—can be reconciled should be a topic of extended debates.

CONCLUSIONS

As discussed in this chapter, the argument about humans having infinite, and therefore equal, potential at the start of life—not the same as in exactly a replica of each other, but *equal precisely in its infinity* and its open-ended character—is supported by scientific discoveries and advances of recent years in various research areas, from biology and epigenetics to neuroscience and developmental psychology. These discoveries and advances testify to the malleability of genetics, the practically infinite plasticity of the brain, the vast potential of cultural mediation to propel development forward, and the "enormous potency" (Nisbett et al., 2012, p. 149), previously unacknowledged, of experience, environment, cultural mediation, and social interactions in development. Given this evidence, Lee (2010) rightfully wonders why we are not doing more to understand the conditions of such plasticity, particularly with regard to those who face biases and obstacles in our society. Reconceptualizing principles of equality on these grounds can be envisioned as a step on the way to promoting education that is based in egalitarian principle that *all* students, with no exception, can learn and develop without any limits or ceilings automatically preimposed by nature, provided that they are given requisite (and individually tailored) access to cultural tools, supports, spaces, and incentives—including, importantly, in remedying structural injustices that have accrued across history and are continuing today—especially for their own agency as actors who contribute to social community practices and coauthor their world and development.

From this perspective, it is imperative to shift major national concerns away from high-stakes testing to instead focus on better and more appropriately distributed learning opportunities (such as cultural tools, spaces, resources, and supports) because these opportunities are *inherent parts of development* that participate in producing its outcomes. This shift requires strong advocacy for major new programs stretched from preschool through college and a major effort to provide families with access to education and economic opportunities and resources including in education. As Orfield (2014) writes, we already know that high-quality preschool can be a powerful factor in school readiness; yet such preschool is largely limited to middle- and upper-class families. Efforts such as Head Start need to be supported if there is to be a real possibility of disrupting inequalities (see Heckman, 2013). As Orfield (2014) further states,

Recent decades have been wasted on hostile social policy and civil rights changes that have diminished and divided our society, with education policy deeply limited by many disruptive and destructive trends of racial and economic polarization, segregation, and economic disinvestment. These policy and changes are built on many unfounded and untrue assumptions. (p. 289)

These unfounded and untrue assumptions include, as argued throughout this chapter, an outright mythology akin to eugenics about biologically determined, inborn talents and predetermined biological limitations rigidly imposed on developmental outcomes. This mythology urgently needs to be dispelled.

REFERENCES

Allen, G. E. (2001). Essays on science and society. Is a new eugenics afoot? *Science, 294,* 59–61.

Anastasi, A. (1984). Aptitude and achievement tests: The curious case of the indestructible strawperson. In B. S. Plake (Ed.), *Social and technical issues in testing: Implications for test construction and usage* (pp. 129–140). Hillsdale, NJ: Erlbaum.

Anderson, J. D. (2007). Race-conscious educational policies versus a "color-blind constitution": A historical perspective. *Educational Researcher, 36,* 249–257.

Anderson, N. B., & Nickerson, K. J. (2005). Genes, race, and psychology in the genome era: An introduction. *American Psychologist, 60,* 5–8.

Bodrova, E., & Leong, D. J. (2007). *Tools of the mind: The Vygotskian approach to early childhood education.* New York, NY: Merrill/Prentice Hall.

Bronfenbrenner, U., & Ceci, S. J. (1994). Nature-nurture reconceptualized: A bioecological model. *Psychological Review, 101,* 568–586.

Burt, C. H., & Simons, R. L. (2015). Heritability studies in the postgenomic era: The fatal flaw is conceptual. *Criminology, 53,* 103–112.

Byrge, L., Sporns, O., & Smith, L. B. (2014). Developmental process emerges from extended brain-body-behavior networks. *Trends in Cognitive Sciences, 18,* 395–403.

Cahan, E. D., & White, S. H. (1992). Proposals for a second psychology. *American Psychologist, 47,* 224–235.

Carter, P. L., & Reardon, S. F. (2014). *Inequality matters: Framing a strategic inequality research agenda.* Retrieved from http://wtgrantfoundation.org/inequality-matters-framing-a-strategic-inequality-research-agenda

Ceci, S. J., & Papierno, P. B. (2005). The rhetoric and reality of gap closing: When the "have-nots" gain but the "haves" gain even more. *American Psychologist, 60,* 149–160.

Ceci, S. J., & Williams, W. M. (2010). *The mathematics of sex: How biology and society conspire to limit talented women and girls.* Oxford, England: Oxford University Press.

Charney, E. (2008). Genes and ideologies. *Perspectives on Politics, 6,* 299–319.

Charney, E. (2012). Behavior genetics and post genomics. *Behavioral and Brain Sciences, 35,* 331–410.

Chávez, K., Nair, Y., & Conrad, R. (2015). Equality, sameness, difference: Revisiting the equal rights amendment. *Women's Studies Quarterly, 43,* 272–276.

Collins, F. S. (2004). What we do and don't know about race, ethnicity, genetics and health at the dawn of the genome era. *Nature Genetics, 36*(11 Suppl.), 1–3.

Cooper, R. S. (2005). Race and IQ: Molecular genetics as deus ex machina. *American Psychologist, 60,* 71–76.

Danforth, S. (2008). John Dewey's contributions to and educational philosophy of intellectual disability. *Educational Theory, 58,* 45–62.

Darling-Hammond, L. (2007a). The flat earth and education: How America's commitment to equity will determine our future. Third Annual Brown Lecture in Education Research. *Educational Researcher, 36,* 318–334.

Darling-Hammond, L. (2007b). Race, inequality and educational accountability: The irony of "No Child Left Behind." *Race Ethnicity and Education, 10,* 245–260.

Dar-Nimrod, I., & Heine, S. J. (2011). Genetic essentialism: On the deceptive determinism of DNA. *Psychological Bulletin, 137,* 800–818.

Delgado, R., & Stefancic, J. (2012). *Critical race theory: An introduction* (2nd ed.). New York: New York University Press.

Diamond, A., Barnett, W. S., Thomas, J., & Munro, S. (2007). Preschool program improves cognitive control. *Science, 318,* 1387–1388.

Dickens, W. T., & Flynn, J. R. (2001). Great leap forward: A new theory of intelligence. *New Scientist, 21,* 44–47.

Doane, A. W., & Bonilla-Silva, E. (2003). *White out: The continuing significance of racism.* New York, NY: Routledge.

Dupré, J. (2012). *Processes of life: Essays in the philosophy of biology.* Oxford, England: Oxford University Press.

Eaton, S., & Black, D. (2016). *How public scholarship helped put school integration back on the public agenda.* Presidential Session at the AERA Annual Meeting, Washington, DC.

Eisenberg, L. (1995). The social construction of the human brain. *American Journal of Psychiatry, 152,* 1563–1575.

Ericsson, K. A. (2014). *The road to excellence: The acquisition of expert performance in the arts and sciences, sports and games.* New York, NY: Psychology Press.

Fischer, K. W., Goswami, U., & Geake, J. (2010). The future of educational neuroscience. *Mind, Brain, and Education, 4,* 68–80.

Fox, S., Levitt, P., & Nelson, C. A. (2010). How the timing and quality of early experiences influence the development of brain architecture. *Child Development, 81,* 28–40.

Gabel, S. L., & Danforth, S. (Eds.). (2008). *Disability and the policy of education: An international reader.* New York, NY: Peter Lang.

Gottlieb, G. (2003). On making behavioral genetics truly developmental. *Human Development, 46,* 337–355.

Gould, S. J. (1996). *The mismeasure of man* (Rev. ed.). New York, NY: W. W. Norton.

Graves, J. L. (2001). *The emperor's new clothes: Biological theories of race at the millennium.* New Brunswick, NJ: Rutgers University Press.

Guthrie, R. (1998). *Even the rat was white: A historical view of psychology.* Needham, MA: Allyn & Bacon.

Gutiérrez, C. D., & Rogoff, B. (2003). Cultural ways of learning: Individual traits and repertoire of practice. *Educational Researcher, 32,* 19–25.

Haslam, N. (2011). Genetic essentialism, neuroessentialism, and stigma: Commentary on Dar-Nimrod and Heine (2011). *Psychological Bulletin, 137,* 819–824.

Heckman, J. J. (2013). *Giving kids a fair chance.* Cambridge: MIT Press.

Herrnstein, R. J., & Murray, C. (1994). *The bell curve: Intelligence and class structure in American life.* New York, NY: Free Press.

Hirsh-Pasek, K., Bruer, J., Kuhl, P., Goldin-Meadow, S., Stern, E., Galles, N. S., . . . Byers-Heinlein, K. (2007). *The Santiago declaration.* Retrieved from http://www.jsmf.org/santiagodeclaration

Howe, K. R. (2010). Educational equality in the shadow of the Reagan era. In G. Haydon (Ed.), *Educational equality* (pp. 71–95). London, England: Continuum.

Howe, K. R. (2015). The meritocratic conception of educational equality: Ideal theory run amuck. *Educational Theory, 65,* 183–201.

Hruby, G. G. (2012). Three requirements for justifying an educational neuroscience. *British Journal of Educational Psychology, 82,* 1–23.

Huttenlocher, P. R. (2002). *Neural plasticity: The effect of environment on the development of cerebral cortex.* Cambridge, MA: Harvard University Press.

Ingold, T. (2008). Bindings against boundaries: Entanglements of life in an open world. *Environment and Planning A, 40,* 1796–1810.

Ingold, T. (2011). *Being alive: Essays on movement, knowledge and description.* Abingdon, England: Routledge.

Johnson, M. H., Grossmann, T., & Cohen-Kadosh, K. (2009). Mapping functional brain development: Building a social brain through interactive specialization. *Developmental Psychology, 45,* 151–159.

Joseph, J. (2010). Genetic research in psychiatry and psychology. A critical overview. In K. E. Hood, C. Tucker Halpern, G. Greenberg, & R. M. Lerner (Eds.), *Handbook of developmental science, behavior, and genetics* (pp. 557–625). Hoboken, NJ: Wiley-Blackwell.

Kaufman, J. S., & Cooper, R. S. (2001). Considerations for use of racial/ethnic classification in etiologic research. *American Journal of Epidemiology, 154,* 291–298.

Keller, F. E. (2010). Foreword: Gilbert Gottlieb and the developmental point of view. In K. E. Hood, C. Tucker Halpern, G. Greenberg, & R. M. Lerner (Eds.), *Handbook of developmental science, behavior, and genetics* (pp. xi–xiv). Hoboken, NJ: Wiley-Blackwell.

King, M. L., Jr. (1968). *Speech at Western Michigan University,* December 18, 1963. Kalamazoo, Michigan. Retrieved from http://wmich.edu/sites/default/files/attachments/MLK.pdf

Kolb, B., & Gibb, R. (2011). Brain plasticity and behaviour in the developing brain. *Journal of the Canadian Academy of Child and Adolescent Psychiatry, 20,* 265–276.

Kucsera, J., & Orfield, G. (2014). *New York State's extreme school segregation: Inequality, inaction and a damaged future.* Los Angeles: University of California, Los Angeles.

Ladson-Billings, G. (2006). From the achievement gap to the education debt: Understanding achievement in U.S. schools. *Educational Researcher, 35*(7), 3–12.

Lawlor, L. (2014). Jacques Derrida. In E. N. Zalta (Ed.), *The Stanford encyclopedia of philosophy* (Spring 2014 ed.). Retrieved from http://plato.stanford.edu/archives/spr2014/entries/derrida/

Lee, C. D. (2010). Soaring above the clouds, delving the ocean's depths: Understanding the ecologies of human learning and the challenge for education science. *Educational Researcher, 39*, 643–655.

Lehrman, D. S. (1953). A critique of Konrad Lorenz's theory of instinctive behavior. *The Quarterly Review of Biology, 28*, 337–363.

Leontiev, A. N. (1979). The problem of activity in psychology. In J. V. Wertsch (Ed.), *The concept of activity in Soviet psychology* (pp. 37–71). Armonk, NY: Sharpe.

Lerner, R. M. (2006). Developmental science, developmental systems, and contemporary theories of human development. In R. M. Lerner (Vol. ed.), *Handbook of child psychology. Vol. 1: Theoretical models of human development* (6th ed., pp. 1–17). Hoboken, NJ: Wiley.

Lewontin, R. (1995). Genes, environment, and organisms. In R. Silvers (Ed.), *Hidden histories of science* (pp. 115–140). New York: New York Review of Books.

Li, S.-C. (2009). Brain in macro experiential context: Biocultural coconstruction of lifespan neurocognitive development. *Progress in Brain Research, 178*, 17–29.

Li, S.-C. (2013). Neuromodulation and developmental contextual influences on neuraland cognitive plasticity across the lifespan. *Neuroscience & Biobehavioral Reviews, 37*, 2201–2208.

Lickliter, R., & Honeycutt, H. (2003a). Developmental dynamics: Towards a biologically plausible evolutionary psychology. *Psychological Bulletin, 129*, 819–835.

Lickliter, R., & Honeycutt, H. (2003b). Evolutionary approaches to cognitive development: Status and strategy. *Journal of Cognition and Development, 4*, 459–473.

Lickliter, R., & Honeycutt, H. (2013). A developmental evolutionary framework for psychology. *Review of General Psychology, 17*, 184–189.

Lickliter, R., & Honeycutt, H. (2015). Biology, development, and human systems. In R. M. Lerner (Ed.), *Handbook of child psychology and developmental science* (pp. 162–207). New York, NY: Wiley.

Luria, A. R. (1973). *The working brain: An introduction to neuropsychology.* New York, NY: Penguin Books.

Lynch, K., & Lodge, A. (2002) *Equality and power in schools: Redistribution, recognition and representation.* London, England: Routledge/Falmer.

MacLeod, D. I. A. (2010). Into the neural maze. In J. Cohenand, & M. Matthen (Eds.), *Color ontology and color science* (pp. 151–178). Cambridge: MIT Press.

Mausfeld, R. (2012). On some unwarranted tacit assumptions in cognitive neuroscience. *Frontiers in Psychology, 3*, 67.

McCabe, D. P., & Castel, A. D. (2008). Seeing is believing: The effect of brain images as judgments of scientific reasoning. *Cognition, 107*, 343–352.

McDermott, M., & Samson, F. L. (2005). White racial and ethnic identity in the United States. *Annual Review of Sociology, 31*, 245–261.

Miller, G. (2008). Growing Pains for fMRI. *Science, 320*, 1412–1414.

Mohammed, A. (2014). *Why inequality is 2015's most worrying trend* (The World Economic Forum Report). Retrieved from https://www.weforum.org/agenda/2014/11/inequality-2015s-worrying-trend/ion

Morawski, J. G. (2005). Moving gender, positivism and feminist possibilities. *Feminism & Psychology, 15*, 408–414.

Moss, L. (2006). Redundancy, plasticity, and detachment: The implications of comparative genomics for evolutionary thinking. *Philosophy of Science, 73*, 930–946.

Nash, R. (2004). Equality of educational opportunities: In defense of traditional concept. *Educational Philosophy and Theory, 36*, 361–377.

Nelson, C. A., & Luciana, M. (2001). *Handbook of developmental cognitive neuroscience.* Cambridge: MIT Press.

Nisbett, R. E., Aronson, J., Blair, C., Dickens, W., Flynn, J., Diane, F., . . . Turkheimer, E. (2012). Intelligence: New findings and theoretical developments. *American Psychologist, 67*, 130–159.

Oakes, J. (2005). *Keeping track: How schools structure inequality* (2nd ed.). New Haven, CT: Yale University Press.

Orfield, G. (2014). Tenth annual *Brown* lecture in educational research: A new civil rights agenda for American education. *Educational Researcher, 43*, 273–292.

Organization for Economic Cooperation and Development. (2002). *Understanding the brain: Towards a new learning science.* Paris, France: Author.

Overton, W. F. (2006). Developmental psychology: Philosophy, concepts, methodology. In W. Damon (Series ed.) & R. M. Lerner (Vol. ed.), *Theoretical models of human development: Vol. 1, Handbook of child psychology* (6th ed., pp. 18–88). Hoboken, NJ: Wiley.

Oyama, S. (2000). *Evolution's eye.* Durham, NC: Duke University Press.

Oyama, S., Griffiths, P. E., & Gray, R. D. (2001). (Eds.). *Cycles of contingency: Developmental systems and evolution.* Cambridge: MIT Press.

Papierno, P. B., Ceci, S. J., Makel, M. C., & Williams, W. M. (2005). The nature and nurture of talent: A bioecological perspective on the ontogeny of exceptional abilities. *Journal for the Education of the Gifted, 28*, 312–332.

Racine, E., Bar-Ilan, O., & Illes, J. (2005). fMRI in the public eye. *Nature Reviews Neuroscience, 6*, 9–14.

Reardon, S. (2015, 9 December). Brain-manipulation studies may produce spurious links to behaviour. *Nature.* Retrieved from http://www.nature.com/news/brain-manipulation-studies-may-produce-spurious-links-to-behaviour-1.19003

Rees, T. (2010) Being neurologically human today. Life and science and adult cerebral plasticity. *American Ethnologist, 37*, 150–166.

Richardson, K., & Norgate, S. (2005). The equal environments assumption of classical twin studies may not hold. *Journal of Educational Psychology, 75*, 339–350.

Robert, J. S. (2004). *Embryology, epigenesis, and evolution: Taking development seriously.* New York, NY: Cambridge University Press.

Sefa Dei, G. J., Mazzuca, J., McIssac, E., & Zine, J. (1997). *Reconstructing dropout: A critical ethnography of the dynamics of black students' disengagement from school.* Toronto, Ontario, Canada: University of Toronto Press.

Sen, A. (1999). *Development as freedom.* Oxford, England: Oxford University Press.

Shifferman, E. (2015). More than meets the fMRI: The unethical apotheosis of neuroimages. *Journal of Cognition and Neuroethics, 3*, 57–116.

Smagorinsky, P. (2016). (Ed.). *Creativity and community among autism-spectrum youth: Creating positive social updrafts through play and performance.* New York, NY: Palgrave Macmillan.

Smedley, A., & Smedley, B. D. (2005). Race as biology is fiction, racism as a social problem is real: Anthropological and historical perspectives on the social construction of race. *American Psychologist, 60*, 16–26.

Stenberg, A. (2013). Interpreting estimates of heritability: A note on the twin decomposition. *Economics & Human Biology, 11*, 201–205.

Sternberg, R. J., Grigorenko, E. L., & Kidd, K. K. (2005). Intelligence, race, and genetics. *American Psychologist, 60*, 46–59.

Stetsenko, A. (2003). Alexander Luria and the cultural-historical activity theory: Pieces for the history of an outstanding collaborative project in psychology. Review of E. D. Homskaya (2001), *Alexander Romanovich Luria: A scientific biography. Mind, Culture, and Activity, 10*, 93–97.

Stetsenko, A. (2008). From relational ontology to transformative activist stance on development and learning: Expanding Vygotsky's (CHAT) project. *Cultural Studies of Science Education, 3*, 471–491.

Stetsenko, A. (2009). Vygotsky and the conceptual revolution in developmental sciences: Towards a unified (non-additive) account of human development. In M. Fleer, M. Hedegaard, J. Tudge, & A. Prout (Eds.), *World yearbook of education. Constructing childhood: Global–local policies and practices* (pp. 125–142). New York, NY: Routledge.

Stetsenko, A. (2016). *The transformative mind: Expanding Vygotsky's approach to human development and education.* New York, NY: Cambridge University Press.

Stetsenko, A. (2016). Moving beyond the relational worldview: Exploring the next steps premised on agency and a commitment to social change. *Human Development, 59*, 283–389.

Stetsenko, A., & Arievitch, I. M. (2010). Cultural-historical activity theory: Foundational worldview and major principles. In J. Martin, & S. Kirschner (Eds.), *The sociocultural turn in psychology: The contextual emergence of mind and self* (pp. 231–253). New York, NY: Columbia University Press.

Taylor, P. J. (2007). Unreliability of high human heritability estimates and small shared effects of growing up in the same family. *Biological Theory, 2*, 387–397.

Thelen, E. (1995). Motor development: A new synthesis. *American Psychologist, 50*, 79–95.

Thelen, E. (2000). Grounded in the world: Developmental origins of the embodied mind. *Infancy, 1*, 3–28.

Thelen, E. (2005). Dynamic systems theory and the complexity of change. *Psychoanalytic Dialogues, 15*, 255–283.

Tobach, E., & Rosoff, B. (Eds.). (1994). *Challenging racism and sexism: Alternatives to genetic explanations.* New York: Feminist Press, City University of New York.

Tucker, W. H. (1994). *The science and politics of racial research.* Urbana: University of Illinois Press.

Varma, S., McCandliss, B., & Schwartz, D. (2008). Scientific and pragmatic challenges for bridging education and neuroscience. *Educational Researcher, 37*, 140–152.

Vygotsky, L. S. (1993). *The collected works. Volume 2: The fundamentals of defectology* (R. W. Rieber & A. S. Carton, Eds.). New York, NY: Plenum.

Vygotsky, L. S. (1997). *The collected works. Volume 4: The history of the development of higher mental functions* (R. W. Rieber, Ed.). New York, NY: Plenum.

Weisberg, D. S., Keil, F. C., Goodstein, J., Rawson, E., & Gray, J. (2008). The seductive allure of neuroscience explanations. *Journal of Cognitive Neuroscience, 20*, 470–477.

Willingham, D. T., & Dunn, E. W. (2003). What neuroimaging and brain localization can do, cannot do, and should do for social psychology. *Journal of Personality and Social Psychology, 85*, 662–671.

Winston, A. S. (Ed.). (2004). *Defining difference: Race and racism in the history of psychology.* Washington, DC: American Psychological Association.

Witherington, D. C. (2007). The dynamic systems approach as metatheory for developmental psychology. *Human Development, 50*, 127–153.

Chapter 6

Civic Participation Reimagined: Youth Interrogation and Innovation in the Multimodal Public Sphere

Nicole Mirra

The University of Texas at El Paso

Antero Garcia

Colorado State University

This chapter challenges dominant narratives about the civic disengagement of youth from marginalized communities by reconceptualizing what counts as civic participation in public life and how youth are positioned as civic agents. We examine ideologies that undergird traditional forms of civic education and engagement in the United States and offer an alternative vision of civic life grounded in recognition of systemic inequality and struggle for social justice. We consider the ways in which digital media has fundamentally transformed the public sphere and expanded opportunities for youth civic expression and action, as well as the ways that youth participatory action research literature offers a framework for civic education that forefronts youth experience and voice. Our analysis culminates in the development of a new conceptual model for civic learning and engagement that pushes past participation into the realms of interrogation and innovation.

This is the foundation of the [American] Dream—its adherents must not just believe in it but believe that it is just, believe that their possession of the Dream is the natural result of grit, honor, and good works. There is some passing acknowledgement of the bad old days, which, by the way, were not so bad as to have any ongoing effect on our present. The mettle that it takes to look away from the horror of our prison system, from police forces transformed into armies, from the long war against the black body, is not forged overnight. This is the practiced habit of jabbing out one's eyes and forgetting the work of one's hands. To acknowledge these horrors means turning away from the brightly rendered version of your country as it has always declared itself and turning toward something murkier and unknown. It is still too difficult for most Americans to do this.

—Ta-Nehisi Coates, *Between the World and Me* (2015, pp. 98–99)

Review of Research in Education
March 2017, Vol. 41, pp. 136–158
DOI: 10.3102/0091732X17690121
© 2017 AERA. http://rre.aera.net

From the perspective of African American writer and journalist Ta-Nehisi Coates, the American Dream represents more than simply economic opportunity or material success; it also signifies a fundamental belief in the virtue of this country. According to the "Dream," the American narrative is one of triumphant progress and any behavior contrary to this ideal—including oppression, brutality, or hate—is a mere aberration from American character rather than a manifestation of it.

The Dream is powerful; indeed, much of the formal education provided to U.S. youth about what it means to be a citizen is built on its vision. Many state civic learning standards focus "almost exclusively on patriotic observances" (Torney-Purta & Vermeer, 2006, p. 16), and students are over twice as likely to study "great American heroes and the virtues of the American form of government" in their social studies and civic courses than problems facing the country (Lopez & Kirby, 2007, p. 1).

Consider the National Assessment of Educational Progress Civics Project, the most comprehensive and influential measure of civic knowledge and skills in the nation. In the framework for the 2014 exam, the governing board lays out a specific blueprint for how students should be taught to see their nation that fits strikingly well into the vision Coates (2015) critiques. They make passing reference to the bad old days when we experienced a "gap between the nation's ideals and reality" but highlight the progress Americans have made to "abolish slavery" and "remove legal support for segregation," concluding with glowing praise for "Americans [who] have joined forces to work toward the achievement of their shared ideals" (National Assessment of Educational Progress Civics Project, 2014, p. 19).

Thus, much of the civic education young people experience in school encourages them to engage in public life based on the core assumption that the infrastructure of our democracy is sound—that all citizens enjoy equitable access to opportunity and can use the tools of self-governance to remedy any threats to such opportunity. Our schools largely educate toward the Dream.

But for those, like Coates (2015), who see the agency of their communities stripped away by systemic inequities in multiple areas of public life, including criminal justice and law enforcement, citizenship is a much more fraught proposition. As the lived experiences of many Americans of color contradict the inherent logic of the Dream, these citizens must continuously negotiate the extent of their identification and engagement with a society in which they have experienced "horrors"—a painful process that W. E. B. Du Bois (1903) described over a century ago as the struggle of "double-consciousness" (p. 5). Indeed, the term *citizen* itself becomes problematic when considering the tenuous status of undocumented immigrant students in this country who find their access to public services and voice in public life in constant limbo. While we use the terms *citizen* and *civic* in this chapter, we conceptualize them not as markers of legal status but as signifiers of the rights of individuals to participate fully in civic communities at local, national, and global levels regardless of age or legal residency. While we recognize citizenship as a concept that can complicate, challenge, or even transcend national borders, our primary focus here remains on civic engagement and disparities in the U.S. context.

The contested nature of the civic sphere for all youth, but particularly for youth from historically marginalized communities, raises questions for us about the traditional purposes and practices of civic education. We feel compelled to ask, What does it mean to educate toward civic engagement in a society in which progress occurs not inevitably or in a straight line but instead in stops, starts, and retreats? Whose perspectives and cultural values define progress today? What story lines can inspire civic action when the narrative of the Dream does not resonate?

Young people are offering answers to these questions but in forms that much civic education scholarship has a difficult time characterizing. For instance, in the wake of the unrest in Ferguson, Missouri, in 2014, which was sparked when a White police officer shot and killed African American teenager Michael Brown, a young Black man posted a tweet using hashtag #IfTheyGunnedMeDown in which he asked, "Which photo does the media use if the police shot me down?" One showed him in cap and gown at a graduation ceremony, while the other showed him in informal clothing and sunglasses dancing in a house with a bottle in his hand. The hashtag went viral as hundreds of thousands of Twitter users posted photos that expressed their outrage not only at the "horror" of the shooting itself but also at the role that media outlets play in portraying people of color in stereotypical and victim-blaming fashion.

These tweets represent complex responses to a serious civic issue but do not conform to established categories of civic engagement because they are youth-generated, explicitly critical of the Dream, and representative of the new communicative possibilities opened up by digital technologies. We argue that to better capture the range of civic experiences of young people in America, the future of civic education scholarship must engage more forcefully with youth agency, critical perspectives, and digital forms of expression.

In this chapter, we counter the "brightly rendered" vision of our country that undergirds mainstream models of civic education and engagement in the United States and take Coates's (2015) challenge to turn toward a "murkier and unknown" understanding of America that arises from and builds on experiences of struggle and oppression. We aim to recast civic learning by examining a range of community-based civic education initiatives in both formal and informal learning spaces to demonstrate how they amplify youth voice from a redefined vision of civic participation focused on creation and criticality. We characterize these initiatives not simply as new practices within the field of civic education as it currently exists but as a provocation for this entire body of scholarship to focus on reimagining and rearticulating what citizenship and civic participation mean for young people in an era of broader social media use, interest-driven collaboration, and research-driven activism. In fact, our analysis suggests the need to actually move *beyond* practices of civic participation and toward practices of civic interrogation and innovation.

We begin by offering a conceptualization of the "civic" that structures our discussion of civic learning and development. We continue with a brief review of current data about civic engagement and education among communities of color and then step back to determine how these scholars theorize inequity and the nature of the public sphere itself. Next, we turn to a deeper examination of our current context of civic inequity and offer examples of how research in digital social movements and participatory action research is extending notions of the "who" and "how" of civic participation. We outline the key contributions of this "participatory turn" in civic education while raising questions about the extent to which simply *participating* within existing inequitable power structures can ever truly offer redress for the injustices that marginalized communities have experienced in public life. These questions lead us to ultimately reject participation as an adequate frame for civic engagement and offer new ways forward in the field through the practices of civic interrogation and innovation.

Throughout this chapter, we focus on selected literature that is representative of and offers clear perspectives on the dominant paradigms of civic education as well as new models of participation emerging throughout the field of education research writ large. We do not seek to present a meta-analysis of the entire field of civic education in the United States; rather, our intent is to expose the normative ideas that inform policy, practice, and research in civic education as a basis for problematizing them and offering new competencies that can lead us toward a more inclusive and critical vision of civic life.

DEFINING THE CIVIC

Our understanding of the "civic" throughout this chapter hinges on the idea of democratic community—both the formal communities of local, state, and national politics and the informal communities of fellow citizens united by shared interests and concerns (Flanagan & Faison, 2001). We hearken back to John Dewey's (1916) understanding of democracy as not only a system of representative government but also "a form of associated living" (p. 16). From this perspective, civic engagement includes not only explicitly political acts such as voting but also behaviors representative of what Harry Boyte (2003) calls a "different" kind of politics—one that "builds the commonwealth" between individuals of various backgrounds, experiences, and beliefs by being "productive and generative, not simply a bitter distributive struggle over scarce resources" (p. 9). In turn, civic education involves the process by which young people gain knowledge, skills, and identities that they use to understand and participate in these forms of community life.

Of course, tensions lurk under the surface of these general definitions as scholars debate the exact sorts of knowledge, skills, and identities that spur decisions to

TABLE 1

Normative Characteristics of Citizenship

- Belonging to at least one group
- Attending religious services at least monthly
- Belonging to a union
- Reading newspapers at least once per week
- Voting
- Being contacted by a political party
- Working on a political project
- Attending club meetings
- Believing that people are trustworthy
- Volunteering

become civically engaged, what engagement looks like, and whether and how it can be fostered through specific learning experiences. We now turn to examine some of the prevailing understandings in the field.

INEQUALITIES IN CIVIC ENGAGEMENT AND EDUCATION

The dominant narrative about youth civic engagement in the United States today is one of crisis. Political and social scientists generally support this narrative by comparing the actions and attitudes of today's youth (as represented through large-scale survey responses) to their counterparts from previous decades. For instance, Constance Flanagan and Peter Levine (2010) reference the results of General Social Survey and the American National Election Study to demonstrate decreases among Americans ages 18 to 29 in almost all of the major "characteristics of citizenship" since the 1970s (p. 161). Various combinations of these characteristics (see Table 1) have been cited by a wide array of scholars over time (e.g., Levine & Lopez, 2002; Macedo et al., 2005; McFarland & Thomas, 2006; Zukin, Keeter, Andolina, Jenkins, & Delli Carpini, 2006) to become commonly accepted as normative attributes of civic engagement.

The general narrative of youth civic crisis is accompanied by a specific story line of inequality, as analyses of most of these indicators reveal stark differences in youth participation along lines of race, class, and educational attainment (Wray-Lake & Hart, 2012). According to this story line, young people who are White, come from more privileged backgrounds, and expect to attend college demonstrate higher levels of engagement in many of the actions detailed in Table 1 than young people of color who come from communities with lower incomes and less formal educational attainment (Foster-Bey, 2008; Verba, Schlozman, & Brady, 1995).

While the overall decline in youth civic engagement is often connected to broad social trends such as "a loss of trust in government" (American National Election Study, 2010) or a diminishing sense of community life across the United States

(Putnam, 2000), race- and class-based inequalities in engagement are largely attributed to two factors: deficits within marginalized communities and/or the inequitable distribution of civic learning opportunities.

While scholars who take a deficit approach to inequalities in civic engagement often acknowledge the intersection of various social structures that act on members of marginalized groups to suppress participation, they nonetheless locate the failure of engagement in those communities themselves. For instance, Meira Levinson (2007) conceptualizes the inequalities in engagement as a "civic achievement gap." She attributes lower levels of civic participation among minoritized communities to lack of education, failure to join voluntary organizations, and low-status employment opportunities (p. 5). She does acknowledge that race- and class-based inequalities create distinct civic experiences for members of these groups but persists in placing the onus of responsibility on *them* for not "achieving" civically (pp. 7–8). Similarly, Atkins and Hart (2003) argue that low-income youth living in urban areas fail to "acquire" civic identities because of the effects of poverty, including lower densities of adults, adults with fewer civic resources due to lack of income and education, and adults who fail to model civic behaviors like voting (p. 159).

Conversely, scholars who concentrate on the inequitable distribution of civic learning opportunities locate the root cause of civic inequalities in public institutions such as schools and community organizations that fail to educate all communities equally. This argument is grounded in the belief that civic education is a crucial catalyst for civic engagement. Research indicates that levels of civic engagement increase steadily along with levels of formal education (Nie, Junn, & Stehlik-Barry, 1996); however, beyond the positive effects of schooling generally, concerted efforts to provide targeted civic learning opportunities in both formal and informal learning environments have been found to demonstrate positive effects on young people's knowledge, skills, and commitments to participation in public life (Delli Carpini & Keeter, 1996).

Yet Joseph Kahne and Ellen Middaugh (2008), in their work studying the opportunities afforded to high school students across the state of California, found that students in higher tracked classes and those from high-income families consistently received more civic learning opportunities than students who did not attend well-resourced schools or experience the benefits of family wealth. They conclude,

Schools, rather than helping to equalize the capacity and commitments needed for democratic participation, appear to be exacerbating this inequality by providing more preparation for those who are already likely to attain a disproportionate amount of civic and political voice. (p. 18)

The American Political Science Association Task Force on American Inequality (2004) details the consequences of these educational inequalities, noting that "Citizens with lower or moderate incomes speak with a whisper that is lost on the ears of inattentive government officials, while the advantaged roar with a clarity and consistency that policy-makers readily hear and routinely follow" (p. 1).

Therefore, while existing scholarship takes competing perspectives on who bears responsibility for inequalities in civic engagement (communities or institutions), it is largely united in its enduring faith in the normative constructs of civic engagement laid out in Table 1 and calls for civic learning opportunities that move students toward these behaviors. Best practices in civic education—as synthesized by a partnership of business, foundation, and research groups—include formal instruction in government and civics, discussion of controversial social issues, service learning, and participation in school governance (Gould, 2011).

Yet we find it necessary to problematize the consensus that these particular skills embody "good" civic engagement; indeed, relying on these skills as measures of engagement is an ideological choice that inevitably minimizes or ignores the value of other skills and, in turn, contributes to a narrow and exclusionary vision of who does and does not count as a good citizen. While it may appear on the surface that behaviors like working on a political project or following the news are skills unrelated to any particular ideological perspective, they cannot be separated from the narratives that educators construct about what it means to be a good citizen (Westheimer, 2015; Westheimer & Kahne, 2004)—narratives that, as we indicated earlier, are often tied to ideas of the American Dream. The skills listed in Table 1 are not neutral; rather, they conform to a particular vision of civic identity that we argue fails to take into account the systemic inequalities faced by young citizens of color. Thus, characterizing their civic engagement based on these measures fails to accurately capture their experiences of civic life.

We do not believe that this situation can be rectified by simply offering students of color more access to normative skills or adding a few new skills to the list; research in academic literacy and youth culture indicates that this approach often contradicts and impedes the pursuit of equity (Azevedo, 2011; Gutierrez, 2007). Instead, we argue for a critical vision of citizenship that can counter the dominant perspective that young American of color are civically disengaged and instead acknowledge the innovative ways in which they are participating in civic life.

In the next section, we move toward this vision by delving into how conceptualizations of civic identity based on the American Dream come up short in the face of the systemic civic inequalities faced by marginalized communities and demonstrating how researchers are beginning to develop new theoretical frameworks for civic education.

DISCONNECT BETWEEN CIVIC IDEALS AND CIVIC REALITY

As we discussed earlier, a powerful current exists in civic education scholarship that equates citizenship to a common understanding of the United States as an exceptional nation. William Damon (2001) argues that young people need to develop a shared sense of pride and patriotism in the best traditions of their country in order to realize a *civil* identity, a term that he uses to stress the traits of honesty, fairness, and common decency that he sees as crucial to good citizenship (pp. 130, 137). William

Galston (2003) attributes low levels of youth civic engagement to the failure of schools to specify a required core of civic knowledge and provide common, standardized civics assessments.

James Banks (2008) warns against this universal conception of citizenship precisely because of its propensity to minimize and suppress the experiences of minoritized groups; as he describes the consequences, "Groups with power and influence often equate their own interests with the public interest" (p. 131). A normative vision of citizenship does not comport with a society structured by systemic racial inequalities.

And these inequalities exist in almost every aspect of American public life. In 2013, the Pew Research Center calculated the wealth of White American households to be 13 times the median wealth of African American households and 10 times the median wealth of Hispanic American households (Kochhar & Fry, 2014). Meanwhile, according to the 2010 Census, African American and Hispanic families are more than twice as likely as White families to be living below the federal poverty line (Macartney, Bishaw, & Fontenot, 2013). Scholars have exhaustively documented the discriminatory treatment that minoritized populations continue to experience in public systems of criminal justice (Alexander, 2010), health (Centers for Disease Control and Prevention, 2013), housing (Desmond, 2016), and education (Lipman, 2011).

In the face of these experiences in public life, appeals to patriotism and calls to participate in a responsive and inherently virtuous democratic system can ring hollow. While civic education is one influence on civic engagement, so are interactions with government representatives and agencies, and research shows that negative contact with public officials can have a dampening effect on willingness to participate in public life (Soss, 2005; Weaver & Lerman, 2010). Cathy Cohen (2010) argues that many young people respond to the danger they sense from public officials such as police officers by engaging in a "politics of invisibility" that involves staying under the radar and disengaging from public life as a civic adaptation geared at ensuring their literal survival (pp. 195–196). Over 20 years before Ta-Nehisi Coates published his memoir, philosopher Cornel West (1993) argued that those who study American democracy must "face up to the monumental eclipse of hope [and] unprecedented collapse of meaning" (p. 12) experienced by the Black community, and fellow philosopher Eddie Glaude (2007) asserts that democracy in the United States "must begin by engaging the historical legacies of racism that threaten democracy's realization" (p. 40).

Community psychologists Roderick Watts and Constance Flanagan (2007) lay bare the civic education dilemma created by a context of systemic civic, political, and economic inequality—they contend that traditional notions of political socialization "implicitly encourage investment in or identification with the prevailing social order and replication of it" and ask, "Are young members of marginalized groups as likely as more socially integrated youth to replicate or buy into a system where they feel excluded?" (p. 781).

Anger and disengagement from traditional channels of political participation emerge as reasonable responses to Watts and Flanagan's (2007) question about the civic atmosphere in the United States for people of color. Educators face the daunting task of instead developing an alternative vision of civic engagement with their students that can inspire hope and action. Deep exploration of the root causes of racial inequality in this country requires that educators refuse to force youth to conform to dominant systems of civic participation and instead create space for interrogation and innovation.

Many of the efforts to find a way forward involve reconceptualizing citizenship, moving away from viewing it as a possession or status to be achieved and toward a practice to be constantly negotiated based on the contexts that young people are experiencing (Lawy & Biesta, 2007). Drawing on sociocultural learning theory, Nasir and Kirshner (2003) argue that civic identity development must be analyzed through three overlapping lenses—the social interactions that occur between individuals, the cultural practices that structure these interactions, and the institutions in which these interactions occur (p. 141).

Scholars operating from this practice-oriented, sociocultural view of citizenship have been advancing youth civic education and participation on two fronts: pushing on the modalities of civic participation by focusing on new possibilities offered by digital media tools and expanding views on the agency of young people as participants in public life. We turn now to these literatures in order to demonstrate how they move us toward a new critical framework for understanding and educating for civic life.

THE PARTICIPATORY TURN: NEW AFFORDANCES OF DIGITAL TECHNOLOGIES

When it comes to understanding civic participation, research too often becomes bogged down by privileging adult perspectives on what youth should be doing as civic agents rather than asking young people what actually engages them or what kinds of civic learning opportunities they may already be experiencing.

Before exploring examples of how civic participation and civic learning could be broadened in contemporary contexts, we find it necessary for education researchers to take a step back and assess what our field means when we discuss participation. As noted earlier, a litany of traditionally defined markers of civic participation exist and currently dominate the field; however, these skills do not take a full account of the practices in which youth are presently engaged. In considering the skills that are presently valued within the public sphere and the gaps that exist, we in the civic research community must ask ourselves several key questions:

- What does it mean to participate?
- Who participates in civic acts?
- What outcomes are sought and gained by participation?
- What stances must researchers take when studying the civic participation of youth and communities?

Looking beyond traditional measurements of civic action, youth are participating in civic activities that dive deeper into issues of equity and localized politics and that represent broader contexts for civic action. By moving from traditional forms of civics that focus on voting and individual responsibility to more justice-oriented understandings of civics that capitalize upon advances in multimodality and connected forms of learning, we see possibilities for deeper and more resonant approaches to civic learning. If we are to continue to trust in institutions of public education to foster commitments to civic participation, we argue that they must be willing to explore the varied experiences of citizenship that students bring to school. Furthermore, while much of the language around digital civic engagement focuses on increasing youth participation in public life, we argue that students' use of social media tools can start to change the conversation from one about merely participating toward one about interrogating normative civic practices and structures and innovating new forms of civic action.

In looking at youth socialization, engagement, and forms of shared governance in interest-driven spaces like online gaming and fandom communities, Mimi Ito et al. (2015) describes the value of understanding the "little p" politics that youth engage in regularly (p. 162). Considering that youth and adults alike are now participating, socializing, and demonstrating civic agency in both the physical world and in online spaces (Bennett, 2007), the contexts in which participation happens and civic engagement occurs are much more flexible than ever before.

Participatory Culture as a Disruption of Traditional Civic Engagement

Broadening definitions of participation to consider how youth organize, socialize, and produce complex media in, for example, online gaming communities demonstrate how civic engagement is fundamentally different in today's "participatory culture." As Jenkins, Clinton, Purushotma, Robison, and Weigel (2009) explain, "Participatory culture is emerging as the culture absorbs and responds to the explosion of new media technologies that make it possible for average consumers to archive, annotate, appropriate, and recirculate media content in powerful new ways" (p. 8). Though remix culture and fan fiction are seen as some of the main aspects of how participatory culture shapes youth experiences (Jenkins, 2008), this includes an important civic shift for youth as well; if youth today possess the tools for producing, distributing, and coordinating civic messages via digital technologies, the opportunities for learning about civic engagement are no longer tethered to traditional spaces like classrooms.

Furthermore, expanding on the value of understanding participatory culture, a group of recent researchers have described the ecosystem of extracurricular participation that youth engage in as "connected learning" (Ito et al., 2013). Connected learning is realized when a young person pursues a personal interest or passion with the support of friends and caring adults and is in turn able to link this learning and interest to academic achievement, career possibilities, or civic engagement (p. 6).

By looking at how individuals might collaborate when socializing in virtual worlds like *World of Warcraft* or *Second Life* (Boellstorff, 2008, Chen 2011; Nardi, 2010) or online knitting communities (Pfister, 2014) or video game design (Rafalow and Tekinbas, 2014) or fan fiction production (Hellekson & Busse, 2014), connected learning points to powerful forms of participation, engagement, and production that—while academically robust—often happen far away from the gaze of schooling and traditional measures of civic participation.

At the same time, as connected learning points to forms of extracurricular participation that are "socially embedded, interest-driven, and oriented toward educational, economic, or political opportunity" (Ito et al., 2013, p. 6), engagement in online gaming, fan fiction production, and distribution of remixes of popular songs can potentially highlight how youth understand their role in broader civic, public spheres. Youths' lives are spent socializing in digital spaces just as much as they are in their physical environments, and as such, the connected ecosystem must consider how civic learning opportunities occur across these spaces.

Though youth may learn forms of participation in digital spaces that can be taken up for civic and political purposes, the online context is not inherently political. For example, though some studies have noted that games can foster spatial awareness and civic learning (Kahne, Middaugh, & Evans 2008; Ondrejka, 2008; Squire, 2008, 2010), most digital games that youth consume do not explicitly engage with civic agency. However, the Internet can become a means of civic learning if we look beyond traditional measurements found in civic education literature. For example, as portals for socialization, group coordination, and production of fan fiction, games can foster youth participation in "affinity spaces" (Gee, 2004) for civic learning opportunities. As Salen (2008) notes, "Beyond their value as entertainment media, games and game modification are currently key entry points for many young people into productive literacies, social communities, and digitally rich identities" (pp. 14–15). As we look toward new avenues of youth civic engagement, youth interests and online social forums have the potential to become the seeds of 21st-century collaboration and organization around political interests.

Connected Politics and Civics That #Matter

Connected learning is also tied to more familiar contexts of political engagement. Most usefully, Cohen, Kahne, Bowyer, Middaugh, and Rogowski (2012) describe "participatory politics" as "interactive, peer-based acts through which individuals and groups seek to exert both voice and influence on issues of public concern" (p. vi). Considering how information can circulate, inform, and lead to action, participatory politics can mobilize networks—both online and off—sustain dialogue for agenda setting, and "enable participant to exert greater agency through the circulation" and production of political content (Cohen et al., 2012, p. vi).

One aspect of civic engagement in today's participatory culture that youth have shaped is the role of activism and organizing vis-à-vis online hashtags. In terms of sustaining circulated, politicized content, hashtags have played a significant role in how youth engage in participatory politics. As such, the hashtag has quietly become a feature of recent social networking software that elevates it to a tool for powerful civic participation. As a nod to the ability of media to shift based on the needs of consumers and producers in a participatory age, the rise of the hashtag as a tool for organizing was initially a "hack" of existing search functions within Twitter (Parker, 2011). In 2007, Chris Messina tweeted, "How do you feel about using # (pound) for groups. As in #barcamp [msg]?" Messina's tweet points to the ability of search engines to neatly organize all tweets that include the same appended text (e.g., #BlackLivesMatter; #Occupy, etc.). Using hashtags for youth civic engagement can "help amplify individual voice through aggregation and dialogue. These two contemporary examples build off of global uses of hashtags on Twitter for civic action across the globe from Greece to the Arab Spring" (Garcia, in press). While important critiques exist regarding the ways that social media can create new opportunities for surveillance and harassment and perpetuate capitalistic corporate interests, we find it important to highlight its potential to instigate sociopolitical innovation. Though some pundits have dismissed the uses of online media for civic change as "clicktivism" or "slacktivism" (Gladwell, 2010; Morozov, 2011), its ability to sustain civic solidarity is perhaps most visible as a result of recent and ongoing movements such as #BlackLivesMatter.

Originally seen on Twitter in response to the unceasing murder of unarmed young men and women of color at the hands of police officers, #BlackLivesMatter is an ongoing movement to end violence—both literal and symbolic—that people of color continue to experience. As such, we are intentional in noting that #BlackLivesMatter is not simply a "trending" phrase or a "dialogue." As a movement, #BlackLivesMatter has persevered in public consciousness over the past 3 years largely due to its ability to sustain participation in both online spaces and in physical demonstrations like "die ins" (Levenson, 2014) held during holiday shopping seasons.

Young people, and particularly young people from historically marginalized communities, have been spearheading one of the most prominent civil rights movements taking place online and in the streets of the United States today (Abber, 2014). Unlike conventional models of civic education, the #BlackLivesMatter movement critiques the root causes of policies affecting young people's daily lives; rather than working within the system, the movement is calling out the system itself. In considering how these efforts reflect youth expertise around forms of connected learning and a fluency in the mechanisms that drive participatory politics, #BlackLivesMatter can be seen as a form of "connected civics." Ito et al. (2015) define connected civics as "a form of learning fostered via participatory politics that emerges when young people achieve civic agency linked to their deeply felt interests, identities, and affinities" (p. 17).

Looking across the possibilities of participatory politics and youth civic development vis-à-vis connected learning, it is important to emphasize that these disruptions to traditional understandings of civic opportunities are not simply built on the premise that technology "solves" issues of equity. In fact, though many examples of disruptive participatory politics or youth engagement in connected learning point to positive aspects of digital technologies, the affordances of tech are not the root of these disruptive practices; youth interests, concerns, and passions are what drive civic learning—be these interests in online or off-line contexts. Likewise, not all games (digital or nondigital) are useful for civic learning. Though U.S. Supreme Court Justice Sandra Day O'Connor made headlines in 2016 for launching an "iCivics" videogame (Singer, 2016), such digital tools largely reify traditional understanding of civic learning. The kinds of civic learning that youth are already doing in online games like Minecraft or in virtual communities like Twitter are leading to new disruptions of old civics. As Jenkins, Ito, and boyd (2015) note,

Connected civics begins with an appreciation of how young people are developing political and civic capacity when they run their own World of Warcraft guilds, Minecraft servers, or fan conventions, a kind of "little p" politics that contrasts with the more adult-centered 'big P' Politics. This kind of organizing may not be about the government, but it is about governance, and it involves trial by fire in experiencing what happens when you have power and authority. (p. 162)

The "trial by fire" of youth civic participation in online and off-line contexts is largely ignored in how adults are considering the possibilities of youth as leaders today. And while some digital games, resources, and curriculum are developed to support youth civic learning, these tools often funnel individuals into traditional metrics of civic participation and are frequently advertised in ways that reinforce dominant, capitalist markets that do not sustain the cultural wealth of youth of color. These issues contribute to our desire to further the conversation about youth civic action in ways that push past mere participation and toward critical practices of interrogation and innovation.

Thus far we have considered the affordances of the participatory turn as related to youth socialization, play, and connected civics in digital spaces. In what follows we consider specific models of youth-led research and codesigned activism and consider the contributions of critical theory to transforming how young people are viewed as civic actors.

THE PARTICIPATORY TURN EXTENDED: SITUATING YOUTH AS CIVIC LEADERS

Alongside our field's need to challenge what counts as participation, we must consider what kinds of epistemological stances and methodological approaches ground how we work alongside and within youth-driven civic communities. While much civic education research treats young people as citizens in training and attempts to measure future commitments to participation in public life rather than honoring their current forms of public engagement, the expanded view of participation that we have presented insists on highlighting youth civic agency in its own right and on its own terms.

A variety of educational practices in formal and informal educational spaces, running the gamut from ethnic studies courses (Sleeter, 2011) to spoken word poetry slams (Fisher, 2005) to youth organizing collaboratives (Rogers, Mediratta, & Shah, 2012), are seeking to reorient civic learning from the perspective of young people and build opportunities for action out of the contexts and experiences of their daily lives.

We propose that these practices can be usefully grouped together and understood as forms of civic education under the umbrella of what has come to be known as youth participatory action research (YPAR)—a form of inquiry that situates young people as the primary drivers of the research process and situates the issues about which they care most as the primary subjects of that research (Cammarota & Fine, 2008; Duncan-Andrade & Morrell, 2008). While the word "research" implies that YPAR is primarily a methodology, its openness in terms of the practices that can be included in this term show that its overriding contribution is primarily an epistemological one—challenging traditional notions of who can produce knowledge and who can drive social action and change (Mirra, Garcia, & Morrell, 2015).

YPAR happens in a variety of learning contexts, from classrooms and after-school programs to community organizations and universities, and amplifies the voices of young people from elementary school to college and beyond through a range of activities. Our purpose in this chapter is not to parse exactly which activities should be considered YPAR according to any strict definition but instead to use YPAR as a broad framework that expands the nature and purpose of civic participation. YPAR addresses key concerns about what "counts" as research, who gets a voice within the research arena, and what role research plays in the daily lives of youth.

Figure 1 highlights a set of competencies distilled from our review of YPAR scholarship that comprise a cycle of critical civic learning and development. While these competencies are inextricably linked in practice, we tease them apart here in order to foreground their unique contributions to challenging traditional models of civic learning and supporting youth agency.

As we unpack each of these competencies, we reiterate they comprise a process that can be used to interrogate the civic world youth and adults inhabit—there is no beginning or end or linear progression of steps to be followed. A comparison of these competencies to the normative skills presented earlier in Table 1 offers a clear illustration of the contributions YPAR makes to establishing an innovative, critical vision of civic engagement that honors the experiences of youth from marginalized communities.

Developing Critical Consciousness

One of the key processes involved in YPAR is the deconstruction of traditional narratives of meritocracy and equality that undergird the American Dream and foster deficit ideology about minoritized communities. Unlike most civic education research, YPAR is built on a critical theoretical tradition—specifically Paulo Freire's (1970) theory of conscientization, in which oppressed communities engage in critical social analysis to expose and dismantle unjust power hierarchies and ideologies and imagine alternative possibilities. Instead of taking at face value the idea that cultural

FIGURE 1
Cycle of Critical Civic Learning and Development

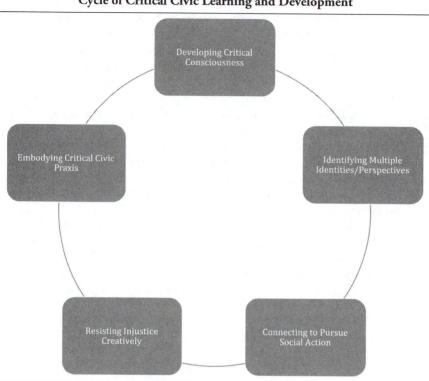

capital is concentrated within dominant communities (Bourdieu, 1985), YPAR draws on theories that highlight the funds of knowledge (Moll, Amanti, Neff, & Gonzalez, 1992) and cultural wealth (Yosso, 2005) of working-class communities of color.

In their description of their work with Latina/Latino youth in Tucson, Arizona, Julio Cammarota and Augustine Romero (2011) explain that the development of critical consciousness helps youth move past feelings of powerlessness in the face of civic inequities by helping them "name the practices that counter and address the oppressive social and economic forces impeding the development of a healthy identity, neighborhood, and world" (p. 494). Coming to understand society from a critical perspective is the foundation on which political efficacy and civic praxis can be built (Watts, Diemer, & Voight, 2011).

Identifying Multiple Identities/Perspectives

Part of the process of developing critical consciousness involves making explicit the pluralism of American society—the variety of cultures, experiences, and beliefs that are contained within the label of "American citizen." Sonia Nieto and Patty Bode (2008) define multicultural education as the explicit application of critical consciousness to formal and informal learning contexts, transforming not only curriculum and instruction to include diverse perspectives but also "the interactions among students, teachers, and families and the very way that schools conceptualize the nature of teaching and learning" (p. 44). Critical multicultural education, with its explicit anti-racist orientation and commitment to honoring students' lived experiences, sets the stage for characterizing young people as active civic agents with the power to challenge historical power hierarchies and create knowledge on their own terms.

Jason Irizarry (2009) characterizes YPAR as a vehicle for connecting multicultural education to social action in order to counter civic inequities. He highlights youth research as a model that can help young people develop "the skills necessary to positively shape their life trajectories, while simultaneously challenging the multiple forms of oppression that delimit them and reproduce social inequality" (p. 198). This model of civic learning resists conceptualizing Americans as an undifferentiated group and instead celebrates differentiated experience as a catalyst for recognizing oppression and pursuing justice.

Connecting to Pursue Social Action

The concept of critical consciousness holds that the key element that bridges critical social analysis with social action is a sense of collective efficacy (Watts & Hipolito-Delgado, 2015). YPAR promotes a sense of solidarity and trust between young people and stresses the key role that relationships play in struggles for social justice. YPAR, whether it takes place in schools or community organizations, gives young people opportunities to connect with each other as well as to adults, resources, and experiences that enable them to realize their civic potential and take action on issues that matter to them (Ginwright, Noguera, & Cammarota, 2006). The collective nature of YPAR offers a source of community social capital based in mutual trust and shared interest (Sampson, Morenoff, & Earls, 1999).

Resisting Injustice Creatively

In the face of oppression, young people can choose to respond in a variety of ways. Daniel Solorzano and Dolores Delgado-Bernal (2001) offer a typology for responses—progressing from reactionary behavior through conformity toward resistance—that is organized by the extent to which young people possess a critique of social oppression and an orientation toward social justice. Without an understanding of oppression created by the ongoing development of critical consciousness, students may veer toward taking action within the constraints of existing civic structures, a choice that the authors claim has little chance of fostering social justice. Transformational resistance is achieved only when young people channel their awareness of oppression and passion for justice into pursuing action that is "political, collective, conscious, and motivated by a sense that individual and social change is possible" (p. 320).

YPAR represents a model of civic engagement that has the potential to foster transformational resistance. Cerecer, Cahill, and Bradley (2011) highlight the space that YPAR creates for young people to express themselves creatively through a variety of modalities in pursuit of justice.

Embodying Critical Civic Praxis

Shawn Ginwright and Julio Cammarota (2007) bring together all of the elements of this alternative vision of civic learning in their model of critical civic praxis, which they define as "the organizational processes that promote civic engagement among youth and elevate their critical consciousness and capacities for social justice activism" (p. 699). This commitment to continuous collective action and reflection through YPAR offers a pathway forward in our understanding of how to structure civic learning experiences that resonate with the experiences of young people of color.

YPAR engages productively with the ideas of connected learning and participatory politics considering its commitment to building on shared youth interests and using digital media tools in the service of amplifying youth voice about issues of civic concern. YPAR scholarship often highlights the use of multimedia as a favored strategy among young people for conducting data collection and sharing their research findings (Garcia, Mirra, Morrell, Martinez, & Scorza, 2015; Yang, 2009). More important, YPAR also reinforces the idea that the stance we take toward youth civic participation is just as, if not more important than, as the modalities we use; positioning youth as knowledge-makers necessitates a more creative and production-centered relationship with digital technologies.

We argue that these advances in the modalities and stances of civic learning also necessitate new language to describe civic action. We now turn to consider whether the terms *participation* and *engagement* are strong enough to capture the intents and purposes of critical civic praxis and offer new terminology to guide future research in this field.

MOVING FROM PARTICIPATION AND ENGAGEMENT TO INTERROGATION AND INNOVATION

We find it problematic to characterize the critical youth production embodied by participatory culture and YPAR as examples of mere civic participation or engagement, largely because those terms signify action that is circumscribed by and beholden to a larger system that, in the case of our civic context, is too often attached to patriotic and outdated ideologies and behaviors. While we could be content to claim that these forms of civic learning serve to expand what counts as participation, we feel that the power and potential of these practices call for stronger terminology.

Young people who recognize that their lived experiences do not comport to the narrative of the American Dream and who take social action based on critical social analysis are engaged in the crucial work of interrogating the public sphere. They are disrupting dominant ideas and exposing the bedrock inequities behind the assumptions of fairness and equality in American life. They, like Ta-Nehisi Coates, are taking up the difficult task of moving past the brightly rendered version of their country but finding hope and change in the process of agitation.

And they do not stop there. They are not content to ask their questions to those in traditional positions of authority; instead, they turn to the communicative possibilities of new media and raise their voices as researchers to engage in civic innovation. They are remixing tools like Twitter through hashtag activism and are beginning to develop their own apps and programs. They are asking adults to take up positions as audience members as they take the mic to profess their expertise. And as quickly as new modes of expression are developed, young people are finding ways to manipulate them to broadcast their civic ideas and beliefs.

These youth practices offer huge promise for challenging systemic inequalities in civic life and for challenging deficit narratives of youth of color in the public sphere. They situate struggle as just as powerful a catalyst for civic action as patriotism and expand our conceptualizations of civic agency. Future research is needed that offers more responsive methodological frameworks for capturing these forms of agency and more innovative analytical frameworks for synthesizing the impacts, but we are encouraged by the possibilities.

CONCLUSION: REIMAGINING CIVIC PATHWAYS ALONGSIDE YOUTH

If we are to look for ways to better engage youth of color in meaningful civic learning opportunities, it is not enough to simply hew to the pathways of participation that have largely disenfranchised these students for decades. As Kirshner (2015) writes, "Too many interventions that target students of color–despite decades of critiques of deficit-based approaches–continue to be designed without their input and to be based on carefully elaborated accounts of what they lack" (p. 172). Clearly, the traditional measures of civic participation that have been foundational for education research are not dramatically transforming the civic life experiences of youth of color today. With no end in sight, it is time to rethink the civic educational approaches currently implemented and researched and, perhaps, look at how youth anger, sense of disenfranchisement, and disappointment in the current socioeconomic landscape can open up the space to reimagine civic possibilities today.

As there are widespread precedents of how national electoral forms of civic participation have intentionally placed communities of color at distinct disadvantage through voter suppression and gerrymandering; as there are numerous examples of how communities of color in the U.S. experience systemic social inequities; as civic education research is often done in the silos of tenure track academia such that little benefit or insight is gleaned by those communities most disenfranchised by the sociopolitical and educational system, ours is a field that is overdue to more critically question how and why civic participation reinforces existing power structures.

Current popular media—from fictional worlds of Harry Potter and the Hunger Games to real-world examples like #BlackLivesMatter—illustrate youth leading in powerful and world-realigning ways. It is time to stop dictating pathways of civic participation and following the powerful examples young people are providing of what embodied civic leadership looks like both online and off-line. Fundamentally, a movement moves. Embracing the flux and responsiveness of civic participation in new contexts—whether contained in online, off-line, or hybrid spaces—youth movements are led by processes of innovation today. Largely, civic education does not sustain the participatory politics of youth involved in *World of Warcraft* guilds or organizing #BlackLivesMatter because these are foreign to the familiar "Characteristics of Citizenship" that have been replicated in schools for generations.

As a field that must advance forms of youth civic engagement that value youth interests and expertise, we argue that we must rely on two dimensions of disruption. First, we must answer Cohen's (2010) call to interrogate what counts as civic participation and engagement today. Rather than dictate the pathways for civic participation for youth—and particularly disenfranchised youth of color—the paradigms of what citizenship looks like and how it is enacted must be thoroughly reevaluated. Second, we must innovate participatory pathways forward alongside the youth that have been primarily kept at a clinical distance for scrutiny.

The book-length dialogue between Paulo Freire and Myles Horton (1990) lifts its title from the work of Spanish poet Antonio Machado: *We Make the Road by Walking.* As we tread through the "murkier and unknown" context of the United States today, our civic pathways require innovating new methods of participation and reexamining our assumptions about the civic roads we have trusted in the past.

REFERENCES

Abber, C. (2014). These teens and 20-somethings are organizing the Civil Rights Movement that will change our country. *MTV News.* Retrieved from http://www.mtv.com/news/2031498/meet-young-people-organizing-2014-protests-civil-rights-movement/

Alexander, M. (2010). *The new Jim Crow: Mass incarceration in the age of colorblindness.* New York, NY: New Press.

American National Election Studies. (2010). *Trust in government index, 1958-2008.* Ann Arbor, MI: Center for Political Studies.

American Political Science Association Task Force on American Inequality. (2004). *American democracy in an age of rising inequality. Report of the Task Force on Inequality and American Democracy.* Washington, DC: Author.

Atkins, R., & Hart, D. (2003). Neighborhoods, adults, and the development of civic identity in urban youth. *Applied Developmental Science, 7,* 156–164.

Azevedo, F. S. (2011). Lines of practice: A practice-centered theory of interest relationships. *Cognition and Instruction, 29,* 147–184.

Banks, J. A. (2008). Diversity, Group identity, and citizenship education in a global age. *Educational Researcher, 37,* 129–139.

Bennett, W. L. (Ed.). (2007). *Civic life online: Learning how digital media can engage youth.* Cambridge: MIT Press.

Boellstorff, T. (2008). *Coming of age in second life: An anthropologist explores the virtually human.* Princeton, NJ: Princeton University Press.

Bourdieu, P. (1985). The forms of capital. In J. Richardson (Ed.), *Handbook of theory and research for the sociology of education* (pp. 241–258). New York, NY: Greenwood.

Boyte, H. (2003). A different kind of politics: John Dewey and the meaning of citizenship in the 21st century. *The Good Society, 12*(2), 1–15.

Cammarota, J., & Fine, M. (2008). *Revolutionizing education: Youth participatory action research in motion.* New York, NY: Routledge.

Cammarota, J., & Romero, A. (2011). Participatory action research for high school students: Transforming policy, practice, and the personal with social justice education. *Educational Policy, 25*, 488–506.

Centers for Disease Control and Prevention. (2013). CDC health disparities and inequalities report-United States, 2013. *Morbidity and Mortality Weekly Report, 62*(3 Suppl.). Retrieved fromhttps://www.cdc.gov/mmwr/pdf/other/su6203.pdf

Cerecer, D., Cahill, C., & Bradley, M. (2011). Resist this! Embodying the contradictory positions and collective possibilities of transformative resistance. *International Journal of Qualitative Studies in Education, 24*, 587–593.

Chen, M. (2011). *Leet Noobs: The life and death of an expert player group in World of Warcraft.* New York, NY: Peter Lang.

Coates, T. (2015). *Between the world and me.* New York, NY: Random House.

Cohen, C. (2010). *Democracy remixed: Black youth and the future of American politics.* New York, NY: Oxford University Press.

Cohen, C., Kahne, J., Bowyer, B., Middaugh, E., & Rogowski, J. (2012). *Participatory politics: New media and youth political action.* Irvine, CA: DML Research Hub. Retrieved from http://ypp.dmlcentral.net/sites/default/files/publications/Participatory_Politics_New_Media_and_Youth_Political_Action.2012.pdf

Damon, W. (2001). To not fade away: Restoring civil identity among the young. In D. Ravitch, & J. Vitteriti (Eds.), *Making good citizens: Education and civil society* (pp. 122–141). New Haven, CT: Yale University Press.

Delli Carpini, M., & Keeter, S. (1996). *What Americans know about politics and why it matters.* New Haven, CT: Yale University Press.

Desmond, M. (2016). *Evicted: Poverty and profit in the American city.* New York, NY: Crown.

Dewey, J. (1916). *Democracy and education: An introduction to the philosophy of education.* New York, NY: Macmillan.

Du Bois, W. E. B. (1903). *Souls of black folk.* New York, NY: Modern World Library.

Duncan-Andrade, J. M. R., & Morrell, E. (2008). *The art of critical pedagogy: Possibilities for moving from theory to practice in urban schools.* New York, NY: Peter Lang.

Fisher, M. (2005). From the coffee house to the school house: The promise and potential of spoken word poetry in school contexts. *English Education, 37*, 115–131.

Flanagan, C., & Faison, N. (2001). Youth civic development: Implications of research for social policy and programs. *Social Policy Report, 15*, 1–14.

Flanagan, C., & Levine, P. (2010). Civic engagement and the transition to adulthood. *The Future of Children, 20*, 159–179.

Foster-Bey, J. (2008). *Do race, ethnicity, citizenship and socioeconomic status determine civic engagement?* (CIRCLE Working Paper No. 62). College Park, MD: Center for Information & Research on Civic Learning and Engagement.

Freire, P. (1970). *Pedagogy of the oppressed.* New York, NY: Seabury Press.

Freire, P., & Horton, M. (1990). *We make the road by walking: Conversations on education and social change* (B. Bell, J. Gaventa, & J. Peters, Eds.). Philadelphia, PA: Temple University Press.

Galston, W. (2003). Civic education and political participation. *Phi Delta Kappan, 85*(1), 29–33.

Garcia, A. (in press). Networked teens and YA literature: Gossip, identity, and what really #matters. *The ALAN Review.*

Garcia, A., Mirra, N., Morrell, E., Martinez, A., & Scorza, D. (2015). The Council of Youth research: Critical Literacy and civic agency in the digital age. *Reading & Writing Quarterly, 31,* 151–167.

Gee, J. P. (2004). *Situated language and learning: A critique of traditional schooling.* New York, NY: Routledge.

Ginwright, S., & Cammarota, J. (2007) Youth activism in the urban community: Learning critical civic praxis within community organizations. *International Journal of Qualitative Studies in Education, 20,* 693–710.

Ginwright, S., Noguera, P., & Cammarota, J. (2006). *Beyond resistance! Youth activism and community change: New democratic possibilities for practice and policy for America's youth.* New York, NY: Routledge.

Gladwell, M. (2010). Small change: Why the revolution will not be tweeted. *The New Yorker.* Retrieved from: newyorker.com/reporting/2010/10/04/101004fa_fact_gladwell? currentPage=all

Glaude, E. (2007). *In a shade of blue: Pragmatism and the politics of black America.* Chicago, IL: The University of Chicago Press.

Gould, J. (2011). *Guardian of democracy: The civic mission of schools.* Philadelphia: Leonore Annenberg Institute for Civics of the Annenberg Public Policy Center at the University of Pennsylvania.

Gutierrez, K. (2007). "Sameness as fairness": The new tonic of equality and opportunity. In J. Larson (Ed.), *Literacy as snake oil: Beyond the quick fix* (pp. 108–122). New York, NY: Peter Lang.

Hellekson, K., & Busse, K. (2014). *The fan fiction studies reader.* Iowa City: University of Iowa Press.

Ito, M., Gutiérrez, K., Livingstone, S., Penuel, B., Rhodes, J., Salen, K., . . . Craig Watkins, S. (2013). *Connected learning: An agenda for research and design.* Irvine, CA: Digital Media and Learning Research Hub.

Ito, M., Soep, E., Kliger-Vilenchik, N., Shresthova, S., Gamber-Thompson, L., & Zimmerman, A. (2015). Learning connected civics: Narratives, practices, and infrastructures. *Curriculum Inquiry, 45,* 10–29.

Irizarry, J. (2009). Reinvigorating multicultural education through youth participatory action research. *Multicultural Perspectives, 11,* 194–199.

Jenkins, H. (2008). *Convergence culture: Where old and new media collide.* New York: New York University Press.

Jenkins, H., Clinton, K., Purushotma, R., Robison, A. J., & Weigel, M. (2009). *Confronting the challenges of participatory culture: Media education for the 21st century.* Chicago, IL: MacArthur Foundation.

Jenkins, H., Ito, M., & boyd, d. (2015). *Participatory culture in a networked era.* Cambridge, England: Polity.

Kahne, J., & Middaugh, E. (2008). *Democracy for some: The civic opportunity gap in high school* (Circle Working Paper No. 59). College Park, MD: Center for Information & Research on Civic Learning and Engagement.

Kahne, J., Middaugh, E., & Evans, C. (2008). *The civic potential of video games.* Cambridge: MIT Press.

Kirshner, B. (2015). *Youth activism in an era of education inequality.* New York, NY: New York University Press.

Kochhar, R., & Fry, R. (2014). *Wealth inequality has widened along racial, ethnic lines since end of Great Recession.* Washington, DC: Pew Research Center. Retrieved from http://www. pewresearch.org/fact-tank/2014/12/12/racial-wealth-gaps-great-recession/

Lawy, R., & Biesta, G. (2007). Citizenship-as-practice: The educational implications of an inclusive and relational understanding of citizenship. *British Journal of Educational Studies, 54,* 34–50.

Levenson, E. (2014). "Die-in" protest of Ferguson decision blocks Mass Ave. traffic. *Boston. com*. Retrieved from http://www.boston.com/news/local/massachusetts/2014/12/01/die-protest-ferguson-decision-blocks-mass-ave-traffic/ykpJKgLbiiLA1GPy20xrEL/story.html

Levine, P., & Lopez, M. H. (2002). *Youth voter turnout has declined, by any measure.* College Park, MD: Center for Information & Research on Civic Learning and Engagement.

Levinson, M. (2007). *The civic achievement gap* (CIRCLE Working Paper No. 51). College Park, MD: Center for Information & Research on Civic Learning and Engagement.

Lipman, P. (2011). *The new political economy of urban education: Neoliberalism, race, and the right to the city.* New York, NY: Routledge.

Lopez, M., & Kirby, E. (2007). *U.S. civics instruction: Content and teaching strategies (CIRCLE fact sheet).* College Park, MD: Center for Information & Research on Civic Learning and Engagement.

Macartney, S., Bishaw, A., & Fontenot, K. (2013). *Poverty rates for selected detailed race and Hispanic groups by state and place: 2007-2011.* Washington, DC: U.S. Census Bureau.

Macedo, S., Assensoh, Y., Berry, J., Brintnall, M., Cambell, D., Fraga, L., . . . Walsh, K. (2005). *Democracy at risk: How political choices undermine political participation and what we can do about it.* Washington, DC: Brookings Institution Press.

McFarland, D. A., & Thomas, R. J. (2006). Bowling young: How youth voluntary associations influence adult political participation. *American Sociological Review, 71,* 401–425.

Messina, C. (2007). *How do you feel about using # (pound) for groups. As in #barcamp [msg]?* [Tweet]. Retrieved from https://twitter.com/chrismessina/status/223115412

Mirra, N., Garcia, A., & Morrell, E. (2015). *Doing youth participatory action research: Transforming inequity with researchers, educators, and youth.* New York, NY: Routledge.

Moll, L., Amanti, C., Neff, D., & Gonzalez, N. (1992). Funds of knowledge for teaching: Using a qualitative approach to connect homes and classrooms. *Theory Into Practice, 31,* 132–141.

Morozov, E. (2011). *Net delusion: The dark side of internet freedom.* New York, NY: PublicAffairs.

Nardi, B. (2010). *My life as a night elf priest: An anthropological account of World of Warcraft.* Ann Arbor: University of Michigan Press.

Nasir, N., & Kirshner, B. (2003). The cultural construction of moral and civic identities. *Applied Developmental Science, 7,* 138–147.

National Assessment of Educational Progress Civics Project. (2014). *Civics framework for the 2014 National Assessment of Educational Progress.* Washington, DC: National Assessment Governing Board.

Nie, N. H., Junn, J., & Stehlik-Barry, K. (1996). *Education and democratic citizenship in America.* Chicago, IL: University of Chicago Press.

Nieto, S., & Bode, P. (2008). *Affirming diversity: The sociopolitical context of multicultural education* (5th ed.). Boston, MA: Allyn & Bacon.

Ondrejka, C. (2008). Education unleashed: Participatory culture, education, and innovation in Second Life. In K. Salen (Ed.), *The ecology of games: Connecting youth, games, and learning* (pp. 229–252), Cambridge: MIT Press.

Parker, A. (2011). Twitter's secret handshake. *The New York Times*. Retrieved from http://www.nytimes.com/2011/06/12/fashion/hashtags-a-new-way-for-tweets-cultural-studies.html?_r=1&pagewanted=all

Pfister, R. C. (2014). *Hats for house elves: Connected learning and civic engagement in Hogwarts at Ravelry.* Irvine, CA: Digital Media and Learning Research Hub.

Putnam, R. D. (2000). *Bowling alone: The collapse and revival of American community.* New York, NY: Simon & Schuster.

Rafalow, M. H., & Tekinbas, K. S. (2014). *Welcome to Sackboy Planet: Connected learning among LittleBigPlanet 2 players.* Irvine, CA: Digital Media and Learning Research Hub.

Rogers, J., Mediratta, K., & Shah, S. (2012). Building power, learning democracy: Youth organizing as a site of civic development. *Review of Research in Education, 36*, 43–66.

Salen, K. (2008). *The ecology of games: Connecting youth, games, and learning.* Cambridge: MIT Press.

Sampson, R. J., Morenoff, J. D., & Earls, F. (1999). Beyond social capital: Spatial dynamics of collective efficacy for children. *American Sociological Review, 64*, 633–660.

Singer, N. (2016). A Supreme Court pioneer, now making her mark on video games. *The New York Times.* Retrieved from http://www.nytimes.com/2016/03/28/technology/sandra-day-oconnor-supreme-court-video-games.html?_r=0

Sleeter, C. (2011). *The academic and social value of ethnic studies: A research review.* Washington, DC: National Education Association.

Solorzano, D., & Delgado-Bernal, D. (2001). Examining transformational resistance through a critical race and LatCrit theory framework: Chicana and Chicano students in an urban context. *Urban Education, 36*, 308–342.

Soss, J. (2005). Making clients and citizens: Welfare policy as a source of status, belief, and action. In A. Schneider, & H. Ingram (Eds.), *Deserving and entitled: Social constructions and public policy* (pp. 291–328). Albany: State University of New York Press.

Squire, K. (2008). Open-ended video games: A model for developing learning for the interactive age. In K. Salen (Ed.), *The ecology of games: Connecting youth, games, and learning* (pp. 167–198) Cambridge: MIT Press.

Squire, K. (2010). From information to experience: Place-based augmented reality games as a model for learning in a globally networked society. *Teachers College Record, 112*, 2565–2602.

Torney-Purta, J., & Vermeer, S. (2006). *Developing citizenship competencies from kindergarten through Grade 12: A background paper for policymakers and educators.* Denver: Education Commission of the States.

Verba, S., Schlozman, K. L., & Brady, H. E. (1995). *Voice and equality: Civic voluntarism in American politics.* Cambridge, MA: Harvard University Press.

Watts, R., Diemer, M. A., & Voight, A. M. (2011). Critical consciousness: Current status and future directions. *New Directions for Child and Adolescent Development, 134*, 43–57.

Watts, R., & Flanagan, C. (2007). Pushing the envelope on civic engagement: A developmental and liberation psychology perspective. *Journal of Community Psychology, 35*, 779–792.

Watts, R., & Hipolito-Delgado, C. (2015). Thinking ourselves to liberation? Advancing sociopolitical action in critical consciousness. *Urban Review, 47*, 847–867.

Weaver, V., & Lerman, A. (2010). Political consequences of the carceral state. *American Political Science Review, 104*, 817–833.

West, C. (1993). *Race matters.* New York, NY: Beacon Press.

Westheimer, J. (2015). *What kind of citizen? Educating our children for the common good.* New York, NY: Teachers College Press.

Westheimer, J., & Kahne, J. (2004). What kind of citizen? The politics of educating for democracy. *American Educational Research Journal, 41*, 237–269.

Wray-Lake, L., & Hart, D. (2012). Growing social inequalities in youth civic engagement? Evidence from the National Election Study. *Political Science & Politics, 45*, 456–461.

Yang, K. W. (2009). Mathematics, critical literacy, and youth participatory action research. *New Directions for Youth Development, 123*, 99–118.

Yosso, T. (2005). Whose culture has capital? A critical race theory discussion of community cultural wealth. *Race, Ethnicity and Education, 8*, 69–91.

Zukin, C., Keeter, S., Andolina, M., Jenkins, K., & Delli Carpini, M. (2006). *A new engagement? Political participation, civic life, and the changing American citizen.* New York, NY: Oxford University Press.

Chapter 7

Permission Not Required: The Power of Parents to Disrupt Educational Hypocrisy

BEATRICE S. FENNIMORE
Indiana University of Pennsylvania

This review is focused on literature documenting the experiences of nondominant and minoritized parents who challenge injustice and inequity in the public schools attended by their children. It interrogates hegemonic approaches to parent involvement favoring dominant groups and silencing efforts of nondominant parents to confront discriminatory assumptions and unequal opportunities. Research studies generally published between 1995 and 2016 reflecting grassroots parent activism encountering conflict and tension and exposing racism, classism, and discrimination in public school practices and policies were selected. Using the lens of critical race and social justice theories, the review is structured on three major public school hypocrisies: (1) hegemonic traditional school-controlled parent involvement that privileges dominant groups and devalues contributions of nondominant groups, (2) false claims of equity in schools characterized by stratified and differential opportunities, and (3) discriminatory market-based choice and privatization schemes. Ultimately the review calls on researchers to acknowledge ethical issues that arise when their work "confirms" nondominant parent and child inferiority. Further, it calls for observer–activist–participant research paradigms that acknowledge school-based resistance to critical nondominant parent activism and respectfully document the continuing struggle of nondominant parents for equal educational opportunities.

We don't have the power to hire lawyers, we don't have the power to mobilize hundreds of people, but we have the power to make things difficult for you. We know enough to keep you occupied and answer our questions one way or another. We may not get the answers we want, but you can be assured that there's always someone out there watching your decision. And that's the way we see it. We are not powerful people.
—Martinez-Cosio (2010, p. 295)

In this chapter, I examine the literature on parent-initiated advocacy and activism for equal educational opportunities for their children in the public schools of the

Review of Research in Education
March 2017, Vol. 41, pp. 159–181
DOI: 10.3102/0091732X16687974
© 2017 AERA. http://rre.aera.net

United States. The activism may have had initial roots in traditional parent involvement, but at some point, it entered the contentious and contested terrain of conflict between the interests of parents and those of the school (Martinez-Cosio, 2010). Traditional parent involvement is widely considered to have a positive impact on the academic success of children (Comer & Haynes, 1991; Delgado-Gaitan, 1991; Epstein, 2005; Valdes, 1996), and to be a useful first step in understanding the structure of educational institutions (Ishimaru, 2014b; Warren, Hong, Rubin, & Uy, 2009). While acknowledging potential positive benefits of parent involvement, this review is aligned with the critical stance that the prominent hegemonic approaches to parent involvement, meaning those shaped by dominant social groups, are biased toward the White middle-class culture and dismissive of the strengths and potential contributions of nondominant families (Baquedano-Lopez, Alexander, & Hernandez, 2013; Lareau & Munoz, 2012; Olivos, 2004; Posey-Maddox, 2013; Souto-Manning & Swick, 2006; Yosso, 2005; Zulmara & Necochea, 2001). Furthermore, it recognizes the unfinished work of the court decisions that challenged and ultimately overturned the "separate but equal" doctrine of *Plessy v. Ferguson*—begun by *Mendez v. Westminster* in the state of California in 1946 and completed by *Brown v. Board of Education* in the Supreme Court in 1954—in the ongoing struggle for equal educational opportunity in the United States (Ladson-Billings, 2004; Orfield, 2014; Strum, 2010). Although the courageous and persistent forward movement of nondominant parent activists are highlighted, this review ultimately compares their ongoing struggle for change and equal opportunity in dismissive schools with the constant privilege-based concessions made to self-interested dominant parents in the choice arena.

It is the nondominant parents fighting for their constitutional right to equal opportunity rather than elite parents fighting to retain their domination of educational resources who represent the democratic ideals of the United States. Thus, this review calls on education researchers to challenge hypocrisies embedded in traditional hegemonic forms of parent involvement, to interrupt the deficit-based research that serves to justify the denigration and dismissal of nondominant parents in schools, and to participate with nondominant parents in activist-participant research methods that support them in their ongoing independent struggle for civil rights and equal educational opportunities in the United States. This commitment on the part of researchers will require them to reflect and act ethically in consideration of the benefits they may enjoy through connection with selective, elite educational institutions or the ways in which their own children may be valued and provided with more resources in schools favoring and privileging dominant over nondominant students. An ethical resolution to the question of how researchers should balance their ambition and desire for the best opportunities for their own families with a commitment to equal educational opportunities in an unequal society is essential to the integrity of the profession.

The young Latino coalition leader whose words begin this review was representing parents from immigrant and working-class backgrounds initially believed by school administrators to "lack the social and cultural resources . . . to engage effectively in education reform" (Martinez-Cosio, 2010, p. 284). Angered by the dismissal of their concerns about bilingual education, these self-empowered parents realized that mobilization for political resistance was their only hope for school change. Parent-led resistance that disrupts inequality tends to be excluded from the traditional hegemonic view that parent involvement should be focused on school-based support activities such as volunteering, fund-raising, attendance at school meetings and functions, and supervision of homework (Grau, 2005).

The hegemonic focus on parent participation in school support activities presumes ideologically neutral public schools that hold all parents in equal regard. This false presumption ignores the damage done by deficit-based educational scholarship labeling nondominant families as deficient and inferior. Education research fostering beliefs that nondominant children enter school behind their privileged peers, and inevitably continue to fall behind their privileged peers, has persisted in educational literature since the War on Poverty in the 1960s (Hunt, 1968; Jensen, 1969; Reissman, 1962; Wesley-Gibson, 1969). Hunt (1968), whose research is considered central to the development of the Head Start program, described the difference between culturally privileged and culturally deprived children as ". . . analogous to cage-reared and pet-reared rats and dogs" (p. 323). Harmful implications of inferiority in poor and marginalized families remain just as powerful today. Richard Rothstein (2004), for example, in his book *Class and Schools: Using Social, Economic, and Educational Reform to Close the Black-White Achievement Gap*, suggests that people from the "lower class" can be presumed to have specific (deficient) characteristics and that "the influence of (these) social class characteristics is probably so powerful that schools cannot overcome it, no matter how well trained are their teachers and no matter how well designed are their instructional programs and climates" (p. 5).

Given the persistence of educational scholarship reinforcing deficit views of nondominant families, I consider any implications that all parents are equally welcomed and have equal access to benefits of school-based involvement to represent a significant hypocrisy. In reality, parent involvement in schools is "a privileged domain signified by certain legitimate acts" (Lopez, 2001, p. 417) that are mediated either by the validation or dismissal of the parents' social, economic, and cultural attributes in school districts (Martinez-Cosio, 2010). The dismissal of nondominant parents is rationalized through "neodeficit discourses" that focus on race, class, and immigration, and that shape "parent involvement programs, practices, and ideologies" (Baquedano-Lopez et al., 2013, p. 150).

Perspective and Structure of the Review

The perspective of this review emerges from the work of Ron Edmonds (1979), whose scholarly activism focused on damage done by education research fostering deficit models of poor and minoritized families and children. Edmonds (1979), in his critique of such research, argued that repudiation "of the social science notion that family background is the principal cause of pupil acquisition of basic school skills is probably prerequisite to successful reform of public schooling for the children of the poor" (p. 23). He believed that educators embraced such deficit-based social science notions in order to absolve themselves of responsibility to offer equal and effective schooling to all children. Edmonds's response to this affront of justice was the proposal that parents be encouraged to see that *"politics are the greatest form of school reform extant"* (p. 23, italics added).

This review examined research on independent, parent-initiated, and inherently political, activism. It excluded parent activism overseen by community organizations or organized legislative initiatives to focus specifically on ways in which independent nondominant parents initiate resistance to inequity in their public schools. While recognizing that there is research highlighting the success of nondominant parent initiatives in public schools, this review was constructed with a specific focus on ways in which schools dismiss and resist the activism of nondominant parents. To organize the review, I focused on parent activism related to three educational hypocrisies: (a) the hypocrisy of hegemonic school-controlled parent involvement that privileges the White middle-class culture, devalues the cultures and contributions of nondominant parents, and then blames the unequal school outcomes of nondominant children on failure of their parents to be involved; (b) the hypocritical claims of equal educational opportunity in schools actually characterized by differential, stratified opportunities offered to privileged and nondominant children; and (c) the hypocrisy of neoliberal market–based approaches to school choice and privatization that claim to increase equity for nondominant families while constructed to exclude or marginalize them in favor of dominant groups. This section of the chapter shifts to the increased power of dominant parents to compete for resources and points to the increased knowledge and support needed by nondominant parents in new complicated choice arenas. Analysis of activist strategies of dominant parents is also included.

This review includes primary research studies generally published between 1995 and 2016 and selected with the following criteria: (a) they reflected independent forms of localized grassroots parent activism that broke free of hegemonic school control, (b) they revealed the conflict and tension that arose when marginalized or nondominant parents challenged forms of inequality in public schooling, and (c) they exposed underlying racism, classism, and discrimination in the practices and outcomes of public education. The initial literature search was focused on the following keywords: parent activism, parent involvement, parent advocacy, parent engagement, and family engagement in the contexts of public school equity, public school choice, and public school access to equal educational opportunity. I use the term *parent involvement* most frequently as it was most commonly used in the articles I reviewed. Targeted journals were those focused on general education, teacher education, early childhood education, sociology of education, political science and education, and policy studies in education, in order to provide a broad examination of issues of parent engagement, involvement, and resistance to inequality in the public schools of the United States. The following guided research questions were used to locate articles for the review:

Research Question 1: How does education research document hypocrisies in school-controlled and traditional schemes of parent involvement?

Research Question 2: How does education research document the resistance of schools to efforts of nondominant parents to confront hypocrisy and inequality?

Research Question 3: How does education research document hypocrisy in "school choice," which empowers dominant parents and disempowers nondominant parents?

Research Question 4: How should education research support nondominant parents in their self-initiated disruption of educational hypocrisies?

While the search was constructed to locate studies across methodologies, ultimately only qualitative studies met the selection criteria. Parent activism is often difficult to measure ". . . in terms of objective data because of the absence of parameters, elusiveness of the concept, and unclear quantifiable definitions" (Cline & Necochea, 2001). Resistance to inequality appears to be a personal and relational construct best documented in qualitative contexts.

I broadly defined the term *parent(s)* as the adult(s) who have major responsibility for a child and who are the primary source of communication between home and school. I considered *diversity* to be the *norm* in the United States (Genishi & Dyson, 2009); specifically neither White, married, heterosexual, nor were economically advantaged families considered the norm, with "othered" families discussed as diverse (Fennimore, 2016). The terms *nondominant* and *minoritized* were used to identify individuals or groups who, in the context of social and educational institutions, were marginalized or stratified through deeply embedded forms of racism, exclusion, and discrimination. The terms *dominant* and *nondominant* were derived from the social dominance theory that nearly all societies maintain group-based dominance in which one group holds disproportionate power. Discrimination results from the tendency of dominant groups to maintain their power through the sustained oppression of nondominant groups (Hummel, 2012; Pratto & Stewart, 2012).

The term *minoritized* refers to the objective outcomes of the exclusionary practices of dominant groups and reflects an ongoing social experience of marginalization even when the groups subjected to discrimination achieve a numerical majority in a population (Chase, Dowd, Pazich, & Bensimon, 2014). The term *elite* is used to describe parents who have attained status, power, and economic gain, often in great part through their attendance in and association with highly selective educational institutions; their aspirations include the future admission of their children to similar institutions in order to gain similar social and economic status (Deresiewicz, 2015).

While elite parents sometimes choose public education for their children, their willingness to utilize public schools may depend on demands for access to special programs, classrooms separate from nondominant children, and increased resources that will create advantage in future selective admission situations (Rhoda & Wells, 2013). Traditional (hegemonic) parent involvement was defined as seemingly noncontroversial and ideologically neutral school-based activities such as Epstein's (1992, 1995) much cited framework of parent involvement focused on parenting, communicating, volunteering, learning at home, and participating in decisions. This article seeks to problematize traditional parent involvement frameworks that silence the need for nondominant parents to actively resist school-based inequities.

THEORY

The theoretical lens through which this review was developed is an integration of perspectives focused on the moral purpose of achieving social justice and interrupting oppression and inequality in public education. Rawls (1971, 2001) considered social justice as "the first virtue of social institutions" (Rawls, 1971, p. 3) with fairness as the ultimate moral guide (Rawls, 2001). Critical race theory centers and strengthens this social justice perspective through explicit attention to race and racism (Howard & Reynolds, 2008), considering educational inequalities to be a "logical and predictable result of a racialized society" (Ladson-Billings & Tate, 1995, p. 47). In critical race theory, racism is viewed not as an individualized act but as a generalized manifestation of the ways in which race, class, privilege, and power are deeply ingrained and enacted in social institutions (Ladson-Billings & Tate, 1995; Watson & Bogotch, 2015).

Once racism is explicitly visible, all responsible citizens in a democracy must seek racial and social justice. Bakhtin (1993) emphasized the moral dialogue maintained by each individual with the world, and the impossibility of remaining neutral toward the moral and ethical demands of which we become aware. This would underscore, in the theory of Habermas, the importance of collective social negotiations through discourse that is transparent, accessible, and equally inclusive of all involved persons (Head, 2008). Such discourse is problematic in a racialized society because of the tendency of the dominant class to protect and maintain inequality of privilege and access to resources (Bakhtin, 1993; McKnight & Chandler, 2012; Trainor, 2010). This is often accomplished through constructs of discourse that make discriminatory stratifications appear natural and inevitable in social institutions (Bourdieu, 1991; Fennimore, 2000; MacKinnon, 1992). Critical race theory recognizes discriminatory and racist constructs of discourse, which are often couched in claims of neutrality and colorblindness (Ladson-Billings & Tate, 1995). Thus, critical race theory calls for counterstorytelling that disrupts persistent rationalizations for unequal treatment of social groups (Howard, 2008, Ladson-Billings & Tate, 1995).

TRADITIONAL PARENT INVOLVEMENT, POLICY, AND BARRIERS TO PARENT INVOLVEMENT

This section will focus on the frequently silenced hypocritical barriers and exclusions faced by nondominant parents in traditional approaches to parent involvement. Extensive parent involvement research points to evidence linking it to positive educational outcomes (Baquedano-Lopez et al., 2013; Epstein, 2005; Olivos, 2004; Martinez-Cosio, 2010). A focus on parent involvement has concurrently evolved as important in educational policy and legislation. The Head Start federally funded preschool program emphasized parent involvement as a central construct from its start in 1965 (Duch, 2005). Legislative emphasis on parent involvement is reflected in the reauthorization of the Individuals with Disabilities Act (Stanley, 2015), which maintains the expectations of parents in participatory partnerships with schools. No Child Left Behind indicated a policy shift with its expanded view of the engagement of parents from diverse backgrounds (Baquedano-Lopez et al., 2013). The Every

Child Succeeds Act further stresses inclusive, collaborative engagement with all families (Lectura Books, 2015).

Silencing Race and Poverty

Legislative and policy initiatives focus on parent involvement for improved academic achievement of their children, but policy rhetoric tends to ignore not only income inequality but the cuts in funding and lack of school resources that place extra burdens on low-income families. This creates a commonsense approach to parent involvement that shifts a critical lens away from poverty and social injustice and makes it easier to blame unequal school outcomes on uninvolved parents (Kainz & Aikens, 2007). I argue that this unfair blaming of families in the context of unequal schools constitutes a significant educational hypocrisy. Added to this hypocrisy is the commonly heard phrase that "parents are the first teachers," which serves to further shift the blame for unequal school outcomes onto families. In truth, it is educational professionals who are the "first teachers" because only they have bordered professional expertise designated by public certification and guided by established codes of ethics. Parents are carrying widely generalized and undefined responsibilities that fall outside the realm of professionalism and are often undermined by a lack of access to adequate resources (Fennimore, 2016).

Barriers to traditional parent involvement often overlooked in the literature are entry requirements for fingerprinting, child abuse clearances, and criminal clearances in many school districts. Combined with language differences and current U.S. immigration policies and practices, these requirements can restrict the participation of many parents in schools (Olivos & Mendoza, 2009). Parents who are recent immigrants may also be challenged by lack of knowledge of the school culture, feelings of inadequacy, and an all-consuming focus on provision for the family (Cline & Necochea, 2001; Quin & Han, 2014). Teachers may expect them to "step up and be parents" (Wassell, Hawrylak, & Scantlebury, 2015, p. 13) in terms of traditional involvement when hours of necessary employment make them unavailable to their children.

Lack of access to technology is a significant barrier in an era when privileged parent involvement includes Facebook, Twitter, e-mail, and online petitions (Blumenreich & Jaffe-Walter, 2015, Yoder & Lopez, 2013). Cultural misunderstandings may arise when schools accustomed to the individualistic concerns of privileged parents encounter collective or relational forms of participation in nondominant groups (Warren et al., 2009). For example, Cooper (2009) explored the unique qualities of "Black womanist identities" linked to African American gendered parent activism characterized by collective uplifting of the group, care, and resistance to historic and present inequality.

The hegemonic, socially dominant approach to parent involvement falters in the inner political workings of the current decline in support for public education. Fine (1993) notes the irony that "parents are being promiscuously invited into the now deficit-ridden sphere of public education . . . 'as if' this were a power-neutral partnership" (p. 682). In truth, as Noguera (2004) argues, public education reflects the current fracture in our civil society more than any other sector in the United States.

Schools have become the "battleground over cultural, social, and political debates about visions for America" (Kretchmar, 2014, p. 22). It is within this highly contentious social, economic, political, and cultural backdrop that nondominant parents must now step forward as activists to challenge educational hypocrisies and work for school reform.

Parent Involvement as Activism for Equal Opportunity

Inequitable school and social hierarchies have not deterred nondominant parents from the struggle to resist inequalities created by dominant power groups in schools (Abrams & Gibbs, 2002). Such parent activism can be defined as "efforts of caregivers to promote, advocate, mobilize, or direct social, political, or institutional change in schools . . . an expression of public engagement at the grassroots level" (Jasis, 2013, p. 114). This activism is often contentious and controversial; nondominant parents face an uphill battle when they defy the deficit views that school administrators hold, challenge traditional conceptions of parent involvement, and fight for their rights.

Historic models of nondominant parent activism include the 1958 Harlem School Boycott during which parents who were motivated by "shared and individual histories of racial discrimination, gender, inequality, and economic discrimination" (Back, 2003, p. 66) demonstrated organizational savvy and left the enduring legacy of "powerful affirmation of a parent's right to confront the educational bureaucracy over perceived inequalities" (de Forest, 2008, p. 39). The conflict and tension these parents experienced in their boycott of their children's assignment to segregated schools in New York City was eventually vindicated by the decision of Judge Justine Polier who argued that the segregated schools were inferior (Back, 2003). Ten years later, in 1968, parents rose up in the Brooklyn Ocean Hill–Brownsville era of experimental community control to call for more Black and Hispanic teachers and more control over personnel, curriculum, and school finances (Song-Ha Lee, 2014). These models of powerful resistance enacted by minoritized parents took place during the Civil Rights era, a time when egregious legally sanctioned forms of racism were documented and resisted. Courageous forms of public protest during that era were highly contentious but, through constant media exposure, they had become something of a social norm.

In current society, however, we encounter what Dryness (2011) has described as "the era of good intentions" (p. 37) in which unequal treatment of groups may be less evident than it was in the Jim Crow era. Racism and related injustices are now deeply embedded in complex social and legal constructs such as court decisions that ignore apartheid schools and eliminate race from legal equations. Privileged groups have a sense of comfort in their "good intentions," which serve as vehicles for "benevolence or passivity" (p. 37).

Nondominant parents who engage in protest against current injustices tend to fall into the disfavor of those who see themselves as well-meaning but deny the relationship between racism, classism, and school exclusions (Dryness, 2011). The nondominant parents who ask questions, demand answers, and challenge current school programs and policies are made to feel unwelcome (Abrams & Gibbs, 2002) in direct contrast to the privileged parents whose demands for superior school resources tend to be well received (Wells & Serna, 1996). Pollock (2008) describes the current situation as a new civil rights era in which parents who raise issues of racism and discrimination are discounted or rebuffed.

Biased school-based assumptions that nondominant parents lack interest in the schooling of their children are rarely based on the voices of parents themselves.

Parents who have experienced marginalization because of their race, social class, language, or immigrant status have a rich critique of the structures of inequality that disadvantage their children but they are seldom invited to express or act on this critique. (Dryness, 2011, p. 36)

Qualitative research documents the gaps between parent awareness of inequalities and the lack of receptiveness to subsequent activism on the part of schools. When the voices of nondominant parents are raised, their "critique is censored, silenced, or condemned" (Dryness, p. 36). Lareau and Horvat (1999), in a study of the ways in which the social capital of nondominant parents was activated in schools, noted the preference of teachers for positive and deferential behaviors. The African American parents who voiced racism-based school critique experienced what the researchers termed "dismissive events" and "moments of exclusion" (p. 38). Similarly, Stanley (2015) studied African American rural mothers of children with disabilities who initially organized as advocates but became frustrated when their concerns were neither heard nor validated by the educators they considered to be experts. Luet's (2016) 3-year qualitative study of the navigational and aspirational capital (Yosso, 2005) of economically stressed parents documented creative familial interactions with school staff outside the formally established venues. These were obscured by a constant discourse of parent disengagement—a paralysis created by blaming parents and reframing systemic educational problems as parental failures. Greene (2013) also studied ways in which nondominant parents constructed extraordinary supporting roles that often extended outside the borders of what the school considered to be involvement; his analysis revealed the ways in which schools neglected to consider their voices and perspectives.

In spite of the considerable challenges that exist, nondominant parents persist against the odds as advocates and activists. Martinez-Cosio (2010) documented ways in which Latino and African American parents developed activist competencies and "strategies . . . within the space of possibility" (p. 284) even while impeded by structural barriers within the school. Lareau and Horvat (1999) also documented voices of African American parents who were able to successfully counter teacher resistance to elevate awareness of patterns of injustice. They protested, for example, the far greater emphasis on Halloween in the school than on Dr. Martin Luther King's birthday. In a related case study (Wallace, 2013), the efforts of a group of African American high school parents who banded together to create new resources for a parent-run academic enrichment center and other student resources were not considered legitimate by teachers in the building. In spite of roadblocks, the parents successfully developed stronger support systems for themselves and the students through their initiatives. Jasis and Marriott (2010) completed an ethnographic analysis of the process of parent actualization within a community-based adult education program, *Project Avanzando*, constructed for a particularly underserved group of migrant and seasonal farmworkers. The growth of the parents was later connected to engagement and activism in their children's school. Ishimaru's (2014b) related ethnographic case study examined a collaboration that evolved within a low-income Latino parent organizing group that "actively validated the parents' own way of knowing, engaged them in active learning from one another, and improved their capacity to advocate for themselves and their children" (p. 198). These studies make visible the desire and ability of nondominant parents to counter hegemonic processes to advocate for their children but also document the ways in which they are undermined through school-based constructs of their generalized deficiencies.

HYPOCRISIES IN SCHOOL RESPONSES TO PARENTAL ACTIVISM FOR EQUALITY

This section focuses on the escalating tensions that arise when involved parents are involved in challenging hypocritical school-based claims of equity. Efforts of nondominant parents to gain equal resources for their children have long existed in educational history. Siddle Walker (2000) documents African American parents in segregated southern schools in the 1950s who were activists and advocates seeking better educational opportunities for their children. This trend continued in Head Start in the 1960s, which focused on parent involvement that included decision making and social activism (Lubeck & deVries, 2000) helping parents "develop an alternative power structure" that might challenge future discriminatory educational institutions (Ziegler & Muenchow, 1992). The strengthened focus of Every Child Succeeds Act (2015) on family engagement includes advocacy and activism for new learning opportunities for their children (Lectura Books, 2015). However promising this legislative focus may be, little is currently known about the actual implementation of federal policy initiatives or the grassroots organizing of nondominant parents in individual school districts with a pattern of rebuffing their critique (Auerbach, 2007; Jasis, 2013; Martinez-Cosio, 2010).

The activism of nondominant parents requires negotiation with institutional scripts (Ishimaru, 2014a) that demean minoritized parents and privilege the upper middle–class parents who use their social assets to secure superior advantages for their own (Wells & Oakes, 1996). Nondominant parents who assume the expected subordinate position of accepting the prescriptions and decisions of school-based educators (Valdes, 1996) will not be able to confront the discriminations that undermine the access of their children to an equal educational opportunity. Yet "parents are not usually welcomed, by schools, to the critical and serious work of rethinking educational structures and practices" (Fine, 1993, p. 682). In fact, parents who challenge the hypocrisy of discriminatory scripts may need to engage in a contentious level of resistance met with attempts of schools (and their coopted traditional parent groups) to discredit their efforts (Medeiratta & Fruchter, 2003).

Emergent activist parent roles often begin in traditional involvement that awaken parents to structural inequalities of which they were unaware (Ishimaru, 2014b;

Warren et al., 2009). As parents observe school practices, they may become suspicious, lose confidence in the school, and revert to activism as a way to reverse underrepresentation of culturally diverse students in school programs such as classes offering higher levels of math and science instruction (Abrams & Gibbs, 2002) and preparation for college admissions (Auerbach, 2007). Arriaza (2004) studied a confluence of a few parents defined by the school in deficit terms who became aware of their rights. They were able to awaken other parents to their rights as well; one parent who had been told that she was not allowed to view her child's school record demanded and viewed it after discovering that she had a right to do so.

Schools Undermine Parental Activism

It is when nondominant parents resist and speak out that obstructionist school behaviors become visible. Harry, Klingner, and Hart (2005), studied the discrepancy between the negative stereotyping of African American families by school personnel and actual parent competencies in activism for their children in special education. Through 272 audiotaped interviews and observations of parent–school meetings, the researchers documented rudeness, sarcasm, deficit language, and unethical treatment on the part of school personnel. In a related study of parent advocacy for children with significant disabilities, Nespor and Hicks (2010) documented district efforts to discredit (through "tales of witchcraft") the parent activists who transcended boundaries of pseudoparticipation to engage in ". . . collective action in an institutional climate uniquely constructed to forestall it" (p. 309).

Ishimaru (2014b) also documented a hostile school environment encountered by low-income Latino parents in a new-destination immigrant community; they were nonetheless able to collaborate with the district in some ways that changed the existing school script about their families and children. Another group of parents (Cline & Necochea, 2001) were ignored when they complained to the district about inadequate resources for bilingual children; their persistent tenacity was later resisted by school leaders. Likewise, Dryness (2011), in participant activist research enhanced by her bilingualism, documented disturbing signs of the betrayal of activist parents from a Hispanic community through misleading information, overturned decisions, and broken promises that had originally been made to the parents. In my participatory parent-activist study of a small group that challenged a discriminatory and inequitable gifted program in a large urban area (Fennimore, 1996, 1997, 2005), I documented efforts on the part of the school district to ignore the parent activists, misrepresent information, deny concerns, alter published school board testimony, malign the motives of the parent-resisters, and incite angry counteractivism in parents of children in the gifted program.

The Transformational Process of Parent Activism

While there can be little doubt that the impact of nondominant parent critique is weakened by biased school-based responses, the transformational process of engaging in civically responsible activism can be a significant personal gain in and of itself. Olivos (2004) integrated his own parent activist narrative into a study of the development of political consciousness in parents. Their initial collaboration with school officials was positive but later became oppositional. As the parents experienced tension and resistance, they were transformed in their own sense of participatory power. The "parents were driven by democratic issues of social justice and equity, compelling them to continue their fight in spite of a lack of respect and disdain" (Jasis and Ordonea-Jasis, p. 90). Transformative experiences were also documented by Jasis and Ordonea-Jasis (2012) in their study of the *Tequio* (communal collective work) of a group of Latino immigrant families and by Dryness (2011) who documented ways in which a group of Latino mothers transformed critique of exclusionary school practices into catalyst for change. They transcended tension and resistance to call public attention to "exclusionary terms, practices, and politics" (p. 51) and to initiate a process of dialogue. The parents who transcended traditional involvement to organize for resistance and change experienced personal growth and were able in many cases to make a dent in the institutional scripts considering them to be uninvolved and deficient.

HYPOCRISIES EMBEDDED IN MARKET-BASED "SCHOOL CHOICE" FOR PARENTS

This section is focused on school-controlled "choices" that are said to improve education for all but instead increase inequity and social stratification in schools. School choice has become a catchword for the "neoliberal ideology in which . . . free markets provide society with the most efficient distribution of resources" (Hankins, 2005, p. 43). The concept of educational choice has deep roots in the "storm of controversy" raised by the Brown decision; White resistance to new integration policies was extraordinary (Schofield, 1991). The so-called "freedom of choice" policies in the post-Brown south were designed to retain the segregated status quo. School districts speciously provided registration forms on which Black and White parents could "choose" schools. White parents inevitably chose their White schools; Black parents who chose White schools faced threats, intimidation, and barriers to registration (Fennimore, 2005; Wells, 1993). Voucher-like programs were also created at this time to provide public financial support for White segregationist academies. Although both these strategies were eventually struck down in court (Gill, Timpane, Ross, & Brewer, 2001) the post-Brown educational climate remains fraught with political tension and resistance to the fair distribution of educational resources (Ladson-Billings, 2004; Orfield, 2014; Schofield, 1991).

Over 60 years after Mendez and Brown, racial segregation remains an intractable dilemma in the public schools of the United States and parent choice is now considered a salient factor affecting its persistence (Billingham & Hunt, 2016). Newer forms of colorblind market-based school choices, not constructed to promote racial integration, are correlated with increasing segregation (Rhoda & Wells, 2013). The presence of more charter schools and vouchers than any time in U.S. history has not made a noticeable difference in the performance or efficiency of public schools (Nieto, 2015). Although the words "parent choice" are common in educational discourses, "the mechanisms of choice create a hierarchical system of inequitable distribution that harms nondominant families when that choice does not contest neighborhood segregation, racialized tracking, or inequitable resource/opportunity provisions" (Baquedano-Lopez et al., 2013, p. 156).

School Choice Exacerbates Inequality

Considering the intractable nature of racial segregation to date, the relentless resistance to the equity mandates of Mendez and Brown, and the preponderance of barriers faced by nondominant parents in public schools, I consider any claims that neoliberal school choice is shaped to disrupt the results of centuries of discriminatory practices in public education in the United States (Trent, 1992) to represent a significant hypocrisy. My argument is based on the ways in which choice liberates dominant parents to become more openly manipulative and forceful in their demands for the superior educational resources to which they are accustomed, allows school districts to develop highly discrepant opportunities identified as choice but specifically targeted to elite White populations, and focuses inauthentic blame for poor school outcomes on the "choices" of nondominant parents who were unable to gain access to the best schools.

While support for choice has been documented in minoritized groups, this information is often based on surveys that do not document actual actions or outcomes (Teske & Schneider, 2001). Although some minoritized children have undoubtedly benefitted from school choice options, support for school choice in minoritized groups does not necessarily lead to fair access. White advantaged parents are always more likely to gain admission to the best schools (Rhoda & Wells, 2013). "The ability of individuals to participate in voluntary, privately managed choice . . . is contingent on having the social, cultural, and economic resources to do so (Hankins, 2005, p. 41). Pletz (2001) documents the case of an urban lottery-based magnet program combined with a regional selective gifted program so attractive that elite White parents purchased condominiums and townhouses in the neighborhood so they could send their children to the school.

In a climate where privileged parents are increasingly donating substantial personal funds to the schools their children attend (Posey-Maddox, McDonough, & Cucchiara, 2014), it is not surprising that cash-strapped districts cater to them in choice programs and admission policies. Dominant parents who choose public schools rather than the private schools they can afford are likely to demand forms of differentiation that separate their children from less advantaged populations. Today these demands are expressed not in overt terms of racism but couched in such "colorblind" concerns as nondominant children will have behavior problems and be less motivated toward academic excellence (Rhoda & Wells, 2013; Wells & Serna, 1996).

These elite parents use political and cultural capital to make their children appear more deserving of separate and unequal resources; strategies utilized include threatening flight and accepting district bribes as an assurance that their children will continue to get more than others (Andre-Bechely, 2013; Brantlinger, 2003; Wells & Oakes, 1996).

Schools Acquiesce to Dominant Parents

The nondominant parents who try to expose inequitable choice programs privileging dominant parents may face conflict and intimidation during subsequent public parent battles. For example, I documented in my parent-participant study the school-based resegregation of the Black children who had been transferred to a privileged white school during the desegregation era. Their oversized single class on each grade level was maintained separately from the two magnet classes on each grade level that enjoyed a small class size, additional curriculum, access to trips, and in-school festivals—all of which the resegregated children were aware and from which they were completely excluded. Confronted by a small group of parent activists from the resegregated classes, the embarrassed district first attempted to support its proposal that the entire school be unified in one inclusive program. However, district leaders soon backed down under well-organized pressure from the much larger group of privileged and furious magnet parents. The inequitable status quo was thus retained with a small temporary concession to the resegregated children, who were later quietly transferred back to a segregated school in their home community (Fennimore, 1997, 2005).

Choice weakens district responsibility for implementing equity mandates by allowing highly discrepant opportunities for different groups of children. In this climate, districts are able to manipulate or withhold registration information from undesired candidates or to create selective admission policies that include the right to expel children if they fail to meet academic or behavioral criteria (Fennimore, 1996). Cooper (2005), exploring the claim of critics that less privileged parents face defeat in competitive school markets, conducted interviews with low-income and working-class African American mothers about school choice. The mothers wanted a good education for their children and saw the limitations of low-performing public schools. However, some were unaware of the charter school concept and others had either not heard information about vouchers or knew that the vouchers were not sufficient to cover private school costs for their children.

While some education research suggests that poor and minoritized parents do not know how to navigate the complexity of choosing schools in a free market (DeLuca & Rosenblatt, 2010), my studies document nondominant parents who trusted the expertise of the schools and did not understand that new choice-based ground rules created winners and losers in program availability. In contrast, the elite parents were fully aware of the inequitable choice agendas and determined to take all necessary steps to win the fight for the best school resources for their own children (Fennimore, 1996, 1997, 2005).

Parent Conflict as Hypocritical Policy Strategy

Nondominant parents who have experienced conflict as advocates in their schools may now face escalated district-wide public contention with privileged parents over school choice. For example, nondominant parents who plan to challenge unequal access to popular choice programs at a school board meeting may find themselves greatly outnumbered at the meeting by the dominant parents in the programs under question. School board requirements for advance registration of testimony and topic provides district leaders with the opportunity to alert opposing parents. When this occurs, school districts can strategically sidestep their own responsibility for constructing equal education for all by pitting parents against parents in the fight over choice-based inequalities that should not exist in the first place (Pappas, 2012; Rhoda & Wells, 2013). Also, as privatization creates competing financial interests, parents may be used as "pawns" and "puppets" in charter school deliberations (Marsh, Strunk, Bush-Mecenas, & Huguet, 2015). Current efforts to mobilize low-income parents to support competing market agendas can be misleading and may ultimately lead to programs from which the parents are excluded (McAlister & Catone, 2013). Although the Brown and Mendez decisions created constitutional protections for nondominant parents who fight for their educational rights, these have been steadily eliminated by the courts. There is now danger that the intentions of equal educational opportunity are increasingly blurred and diluted in neoliberal choice markets.

THE CALL FOR RESPONSIBLE RESEARCH ON PARENT INVOLVEMENT

This chapter focused on the power of nondominant parents to expose and challenge educational hypocrisies. It has documented ways in which minoritized parents strengthened their determination to challenge inequalities and deficit scripts in public schools. However, it has also documented the ways in which schools their children attend resisted their efforts. Furthermore, the review has examined ways in which the complex systemic structures supported by neoliberal market strategies in public education have strengthened the dominance of elite parents.

New related frontiers, such as increasing urban gentrification and the entry of upper-middle class parents into predominantly low-income neighborhood schools, are exacerbating new inequalities. A critical mass of dominant parents in a newly gentrified area can seek to improve a local public school for their own children in ways that exclude the interests of the low-income children still in attendance. Elite parents are increasingly making significant financial donations to the public schools their children attend; in return, they expect to direct those donations toward initiatives targeted for selected classes and activities (Posey-Maddox et al., 2014). In the context of new as well as long-standing inequalities, I believe that education researchers must recognize the urgent need for their participation in a movement to rearticulate commitment to the mandates of Brown and Mendez and confront the forces that increasingly undermine the promise of democratic schooling in the United States.

Interrupting Hypocrisy Through Research on Parental Activism

I believe that escalated study of nondominant parent advocates and activists holds promise for research that interrupts educational hypocrisies undermining equity. The important first step for committed researchers is a rigorous self-examination of personal, educational, or political bias that affects their assumptions about the population of nondominant parents under study. Critical race theory essentializes acknowledgment that racism is always present in society. Researchers must thus accept responsibility to "make it as visible and open to scrutiny as possible" (Greene & Abt-Perkins, 2003). Perhaps a more sensitive and difficult critical analysis must be applied to the conflict of interest that can exist when researchers claim to seek more equal educational opportunities for marginalized children while rationalizing (and possibly benefitting from) privileges provided for the elite in a deeply unequal system of public education.

As stated at the outset of this article, my approach to parent involvement is informed by the assertion of Ron Edmonds (1979) that political activism on the part of nondominant parents is needed to derail the school-based scripts of deficiency and bring about true educational reform. Admittedly, Edmonds (1979) was highly skeptical of education research:

Schools teach those they think they must, and when they think they needn't they don't. This has nothing to do with social science, except that the children of social scientists are among those that the schools feel compelled to teach effectively. (p. 16)

Edmonds's research, which was controversial, incites a fundamental question: Are the researchers who are often among the educationally privileged willing and able to challenge unequal schools in solidarity with the educationally underserved?

I would argue that such resistance to inequality is eminently possible for education researchers because they study "human attributes, interactions, organizations, and institutions that shape educational outcomes" (American Educational Research Association, n.d.). Such research thus can enable them to critique the social and political forces underlying the historic pattern of social science research "confirming" the deficiencies of nondominant families. By joining forces with parents and communities, qualitative researchers can be "worthy witnesses" who humanize research on those historically and presently oppressed with racist and classist social science constructions of inferiority (Paris & Winn, 2014).

The Need for Ethical and Humane Research

Activist research with nondominant parents is supported by the American Educational Research Association (2011) Code of Ethics particularly in terms of *nondiscrimination* and *conflict of interest*. The racialized misalignments between nondominant families and education researchers, where they are in evidence, must be vigorously addressed through critical analysis of the ways in which deficit discourse about nondominant families in education research literature empowers and validates dismissive practices in schools. Such discourse ignores existing research documenting the commitment of nondominant families to the educational welfare of their children. Furthermore, it ignores the very different ways in which the attempted involvement of nondominant parents may be enacted and received in schools.

I pose that activist-participant-observer paradigms offer resolution to issues of discrimination and conflict of interest in research on nondominant family involvement. Through such paradigms, researchers share the experience of school-based resistance and dismissal faced by parents who are struggling for their educational rights. In partnership with parents, they can encourage them to "enter into discourses of power, (re) frame their experiences, and challenge the ways in which social science research has historically excluded and denigrated them" (Irizarry & Brown, 2014, p. 65).

Furthermore, participant-activist research provides the opportunity for researchers to share information on educational rights and support parents as they use their own experience and cultural knowledge (Yosso, 2005) at effective points of intersection with educators, administrators, and school boards (Hoover-Dempsey & Sandler, 1995; Jasis & Ordana-Jasis, 2012; Lareau & Munoz, 2012; Matthews & Hastings, 2013). Working together, researchers and nondominant parents can move conceptualizations of parent involvement and engagement to a new level—one which recognizes the challenges faced by nondominant parents in an inequitable school system and encourages advocacy and activism as an essential component of engagement with schools.

Such studies might, for example, focus on the localized school district responses to grassroots parent activism related to specific mandates of state or federal equity–based legislation. Education researchers can thus document the work of parents seeking to break silences that hide inequalities, denaturalize practices that appear natural or inevitable, and build a vision of what is possible (Fine, 1994)—even for those for whom the struggle is most daunting. Education research does have the power to disrupt inequalities, expose hypocritical educational practices, document inauthenticity in school choice, and interrupt the unjust dominance of parent-elites.

Kretchmar (2014), in his critical analysis of parent testimony over school closings in a large urban area, documented the ways in which parents challenged the school administration in terms of inconsistent information, misinformation, and ways in which the financial interests of charter schools were influencing district decisions. At the end of his study, he noted not only the ways in which the voices of parents were ignored but also the absence of participation of academics in the volatile district conflict.

Given that these (parent) voices go unheard, and given that many academics profess commitments about social justice, equity, and democracy, we cannot let communities stand alone. Academics must raise our voices in solidarity. We must demand that the arguments of parents . . . are heard. (Kretchmar, 2014, p. 24)

Education researchers who join collaboratively with nondominant parent activists to resist existing hypocrisies can contribute to progress in the construction of equal educational opportunity while strengthening their own democratic scholarly agendas. Furthermore, they can raise awareness and concern in the academy and in society at large about the continuing struggle for educational and civil rights and the critical role that nondominant parents and communities can play in strengthening equity and justice in public education.

ACKNOWLEDGMENTS

The author extends gratitude to Kelsey Darity, doctoral student at Teachers College, Columbia University, for her outstanding research assistance. Further gratitude is extended to Marvin Fein, Laurie Nicholson, and Beth Wassell for their helpful comments on earlier versions of this chapter.

REFERENCES

Abrams, L. S., & Gibbs, J. T. (2002). Disrupting the logic of home-school relations: Parent involvement strategies and practices of inclusion and exclusion. *Urban Education, 37*, 384–407.

American Educational Research Association. (n.d.). *What is education research?* Retrieved from http://www.aera.net/About-AERA/What-is-Education-Research

American Educational Research Association. (2011). AERA code of ethics. *Educational Researcher, 40*, 145–156.

Andre-Bechely, A. (2013). *Could it be otherwise? Parents and the inequalities of school choice.* New York, NY: Routledge.

Arriaza, G. (2004). Making changes that stay made: School reform and community involvement. *High School Journal, 87*(4), 10–24.

Auerbach, S. (2007). From moral supporters to struggling advocates: Reconceptualizing parent roles in education through the experience of working-class families of color. *Urban Education, 42*, 250–283.

Back, A. (2003). Exposing the "whole segregation myth": The Harlem Nine and New York City's school desegregation battles. In J. F. Theoharis, & K. Woodard (Eds.), *Freedom north: Black freedom struggles outside the south 1940–1980* (pp. 65–91). Gordonsville, VA: Palgrave Macmillan.

Bakhtin, M. M. (1993). *Toward a philosophy of the act.* Austin, TX: Austin University Press.

Baquedano-Lopez, P., Alexander, R. A., & Hernandez, S. (2013). Equity issues in parental and community involvement in schools: What teacher educators need to know. *Review of Research in Education, 37*, 149–182.

Billingham, C. M., & Hunt, M. O. (2016). School racial composition and parental choice: New evidence on the preferences of White parents in the United States. *Sociology of Education, 89*(2), 99–117.

Blumenreich, M., & Jaffe-Walter, R. (2015). Social media illuminates: Some truths about school reform. *Phi Delta Kappan, 97*, 25–28.

Bourdieu, P. (1991). *Language and symbolic power.* Cambridge, MA: Harvard University Press.

Brantlinger, E. (2003). *How the middle class negotiates and rationalizes school advantage.* New York, NY: Routledge.

Chase, M. M., Dowd, A. C., Pazich, L. B., & Bensimon, E. (2014). Transfer equity for "minoritized" students: A critical policy analysis of seven states. *Educational Policy, 28*, 669–717.

Cline, Z., & Necochea, J. (2001). !Basta Ya! Latino parents fighting entrenched racism. *Bilingual Research Journal, 25*(1–2), 89–114.

Comer, J. P., & Haynes, N. M. (1991). Parent involvement in schools: An ecological approach. *Elementary School Journal, 91*, 271–277.

Cooper, C. W. (2005). School choice and the standpoint of African American mothers: Considering the power of positionality. *Journal of Negro Education, 74*, 174–189.

Cooper, C. W. (2009). Parent involvement, African American mothers, and the politics of educational care. *Equity & Excellence in Education, 42*, 379–394.

de Forest, J. (2008). The 1958 Harlem school boycott: Parental activism and the struggle for educational equity in New York City. *Urban Review, 40*, 21–41. doi:10.1007/s11256-007-0075-5

Delgado-Gaitan, C. (1991). Involving parents in the schools: A process of empowerment. *American Journal of Education, 100*, 20–46.

DeLuca, S., & Rosenblatt, P. (2010). Does moving to better neighborhoods lead to better schooling opportunities? Parental school choice in an experimental housing voucher program. *Teachers College Record, 112*, 1443–1491.

Deresiewicz, W. (2015). *Excellent sheep: The miseducation of the American elite and the way to a meaningful life*. New York, NY: Free Press.

Dryness, A. (2011). Cultural exclusion and critique in the era of good intentions: Using participatory research to transform parent roles in urban school reform. *Social Justice, 36*(4), 36–53.

Duch, H. (2005). Redefining parent involvement in Head Start: A two generation approach. *Early Childhood Development and Care, 175*, 23–35.

Edmonds, R. (1979). Effective schools for the urban poor. *Educational Leadership, 31*, 15–23.

Epstein, J. L. (1992). School and family partnerships. In M. Alkin (Ed.), *Encyclopedia of educational research* (pp. 1139–1151), New York, NY: Macmillan.

Epstein, J. L. (1995). School/family/community partnerships: Caring for the children we share. *Phi Delta Kappan, 76*, 701–712.

Epstein, J. L. (2005) Attainable goals? The spirit and letter of the No Child Left Behind Act on parental involvement. *Sociology of Education, 78*, 179–182.

Fennimore, B. S. (1996). Equity is not an option in public education. *Educational Leadership, 54*, 53–55.

Fennimore, B. S. (1997). When mediation and equity are at odds: Potential lessons in democracy. *Theory Into Practice, 1*, 59–64.

Fennimore, B. S. (2000). *Talk matters: Refocusing the language of public schooling*. New York, NY: Teachers College Press.

Fennimore, B. S. (2005). Brown and the failure of civic responsibility. *Teachers College Record, 107*, 1905–1932.

Fennimore, B. S. (2016). A social justice approach to families. In L. J. Couse, & S. L. Recchia (Eds.), *Handbook of early childhood teacher education* (pp. 304–316). New York, NY: Routledge.

Fine, M. (1993). [Ap]parent Involvement: Reflections on parents, power, and urban public schools and responses. *Teachers College Record, 94*, 682–729.

Fine, M. (1994). Dis-stance and other stances: Negotiations of power inside feminist research. In A. Gitlin (Ed.), *Power and method: Political activism and educational research* (pp. 13–35). London, England: Routledge.

Genishi, C., & Dyson, A. H. (2009). *Children, language, and diversity: Diverse learners in diverse times*. New York, NY: Teachers College Press.

Gill, B. P., Timpane, P. M., Ross, K., & Brewer, D. J. (2001). *Rhetoric versus reality: What we know and what we need to know about vouchers and charter schools*. Santa Monica, CA: Rand Corporation.

Grau, E. (2005). Theorizing and describing preservice teachers' images of families and schooling. *Teachers College Record, 907*, 157–185.

Greene, S. (2013). Mapping low-income African American Parents' roles in their children's education in a changing political economy. *Teachers College Record, 15*(10), 1–33.

Greene, S., & Abt-Perkins, D. (2003). How can literacy research contribute to racial understanding. In S. Greene, & D. Abt-Perkins (Eds.), *Making race visible: Literacy research for cultural understanding* (pp. 1–31). New York, NY: Teachers College Press.

Hankins, K. B. (2005). Practicing citizenship in new spaces: Rights and realities of charter school activism. *Space and Polity, 9*, 41–60.

Harry, B., Klingner, J. K., & Hart, J. (2005). African American families under fire. *Remedial and Special Education, 26*, 101–112.

Head, N. (2008). Critical theory and its practices: Habermas, Kosovo, and international relations. *Politics, 23*, 150–159.

Hoover-Dempsey, K. V., & Sandler, H. M. (1995). Parental involvement in children's education: Why does it make a difference? *Teachers College Record, 97*, 310–331.

Howard, T. C. (2008). Who really cares? The disenfranchisement of African American males in PreK-12 schools: A critical race theory perspective. *Teachers College Record, 110*, 954–985.

Howard, T. C., & Reynolds, R. (2008). Examining parent involvement in reversing underachievement of African American Students in middle class schools. *Educational Foundations, 22*, 79–88.

Hummel, D. (2012). Principles over prejudice: Social dominance theory and the mosques' controversy in American cities. *Journal of Muslim Minority Affairs, 32*, 32–46.

Hunt, J. M. (1968). Environment, development and scholastic achievement. In M. Deutsch, I. Katz, & A. R. Jensen (Eds.), *Social class, race, and psychological development* (pp. 293–336). New York, NY: Holt, Rinehart & Winston.

Irizarry, J. G., & Brown, T. M. (2014). Humanizing research in dehumanizing spaces: The challenges and opportunities of conducting research with youth in schools. In D. Paris, & M. T. Winn (Eds.), *Humanizing research: Decolonizing qualitative inquiry with youth and communities* (pp. 63–80). Thousand Oaks, CA: SAGE.

Ishimaru, A. M. (2014a). Rewriting the rules of engagement: Elaborating a model of district-community collaboration. *Harvard Educational Review, 84*, 188–216.

Ishimaru, A. M. (2014b). When new relationships meet old narratives: The journey towards improving parent-school relations in a district-community organizing collaboration. *Teachers College Record, 116*(2). Retrieved from http://www.tcrecord.org/library/abstract.asp?contentid=17350

Jasis, P. (2013). Latino families challenging exclusion in a middle school: A story from the trenches. *School Community Journal, 23*, 111–130.

Jasis, P. M., & Ordonea-Jasis, R. (2012) Latino parent involvement: Examining commitment and empowerment in schools. *Urban Education, 47*, 65–89.

Jasis, P., & Marriott, D. (2010). All for our children: Migrant families and parent participation in an alternative education program. *Journal of Latinos and Education, 9*, 126–140.

Jensen, A. R. (1969). How much can we boost IQ and scholastic achievement? *Harvard Educational Review, 39*, 1–123.

Kainz, K., & Aikens, N. L. (2007). Governing the family throughout education: A genealogy on the home-school relation. *Equity & Excellence in Education, 40*, 301–310. doi:10.1080/10665680701610721

Kretchmar, K. (2014). Democracy (in) action: A critical policy analysis of New York City public school closings by teachers, students, administrators, and community members. *Education and Urban Society, 46*, 3–29.

Ladson-Billings, G. (2004). Landing on the wrong note: The price we paid for Brown. *Educational Researcher, 33*(7), 3–13.

Ladson-Billings, G., & Tate, W. F. (1995). Toward a critical race theory of education. *Teachers College Record, 97*, 47–68.

Lareau, A., & Horvat, E. M. (1999). Moments of social inclusion and exclusion: Race, class, and cultural capital in family-school relationships. *Sociology of Education, 72*, 37–53.

Lareau, A., & Munoz, V. L. (2012). "You're not going to call the shots": Structural conflicts between the principal and the PTO at a suburban public elementary school. *Sociology of Education, 85*, 201–218. doi:10.1177/00380407114435855

Lectura Books. (2015). *The Latino Family Literacy Project Parent Involvement and the new Every Child Succeeds Act (ESSA)*. Retrieved from http://www.latinoliteracy.com/12915-2/

Lopez, G. R. (2001). The value of hard work: Lessons on parent involvement from an (im)migrant household. *Harvard Educational Review, 71*, 416–437.

Lubeck, S., & deVries, M. (2000). The social construction of parent involvement in Head Start. *Early Education and Development, 11*, 633–658.

Luet, K. M. (2016). Disengaging parents in urban schooling. *Educational Policy*. Advance online publication. doi:10.1177/0895904815616481

MacKinnon, C. A. (1992). *Only words*. Cambridge, MA: Harvard University Press.

Marsh, J. A., Strunk, K. O., Bush-Mecenas, S. C., & Huguet, A. (2015). Democratic engagement in district reform: The evolving role of parents in the Los Angeles public school choice initiative. *Educational Policy, 29*, 51–84.

Martinez-Cosio, M. (2010). Parents' roles in mediating and buffering the implementation of an urban school reform. *Education and Urban Society, 42*, 283–306.

Matthews, P., & Hastings, A. (2013). Middle-class political activism and middle-class advantage in relation to public services: A realist synthesis of the evidence base. *Social Policy & Administration, 47*, 72–92.

McAlister, S., & Catone, K. C. (2013). Real parent power: Relational organizing for sustainable school reform. *National Civic Review, 102*, 26–32.

McKnight, D., & Chandler, P. (2012). The complicated conversation of class and race in social and curricular analysis: An examination of Pierre Bourdieu's interpretive framework in relation to race. *Educational Philosophy and Theory, 44*(1), 74–97.

Medeiratta, K., & Fruchter, N. (2003). *From governance to accountability: Building relationships that make schools work*. New York, NY: Drum Major Institute for Public Policy.

Nespor, J., & Hicks, D. (2010). Wizards and witches: Parent advocates and contention in special education in the USA. *Journal of Education Policy, 25*, 309–334.

Nieto, S. (Ed.). (2015). *Why we teach now*. New York, NY: Teachers College Press.

Noguera, P. (2004). Racial isolation, poverty, and the limits of local control in Oakland. *Teachers College Record, 106*, 2146–2170.

Olivos, E. M. (2004). Tensions, contradictions, and resistance: An activist's reflection on the struggles of Latino parents in the public school system. *High School Journal, 87*(4), 25–36.

Olivos, E. M., & Mendoza, M. (2009). Immigration and educational inequity: An examination of Latino immigrant parents' inclusion in the public school context. *Journal of Latino/Latin American Studies, 3*(3), 38–53.

Orfield, G. (2014). Tenth Brown lecture in educational research a new civil rights agenda. *Educational Researcher, 43*, 273–292.

Pappas, L. N. (2012). School closings and parent engagement. *Peace and Conflict, 18*, 165–172.

Paris, D., & Winn, M. T. (2014). Preface: To humanize research. In D. Paris, & M. T. Winn (Eds.), *Humanizing research: Decolonizing qualitative inquiry with youth and communities* (pp. xiii-xx). Thousand Oaks, CA: SAGE.

Pletz, J. (2001). Huge impact and dramatic results when parents get involved in schools. *Crain's Chicago Business, 35*, 0008.

Pollock, M. (2008) *Because of race: How Americans debate harm and opportunity in our schools*. Princeton, NJ: University of Princeton Press.

Posey-Maddox, L. (2013). Professionalizing the PTO: Race, class, and shifting norms of parental engagement in a city public school. *American Journal of Education, 119*, 235–260.

Posey-Maddox, L., McDonough, S., & Cucchiara, M. (2014). Middle class parents and urban public schools: Current research and future directions. *Sociology Compass, 8,* 446–456.

Pratto, F., & Stewart, A. L. (2012). Group dominance and the half-blindness of privilege. *Journal of Social Issues, 68,* 28–45.

Quin, D. B., & Han, E. J. (2014). Tiger parents or sheep parents: Struggles of Parental involvement in working-class Chinese immigrant families. *Teachers College Record, 116*(8), 1–32.

Rawls, J. (1971). *A theory of justice.* Cambridge, MA: Harvard University Press.

Rawls, J. (2001). *Justice as fairness: A restatement.* Cambridge, MA: Belknap Press of Harvard University Press.

Reissman, F. (1962). *The culturally deprived child.* New York, NY: Harper.

Rhoda, A., & Wells, A. S. (2013). School choice policies and racial segregation: Where White parents' good intentions, anxiety, and privilege collide. *American Journal of Education, 119,* 261–293.

Rothstein, R. (2004). *Class and schools: Using social, economic, and education reform to close the black-white achievement gap.* New York, NY: Economic Policy Institute and Teachers College.

Schofield, J. (1991). School desegregation and intergroup relations: A review of the literature. *Review of Research in Education, 17,* 335–409.

Siddle Walker, V. (2000). *Their highest potential: An African American school community in the segregated south.* Chapel Hill: University of North Carolina Press.

Song-Ha Lee, S (2014). *Building a Latino civil rights movement: Puerto Ricans, African Americans, and the pursuit of racial justice in New York City.* Chapel Hill: University of North Carolina Press.

Souto-Manning, M., & Swick, K. J. (2006). Teachers' beliefs about parent and family involvement: Rethinking our family involvement paradigm. *Early Childhood Education Journal, 34,* 187–193.

Stanley, S. L. G. (2015). The advocacy efforts of African American mothers of children with disabilities in rural special education: Considerations for school professionals. *Rural Special Education Quarterly, 34*(4), 3–17.

Strum, P. (2010). *Mendez v. Westminster: School desegregation and Mexican American rights.* Lawrence: University of Kansas Press.

Teske, P., & Schneider, M. (2001). What research can tell policymakers about school choice. *Journal of Policy Analysis and Management, 20,* 609–631.

Trainor, A. A. (2010). Diverse approaches to parent advocacy during special education home-school interactions: Identification and use of cultural and social capital. *Remedial and Special Education, 31,* 34–47.

Trent, S. C. (1992). School choice for African-American children who live in poverty: A commitment to equity or more of the same? *Urban Education, 27,* 291–307.

Valdes, G. (1996). *Con Respecto: Bridging the distances between culturally diverse families and schools.* New York, NY: Teachers College Press.

Wallace, M. (2013). High school teachers and African American parents: A (not so) collaborative effort to increase student success. *High School Journal, 96,* 195–208.

Warren, M. R., Hong, S., Rubin, C. L., & Uy, P. S. (2009). Beyond the bake sale: A community-based relational approach to parent engagement in schools. *Teachers College Record, 111,* 2209–2254.

Wassell, B., Hawrylak, M. F., & Scantlebury, K. (2015). Barriers, resources, frustrations, and empathy: Teachers' expectations for family involvement for Latino/a ELL students in urban STEM classrooms. *Urban Education.* Advance online publication. doi:10.1177/0042085915602539

Watson, T. L., & Bogotch, I. (2015). Reframing parent involvement: What should urban school leaders do differently? *Leadership and Policy in Schools, 14,* 257–258.

Wells, A. S. (1993). *Time to choose: America at the crossroads of school choice policy* (New Frontiers of Education). East Rutherford, NJ: Putnam.

Wells, A. S., & Oakes, J. (1996). Potential pitfalls of systems reform: Early lessons from research on detracking. *Sociology of Education, 69*, 135–143.

Wells, A. S., & Serna, I. (1996). The politics of culture: Understanding local political resistance to detracking in racially mixed schools. *Harvard Educational Review, 66*, 93–118.

Wesby-Gibson, D. (1969). The disadvantaged child. In D. L. Barclay (Ed.), *Art education for the disadvantaged child* (pp. 6–9)? Washington, DC: National Art Education Foundation.

Yoder, J. R., & Lopez, A. (2013). Parent's perceptions of involvement in children's education: Findings from a qualitative study of public housing residents. *Child and Adolescent Social Work Journal, 30*, 415–433.

Yosso, T. J. (2005). Whose culture has capital? A critical race theory discussion of community cultural wealth. *Race Ethnicity and Education, 8*, 69–91.

Ziegler, E., & Muenchow, S. (1992). *Head Start: The inside story of America's most successful educational experiment.* New York, NY: Basic Books.

Zulmara, C., & Necochea, J. (2001). !Basta Ya! Latino parents fighting entrenched racism. *Bilingual Research, 25*, 89–114.

Chapter 8

The "New Racism" of K–12 Schools: Centering Critical Research on Racism

Rita Kohli
University of California, Riverside

Marcos Pizarro
San José State University

Arturo Nevárez
University of California, Riverside

While organizing efforts by movements such as Black Lives Matter and responses to the hate-filled policies and rhetoric of President Donald Trump are heightening public discourse of racism, much less attention is paid to mechanisms of racial oppression in the field of education. Instead, conceptualizations that allude to racial difference but are disconnected from structural analyses continue to prevail in K–12 education research. In this chapter, our goal is to challenge racism-neutral and racism-evasive approaches to studying racial disparities by centering current research that makes visible the normalized facets of racism in K–12 schools. After narrowing over 4,000 articles that study racial inequity in education research, we reviewed a total of 186 U.S.-focused research studies in a K–12 school context that examine racism. As we categorized the literature, we built on a theory of the "new racism"—a more covert and hidden racism than that of the past—and grouped the articles into two main sections: (1) research that brings to light racism's permanence and significance in the lives of students of Color through manifestations of what we conceptualize as (a) evaded racism, (b) "antiracist" racism, and (c) everyday racism and (2) research focused on confronting racism through racial literacy and the resistance of communities of Color. In our conclusion, we articulate suggestions for future directions in education research that include a more direct acknowledgement of racism as we attend to the experiences and needs of K–12 students of Color.

Review of Research in Education
March 2017, Vol. 41, pp. 182–202
DOI: 10.3102/0091732X16686949
© 2017 AERA. http://rre.aera.net

In October 2015, a video of a police officer slamming a young Black[1] girl to the ground in a South Carolina high school classroom as a method of discipline went viral (Dana Ford, Botelho, & Conlon, 2015). Part of a larger national conversation of anti-Blackness (Cullors, Garza, & Tometi, 2015), this incident brought to light current manifestations of racism—overt and subtle—that have been part of schools since the inception of the U.S. educational system (Spring, 1994). While organizing efforts by movements such as Black Lives Matter and responses to the hate-filled presidential campaign of Donald Trump are heightening public discourse of racism, in the field of education much less attention is paid to mechanisms of racial oppression. Instead, conceptualizations that allude to racial difference but are disconnected from structural analyses prevail (May & Sleeter, 2010; Patel, 2015). In a recent search of peer-reviewed educational scholarship over the past decade using Education Source and the Educational Resources Information Center, words such as "achievement gap," "diversity," and "multicultural(ism)" are included up to 8 times more frequently than concrete discussions of racism.

Brayboy, Castagno, and Maughan (2007) wrote a chapter in the *Review of Research in Education* that called for a centering of equity and justice in education research on race. As they point out, even within scholarship that names racial inequity, conceptualizations are often cursory or incomplete or avoid direct analyses of power altogether. In 2012, Harper reviewed 255 articles to illuminate how contemporary higher education research on race neglects critical discussions of racism. These scholars argue that until we concretely name racism as a problem, we will be challenged to resolve the glaring racial disparities of our educational system. With racial inequity as heightened as ever, we write to hone their call through a close examination of scholarship that directly examines racism in K–12 schools. While it is a small subfield in education, key studies over the past decade have deepened our understanding of the mechanisms by which schools systematically racialize, marginalize, and thwart the opportunities of students of Color.[2] In this chapter, our goal is to challenge racism-neutral and racism-evasive approaches to studying racial disparities by centering current research that makes visible the normalized facets of racism in K–12 schools.

In consonance with the theme of this volume, "Disrupting Inequality Through Education Research," we begin by introducing our rationale for centering scholarship that takes a structural analysis of racism (Ladson-Billings, 1998). Guided by our research questions, we narrowed over 4,000 education studies from the last decade that focus on racial inequity, to review and analyze 186 articles that explicitly examine racism:

Research Question 1: What insight does current research on racism in K–12 schools offer about the experiences of students of Color?

Research Question 2: What gaps and directions does this scholarship point to in education research?

As we categorized the literature, we built on a theory of the "new racism"—a more covert and hidden racism than that of the past (Bonilla-Silva, 2006; Cross, 2005;

Fiske, 1993)—and grouped the articles into two main sections: (1) research that brings to light racism's permanence and significance in the lives of students of Color through manifestations of what we conceptualize as (a) evaded racism, (b) "antiracist" racism, and (c) everyday racism and (2) research focused on confronting racism through racial literacy and the resistance of communities of Color. In our conclusion, we offer an analysis of the collective literature and articulate suggestions for future directions of research that include a more direct acknowledgement of racism as we attend to the experiences and needs of K–12 students of Color.

THE NORMALIZATION OF RACISM IN K–12 SCHOOLS

Racism is the creation or maintenance of a racial hierarchy, supported through institutional power (Solorzano, Allen, & Carroll, 2002). Schooling in the United States has a history driven by racialization and racism. From Americanization schools and Native American boarding schools that spanned the 19th and much of the 20th century (Spring, 1994), to a socialization of inferiority in segregated schools serving African Americans (Du Bois, 1935; Irons, 2002; Woodson, 1933) and Mexican Americans (Drake, 1927; Gould, 1932), students of Color have been subjected to institutionalized conditions that contradict their interests and their humanity.

Despite the discourse of racial progress through integration, Judge Robert L. Carter (1968), who presented part of the oral argument in *Brown v. Board of Education of Topeka*, lamented the persistence of racism:

Few in the country, black or white, understood in 1954 that racial segregation was merely a symptom, not the disease; that the real sickness is that our society in all its manifestations is geared to the maintenance of white superiority. (p. 247)

Judge Carter argued that the changes in policy and practice that emerged from Brown and other civil rights legislation addressed superficial symptoms, leaving the disease of White supremacy/racism embedded in U.S. institutions. Starting in the late 1970s, critical race legal scholars echoed R. L. Carter's (1968) sentiment, arguing that institutional racism is an ever-present barrier to U.S. racial progress, as it protects and serves White interests (Crenshaw, 1995; Harris, 1993).

In the 1990s, key education scholars of race built on critical race theory legal arguments to deconstruct the ways that schooling, fraught with institutionalized racism, affirmed the racial status quo (Dixson & Rousseau, 2005; Ladson-Billings & Tate, 1995; Solorzano 1997; Solorzano, Ceja, & Yosso, 2000; Parker & Lynn, 2002). These and other race scholars have illuminated institutional culpability in inequitable schooling outcomes by challenging ideologies, policies, and practices steeped in deficit thinking (Valencia, 2012; Valencia & Solorzano, 1997), colorblindness—the ignoring of race or racial difference (Bonilla-Silva, 2006)—and meritocracy—the belief that success is always the product of individual merit (Au, 2013; 2016).

In essence, as this trajectory of research points out, the post-Brown era has bred a "new racism" (Bonilla-Silva, 2006; Fiske, 1993) that has replaced the overt and blatant discriminatory policies and practices of the past with covert and more subtle beliefs and behaviors, reflecting the persistent and pervasive nature of racism that R. L. Carter (1968) described. Through this process, racial inequality has become normalized and even accepted. Cross (2005), who applies the framework of "new racism" to teacher education, explains, "White privilege is maintained through invisible, insidious operations of power that foster whiteness and racism. This power is no longer enacted primarily through physical violence but is mostly achieved through more symbolic power" (p. 267). In this chapter, we use the concept of the "new racism" to shift our attention away from K–12 research that evades concrete discussions of racism toward scholarship that centers a direct and structural analysis of racism.

METHOD

As we are in yet another moment of heightened racial awareness nationally, it is important to understand how current education research is assisting in efforts to address racism. The articles selected for this chapter are peer-reviewed, U.S.-based, educational scholarship published between 2005 and 2016 that explicitly examine racism in a K–12 school context. We undertook a systematic inquiry and examination using the Education Source and the Educational Resources Information Center databases. We used the keywords *racial inequity/racial equity, racism, racial justice/racial injustice*, and *racial inequality/racial equality* to capture a range of scholarship that considers racism and related issues. We limited this search by excluding keywords such as *higher education, teacher preparation, adult education*, and *international*. This broad search yielded over 4,000 articles studying race, racial disparities, and racial inequity in education. We then sifted through those articles, eliminating those that did not directly name and center an analysis of racism.

To ensure that we carefully accounted for the scholarship that uses racism as a primary tool of analysis, we conducted a second search for articles that included the word *racism* in their titles, keywords and abstracts, and compared our results with our original search. Recognizing that there are other terms intimately associated with racism, we also searched *White supremacy, anti-Blackness, critical race theory*, and *racial microaggressions*. While there may have been a related body of work that we could have found by searching other terms such as *race* or *Whiteness*, we chose to exclude those terms to avoid research divorced from specific analyses of racism.

There are obvious limitations to our process because there is likely research that includes racism in its analysis but does not use the word (or related words) in the title, keywords, or abstracts. Additionally, there is work that discusses systems of racialized oppression in important ways but that because it does not explicitly name racism falls outside of the scope of our search. It is also probable that there is scholarship in other fields such as psychology, sociology, and ethnic studies that consider racism in K–12 schools but may not show up in an education research search engine. Thus, this chapter has boundaries to its scope and generalizability that are important to recognize.

After we narrowed the articles of both searches along our criteria, we were left with a total of 186 articles. These articles were then coded and organized along two distinct categories: (1) research that examined racism in K–12 schools (140 articles) and (2) research that explored examples of confronting racism in K–12 schools (46 articles). These categories, the deeper subtopics that emerged, and our analysis were developed using grounded theory (Glaser & Strauss, 1967). The 18 articles that focus on racism in K–12 schools were not included in this review because they were either surface level in their consideration of racism, took a historical approach, and thus were outside the scope of this study or because they were theoretical and related to K–12 schools yet were not directly situated there. While we reviewed and coded each article in our process, we do not discuss every piece from our search here. Thus, this chapter more accurately represents our analysis of important trends in the field of education research rather than an exhaustive survey of the literature.

THE "NEW RACISM" OF K–12 SCHOOLS

The purpose of this chapter is to draw attention to education research that examines how contemporary racism disrupts the educational opportunities of students of Color in K–12 schools. As we reviewed the scholarship, we found three main patterns to how researchers identified racism in schools, which we theorize as (1) evaded racism (10 articles), where equity-explicit discourse is divorced from institutional analyses or concrete discourse on race and racism (this type of racism is often used to avoid, silence, or invisibilize racism); (2) "antiracist" racism (66 articles), where racially inequitable policies and practice are actually masked as the solution to racism; and (3) everyday racism (64 articles), where the racism manifests on a micro or interpersonal level, and thus is often unrecognized or viewed as insignificant. Our analysis of the research collectively points to the "new racism" of K–12 schools, a system of institutionalized power and domination that works best when invisible. In this section, we review research that illuminates the specific mechanisms of how this 'new racism' manifests in K–12 schooling policy and practices.

Evaded Racism

Prominent race scholar, Richard Valencia (2012) argues that while in the past intellectual inferiority and cultural deprivation were prominent theories used to uphold racial inequity in schooling, today, individualized analysis of underachievement are tools that maintain the status quo. K. D. Brown & Brown (2012) contend that dominant rhetoric blames students of Color and their families for a lack of academic success, promoting a shift in their behavior as the solution (e.g., reminding parents to read more to their children; advocating for a growth mind-set), rather than suggesting shifts to structures or policies that systematically fail students of Color (e.g., limited resources, racial profiling; Malagon & Alvarez, 2010). Blaming communities of Color for educational inequality at the individual level invisiblizes institutional responsibility, thus providing a rationale to study race yet evade concrete analyses of racism (Bonilla Silva, 2006).

There is a body of current scholarship that draws attention to this practice of evading racism in K–12 schooling, and its negative impact on students of Color. The focus on the achievement gap in education research is one clear example. In a conceptual article, Ladson-Billings (2006) argues that the framing of the achievement gap serves as a distraction from "the historical, economic, sociopolitical, and moral decisions and policies that characterize our society [and] have created an education debt" (p. 5) owed to Black and Latinx[3] students. While recognizing racial disparities in the success of students is important, without understanding the critical role of structural racism in the outcomes being analyzed, as Ladson-Billings (2006) points out, "this all-out focus on the 'Achievement Gap' moves us toward short-term solutions that are unlikely to address the long-term underlying problem" (p. 4).

In addition to the achievement gap, the literature points to other equity framed concepts used to avoid racism. For example, there is widespread acknowledgment of the importance and reality of diversity in schools. However, as Doucet and Keys Adair (2013) explain in their review of research on early childhood classrooms, much of the work emphasizing "diversity" does so as an undeveloped afterthought rather than through an actual paradigm shift that weaves diverse histories and perspectives into the school, thus reifying racism. In critiquing this approach, they argue,

The underlying message, then, is that from day to day, the classroom reflects White, middle-class, mainstream events, foods, attire, but, say, for Chinese New Year or Rosh Hashanah, the curriculum pauses to focus on how a culture or a child or a family is different from the norm. (p. 90)

A superficial response to changing demographics in public schools, additive frames of diversity that maintain Whiteness as central often serve as substitutes for concrete discussions of race or racism, thus maintaining or exacerbating racial inequity in schools.

Similarly, while McGee Banks and Banks's (1995) original framing of multiculturalism was intended to combat the effects of racism on students of Color in schools, a cluster of studies we reviewed argue that much of current multicultural research and practice is used as a mechanism to evade discussions of power or inequity in education policy and practice. Analyzing a unit taught in a New England school under a multicultural framework, Bery (2014) argues, "Multiculturalism, when combined with color blind ideology, results in a reassertion of racism and racist hierarchies" (p. 334). She concludes, "Multiculturalism is, simultaneously, the consequence and the materialization of white supremacy" (p. 350), as it is often lauded as a challenge to racism while it replaces any critical or structural approach to thinking about racially marginalized communities. In the literature, we also see key studies that critique how well intended practices such as "antibias" teaching and "culturally responsive pedagogy" can work to affirm Whiteness in the education of students of Color when divorced from a clear analysis of racism (Castagno & Brayboy, 2008; Epstein, Mayorga, & Nelson, 2011; Lindsay, 2007).

We see a push in the scholarship to problematize frameworks and practices that subvert or overlook the multifaceted realities of racism in contemporary schooling.

These studies demonstrate how evaded racism in education research, policy, and practice results in deficit-minded or superficial approaches to reform that center Whiteness rather than improve the educational opportunities of students of Color.

"Antiracist" Racism

Another body of current scholarship demonstrates that much of the racism we experience in K–12 schools today is not evaded but is actually framed through equity, justice, and antiracist rhetoric. Three subcategories of this research emerged within our review, articles that discuss: (1) neoliberal racism and its influence on policy, (2) hostile school racial climates, and (3) racist processes of designation that serve to further marginalize working-class students of Color.

Neoliberal Racism and Policy

As privatization practices have increased in K–12 schools over the past decade, so have racial disparities. In recent years, a growing body of education research has documented neoliberal-driven policies that exacerbate what the racialization and racism communities of Color endure in K–12 education through issues such as testing, school choice, charter school development, and a divestment from public education (Buras, 2009; Gay, 2007; Prins, 2007). Through a policy analysis of recent federal education reforms such as No Child Left Behind and Race to the Top, Au (2016) argues that high-stakes, standardized testing policies increase racism by centering individual achievement without any structural analysis—what he calls "Meritocracy 2.0." Masked as an accountability narrative for achieving racial equality in schools, corporate-driven testing practices affirm racial hierarchies of student success (Au, 2013; 2016). Urrieta (2006), in a case study of a predominantly White charter school, and Roda and Stuart Wells (2013), through interviews with kindergarten parents, argue that school choice policies, which often take a colorblind stance, advantage White and affluent parents and increase segregation. Through an ethnographic case study (Stovall, 2013), and critical race discourse analysis of newspaper articles, community forum transcripts, and school board meeting notes (Briscoe & Khalifa, 2015), two key studies illuminate how school closures disproportionately and negatively affect working-class urban Black neighborhoods. A parent from a community forum explained, "You know if you kill the school, you know you're killing the community, right?" (Briscoe & Khalifa, p. 748). Recognizing schools are an extension of communities, the authors argue that school leaders driven by neoliberal mandates pay less and less attention to the community's voice and needs, exacerbating educational inequity (Briscoe & Khalifa, 2015).

As many public schools are being closed, research also points to the insurgence of charter schools as a form of contemporary racism. In semistructured interviews with educational stakeholders and through policy analyses, Henry and Dixson (2016) critique the discourse of charter schools as the "common sense" solution to inequity by pointing to charter authorization and application processes in post-Katrina New Orleans that resulted in an influx of White-dominated corporate charters and the marginalization of Black school leaders. Buras (2015) echoes the sentiment in her New Orleans study, arguing that many corporate charter schools and alternative teacher recruitment reforms displace veteran Black teachers for young White teachers and are funded by White philanthropists whose purpose is to align public education to business. Other charter school critics point to racist, deficit-minded pedagogies masked as classroom management (Casey, Lozenski, & McManimon, 2013) that stratify and limit the learning opportunities of students of color (Foiles Sifuentes, 2015).

A collective analysis of these studies pushes us to understand a new form of educational racism that is masked by equity language and driven by capitalist, market-driven goals. This literature reveals how rhetoric of equity and justice is being used to promote neoliberal-driven educational laws, policies and institutions that, in fact, protect and exacerbate racial inequity in and through K–12 schools.

Colorblind Racism

Another prominent theme to emerge from the literature was the manifestation of colorblind racism in schools. Despite attempts to equate colorblindness to equity, qualitative and conceptual studies demonstrate how silence around race maintains and legitimates racism, thus constructing hostile racial climates for students of Color (Castagno, 2008; Chapman, 2013; Love, 2014) and teachers of Color (Amos, 2016; Kohli, 2016; Souto-Manning & Cheruvu, 2016). Steeped in deficit thinking, colorblindness reduces any visible racism to the actions of a few ignorant individuals (Hardie & Tyson, 2013). This allows systemic mechanisms of racism (e.g., tracking, curriculum, student surveillance) to be ignored as explanations for racial inequality and replaced by individual-based rationales (i.e., students of Color are lazy, behaviorally challenged, intellectually deficient; Donna Y. Ford, 2014; Rozansky-Lloyd, 2005; Tarca, 2005).

The reviewed research is critical of colorblind understandings of school punishment, which obscure structural analyses of the severity and frequency of discipline faced by students of Color (Milner, 2013). From the racial and gender profiling of Black students in integrated suburban schools (Chapman, 2013; Gordon, 2012; Modica, 2015), to teachers' criminalizing and deficit perceptions of Black male students (Love, 2014), and the hypersurveillance of Black girls (Wun, 2015), while they do not all represent "colorblind" ideology, these studies all illuminate school practices that explicitly purport to not consider race and, yet, do exactly that.

Several studies employed textual analyses to reveal colorblindness in schools. Through a surface-level or distorted representation of racism in the history standards (Heilig, Brown, & Brown, 2012), social studies textbooks, and the pedagogies of history teachers (Chandler, 2009), representations of racial violence against African Americans and their resistance are typically individualized and detached from larger structural and institutional factors (A. L. Brown & Brown, 2010; K. D. Brown & Brown, 2010; Chandler & McKnight, 2009). Suh, An, and Forest (2015), in their content analysis of high school history textbooks, found that Asian American experiences and histories are portrayed through the model minority myth, which ignores racism and exacerbates the deficit framing of other communities of Color.

Masked as equity discourse, colorblind ideology is actually a form of racism that erases the contemporary, lived, and systemic oppression of communities of Color. The literature that names colorblindness as racism, as manifested in school policies such as punishment and curriculum, shifts the analyses from individualizing explanations of inequity back to institutionally driven, systemic patterns of displacement, dehumanization, and criminalization.

Racist Policies of Designation

A third focus in the literature that examined institutional racism in K–12 schools was a critique of policies and practices that label and serve two frequently marginalized student groups—*dual-language learners* (DLLs), often referred to as English Learners; and students labeled with disabilities. There is a body of literature that illuminates the White supremacy of language policies and practices that devalue DLLs and their families. While there is a history of English-only impositions on immigrant youth, masked as a social good to remedy the supposed deficiencies of DLLs (Briscoe, 2014), English-only campaigns were reinstitutionalized in 2001 through the No Child Left Behind policy (Lapayese, 2007). Research illuminates trauma that immigrant, bilingual students of Color experience through policies that affirm White racial privilege (Lapayese, 2007; Malsbary, 2014), noting that English dominance in schools is actually a racializing process that undermines student potential and success (Pimentel, 2011), particularly for those labeled *long-term English learners* (Flores, Kleyn, & Menken, 2015). Perez Huber (2011) builds on the narratives of both documented and undocumented Chicanas to show how the English-language hegemony of California public schools institutionalizes racist nativism: "the institutionalized ways people perceive, understand and make sense of contemporary U.S. immigration that justifies *native* (*white*) dominance, and reinforces hegemonic power" (p. 380). Uncovering the racist, nativist microaggressions of teachers, she argues that as students are shamed for their Spanish, they are also socialized to understand themselves as outsiders in the United States, regardless of their immigration status or years of residence (Perez Huber, 2011; Perez Huber & Cueva, 2012). Simultaneous to the degradation of Spanish for Latina/o students, D. Palmer's (2010) qualitative study in a second-grade dual-language classroom points to a newly emerging trend of dual-language education that benefits middle-class White students. Bilingualism is thus gentrified as Latina/Latino, and Black students are prevented from enrolling in these specialized programs in their own schools (D. Palmer, 2010).

Collectively, this literature exposes language policy and practice as a racializing force that, as it stands, serves to perpetuate racial inequity. Interestingly, there is a parallel body of research that examined the racialization of students of Color through (dis)ability-focused policies and practices (Artiles, 2011). Because of intersecting forms of ableism and racism embedded in the Individuals With Disabilities Education

Act (2004) and the associated policies and practices (Beratan, 2006; Liasidou, 2014), schooling often results in the forced segregation and racist exclusion of (mostly Black male) students with special needs (Ferri & Connor, 2005). The research delineates the overrepresentation of Black and Latinx students in special education as guided by assumptions of cultural deficits and pseudoscientific placement processes that result in misguided conceptualizations of disability (Ahram, Fergus, & Noguera, 2011), as well as inequitable resource allocation, inappropriate curriculum and pedagogy, and inadequate teacher preparation (Blanchett, 2006). As a challenge to the rationalization that disproportionality occurs because there is something inherently wrong with Black bodies (i.e., their behavior, their cognition; Artiles, 2011), Fitzgerald (2006, 2009), through an analysis of school records in an integrated public school district, problematizes disproportionate behavior designations and the use of psychotropic medications (e.g., Ritalin) as a racialized process used to control the academic and social behavior of Black boys. Thus, without addressing racism—the need to pacify, control, and exclude Black and brown bodies—alongside ableism, students of Color continue to be overrepresented, segregated, and prevented from reaching their academic potential (Zion & Blanchett, 2011). Building on DisCrit, the union of disability studies and critical race theory (Annamma, Connor, & Ferri, 2013), Annamma, Morrison, and Jackson (2014) use policy and spatial analysis to make groundbreaking connections between disproportionality, racist school discipline practices, and the school to prison pipeline.

While programs serving DLLs and students labeled with disabilities have been framed as a benefit to these student subgroups, when examined through a structural analysis of racism, the literature reveals how these programs systematically exacerbate racial inequity. Understanding the racism associated with processes of designation alongside neoliberal policies and colorblind discourse, there is a pattern in K–12 schools where antiracist discourse is often misappropriated by policies and practices that racialize and further marginalize students of Color.

Everyday Racism

Historical scholar Thomas Holt (1995) theorizes,

The everyday acts of name calling and petty exclusions are minor links in a larger historical chain of events, structures, and transformations anchored in slavery and the slave trade. Together, they nourish the racial knowledge that produces and sustains the mentalities or subjectivities capable of engaging in the brutal, wholesale destruction of other human beings. (p. 7)

Holt and other scholars argue that we must pay attention to racialized microevents and how they connect to macrostructures of racial injustice, particularly because the normalizing everydayness serves as a barrier to dismantling racism (Essed, 1997; Holt, 1995; Lewis, 2003). Given the powerful evidence of racism in K–12 educational policy and practice, it is surprising that there is but a small body of research that unpacks the everyday racism of schools. This scholarship, focused primarily on the practices of teachers and administrators, reveals interpersonal manifestations of institutionally driven racism.

A primary theme that emerged from this literature was the manner by which White teachers perpetuate racism in schools. In a 3-year ethnography, Buehler (2013) pointed to the ways in which White staff racialized students of Color and teachers of Color, while acting as barriers in efforts to improve school racial climate. And while White teacher racism can be overt, it is often upheld through colorblind or racism-neutral approaches to their daily work with students of Color (Chandler, 2009; Stoll, 2014). Several studies found that White teachers positioned themselves as "good teachers" while simultaneously reifying Whiteness by resisting an awareness of racism (Hyland, 2005; Vaught & Castagno, 2008, Young, 2011). Being "good" at teaching content but having no structural or social analysis for inequity was a prevalent blind spot of White teachers who maintained racism in K–12 schools.

Another significant contribution from scholars who study K–12 school racism was an in-depth exploration of student experiences with racism. From studies of Korean and Korean American students in the Midwest (J. D. Palmer & Eun-Young, 2005) to Puerto Rican students in the Northeast and Midwest (Irizarry & Antrop-González, 2013) and Native Hawaiian students (Borrero, Yeh, Cruz, & Suda 2012), the literature demonstrates how nuanced, yet universal, racism is experienced by students of Color in U.S. schools. Cammarota (2014) studied a process whereby Latina/Latino students researched their encounters with racism in a Tucson high school. They uncovered significant experiences with not only "direct racist statements" but also racial microaggressions—subtle racial assaults or insults (Kohli & Solorzano, 2012). Primarily studied in psychology, there is now a small but growing body of K–12 school research that analyzes the impact of racial microaggressions on students of Color in K–12 schools (A. Allen, Scott, & Lewis, 2013; Q. Allen, 2010, 2012). Kohli and Solorzano (2012) demonstrate the way that teachers enact racial microaggressions, through their treatment of the names of students of Color. They argue that situated within multiple policies and practices, the cumulative impact of these subtle manifestations of racism had lasting and damaging impact on the self-perceptions of students. Perez Huber and Cueva (2012) use the *testimonio* research method to understand how undocumented and U.S.-born Chicana/Latina students experience racial microaggressions as embodied systemic oppression. Q. Allen (2010) details the ways in which microaggressions define Black student experiences in predominantly White schools, resulting in feelings of invisibility and being devalued along with interracial conflict with Latino students.

As Black families move to the suburbs in search of quality educational experiences, a growing body of research identifies the constant racialization and racism they experience in predominantly White schools (Q. Allen, 2012; Carter Andrews, 2009, 2012; Frazier, 2012). Gordon (2012) argued that while one third of African Americans now attend suburban schools, the social mobility and aspirations of their families are not enough to protect them from the "othering" that they experience in these spaces. Matrenec's (2011) study affirms this finding, arguing that Black students are challenged by the dominance of racist stereotypes, manifested by the "constant and inescapable, racist, hegemonic fog in the air of the school" (p. 230), a helpful metaphor to understand the persistence of racism in Black student schooling experiences. There is also a small body of work that considers how parents of Color experience racism in middle-class schools, providing a deeper understanding of the pervasive ways the primacy of Whiteness is maintained (Howard & Reynolds, 2008; Yull, Blitz, Thompson, & Murray, 2014).

Given the challenges of effectively confronting racist beliefs and practices among teachers and administrators, one of the most critical issues that must be understood regarding the schooling of students of Color is the impact racism has on their lives. Perez Huber, Johnson, and Kohli (2006) connect the construct of internalized racism to historical and contemporary experiences with racism in schools in terms of curriculum, resources disparities, and teacher competency, arguing that it has a deep psychological impact on students of Color. Other researchers have explored related impacts by considering internalized oppression (Irizarry & Raible, 2014) and, perhaps most important, racial trauma and the need for holistic models of counseling (Curry, 2010).

Of course, the impacts of racism do not exist in a vacuum and are often intimately connected to other vectors of oppression in school. A critical theme that emerged from the literature is the necessity for intersectional frameworks and analyses to understand how students of Color experience racism alongside other forms of oppression, and their complex and cumulative effects. In a 2-year ethnographic study of a public school, Cruz (2008) explored homophobia and heteronormativity faced by lesbian, gay, bisexual, transgender, and queer migrant students, many of who were undocumented. Malagon and Alvarez (2010), through extensive oral history interviews, examined the intersectionality of gender, race, and class of five Chicana women enrolled in a continuation high school. Several qualitative studies also examined the racialized and gendered experiences of Black female students (Ricks, 2014), Mexican American female students (K. A. Taylor & Fernandez-Bergersen, 2015), and Chicana students (Malagon & Alvarez, 2010).

The most poignant and revelatory research in this area uncovers the hidden and typically unacknowledged ways that institutional racism manifests in intersectional, mundane, interpersonal interactions in K–12 schools. The researchers addressing covert racism often acknowledge the challenges of highlighting racism in what many have wrongly deemed postracial times. Thus, the insights gained from these analyses help uncover the often unseen ways everyday racism along with evaded racism and "antiracist" racism serve as collective and systemic mechanisms to maintain the status quo of racial inequity.

CONFRONTING RACISM

In light of the continuing severity the covert nature of the "new racism" of K–12 schools revealed in the literature, it is troubling to us that only 45 articles focused on confronting racism emerged in our search. As we draw attention to the need for research on applied approaches, we highlight scholarship that conceptualizes responses to racism in K–12 contexts. Two interrelated bodies of research emerged in our review of the literature: (1) articles that examine curriculum and pedagogy to develop K–12 students' racial literacy—the ability to name and examine the effects of structural racism on society, institutions, and people (Skerrett, 2011) and (2) studies focused on resistance and resilience of students of Color to racism in K–12 schools.

Considering the need for students to critically engage with a world structured by an insidious new form of racism that covertly diminishes their educational opportunities and life chances, the literature points to the importance of racial literacy for both students and teachers, shifting their understanding from an individualized to an institutional analysis of racism (K. D. Brown & Brown, 2011; Epstein & Gist, 2015). A primary component to developing students' racial literacy articulated in the research was their teachers' ability to understand and discuss racism. Rogers and Mosley (2006), in their study with second graders, demonstrated how racial literacy development is an interactive process requiring teachers adept at guiding students through a development of race and racism discourse. Teachers with high racial literacy were able to support students' recognition of institutionalized racism. As Skerrett (2011) illustrates in a study with English teachers, teachers' racial literacy ranged widely, from "ill-informed" practices that poorly prepared students to confront and process the racialized experiences they faced to approaches that helped students expose, critique, and take action against racial inequity. A teacher's racial literacy, as infused in his or her pedagogy, made a considerable difference in students' ability to process and confront racism, something that the literature conveyed in the previous sections suggests is necessary. Taken together, studies on racial literacy highlight the need for professional development support, antiracist school environments, as well as teaching and curriculum focused on race and racism (K. D. Brown & Brown, 2011; Epstein & Gist, 2015; Rogers & Mosley, 2006; Skerrett, 2011).

Beyond teachers' comfort and skill with racial discourse, critical pedagogy emerged in the literature as a prominent mechanism for developing students' ability to navigate and deflect racism. From dialogic spaces for students to increase their understanding of racism (Flynn, 2012; M. Taylor & Otinsky, 2006), to critical engagement with storytelling (Bell & Roberts, 2010; Castagno, 2008), and the use of theatre and the arts to teach students about human rights, immigration, and internalized racism (Hanley, 2011; Gutiérrez-Vicario, 2016), the research provided classroom-level illustrations of curricula that opened possibilities for productive conversations and engagement around race, racism, and antiracism.

In addition to students' ability to name, navigate, and process racism, scholarship draws attention to the resilience and resistance of students of Color. Research highlights the instrumental role of positive racial identity and positive self-concept in the academic achievement and resilience of students of Color in the face of racialized experiences (Ani, 2013; Berry, 2005; D. J. Carter, 2008). On a school level, Pulido (2008) highlights Mexican-descent and Puerto Rican students' use of hip-hop to understand their racialized experiences in the United States and as a means of resistance to official school discourses that relegate them to the margins. Other studies centered K–12 students as researchers of racism and as agents of change for their communities, using the frame of youth participatory action research (Cammarota, 2014; Cammarota & Aguilera, 2012). Recognizing the power of parents' resistance alongside their children's, Stovall (2013) highlights the hunger strike activism of Black and Latinx families in Chicago, used to challenge systematic and racist divestment from the community manifested in the form of a school closure.

From storytelling, theater, and art to explicitly teaching racial literacy, as well as student and community-based resistance, much of the scholarship was focused on naming, navigating, healing from, and resisting racism. And while this research, rightfully, does not articulate how to dismantle the complex and hegemonic "new racism" of K–12 schools, these articles serve as models of the collective power that students and communities of Color have in reclaiming access to an education that is both humanizing and empowering.

ANALYSIS AND FUTURE DIRECTIONS

Over the past decade of K–12 education research, there are relatively few articles that center racism in the analysis of educational inequity. And while there are many research areas that can support efforts to improve educational conditions for students of Color, because racism is persistent and central in our society and our schools, it is essential that there is a strong body of literature that acknowledges and confronts its detrimental impact. The scholarship reviewed in this chapter, although few and far between in the broader field of education research, brings light to such important insights about the role of racism in maintaining racial inequities in K–12 schools. We see nuances of racial injustice from school closures in Chicago, to post-Katrina displacement of Black teachers through charterization in New Orleans, to the hostile racism students of Color experience in Tucson schools. Collectively, these articles help us understand how racism currently operates in K–12 schools.

Through this review, we see manifestations in the past decade of a "new racism" in K–12 schools that is evasive, subtle, and challenging to identify because it is normalized and hidden under the guise of multiculturalism, colorblindness, and everyday individualized interpretations of policy and practices. However, this does not make the racism any less painful for students of Color. Instead, legalized racial violence has now been institutionalized through school policing and excessive school punishment, while the inequitable resources of de facto and even de jure segregation are now invisibilized by "equity" discourse in neoliberal policies such as "school choice." Overt racial slurs, while still present, have overwhelmingly turned to racial microaggressions, subtle yet powerful in their impact. In these hostile racial climates, students of Color—like the young Black girl from South Carolina we center at the start of this chapter—continue to be dehumanized and disproportionately denied academic and economic opportunities.

The research we highlight exposes the way in which racial equity discourse, when divorced from a structural analysis of racism, serves to maintain the systemic oppression of students of Color. Thus, this review calls into question the ongoing trend in research to ignore the role of racism in shaping school experiences. There is a large body of work, which for a host of reasons, alludes to racism without discussing it directly. It is not our purpose to denounce the utility of this scholarship or dichotomize the field into "good" or "bad" scholarship. To be clear, it is important that research is drawing attention to racial inequity. The insidiousness of this 'new racism' of K–12 schools, however, demonstrates why it is even more significant that education researchers must name racism.

While the critical scholarship analyzed in this review exposed mechanisms of racism in K–12 schools, there is still much work to be done. The majority of the existing literature is focused on the racism that Black students, particularly Black boys, face. Not only must education research improve its articulation of the prominence and impact of anti-Black racism on school policies and structures (Dumas, 2016), it must also strengthen its intersectional analyses of racism (Hopson & Dixson, 2011), as well as specific and nuanced analyses of the racialized educational experiences of Latinx, indigenous, Pacific Islander, and Asian American students. Very little research exists on issues such as the racial and gendered violence that young women of Color experience in schools, the denied opportunities of K–12 undocumented students of Color, the almost complete erasure of indigenous student experiences in mainstream educational discourse, or the obscured racism of the model minority myth. Additionally, it seems the insidious and mundane pervasiveness of racism in schools leaves those committed to confronting racism forced to focus on preparing students and/or teachers to address this reality, as institutional and systemic shifts seem insurmountable. And while the tools to confront racism are also far understudied, there is little research analyzing systemic shifts in racism.

Through this review of research, we argue for an enhanced commitment of practitioners and researchers to more frankly discuss, critically analyze, and challenge structural racism. Many of the concepts in the reviewed scholarship were developed within other disciplines such as law, ethnic studies, higher education, and psychology and have been borrowed into K–12 scholarship. Rather than continuing the trend of evading racism in K–12 school research, we argue that there is a utility in an interdisciplinary approach to racism research in schools, as improved tools are needed to name, challenge, and transform the racializing conditions in which students of Color are educated. With these tools, education scholars, policymakers, practitioners, and activists will be better equipped to disrupt the "new racism" of K–12 schools and move us further toward a racially just educational system.

NOTES

[1]We primarily use the term *Black* but do use *Black* and *African American* interchangeably, selecting the term of a selected author whenever possible.

[2]We use the term *of Color* throughout to reference African Americans, Asian Americans, Pacific Islanders, Latinxs, and Native Americans to identify their shared racialization in the United States.

[3]We use the term *Latinx* to reference all people of Latin American descent in the United States but adopt the term used by specific authors when appropriate. This term is increasingly being used to address the gender norming implicit in other ethnic labels derived from Spanish.

REFERENCES

Ahram, R., Fergus, E., & Noguera, P. (2011). Addressing racial/ethnic disproportionality in special education: Case studies of suburban school districts. *Teachers College Record, 113,* 2233–2266.

Allen, A., Scott, L. M., & Lewis, C. W. (2013). Racial microaggressions and African American and Hispanic students in urban schools: A call for culturally affirming education. *Interdisciplinary Journal of Teaching and Learning, 3,* 117–129.

Allen, Q. (2010). Racial microaggressions: The schooling experiences of black middle-class males in Arizona's secondary schools. *Journal of African American Males in Education, 1,* 125–143.

Allen, Q. (2012). "They think minority means lesser than": Black middle-class sons and fathers resisting microaggressions in the school. *Urban Education, 48,* 117–197.

Amos, Y. T. (2016). Wanted and used: Latina bilingual education teachers at public schools. *Equity & Excellence in Education, 49*(1), 41–56.

Ani, A. (2013). In spite of racism, inequality, and school failure: Defining hope with achieving Black children. *Journal of Negro Education, 82,* 408–421.

Annamma, S., Morrison, D., & Jackson, D. (2014). Disproportionality fills in the gaps: Connections between achievement, discipline and special education in the school-to-prison pipeline. *Berkeley Review of Education, 5*(1), 53–87.

Annamma, S. A., Connor, D., & Ferri, B. (2013). Dis/ability critical race studies (DisCrit): Theorizing at the intersections of race and dis/ability. *Race, Ethnicity and Education, 16*(1), 1–31.

Artiles, A. J. (2011). Toward an interdisciplinary understanding of educational equity and difference: The case of the racialization of ability. *Educational Researcher, 40,* 431–445.

Au, W. (2013). Hiding behind high-stakes testing: Meritocracy, objectivity and inequality in U.S. education. *International Education Journal: Comparative Perspectives, 12*(2), 7–20.

Au, W. (2016). Meritocracy 2.0.: High-stakes, standardized testing as a racial project of neoliberal multiculturalism. *Educational Policy, 30*(1), 39–62.

Bell, L. A., & Roberts, R. A. (2010). The storytelling project model: A theoretical framework for critical examination of racism through the arts. *Teachers College Record, 112,* 2295–2319.

Beratan, G. D. (2006). Institutionalizing inequity: Ableism, racism and IDEA 2004. *Disability Studies Quarterly, 26*(2), 3–3.

Berry, R. Q. (2005). Voices of success: Descriptive portraits of two successful African American male middle school mathematics students. *Journal of African American Studies, 8,* 46–62.

Bery, S. (2014). Multiculturalism, teaching slavery, and white supremacy. *Equity & Excellence in Education, 47,* 334–352.

Blanchett, W. J. (2006). Disproportionate representation of African American students in special education: Acknowledging the role of white privilege and racism. *Educational Researcher, 35*(6), 24–28.

Bonilla-Silva, E. (2006). *Racism without racists: Color-blind racism and the persistence of racial inequality in the United States.* New York, NY: Rowman & Littlefield.

Borrero, N. E., Yeh, C. J., Cruz, C. I., & Suda, J. E. (2012). School as a context for "othering" youth and promoting cultural assets. *Teachers College Record, 114*(2), 1–37.

Brayboy, B. M. J., Castagno, A. E., & Maughan, E. (2007). Equality and justice for all? Examining race in education scholarship. *Review of Research in Education, 31*(1), 159–194.

Briscoe, F. M. (2014). "The biggest problem": School leaders' covert construction of Latino ELL families—institutional racism in a neoliberal schooling context. *Journal of Language, Identity & Education, 13*, 354–373.

Briscoe, F. M., & Khalifa, M. A. (2015). "That racism thing": A critical race discourse analysis of a conflict over the proposed closure of a black high school. *Race, Ethnicity and Education, 18*, 739–763.

Brown, A. L., & Brown, K. D. (2010). Strange fruit indeed: Interrogating contemporary textbook representations of racial violence toward African Americans. *Teachers College Record, 112*, 31–67.

Brown, K. D., & Brown, A. L. (2010). Silenced memories: An examination of the sociocultural knowledge on race and racial violence in official school curriculum. *Equity & Excellence in Education, 43*, 139–154.

Brown, K. D., & Brown, A. L. (2011). Teaching K-8 students about race. *Multicultural Education, 19*, 9–13.

Brown, K. D., & Brown, A. L. (2012). Useful and dangerous discourse: Deconstructing racialized knowledge about African-American students. *Educational Foundations, 26*(1/2), 11–25.

Buehler, J. (2013). 'There's a problem, and we've got to face it': How staff members wrestled with race in an urban high school. *Race, Ethnicity and Education, 16*, 629–652.

Buras, K. L. (2009). "We have to tell our story": Neo-griots, racial resistance, and schooling in the other south. *Race, Ethnicity and Education, 12*, 427–453.

Buras, K. L. (2015). "Thank God for Mississippi!" How disparagement of the south has destroyed public schooling in New Orleans—and beyond. *Peabody Journal of Education, 90*, 355–379.

Cammarota, J. (2014). Challenging colorblindness in Arizona: Latina/o students' counternarratives of race and racism. *Multicultural Perspectives, 16*(2), 79–85.

Cammarota, J., & Aguilera, M. (2012). "By the time I get to Arizona": Race, language, and education in America's racist state. *Race, Ethnicity and Education, 15*, 485–500.

Carter, D. J. (2008). Cultivating a critical race consciousness for African American school success. *Journal of Educational Foundations, 22*(1/2), 11–28.

Carter, R. L. (1968). The Warren Court and desegregation. *Michigan Law Review, 67*, 237–248.

Carter Andrews, D. J. (2009). The construction of Black high-achiever identities in a predominantly white high school. *Anthropology & Education Quarterly, 40*, 297–317.

Carter Andrews, D. J. (2012). Black achievers' experiences with racial spotlighting and ignoring in a predominantly white high school. *Teachers College Record, 114*(10), 1–46.

Casey, Z. A., Lozenski, B. D., & McManimon, S. K. (2013). From neoliberal policy to neoliberal pedagogy: Racializing and historicizing classroom management. *Journal of Pedagogy/ Pedagogický Casopis, 4*(1), 36–58.

Castagno, A. E. (2008). Flipping the script: Analyzing youth talk about race and racism. *Anthropology & Education, 39*, 334–354.

Castagno, A. E., & Brayboy, B. M. J. (2008). Culturally responsive schooling for indigenous youth: A review of the literature. *Review of Educational Research, 78*, 941–993.

Chandler, P., & McKnight, D. (2009). The failure of social education in the United States: A critique of teaching the national story from "white" colourblind eyes. *Journal for Critical Education Policy Studies, 7*, 217–248.

Chandler, P. T. (2009). Blinded by the white: Social studies and raceless pedagogies. *Journal of Educational Thought, 43*, 259–288.

Chapman, T. K. (2013). You can't erase race! Using CRT to explain the presence of race and racism in majority white suburban schools. *Discourse: Studies in the Cultural Politics of Education, 34*, 611–627.

Crenshaw, K. (Ed.). (1995). *Critical race theory: The key writings that formed the movement.* New York, NY: The New Press.

Cross, B. E. (2005). New racism, reformed teacher education, and the same ole' oppression. *Educational Studies, 38,* 263–274.

Cruz, C. (2008). Notes on immigration, youth, and ethnographic silence. *Theory Into Practice, 47,* 67–73.

Cullors, P., Garza, A., & Tometi, O. (2016). *A herstory of the #BlackLivesMatter movement.* Retrieved from http://blacklivesmatter.com/herstory

Curry, J. R. (2010). Addressing the spiritual needs of African American students: Implications for school counselors. *Journal of Negro Education, 79,* 405–415.

Dixson, A. D., & Rousseau, C. K. (2005). And we are still not saved: Critical race theory in education ten years later. *Race, Ethnicity and Education, 8,* 7–27.

Doucet, F., & Keys Adair, J. (2013). Addressing race and inequity in the classroom. *YC: Young Children, 68*(5), 88–97.

Drake, R. (1927). *A comparative study of the mentality and achievement of Mexican and white children* (Unpublished master's thesis). University of Southern California, Los Angeles.

Du Bois, W. B. (1935). Does the Negro need separate schools? *Journal of Negro Education, 4,* 328–335.

Dumas, M. J. (2016). "Be real Black for me": Imagining BlackCrit in education. *Urban Education, 51,* 415–442.

Epstein, T., & Gist, C. (2015). Teaching racial literacy in secondary humanities classrooms: Challenging adolescents' of color concepts of race and racism. *Race, Ethnicity & Education, 18*(1), 40–60.

Epstein, T., Mayorga, E., & Nelson, J. (2011). Teaching about race in an urban history class: The effects of culturally responsive teaching. *Journal of Social Studies Research, 35*(1), 2–21.

Essed, P. (1997). Racial intimidation: Sociopolitical implications of the usage of racist slurs. In S. H. Riggins (Eds.), *The language and politics of exclusion* (pp. 131–152). Thousand Oaks, CA: Sage.

Ferri, B. A., & Connor, D. J. (2005). Tools of exclusion: Race, disability, and (re)segregated Education. *Teachers College Record, 107,* 453–474.

Fiske, S. T. (1993). Controlling other people: The impact of power on stereotyping. *American Psychologist, 48,* 621–628.

Fitzgerald, T. (2006). Control, punish, and conquer: US public schools' attempts to control Black males. *Challenge (Atlanta): A Journal of Research on African American Men, 12*(1), 38–55.

Fitzgerald, T. D. (2009). Controlling the Black school age male: Psychotropic medications and the circumvention of public law 94-142 and section 504. *Urban Education, 44,* 225–227.

Flores, N., Kleyn, T., & Menken, K. (2015). Looking holistically in a climate of partiality: Identities of students labeled long-term English Language Learners. *Journal of Language, Identity & Education, 14,* 113–132.

Flynn, J. E. (2012). Critical pedagogy with the oppressed and the oppressors: Middle school students discuss racism and white privilege. *Middle Grades Research Journal, 7,* 95–110.

Foiles Sifuentes, A. M. (2015). Performing the grade: Urban Latino youth, gender performance, and academic success. *Race, Ethnicity and Education, 18,* 764–784.

Ford, D., Botelho, G., & Conlon, K. (2015). *Spring Valley high school officer suspended after violent classroom arrest.* Retrieved from http://www.cnn.com/2015/10/27/us/south-carolina-school-arrest-video/

Ford, D. Y. (2014). Segregation and the underrepresentation of Blacks and Hispanics in gifted education: Social inequality and deficit paradigms. *Roeper Review, 36,* 143–154.

Frazier, A. D. (2012). The possible selves of high-ability African males attending a residential high school for highly able youth. *Journal for the Education of the Gifted, 35,* 366–390.

Gay, G. (2007). Teaching children of catastrophe. *Multicultural Education, 15*(2), 55–61.

Glaser, B. G., & Strauss, A. L. (1967). *The discovery of grounded theory.* Chicago, IL: Aldine.

Gordon, B. M. (2012). "Give a brotha a break!" The experiences and dilemmas of middle-class African American male students in white suburban schools. *Teachers College Record, 114*(5), 1–26.

Gould, B. (1932). *Methods of teaching Mexicans* (Unpublished master's thesis). University of Southern California, Los Angeles.

Gutiérrez-Vicario, M. A. (2016). More than a mural: The intersection of public art, immigrant youth, and human rights. *Radical Teacher, 104*, 55–61.

Hanley, M. S. (2011). You better recognize! The arts as social justice for African American students. *Equity & Excellence in Education, 44*, 420–444.

Hardie, J. H., & Tyson, K. (2013). Other people's racism: Race, rednecks, and riots in a southern high school. *Sociology of Education, 86*, 83–102.

Harper, S. R. (2012). Race without racism: How higher education researchers minimize racist institutional norms. *Review of Higher Education, 36*(1), 9–29.

Harris, C. I. (1993). Whiteness as property. *Harvard Law Review, 106*, 1707–1791.

Heilig, J. V., Brown, K. D., & Brown, A. L. (2012). The illusion of inclusion: A critical race theory textual analysis of race and standards. *Harvard Educational Review, 82*, 403–424.

Henry, K. L., & Dixson, A. D. (2016). "Locking the door before we got the keys": Racial realities of the charter school authorization process in post-Katrina New Orleans. *Educational Policy, 30*(1), 218–240.

Holt, T. C. (1995). Marking: Race, race-making, and the writing of history. *American Historical Review, 100*(1), 1–20.

Hopson, R. K., & Dixson, A. D. (2011). Intersections, theories, and meanings of race, racism, and educational ethnography. *Ethnography and Education, 6*, 1–7.

Howard, T. C., & Reynolds, R. (2008). Examining parent involvement in reversing the underachievement of African American students in middle-class schools. *Journal of Educational Foundations, 22*(1/2), 79–98.

Hyland, N. E. (2005). Being a good teacher of Black students? White teachers and unintentional racism. *Curriculum Inquiry, 35*, 429–459.

Irizarry, J. G., & Antrop-González, R. (2013). RicanStruction sites: Race, space, and place in the education of DiaspoRican youth. *Taboo: Journal of Culture and Education, 13*(1), 77–96.

Irizarry, J. G., & Raible, J. (2014). "A hidden part of me": Latino/a students, silencing, and the epidermalization of inferiority. *Equity & Excellence in Education, 47*, 430–444.

Irons, P. (2002). *"Cut yer thumb er Finger off." Jim Crow's children: The broken promise of the Brown decision*. New York, NY: Penguin Putnam,

Kohli, R. (2016). Behind school doors: The racialization of teachers of color in urban public schools. *Urban Education*. Advance online publication.

Kohli, R., & Solorzano, D. G. (2012). Teachers, please learn our names! Racial microaggressions and the K-12 classroom. *Race, Ethnicity and Education, 15*, 441–462.

Ladson-Billings, G. (1998). Just what is critical race theory and what's it doing in a nice field like education? *International Journal of Qualitative Studies In Education, 11*(1), 7–24.

Ladson-Billings, G. (2006). From the achievement gap to the education debt: Understanding achievement in US schools. *Educational Researcher, 35*(7), 3–12.

Ladson-Billings, G., & Tate, W., IV. (1995). Toward a critical race theory of education. *Teachers College Record, 97*(1), 47–68.

Lapayese, Y. V. (2007). Understanding and undermining the racio-economic agenda of No Child Left Behind: Using critical race methodology to investigate the labor of bilingual teachers. *Race, Ethnicity and Education, 10*, 309–321.

Lewis, A. E. (2003). Everyday race-making: Navigating racial boundaries in schools. *American Behavioral Scientist, 47*, 283–305.

Liasidou, A. (2014). The cross-fertilization of critical race theory and disability studies: Points of convergence/divergence and some education policy implications. *Disability & Society, 29*, 724–737.

Lindsay, J. L. (2007). Talking whiteness: Representations of social justice in one school. *Urban Review, 39,* 425–453.

Love, B. B. (2014). "I see Trayvon Martin": What teachers can learn from the tragic death of a young Black male. *Urban Review, 46,* 292–306.

Malagon, M., & Alvarez, C. (2010). Scholarship girls aren't the only Chicanas who go to college: Former Chicana continuation high school students disrupting the educational achievement binary. *Harvard Educational Review, 80,* 149–174.

Malsbary, C. (2014). "Will this hell never end?" Substantiating and resisting race-language policies in a multilingual high school. *Anthropology & Education Quarterly, 45,* 373–390.

Matrenec, R. H. (2011). The struggle for identity for African American adolescent males in a predominantly white, affluent school. *Journal of Poverty, 15,* 226–240.

May, S., & Sleeter, C. E. (Eds.). (2010). *Critical multiculturalism: Theory and praxis.* New York, NY: Routledge.

McGee Banks, C. A., & Banks, J. A. (1995). Equity pedagogy: An essential component of multicultural education. *Theory Into Practice, 34,* 152–158.

Milner, H. R. (2013). Why are students of color (still) punished more severely and frequently than white students? *Urban Education, 48,* 483–489.

Modica, M. (2015). Unpacking the "colorblind approach": Accusations of racism at a friendly, mixed-race school. *Race, Ethnicity and Education, 18,* 396–418.

Palmer, D. (2010). Race, power, and equity in a multiethnic urban elementary school with a dual-language "Strand" program. *Anthropology & Education Quarterly, 41,* 94–114.

Palmer, J. D., & Eun-Young, J. (2005). Korean born, Korean-American high school students' entry into understanding race and racism through social interactions and conversations. *Race, Ethnicity and Education, 8,* 297–317.

Parker, L., & Lynn, M. (2002). What's race got to do with it? Critical race theory's conflicts with and connections to qualitative research methodology and epistemology. *Qualitative Inquiry, 8,* 7–22.

Patel, L. (2015). Desiring diversity and backlash: White property rights in higher education. *Urban Review, 47,* 657–675.

Perez Huber, L. (2011). Discourses of racist nativism in California public education: English dominance as racist nativist microaggressions. *Educational Studies, 47,* 379–401.

Perez Huber, L., & Cueva, B. M. (2012). Chicana/Latina testimonios on effects and responses to microaggressions. *Equity & Excellence in Education, 45,* 392–410.

Perez Huber, L., Johnson, R. N., & Kohli, R. (2006). Naming racism: A conceptual look at internalized racism in US schools. *Chicano/Latino Law Review, 26,* 183–206.

Pimentel, C. (2011). The color of language: The racialized educational trajectory of an emerging bilingual student. *Journal of Latinos and Education, 10,* 335–353.

Prins, E. (2007). Interdistrict transfers, Latino/white school segregation, and institutional racism in a small California town. *Journal of Latinos and Education, 6,* 285–308.

Pulido, I. B. (2008). *Knowledge—the fifth element of hip hop music: Mexican and Puerto Rican youth engagement of hip hop as critically rac(ed) Education discourse* (Unpublished doctoral dissertation). University of Illinois at Urbana-Champaign.

Ricks, S. A. (2014). Falling through the cracks: Black girls and education. *Interdisciplinary Journal of Teaching and Learning, 4*(1), 10–21.

Roda, A., & Stuart Wells, A. M. Y. (2013). School choice policies and racial segregation: Where white parents' good intentions, anxiety, and privilege collide. *American Journal of Education, 119,* 261–293.

Rogers, R., & Mosley, M. (2006). Racial literacy in a second-grade classroom: Critical race theory, whiteness studies, and literacy research. *Reading Research Quarterly, 41,* 462–495.

Rozansky-Lloyd, C. (2005). African Americans in schools: Tiptoeing around racism. *Western Journal of Black Studies, 29,* 595–604.

Skerrett, A. (2011). English teachers' racial literacy knowledge and practice. *Race, Ethnicity and Education, 14*, 313–330.

Solorzano, D., Allen, W. R., & Carroll, G. (2002). Keeping race in place: Racial microaggressions and campus racial climate at the University of California, Berkeley. *Chicano/Latino Law Review, 23*, 15.

Solorzano, D., Ceja, M., & Yosso, T. (2000). Critical race theory, racial microaggressions, and campus racial climate: The experiences of African American college students. *Journal of Negro Education, 69*, 60–73.

Solorzano, D. G. (1997). Images and words that wound: Critical race theory, racial stereotyping, and teacher education. *Teacher Education Quarterly, 24*(3), 5–19.

Souto-Manning, M., & Cheruvu, R. (2016). Challenging and appropriating discourses of power: Listening to and learning from early career early childhood teachers of color. *Equity & Excellence in Education, 49*(1), 9–26.

Spring, J. (1994). *Deculturalization and the struggle for equality: A brief history of the education of dominated cultures in the United States.* Boston, MA: McGraw-Hill.

Stoll, L. C. (2014). Constructing the color-blind classroom: Teachers' perspectives on race and schooling. *Race, Ethnicity and Education, 17*, 688–705.

Stovall, D. (2013). 14 souls, 19 days and 1600 dreams: Engaging critical race praxis while living on the "edge" of race. *Discourse: Studies in the Cultural Politics of Education, 34*, 562–578.

Suh, Y., An, S., & Forest, D. (2015). Immigration, imagined communities, and collective memories of Asian American experiences: A content analysis of Asian American experiences in Virginia US history textbooks. *Journal of Social Studies Research, 39*(1), 39–51.

Tarca, K. (2005). Colorblind in control: The risks of resisting difference amid demographic change. *Educational Studies, 38*, 99–120.

Taylor, K. A., & Fernandez-Bergersen, S. L. (2015). Mexican American women's reflections from public high school. *Journal of Latinos and Education, 14*(1), 6–24.

Taylor, M., & Otinsky, G. (2006). Embarking on the road to authentic engagement: Investigating racism through interactive learning centers. *Voices From the Middle, 14*(1), 38–46.

Urrieta, L., Jr. (2006). Community identity discourse and the heritage academy: Colorblind educational policy and white supremacy. *International Journal of Qualitative Studies in Education, 19*, 455–476.

Valencia, R. R. (Ed.). (2012). *The evolution of deficit thinking: Educational thought and practice.* New York, NY: RoutledgeFalmer.

Valencia, R. R., & Solorzano, D. G. (1997). Contemporary deficit thinking. In R. Valencia (Ed.), *The evolution of deficit thinking: Educational thought and practice* (pp. 160–210). New York, NY: RoutledgeFalmer.

Vaught, S. E., & Castagno, A. E. (2008). "I don't think I'm a racist": Critical race theory, teacher attitudes, and structural racism. *Race, Ethnicity and Education, 11*, 95–113.

Woodson, C. G. (1933). *The mis-education of the Negro.* Trenton, NJ: Africa World Press.

Wun, C. (2015). Against captivity: Black girls and school discipline policies in the afterlife of slavery. *Educational Policy, 30*, 171–196.

Young, E. Y. (2011). The four personae of racism: Educators' (mis)understanding of individual vs. systemic racism. *Urban Education, 46*, 1433–1460.

Yull, D., Blitz, L. V., Thompson, T., & Murray, C. (2014). Can we talk? Using community-based participatory action research to build family and school partnerships with families of color. *School Community Journal, 24*(2), 9–31.

Zion, S., & Blanchett, W. (2011). [Re]conceptualizing inclusion: Can critical race theory and interest convergence be utilized to achieve inclusion and equity for African American students? *Teachers College Record, 113*, 2186–2205.

Chapter 9

Black Women's and Girls' Persistence in the P–20 Mathematics Pipeline: Two Decades of Children, Youth, and Adult Education Research

NICOLE M. JOSEPH
Vanderbilt University

MESERET HAILU
University of Denver

DENISE BOSTON
University of Illinois at Chicago

Like other women and girls of color in the U.S. education system, Black[1] women and girls negotiate and integrate multiple marginalized identities in mathematics. As such, this integrative review used critical race theory (CRT) and Black feminism as interpretive frames to explore factors that contribute to Black women's and girls' persistence in the mathematics pipeline and the role these factors play in shaping their academic outcomes. A synthesis of 62 research studies reveals that structural disruptions, community influences, and resilience strategies significantly influence Black women's and girls' persistence in mathematics, and that combined, these factors can culminate into a more robust mathematics identity for Black women and girls. A robust mathematics identity, in turn, is an aspect of self-actualization that is needed for persistence, engagement, and sustained success in the pursuit of a mathematics doctoral degree. New questions, paradigms, and ways of examining the experiences of Black women and girls in mathematics to advance further knowledge that will inform policy are identified and discussed as a future research agenda.

MAKING #BLACKGIRLMAGIC[2] COUNT IN MATHEMATICS AND MATHEMATICS EDUCATION

There is a national movement in the United States that emphasizes the importance of Black women's and girls' lives. Although widespread focus on the importance of Black women's lives is not a new phenomenon, the confluence of social media, federal

Review of Research in Education
March 2017, Vol. 41, pp. 203–227
DOI: 10.3102/0091732X16689045
© 2017 AERA. http://rre.aera.net

TABLE 1
Math Doctorates Awarded to Black and White Females and White Males: 2003 to 2012

	2003	2004	2005	2006	2007	2008	2009	2010	2011	2012
Total	513	508	540	583	645	671	788	863	849	852
Black females	4	1	9	5	5	11	16	9	9	10
White females	108	118	101	102	132	161	154	168	155	163
White males	281	270	297	326	326	329	405	466	472	473

Source. National Science Foundation (2015).

attention, and research funding is driving the increased visibility. For example, #BlackGirlMagic is a social media campaign about increasing the positive identity of Black girls and women (Thomas, 2016). On March 29, 2016, the NoVo Foundation announced the largest commitment ever made ($90 million) by a private foundation to address the structural inequalities facing girls and young women of color in the United States. The foundation is partnering with other leading advocates and organizers, a large majority of whom are women of color, such as the African-American Policy Forum and Girls for Gender Equity. Additionally, the White House Council of Women and Girls recently announced commitments totaling $118 million from various women's foundations and academic institutions across the country to improve the lives of young women of color through new programs and research (NoVo Foundation, 2016).

Similarly, the Congressional Caucus on Black Women and Girls recently hosted *Black Girl Movement: A National Conference*. This 3-day convening at Columbia University in 2016 focused on how to strategically address disadvantages that Black girls face, while "creating the political will to publicly acknowledge their achievements, contributions, and leadership" (NoVo Foundation, 2016, A Growing Movement, para. 3). These national efforts—spanning the public and private sector, including academe—are important because they acknowledge racism, sexism, and other structural inequalities that affect Black women's lives. Despite all of this attention, none of these initiatives is addressing the underrepresentation of Black women and girls in mathematics and mathematics education specifically, which is a phenomenon inextricably connected to issues of race, racism, and sexism (Joseph, 2017; Joseph, Haynes, & Cobb, 2016; Kenschaft, 1981; Martin, 2012; Walker, 2014). Problematizing the experience of Black women and girls and their underperformance and underrepresentation in mathematics across the P–20 pipeline is imperative (see Table 1). Such an examination is significant because, until very recently, the national discourse about Black girls' and women's academic mathematics performance has come from a deficit-based perspective, exacerbating poor performance and underrepresentation (Solorzano & Yosso, 2001), and creating and sustaining a negative master narrative (Giroux, 1991). The authors of this article argue that a more complex and nuanced narrative that accounts for social and historical processes is needed.

In this literature review, there are three guiding research questions: (a) What are the malleable factors that contribute to the persistence of Black women and girls in the mathematics pipeline? (b) How do these factors shape academic outcomes for Black women and girls? (c) Based on these findings, what should a future research agenda include to advance further knowledge that will inform policy? We define the primary academic outcome as the attainment of a terminal mathematics degree (specifically, a PhD in mathematics). Correspondingly, we define persistence as the progression of a student through primary, secondary, and postsecondary mathematics education in the United States.

The rest of this review is organized as follows. First, we begin by presenting and discussing our interpretive framing for analysis of the literature. We point out that the nature of mathematics and mathematics education is embedded in White supremacy; therefore, critical perspectives are necessary. As such, we take up critical race theory and Black feminism perspectives. This discussion is followed by our methods for how we conducted the review. Next, we consider the key findings that influence persistence in mathematics for Black women and girls despite mostly exclusionary and unwelcoming environments of the discipline. We conclude by speaking to scholars and practitioners who want to conduct research in this area. We identify and discuss new sets of questions, new paradigms, and new ways of examining Black women and girls in mathematics and mathematics education moving forward.

INTERPRETIVE FRAMING AND METHODOLOGY

The Nature of Mathematics and Mathematics Education: Exclusion, Gatekeeping, and White Supremacy

Mathematics, as a subject domain, is not a-racial, a-cultural, apolitical, or a-historical (Joseph, 2017; Joseph, Haynes, & Cobb, 2016; Joseph & Jordan-Taylor, 2016; Leonard, 2008; Martin, 2012; Martin, Gholson, & Leonard, 2010; McGee, 2013; Stinson, 2004; Walker, 2014). In fact, we suggest that mathematics is embedded in White supremacy (Joseph, Haynes, & Cobb, 2016; Martin, 2009; Stinson, 2004) and thrives on exclusion (Harris, 1993). In Western education, ideas related to tracking in mathematics can be traced back to Plato (see full argument in Joseph, 2017; Stinson, 2004) and tracking in mathematics in modern times can begin in early primary grades (Oakes, 1985). And while Oakes (1990a, 1990b) has warned the field about tracking and its restrictive and negative effects on opportunities to learn and college access, most public schools continue to track (Domina, Hanselman, Hwang, & McEachin, 2016; Minor, 2016; Tyson & Roksa, 2016). As such, Black girls are most likely to attend tracked public primary and secondary schools (National Center for Education Statistics, 2015). There are serious consequences for racial minorities who find themselves in low-tracked mathematics courses (Oakes, 1990a, 1990b) because once a student is on the low track, it is plausible that she or he will stay on that low track through high school. We know that the instruction that occurs in the low-tracked mathematics classes is subpar and does not prepare students for advanced mathematics (Oakes, Joseph, & Muir, 2004). In addition, this problem is exacerbated by a shortage of qualified mathematics teachers and a consistent staffing pattern of giving the most unprepared teachers to the most underserved students

(Ingersoll, 2001). Nearly 16 years ago, mathematics education leader Robert Moses suggested that in order for all students to be adequately prepared for advanced mathematics, taking Algebra in middle school is imperative (Moses & Cobb, 2001). Moses argues that all children should have access to the college preparatory mathematics curriculum of the high schools, because children without access to such programs are barred from acquiring the knowledge and skills necessary for participation in an economy driven by rapid technological change. More pointedly, Moses views mathematics literacy as a Civil Rights issue (Moses, Kamii, Swap, & Howard, 1989), especially for racial minorities who desire to take advanced mathematics courses at the secondary level but are unable to because many of the schools they attend do not offer such courses (Oakes et al., 2004). As students continue along the pipeline, adequate prior preparation in high school, as measured by indicators such as American College Testing scores, is a key factor that can predict persistence in undergraduate mathematics and other STEM (science, technology, engineering and mathematics) disciplines (Griffith, 2010; Price, 2010). For those few racial minorities who do make it to graduate mathematics (masters or doctorate), they continue to have to work through the lived reality of exclusion (i.e., "weed-out" courses and comprehensive exams; Herzig, 2004) and attempt to establish robust mathematics identities in unwelcoming environments (McGee, 2015).

Critical Race Theory, Black Feminism, and Black Women and Girls in Mathematics

Although the numbers are small (see Table 1), Black women and girls do persist in the mathematics education pipeline (Joseph, 2017; Kenschaft, 1981; Walker, 2014). Naturally, their pathways to the mathematics doctorate are not monolithic, as Walker (2014) points out in her seminal text, *Beyond Banneker: Black Mathematicians and the Paths to Excellence*. However, their formation to becoming mathematicians continues to be hampered by racism and sexism. Racism and sexism are social oppressions that have historical roots and contemporary lived implications, including the underrepresentation and underperformance of Black women and girls in the mathematics pipeline. For example, African Americans are less likely than White students to have teachers who emphasize high-quality mathematics instruction such as reasoning and nonroutine problem solving (Flores, 2007).

Critical race theory (CRT) aids us to interpret the literature about Black women and girls in mathematics education. As a heuristic for research, CRT has a variety of undergirding tenets. First, CRT scholars posit that race and racism is an everyday occurrence in American society and its institutions (Delgado & Stefancic, 2001). Black women and girls comprise about 6% of the U.S. population (U.S. Census Bureau, 2014), and they live as racialized beings, particularly in schools (Evans-Winters, 2005; Evans-Winters & Esposito, 2010; Joseph, Viesca, & Bianco, 2016; Rowley, Kurtz-Costes, & Cooper, 2011). For example, because Black women and girls are often depicted as loud, hypersexual, and disrespectful in popular media (Gordon, 2008; Muhammad & McArthur, 2015), this portrayal can influence how they get viewed and perceived by teachers (Joseph, Viesca, & Bianco, 2016). Many of the ways teachers, particularly

White teachers, come to understand their Black girls are via social media, the teachers' lounge, and other spaces that do not validate or affirm Black girls (Yoon, 2012).

Because race and racism are entrenched constructs in American life, our analyses deconstruct and disrupt ideas of meritocracy, colorblindness, neutrality, and objectivity (Chavous & Cogburn, 2007). CRT gives us permission to claim that mathematics spaces are not neutral, thereby making learning mathematics while Black a complex phenomenon (Alexander & Hermann, 2015; Gholson & Martin, 2014; Joseph, 2017; Martin, 2012; McGee, 2013). There are racial disparities in how educators organize mathematics learning, teaching, and assessment (Cobb & Russell, 2015). Nothing about the places in which Black women and girls learn mathematics reflects colorblindness and objectivity (Borum & Walker, 2011; Joseph, 2017; Walker, 2014). Black women are usually the only one of a few Black people in their advanced mathematics courses and programs and have to constantly prove their worth and value to the mathematics community, all while enduring isolation (Joseph, 2017; McGee, 2013; Walker, 2014).

Second, CRT in education underscores the need for counternarratives from students of color (Tate, 1997). Martin (2000, 2006a, 2006b) has written extensively about sociohistorical, community, school, and intrapersonal forces contributing to resilience and success in mathematics, but that work has not specifically focused on Black women and girls. As a result, we use the CRT tenet of counternarratives to frame counterstories of Black women and girls' achievement in mathematics to disrupt normative discourse about their underachievement and unpreparedness. Additionally, CRT elevates the importance of praxis based on the notion that researchers should be working toward social justice—the elimination of racism and sexism; as well as the empowerment of people of color and other subordinated groups (Solórzano & Delgado Bernal, 2001). In addressing underrepresentation and underperformance of Black women and girls in the mathematics pipeline, the understanding of theory is important but not sufficient. By pushing for a transformative policy agenda, we engage in praxis. This means that we, as education researchers, not only use theory and reflection to understand the complexities of Black women's and girls' persistence in mathematics but we also take action that embodies the commitment to human well-being, the search for truth, and respect for others (Freire, 2000).

In tandem with CRT, we also draw from Black feminism in our analyses and recommendations for further research. Although CRT gives researchers language to analyze, explain, and critique accepted norms and standards in education practice that claim to emphasize neutrality, objectivity, and truth related to race, it is limited for our population of interest because it does not explicitly account for gender. Critical race feminism (CRF; Wing, 1999), meanwhile, is another important framework, for studies examining the experiences of women of color in general. Although, CRF points out that women of color have different experiences from men of color, and that these women are often devalued in American society, rendering them voiceless and invisible, CRF is also limited in that it does not take into account the nuances of distinct experiences of Black women and girls in the United States; and one of those nuanced experiences is the legacy of slavery (Collins, 2000). Since our study is interrogating the literature related to Black women's and girls' experiences across the P–20 mathematics pipeline, we recognize the need for a framework that incorporates Black feminism. Black feminist thought critiques the broader feminist notion that there is an essential female voice regardless of race or class, and that the essentialized feminist voice actually represents that of middle- or upper-middle-class White women (Collins, 2000; hooks, 2000). Black feminism foregrounds Black women's and girls' lived experiences, which may not conform to the essentialist view of feminism or normative female experiences.

Hence, it is counterproductive to explore issues of equity in the mathematics and mathematics education pipeline by solely considering race, in large part because for women of color, race and gender identities intersect and cannot be divorced from each other (Crenshaw, 1991; Evans-Winters & Esposito, 2010). Black feminism points out that the two socially constructed categories of race and gender generate unique histories and experiences at the point of intersection (Collins, 1998). Without this type of intersectional analysis, sufficiently addressing the manner in which Black women and girls are subordinated and engage in resistance and self-actualization in mathematics and mathematics education is difficult. Furthermore, mathematics is uniquely primed for the use of this tool because it is considered a male-dominated domain, as well as a White institutional space (Joseph, 2017; Joseph, Haynes, & Cobb, 2016; Martin, 2008).

Methodology

We implemented a systematic approach to identifying, appraising, and synthesizing the results of relevant studies to arrive at conclusions about the body of literature related to Black women's and girls' persistence in the mathematics pipeline. We examined the literature from the past 20 years through electronic searches, manual searches of relevant journals, and consultation with experts in the field. By including research studies from 1996 to 2016, we investigated scholarship that critically examines educational systems and views minoritized populations from an asset-based theoretical lens (King, 1995; Ladson-Billings & Tate, 1995; Tate, 1997). We searched databases such as ERIC, JSTOR, PsycINFO, Google Scholar, Summon, and ProQuest. A combination of search terms that describe our population of interest (i.e., Black* girls* women* mathematics*females*achievement* success* persistence*) was used to maximize the number of peer-reviewed articles located. These searches yielded over 500 potential studies. Abstracts were read and citations were imported into an Excel spreadsheet if the study met the following criteria: (a) the title or abstract alluded to an examination of mathematics or STEM success; (b) the study appeared to contain original data—primary or secondary; and (c) the sample included racial minorities.

We include 62 peer-reviewed articles in this synthesis. Studies that investigated all racial minority populations (Black, Native American, Latino/a) and educational success factors and/or persistence in mathematics or STEM broadly[3] included an $n = 25$. Sixteen of the studies examined similar issues related to success but focused specifically on *Black students* (males and females). Studies that examined all racially minoritized women and girls (Black, Native American, Latino/a) included an $n = 9$. Finally, articles that were the focus of this literature review, Black women and girls and persistence in mathematics across the P–20 pipeline, included 12 studies. Of these 12 studies, one used a quantitative methodology, one used mixed methods, and the rest had qualitative approaches. In our conclusion, we discuss the future work that is required to fill this gap in the literature to inform theory and practice.

FINDINGS

In the United States, mathematics represents a White institutional space (Martin, 2008). As such, the study of mathematics is tied to physical and emotional places that are dominated by White ideology and traditions that do not include African American scholarship and thought (Martin, 2008), and this way of thinking is embedded in White supremacy (Joseph, 2017; Martin, 2008; Stinson, 2004). While there are many programs that aim to address STEM persistence broadly, our analysis of the literature suggests three interrelated themes that contribute to Black women's and girl's persistence in the P–20 mathematics pipeline, including (a) structural disruptions, (b) community influences, and (c) resilience strategies. Combined, these factors can culminate into a more robust mathematics identity for Black women and girls—an aspect of self-actualization that is needed for persistence, engagement, and sustained success (Boaler & Greeno, 2000). A stronger mathematics identity, in turn, helps Black women and girls see themselves not as just mathematics learners, but also as mathematics doers and creators of mathematics knowledge (Martin, 2010). We organize this section by first reporting and discussing these themes, and then we discuss what the findings suggest for the education field moving forward.

Structural Disruptions

CRT and Black feminism help us understand that structural disruptions are fundamental to supporting Black women's and girls' persistence through the mathematics pipeline because structural disruptions combat the constant erasure or invisibility (Crenshaw, 1989) that Black women and girls are subject to in many institutions. We define structural disruptions to mean interruptions in the basic ways the education system operates. It is well documented in the literature that since the beginning of the formation of common, compulsory schools in the early 19th century, the U.S. system of education has been set up to serve White middle-class students and that "other" students should assimilate and take on White, middle-class values and learning styles (Tyack, 1974). In contemporary times, these ideas are still ubiquitous, as we see in the pervasiveness of tracking (Oakes, 1985, 1990a, 1990b). Structural disruptions can be permanent, but many are short-lived in part because of limited funds (i.e., National Science Foundation funding) or political unwillingness to change age-old policies (i.e., tracking and curriculum adoptions). Structural disruptions can take the form of access to physical capital (like books, a clean and safe classroom, and adequate writing materials), availability of human capital (i.e., culturally responsive teachers, professors, and tutors), and administrative policies and programs that enhance the success of historically underserved student populations (Gutiérrez, 2013; Ladson-Billings, 2000; Noddings, 2005).

Structurally, many forces have increased the participation of Black women and girls in mathematics, including cocurricular programs, single-sex classrooms, a rise in the number of equity-focused mathematics teachers, learning centers, affirmative action policies, and education pipeline programs. Cocurricular programs are extensions of the formal learning space and generally occur outside of school and sometimes are operated by outside organizations (Bresciani, 2006). Additionally, cocurricular programs do not usually grant academic credit but provide students the opportunity to engage in learning without penalty (grades, etc.). For example, the GO-GIRL (Gaining Options: Girls Investigate Real Life) program for seventh-grade girls is a Saturday mathematics enrichment program that aims to build mathematical confidence, skills, and conceptual understanding by integrating mathematics and social science research and has shown an increase in mathematics achievement (Reid & Roberts, 2006). The Rural and Urban Images: Voices of Girls in Science, Mathematics, and Technology program is another cocurricular learning experience that has been found to be effective for Black girls and their families in rural areas (Kusimo, Carter, & Keyes, 1999). Elementary school–aged girls who participate in afterschool programs, compared with their male peers, benefit more from the academic activities and socialization offered in these spaces (Posner & Vandell, 1999).

In primary and secondary education, single-sex classrooms enhance achievement of female students because of the increased presence of same-sex role models and peer mentors (Bowe, Desjardins, Clarkson, & Lawrenz, 2015; Mael, 1998). As such, increasing the percentage of Black high school mathematics teachers overall has a positive impact on the likelihood that Black students will take additional rigorous mathematics (Klopfenstein, 2005). We know that Black mathematics teachers are rare; however, a rise in equity-focused mathematics teachers in general can influence persistence. Scholars who have studied racially diverse high schools have demonstrated that mathematics instructors can learn on the job and work collaboratively to create more equitable classrooms (Boaler & Staples, 2008; Horn, 2005). Some examples of strategies that equity-minded teachers utilize include having high expectations for their students, implementing mixed-ability grouping, and using reform-oriented mathematics experiences, such as focusing on conceptual problems, questioning, and group work (Cohen & Lotan, 2014; Horn, 2012). These practices can help racially diverse students succeed. Overall, teachers who hold high expectations generally send affirming messages to their students, and these equity-focused teacher moves have been found to make a significant difference in the lives of their students and mediate access to mathematics content (Battey, 2013; Wood, Kaplan, & McLoyd, 2007).

Learning centers that provide mathematics tutoring for standardized examinations have also proven useful (Knight-Diop, 2010). In postsecondary settings, summer research enrichment programs for undergraduate students have supported many Black women on their journey to becoming mathematics doctorate degree holders (Borum & Walker, 2011). Analogously, affirmative action and education pipeline programs help retain Black women and girls in mathematics programs as they navigate college and postgraduate mathematics education. The Meyerhoff Scholars

Program at the University of Maryland, Baltimore County, is an example of an affirmative-action support program that has increased the number of Black women who receive higher education degrees in mathematics (Fries-Britt, 1998). Structurally, the Meyerhoff Program supports enrolled students through financial support, academic advising, access to a network of professional liaisons, and tutoring (Fries-Britt, 1998). The Academic Investment in Mathematics and Science program at Bowling Green State University has a similar impact on educational attainment for Black women in undergraduate education (Gilmer, 2007). Participants in the Academic Investment in Mathematics and Science program are expected to complete a 5-week Summer Bridge Program (prior to starting their first year of college), enroll in mini courses that focus on mathematics and computer science, and attend excursions to professional facilities like National Aeronautics and Space Administration (Gilmer, 2007). The Early Scholars Program at the University of Texas at Austin, supports Black students enrolled in Calculus I in that they get to exchange mathematics knowledge with other racially diverse students, attend additional mathematics lectures, and receive mentoring. This program found that Black students who participated earned at least one letter grade higher in Calculus I than non–Early Scholars Program students and increased their likelihood of choosing mathematics, science, or engineering majors (Moreno & Muller, 1999). Broadly, Price (2010) found that undergraduate Black students who enroll in STEM courses taught by Black faculty are more likely to persist in their STEM major after the first year.

Traditionally, Historically Black Colleges and Universities have likewise focused on the institutional structures that support Black student's persistence to terminal degrees. In the period between 1997 and 2006, Historically Black Colleges and Universities were ranked as the top eight highest producers of Black mathematics and science graduates that persisted to PhDs (Lederman, 2008). Spelman College, in particular, is often touted for its historical reputation, constitution as a Black women's college and its success in awarding bachelor degrees in STEM fields to Black women. In this way, Spelman's institutional structure fosters a sense of collaboration and cooperative peer relationships that promotes academic achievement and success for Black women at the undergraduate level (Perna et al., 2009). Continuing the structure of intuitional support to graduate-level education and degree attainment, Sylvia Bozeman of Spelman College and Rhonda Hughes of Bryn Mawr College collaborated in the creation of the Enhancing Diversity in Graduate Education (EDGE) program to support women's transition from undergraduate to graduate programs. EDGE program activities include structural supports of a 4-week summer session of enrichment activities, attendance at annual conferences, and financial support for research travel as well as social interactions through collaborations, peer networking, and establishing mentoring relationships (Adam, 2006; "EDGE", 2016; Schroen, 2013). Collectively, structural disruptions like these have provided formalized ways for Black women and girls to enter and remain in the mathematics pipeline. By providing support for rigorous participation in mathematics learning, these instances of physical capital, human capital, and administrative policies and programs positively shape Black women's and girls' academic outcomes.

Community Influences

In ways similar to structural disruptions, community influences of family, peers, and social networks are important for Black women's and girls' persistence in mathematics. This persistence factor is also important in the context of Black feminism because African American women tend to have a unique camaraderie with one another that is not accessible for those who are not both female and Black (Collins, 1989). For example, in their study of the experiences of Black women in a same-sex and same-race graduate mentoring program, the *Sistah Network*, 18 Black women reported that their identities were affirmed and strengthened (Allen & Joseph, in press). They felt affirmed because Black women came together to celebrate being Black women, acknowledge their unique contributions, and see other successful Black women in graduate programs. Community factors are also important in the context of CRT because Black women co-construct and engage in praxis to disrupt social injustice. Black women engaging in community work for social justice is historical. The authentic intellectual work of the National Council of Negro Women founded in 1935 by Mary McLeod Bethune is an important example. In this organization, Black women collaborated, and continue to collaborate, to address challenges facing Black families and communities in rural and urban areas (Mueller, 1954).

Community influences on student persistence are those dynamic interactive relationship forces that support students as they persist through the mathematics pipeline. The process of communities influencing curriculum, student agency, and persistence is not novel, but are again historical in the African American community (Perlstein, 2004). Relationships with teachers, classmates, and families require community engagement and can shape the educational experience of Black women and girls pursuing mathematics (Trusty, 2002). For instance, Castagno and Brayboy (2008) argue that culturally responsive schooling is an important element of education, particularly for marginalized students who are part of socially, culturally distinct and subjugated communities. Across states in the United States, Black students are more likely to attend schools located in economically disadvantaged urban areas (Byrnes, 2003). As a result, teachers' ability to implement culturally responsive schooling is vital for Black girls because these students need to constantly negotiate academic demands while exhibiting cultural competence (Carter, 2005; Ladson-Billings, 1995). Moreover, since students' self-perception of mathematics ability can predict mathematics achievement, teachers who build on the cultural knowledge of Black girls can influence that self-perception, which then can increase the likelihood of positive views of mathematics among Black women and girls (Byrnes, 2003; Castagno & Brayboy, 2008).

Furthermore, the presence of same-race and same-gender peers normalizes the presence of Black women and girls in educational spaces (Borum & Walker, 2011). In the context of mathematics learning, a sense of belonging (mediated by same-race and same-gender peers) can help Black women and girls become high achievers and combat the social stereotype of male superiority in mathematics in primary and secondary schooling (Brown & Josephs, 1999; Evans, Copping, Rowley, & Kurtz-Costes, 2011). Additionally, the use of effective cooperative groups in classroom-sustained mentorship from more seasoned Black women scholars also contributes to the persistence of women in secondary and higher education (Blickenstaff, 2005; Wallace, Moore, & Curtis, 2014).

Like academic peer milieu, familial milieu matters because parent education is a predictor of student success in mathematics (Byrnes, 2003). Ing (2014) posits that parental influence is evident in students' successful mathematics achievement and that it outweighs the influences of teachers, counselors, and peers in career selection. Parental involvement is most influential in middle school and the first half of high school (Muller, 1998). Black girls whose parents are actively involved in school meetings (including parent–teacher conferences and parent–teacher association gatherings) have significantly higher math achievement than Black girls who do not (Strayhorn, 2010). Sometimes, what the field understands as parent involvement can be misunderstood. In their analysis of Black STEM high achievers at the college level, McGee and Spencer (2015) conceptualized parent involvement in support of mathematics participation and learning as being more complex than traditional notions of parental support. They highlight that Black parents are aware of inequities in schools and that they actively respond by becoming advocates, motivators, and even early teachers of mathematics for their children. Thus, parents who explicitly communicate their expectations to their daughters and support their daughters' critical consciousness improve their academic achievement (Gill & Reynolds, 2000).

The impact made by institutional figures is not to be underestimated at the primary, secondary, and tertiary levels. Encouragement from teachers plays a significant role in the development of and resilience for students to pursue STEM careers (Borum & Walker, 2012). Just as elementary and secondary school teachers and administrators shape the development of Black girls, postsecondary faculty and staff have dramatic longstanding influences on undergraduates and graduate students (Borum & Walker, 2012). That is to say, role models, mentors, and interactions with teachers and faculty are crucial for students' development and persistence. One study reported "African Americans tend to select occupations in which they have had contact with successful role models" (Hall & Post-Kammer, 1987, as cited in Borum & Walker, 2012, p. 368). This is a declaration of the importance of role models for Black women and girls to persist in mathematics (Joseph, 2017). Furthermore, it has been found that Black women at the graduate level benefit from the mentorship of Black women faculty, who often provide instrumental and psychosocial support (Allen & Joseph, in press; Williams, Brewley, Reed, White, & Davis-Haley, 2005) as well as socialization facilitators for entry into mathematics professions (Borum, Hilton, & Walker, 2016). Each of these community examples can be summed into what Morganson, Jones, and Major (2010) called social support coping—the looking to others for emotional support as a way of dealing with challenges and seeking aid from others to overcome stressors. In their examination of undergraduate Black women in STEM majors, the women reported that when they used social coping skills, it influenced their persistence. It is important to note that the programs mentioned in the structural disruptions section also have components of community forces at work. In the case of the Meyerhoff program, 13 of the 14 components listed as support for students' persistence were community building related (Maton & Hrabowski, 2004).

Resilience Strategies

Resilience is also a construct the field should consider related to persistence in the mathematics pipeline. Black women and girls take on an active role in the ways that they respond to and interact with their environments, particularly in mathematics spaces. This aspect of persistence is aligned with Black feminism, which asserts that Black women can produce knowledge, independent of Eurocentric oppressors (Collins, 1989). How do constructs such as belonging, attitudes, or aspirations play out in Black women's and girls' thought processes as they make decisions and solve problems in spaces that were not necessarily designed for them to be affirmed, validated, or function successfully? Studies show that from elementary through high school, Black girls have positive mathematics attitudes despite their low level of academic performance (Else-Quest, Mineo & Higgins, 2013; Riegle-Crumb, 2006). Some high-achieving Black girls view mathematics work as normative because they enjoy both procedural and conceptual mathematics that have direct applications in their daily lives (Lim, Chae, Schinck-Mikel, & Watson, 2013). Research suggests that when mathematics content is in conflict with one's sense of self or who she wants to be (disconnected), high-achieving students can dislike mathematics (Boaler, William & Zevenbergen, 2000). Consequently, scholars in the field should view high-achieving students who do not study mathematics or leave the field as an issue of belonging, rather than ability (Boaler et al., 2000; Herzig, 2004).

Even for Black women and girls who are high achieving and pursue advanced mathematics, perceptions of belonging or social and academic integration can be important for persistence (Herzig, 2004). For example, analysis of the archival documents of Drs. Euphemia Haynes, Evelyn Granville, Marjorie Brown, Vivienne Malone Mayes, and Gloria Hewitt, the first five Black women to receive doctorates in mathematics in the United States between the 1940s and 1960s, suggest that "complete isolation" and limited access to participate in the White male-dominated mathematics community of practice (due to racism and gender issues) were key factors that played a role in their discouragement from, but not failure in, pursuing a PhD in mathematics (Joseph, 2017). The strategies that these Black women employed could be explained by a more contemporary construct called stereotype management (McGee, 2013; McGee & Martin, 2011). High-achieving Black women and girls are isolated and experience feelings of not belonging in mathematics in part because of societal stereotypes of being perceived as "less than" and not capable. Additionally, racism and racialized experiences also contribute to feelings of isolation (Acosta, Duggins, Moore, Adams, & Johnson, 2016; McGee & Martin, 2011; Steele, 1997). Stereotype threat (Steele, 1997) is a key idea associated with mathematics performance. McGee and Martin (2011) extend Steele's (1997) work on stereotype threat because they include the everyday microaggressions inside and outside of the mathematics classroom. Additionally, while *stereotype threat* leads to academic disengagement, *stereotype management*—per McGee's and Martin's (2011) conceptualizations—moves toward additional motivation and high achievement, suggesting that the negative outcomes related to stereotype threat are not permanent.

Belonging is also an important aspect of identity and self-efficacy for Black female adolescents, especially for those who attend urban middle and high schools (Matthews, Banerjee, & Lauermann, 2014) or postsecondary predominately White institutions (Strayhorn, 2012). Faircloth and Hamm (2005) found that school belonging played a stronger role between self-efficacy and academic performance for African Americans than Whites. In fact, a sense of school belonging even showed enduring achievement and mental health benefits. Therefore, belonging among African Americans in urban schools is not only an essential motivational construct as Matthews et al. (2014) point out, but a unique scaffold for struggling Black children because it can keep them engaged in their academic efforts and can buffer against disengagement despite feelings of low efficacy.

Other studies have shown that Black girls have higher mathematics career aspirations than their White and Latina female peers (Riegle-Crumb, Moore, & Ramos-Wada, 2011), but over time structural obstacles limit access to higher level mathematics courses (Oakes, 1990b). Additionally, teachers' low expectations and the overall assumptions about Black girls in society impede the opportunity for Black girls to learn in mathematics classrooms (Rist, 2000). Given these realities, Black girls have learned how to be resilient and employ critical agency to persist in mathematics (Ellington & Frederick, 2010).

Black women and girls engage in the process of academic resilience in different ways. We adopt Rigsby's (1994) notion of resilience that suggests that resilience is not just individual characteristics, temperament, or natural abilities, but instead "is the response to a complex set of interactions involving person, social context, and opportunities" (p. 89). In her review of literature on Black women's college success, Winkle-Wagner (2015) pointed out the importance of moving beyond individual characteristics and more toward the role of relationships and institutions in fostering academic success among Black women. In their study of academic resilience in mathematics among poor and minority students at the elementary level, Borman and Overman (2004) found that the most powerful school models for promoting resiliency appear to be those that include elements that actively shield children from adversity. In addition to safe and orderly environments and positive teacher–student relationships, they also found that efficaciousness in mathematics, positive outlooks toward school, and greater engagement with schools were all associated with academic resilience.

Black women and girls who persist in the mathematics pipeline often have to overcome gender role cultural expectations and seek esteem through their own sense of achievement (Kenschaft, 1981,[4] 2005; Morales, 2008). Many of the gender role expectations come from their own families as some families view Black women as not having time to pursue a highly competitive discipline like mathematics (Case & Leggett, 2005; Kenschaft, 2005). For example, how does being a mathematician support a family or uplift the community or race? Focusing her time working on and solving important mathematics problems, reading books and spending long hours in a library are aspects of the life of a mathematician (Kenschaft, 2005). Thus, Black women, in general, are viewed more as caregivers and nurturers, rather than as individually ambitious mathematicians recognized for their own academic or professional pursuits (Joseph, 2017; Kenschaft, 2005). Such literature suggests that there is a heavy cost that high-achieving Black women must pay to remain successful.

Quality mentorship for Black women and girls across the pipeline is another factor contributing to resilience (Morales, 2008). The first author has written elsewhere about the recommendation to include White male mathematics faculty with social justice orientations and strong racial consciousness as important mentors, specifically for Black women at the graduate level (Joseph, 2017). One such faculty member was Lee Lorch (1915–2014), a mathematician from New York who worked at highly selective universities such as the University of Pennsylvania (Mathematicians of the African Diaspora, n.d.). Lorch held an egalitarian view of mathematics study, in which all scholars should have equal access to the rest of the mathematics community. To this end, he protested a regional Mathematical Association of America (MAA) meeting hosted by Vanderbilt University's Peabody College on March 16 to 17 in 1951 (Falconer, Walton, Wilkins, Shabazz, & Bozeman, 1995) because his Fisk University colleagues, Evelyn Boyd, Walter Brown, and H. M. Holloway, all African Americans (Falconer et al., 1995), were unable to attend the banquet to hear the plenary talk by MAA president, Saunders Mac Lane, titled "What Makes Students Think?" In the first author's study of the first five Black female mathematicians, some of the women spoke of Dr. Lorch's influence on their advancement of getting their PhDs in mathematics. Part of his influence came while teaching in the mathematics department at Fisk University, a historically Black university in Nashville. Lorch was an important advocate and mentor for two of these Black women since he even went so far as to fill out the doctorate application for one of the women without her even knowing (Joseph, 2017). While this can appear extreme, it shows the commitment that a White male mathematics faculty member had in affirming and legitimizing Black women's value and abilities to pursue mathematics to the highest level (Joseph, 2017). This was not an example of a White savior mentality, but a White man who clearly acknowledged the racism that exists in mathematics and who chose to utilize his race and gender privilege to think, to care, and to act.

MOVING FORWARD TO ADVANCE KNOWLEDGE ABOUT BLACK WOMEN AND GIRLS IN MATHEMATICS AND MATHEMATICS EDUCATION

It can be argued that structural disruptions, community influences, and resilience all funnel down to one key idea in mathematics and mathematics education no matter where a Black woman or girl is on the P–20 pipeline: the importance of a positive mathematics identity. Borrowing concepts from Martin's (2006b) mathematics socialization and identity development to orient this portion of the discussion, community influences affect how we see ourselves, how others see us, and how we do things. In this way, these relationships interact to help develop Black women's and girls' sense of mathematics identity in the context of performing mathematically. Additionally, structural disruptions, such as pipeline and cocurricular programs, can influence aspects of mathematics identity (like motivation and persistence) because they are designed to consider ways of learning and teaching for Black girls that can be counter to normative schooling practices and policies that exclude them. The ways in which Black girls engage in mathematics suggests that they take into account their own ways of knowing and learning to view themselves as effective mathematics learners (Jones, 2012). Finally, Black women's and girls' resilience in mathematics suggests that they have strong mathematics identities since they persist in obtaining mathematics knowledge, even though it can come at great personal costs given the prevailing norms of Whiteness or even anti-Blackness (McGee, 2015).

Black women and girls do persist in the P–20 mathematics pipeline, and we can learn from the ones who have succeeded. Like other girls and women of color in academe, they negotiate and integrate multiple marginalized identities (Turner, 2002). Black women and girls succeed because of their individual and communal resilience, and the support they receive through social interactions, structures, policies, and institutions (O'Connor, 2002). Our 20-year review of the literature has shown that the three broad motifs include important structural, community, and resilience factors that facilitate Black women's and girls' success and also have important implications for positive mathematics identity development. Moreover, this literature review shows that there is still much more work to do. In light of the findings from this review, the authors recommend six broad research and practice priorities that can push the discourse about mathematics education policy forward and improve academic outcomes for Black women and girls in mathematics.

Research Priority 1: Asset-Based and Policy-Oriented Research Agendas

Additional asset-based research is needed because it shed lights on effective ways to support Black women and girls. As suggested in CRT, counternarratives of educational success are important tools that can be used to combat inequity (Solorzano & Yosso, 2002). Thus, major research associations, such as the National Council of Teachers of Mathematics and the American Council on Education (ACE), should create distinct divisions that study Black women's and girls' educational attainment in mathematics. For example, ACE's Center for Policy Research and Strategy has a variety of active research projects in which a focus on Black girls and women in mathematics would naturally fit. Projects like "Minority Serving Institutions Issue and Policy Brief Series" and "An Analysis of Minority Serving Institutions using National Student Clearinghouse Data" (ACE, 2016) would be enhanced by a focus or task force on this population. This type of achievement-oriented scholarship, in turn, should inform policy design at the institutional, state, and federal level.

Research Priority 2: Cross-Departmental and Cross-Institutional Collaboration

Collaboration between departments and across institutions is needed to broaden opportunity for Black women and girls in mathematics. Specifically, education researchers need to collaborate across disciplines to better understand success factors that draw from fields such as economics, psychology, sociology, learning sciences, and history. Dr. Melissa Harris-Perry, professor at Wake Forest University, recently hosted a forum that serves as an excellent model for this type of collaboration. During the 2016 annual meeting of a national conference, Dr. Harris-Perry brought together education scholars from a wide range of subdisciplines for the Anna Julia Cooper Center Seminar (American Educational Research Association, 2016). During this luncheon, participants were asked to share their ideas and research agendas that relate to Black women and girls in education. In facilitating this type of conversation, Dr. Harris-Perry underscores the need for bridging disciplinary silos. Creating task forces, invited panels, and working groups is an important way to advance the scholarship about Black women and girls in mathematics. Within the context of Black feminism (Collins, 2000), this type of interdisciplinary conversation contributes to necessary coalition building that will support creative use of resources and reimagining historically exclusionary institutional arrangements.

Research Priority 3: Increased Quantitative Studies

The authors posit that the education field needs more robust quantitative studies that measure success in mathematics for Black women and girls in mathematics from multiple lenses. Moreover, large-scale quantitative studies should also be a priority for scholars and policymakers so that academic support programs can be rigorously evaluated and scaled. Quantitative research on Black women and girls should include multilevel statistical modeling to account for the moderating variables of the experience of Black female students and to allow for the intersections of race, class, and gender. To this end, combining CRT with quantitative analysis would be informative in addressing both intersectionality (Delgado & Stefancic, 2001) and generalization to a broader population.

Practice Priority 1: Curriculum Reform in Teacher Education Programs

In the realm of education practice, the authors call for additional coursework and professional development training about what it means to learn mathematics as a woman or girl of color, particularly a Black woman or girl. Using CRF (Evans-Winters & Esposito, 2010) as a tool, leaders at individual institutions should develop curriculum that reflects the unique intellectual and emotional needs of this student population. Teacher candidates should also be exposed to academic training that provides historical context about Black people's limited access to mathematics education over time (Joseph & Jordan-Taylor, 2014). Regional comprehensive universities, which tend to produce K–12 teachers in high numbers (Vandal & Thompson, 2009), should be especially cognizant of this recommendation.

Practice Priority 2: Curriculum Reform in Doctoral Mathematics Programs

The authors also call for a reform in mathematics doctoral programs. Across institutions, course curricula in doctoral programs for mathematics are almost exclusively focused on mathematics content (Herzig, 2004). While there is not a national accrediting body for mathematics PhD programs, leading professional organizations such as the American Mathematical Society and MAA periodically publish recommendations for what PhD programs should include. Oftentimes, these organizations promote excellence in mathematics content, like linear algebra and differential equations (American Mathematical Society, 2016). Although there is obvious value and a need for this, discussion-based seminar courses that address systemic inequity and sociopolitical contexts in mathematics and mathematics education are also needed. The authors highlight doctoral education because many of these students in these programs will go on to become faculty members in mathematics departments (Herzig, 2002; Reys & Dossey, 2008). As the future producers of mathematics knowledge, mathematics instructors need to be equipped with knowledge of the social, historical, and political contexts of their profession.

The National Alliance for Doctoral Studies in the Mathematical Sciences at the University of Iowa serves as an exemplary program that facilitates curriculum reform in doctoral mathematics programs. The National Alliance for Doctoral Studies in the Mathematical Sciences is a coalition of mathematics/science students and faculty who are committed to increasing the number of people of color with a PhD in mathematics and statistical sciences. In an effort to diversify the mathematics field, the Alliance has worked with mathematical sciences graduate faculty nationally to build Alliance Graduate Program Groups: groups of faculty at mathematical (or math and sciences) sciences graduate programs that have committed themselves to the best practices and community building that have been the hallmark of the Alliance (University of Iowa, 2013).

Practice Priority 3: Support for Pipeline Programs

Last, the authors call for the allocation of funding from White House Council of Women and Girls to support mathematics education pipeline programs. The literature presented in this review demonstrates that programs like the Meyerhoff Scholars Program and the Academic Investment in Mathematics and Science Program help women get into and stay in the mathematics field. Thus, allocating significant funding to enhance and expand programs like these—particularly flagship state institutions and Historical Black Colleges and Universities—would be beneficial.

CONCLUSION

In this literature review, the authors have demonstrated how the mathematics and mathematics education fields have an important opportunity to interrogate educational achievement in more complex ways, in part by leveraging the national Black girls' movement. The extant literature has shown that achievement is not just measured by test scores but also other academic outcomes such as persistence, degree completion, and a robust mathematics identity (McGee, 2015; McGee & Martin, 2011). The review of the literature has also allowed authors to address three guiding questions of the text. The malleable factors that contribute to the persistence of Black women and girls in the mathematics pipeline are structural disruptions to traditional schooling, community support for Black women scholars, and individual and collective resilience that allows Black women to succeed in hostile environments. Though these persistence factors are distinct, they work in tandem to promote mathematics achievement for Black women and girls. Based on these findings, future research should focus on asset-based and policy-oriented research agendas, cross-departmental and cross-institutional collaboration, and increased quantitative studies. Meanwhile, mathematics practitioners should focus on curriculum reform in teacher education programs, curriculum reform in doctoral mathematics programs, and additional support for pipeline programs.

The Black girls' movement provides opportunities for transformation in our education systems, and the way we think in mathematics education specifically. If more Black and other women of color were included as full participants in mathematics, then the communities from which they come could also share in the development of mathematics thought, leading to equity implications that reach far beyond the domain of mathematics (Herzig, 2004). Mastery of mathematics content and learning is the basis for a variety of occupations and industries, including mathematical modeling, engineering, architecture, and biostatistics. Thus, when Black women excel in mathematics throughout the pipeline and become PhD holders, they ultimately gain access to much wider professional and social networks as well.

Secada (1989) stated almost 30 years ago that if large numbers of people perceive that they are outcasts from mathematics and science, they are less likely to support critical societal investments. Mathematics development and the solving of complex problems are important and should be approached by using a collection of diverse individuals rather than a collection of individually capable individuals (Paige, Lloyd, & Chartres, 2008). As such, Black women and girls deserve the opportunity to fully participate by making important contributions in the following ways: solving grand challenges in mathematics, expanding mathematics leadership and decision making, and making mathematics achievements by Black women visible. Black women's and girls' persistence in mathematics and mathematics education matters.

NOTES

[1]*Black* refers to individuals who are multigenerationally born and raised in the United States; a group of people whose families identified themselves as African American for generations and for whom that identification is a crucial part of their sense of themselves, their families, and their communities. Black people have a distinct identity that has been shaped in large measure by a common history of slavery and by the political struggle of the Civil Rights Movement. Multigenerational African Americans have been enculturated in how race and ethnicity are socially constructed in the United States (Clark, 2010).

[2]Black Girl Magic: Retrieved from http://www.huffingtonpost.com/entry/what-is-black-girl-magic-video_us_5694dad4e4b086bc1cd517f4

[3] We note that it is just as important to hear from the women and girls who are experiencing struggle in mathematics and that these studies could also provide insight as to how to improve outcomes for Black women in mathematics; however, the focus of this special issue is about disrupting inequality. Thus by focusing on success, we participate in resistance and disruption.

[4] We include Patricia Kenschaft's (1981) study as one of the 62 even though it is outside of the timeline. We include this work because Kenschaft was the first mathematician to study, center, publish and make public recommendations about American Black women's experiences

in mathematics. In this 1981 study, she provided statistics on the number of Black women holding doctorates in mathematics as well as shared findings from her personal interviews with several of these Black women. She highlighted their plight and promise as Black women in mathematics.

REFERENCES

Acosta, M., Duggins, S., Moore, T. E., Adams, T., & Johnson, B. (2016). From whence cometh my help? Exploring Black doctoral student persistence. *Journal of Critical Scholarship on Higher Education and Student Affairs, 2*(1), 32–48.

Adam, M. (2006). Women, EDGE, and the PhD in math. *Hispanic Outlook in Higher Education, 16*(20), 30–31.

Alexander, Q. R., & Hermann, M. A. (2015). African-American women's experiences in graduate science, technology, engineering, and mathematics education at a predominantly White university: A qualitative investigation. *Journal of Diversity in Higher Education.* Advance online publication. doi:10.1037/a0039705

Allen, E., & Joseph, N. M. (in press). The Sistah Network: Enhancing the educational and social experiences of Black graduate women in the academy. *NASPA Journal About Women in Higher Education.*

American Council on Education. (2016). *Projects.* Retrieved from https://www.acenet.edu/news-room/Pages/CPRS-Select-Ongoing-Projects.aspx

American Educational Research Association. (2016). *Key sessions.* Retrieved from http://www.aera.net/EventsMeetings/AnnualMeeting/Program/KeySessions/tabid/16161/Default.aspx

American Mathematical Society. (2016). *Data on the profession.* Retrieved from http://www.ams.org/profession/data/emp-survey

Battey, D. (2013). "Good" mathematics teaching for students of color and those in poverty: The importance of relational interactions within instruction. *Educational Studies in Mathematics, 82,* 125–144.

Blickenstaff, J. (2005). Women and science careers: Leaky pipeline or gender filter? *Gender and Education, 17,* 369–386.

Boaler, J., & Greeno, J. G. (2000). Identity, agency, and knowing in mathematics worlds. In J. Boaler, & J. G. Greeno (Eds.), *Multiple perspectives on mathematics teaching and learning* (pp. 170–200). Westport, CT: Ablex.

Boaler, J., & Staples, M. (2008). Creating mathematical futures through an equitable teaching approach: The case of Railside School. *Teachers College Record, 110,* 608–645.

Boaler, J., William, D., & Zevenbergen, R. (2000, March). *The construction of identity in secondary mathematics education.* Paper presented at the International Mathematics Education and Society Conference, Montechoro, Portugal.

Borman, G. D., & Overman, L. T. (2004). Academic resilience in mathematics among poor and minority students. *Elementary School Journal, 104,* 177–195.

Borum, V., & Walker, E. (2011). Why didn't I know? Black women mathematicians and their avenues of exposure to the doctorate. *Journal of Women and Minorities in Science and Engineering, 17,* 357–369.

Borum, V., & Walker, E (2012). What makes the difference? Black women's undergraduate and graduate experiences in mathematics. *Journal of Negro Education, 81,* 366–378.

Borum, V., Hilton, A. A., & Walker, E. (2016). The role of Black colleges in the development of mathematicians. *Journal of Research Initiatives, 2*(1). Retrieved from http://digitalcommons.uncfsu.edu/jri/vol2/iss1/6

Bowe, A. G., Desjardins, C. D., Clarkson, L. M. C., & Lawrenz, F. (2015). Urban elementary single-sex math classrooms mitigating stereotype threat for African American girls. *Urban Education.* Advance online publication. doi:10.1177/0042085915574521

Bresciani, M. J. (2006). *Outcomes-based academic and co-curricular program review: A compilation of institutional good practices.* Sterling, VA: Stylus.

Brown, R. P., & Josephs, R. A. (1999). A burden of proof: Stereotype relevance and gender differences in math performance. *Journal of Personality and Social Psychology, 76,* 246–257.

Byrnes, J. P. (2003). Factors predictive of mathematics achievement in White, Black, and Hispanic 12th graders. *Journal of Educational Psychology, 95,* 316–326.

Carter, P. (2005). *Keeping it real: School success beyond Black and White.* New York, NY: Oxford University Press.

Case, B. A., & Leggett, A. M. (Eds.). (2005). *Complexities: Women in mathematics.* Princeton, NJ: Princeton University Press.

Castagno, A. E., & Brayboy, B. M. J. (2008). Culturally responsive schooling for Indigenous youth: A review of the literature. *Review of Educational Research, 78,* 941–993.

Chavous, T., & Cogburn, C. D. (2007). Superinvisible women: Black girls and women in education. *Black Women, Gender + Families, 1*(2), 24–51.

Clark, H. D. (2010). *We are the same but different: Navigating African American and deaf cultural identities* (Doctoral dissertation). Retrieved from ProQuest Dissertations and Theses Global. (Accession Order No. 3421743)

Cobb, F., & Russell, N. M. (2015). Meritocracy or complexity: Problematizing racial disparities in mathematics assessment within the context of curricular structures, practices, and discourse. *Journal of Education Policy, 30,* 631–649. doi:10.1080/02680939.2014 .983551

Cohen, E. G., & Lotan, R. A. (2014). *Designing groupwork: Strategies for the heterogeneous classroom* (3rd ed.). New York, NY: Teachers College Press.

Collins, P. H. (1989). The social construction of Black feminist thought. *Signs, 14,* 745–773.

Collins, P. H. (1998). Intersections of race, class, gender, and nation. Some implications for Black family studies. *Journal of Comparative Family Studies, 29,* 27–34.

Collins, P. H. (2000). *Black feminist thought: Knowledge, consciousness, and the politics of empowerment.* New York, NY: Routledge.

Crenshaw, K. (1989). Demarginalizing the intersection of race and sex: A Black feminist critique of antidiscrimination doctrine, feminist theory and antiracist politics. *University of Chicago Legal Forum, 1*(8), 139–167.

Crenshaw, K. (1991). Mapping the margins: Intersectionality, identity politics, and violence against women of color. *Stanford Law Review, 43,* 1241–1299.

Delgado, R., & Stefancic, J. (2001). *Critical race theory: An introduction.* New York: New York University Press.

Domina, T., Hanselman, P., Hwang, N., & McEachin, A. (2016). Detracking and tracking up mathematics course placements in California middle schools, 2003–2013. *American Educational Research Journal, 53,* 1229–1266.

EDGE: A program for Women in Mathematics. (2016, March 22). Retrieved from http://www.edgeforwomen.org/

Ellington, R. M., & Frederick, R. (2010). Black high achieving undergraduate mathematics majors discuss success and persistence in mathematics. *Negro Educational Review, 61*(1–4), 61–84, 123.

Else-Quest, N. M., Mineo, C. C., & Higgins, A. (2013). Math and science attitudes and achievement at the intersection of gender and ethnicity. *Psychology of Women Quarterly, 37,* 293–309.

Evans, A. B., Copping, K. E., Rowley, S. J., & Kurtz-Costes, B. (2011). Academic self-concept in Black adolescents: Do race and gender stereotypes matter? *Self and Identity, 10,* 263–277.

Evans-Winters, V. E. (2005). *Teaching Black girls: Resiliency in urban classrooms.* New York, NY: Peter Lang.

Evans-Winters, V. E., & Esposito, J. (2010). Other people's daughters: Critical race feminism and Black girls' education. *Journal of Educational Foundations, 24*(1/2), 11–24.

Faircloth, B. S., & Hamm, J. (2005). Sense of belonging among high school students represent 4 ethnic groups. *Journal of Youth and Adolescence, 34*, 293–309.

Falconer, E. Z., Walton, H. J., Wilkins, E. J., Shabazz, A. A., & Bozeman, S. T. (1995, April). *A history of minority participation in the southeastern section. A supplement to Threescore and Ten: A history of the Southeastern Section of the Mathematical Association of America 1922–1992.* Retrieved from http://sections.maa.org/southeastern/minority/

Flores, A. (2007). Examining disparities in mathematics education: Achievement gap or opportunity gap? *High School Journal, 91*(1), 29–42.

Freire, P. (2000). *Pedagogy of the oppressed.* New York, NY: Bloomsbury.

Fries-Britt, S. (1998). Moving beyond Black achiever isolation: Experiences of gifted Black collegians. *Journal of Higher Education, 69*, 556–576.

Gholson, M., & Martin, D. B. (2014). Smart girls, Black girls, mean girls, and bullies: At the intersection of identities and the mediating role of young girls' social network in mathematical communities of practice. *Journal of Education, 194*(1), 19–33.

Gill, S., & Reynolds, A. J. (2000). Educational expectations and school achievement of urban African American children. *Journal of School Psychology, 37*, 403–424.

Gilmer, T. C. (2007). An understanding of the improved grades, retention and graduation rates of STEM majors at the Academic Investment in Math and Science (AIMS) Program of Bowling Green State University (BGSU). *Journal of STEM Education, 8*(1/2), 11–21.

Giroux, H. A. (1991). *Postmodernism, feminism, and cultural politics: Redrawing educational boundaries.* New York: State University of New York Press.

Gordon, M. K. (2008). Media contributions to African American girls' focus on beauty and appearance: Exploring the consequences of sexual objectification. *Psychology of Women Quarterly, 92*, 245–256.

Griffith, A. M. (2010). Persistence of women and minorities in STEM field majors: Is it the school that matters? *Economics of Education Review, 29*, 911–922.

Gutiérrez, R. (2013). The sociopolitical turn in mathematics education. *Journal for Research in Mathematics Education, 44*(1), 37–68.

Hall, E. R., & Post-Kammer, P. (1987). Black mathematics and science majors: Why so few? *Career Development Quarterly, 35*, 206–219.

Harris, C. I. (1993). Whiteness as property. *Harvard Law Review, 106*, 1707–1791.

Herzig, A. H. (2002). Where have all the students gone? Participation of doctoral students in authentic mathematical activity as a necessary condition for persistence toward the PhD. *Educational Studies in Mathematics, 50*, 177–212.

Herzig, A. H. (2004). Becoming mathematicians: Women and students of color choosing and leaving doctoral mathematics. *Review of Educational Research, 74*, 171–214.

hooks, B. (2000). *Feminist theory: From margin to center.* London, England: Pluto Press.

Horn, I. S. (2005). Learning on the job: A situated account of teacher learning in high school mathematics departments. *Cognition and Instruction, 23*, 207–236.

Horn, I. S. (2012). *Strength in numbers: Collaborative learning in secondary mathematics.* Reston, VA: National Council of Teachers of Mathematics.

Ing, M. (2014). Can parents influence children's mathematics achievement and persistence in STEM careers? *Journal of Career Development, 41*, 87–103. doi:10.1177/0894845313481672

Ingersoll, R. M. (2001). Teacher turnover and teacher shortages: An organizational analysis. *American Educational Research Journal, 38*, 499–534.

Jones, J. (2012). *Case stories of mathematical and racial identity among Black girls in a small urban school district.* Retrieved from https://rucore.libraries.rutgers.edu/rutgers-lib/37820/

Joseph, N. M. (2017). What Plato took for granted: Examining the biographies of the first five African American female mathematicians and what that says about resistance to the western epistemological cannon. In B. Polnick, B. Irby, & J. Ballenger (Eds.), *Women of color in STEM: Navigating the workforce* (pp. 3–38). Charlotte, NC: Information Age.

Joseph, N. M., Haynes, C. M., & Cobb, F. (Eds.). (2016). *Interrogating whiteness and relinquishing power: White faculty's commitment to racial consciousness in STEM classrooms.* New York, NY: Peter Lang.

Joseph, N. M., & Jordan-Taylor, D. (2016). The value of a triangle: Mathematics education in industrial and classical schools in the segregated south. *Journal of Negro Education, 85,* 444–461.

Joseph, N. M, & Jordan-Taylor, D. (April, 2014). *The mathematics education of African Americans, 1866–1954.* Paper presented at the American Educational Research Association annual meeting, Philadelphia, PA.

Joseph, N. M., Viesca, K. M., & Bianco, M. (2016). Black female adolescents and racism in schools: Experiences in a colorblind society. *The High School Journal, 100,* 4–25.

Kenschaft, P. C. (1981). Black women in mathematics in the United States. *American Mathematical Monthly, 88,* 592–604.

Kenschaft, P. C. (2005). *Change is possible: Stories of women and minorities in mathematics.* Providence, RI: American Mathematical Society.

King, J. E. (1995). Culture-centered knowledge: Black studies, curriculum transformation, and social action. In J. A. Banks, & C. A. M. Banks (Eds.), *Handbook of research on multicultural education* (pp. 265–292). New York, NY: Macmillan.

Klopfenstein, K. (2005). Beyond test scores: The impact of Black teacher role models on rigorous math taking. *Contemporary Economic Policy, 23,* 416–428.

Knight-Diop, M. G. (2010). Closing the gap: Enacting care and facilitating Black students' educational access in the creation of a high school college-going culture. *Journal of Education for Students Placed at Risk, 15,* 158–172.

Kusimo, P. S., Carter, C. S., & Keyes, M. C. (1999). *I'd like to go to Harvard but I don't know where it is: Bridging the gap between reality and dreams for adolescent African American girls.* Arlington, VA: National Science Foundation.

Ladson-Billings, G. (1995). Toward a theory of culturally relevant pedagogy. *American Educational Research Journal, 32,* 465–491.

Ladson-Billings, G. (2000). Fighting for our lives preparing teachers to teach African American students. *Journal of Teacher Education, 51,* 206–214.

Ladson-Billings, G., & Tate, W.F. (1995). Toward a critical race theory of education. *Teachers College Record, 97,* 47–68.

Lederman, D. (2008). *Who produces Black Ph.D.'s?* Retrieved from https://www.insidehighered.com/news/2008/09/02/phds

Leonard, J. (2008). *Culturally specific pedagogy in the mathematics classroom.* New York, NY: Routledge.

Lim, J. H., Chae, J., Schinck-Mikel, A. G., & Watson, J. (2013). Varied meanings and engagement in school mathematics: Cross-case analysis of three high-achieving young adolescent girls. *School Science and Mathematics, 113,* 191–200.

Mael, F. A. (1998). Single-sex and coeducational schooling: Relationships to socio-emotional and academic development. *Review of Educational Research, 68,* 101–129.

Martin, D. B. (2000). *Mathematics success and failure among African American youth: The roles of socio-historical context, community forces, school influence, and individual agency.* Mahwah, NJ: Lawrence Erlbaum.

Martin, D. (2006a). Mathematics learning and participation as racialized forms of experience: African American parents speak on the struggle for mathematics literacy. *Mathematical Thinking and Learning, 8,* 197–229.

Martin, D. B. (2006b). Mathematics learning and participation in the African American context: The co-construction of identity in two intersecting realms of experience. In N. Nasir, & P. Cobb (Eds.), *Improving access to mathematics: Diversity and equity in the classroom* (pp. 146–158). New York, NY: Teachers College Press.

Martin, D. B. (2008). E (race) ing race from a national conversation on mathematics teaching and learning: The national mathematics advisory panel as white institutional space. *The Montana Mathematics Enthusiast, 5*, 387–398.

Martin, D. B. (2009). *Little Black boys and little Black girls: How do mathematics education research and policy embrace them.* Paper presented at the proceedings of the 31st annual meeting of the North American Chapter of the International Group for the Psychology of Mathematics Education, Atlanta, GA.

Martin, D. B. (Ed.). (2010). *Mathematics teaching, learning, and liberation in the lives of Black children.* New York, NY: Routledge.

Martin, D. B. (2012). Learning mathematics while Black. *Journal of Educational Foundations, 26*(1/2), 47–66.

Martin, D. B., Gholson, M. L., & Leonard, J. (2010). Mathematics as gatekeeper: Power and privilege in the production of knowledge. *Journal of Urban Mathematics Education, 3*(2), 12–24.

Mathematicians of the African Diaspora. (n.d.). *An appreciation to Lee Lorch.* Retrieved from http://www.math.buffalo.edu/mad/special/lorch-lee.html

Maton, K. I., & Hrabowski, F. A., III. (2004). Increasing the number of African American PhDs in the sciences and engineering: A strengths-based approach. *American Psychologist, 59*, 547–556.

Matthews, J. S., Banerjee, M., & Lauermann, F. (2014). Academic identity formation and motivation among ethnic minority adolescents: The role of the "self" between internal and external perceptions of identity. *Child Development, 85*, 2355–2373.

McGee, E. (2013). Young, Black, mathematically gifted, and stereotyped. *High School Journal, 96*, 253–263.

McGee, E. O. (2015). Robust and fragile mathematical identities: A framework for exploring racialized experiences and high achievement among Black college students. *Journal for Research in Mathematics Education, 46*, 599–625.

McGee, E. O., & Martin, D. B. (2011). "You would not believe what I have to go through to prove my intellectual value!" Stereotype management among academically successful Black mathematics and engineering students. *American Educational Research Journal, 48*, 1347–1389.

McGee, E., & Spencer, M. B. (2015). Black parents as advocates, motivators, and teachers of mathematics. *Journal of Negro Education, 84*, 473–490.

Minor, E. C. (2016). Racial differences in mathematics test scores for advanced mathematics students. *High School Journal, 99*, 193–210.

Morales, E. E. (2008). Exceptional female students of color: Academic resilience and gender in higher education. *Innovative Higher Education, 33*, 197–213.

Moreno, S. E., & Muller, C. (1999). Success and diversity: The transition through first-year calculus in the university. *American Journal of Education, 108*, 30–57.

Morganson, V. J., Jones, M. P., & Major, D. A. (2010). Understanding women's underrepresentation in science, technology, engineering, and mathematics: The role of social coping. *Career Development Quarterly, 59*, 169–179.

Moses, R., Kamii, M., Swap, S. M., & Howard, J. (1989). The algebra project: Organizing in the spirit of Ella. *Harvard Educational Review, 59*, 423–444.

Moses, R. P., & Cobb, C. E. (2001). *Radical equations: Math literacy and civil rights.* Boston, MA: Beacon Press.

Mueller, R. C. (1954). National council of Negro women. *Negro History Bulletin, 18*(2), 27.

Muhammad, G. E., & McArthur, S. A. (2015). "Styled by their perceptions": Black adolescent girls interpret representations of Black females in popular culture. *Multicultural Perspectives, 17*, 133–140. Retrieved from http://0-search.proquest.com.bianca.penlib.du.edu/docview/1773229699?accountid=14608

Muller, C. (1998). Gender differences in parental involvement and adolescents' mathematics achievement. *Sociology of Education, 71*, 336–356.

National Center for Education Statistics. (2015). *Back to school statistics.* Retrieved from http://nces.ed.gov/fastfacts/display.asp?id=372

National Science Foundation. (2015). *Women, minorities, and persons with disabilities in science and engineering* (Special Report NSF 15-311). Arlington, VA: Author. Retrieved from http://www.nsf.gov/statistics/wmpd/

Noddings, N. (2005). What does it mean to educate the whole child? *Educational Leadership, 63,* 8–13.

NoVo Foundation. (2016). *NoVo Foundation announces $90 million investment in girls and young women of color across the United States* (Press release). Retrieved from http://novo-foundation.org/pressreleases/novo-foundation-announces-90-million-investment-in-girls-and-young-women-of-color-across-the-united-states/

Oakes, J. (1985). *Keeping track.* New Haven, CT: Yale University Press.

Oakes, J. (1990a). *Multiplying inequalities: The effects of race, social class, and tracking on opportunities to learn mathematics and science.* Santa Monica, CA: Rand.

Oakes, J. (1990b). Opportunities, achievement, and choice: Women and minority students in science and mathematics. *Review of Research in Education, 16,* 153–222.

Oakes, J., Joseph, R. R., & Muir, K. (2004). Access and achievement in mathematics and science: Inequalities that endure and change. In J. A. Banks, & C. A. M. Banks (Eds.), *Handbook of research on multicultural education* (pp. 69–90). San Francisco, CA: Jossey-Bass.

O'Connor, C. (2002). Black women beating the odds from one generation to the next: How the changing dynamics of constraint and opportunity affect the process of educational resilience. *American Educational Research Journal, 39,* 855–903.

Paige, K., Lloyd, D., & Chartres, M. (2008). Moving towards transdisciplinarity: An ecological sustainable focus for science and mathematics pre-service education in the primary/middle years. *Asia-Pacific Journal of Teacher Education, 36,* 19–33.

Perlstein, D. H. (2004). *Justice, justice: School politics and the eclipse of liberalism.* New York, NY: Peter Lang.

Perna, L., Lundy-Wagner, V., Drezner, N. D., Gasman, M., Yoon, S., Bose, E., & Gary, S. (2009). The contribution of HBCUS to the preparation of African American women for stem careers: A case study. *Research in Higher Education, 50,* 1–23 doi:10.1007/s11162-008-9110-y

Posner, J. K., & Vandell, D. L. (1999). After-school activities and the development of low-income urban children: A longitudinal study. *Developmental Psychology, 35,* 868–879.

Price, J. (2010). The effect of instructor race and gender on student persistence in STEM fields. *Economics of Education Review, 29,* 901–910.

Reid, P. T., & Roberts, S. K. (2006). Gaining options: A mathematics program for potentially talented at-risk adolescent girls. *Merrill-Palmer Quarterly, 52,* 288–304.

Reys, R. E., & Dossey, J. A. (2008). *U.S. doctorates in mathematics education: Developing stewards of the discipline.* Providence, RI: American Mathematical Society.

Riegle-Crumb, C. (2006). The path through math: Course sequences and academic performance at the intersection of race-ethnicity and gender. *American Journal of Education, 113,* 101–122. doi:10.1086/506495

Riegle-Crumb, C., Moore, C., & Ramos-Wada, A. (2011). Who wants to have a career in science or math? Exploring adolescents' future aspirations by gender and race/ethnicity. *Science Education, 95,* 458–476.

Rigsby, D. W. (1994). On resilience: Questions of validity. In M. Wang, & E. Gordon (Eds.), *Educational resilience in inner-city America* (pp. 85–94). Mahwah, NJ: Lawrence Erlbaum.

Rist, R. C. (2000). HER classic: Student social class and teacher expectations: The self-fulfilling prophecy in ghetto education. *Harvard Educational Review, 70,* 257–301.

Rowley, S., Kurtz-Costes, B., & Cooper, S. M. (2011). The schooling of African American children. In J. L. Meece, & J. S. Eccles (Eds.), *Handbook of research on schools, schooling, and human development* (pp. 275–292). New York, NY: Routledge.

Schroen, A. (2013). EDGE program helps women complete graduate math programs. *Diverse Issues in Higher Education, 30*(12), 6–7.

Secada, W. G. (1989). Agenda setting, enlightened self-interest, and equity in mathematics education. *Peabody Journal of Education, 66*(2), 22–56.

Solórzano, D. G., & Delgado Bernal, D. (2001). Critical race theory, transformational resistance and social justice: Chicana and Chicano students in an urban context. *Urban Education, 36*, 308–342.

Solorzano, D. G., & Yosso, T. J. (2001). From racial stereotyping and deficit discourse toward a critical race theory in teacher education. *Multicultural Education, 9*(1), 2–8.

Solorzano, D. G., & Yosso, T. J. (2002). Critical race methodology: Counter-storytelling as an analytical framework for education research. *Qualitative Inquiry, 8*, 23–44.

Steele, C. M. (1997). A threat in the air: How stereotypes shape intellectual identity and performance. *American Psychologist, 52*, 613–629.

Stinson, D. W. (2004). Mathematics as "gate-keeper"(?): Three theoretical perspectives that aim toward empowering all children with a key to the gate. *The Mathematics Educator, 14*(1), 8–18.

Strayhorn, T. L. (2010). The role of schools, families, and psychological variables on math achievement of Black high school students. *High School Journal, 93*(4), 177–194.

Strayhorn, T. L. (2012). *College students' sense of belonging: A key to educational success for all students.* New York, NY: Routledge.

Tate, W. F. (1997). Critical race theory and education: History, theory, and implications. *Review of Research in Education, 22*, 195–247.

Thomas, J. (2016, February 24). "Black girl magic" is more than a hashtag; It's a movement. *CNN.* Retrieved from http://www.cnn.com/2016/02/24/living/black-girl-magic-feat/

Trusty, J. (2002). African American's educational expectations: Longitudinal causal models for women and men. *Journal of Counseling & Development, 80*, 332–345.

Turner, C. S. V. (2002). Women of color in academe: Living with multiple marginality. *Journal of Higher Education, 73*, 74–93.

Tyack, D. B. (1974). *The one best system: A history of American urban education.* Cambridge, MA: Harvard University Press.

Tyson, W., & Roksa, J. (2016). How schools structure opportunity: The role of curriculum and placement in math attainment. *Research in Social Stratification and Mobility, 44*, 124–135.

University of Iowa. (2013). *History of the alliance.* Retrieved from http://mathalliance.org/about-the-math-alliance/a-brief-history-of-the-national-alliance/

U.S. Census Bureau. (2014). *Table 10. Projections of the population by sex, Hispanic origin, and race for the United States: 2015 to 2060, population projections.* Washington, DC: Author

Vandal, B., & Thompson, B. (2009). *State partnerships for quality teacher preparation* (Issue Paper). Retrieved from http://www.ecs.org/clearinghouse/80/55/8055.pdf

Walker, E. N. (2014). *Beyond Banneker: Black mathematicians and the paths to excellence.* New York: State University of New York Press.

Wallace, S. L., Moore, S. F., & Curtis, C. M. (2014). Black women as scholars and social agents: Standing in the gap. *Negro Educational Review, 65*(1–4), 44–62.

Williams, M. R., Brewley, D. N., Reed, R. J., White, D. Y., & Davis-Haley, R. T. (2005). Learning to read each other: Black female graduate students share their experiences at a White research I institution. *Urban Review, 37*, 181–199.

Wing, A. K. (1999). Race and gender issues: Critical race feminism. *Journal of Intergroup Relations, 26*(3), 14–25.

Winkle-Wagner, R. (2015). Having their lives narrowed down? The state of Black women's college success. *Review of Educational Research, 85*, 171–204

Wood, D., Kaplan, R., & McLoyd, V. C. (2007). Gender differences in the educational expectations of urban, low-income African American youth: The role of parents and the school. *Journal of Youth and Adolescence, 36*, 417–427.

Yoon, I. H. (2012). The paradoxical nature of whiteness-at-work in the daily life of schools and teacher communities. *Race Ethnicity and Education, 15*, 587–613.

Chapter 10

(Mis)Taken Identities: Reclaiming Identities of the "Collective Black" in Mathematics Education Research Through an Exercise in Black Specificity

MAISIE L. GHOLSON
CHARLES E. WILKES
University of Michigan

This chapter reviews two strands of identity-based research in mathematics education related to Black children, exemplified by Martin (2000) and Nasir (2002). Identity-based research in mathematics education is a burgeoning field that is disrupting narratives around the meanings of mathematical competence and brilliance. We argue that the identities of Black children as doers and knowers of mathematics are often confused (or mistaken) with stereotypical images of various social identities, as well as wrongly confiscated (or mis-taken), in order to perpetuate persistent narratives of inferiority, criminality, and general ineducability of these children. We use Black children as a particular example within the mathematics education research literature and argue that children within a so-called "collective Black" are subject to the same racial scripts that organize mathematics teaching and learning. While we acknowledge that important lines of identity-based research have emerged to reclaim the rightful identities of Black children and those within the collective Black, we conclude with a critique of this recent literature in which we note the troubling exclusion of girls and young children.

I know this girl don't got nobody and I couldn't believe this was happening. I had never seen nothing like that in my life, a man use that much force on a little girl. A big man, like three hundred pounds full of muscle. I was like "no way." You can't do nothing like that to a little girl.
—Niya Kenny, "Student Arrested Says She Was Standing Up for Classmate" (Moyer, 2015)

They didn't read my any rights. They arrested me after sitting in the office for a couple of minutes. They handcuffed me. It cut my wrist, and really hurt sitting on my hands behind my back.
—Kiera Wilmot, "Kiera Wilmot Teen Arrested in Botched Science Experiment, Haunted by Felony Record" (Klein, 2014)

Review of Research in Education
March 2017, Vol. 41, pp. 228–252
DOI: 10.3102/0091732X16686950
© 2017 AERA. http://rre.aera.net

They were like, "So you tried to make a bomb?" I told them no, I was trying to make a clock. He said, "It looks like a movie bomb to me."

—Ahmed Mohamed, "Muslim 9th Grader Ahmed Mohamed Arrested for Bringing Homemade Clock to School" (Visser, 2015)

The Troubling Truth of (Mis)Taken Identities

Ahmed Mohamed, Kiera Wilmot, Niya Kenny, and her unnamed peer are examples of children who have suffered from (mis)taken identities within the domains of science and mathematics. Each of these children was arrested—one charged with a felony—in their *science and mathematics classrooms*. The disciplinary identities of these children were mistaken with stereotypes of being a Black girl or a Muslim boy and, consequently, wrongly taken (i.e., mis-taken), in one case, quite violently. Mistaken identification is not merely a matter of sensational media headlines but has carceral implications. That is, children, like Ahmed, Kiera, Niya, and the unnamed young Black girl, are not only denied labels, such as mathematics doers, tinkerers, knowers, and legitimate observers, but inherit labels of academic disidentification (Osborne & Jones, 2011), such as troublemaker, criminal, and terrorist that serve to naturalize their trajectory out of mathematics and science and into the school-to-prison pipeline. Much has been said about the school-to-prison pipeline (Duncan, 2000; Fasching-Varner, Mitchell, Martin, & Bennett-Haron, 2014; McGrew, 2008; Meiners, 2010; Noguera, 2003; Winn & Behizadeh, 2011), but few have suggested *the infrastructure* that supports and maintains the school-to-prison pipeline is in fact the discipline of mathematics. For example, ninth-grade algebra courses have been described as a primary indicator, if not driver, of high school dropout rates (Helfand, 2006; Rickels et al., 2016), which necessarily increase the likelihood for incarceration (Levin, Belfield, Muennig, & Rouse, 2007; Sum, Khatiwada, McLaughlin, & Palma, 2009). Furthermore, Algebra I course-taking have been shown to correlate more directly with incarceration rates, than future successes (Tate, 2016). Certainly, mathematics has been described as a "gatekeeper" (Moses & Cobb, 2001; Stinson, 2004), but this term understates the pernicious discursive and structural machinations by which mathematics classrooms actively exclude particular groups of children, who some have referred to as part of the *collective Black* (cf. Bonilla-Silva, 2002; Martin, 2015).

Collectives, Racial Scripts, and (in Our Case) the Necessity of Black Specificity

The collective Black has included African American, Latin@, Indigenous, Vietnamese, Hmong, Laotian, West Indian and African immigrant children, and extended to Muslim and poor children, as social groups whose status has been racialized, Blackened, or, more pointedly, positioned as inferior (see Bonilla-Silva, 2004). We note that children within this racialized collective are subject to their identities being confused or confiscated within mathematical contexts in order to perpetuate persistent narratives of criminality or general ineducability and, concomitantly, sustain the prestige of mathematical knowledge. Through racial listing and ordering, hierarchies are formed and maintained, such as the racial hierarchy of mathematics ability (Martin, 2009). These hierarchies are predictable organizing principles that provide shortcuts in thinking about mathematics achievement and participation in racial (and gendered) terms—placing Whites and certain Asian groups at the top and Blacks, Latin@, and Native Americans at the bottom.

Our reference to the collective Black is not to suggest that children within this collective experience marginalization or success in similar ways, but to acknowledge that children within the collective are subject to the same racial scripts. According to Molina (2014), racial scripts "highlight the ways in which the lives of racialized groups are linked across time and space and thereby affect one another, even when they do not directly cross paths" (p. 6). Because the shared processes of racialization among different groups often go unrecognized, our theorization strives toward understanding racial scripts. However, our review of the empirical literature of human experience is necessarily specific to the processes of identification and identity development of African American children in mathematics. Such specificity of African American Blackness is not designed to erase or consume individual racialized groups, rather to avoid a collapsing of the collective Black into an indistinguishable multicultural identity. Nevertheless, there are many reasons to engage in the specificity of Blackness within identity-based research literature—three of which we outline here. First, we view the African American experience as a fulcrum for racialized constructions within the U.S. context (Nakagawa, 2012 as cited by Dumas, 2016), insofar as the African American experience provides particular leverage within racial politics. Second, and important, the preponderance of identity-based studies includes or centers African American learners. Third, as African Americans, we have particular familiarity with the African American counterscripts that alter or challenge dominant racial scripts (Molina, 2014). On a similar note, our theorization of racial scripts is also applicable to the arena of science education—a close cousin to mathematics, but certainly a different family. We again do not wish to collapse our analysis of mathematics into science. However, as the introduction makes clear, we recognize similar processes of misidentification and identity development are at play within these domains.

Racial Scripting of Personhood Through Mathematics

Misidentification in any context can be disconcerting, but the implications in mathematics are particularly dire. Recent work details how the cultural and discursive construction of mathematics, as high status knowledge (Apple, 2004), is enabled by the exclusion of particular social groups (Hottinger, 2016; Shah, 2013). For example, Shah (2013) convincingly argues that both race and mathematics rely on similar foundational conceptions of hierarchy, intelligence, and innateness, which create an inextricable and problematic relationship for classroom learning:

For many students, learning math is about solving equations and graphing parabolas—it is just another course requirement. However, for students from persistently marginalized racial backgrounds, the stakes are much higher. Certainly, mathematics can act as a material gatekeeper, obstructing access to future economic opportunities and full civic participation (Moses & Cobb, 2001). But learning mathematics can also be about identity and personhood. Living in a world where intelligence has become the primary marker of personhood, and where for five hundred years certain racial groups have been considered under evolved and intellectually deficient, mathematics can represent an opportunity for a student to reclaim cognitive status by showing that she or he is "smart" and can think complex thoughts. Mathematics offers a chance to show the social world that you are a full human being. (Shah, 2013, pp. 30–31)

In short, personhood in the U.S. context is granted—at least in part—through mathematical knowing and doing. (We would be remiss here to fail to mention that Black literacy was criminalized in and during the pre-bellum South [Williams, 2009] to further inscribe Black bodies as subhuman.) It is then no surprise that normative mathematical subjectivity in the U.S. context is constructed as White, male, and upper class (Ernest, 1992; Hottinger, 2016; Stinson, 2013).

Now consider, the project for subjugating and criminalizing Black bodies (figuratively and literally) has been at play far longer and with greater force (Muhammad, 2010; Roberts, 1997), than any project for developing mathematicians and scientists from the collective Black. So, if African American children, for example, can be more readily recognized as deviants or criminals to be subdued and constrained versus as mathematicians or scientists to create, invent, and challenge mathematically based ideas, what does this mean for their educational pursuits within the domains of mathematics and science, for their access to citizenship and democratic representation, or for their hopes for personhood in a 21st century that demands mathematical knowledge? Beyond the moral implications, this grim question speaks to the variety of nonmonetary costs incurred (by both the individual and society) due to the misidentification and underutilization of human potential of African Americans—the dampening of intergenerational effects for social mobility, the criminalization of excess labor, the decline in adaptability to technology, and the potential eclipsing of aspirational sentimentality (Freeman, 2005). The denial of mathematical identities also entails material (i.e., monetary) costs and constitutes a theft, that is, a disinvestment in the opportunity for African American children and a possessive investment in White educational opportunity in mathematics (Battey, 2013). For example, Battey (2013) has shown that earning differentials attributable to mathematics education course-taking favors Whites in the hundreds of billions of dollars over other racial groups. Battey describes mathematics education as a system used to stratify society through the availability of advanced courses, tracking systems, and a regime of guidance counselors who refer children within the collective Black to less rigorous coursework (p. 340). Furthermore, to the extent that children within the collective Black are taught mathematics, the pedagogy is lacking in rigor and breadth—narrowed to assessment practices for increasing standardized test scores (Davis & Martin, 2008). Given mathematics content knowledge provides access to elite colleges and higher paying careers, the misidentification of mathematics knowers and doers is also a matter of lifelong earning potential and material well-being. It is no wonder then that the mathematics education of children within the collective Black has been likened to "sharecropping"—as "sharecropper math"

(Moses & Cobb, 2001), that is, a menial mathematics in which children have little to no ownership.

Naming and Claiming: Black Pain and Suffering in Mathematics

We mean not to pivot here to a pithy question that demands a solution (Martin, 2009) and releases ourselves (and the reader) from the gravity of this social and moral problem. Dumas (2014) reminded us that schools and schooling are a site of Black suffering—not merely suffering, but suffering nonetheless. Black, Mendick, Rodd, Solomon, and Brown (2009) have been astute in naming the pain, pleasure, and power located in mathematics. We pause for a moment on the pain and encourage the mathematics education community (i.e., researchers, teachers, policymakers, etc.) to pause with us, acknowledging our role in this suffering and accepting that school mathematics is also a site of Black suffering. Given this sad state of affairs, we endeavor with Dumas (2014), who referenced Tuck (2009), to envision our work in part as an epistemology of mourning that inquires:

> How do subjects understand their own loss? In what ways might they still be grasping to articulate it? How do we as researchers know this loss in our bodies and express it in our words? Following from this, it becomes important for us to create research designs that allow space for participants to reflect on their own suffering, in ways that are safe, and in ways that allow them to remain protagonists of their own narrative and survivors rather than damaged victims. (Tuck, 2009, p. 26)

We revise their questions in relation to (mis)taken identities in mathematics education: How do children and learners within the collective Black author themselves into the narrative of mathematics? How do children and learners within the collective Black claim or reclaim practices, tools, and meanings about mathematics within their local contexts? In what ways have we developed research designs that allow space for participants to reflect on their own mathematical suffering, pleasure, and power in ways that are safe, and in ways that allow them to remain protagonists of their own narrative and brilliant rather than illiterate? We believe extant identity-based research as exemplified by Danny Martin (2000) and Na'ilah Nasir (2002) provide a way forward for authoring narratives and reclaiming–claiming practices in mathematics. Recent identity-based models and frameworks also hold potential for research designs that capture the experiential complexity of learners within (and outside of) the collective Black. The promise of this work inspires us to explore its origins, findings, and possible futures for liberatory projects designed specifically for Black children and, more broadly, within the collective Black.

Identity as a Site for Disruption

We believe identity-based research in mathematics to be a key site of disruption, even in light of the overwhelming macro-structural forces that organize children's learning within the collective Black, such as residential segregation, school funding, and tracking policies. For example, consider that children's lives have been extinguished within micro-scales of time based on readings of an identity, like "Black boy." Think Tamir Rice and Trayvon Martin, two Black boys gunned down due to the perception of their personhood as thugs, predators, and criminals. These are just two recent and tragic examples. In this sense, identities serve as the organizing link between macro-structural forces and the face-to-face moments in which we all live. Identities—really our consumption of children's identities—can be extraordinarily powerful in a child's life trajectory. Our read and interpretation of who children are, what they are doing, and who they are becoming set into motion a constellation of constraints or affordances—at the interpersonal level—that structure interactions, activities, and, ultimately, life opportunities.

Overview of the Chapter

In this chapter, we provide a selective review of the K–12 mathematics education research literature in two parts. The first part is chronology of salient moments for understanding Black mathematics learners. This historical rendering traces the emergence of identity-based research with and about African American children. The second part is a typology that distinguishes between two prominent strands of the identity-based research, exemplified by Martin (2000) and Nasir (2002), respectively. By combining the historical and typological review, we provide an account of how this burgeoning field of identity-research came into being and in what manner it went about disrupting narratives and meanings of mathematical competence and brilliance for African American learners (cf. Leonard & Martin, 2013). Finally, we conclude with our concerns with the paucity of identity research on girls and young children.

THE EMERGENCE OF MATHEMATICS IDENTITY–BASED RESEARCH FOR BLACK CHILDREN

Within identity-based research, children and adolescents' subjectivities are at the root of knowledge production. Children's subjectivities and intersubjectivities with their teacher and classmates are described in detail to make sense of the variance in student learning, participation, and achievement. Subjectivities are the idiosyncratic ways in which individuals make meaning of their contexts in space and time. While subjectivity is critical to identity-related research, studies on identity requires more than attention to subjectivity. Identity-based research also involves the interrogation of processes of becoming, as well as the formation and dissolution of relationships between other children, teachers, the content, practices, discourses and tools as a function of context (Sfard, 1998). In the following section, we recount the emergence of identity-based research in mathematics education pointed to understand the experiences of Black children.

Moments in Mathematics Education Research for Black Children

We use a "methodology of moments" (cf. Stinson & Bullock, 2012a) to trace the position of the Black child in mathematics education research. Differences in achievement and participation of Black children tend to be framed in three

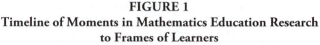

FIGURE 1
Timeline of Moments in Mathematics Education Research
to Frames of Learners

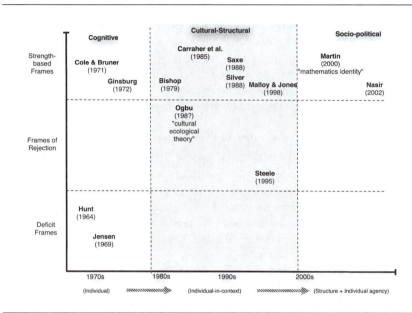

Note. The timeline is divided into three key moments around identity-based research: individual-in-cognition, individual-in-context, and structure + agency.

ways—deficit-based, strength-based, and frames of rejection (Delpit, 2012; Stinson, 2006; Valencia, 2010). Strength-based frames focus on assets in children and their context; whereas deficit frames, while often sympathetic, rather explicitly or implicitly purport that children, their families, or communities are lacking the cognitive, cultural, or structural resources that facilitate learning, well-being, and success. Frames of rejection posit that children and their families are not necessarily lacking resources but seeking coping strategies to maintain cultural and personal autonomy by rejecting the dominant culture or features of their own culture (Stinson, 2006, p. 482). In Figure 1, we juxtapose several decades of mathematics education research with frames of learners to construct a constellation of studies about or critical to the learning of children in the collective Black. By doing so, we find three salient phases for children in the collective Black—*individual-in-cognition, individual-in-context*, and *structure + agency*. Like others who have constructed and named moments (Stinson & Bullock, 2012a), we do not suggest that these periods of research are linear or particularly well defined. To be clear, cognitive-oriented research as we describe below is still the predominant paradigm through mathematics learning and knowledge is understood and validated (Silver & Kilpatrick, 1994). These periods represent shifts, surges, and new ways of imagining children and context of the collective Black. Additionally, the dates on which we rely are those of publication and do not accurately represent a true beginning of ideas and conceptions of learners in the collective Black but serve as a markers and guides. To manage the scope of the history, we highlight some of the research that served as a clear antecedent to the identity-based research of Martin (2000) and Nasir (2002), as well as studies that established discourses, like "oppositional identity theory" (Fordham & Ogbu, 1986), to which identity-based research was poised to respond.

Individual-in-Cognition: Can the Black Child Learn?

The *individual-in-cognition* period serves as the starting point in our timeline and marked a contested space for African American learners in which their intellectual competence was being empirically questioned and justified. For example, "Jensen (1969) proposed that lower-class children and Blacks in particular suffer from an inability to engage in 'conceptual learning,' which involves cognitive activity mediating between stimulus and response, and that this deficit is the result of genetic inheritance" (Ginsburg & Allardice, 1984, pp. 197–198). Herbert Ginsburg, along with others, conducted clinical research that refuted claims of cognitive deficiencies and positioned poor and Black learners as cognitively competent (Cole & Bruner, 1971; Ginsburg, 1972). Ginsburg and Allardice (1984) describe poor and Black children's mathematics learning and development this way:

> Of course, we do not argue that such an environment, specifically lower-class poverty, is beneficial for those growing up in it, nor that it exerts no effects on psychological functioning. Rather, the study demonstrated that basic mathematical thought develops in a robust manner among lower-and middle-class children, black and white. School failure cannot be explained by initial deficit in basic cognitive skills, specifically System 1 [i.e., intuitive mathematical concepts] and 2 [i.e., counting] mathematical skills. Instead, poor children display important cognitive strengths, developed spontaneously before the onset of formal schooling. These strengths should provide a sufficient foundation for later understanding of school mathematics. (p. 203)

This cognitive period coincided with researchers attempts to correlate student behaviors to achievement primarily through quantitative statistical inference (Stinson & Bullock, 2012a).

Individual-in-Context: Under What Conditions Does the Black Child Learn?

In the next period, the individual-in-context, studies were focused on cultural manifestations of learning at the classroom level. This was the longest period in our schema, spanning at least three decades, and includes a variety of research studies. The individual-in-context period was ushered by a methodological shift toward qualitative studies in the late 1970s. Within this methodological and theoretical turn, Lagemann (2000) notes that anthropologists began investigating schools, schooling, and classroom practices, including discourse. However, along with anthropological methods came anthropological explanations for various social differences. In particular, Oscar Lewis's (1966) theory of the *culture of poverty* found traction within educational discourse and was redefined as "cultural deprivation" (Valencia, 2010). While cultural deprivation theories gained traction, there seemed to be little empirical work in mathematics education research to verify such claims with the exception of one study by Kirk, Hunt, and Volkmark (1975), which supported no racial differences between Black and White children (Ginsburg & Allardice, 1984). The culture problem thesis was critiqued by many educational theorists, including John Ogbu— also an anthropologist but in education. Ogbu (1978) put forth his own theory *cultural–ecological theory* or *caste theory*, which argued that based on the numerical or the sociohistorical migratory status (i.e., forced or voluntary) of their racial group, children may resist or capitulate to assimilatory practices in school. For example, African American, Native American, and Hawaiian American children, whose historical communities were enslaved, conquered, or colonialized, resist assimilation into schools as a means to maintain their cultural authenticity and autonomy. Cultural– ecological theory led to the *acting White* hypothesis that suggested Black children construct school success as a White cultural norm (Fordham & Ogbu, 1986). Ogbu's work importantly introduced theorizing about race through various ecological contexts foregrounding the sociohistorical. This work uses a frame of rejection to refute clams of cultural deprivation (Stinson, 2006). Within this period, mathematics education studies about the collective Black leveraged individual-in-context explanations, such as "acting White," which attempted to connect children's everyday decisions within a cultural–historical framework. It is also around this time that Alan Bishop (1988), using anthropological methods, also introduced mathematics as a form of cultural induction or socialization.

The individual-in-context period extended into the mid-1980s. This was a pivotal time in which mathematics learning was considered "products of social activity" and "goes beyond the [cognitivist] ideas that social interactions provide the spark that generates or stimulates an individual's internal meaning-making activity" (Lerman, 2000, p. 23). In other words, while previous moments in mathematics education had included the social activity, the social was subjugated to individual cognitive processes instead of as a phenomenon of interest that requires a telescopic lens for zooming in and out (Stinson & Bullock, 2012a). It was during this time that Vygotsky's work was being utilized by Cole, Engestrom, and Lave to understand mathematics practices. Perhaps the social turn is best represented through the study of child candy sellers in Brazil (Carraher, Carraher, & Schliemann, 1985; Saxe, 1988). For example, Carraher et al. (1985) found that while some children had difficulty solving routine school mathematics problems, they were quite proficient in conducting complex calculations outside of school as candy sellers. Of course, this work does not address the marginalized children within the United States, but exemplifies the affordances of foregrounding social context in mathematics learning, as well specifying, a particularized social group of learners (which in this case comprised Brazilian children candy sellers).

Other studies within the individual-in-context period took an institutional approach. Fueling the mathematics education reform movement, these studies focused on instructional programs, that is, a collection of curricular materials, professional development, and instructional techniques, in mathematics education. Perhaps most notably among this research were the quasar studies, which showed the feasibility of broad scale, high-quality mathematics instructional programs in economically disadvantaged and minoritized communities (Silver, Smith, Nelson, 1995). Furthermore, Silver et al. (1995) note,

A fundamental premise of the project was that low levels of participation and performance in mathematics by females, ethnic minorities, and the poor were not due primarily to a lack of ability and potential but rather to educational practices that denied access to meaningful, high-quality experiences with mathematics learning. (p. 10)

The quasar work was a continuation of strength-based approach, yet unique in its scale. This work broadened the field's imagination for national reform for marginalized children in the collective Black.

Still within the individual-in-context period, Malloy and Malloy (1998) proposed that African American children had different learning preferences that should be honored and leveraged in mathematics learning. Malloy and Jones (1998) conducted clinical interviews with 24 African American eighth-grade children. Their findings describe the African American children as showing characteristics endemic to good problem solvers and "exhibit[ing] other positive characteristics usually not credited to African American students" (Malloy & Jones, 1998, p. 161). Additionally, Malloy and Jones (1998) found that the African American children frequently used holistic reasoning, a stance in which you view the world and problems in their totality. Carol Malloy's work was groundbreaking insofar as little attention until this time had been given to the study of African American learners as a group of learners onto themselves. That is, African American children were generally studied in comparison to White children (McLoyd, 1991).

Of course, this period also marked the introduction of "stereotype threat" (Steele, 1997), as a dampening psychological response to performance within a domain of high salience for fear of enforcing stereotypical images of one's racial group. Steele's work is also situated along the frames of rejection band, because his explanatory model ultimately suggests that the "abiding effect [of stereotype threat] on school achievement" leads to academic disidentification (Stinson, 2006, p. 489).

At this point, we note three things about studies within individual(s)-in-context moment: First, mathematics education studies were providing descriptive accounts of student learning at various scales of time and over various levels of analysis. Second, many of those studies focused on students' individual strengths and competence in their contexts, but these studies failed to provide accounts for the variance of student success or failure. Third, education researchers in anthropology and social psychology were providing explanatory theories of school failure or disengagement, based on frames of rejection of the dominant culture, which in many ways problematically reified deficit notions about Black families, communities, and culture.

Structure + Agency Dialectic: Why Does the Black Child Learn That Way?

In response to the above issues, the *structure + agency* period unfolds via identity-based research. This body of research directed at the collective Black reconceptualized learning by contemplating the discursive construction of context, accounting for individual difference vis-à-vis agency, and disrupting deficit and rejection-oriented frames of learners. Within the structure + agency period, the notion of context is troubled via "sociocultural, sociohistorical, and sociopolitical assumptions, conditions, and power relations," and the individual is reinscribed as an agent left to marshal and "resist the surveilling and disciplining gazes of normalization (cf. Focault, 1977/1995)" (Stinson & Bullock, 2012b, p. 1165). Varelas, Settlage, and Mensah (2015), in science education, describe it this way:

Structures are considered to be the cultural rules, or schemas, that shape and are shaped by social practices in a domain, and are in a dialectical relationship with resources, the sources of power with the domain and its social interactions (Sewell, 1992). Agency is seen as a person's capacity to engage with cultural schemas and mobilize resources in ways that did not exist before, creating new contexts and practices. (p. 439)

Therefore, the structure + agency period rejects the notion of a benign, apolitical, and inanimate context preferring an animated, political, and potentially hazardous or radicalized landscape for learning. Similarly, the individual is reenvisioned as an agent that does not merely respond to a radicalized context, but shapes the very nature of this context in light of their access and utilization of various structures, which Varelas et al. (2015) delineate as "physical, material, symbolic, discursive, social, curricular, etc." (p. 439). Accordingly, the push to grapple with an individual's subjectivities in mathematical contexts made it necessary to reckon with and about the performed practices, meanings, dispositions, values, social positions, and histories—namely, their identity. There have been several theories regarding the mathematics identity of learners (Anderson, 2007; Boaler & Greeno, 2000; Cobb, Gresalfi, & Hodge, 2009; Martin, 2000; Nasir, 2002), although different emphases are placed on students' histories, practices, positions, orientations, statuses, and roles. The emergence of identity-based research about and with Black children was by no means natural or the self-evident "next step." Studying the Black child in this way qualified as a political move to, first, reckon with children's subjectivities, second, capture the sociohistorical and sociocultural discourses that pulse through concentric contexts, such as classrooms, schools, school districts, communities, and the broader society (Stinson & Bullock, 2012b), and, last, provide some theoretical explanation that maintained the humanity, dignity, and educability of children within the collective Black.

Summary of Mathematical Moments of the Black Child's Learning

One simple way to read the three periods in mathematics education research is through three questions: (a) *whether* children in the collective Black can learn mathematics (individual-in-cognition), (b) *how* (under what conditions and through what modes) do the children in the collective Black learn mathematics (individual-in-context), and (c) *why* do children in the collective Black learn mathematics the way that they do (structure + agency; cf. Stinson & Bullock, 2012a)? The exploration of this latter question, to which identity-based research responds, has been the subject of debate in the field, insofar as this question is deemed as mathematically dubious because it does not attend to "the nature of quantitative relationships, the meanings of symbolic representations [in math], conceptions underlying advanced mathematical conceptions, and the meaning of arithmetical expressions" (Heid, 2010, p. 103). (For full context of this debate, see also, Battista, 2010; Confrey, 2010; Harel, 2010; Martin, Gholson, & Leonard, 2010.) However, critiques emanating from this stance construe context as domesticated (vs. radicalized) being more or less fixed and extricable from the domain of mathematics, instead of imbricated by a radicalized context. The question of *why* is imbued with political tensions that "seek not just to better *understand* mathematics education and all of its social forms but *transform* mathematics education in ways that privilege more socially just practices" (Gutierrez, 2010, p. 40).

The Contributions of Martin and Nasir

Of course, all identity-based research is not necessarily political in its orientation (e.g., Cobb et al., 2009) and tend to push and pull with varying force on the structure/agency dialectic. However, for Black children, identity researchers took care to grapple with conceptions regarding what it means to be a math person or doer, along with how holding or enacting a racialized identity constrains or affords the identification in and with mathematics. Two lines of inquiry in mathematics identity research exemplify this work—Martin (2000) and Nasir (2002). At this point, we provide a brief overview of Martin and Nasir's identity-based research in mathematics.

Martin's seminal study explored mathematical success and failure among African Americans. This interdisciplinary work built on a variety of strength-based studies, such as Bishop's work on mathematical enculturation, and responded to studies that used frames of rejection, such as Ogbu's cultural ecological theory. In Martin's study, he conducted interviews with parents, community members, teachers, and African American children (Grades 7 through 9), as well as conducted observations at the children's junior high school. One of the greatest contributions of Martin's work is his multilevel framework. This framework includes several ecological contexts—sociohistorical, community, and school contexts—in which an individual is socialized. The resultant of mathematics socialization is a mathematics identity, which was defined as

beliefs about (a) their ability to perform in mathematical contexts, (b) the instrumental importance of mathematical knowledge, (c) constraints and opportunities in mathematical contexts, and (d) the resulting motivations and strategies used to obtain mathematics knowledge. (Martin, 2000, p. 19)

Martin (2000), along with Moody (2000), was among the first to give voice to African American parents and children about their experiences learning mathematics.

Through the voices of African American children and parents, learning could no longer be conceptualized in terms of mere transmission and reception, but a swirl of multilevel forces, such as the expectations and beliefs of the community members and teachers, that enable mathematics identities.

Nasir's (2002) seminal work builds on the sociocultural studies of mathematics learning in context, similar to the candy sellers' studies by Carraher et al. (1985) and Saxe (1988), and also responds to cultural ecological theory proposed by Ogbu. She conducted two studies that examined the mathematical practices of African American children playing dominoes and basketball, respectively. In the first study, Nasir observed and interviewed African American children at two age levels, elementary and high school. In the second study, Nasir observed and interviewed middle and high school African American, male basketball players. Using two cultural practices (dominoes and basketball), Nasir constructs a mathematics identity-in-practice for African American children. She showed as African American players of dominoes and basketball became more engaged in the practice, they developed goals and identities that were associated with changes in mathematical learning. Nasir (2002) describes it this way:

In dominoes, players shifted from basic matching numbers and addition at the elementary school level to complex inferences of probability and logical (if-then) thinking at the high school level. In basketball, players' mathematical goals shifted from understanding basic statistics involving counts in middle school to calculating relatively complex statistics with percentages and averages in high school. (p. 237)

While the players in Nasir's study experienced an inbound trajectory within the practices of dominoes and basketball, she notes that many African American children experience a trajectory that is different in school mathematics. Nasir argues that the ways children engage, align, and imagine themselves to the mathematical goals and activities in the mathematics classroom influences their learning trajectories.

The studies conducted by Martin and Nasir are quite different in their orientations and offer different explanatory models for African American children's learning and participation in mathematics. However, Nasir and Martin share equally disruptive approaches to the study of African American children, specifically, that allow children within the collective Black to reclaim identities of competence and brilliance. To understand the unique contributions of Martin and Nasir, we situate their seminal studies within the body of identity-based research broadly, leaning on recent analyses of this emergent field.

A TYPOLOGICAL RENDERING OF MARTIN AND NASIR

There has been an explosion of identity-based research in mathematics education (Darragh, 2016). In light of this explosive growth, one can barely imagine the breadth of scholarly interpretations of the seemingly self-evident and colloquial term—identity. The body of identity-based research is broad indeed and imagines children's subjectivities in different scales of time-space (Lemke, 2000); through different disciplinary orientations, such as, sociological, anthropological, and psychological (Varelas et al., 2015); as well as various theoretical approaches, including psychoanalytic, performative, participative, positioning, narrative, and poststructural (Darragh, 2016; Langer-Osuna & Esmonde, in press). Accordingly, one of the challenges facing identity-based research is reigning in the "proliferation of definitions and stances towards the concept of identity" (Edwards, Esmonde, & Wagner, 2011, p. 68). Recent efforts by Darragh (2016) and Langer-Osuna and Esmonde (in press) unpack the multiplicity of theoretical orientations and conceptions of identity, as well as explore the affordances that different methodological approaches entail. We do not endeavor to replicate this work here, but attend to a very specific task of situating the two strands of mathematics identity research, exemplified by Martin and Nasir, within different categories.

Identity-Based Research in Space and Time

We begin with Lemke's (2000) question: "How do *moments* add up to *lives?*" (italics in original, p. 273). This is a question of identities in time but also space. Lemke lobbies for a dynamical view, wherein identity is described over time as a process, that extends beyond confines of mere spatial analysis. That is, Lemke—following Cole (1996)—suggests analysis across multiple scales of time, "from the microgenetic (event scale), meso-genetic (extended activity or project scale), and ontogenetic (developmental-biographical scale) to the historical and evolutionary scales" (p. 287). According to Edwards et al. (2011), Nasir's study includes both microgenetic and mesogenetic scales of time and local contexts through the consideration of "both moment-to-moment shifting of identity (sometimes called positioning; Davies & Harré, 1999; Holland, Lachicotte, Skinner, & Cain, 2001) and longer term trajectories of identity as a relatively stable sense of self (Erikson, 1968)," whereas Martin's study goes "beyond local contexts or practices to develop in a relative enduring fashion over the life span" (p. 66), that is, ontogenetic scale.

Identity-Based Research in the Disciplines

In addition to scales of time, Darragh (2016) draws our attention to the different disciplinary perspectives that imagine identity as an *entity* we possess (i.e., acquisition) or an *action* that we enact as a role. Darragh describes the possession of an identity as a psychological Eriksonian conception (1968) and the enacting of a role as a sociological Meadian (1913/2011) conception. We nuance the latter category of action to include identities formed through goal-directed activity stemming from anthropological perspectives, including Michael Cole (1996), Yrjo Engestrom (1999), and James Wertsch (1991). Nasir's early work is firmly situated within this anthropological space. However, Martin pulls from both psychological and anthropological spaces (and some may include sociological). Darragh (2016, p. 27) describes Martin's work as "bridg[ing] the acquisition-action divide, defining identity as a set of beliefs (something that can be acquired) and also looking at identity in using mathematics to change the conditions of one's life (an action)."

FIGURE 2
Theoretical Connections of Two Lines of Inquiry Related to African American Children, According to Categories of Identity-Based Research in Mathematics Education

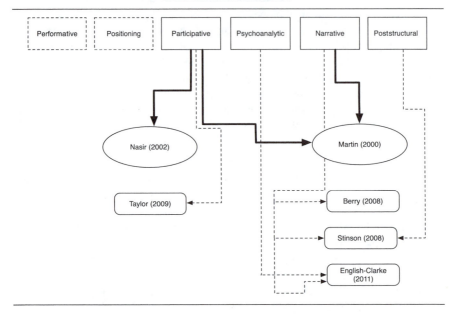

Theoretical Orientations to Identity-Based Research

Of course, the differences in disciplinary perspectives influence the theoretical orientations of both Martin and Nasir. Darragh (2016) and Langer-Osuna and Esmonde (in press) offer a relatively unified set of categories for the sorting identity–based research: psychoanalytic, narrative, poststructural, positioning, participative, and performative. As shown in Figure 2, while these categories are defined separately, studies of mathematics learning and participation often employ multiple definitions and orientations to identity (at times problematically; Darragh, 2016). Beginning with Nasir (2002), this line of inquiry relies on a participative orientation to identity. This work envisions identity as a social construction achieved through the participation in a social group or community and the use of specific cultural practices. Nasir's work also uses positioning to describe the interactional negotiation of identities in real time. The other line of inquiry, exemplified by Martin (2000), relies on participative, narrative, and psychoanalytic definitions of identity. Similar to Nasir, Martin sees identity as part of participation or socialization into a classroom community; however, Martin also included children's (and their parents') narratives to understand how Black learners author themselves in the contexts of mathematics. Martin's first study also goes about teasing apart different beliefs, values, and motivations that children held in his study. Langer-Osuna and Esmonde (in press) emphasize the importance of this psychoanalytic orientation insofar as it outlines the psychic reality in which children live, as well as holds up the "mirror" through which children perceive themselves. (It is worth noting that some do not distinguish between the work of authoring and the perceptions we hold about ourselves, i.e., the stories we tell *are* our identities; Sfard & Prusak, 2005.)

Treatment of Racialized Identities

Within mathematics identity research of Black children, there are two types of social identities—racial and ethnic. "Racial identity," according to Helms (1996), "may be broadly defined as psychological or internalized consequences of being socialized in a racially oppressive environment and the characteristics of self that develop in response to or in synchrony with either benefitting from or suffering under such oppression" (p. 147); while ethnic identity is one's familiarity with and competence in the meanings, values, and artifacts of a culture. An important distinction that Helms (1996) draws between racial and ethnic identity is the locus of inquiry for identity processes. The intrapsychic processes tend to be emphasized by racial identity theorists, like Martin; contrastively, interpersonal processes, such as social role fulfillment, tend to be emphasized by ethnic identity theorist, such as Nasir. This does not suggest that race as a construct only operates intrapsychically or ethnicity does not make its way into the psyche.

Nevertheless, the bifurcation of the mathematics identity research for the collective Black falls along these distinct treatments of one's racialized social identity—as fundamentally ethnic or racial. Finally, acknowledging that a mathematics and a racialized identity are quite different, we note that the complexity in methodology extends to similar categories of: psychoanalytic, narrative, poststructural, positioning, participative, and performative. The racialized identities used by mathematics education research maintain some of its ties to psychology, but also rely generally on racialized signs, significations, and narrations.

NASIR'S IDENTITIES-IN-PRACTICE

When African American children and adolescents were studied in their own community contexts, researchers found that they exhibited mathematical competencies and abilities, which were not reflected in school contexts (Nasir, 2002). Ecologically, this work focuses on proximal processes, that is, people and objects within the child's immediate setting. These studies debunked claims of environmental deprivation attributed to the African American mathematics learner. To the contrary, identities-in-practice studies revealed that African American children and adolescents in their everyday contexts show proficiency in carrying out a variety of mathematical tasks. These studies emphasize the cultural aspects of learning, that is, the use of artifacts, symbols, and meanings, like cultural practice of dominoes, basketball, or purchases at a local store, and conceptualize children's social identities as ethnicity (Nasir, 2002; Taylor, 2009). For example, Edd Taylor's (2009) study, titled, "The Purchasing

Practice of Low-Income Students: The Relationship to Mathematical Development," focuses on *the practice* of African American children's engagement in shopping at liquor stores—a practice typical among some children in low-income, urban communities. Taylor discusses the sociohistorical origins of the liquor store, an edifice born out of structural flight of large supermarkets to "safer" and "more profitable" areas. Taylor (2009) notes, "[A]lthough the term liquor store is descriptive of the role these stores serve in selling alcoholic beverages the stores serve as small markets or convenience stores in these communities" (p. 373). Through this study, Taylor was able to "highlight the distributed nature of students' purchasing practice, the role of whole number understanding (as a form of prior understanding) in purchasing, and multiple levels of students' mathematical engagement during the purchasing practice" (p. 406).

Features of Identities-in-Practice

In these studies, the extent of students' participation within their local communities of practice serves as an indicator of student learning (Lave & Wenger, 1991). Children and adolescents' ability or inability to carry out mathematics tasks in the classroom is considered a function of their cultural relevance and continuity between home-community and school contexts. Restated in terms of identity, African American children and adolescents' ethnic (i.e., home-based) and academic (i.e., school-based) identities are considered to be in tension (Nasir & Saxe, 2003). Within this thread, tensions that students experience between their ethnic and academic identities is negotiated and resolved to some end within social space. Potential drawbacks of identities-in-practice studies include that power, ideology, and racism are not explicitly addressed. However, to this critique, we note (as a rebuttal of sorts) that the cultural practices are necessarily shaped by sociohistorical forces. For example, the examination of purchasing practices at liquor stores *does account for* the effects of structural racism and the allocation of resources in majority-Black, low-income, urban communities. Similarly, the playing of dominoes *does index* the working-class or poor African American communities and marks historical shifts in cultural capital and meanings of agency as individuals take up this practice (Nasir & Saxe, 2003). Consider that dominoes were a game whose history traces back to ancient China and was played by the elite and, at the turn of the century, a game played by the English in pubs. The decision to play dominoes in contemporary United States, however, signals an entirely different affiliation and way of being. Of course, by drawing on practices seemingly endemic to racialized groups may serve to perpetuate stereotypes, if larger structural forces are not considered as part of the analysis *and* all members of a racialized group are assumed to participate in the practice in the same way. While there may be implications for teachers and teaching, these implications are constrained to local communities and are not portable. Yet, this line of work presents concrete actions for teachers to employ in the curriculum and in practice. Another potential drawback, if you will, is identities-in-practice studies do not define a mathematics identity (i.e., commitments to the discipline writ large as a subject matter), only specific practices within the discipline of mathematics. In this sense, identities-in-practice are particularized, pragmatic, and potentially disconnected from mathematics as an intellectual activity, that is, to the extent it can be considered well-defined (cf. Resnick, 1989). The identities-in-practice work, in fact, helps reenvision meanings of what mathematics is and can be in different cultural communities. Said differently, identities-in-practice studies do well to challenge the epistemic value of school mathematics.

There are few studies within the identities-in-practice strand. This work is methodologically complex—requiring ethnographic collection methods and micro-analytical methods of student interactions. The affordances of Nasir's and Taylor's ethnographic work is the approximation of learning in real time. Unfortunately, there are few studies in mathematics education identity–based research that take up this approach for the collective Black. The predominant approach has been Martin's focus on racial identity and socialization. We assume this is in part due to the reduced methodological demands—primarily interviews—and the benefits of the direct confrontation of issues of race and racism to which identities-in-practice only allude.

MARTIN'S RACIAL IDENTITY AND MATHEMATICS SOCIALIZATION

While race and racism are not typically addressed by identities-in-practice studies, this is the explicit focus of empirical work concerning racial identity and mathematics socialization. These studies draw from African American learners' narratives about their mathematical experiences in the classroom and seek to understand how African American learners negotiate racial messages in the context of their mathematics learning. On the one hand, findings from these studies recount African American learners' experiences with racism, negative stereotypes, and lowered expectations; and, on the other hand, these studies provide descriptions of African American student characteristics, relationships, supports, interactions, and management techniques that facilitate success in mathematics learning (Berry, 2008; Martin, 2006; McGee & Martin, 2011; Stinson, 2008). Given the focus on race and racism, studies from this thread consider a broader social and political context and, thus, ecologically, shift between historical, community, school, and home contexts, but primarily distal processes. The two identities under inspection for the African American learner in these studies are racial identity and mathematics identity. For these studies, tension between one's racial and mathematics identity is negotiated intrapsychically manifesting as narrations of experience. Student learning processes are not generally the focus of these studies. However, students' internalization of bias—as expressed through one's racial identity—can be an impediment to learning, that is, most notably through stereotype threat (Steele, 1997).

For brevity's sake, we discuss three studies, but there are many studies that follow in this tradition. We begin with Robert Berry's (2008) work with successful middle school, African American boys in mathematics. Berry, through interviews with eight African American boys, found that early educational experiences, support systems, positive attributions of self as a mathematics doer, and supportive alternative identities facilitated the success of these boys. David Stinson's (2008) study also helps construct the meanings of being an African American, male mathematics doer. In addition to critical race theory as employed by Berry, Stinson uses poststructural and critical theory to analyze four, African American men in their 20s reflecting on their K–12 academic and mathematical experiences. Stinson (2008) found four themes of mathematical success:

(a) Observing or knowing family or community members who had benefited from formal education by achieving financial and societal success; (b) experiencing encouraging and forceful family and community members who made the expectations of academic, and mathematics, success explicit; (c) encountering caring and committed teachers and school personnel who established high academic expectations for students and developed relationships with students that reached beyond the school and academics; and (d) associating with high-achieving peer-group members who had similar goals and interests. (p. 1002)

In the third and final study that we review in this strand, we focus on Traci English-Clarke, Slaughter-Defoe, and Martin's (2012) article titled, "What Does Race Have to do with Math? Relationships between Racial-Mathematical Socialization, Mathematical Identity, and Racial Identity." Clarke developed a series of survey instruments to identify the socialization experiences of African American children in mathematics. Among the many findings of her study, we focus on racial–mathematical stories and messages that the 168 ninth- and tenth-grade Black youth reported. Three kinds of stories and messages were reported by one third of the Black youth. Approximately 45% of those stories and messages related to racism and racial discrimination in mathematics, 18% of the stories and messages focused on persistence in mathematics classes despite being one of the few, and 27% were related to the message that Asian Americans are good at math. As shown in Figure 2, each of these studies rely on narratives, but take up different theoretical conceptualizations of identity.

Features of Racial Identity and Mathematics Socialization

As for potential drawbacks, racial identity and mathematics socialization studies do not explicitly consider interactive performances of identity. These studies tend to emphasize society's influence on the individual via socialization processes and, while the agency of African American learners is shown as possible, this agency is not usually described at the interactional order. In other words, while racial identity and mathematics socialization studies make available student agency, rarely do these studies exhibit how that agency is exercised and negotiated in real-time in the context of mathematics learning. As such, the implications for teachers and teaching is less direct and is situated as knowledge to have and values to possess versus actions teachers can actively take. On the one hand, these studies make clear claims to an identity connected to the discipline of mathematics—a mathematics identity. On the other hand, this leaves mathematics as a subject matter intact and unchallenged. Racism and all of its manifestations structurally and symbolically, however, are clearly brought into focus and challenged with this work.

CHALLENGES WITHIN THE EXTANT IDENTITY-BASED RESEARCH

Identity-based research is not without its challenges. While this work has been critical to disrupting discourses of the collective Black in mathematics education, the disruption has not been equally distributed among subgroups. Particular attention has been paid to Black boys in middle school and beyond in mathematics (e.g., as previously discussed, Berry, 2008; Nasir, 2002; Stinson, 2008). The plight of Black girls and young children (who are occasionally described as not developmentally able to have identities) has received less focus by the field, although there are exceptions at this intersection (Gholson & Martin, 2014; Jones, 2003). The extant mathematics identity–based research is a masculinized narrative of Black adolescence. This raises particular questions about a treatment of race and gender that does not confront the performativity of Blackness and masculinity in the learning of mathematics. That is, how does the performativity of Blackness and femininity by Black girls or boys manifest in mathematics contexts? In the case of Black girls, Dotson (2014), as a philosopher, reminds us that we need epistemological, theoretical, and empirical resources to make Black girls knowable to broader community. Similarly, we need to only look across the disciplinary divide into science education research to see the possibilities of making *young* Black children's identities knowable (Kane, 2012; Varelas et al., 2011). For example, Kane (2012) has found children as young as 7 to 9 years (and perhaps younger) are quite capable of identifying with the discipline of science—through both narration and performance. This example serves as a particular warning to this burgeoning field within mathematics education research to create space and take care not to re-instantiate existing patterns of patriarchy and developmental bias that are dampening our capacity to understand teaching and learning in mathematics.

FINAL NOTES ON RECLAIMING IDENTITIES

The emergence of identity-based research allowed the mathematics education research community to contemplate the Black child in mathematics in a radically new way. For example, Martin's insistence on highlighting Black mathematical success refocused our empirical attention on Black children's competence, capability, and perseverance. Martin's work also helped anchor our understanding of mathematics as a racialized experience, which shifted the empirical gaze away from the child—just enough to begin seeing the waves of race pulsing through mathematics classrooms. Nasir's work was instrumental in naming Black contexts as *mathematical*, a designation that had not been applied to these cultural spaces. Both Martin and Nasir, in their own rigorous way, reclaimed Black children's identities in mathematics and asserted Black children's humanity and competence in mathematical spaces, which had far too long been confused or denied. Given the power of mathematics to confer economic viability on the one hand, and intelligence and personhood on the other, this reclamation of identity is a tremendous disruption to inequalities within mathematics education and beyond.

In this chapter, we have engaged in an exercise of Black specificity out of the necessity to share a particular story—or script if you will—within mathematics education research. However, this script is not unique. It repeats itself among other racialized groups. The script within mathematics education research begins, as all Blackened groups do, with an assertion and then refutation of inferiority followed by an accounting (often quantitative) of the seemingly intractable conditions and outcomes that naturalize hierarchies of mathematics ability. For Black children,

Martin and Nasir have played a pivotal role in rewriting these racial scripts. Parallel scripts are in play for racialized groups, but manifest in relation to various identity markers, like language. The history of mathematics education we told and the strands of identity-based research we reviewed are necessarily specific—not to cloak an array of racialized groups of children, but to highlight the *structures* that enable one to mis(take) Black children and provide fodder for relational (not merely comparative) analysis, among various racialized groups of children (cf. Molina, 2014). Our goal was to call out and name the process of (mis)taking a child's mathematical identity and to provide at least two powerful ways forward in identifying children within the so-called "collective Black." Now that we can see the children, we shall call them mathematician, scientist, and scholar—their rightful names.

REFERENCES

Anderson, R. (2007). Being a mathematics learner: Four faces of identity. *The Mathematics Educator, 17*(1), 7–14.

Apple, M. W. (2004). *Ideology and curriculum.* New York, NY: Routledge.

Battey, D. (2013). Access to mathematics: A possessive investment in Whiteness. *Curriculum Inquiry, 43,* 332–359.

Battista, M. T. (2010). Engaging students in meaningful mathematics learning: Different perspectives, complementary goals. *Journal of Urban Mathematics Education, 3*(2), 34–46.

Bishop, A. (1988). *Mathematical enculturation: A cultural perspective on mathematics education.* Dordrecht, Netherlands: Kluwer Academic Press.

Black, L., Mendick, H., Rodd, M., Solomon, Y., & Brown, M. (2009). Pain, pleasure, and power: Selecting and assessing defended subjects. In L. Black, H. Mendick, & Y. Solomon (Eds.), *Mathematical relationships in education: Identities and participation* (pp. 19–31). New York, NY: Routledge.

Berry, R. Q. (2008). Access to upper-level mathematics: The stories of successful African American middle school boys. *Journal for Research in Mathematics Education, 39,* 464–488.

Boaler, J., & Greeno, J. (2000). Identity, agency, and knowing in mathematics worlds. In J. Boaler (Ed.), *Multiple perspectives on mathematics teaching and learning* (pp. 171–200). Westport, CT: Ablex.

Bonilla-Silva, E. (2002). We are all Americans! The Latin Americanization of racial stratification in the USA. *Race & Society, 5*(1), 3–16.

Bonilla-Silva, E. (2004). From bi-racial to tri-racial: Towards a new system of racial stratification in the USA. *Ethnic and Racial Studies, 27,* 931–950.

Carraher, T. N., Carraher, D., & Schliemann, A. D. (1985). Mathematics in the streets and schools. *British Journal of Developmental Psychology, 3*(1), 21–29.

Cobb, P., Gresalfi, M., & Hodge, L. (2009). An interpretive scheme for analyzing the identities that students develop in mathematics classrooms. *Journal for Research in Mathematics Education, 40,* 40–68.

Cole, M. (1996). *Cultural psychology: A once and future discipline.* Cambridge, MA: Harvard University Press.

Cole, M., & Bruner, J. S. (1971). Cultural differences and inferences about psychological processes. *American Psychologist, 26,* 866–876.

Confrey, J. (2010). "Both and"—Equity and mathematics: A response to Martin, Gholson, and Leonard. *Journal of Urban Mathematics Education, 3*(2), 25–33.

Darragh, L. (2016). Identity research in mathematics education. *Educational Studies in Mathematics, 93,* 19–33.

Davies, B., & Harré, R. (1999). Positioning and personhood. In R. Harré, & L. Van Langenhove (Eds.), *Positioning theory: Moral contexts of intentional action* (pp. 32–52). New York, NY: Wiley.

Davis, J., & Martin, D. B. (2008). Racism, assessment, and instructional practices: Implications for mathematics teachers of African American students. *Journal of Urban Mathematics Education, 1*(1), 10–34.

Delpit, L. (2012). *"Multiplication is for White people": Raising expectations for other people's children.* New York, NY: New Press.

Dotson, K. (2014). *Knowing in space: Three lessons from Black women's social theory* (Unpublished manuscript). Michigan State University, East Lansing.

Dumas, M. (2014). "Losing an arm": Schooling as a site of black suffering. *Race, Ethnicity, and Education, 17*(1), 1–29.

Dumas, M. (2016). *The specificity of Black suffering: Antiblackness and the necessary disordering of educational research.* Ann Arbor: University of Michigan.

Duncan, G. A. (2000). Urban pedagogies and the celling of adolescents of color. *Social Justice, 27*(3), 29–42.

Edwards, A. R., Esmonde, I., & Wagner, J. F. (2011). Learning mathematics. In R. E. Mayer, & P. A. Alexander (Eds.), *Handbook of research on learning and instruction* (pp. 55–77). New York, NY: Routledge.

Engestrom, Y. (1999). Activity theory and individual social transformation. In Y. Engestrom, R. Miettinen, & R. Punamaki (Eds.), *Perspectives on activity theory* (pp. 19–38). New York, NY: Cambridge University Press.

English-Clarke, T., Slaughter-Defoe, D., & Martin, D. B. (2012). "What does race have to do with math?" Relationships between racial-mathematical socialization, mathematical identity, and racial identity. In D. T. Slaughter-Defore (Ed.), *Race and child development contribution to human development* (pp. 57–79). Basel, Switzerland: Karger.

Erikson, E. (1968). *Identity, youth and crisis.* New York, NY: W. W. Norton.

Ernest, P. (1992). The nature of mathematics: Towards a social constructivist account. *Science & Education, 1*, 89–100.

Fasching-Varner, K. J., Mitchell, R. W., Martin, L. L., & Bennett-Haron, K. P. (2014). Beyond school-to-prison pipeline and toward an educational and penal realism. *Equity & Excellence in Education, 47*, 410–429.

Fordham, S., & Ogbu, J. U. (1986). Black students' school success: Coping with the "burden of 'acting white.'" *Urban Review, 18*, 176–206.

Freeman, K. (2005). Black populations globally: The costs of the underutilization of Blacks in education. In J. King (Ed.), *Black education* (pp. 135–156). Washington, DC: American Educational Research Association.

Gholson, M., & Martin, D. B. (2014). Smart girls, black girls, mean girls, and bullies: At the intersection of identities and the mediating role of young girls' social network in mathematical communities of practice. *Journal of Education, 194*, 19–33.

Ginsburg, H. P. (1972). *The myth of the deprived child: Poor children's intellect and education.* Englewood Cliffs, NJ: Prentice-Hall.

Ginsburg, H. P., & Allardice, B. (1984). Children's difficulties with school mathematics. In B. Rogoff, & J. Lave (Eds.), *Everyday cognition: Its development in social context* (pp. 194–219). Cambridge, MA: Harvard University Press.

Gutierrez, R. (2010). The sociopolitical turn in mathematics education. *Journal for Research in Mathematics Education, 44*, 37–68.

Harel, G. (2010, April). *The role of mathematics in mathematics education research: Question for public debate.* Paper presented at the Research Pre-session of the annual meeting of the National Council of Teachers of Mathematics, San Diego, CA.

Heid, M. K. (2010). Where's the math (in mathematics education research)? *Journal for Research in Mathematics Education, 41*, 102–103.

Helfand, D. (2006, January 30). A formula for failure in L.A. schools. *Los Angeles Times*. Retrieved from http://www.latimes.com/local/la-me-dropout30jan30-story.html

Helms, J. (1996). Toward a methodology for measuring and assessing racial as distinguished from ethnic identity. In G. R. Sadowsky, & J. C. Impara (Eds.), *Multicultural assessment in counseling and clinical psychology* (pp. 157–158). Lincoln, NE: Buros Institute of Mental Measurements.

Holland, D., Lachicotte, W. Jr., Skinner, D., & Cain, C. (2001). *Identity and agency in cultural worlds*. Cambridge, MA: Harvard University Press.

Hottinger, S. (2016). *Inventing the mathematician: Gender, race, and our cultural understanding of mathematics*. Albany: State University of New York.

Jensen, A. R. (1969). How much can we boost IQ and scholastic achievement? *Harvard Educational Review, 39*, 1–123.

Jones, S. (2003). Identities of race, class, and gender inside and outside of the classroom: A girls' math club as a hybrid possibility. *Feminist Teacher, 14*, 220–233.

Kane, J. M. (2012). Young African American children constructing academic and disciplinary identities in an urban science classroom. *Science Education, 96*, 457–487.

Kirk, G. E., Hunt, J., & Volkmark, F. (1975). Social class and preschool language skill, Vol. V: Cognitive and semantic mastery of number. *Genetic Psychology Monographs, 92*, 131–153.

Klein, R. (2014, May 30). Kiera Wilmot, teen arrested in botched science experiment, haunted by felony record. *The Huffington Post*. Retrieved from http://www.huffington-post.com/2014/05/30/kiera-wilmot-college_n_5420612.html

Lagemann, E. C. (2000). *An elusive science: The troubling history of education research*. Chicago, IL: University of Chicago Press.

Langer-Osuna, J. M., & Esmonde, I. (in press). Insights and advances in research on identity in mathematics education. In J. Cai (Ed.), *First compendium for research in mathematics education*. National Council of Teachers of Mathematics.

Lave, J., & Wenger, E. (1991). *Situated learning: Legitimate peripheral participation*. New York, NY: Cambridge University Press.

Lemke, J. L. (2000). Across the scales of time: Artifacts, activities, and meanings in ecosocial systems. *Mind, Culture, and Activity, 7*, 273–290.

Leonard, J., & Martin, D. B. (2013). *The brilliance of Black children in mathematics*. Charlotte, NC: Information Age.

Lerman, S. (2000). The social turn in mathematics education research. In J. Boaler (Ed.), *Multiple perspectives on mathematics teaching and learning* (pp. 19–44). Westport, CT: Ablex.

Levin, H., Belfield, C., Muennig, P., & Rouse, C. (2007). *The costs and benefits of an excellent education for all of America's children* (Vol. 9). New York, NY: Teachers College, Columbia University.

Lewis, O. (1966). The culture of poverty. *Scientific American, 215*, 19–25.

Malloy, C. E., & Jones, M. G. (1998). An investigation of African American students' mathematical problem solving. *Journal for Research in Mathematics Education, 29*, 143–163.

Malloy, C. E., & Malloy, W. W. (1998). Issues of culture in mathematics teaching and learning. *Urban Review, 30*, 245–257.

Martin, D. (2000). *Mathematics success and failure among African-American youth*. Mahwah, NJ: Lawrence Erlbaum.

Martin, D. (2009). Researching race in mathematics education. *Teachers College Record, 111*, 295–338.

Martin, D. B. (2006). Mathematics learning and participation as racialized forms of experience: African American parents speak on the struggle for mathematics literacy. *Mathematical Thinking and Learning, 8*, 197–229.

Martin, D. B. (2015). The collective Black and principles to action. *Journal of Urban Mathematics Education, 8*(1), 17–23.

Martin, D. B., Gholson, M., & Leonard, J. (2011). Mathematics as gatekeeper: Power and privilege in the production of knowledge. *Journal of Urban Mathematics Education, 3*(2), 12–24.

McGee, E., & Martin, D. B. (2011). From the hood to being hooded: A case study of a Black male PhD. *Journal of African American Males in Education, 2*(1), 46–65.

McGrew, K. (2008). *Education's prisoners: Schooling, the political economy, and the prison industrial complex* (Vol. 325). Bern, Switzerland: Peter Lang.

McLoyd, V. (1991). What is the study of African American children the study of? In R. L. Jones (Ed.), *Black psychology* (pp. 419–440). Oakland, CA: Cobb & Henry.

Mead, G. H. (2011). The social self. In F. C. da Silver (Ed.), *G. H. Mead: A reader* (pp. 58–62). Oxford, England: Routledge. (Original work published 1913)

Meiners, E. R. (2010). *Right to be hostile: Schools, prisons, and the making of public enemies.* New York, NY: Routledge.

Molina, N. (2014). *American crossroads: How race is made in America.* Berkeley: University of California Press.

Moody, V. R. (2000). African American students' success with school mathematics. In M. E. Strutchens, M. L Johnson, & W. F. Tate (Eds.), *Changing the faces of mathematics: Perspectives on African Americans* (pp. 51–60). Reston, VA: NCTM.

Moses, R. P., & Cobb, C. E. (2001). *Radical equations: Civil rights from Mississippi to the Algebra Project.* Boston, MA: Beacon Press.

Moyer, J. (2015, October 27). Witness to rough South Carolina high school arrest: "I couldn't believe this was happening." *The Washington Post.* Retrieved from https://www.washingtonpost.com/news/morning-mix/wp/2015/10/27/witness-to-spring-valley-high-arrest-i-couldnt-believe-this-was-happening/?utm_term=.72be3cccc2a0

Muhammad, K. G. (2010). *The condemnation of Blackness: Race, crime, and the making of modern urban America.* Cambridge, MA: Harvard University Press.

Nakagawa, S. (2012). *Blackness is the fulcrum.* Retrieved from http://www.racefiles.com/2012/05/04/blackness-is-the-fulcrum/

Nasir, N. (2002). Identity, goals, and learning: Mathematics in cultural practice. *Mathematical Thinking and Learning, 4*, 213–247.

Nasir, N. S., & Saxe, G. B. (2003). Ethnic and academic identities: A cultural practice perspective on emerging tensions and their management in the lives of minority students. *Educational Researcher, 32*(5), 14–18.

Noguera, P. A. (2003). Schools, prisons, and social implications of punishment: Rethinking disciplinary practices. *Theory Into Practice, 42*, 341–350.

Ogbu, J. (1978). *Minority education and caste: The American system in cross-cultural perspective.* New York, NY: Academic Press.

Osborne, J. W., & Jones, B. D. (2011). Identification with academics and motivation to achieve in school: How the structure of self influences academic outcomes. *Educational Psychology Review, 23*, 131–158.

Resnick, L. B. (1989). Treating mathematics as an ill-structured discipline. In R. I. Charles, & E. A. Silver (Eds.), *The teaching and assessing of mathematical problem solving* (pp. 32–60). Mahwah, NJ: Erlbaum.

Rickels, J., Heppen, J., Taylor, S., Allensworth, E., Michelman, V., Sorensen, N., . . . Clements, P. (2016). *Getting back on track: Who needs to recover algebra credit after ninth grade?* Retrieved from http://www.air.org/resource/getting-back-track-who-needs-recover-algebra-credit-after-ninth-grade

Roberts, D. (1997). *Killing the black body: Race, reproduction, and the meaning of liberty.* New York, NY: Random House.

Saxe, G. (1988). Candy selling and math learning. *Educational Researcher, 17*(6), 14–21.

Sfard, A. (1998). On two metaphors for learning and the dangers of choosing just one. *Educational Researcher, 27*(2), 4–13.

Sfard, A., & Prusak, A. (2005). Telling identities: In search of an analytic tool for investigating learning as a culturally shaped activity. *Educational Researcher, 34*(4), 14–22.

Shah, N. (2013). *Racial discourse in mathematics and its impact on student learning, identity, and participation* (Unpublished dissertation). University of California at Berkeley, California.

Silver, E., Smith, M., & Nelson, B. (1995). The QUASAR project: Equity concerns meet mathematics education reform in the middle school. In W. Secada, E. Fennema, & L. Adajain (Eds.), *New directions for equity in mathematics education* (pp. 9–56). New York, NY: Cambridge University Press.

Silver, E. A., & Kilpatrick, J. (1994). E pluribus unum: Challenges of diversity in future of mathematics education. *Journal for Research in Mathematics Education, 25,* 734–754.

Steele, C. M. (1997). A threat in the air: How stereotypes shape intellectual identity and performance. *American Psychologist, 52,* 613–629.

Stinson, D. W. (2004). Mathematics as "gate-keeper" (?): Three theoretical perspectives that aim toward empowering all children with a key to the gate. *The Mathematics Educator, 14*(1), 8–18.

Stinson, D. W. (2006). African American male adolescents, schooling (and mathematics): Deficiency, rejection, and achievement. *Review of Educational Research, 76,* 477–506.

Stinson, D. W. (2008). Negotiating sociocultural discourses: The counter-storytelling of academically (and mathematically) successful African American male students. *American Educational Research Journal, 45,* 975–1010.

Stinson, D. W. (2011). When the 'burden of acting white' is not a burden: School success and African American male students. *Urban Review, 43,* 43–65.

Stinson, D. W., & Bullock, E. C. (2012a). Critical postmodern theory in mathematics education research: A praxis of uncertainty. *Educational Studies in Mathematics, 80*(1), 41–55.

Stinson, D. W., & Bullock, E. C. (2012b). Transitioning into contemporary theory: Critical postmodern theory in mathematics education research. In L. R. Van Zoest, J.-J. Lo, & J. L. Kratky (Eds.), *Proceedings of the 34th annual meeting of the North American Chapter of the International Group for the Psychology of Mathematics Education* (pp. 1163–1169). Kalamazoo, MI: Western Michigan University.

Sum, A., Khatiwada, I., McLaughlin, J., & Palma, S. (2009). *The consequences of dropping out of high school.* Retrieved from https://www.prisonpolicy.org/scans/The_Consequences_of_Dropping_Out_of_High_School.pdf

Tate, W. (2016, April). *Divergent: Supporting "factionless" and underserved students in mathematics education.* Iris M. Carl Equity Address presented at the meeting of the National Council of Mathematics Teachers, San Francisco, CA.

Taylor, E. V. (2009). The purchasing practice of low-income students: The relationship to mathematical development. *Journal of the Learning Sciences, 18,* 370–415.

Tuck, E. (2009). Suspending damage: A letter to communities. *Harvard Educational Review, 29,* 409–427.

Valencia, R. R. (2010). *Dismantling contemporary deficit thinking: Educational thought and practice.* New York, NY: Routledge.

Varelas, M., Settlage, J., & Mensah, F. M. (2015). Explorations of the structure-agency dialectic as a tool for framing equity in science education. *Journal of Research in Science Teaching, 52,* 439–447.

Visser, N. (2015, September 16). Muslim 9th grader Ahmed Mohamed arrested for bringing homemade clock to school. *The Huffington Post.* Retrieved from http://www.huffington-post.com/entry/9th-grader-arrested-clock_us_55f96557e4b0b48f6701519c

Wertsch, J. V. (1991). *Voices of the mind.* Cambridge, MA: Harvard University Press.

Williams, H. A. (2009). *Self-taught: African American education in slavery and freedom.* Chapel Hill: University of North Carolina Press.

Winn, M. T., & Behizadeh, N. (2011). The right to be literate: Literacy, education, and the school-to-prison pipeline. *Review of Research in Education, 35,* 147–173.

Chapter 11

Eliminating Disparities in School Discipline: A Framework for Intervention

ANNE GREGORY
Rutgers University

RUSSELL J. SKIBA
Indiana University

KAVITHA MEDIRATTA
Atlantic Philanthropies

Race and gender disparities in school discipline and associated harms have been well documented for decades. Suspension from school can reduce instructional time and impede academic progress for students who may already be lagging in their achievement. This chapter offers a research-based framework for increasing equity in school discipline. The framework is composed of ten principles that hold promise for helping educators to address student behavior in a developmentally appropriate manner and reduce race and gender disparities in school discipline. The framework also informs directions for future research in school discipline.

Federal and state actions to reduce racial disparities in discipline respond to a decade of findings (e.g., American Psychological Association Task Force, 2008) on the ineffectiveness of exclusionary discipline in improving educational outcomes and their disparate impact on students based on their racial/ethnic group membership, thereby violating civil rights protections. Male and female Black students disproportionately receive discipline referrals and out-of-school suspension (Fabelo et al., 2011), most often at a rate two to three times greater than White students. Disproportionate discipline has also been documented for males, Latinos, American Indians, and students in special education (U.S. Department of Justice/Department of Education, 2014). Recent research has raised concerns that lesbian, bisexual, gay, and transgender students are also at heightened risk of receiving discipline sanctions (Himmelstein & Bruckner, 2011; Poteat, Scheer, & Chong, 2015).

Review of Research in Education
March 2017, Vol. 41, pp. 253–278
DOI: 10.3102/0091732X17690499
© 2017 AERA. http://rre.aera.net

Findings such as these have led policymakers and educators in school districts across the country to examine how best to reduce the use of exclusionary discipline, especially for students from marginalized groups. The rapid pace of reform has outstripped research and documentation. While some evaluations of district-level efforts show significant reductions in rates of exclusionary discipline across racial–ethnic groups (e.g., González, 2015; Osher, Poirier, Jarjoura, Brown, & Kendziora, 2015), few investigations have focused specifically on the discipline gap and even fewer have demonstrated a shrinkage of that gap.

We seek to inform current reforms through a systematic synthesis of promising policies and practices for reducing disciplinary disparities. We draw on naturalistic research and the few extant published intervention studies to propose the Framework for Increasing Equity in School Discipline. The Framework includes 10 school principles that hold promise for reducing race and gender disparities in school discipline. We intentionally offer numerous principles that span many aspects of the ecology of schooling. Narrow, singular interventions targeting only one aspect of schooling will not likely disrupt entrenched patterns of racial and gender inequality. Thus, the principles address varying levels of the school ecology including intrapersonal (educator beliefs and attitudes), interpersonal (quality of individual and group interactions), instructional (academic rigor, cultural relevancy and responsiveness of instruction), and systems levels (access to behavioral supports and avenues for collaborative approaches to resolving conflicts).

In describing the Framework's principles, we distinguish between prevention and intervention-oriented action. Schools that successfully develop communities of responsive and supportive adults and motivated and engaged learners typically prevent disciplinary incidents and punitive responses to behavior from occurring in the first place (Emmer & Sabornie, 2014). Yet, as with all communities, some conflict is inevitable. When conflict happens, it can be addressed in a constructive and equitable manner. Thus, 5 of the 10 principles address prevention, four are intervention oriented, laying the groundwork for constructive responses to conflict and reduced unnecessary discipline, and one addresses both prevention and intervention (see Table 1).

Without what might be called "culturally conscious implementation," there is the risk that advantaged students will reap the rewards of less punitive discipline policies and practices while marginalized students continue to receive more punitive treatment. Thus, we posit the need for culturally conscious implementation of the Framework's 10 principles. This means educators need to explicitly consider issues of culture, race, gender, power, and privilege in addressing inequality in schooling (Gay, 2010, Ladson-Billings, 2009; C. S. Weinstein, Tomlinson-Clarke, & Curran, 2004; Winn, 2016).

We begin by reviewing emerging federal, state, and district reforms to describe the current context for intervention. We then discuss the typical approaches to intervention and argue the racial and gender gaps will only substantially reduce when educators undertake culturally conscious implementation of reforms. We then synthesize available research that supports our selection of each of the 10 principles in the Framework for Increasing Equity in School Discipline, and we offer some preliminary considerations about their culturally conscious implementation.

TABLE 1
Framework for Increasing Equity in School Discipline

Prevention	1. Supportive Relationships	Authentic connections are forged between and among teachers and students.
	2. Bias-Aware Classrooms and Respectful School Environments	Inclusive, positive classroom and school environments are established in which students feel fairly treated.
	3. Academic Rigor	The potential of all students is promoted through high expectations and high-level learning opportunities.
	4. Culturally Relevant and Responsive Teaching	Instruction reflects and is respectful of the diversity of today's classrooms and schools.
	5. Opportunities for Learning and Correcting Behavior	Behavior is approached from a nonpunitive mind-set, and instruction proactively strengthens student social skills, while providing structured opportunities for behavioral correction within the classroom as necessary.
Intervention	6. Data-Based Inquiry for Equity	Data are used regularly to identify "hot spots" of disciplinary conflict or differential treatment of particular groups.
	7. Problem-Solving Approaches to Discipline	Solutions aim to uncover sources of behavior or teacher–student conflict and address the identified needs.
	8. Inclusion of Student and Family Voice on Conflicts' Causes and Solutions	Student and family voice are integrated into policies, procedures, and practices concerning school discipline.
	9. Reintegration of Students after Conflict or Absence	Students are supported in reentering the community of learners after conflict or long-term absence has occurred.
Prevention and Intervention	10. Multitiered System of Supports	Schools use a tiered framework to match increasing levels of intensity of support to students' differentiated needs.

Note. The numerical ordering of principles is not meant to suggest their relative importance.

THE CONTEXT FOR INTERVENTION

Evidence of the deleterious correlates of exclusionary discipline has continued to grow. Multivariate and longitudinal studies demonstrate that exclusionary discipline is a risk factor for a host of short- and long-term negative consequences, including academic disengagement, depressed academic achievement, school dropout, and increased involvement in the juvenile justice system (Skiba, Arredondo, & Williams,

2014). A recent meta-analysis of 24 studies found evidence of a link between in-school and out-of-school suspension and low achievement (Noltemeyer, Ward, & Mcloughlin, 2015).

Although concerns about racial disproportionality go back at least to the 1970s, when the Children's Defense Fund (1975) published a report on disparities in suspensions for children of color, it was not until the late 1990s that the issue began to attract wider notice. The current wave of reform has been field-driven in many ways. Young people, parents, and civil rights advocates began documenting growing rates of suspensions, expulsions and arrests in schools, and their disproportionate impact on students of color (Mediratta, 2012) using the term *school-to-prison pipeline* to describe a pattern of educational exclusion and justice system involvement (Ginwright, 2004). Efforts by grassroots community groups such as *Padres y Jóvenes Unidos* in Denver, CADRE in Los Angeles, and Voices of Youth in Chicago Education demonstrated not only the need for reform but also how partnerships could be built with local schools and districts to develop positive interventions and supports to manage student behavior (Padres y Jóvenes Unidos & Advancement Project, 2010; Rogers & Terriquez, 2013).

By 2014, research and advocacy had established that exclusionary discipline in U.S. public schools constituted a problem of serious proportions. Faced with evidence of the widespread use of these sanctions and the extreme disparities for students of color, policymakers have begun to implement national, state, and local initiatives to reduce rates of suspension and expulsion and increase the use of alternatives (Losen & Martinez, 2013; Morgan, Salomon, Plotkin, & Cohen, 2014).

National Level

The U.S. Departments of Justice and Education launched the national Supportive School Discipline Initiative to improve data collection, expand technical assistance, and inform reform efforts by state and local officials (U.S. Department of Justice/Department of Education, 2011). In January 2014, the two agencies jointly released a two-part federal guidance document with recommended practices for fostering supportive and equitable school discipline. Most recently, Congress passed the *Every Student Succeeds Act* (ESSA S. 1177), which reauthorizes the Elementary and Secondary School Act and includes a number of provisions intended to reduce disciplinary exclusion and disparities in exclusion. Every Student Succeeds Act identifies school climate as an indicator of student success, requires local education agencies to detail how they will reduce the overuse of exclusionary discipline, and permits districts to use federal funding for intervention services such as parent engagement, school-based mental health services, and multitiered systems of support (Capatosto, 2015).

State-Level Changes

States and school districts across the nation have taken action concurrently with the federal-level changes. Often driven by local advocates, at least 17 states have passed legislation on discipline and climate in recent years (Colombi & Osher, 2015). Provisions in state law aim to do the following:

- *Limit out-of-school suspension and expulsion*: California passed measures to curtail the use of suspension, expulsion and referral to law enforcement, and most recently a bill (AB420) that eliminates *willful defiance* as a reason for suspension, which has been associated with particularly extreme levels of disparities (California Department of Education, 2015).
- *Collect disaggregated data and reduce disparities in exclusionary discipline*: In 2014, Illinois mandated the reporting of disaggregated data on discipline and, beginning in 2017, requires districts in the top 20% of use of exclusionary discipline to submit an improvement plan for reducing exclusion and racial disparities (State of Illinois, 2014).
- *Implement alternatives to suspension and expulsion*: Building on a pilot program in Denver, the state of Colorado has expanded the use of restorative justice (RJ) in programs throughout the state (Restorative Justice Colorado, 2015).

School District Reform Efforts

Attempts to reform school disciplinary practices have also made their way to the district level. District-wide reform has been documented in numerous school districts across the country, including the following:

- *Denver*: Beginning in 2005, the Denver Public Schools, in partnership with the advocacy group *Padres & Jovenes Unidos*, implemented RJ practices in selected pilot schools and later expanded them to much of the district (Padres y Jóvenes Unidos & Advancement Project. 2005). Between 2006 and 2013, the overall suspension rate dropped from 10.58% to 5.63%, and the gap between Black and White students decreased from a 12- to 8-point gap (González, 2015).
- *Oakland*: In 2005, the Oakland Unified School District initiated a pilot program of RJ at Cole Middle School and saw an 87% decrease in suspensions in three years (Sumner, Silverman, & Frampton, 2010). By 2014, they expanded the program to 24 schools. In the middle and high schools with RJ programming, suspensions decreased by 23% between 2010 and 2013, and dropout rates declined by 56% (Jain, Bassey, Brown, & Kalra, 2014).
- *Los Angeles Unified School District*: This was among the first large urban districts to substantially revise its Code of Conduct, and data show declines in suspension and expulsion (http://www.publicintegrity.org/2014/01/31/14201/new-california-data-show-drop-overall-school-suspensions-expulsions).

TYPICAL APPROACHES TO REFORM

Stokes and Baer (1977) first identified the strategy of "train and hope" to describe the faulty assumptions behind efforts to generalize individual's behavior change, arguing that attempting to teach an individual a new behavior and then hoping it will generalize to other settings, times, or individuals is not an effective strategy for ensuring generalizable change. In the same way, many strategies for addressing disparate outcomes in school might be termed "implement and hope"—taking a strategy that has shown positive outcomes for students in general, and assuming it will be equally effective in (that is, generalize to) reducing racial/ethnic disparities. The "implement and hope" strategy is so deeply engrained that data often are not disaggregated, precluding tracking, and assessment of implementation effects on target populations. Indeed, one recent report described how fewer than half of Schoolwide Positive Behavior Intervention Support (SWPBIS) schools that entered ethnicity enrollment information into their SWPBIS data system examined disaggregated discipline data by group even once during the school year (McIntosh, Eliason, Horner, & May, 2014).

Evidence suggests that, even in the case of empirically based interventions, implementation without explicit attention to addressing disparities is like its individual analogue, unlikely to reduce discipline disparities. Studying a nationally representative sample of 346 elementary and middle schools implementing SWPBIS for at least 1 year, Skiba et al. (2011) found that Black students remained twice as likely as their White peers to be referred to the office, and that Latino and Black students were more likely than White students to receive suspensions or expulsions as a consequence for similar behaviors, especially for minor misbehavior. Vincent, Swain-Bradway, Tobin, and May (2011) found that, even in schools in which SWPBIS decreased overall school rates of out-of-school suspension, Black students continued to be overrepresented in out-of-school suspensions, particularly suspensions longer than 10 days. Such data underscore the need for explicit consideration of issues of culture, power, and privilege in addressing inequality in schooling (Gay, 2010, Ladson-Billings, 2009; C. S. Weinstein et al., 2004; Winn, 2016). The failure to create equitable outcomes for students of all racial/ethnic backgrounds has led to recommendations for better integration of sociocultural aspects in the design, implementation, and interpretation of interventions (Olmeda & Kauffman, 2003; Harris-Murri, King, & Rostenberg, 2006).

CULTURALLY CONSCIOUS IMPLEMENTATION

Carter, Skiba, Arredondo, and Pollock (2015) argue that schools cannot effectively target racial disparities in discipline without addressing longstanding issues of race and power. They write,

It is impossible to tell the full story of racial discipline disparities without considering the full range of racialized historical and current factors that shape school life in the United States. The ravages of slavery and Jim Crow, forced migration, and policies that enforced unequal treatment placed African Americans and most people of color at an economic and social disadvantage that persists to this day. (p. 2)

They continue,

Regrettably, our history also left us with pervasive and false ideas about "races" that have shaped our perceptions of who is valued and who is not, who is capable and who is not, and who is "safe" and who is "dangerous." (p. 2)

Winn (2011) and Morris (2016) also point out that efforts to disrupt the school-to-prison pipeline need to address the varying forms of discrimination that thwart the positive development of youth depending on their identities and social locations (e.g., race, gender, social class, sexual and gender identity). Together, these scholars raise the importance of considering the interacting sociohistorical forces that contribute to the current disparities in school discipline. According to Carter et al. (2015), such considerations extend to how we approach affecting change. Specifically, they call for a race-conscious approach to intervention. We expand on their call and posit the need for a "culturally conscious" approach to implementing reforms. A handful of tenets underlie our conceptualization of "culturally conscious implementation":

1. We use the term "culture" broadly, referencing the beliefs and behaviors of groups that are bound to history and are passed down from generation to generation. We also see that students and educators in schools perpetuate beliefs and behavior through their own shared culture. For instance, educators can share implicit beliefs that punishment is the appropriate response to student rule-breaking.

2. Interactions among educators, family, and students are sociohistorically situated within a longstanding history of racial and class segregation and unequal schooling (Carter et al., 2015). As Ladson-Billings (2006) describes, achievement gaps reflect the "educational debt" that has accrued over time. Thus, culturally conscious implementation considers the *differential access* marginalized groups have had to high quality schooling given the current and historical legacy of racial and socioeconomic segregation in neighborhoods and schools.

3. Sociocultural and historical narratives shape perceptions and judgements about the "appropriateness" of behavior. Bal, Thorius, and Kozleski (2012) write, "Racial minority students' experiences and cultural and linguistic practices (i.e., ways of knowing, behaving, and being) are often devalued and/or pathologized . . ." (p. 4). In terms of discipline, this means that students of color can be subject to *differential selection*—their behavior can be "selected" for punishment (Gregory, Skiba & Noguera, 2010). For example, teachers' culturally based judgments about dress, speech, vocal tone, and body language can fuel whether or not a teacher "reads" Black students' behavior as defiant or disruptive (Neal, McCray, Webb-Johnson, & Bridgest, 2003). Dominant beliefs about what it means to display appropriate female behavior can also affect treatment toward students. For example, Morris (2016) describes adults' negative appraisals of Black females who are loud or have an "attitude"—negative appraisals which, according to Morris, come from a lack of understanding of Black girls' desire to be heard and seen in the context of gender and race oppression.

4. While Black/White disparities in school discipline have been documented in U.S. public schools for over four decades (Children's Defense Fund, 1975), disproportionate discipline has also been documented for a range of other groups including males, Latinos, American Indians, students in special education, and lesbian, bisexual, gay, and transgender students (Anyon et al., 2014; Himmelstein & Bruckner, 2011; Poteat et al., 2015; Wallace, Goodkind, Wallace, & Bachman, 2008). This raises concerns about how "difference" is policed in schools and

indicates the need for an intersectional lens to understand how expectations/ norms for "respectable" behavior span varying aspects of identity (Snapp & Russell, 2016). For instance, gender–non-conforming girls of color who identify as a lesbian, gay, bisexual, or queer may challenge many adults' behavioral expectations based on White, heterosexual, hyperfeminine forms of self-presentation (Chmielewski, Belmonte, Stoudt, & Fine, 2016).

5. Racism and negative stereotypes are powerful influences on the punitive treatment of students of color. Indeed, Black male and female students are subject to harsher sanctions than their White peers, even when controlling for the seriousness of their infractions (Skiba et al., 2014), the frequency of being involved in discipline incidents (Anyon et al., 2014), and the levels of teacher-reported misbehavior (Bradshaw, Mitchell, O'Brennan, & Leaf, 2010). Moreover, a recent statewide study showed that Black females had 13% higher odds of discipline in a year than White males, accounting for student grade retention and student- and school-level poverty (Blake et al., 2016). This body of research demonstrates that Black students are treated more harshly when compared to similar students, suggesting that race, in the form of stereotypes and implicit bias, affects everyday interactions in school (Carter et al., 2015). Thus, culturally conscious implementation efforts need to further recognize *differential sanction* of marginalized groups.

FRAMEWORK FOR INCREASING EQUITY IN SCHOOL DISCIPLINE

Studies of the effects of interventions currently are too few in number to support a meta-analysis. Yet the extensive research on the existence and causes of disparities in discipline (Losen, 2015; Skiba, Mediratta, & Rausch, 2016) makes it possible to identify *research-based* principles on which intervention to reduce disciplinary data can be based. Below, we present a framework of 10 research-based principles for disparity-reducing intervention in schools. The following 10 principles were identified in a review of research by the Discipline Disparities Research-to-Practice Collaborative, a group of 26 researchers, policymakers, educators, and advocates (Discipline Disparities Collaborative, 2015). Eight of these 10 principles were presented in prior publications from the Discipline Disparities Collaborative (Gregory, Bell, & Pollock, 2016).

The Framework's principles are not exhaustive, and future theory and research may augment or condense them. With that caveat in mind, we explore the extent of empirical support for each of the 10 principles, drawing findings from studies using a wide range of methodologies (ethnography to randomized controlled trials). In addition, we consider how each practice relates specifically to disparities in school discipline for marginalized groups. We draw on the extant research which largely compares the experience of Black and White students, but when possible, we also draw from more recent research which identifies disparities in rates of exclusionary discipline for other racial/ethnic categories (e.g., Latino, American Indian), and by gender, disability status, and sexual orientation and gender identity (Skiba et al., 2016). We also offer some preliminary ideas that relate to the culturally conscious implementation of each principle in the Framework.

Principle 1: Supportive Relationships

A convincing accumulation of research has shown that students who feel supported by their teachers tend to be more engaged in academic work and have fewer disciplinary interactions with adults in school, relative to their peers who experience less support. Two meta-analyses have substantiated the link between the affective dimension of teacher–student relationships and student engagement in school. Examining results across 119 studies, Cornelius-White (2007) found that teacher empathy ($r = .32$) and warmth ($r = .32$) were associated with positive student outcomes. In a meta-analysis of 99 studies, Roorda, Koomen, Spilt, and Oort (2011) found medium to large effects for both positive relationships and engagement ($r = .39$, $p < .01$) and negative relationships and engagement ($r = -.32$, $p < .01$). Of particular concern is the likelihood that negative relationships with teachers in the early years of schooling may have cumulative adverse effects across grade levels (Hamre & Pianta, 2001; Rubie-Davies et al., 2014).

A recent randomized control trial of a teacher coaching program demonstrated that strengthening relationships made a difference for students in groups who receive high rates of discipline. In the My Teaching Partner–Secondary (MTP-S) program, teachers were randomly assigned to a business-as-usual or a coaching condition (Gregory, Hafen, et al., 2016). Coaches worked individually with teachers to increase the emotional, organizational, and instructional supports in their classrooms. During the 2 years of coaching and the year after coaching was discontinued, the MTP-S teachers issued discipline referrals to Black and non-Black students at similarly low rates. The control teachers, in contrast, had a large racial gap in discipline referrals. In classrooms where teachers improved in observed sensitivity to students' social and emotional needs, Black students were less likely to be issued a disciplinary referral than their peers in classrooms where teachers showed less improvement. We might speculate that MTP-S teachers developed trusting relationships with their Black students—treating them as individuals and possibly disrupting negative behavioral stereotypes about Black students.

Culturally Conscious Implementation

Given that the teaching force in the United States is predominantly White and female (Goldring, Gray, & Bitterman, 2013), educators need to ensure that they are attuned to the social and emotional experiences of students of color in an intentional manner. This is underscored by the growing body of evidence demonstrating that Latino and Black students are less likely than White students to report feeling cared about by an adult at school (Bottiani, Bradshaw, & Mendelson, 2014; Fan, Williams, & Corkin, 2011; Voight, Hanson, O'Malley, & Adekanyel, 2015).

Principle 2: Bias-Aware Classrooms and Respectful School Environments

Emerging findings raise the possibility that educators' disciplinary decision making may be influenced by implicit racial bias—unconsciously held negative associations linked to racial stereotypes. A meta-analysis of 184 studies of implicit bias concluded that, generally speaking, implicit bias predicts differential treatment of dissimilar individuals (Greenwald, Poehlman, Uhlmann, & Banaji, 2009). A recent experimental study found a link between race and teacher perceptions of student behavior. Teachers were shown an office discipline referral for a student with two incidents of misconduct, the name of the disciplined student varied between those that are stereotypically Black (Darnell or Deshawn) and White (Greg or Jake; Okonofua & Eberhardt, 2015). Teachers responded with more severe disciplinary actions to students with stereotypically Black names than those with names that are stereotypically White. Okonofua and Eberhardt (2015) also found that the more likely teachers were to think the student was Black, the more likely they were to label the student a troublemaker. Goff, Jackson, Di Leone, Culotta, and DiTomasso (2014) found that Black boys are generally viewed as older and more culpable than White peers, and that the characteristic of innocence, typically associated with childhood, is less frequently applied to Black boys relative to White boys.

A recent randomized field experiment demonstrates how respectful teacher interactions may reduce negative disciplinary outcomes of marginalized students (Okonofua, Paunesku, & Walton, 2016). Okonofua et al. (2016) randomly assigned 39 math teachers to an empathic mind-set intervention or a control condition (an intervention about the use of technology to promote learning). In the empathic mind-set intervention, teachers read an article and student testimonials on a range of nonpejorative factors that affect student misconduct and how positive relationships with teachers help students thrive. The teachers were then asked to write about how they use these ideas in their own practice and were told their written contributions would be integrated into the teacher training program. The aim of the empathic mind-set intervention was to increase teachers' perspective taking about student misconduct and promote a context of trust and understanding. Findings showed that males and Black and Latino students in classrooms of teachers in the empathic mind-set intervention were half as likely to receive a suspension relative to their peers in the control teachers' classrooms that school year (boys 8.4% vs. 14.6% and Black/Latinos: 6.3% vs. 12.3%, respectively). Importantly, students with histories of suspension felt more respected by math teachers in the empathic mind-set intervention versus the control intervention.

Culturally Conscious Implementation

Adolescents may be particularly adept at detecting unfair treatment based on implicit bias and negative stereotyping (Brown & Bigler, 2005), and these perceptions may in turn affect their disengagement or active resistance to authority in school (Yeager et al., 2014). This may be particularly salient for students of color. Based on interviews with Black girls, Morris (2016) discusses how their behavior can be a demonstration of resistance to gender and racial oppression. She writes, "The 'attitude' often attributed to Black girls casts as undesirable the skills of being astute at reading their location—where they sit along the social hierarchy—and overcoming the attendant obstacles" (p. 19). She further states, "To be 'loud' is to be heard. To have 'attitude' is to reject a doctrine of invisibility and mistreatment" (p. 19). Morris's theorizing suggests that efforts to raise awareness about bias should include considering how deeply ingrained culturally bound notions of "appropriate" behavior may impact everyday interactions.

Principle 3: Academic Rigor

When students are engaged in and excited about academic activities, school discipline referrals are typically rare (Emmer & Sabornie, 2014). Cornelius-White's (2007) meta-analysis of 199 studies found that teachers' encouragement of higher order thinking (r = .29) and learning (r = .23) was associated with positive student outcomes. Access to instructionally rich and motivating classrooms, however, are not evenly distributed across student groups (e.g., Kena et al., 2015). Comparing the experiences of high- and low-tracked students, Wing (2006) found that high-achieving classrooms, composed of predominantly White and Asian students, had lively teacher and student engagement with interactive teaching styles and student autonomy, while more remedial classes, composed of predominantly Black and Latino students, emphasized tight management of behavior over student autonomy.

The results from two recent studies indicate that efforts to reduce racial disparities in discipline need to include providing more equitable access to rigorous and interactive curriculum and instruction (Card & Giuliano, 2016; Gregory et al., 2016). Evaluating the effects of a tracking program using a regression discontinuity research design, Card and Giuliano (2016) compared outcomes between fourth- and fifth-grade students who were placed into gifted/high-achiever classrooms or into general education classrooms in a large urban school district. Relative to similar peers, Black students in the gifted/high-achiever classrooms made greater achievement gains and were less likely to receive suspension through sixth grade. Gregory et al.'s (2016) randomized control trial of MTP-S further corroborates the finding that access to cognitively rich and motivating instruction reduces students' risk of receiving a discipline sanction. Teachers in the MTP-S coaching condition had no significant racial disparities in office discipline referrals compared with a large racial gap in discipline referrals among teachers in the control condition. Mediational analyses showed that the degree to which teachers were observed facilitating higher level thinking skills, problem solving, and metacognition was significantly linked to their equitable and infrequent use of discipline referrals.

Culturally Conscious Implementation

Efforts to increase access to academic rigor often take the form of ensuring students from marginalized groups have opportunities to enroll in advanced or honors-level coursework in high school (Handwerk, Tognatta, Coley, & Gitomer, 2008). While important, this singular focus is narrow and does not address the subtle ways marginalized students can be denied access to academic rigor in special education and general education classrooms. Culturally conscious efforts to increase academic rigor, therefore, should address how teacher beliefs about marginalized students' academic potential can impact everyday interactions that result in their receiving subpar instructional opportunities and content (R. S. Weinstein, 2002).

Principle 4: Culturally Relevant and Responsive Teaching

Culturally relevant and responsive instruction has been identified as a positive predictor of student outcomes in increasingly diverse classrooms. Gay (2010) argues that culturally responsive teachers acquire knowledge about their students' cultural and social history and build trust with their students by communicating an understanding of their lives. This in turn helps them both understand student behavior and design instruction that helps students process their experiences of inequality and marginalization. C. S. Weinstein et al.'s (2004) model of culturally responsive classroom management consists of five components: (a) teacher recognition of their own ethnocentrism, (b) development of caring classroom communities, (c) incorporation of students' cultural backgrounds in classroom learning experiences, (d) classroom management strategies that are in synch with those backgrounds, and (e) teacher understanding of the social, economic, and political issues facing their students.

Empirical evidence for the promise of culturally relevant and responsive teaching in reducing disparities in school discipline primarily arises from small-scale qualitative studies of classrooms and small groups of teachers. Researchers have provided rich descriptions of how culturally responsive relationships elicit student engagement and cooperation (Aronson & Laughter, 2016; Howard, 2010). Ethnographic research with eight female teachers of mostly Black youth by Ladson-Billings (2009) found that teachers who most effectively engaged their Black male students in a culturally responsive manner were those that (a) affirmed and celebrated their culture, (b) integrated students' life experiences into the curriculum, and (c) communicated high academic expectations while scaffolding rigorous academic work. Using this perspective, the Oakland Unified School District developed the Manhood Development Program, an in-school elective for Black male students, which aims to foster positive cultural identities, social and emotional competence, and academic skills (Watson, 2014).

Although theory has outpaced empirical studies in this area, a growing number of related studies link student participation in culturally relevant coursework with subsequent academic outcomes. Kisker et al. (2012) argue that culturally relevant coursework, such as ethnic studies, is meaningful and engaging to students whose cultural heritage is not recognized or honored in typical curricula. Using data from a large urban district in a regression discontinuity design study, Dee and Penner (2016) compared the trajectories of similarly low-achieving ninth graders who were or were not assigned to an ethnic studies course. Their sample consisted of 1,405 students (60% Asian, 23% Latino, 6% Black) in five unique school-year cohorts enrolled in three high schools in San Francisco. They found that assignment to ethnic studies increased attendance, grade point average, and ninth-grade credits earned. Importantly, the findings held for students with prior school suspensions, offering compelling evidence that culturally relevant courses can actually shift students' educational trajectories.

Culturally Conscious Implementation

School curricula, schoolwide events, and library resources are forums for educators to present content that is relevant to students' lives. A culturally conscious approach is not limited to making content relevant to only one aspect of students' identity (e.g., ethnicity). Instead, it considers the need to connect with the range of racial, ethnic, cultural, gender, and sexual identities and experiences of students and communities (e.g., Gay, Lesbian & Straight Education Network, 2011). Also, it is not limited to increasing the relevancy of content. A culturally conscious approach includes reflecting on how interactions in classrooms have a cultural basis that aligns or misaligns with varying student communities (e.g., Boykin, Tyler, & Miller, 2005). For example, the Double Check teacher coaching program aims to support teachers in such critical reflection and is currently being evaluated in a randomized controlled trial in elementary and middle schools (Bradshaw, Pas, & Debnam, 2015; Hershfeldt et al., 2010).

Principle 5: Opportunities for Learning and Correcting Behavior

A stream of professional development programming draws on behavioral theory and the strategic use of extrinsic rewards to help schools utilize a behavioral-supports approach to student behavior (Kamps et al., 2015; Sugai & Horner, 2010). When educators respond with specific praise to desired behavior, students tend to decrease disruptive behavior and increase the reinforced behavior (e.g., Walker, Ramsey, & Gresham, 2004). For example, in the Class Wide Function–related Intervention Teams program (CW-FIT), teachers use a social skills game format and reward teams of students who demonstrate social skills taught through direct instruction (Kamps et al., 2015). Similarly, in SWPBIS, school staff teach all students jointly agreed-on, schoolwide expectations for behavior (e.g., be respectful) and issue students tangible reinforcers for positive behavior such as tickets that earn them special privileges. Both CW-FIT and SWPBIS have been shown to reduce disruptive behavior (Bradshaw, Mitchell, & Leaf, 2010; Kamps et al., 2015). Through such programming, adult behavior may also change. When educators intentionally increase their focus on, and praise of, positive student behavior they may shift away from reprimands and punitive mind-sets (Bradshaw, Mitchell, O'Brennan, et al., 2010).

Social and emotional learning (SEL) programs draw on theory about the development of self-discipline through social and emotional competencies (Bear, Whitcomb, Elias, & Blank, 2015). Evidence that students' SEL skills in early childhood are closely tied to their later well-being (Jones, Greenberg, & Crowley, 2015) has provided momentum for revised discipline policies and new practices that offer students greater opportunities to learn and practice social and emotional "literacies." A meta-analysis found that SEL programs can strengthen students' SEL skills which in turn relate to a range of positive outcomes (Durlak, Weissberg, Dymnicki, Taylor, & Schellinger, 2011).

Culturally Conscious Implementation

When schools offer more opportunities for students to learn SEL skills and correct behavior, it needs to be recognized that the selected SEL skills and expectations are culturally based and infused with a value system. Educators prioritize culturally laden types of SEL skills and, therefore, may unintentionally marginalize certain forms of cultural expression (Morris, 2016). In addition, while schools often focus on developing students' social and emotional competencies, there is a growing recognition that educators need support to deepen their own social emotional competencies as well as their skills in developing prosocial classrooms (Jennings & Frank, 2015, Milner, 2014). Jennings and Frank (2015) argue that teachers with high social and emotional competence have strong relationship-building skills and are better able to develop mutual understanding with their students, consider multiple perspectives during conflict, and resolve disputes with skill. Doing so in a culturally responsive manner may help educators navigate diverse cultural norms and defuse or prevent disciplinary interactions with marginalized students (Morris, 2016).

Principle 6: Data-Based Inquiry for Equity

Every Student Succeeds Act requires that state education agencies collect data from local education agencies on a range of discipline-related issues, including "rates of in-school suspensions, out-of-school suspensions, expulsions, school-related arrests, referrals to law enforcement . . ." (Mandinach & Jackson, 2012, p. 47). While the collection and examination of accountability data in schools is not new to federal policy (Mandinach & Jackson, 2012), this is the first time that discipline outcomes have been integrated into federal accountability efforts.

What is measured and tracked in accountability systems is an indicator of outcomes that are valued. McIntosh et al.'s (2013) correlational study of 217 schools across 14 states showed that SWPBIS teams' use of data was a statistically significant predictor of sustained SWPBIS implementation. The authors observe that the practice of regularly sharing data with the entire school staff likely communicated administration's commitment to high-quality SWPBIS implementation to achieve improved student outcomes.

Culturally Conscious Implementation

States and localities that collect, disaggregate, and share discipline data signal the importance of identifying and addressing discipline disparities. In response to advocates' demands for greater transparency, state legislatures are increasing public access to disaggregated discipline data (e.g., Washington State, 2015) and districts are beginning to use data in a process of goal setting and continuous improvement (e.g., Meridian Consent Order, 2013). To support these efforts, the federally funded National Center on Safe Supportive Learning Environments recently issued recommendations on using data to reduce discipline disparities that include data analysis, identifying root causes and developing an action plan (Osher et al., 2015). Identifying patterns in the data can help educators strategically direct their intervention efforts to address the specific issues that are causing high racial and gender disparities in disciplinary referrals (Scott, Hirn, & Barber, 2012).

Principle 7: Problem-Solving Approaches to Discipline

When school community members come together to identify contributors to discipline incidents and jointly develop plans to help resolve those incidents, they are engaging in a problem-solving approach to discipline. For example, teachers, specialists, and/or parents might collaborate in a problem-solving process to understand individual students' academic or behavioral challenges (Sheridan et al., 2012). Moreover, inquiry into what drives student behavior may, in itself, build trust and shared respect when students are given the opportunity to offer their "side of the story" (Sheets, 1996). Problem-solving approaches also may help uncover unaddressed learning or mental health needs of students who are typically "criminalized" or punished, resulting in more appropriate supports or trauma-informed care (Phifer & Hull, 2016; Ramey, 2015).

Research on problem-solving processes has been conducted on a schoolwide program, Virginia Threat Assessment Guidelines (e.g., Cornell, 2013). A recent study found that the suspension gap between Black and White students narrowed when schools implemented a threat assessment team, which is a multidisciplinary team of school staff available to help students involved in a crisis or a conflict that included a threat of violence (Cornell, 2013). More recently, a statewide study of schools using the threat assessment protocol in Virginia found no racial disparities in suspension, expulsion, or arrest among students whose behavior prompted threat assessments (Cornell et al., 2016).

School community members also might engage in RJ or restorative practice (RP), which provides a structured process for problem solving in schools. For example, in a responsive circle or restorative conference, participants typically answer a series of restorative questions about a discipline incident (e.g., "Who has been affected by the incident?"; "What do you think needs to happen to make things right?" Wachtel, Costello, & Wachtel, 2009). Winn (2016) has proposed that RJ in the classroom may not only disrupt punitive practices and racial inequality but also engage students, their families, and school staff in critical dialogue about "notions of citizenship, belonging, and worthiness that can impact teacher practice and student learning" (p. 5).

Case studies of schools implementing RJ/RP in the United States and internationally document schoolwide reductions in exclusionary discipline (e.g., Anyon et al., 2014; International Institute of Restorative Practices, 2014). As of yet, however, there is not enough empirical evidence to claim that RJ/RP, as currently implemented, results in substantial reductions in race and gender discipline disparities. A few studies of districts using RJ have shown that Black students had the greatest decline in the suspension rates, relative to other student groups (González, 2015; Jain et al., 2014). Yet, persistent and large Black/White suspension gaps in these districts and the uneven implementation across district schools suggests that more research is needed to understand the potential of RJ and how to implement it with high fidelity across schools (Anyon et al., 2014; Gregory & Clawson, 2016).

Culturally Conscious Implementation

When implementing problem-solving approaches to conflict educators need to vigilantly watch for how such reforms can revert to shaming, punitive processes that do not authentically engage the voices of marginalized youth and their families. In other words, collaborative problem solving may become part of discipline policy, but in the day-to-day, they may be implemented in a superficial manner that masks hidden agendas reflecting the traditional, underlying stance toward punishment and exclusion. Moreover, culturally conscious implementation of problem-solving approaches need to explicitly address issues of power and privilege. For example, the Oakland Unified School District's RJ implementation guide indicates that a social justice orientation to RJ includes acknowledging that race, gender, and sexual orientation inequities of the larger society impact students' academic and life outcomes, recognizing historical harms when appropriate, and ensuring students in marginalized groups have forums where their concerns can be effectively addressed (Yusem et al., 2016).

Principle 8: Inclusion of Student and Family Voice on Causes and Solutions of Conflicts

A number of school districts are revising their school discipline policies to improve student and family engagement in the disciplinary process (e.g., Syracuse City School District, *Student Code of Conduct, Character, and Support*). This area of policy reform is supported by a diverse body of research demonstrating the feasibility of student and family engagement in addressing discipline incidents and behavioral challenges (e.g., Patton, Jolivette, & Ramsey, 2006). Schools can integrate student voice and family perspectives in many different ways—for example, students might set their own behavioral goals and self-monitor their progress (Patton et al., 2006) or lead a restorative circle with their classmates to address a problem in the classroom (Wachtel et al., 2009). Research has demonstrated that students are more likely to cooperate when they feel fairly treated by teachers (Gregory & Ripski, 2008; Sheets, 1996). Moreover, they tend to be more engaged and motivated in classrooms where they are allowed to express their opinions and exhibit autonomy (Reeve, 2009). Similarly, respectfully engaging family perspectives to help address discipline incidents can build trust and increase the likelihood of a positive resolution to disciplinary incidents (Sheridan et al., 2012).

Culturally Conscious Implementation

Integrating student and family perspectives into the disciplinary process may be especially important for building trust between educators and students from marginalized groups. Several recent studies show that Black and Latino students report less adult support in school compared with their White peers (Bottiani et al., 2014; Voight et al., 2015). Ethnic minority parents also have reported the need for educators to engage them in a respectful and culturally competent manner (National Education Association of the United States, 2010). Respectful and regular engagement of historically disenfranchised voices in school could engender the type of trust needed for constructive collaboration to prevent or diffuse disciplinary interactions that fuel race and gender disparities in discipline (Bryk & Schneider, 2002; Winn, 2016).

Principle 9: Reintegration of Students After Conflict or Absence

Rearrest rates of youth released from the juvenile justice system have highlighted the need for "reentry programs" (Bonnie, Johnson, Chemers, & Schuck, 2013). Osher, Amos, and Gonsoulin (2012) recommend that supports for formerly incarcerated youth engage members from the student's "ecology" to help them successfully reintegrate into their schools and communities. Bullis, Yovanoff, Mueller, and Havel (2002) followed youth after their release and found that those who received appropriate aftercare services—mental health, substance abuse treatment, educational supports, and others—were more than three times as likely to be positively engaged in their community after 12 months, relative to their released peers without such services.

Disrupting the school-to-prison pipeline requires reducing students' odds of rearrest and repeated suspensions. This is especially important since state rearrest rates can be as high as 50% to 80% for high-risk youth over a 1- to 3-year follow-up period (Seigle, Walsh, & Weber, 2014). Reductions in rearrest would be especially beneficial to students in groups who are overrepresented in the juvenile justice system, including Black youth, who account for half of all juvenile arrests for violent crimes (U.S. Department of Justice/Department of Education, 2014).

Culturally Conscious Implementation

Recognizing the risk associated with transitions back to school, some districts have taken steps to create formal reentry procedures for students returning from long-term suspensions. From 2013 to 2014, the Oakland Unified School District provided RJ programming to students as part of a formal reentry procedure after incarceration, involuntary transfer, or suspension (Jain et al., 2014). Students were offered individual meetings or reentry circles including teachers, counselors, friends, and family to welcome them back into the school community and proactively provide wraparound supports. Culturally conscious supports need to also consider the multiple interacting stressors students face as relate to their social positioning. For example, gender-conscious reentry programs for girls released from juvenile detention might address girls' needs for reproductive health education/support or treatment for sexual abuse (Winn, 2011).

Principle 10: Multitiered System of Supports

Finally, schools across the nation are implementing multitiered systems of support (MTSS) to provide a comprehensive approach to prevention and intervention (MTSS; Vincent, Inglish, Girvan, Sprague, & McCab, 2016). The MTSS approach offers districts a systematic way to track data and provide prevention and intervention services that reduce exclusionary responses to student behavior. The emphasis on providing access to supports when students exhibit behaviors that violate school rules and expectations is especially needed for students in groups overrepresented in discipline sanctions (Ramey, 2015).

MTSS is characterized by a tiered framework, drawn from public health, that calibrates the intensity of behavioral supports to students' behavioral needs, with more intensive supports offered when more general strategies fail to resolve the problem. For example, when students are not responsive to Tier 1 social and behavioral programs in the classroom, they can be referred to Tier 2 interventions in small groups or individual sessions outside of the classroom (Bradshaw et al., 2014). SWPBIS is the most widely disseminated and extensively studied MTSS (Vincent et al., 2016), but the multitiered framework has also been used with other types of positive discipline programming such as RJ/RP programming (Jain et al., 2014).

The most extensive research on the promise of MTSS frameworks for reducing disparities has been conducted within the SWPBIS framework. Experimental trials have shown that implementing SWPBIS with fidelity can lead to reductions in negative student behavior and discipline referrals and suspensions (Bradshaw, Mitchell, & Leaf, 2010; Horner et al., 2009). Despite the general positive outcomes associated with SWPBIS, there have been inconsistent findings regarding discipline outcomes for marginalized students (Vincent et al., 2016). For example, Black elementary students have been found to have significantly greater odds of receiving a discipline referral than White students in schools with SWPBIS, even as those schools reduce disciplinary referrals in general (Bradshaw, Mitchell, O'Brennan, et al., 2010; Kaufman et al., 2010).

Culturally Conscious Implementation

The inconsistent results from SWPBIS in reducing disparities have led researchers to highlight the promising results of SWPBIS when it is integrated with explicitly culturally conscious practices. For example, in five Canadian schools implementing SWPBIS, Greflund, McIntosh, Mercer, and May (2014) found that students with aboriginal status were no more likely to receive office disciplinary referrals than their peers. Similarly, Vincent, Sprague, CHiXapkaid, Tobin, and Gau (2015) identified several SWPBIS schools that had low suspension rates of American Indian students, a group historically over-represented in exclusionary discipline. The authors of both studies speculate that the racial equity in discipline in those schools may be due to the culturally responsive adaptations to SWPBIS which emphasized teacher training in cultural sensitivity, culturally relevant instruction, and strong school relationships with parents and families (McIntosh, Moniz, Craft, Golby, & Steinwand-Deschambeault, 2014).

Another promising direction is the integration of SWPBIS and RJ/RP. This blended approach, School-Wide Positive and Restorative Discipline includes teacher training about students' need for positive relationships, fair treatment, and procedural justice. School-Wide Positive and Restorative Discipline recently was piloted in a high school that had been implementing SWPBIS with fidelity, yet had persistent racial disparities in discipline (Vincent et al., 2016). Through online materials and workshops, teachers learned about RJ/RP concepts (e.g., social capital, procedural justice, restoring relationships), and building community through active listening, classroom circles, and delivery of behavior-specific affective statements. Examining end-of-year discipline referral rates, Vincent et al. (2016) reported reductions in schoolwide referrals and racial disparities relative to the year prior.

CONCLUSION

We see the 10 principles in the Framework for Increasing Equity in School Discipline as important considerations for parents, students, educators, and support personnel who wish to shift disciplinary conflicts and consequences toward a more positive school climate. For researchers, the 10 principles are launching points from which to consider the possible "mechanisms of action" in current reform initiatives. Researchers might examine whether select principles from the Framework mediate the program impacts on reducing discipline gaps. In other words, it will be informative to know if a program's success is explained by its inclusion of one or more of the principles (e.g., increasing bias awareness or access to academic rigor).

As of yet, there is insufficient empirical evidence to indicate which combination of the 10 principles from the Framework should be implemented together, or which principles might be prioritized over others to reduce gender and race disparities in school discipline. Similarly, it is unknown whether principles from the multiple levels of the school ecology combine in a synergistic manner or whether addressing one level would "ripple out" and affect another level of the ecology. For example, does increasing awareness of bias (intrapersonal level) lead to change at the interpersonal level or at the systems level whereby punitive treatment of marginalized students is reduced through changes in disciplinary practices and policies?

As relates to culturally conscious implementation of the principles, it is not yet clear *what level of attention* to issues of gender, race, class, culture, power, and privilege will be necessary to effectively close discipline gaps. Research on both positive behavior supports (Vincent et al., 2016) and restorative justice (Gregory & Clawson, 2016; Winn, 2016) has begun to explore the extent to which explicit, culturally conscious modifications to standard models of those interventions are likely to have an impact on discipline gaps. Moreover, it will be essential to identify the best ways to undertake culturally conscious implementation given the research that shows diversity-related initiatives do not necessarily lead to anticipated changes in attitudes, beliefs, or behaviors (e.g., Dover, Major, & Kaiser, 2016).

REFERENCES

American Psychological Association Task Force. (2008). Are zero tolerance policies effective in the schools? An evidentiary review and recommendations. *American Psychologist, 63,* 852–862.

Anyon, Y., Jenson, J., Altschul, I., Farrar, J., McQueen, J., Greer, E., . . . Simmons, J. (2014). The persistent effect of race and the promise of alternatives to suspension in school discipline outcomes. *Children and Youth Services Review, 44,* 379–386.

Aronson, B., & Laughter, J. (2016). The theory and practice of culturally relevant education: A synthesis of research across content areas. *Review of Educational Research, 86,* 163–206.

Bal, A., Thorius, K. K., & Kozleski, E. (2012). *Culturally responsive positive behavioral support matters.* Retrieved from http://www.equityallianceatasu.org/sites/default/files/CRPBIS_Matters.pdf

Bear, G. G., Whitcomb, S. A., Elias, M. J., & Blank, J. C. (2015). SEL and schoolwide positive behavioral interventions and supports. In J. A. Durlak, & C. E. Domintrovich (Eds.), *Handbook of social and emotional learning (SEL): Research and practice* (pp. 453–467). New York, NY: Guilford.

Blake, J. J., Smith, D. M., Marchbanks, M. P. III, Seibert, A. L., Wood, S. M., & Kim, E. S. (2016). Does student teacher racial/ethnic match impact Black students' discipline risk? A test of the cultural synchrony hypothesis. In R. J. Skiba, K. Mediratta, & M. K. Rausch (Eds.), *Inequality in school discipline: Research and practice to reduce disparities* (pp. 79–98). New York, NY: Palgrave MacMillan.

Bonnie, R. J., Johnson, R. L., Chemers, B. M., & Schuck, J. (2013). *Reforming juvenile justice: A developmental approach.* Washington, DC: National Academies Press.

Bottiani, J. H., Bradshaw, C. P., & Mendelson, T. (2014). Promoting an equitable and supportive school climate in high schools: The role of school organizational health and staff burnout. *Journal of School Psychology, 52,* 567–582.

Boykin, A. W., Tyler, K. M., & Miller, O. (2005). In search of cultural themes and their expressions in the dynamics of classroom life. *Urban Education, 40,* 521–549.

Bradshaw, C. P., Mitchell, M. M., & Leaf, P. J. (2010). Examining the effects of schoolwide positive behavioral interventions and supports on student outcomes: Results from a randomized controlled effectiveness trial in elementary schools. *Journal of Positive Behavior Interventions, 12,* 133–148.

Bradshaw, C. P., Mitchell, M. M., O'Brennan, L. M., & Leaf, P. J. (2010). Multilevel exploration of factors contributing to the overrepresentation of Black students in office disciplinary referrals. *Journal of Educational Psychology, 102,* 508–520.

Bradshaw, C. P., Pas, E. T., & Debnam, K. (2015). *Increasing cultural proficiency and student engagement in the Double Check program: Preliminary findings from a randomized trial.* Presentation at the Society for Research on Child Development Conference, Philadelphia, PA.

Brown, C. S., & Bigler, R. S. (2005). Children's perceptions of discrimination: A developmental model. *Child Development, 76,* 533–553. doi:10.1111/j.1467-8624.2005.00862.x

Bryk, A. S., & Schneider, B. L. (2002). *Trust in schools: A core resource for improvement.* New York, NY: Russell Sage Foundation.

Bullis, M., Yovanoff, P., Mueller, G., & Havel, E. (2002). Life on the outs: Examination of the facility-to-community transition of incarcerated adolescents. *Exceptional Children, 69,* 7–22.

California Department of Education. (2015, January 14). *State schools' Chief Tom Torlakson reports significant drops in suspensions and expulsions for second year in a row* [Press Release]. Retrieved from http://www.cde.ca.gov/nr/ne/yr15/yr15rel5.asp

Capatosto, K. (2015). *School discipline policy: Updates, insights, and future directions* (Kirwan Institute Policy Brief). Retrieved from http://kirwaninstitute.osu.edu/wp-content/uploads/2015/06/ki-interventions2015-02.pdf

Card, D., & Giuliano, L. (2016). *Can tracking raise the test scores of high-ability minority students?* (NBER Working Paper No. 22104. JEL No. I21). Retrieved from http://david-card.berkeley.edu/papers/card-giuliano-tracking.pdf

Carter, P., Skiba, R., Arredondo, M., & Pollock, M. (2015). *You can't fix what you don't look at: Acknowledging race in addressing racial discipline disparities* (Discipline Disparities Research-to-Practice Briefing Paper Series #4). Retrieved from http://rtpcollaborative. indiana.edu/briefing-papers/

Children's Defense Fund. (1975). *School suspensions: Are they helping children?* Cambridge, MA: Washington Research Project.

Chmielewski, J., Belmonte, K., Stoudt, B., & Fine, M. (2016). Intersectional inquiries with LGBTQ and gender noncomforming youth of color: Participatory research on discipline disparities at the race/sexuality/gender nexus. In R. J. Skiba, K. Mediratta, & M. K. Rausch (Eds.), *Inequality in school discipline: Research and practice to reduce disparities* (pp. 171–188). New York, NY: Palgrave MacMillan.

Colombi, G., & Osher, D. (2015). Advancing school discipline reform. *Education Leaders Report.* Retrieved from http://www.air.org/sites/default/files/downloads/report/ Advancing-School-Discipline-Reform-Sept-2015.pdf

Cornelius-White, J. (2007) Learner-centered teacher–student relationships are effective: A meta-analysis. *Review of Educational Research, 77,* 113–143.

Cornell, D. (2013). *Prevention v. punishment: Threat assessment, school suspensions, and racial disparities.* Retrieved from http://curry.virginia.edu/uploads/resourceLibrary/UVA_and_ JustChildren_Report_-_Prevention_v._Punishment.pdf

Cornell, D., Maeng, J., Burnette, A. G., Datta, P., Huang, F., & Jia, Y. (2016). *Threat assessment in Virginia schools: Technical report of the Threat Assessment Survey for 2014–2015.* Charlottesville: Curry School of Education, University of Virginia.

Dee, T., & Penner, E. (2016). *The causal effects of cultural relevance: Evidence from an ethnic studies curriculum* (NBER Working Paper No. 21865. JEL No. I0). Retrieved from http://www.nber.org/papers/w21865

Discipline Disparities Collaborative. (2015). Retrieved from http://rtpcollaborative.indiana. edu/

Dover, T. L., Major, B., & Kaiser, C. R. (2016). Members of high-status groups are threatened by pro-diversity organizational messages, *Journal of Experimental Social Psychology, 62,* 58–67.

Durlak, J., Weissberg, R. P., Dymnicki, A. B., Taylor, R. D., & Schellinger, K. B. (2011). The impact of enhancing students' social and emotional learning: A meta-analysis of school-based universal interventions. *Child Development, 82,* 405–432.

Emmer, E. T., & Sabornie, E. (2014). *The handbook of classroom management: Research, practice & contemporary issues* (2nd ed.). Mahwah, NJ: Lawrence Erlbaum.

Fabelo, T., Thompson, M. D., Plotkin, M., Carmichael, D., Marchbanks, M. P. III, & Booth, E. A. (2011). *Breaking schools' rules: A statewide study of how school discipline relates to students' success and juvenile justice involvement.* Retrieved from http://justicecenter.csg. org/resources/juveniles

Fan, W., Williams, C. M., & Corkin, D. M. (2011). A multilevel analysis of student perceptions of school climate: The effect of social and academic risk factors. *Psychology in the Schools, 48,* 632–647.

Gay, G. (2010). *Culturally responsive teaching: Theory, research, and practice* (2nd ed.). New York, NY: Teachers College Press.

Gay, Lesbian & Straight Education Network. (2011). *Teaching respect: LGBT-inclusive curriculum and school climate* (Research Brief). Retrieved from http://www.glsen.org/press/ teaching-respect-finds-having-lgbt-inclusive-curriculum

Ginwright, S. (2004). *Black in school: Afrocentric reform, urban youth and the promise of hip-hop culture.* New York, NY: Teachers College Press.

Goff, P. A., Jackson, M. C., Di Leone, B. A., Culotta, C. M., & DiTomasso, N. A. (2014). The essence of innocence: Consequences of dehumanizing black children. *Journal of Personality and Social Psychology, 106,* 526–545.

Goldring, R., Gray, L., & Bitterman, A. (2013). *Characteristics of public and private elementary and secondary school teachers in the United States: Results from the 2011–12 Schools and Staffing Survey* (NCES 2013-314). Retrieved from http://nces.ed.gov/pubsearch

González, T. (2015). Socializing schools: Addressing racial disparities in discipline through restorative justice. In D. J. Losen (Ed.), *Closing the discipline gap: Equitable remedies for excessive exclusion* (pp. 151–165). New York, NY: Teachers College Press.

Greenwald, A. G., Poehlman, T. A., Uhlmann, E. L., & Banaji, M. R. (2009). Understanding and using the Implicit Association Test: Meta-analysis of predictive validity. *Journal of Personality and Social Psychology, 97,* 17–41.

Greflund, S., McIntosh, K., Mercer, S. H., & May, S. L. (2014). Examining disproportionality in school discipline for Aboriginal students in schools implementing PBIS. *Canadian Journal of School Psychology, 29,* 213–235.

Gregory, A., Bell, J., & Pollock, M. (2016). How educators can eradicate disparities in school discipline: Issues in intervention. In R. J. Skiba, K. Mediratta, & M. K. Rausch (Eds.), *Inequality in school discipline: Research and practice to reduce disparities* (pp. 39–58). New York, NY: Palgrave MacMillan.

Gregory, A., & Clawson, K. (2016). The potential of restorative approaches to discipline for narrowing racial and gender disparities. In R. J. Skiba, K. Mediratta, & M. K. Rausch (Eds.), *Inequality in school discipline: Research and practice to reduce disparities* (pp. 153–170). New York, NY: Palgrave MacMillan.

Gregory, A., Hafen, C. A., Ruzek, E. A., Mikami, A. Y, Allen, J. P., & Pianta, R. C. (2016). Closing the racial discipline gap in classrooms by changing teacher practice. *School Psychology Review, 45,* 171–191.

Gregory, A., & Ripski, M. (2008). Adolescent trust in teachers: Implications for behavior in the high school classroom. *School Psychology Review, 37,* 337–353.

Gregory, A., Skiba, R. J., & Noguera, P. A. (2010). The achievement gap and the discipline gap: Two sides of the same coin? *Educational Researcher, 39,* 59–68.

Hamre, B. K., & Pianta, R. C. (2001). Early teacher-child relationships and the trajectory of children's school outcomes through eighth grade. *Child Development, 72,* 625–638.

Handwerk, P., Tognatta, N., Coley, R. J., & Gitomer, D. H. (2008). *Access to success: Patterns of advanced placement participation in U.S. high schools.* Retrieved from https://www.ets.org/research/policy_research_reports/publications/report/2008/hbxz

Harris-Murri, N., King, K., & Rostenberg, D. (2006). Reducing disproportionate minority representation in special education programs for students with emotional disturbances: Toward a culturally responsive response to intervention model. *Education & Treatment of Children, 29,* 779–799.

Hershfeldt, P. A., Sechrest, R., Pell, K. L., Rosenberg, M. S., Bradshaw, C. P., & Leaf, P. J. (2010). Double-check: A framework of cultural responsiveness applied to classroom behavior. *Teaching Exceptional Children Plus, 6,* 1–18.

Himmelstein, K. E. W., & Bruckner, H. (2011). Criminal-justice and school sanctions against non-heterosexual youth: A national longitudinal study. *Pediatrics, 127,* 49–57.

Horner, R. H., Sugai, G., Smolkowski, K., Eber, L., Nakasato, J., Todd, A. W., & Esperanza, J. (2009). A randomized, wait-list controlled effectiveness trial assessing school-wide positive behavior support in elementary schools. *Journal of Positive Behavior Interventions, 11,* 133–144.

Howard, T. C. (2010). *Why race and culture matter in schools: Closing the achievement gap in America's classrooms.* New York, NY: Teachers College Press.

Illinois, 105 ILCS 5/10-17a. (2014).

International Institute of Restorative Practices. (2014). *Improving school climate: Findings from schools implementing restorative practices.* Retrieved from http://www.iirp.edu/pdf/IIRP-Improving-School-Climate.pdf

Jain, S., Bassey, H., Brown, M. A., & Kalra, P. (2014). *Restorative justice in Oakland Schools. Implementation and impact: An effective strategy to reduce racially disproportionate discipline, suspensions, and improve academic outcomes.* Retrieved from www.ousd.k12.ca.us/

Jennings, P. A., & Frank, J. L. (2015). Inservice preparation for educators. In J. A. Durlak, C. E. Domintrovich, R. P. Weissberg, & T. P. Gullotta (Eds.), *Handbook of social and emotional learning: Research and practice* (pp. 422–437). New York, NY: Guilford Press.

Jones, D. E., Greenberg, M., & Crowley, M. (2015). Early social-emotional functioning and public health: The relationship between kindergarten social competence and future well-ness. *American Journal of Public Health, 105,* 2283–2290.

Kamps, D., Wills, H., Bannister, H. D., Heitzman-Powell, L., Kottwitz, E., Hansen, B., & Fleming, K. (2015). Class-wide function-related intervention teams "CW-FIT" efficacy trial outcomes. *Journal of Positive Behavior Interventions, 17,* 134–145. doi:10.1177/1098300714565244

Kaufman, J. S., Jaser, S. S., Vaughan, E. L., Reynolds, J. S., Di Donato, J., Bernard, S. N., & Hernandez-Brereton, M. (2010). Patterns in office referral data by grade, race/ethnicity, and gender. *Journal of Positive Behavior Interventions, 12,* 44–54.

Kena, G., Musu-Gillette, L., Robinson, J., Wang, X., Rathbun, A., Zhang, J., . . . Dunlop Velez, E. (2015). *The condition of education 2015* (NCES 2015-144). Retrieved from https://nces.ed.gov/pubs2015/2015144.pdf

Kisker, E. E., Lipka, J., Adams, B. L., Rickard, A., Andrew-Ihrke, D., Yanez, E. E., & Millard, A. (2012). The potential of a culturally based supplemental mathematics curriculum to improve the mathematics performance of Alaska Native and other students. *Journal for Research in Mathematics Education, 43,* 75–113.

Ladson-Billings, G. (2006). From the achievement gap to the education debt: Understanding achievement in U.S. schools. *Educational Researcher, 35*(7), 3–12.

Ladson-Billings, G. (2009). *The dream-keepers: Successful teachers of African American children.* San Francisco, CA: Jossey-Bass.

Losen, D. J. (2015). *Closing the school discipline gap: Equitable remedies for excessive exclusion.* New York, NY: Teachers College Press.

Losen, D. J., & Martinez, T. E. (2013). *Out of school and off track: The overuse of suspensions in middle and high schools.* Retrieved from http://files.eric.ed.gov/fulltext/ED541735.pdf

Mandinach, E. B., & Jackson, S. S. (2012). *Transforming teaching and learning through data driven decision making.* Thousand Oaks, CA: SAGE.

McIntosh, K., Eliason, B. M., Horner, R. H., & May, S. L. (2014). *Have schools increased their use of the SWIS school ethnicity report?* Retrieved from http://www.pbis.org/common/cms/files/pbisresources/EthnicityBrief.pdf

McIntosh, K., Mercer, S. H., Hume, A. E., Frank, J. L., Turri, M. G., & Mathews, S. (2013). Factors related to sustained implementation of schoolwide positive behavior support. *Exceptional Children, 79,* 293–311.

McIntosh, K., Moniz, C. A., Craft, C. B., Golby, R., & Steinwand-Deschambeault, T. (2014). Implementing school-wide positive behavioural interventions and supports to better meet the needs of indigenous students. *Canadian Journal of School Psychology, 29,* 236–257.

Mediratta, K. (2012). Grassroots organizing and the school-to-prison pipeline: The emerging national movement to roll back zero tolerance policies in U.S. public schools. In K. Mediratta (Ed.), *Disrupting the school to prison pipeline* (pp. 211–236). Cambridge, MA: Harvard Education Press.

Meridian Consent Order. (2013). *United States Department of Justice.* Retrieved from https://www.justice.gov/iso/opa/resources/850201332211248646502.pdf

Milner, H. R. (2014). Research on classroom management in urban schools, In E. T. Emmer, & E. Sabornie (Eds.), *The handbook of classroom management: Research, practice & contemporary issues* (2nd ed., pp. 167–185). Mahwah, NJ: Lawrence Erlbaum.

Morgan, E., Salomon, N., Plotkin, M., & Cohen, R. (2014). *The school discipline consensus report: Strategies from the field to keep students engaged in school and out of the juvenile justice system.* New York, NY: Council of State Governments Justice Center.

Morris, M. (2016). *Pushout: The criminalization of Black girls in school.* New York, NY: New Press.

National Education Association of the United States. (2010). *Minority parent and community engagement: Best practices and policy recommendations for closing the gaps in student achievement.* Washington, DC: Author.

Neal, L. I., McCray, A. D., Webb-Johnson, G., & Bridgest, S. T. (2003). The effects of African American movement styles on teachers' perceptions and reactions. *Journal of Special Education, 37,* 49–57.

Noltemeyer, A., Ward, R. M., & Mcloughlin, C. S. (2015). Relationship between school suspension and student outcomes: A meta-analysis. *School Psychology Review, 44,* 224–240.

Okonofua, J. A., & Eberhardt, J. L. (2015). Two strikes: Race and the disciplining of young students. *Psychological Science, 26,* 617–624.

Okonofua, J. A., Paunesku, D., & Walton, G. M. (2016). Brief intervention to encourage empathic discipline cuts suspension rates in half among adolescents. *Proceedings of the National Academy of Sciences of the United States of America.* Advance online publication. doi:10.1073/pnas.1523698113

Olmeda, R. E., & Kauffman, J. M. (2003). Sociocultural considerations in social skills training research with African American students with emotional or behavioral disorders. *Journal of Developmental and Physical Disabilities, 15,* 101–121.

Osher, D., Amos, L. B., & Gonsoulin, S. (2012). *Successfully transitioning youth who are delinquent between institutions and alternative and community schools.* Retrieved from http://www.neglecteddelinquent.org/nd/docs/successfully_transitioning_youth.pdf

Osher, D., Fisher, D., Amos, L., Katz, J., Dwyer, K., Duffey, T., & Colombi, G. D. (2015). *Addressing the root causes of disparities in school discipline: An educator's action planning guide.* Retrieved from https://safesupportivelearning.ed.gov/sites/default/files/15-1547%20NCSSLE%20Root%20Causes%20Guide%20FINAL02%20mb.pdf

Osher, D., Poirier, J., Jarjoura, R., Brown, R., & Kendziora, K. (2014). Avoid simple solutions and quick fixes: Lessons learned from a comprehensive districtwide approach to improving student behavior and school safety. *Journal of Applied Research on Children: Informing Policy for Children at Risk, 5.* Retrieved from http://digitalcommons.library.tmc.edu/childrenatrisk/vol5/iss2/16

Padres y Jóvenes Unidos & Advancement Project. (2005). *Education on lockdown: The schoolhouse to jailhouse track.* Retrieved from http://b.3cdn.net/advancement/5351180e24cb166d02_mlbrqgxlh.pdf

Padres y Jóvenes Unidos & Advancement Project. (2010). *Victory at last: The struggle to end the schoolhouse to jailhouse track in Denver Public Schools.* Washington, DC: Author.

Patton, B, Jolivette, K., & Ramsey, M. (2006). Students with emotional and behavioral disorders can manage their own behavior. *Teaching Exceptional Children, 39*(2), 14–21.

Phifer, L., & Hull, R. (2016). Helping students heal: Observations of trauma-informed practices in the schools. *School Mental Health, 8,* 201–205.

Poteat, V. P., Scheer, J. R., & Chong, E. S. K. (2015). Sexual orientation-based disparities in school and juvenile justice discipline: A multiple group comparison of contributing factors. *Journal of Educational Psychology, 108,* 229–241.

Ramey, D. M. (2015). The social structure of criminalized and medicalized school discipline. *Sociology of Education, 88,* 181–201.

Reeve, J. (2009). Why teachers adopt a controlling motivating style toward students and how they can become more autonomy supportive. *Educational Psychologist, 44,* 159–175.

Restorative Justice Colorado. (2015, March 10). *2015 Colorado RJ Bill passes both chambers unanimously!* Retrieved from http://www.rjcolorado.org/blog/2015-colorado-rj-bill-passes-both-chambers-unanimouslyc

Rogers, J., & Terriquez, V. (2013). *Learning to lead: The impact of youth organizing on the educational and civic trajectories of low-income youth.* Los Angeles, CA: Institute for Democracy, Education, and Access.

Roorda, D. L., Koomen, H. M. Y., Spilt, J. L., & Oort, F. J. (2011). The influence of affective teacher-student relationships on students' school engagement and achievement: A meta-analytic approach. *Review of Educational Research, 81,* 493–529.

Rubie-Davies, C. M., Weinstein, R. S., Huang, F. L., Gregory, A., Cowan, P., & Cowan, C. (2014). Successive teacher expectation effects across the early school years. *Journal of Applied Developmental Psychology, 35,* 181–191.

Scott, T. M., Hirn, R. G., & Barber, H. (2012). Affecting disproportional outcomes by ethnicity and grade level: Using discipline data to guide practice in high school. *Preventing School Failure: Alternative Education for Children and Youth, 56,* 110–120.

Seigle, E., Walsh, N., & Weber, J. (2014). *Core principles for reducing recidivism and improving other outcomes for youth in the Juvenile Justice System.* New York, NY: Council of State Governments Justice Center.

Sheets, R. H. (1996). Urban classroom conflict: Student–teacher perception ethnic integrity, solidarity and resistance. *Urban Review, 28,* 165–183.

Sheridan, S. M., Bovaird, J. A., Glover, T. A., Garbacz, S. A., Witte, A., & Kwon, K. (2012). A randomized trial examining the effects of conjoint behavioral consultation and the mediating role of the parent-teacher relationship. *School Psychology Review, 41,* 23–46.

Skiba, R. J., Arredondo, M., & Williams, N. T. (2014). More than a metaphor? The contribution of exclusionary discipline to a School-to-Prison Pipeline. *Equity & Excellence in Education, 47,* 546–564.

Skiba, R. J., Chung, C., Trachok, M., Baker, T. L., Sheya, A., & Hughes, R. L. (2014). Parsing disciplinary disproportionality: Contributions of infraction, student, and school characteristics to out-of-school suspension and expulsion. *American Educational Research Journal, 51,* 640–670.

Skiba, R. J., Horner, R. H., Chung, C., Rausch, M. K., May, S., & Tobin, T. (2011). Race is not neutral: A national investigation of African American and Latino disproportionality in school discipline. *School Psychology Review, 40,* 85–107.

Skiba, R. J., Mediratta, K., & Rausch, M. K. (2016), *Inequality in school discipline: Research and practice to reduce disparities.* New York, NY: Palgrave MacMillan.

Snapp, S., & Russell, S. (2016). Discipline disparities for LGBTQ youth: Challenges that perpetuate disparities and strategies to overcome them. In R. J. Skiba, K. Mediratta, & M. K. Rausch (Eds.), *Inequality in school discipline: Research and practice to reduce disparities* (pp. 207–233). New York, NY: Palgrave MacMillan.

Sugai, G., & Horner, R. H. (2010). School-wide positive behavior support: Establishing a continuum of evidence based practices. *Journal of Evidence-based Practices for Schools, 11,* 62–83.

Sumner, M. D., Silverman, C. J., & Frampton, M. L. (2010) *School-based restorative justice as an alternative to zero-tolerance policies: Lessons from West Oakland.* Berkeley: Thelton E. Henderson Center for Social Justice, University of California.

Stokes, T. F., & Baer, D. M. (1977). An implicit technology of generalization. *Journal of Applied Behavior Analysis, 10,* 349–367.

U.S. Department of Justice/Department of Education. (2011). *Attorney General Holder, Secretary Duncan announce effort to respond to school-to-prison pipeline by supporting good discipline practices* [Press release]. Retrieved from https://www.justice.gov/opa/pr/attorney-general-holder-secretary-duncan-announce-effort-respond-school-prison-pipeline

U.S. Department of Justice/Department of Education. (2014). *Juvenile arrests 2012*. Retrieved from http://www.ojjdp.gov/pubs/248513.pdf

Vincent, C. G., Inglish, J., Girvan, E. J., Sprague, J. R., & McCab, T. (2016). School-wide Positive and Restorative Discipline (SWPRD): Integrating school-wide positive behavior interventions and supports and restorative discipline. In R. Skiba, K. Mediratta, & K. M., Rausch (Eds.), *Inequality in school discipline: Research and practice to reduce disparities* (pp. 115–134). New York, NY: Palgrave MacMillan.

Vincent, C. G., Sprague, J. R., CHiXapkaid, M., Tobin, T. J., & Gau, J. M. (2015). Effectiveness in Schoolwide Positive Behavior Interventions and Supports, in reducing racially inequitable discipline exclusion. In. D. Losen (Ed.), *Closing the school discipline gap: Equitable remedies for excessive exclusion* (pp. 207–221). New York, NY: Teachers College Press.

Vincent, C. G., Swain-Bradway, J., Tobin, T. J., & May, S. (2011). Disciplinary referrals for culturally and linguistically diverse students with and without disabilities: Patterns resulting from school-wide positive behavior support. *Exceptionality, 19*, 175–190.

Voight, A., Hanson, T., O'Malley, M., & Adekanye1, L. (2015). The racial school climate gap: Within-school disparities in students' experiences of safety, support, and connectedness. *American Journal of Community Psychology, 56*, 252–267.

Yeager, D. S., Purdie-Vaughns, V., Garcia, J., Apfel, N., Brzustoski, P., Master, A., . . . Cohen, G. L. (2014). Breaking the cycle of mistrust: Wise interventions to provide critical feedback across the racial divide. *Journal of Experimental Psychology, 143*, 804–824.

Yusem, D., Curtis, D., Johnson, K., McClung, B., Davis, F., Kumar, S., . . . Hysten, F. (2016). *Oakland Unified School District restorative justice implementation guide: A whole school approach*. Retrieved from http://rjoyoakland.org/wp-content/uploads/OUSDRJOY-Implementation-Guide.pdf

Wachtel, T., Costello, B., & Wachtel, J. (2009). *The restorative practices handbook for teachers, disciplinarians and administrators*. Bethlehem, PA: International Institute of Restorative Practices.

Walker, H., Ramsey, E., & Gresham, F. (2004). *Antisocial behavior in schools: Evidence-based practices* (2nd ed.). Belmont, CA: Wadsworth.

Wallace, J. M. Jr., Goodkind, S., Wallace, C. M., & Bachman, J. G. (2008). Racial, ethnic, and gender differences in school discipline among U.S. high school students: 1991–2005. *Negro Educational Review, 59*, 47–62.

Washington State. (2015). *Senate Bill ESSB 5946*. Retrieved from http://apps.leg.wa.gov/billinfo/summary.aspx?bill=5946

Watson, V. (2014). *The Black sonrise: Oakland Unified School District's commitment to address and eliminate institutionalized racism: An evaluation report prepared for the Office of African American Male Achievement*. Retrieved from http://www.ousd.org/cms/lib07/CA01001176/Centricity/Domain/78/TheBlackSonrise_WebV2_sec.pdf

Weinstein, C. S., Tomlinson-Clarke, S., & Curran, M. (2004). Toward a conception of culturally responsive classroom management. *Journal of Teacher Education, 55*, 25–38.

Weinstein, R. S. (2002). *Reaching higher: The power of expectations in schooling*. Cambridge, MA: Harvard University Press.

Wing, J. Y. (2006). Integration across campus, segregation across classrooms: A close-up look at privilege. In J. Y. Wing, & P. A. Noguera (Eds.), *Unfinished business: Closing the achievement gap in our schools* (pp. 84–121). San Francisco, CA: Wiley.

Winn, M. T. (2011). *Girl time: Literacy, justice, and the school-to-prison pipeline*. New York, NY: Teachers College Press.

Winn, M. T. (2016). *Transforming justice: Transforming teacher education*. Retrieved from http://www.teachingworks.org/images/files/TeachingWorks_Winn.pdf

Chapter 12

Challenging Popularized Narratives of Immigrant Youth From West Africa: Examining Social Processes of Navigating Identities and Engaging Civically

Vaughn W. M. Watson
Michigan State University

Michelle G. Knight-Manuel
Teachers College, Columbia University

Given polarizing popular-media narratives of immigrant youth from West African countries, we construct an interdisciplinary framework engaging a Sankofan approach to analyze education research literature on social processes of navigating identities and engaging civically across immigrant youth's heritage practices and Indigenous knowledges. In examining social processes, we disrupt three areas of inequalities affecting educational experiences of immigrant youth: (a) homogenizing notions of a monolithic West Africa and immigrant youth's West African countries, (b) deficit understandings of identities and the heterogeneity of Black immigrant youth from West African countries living in the United States, and (c) singular views of youth's civic engagement. We provide implications for researchers, policymakers, and educators to better meet youth's teaching and learning needs.

Amid increasing immigration to the United States since 1990 (Roberts, 2005), social science and education research on immigrant youth from West African countries has only recently begun to address how immigrant youth are viewed in polarizing ways in dominant public discourses such as popular-media narratives. For example, the positioning of immigrant youth from West African countries as highly educated appears in research literature (Zong & Batalova, 2014) and news stories of high school seniors accepted to prestigious universities. In three successive years,

Review of Research in Education
March 2017, Vol. 41, pp. 279–310
DOI: 10.3102/0091732X16689047
© 2017 AERA. http://rre.aera.net

2014 to 2016, immigrant youth from Ghana and Nigeria, attending high schools in Long Island, New York, were accepted for admission to all eight Ivy League schools. Acceptances by Kwasi Enin, Harold Ekeh, and Augusta Uwamanzu Nna underscore a popular-media narrative of educational attainment and success of immigrant youth from West African countries in stark contrast to popular-media news headlines declaring immigrant youth in polarizing ways—as threats to be feared, isolated, assaulted, and banned from the United States (Cooper, 2015; W. Lee, 2016). In November 2014, for example, reports circulated about assaults against two boys who had recently visited Senegal, their father's home country, then returned to their Bronx, New York, school. The brothers, in sixth and eighth grades, were "pushed and shoved" in the school cafeteria by classmates who yelled "Africa" and "We're done playing with you. You have Ebola" (Lacey-Bordeaux, 2014). Yet the assaults came a month after the World Health Organization (2014) had declared, "The outbreak of Ebola virus disease in Senegal is over."

Popular-media narratives, such as coverage of the boys' experiences, call attention to how, for some, the physical presence of immigrant youth from countries in West Africa evokes, as Obiakor and Afolayan (2007) assert, an "unfounded fear of excessive immigration of Africans to the United States" (pp. 265–266). Moreover, anti-immigrant public discourses intensify a "negation" of past, present, and future lived-experiences and perspectives as "persistent and continuing struggles against [. . .] dehumanization" (Dei, 2012, p. 111) of narratives of youth. This review of education research offers an examination of social processes of immigrant youth from West African countries, to render visible to researchers, policymakers, and educators daily realities of immigrant youth. Specifically, examining social processes of navigating identities and engaging civically allows us to disrupt three areas of inequalities impeding immigrant youth from accessing high-quality, rigorous, and equitable educational experiences across educational settings in the United States: (a) homogenizing notions of a monolithic West Africa and immigrant youth's West African countries, (b) deficit understandings of identities and the heterogeneity of Black immigrant youth from West African countries living in the United States, and (c) singular views of youth's civic engagement.

This review is divided into four sections. First, we focus on contemporary migration contexts for immigrant youth from West African countries. Second, we put forth an interdisciplinary framework grounded in social science and education research to examine immigrant youth from West African countries, navigating identities and engaging civically across what we define as practices of decolonizing knowledge—using "heritage practices" (Paris, 2012) and attending to Indigenous knowledges (Dei, 2000). Third, we engage what we call a *Sankofan approach* in an analysis of selected education research examining social processes of immigrant youth from West African countries navigating identities and engaging civically. Fourth, we conclude with implications for researchers, policymakers, and educators to better meet youth's teaching and learning needs.

Across this review, we refer to "immigrant youth from West African countries" to indicate youth from 17 countries comprising the Western Africa geographic region— Benin, Burkina Faso, Cape Verde, Gambia, Ghana, Guinea, Guinea-Bissau, Ivory Coast, Liberia, Mali, Mauritania, Niger, Nigeria, Senegal, Sierra Leone, St. Helena, and Togo (McCabe, 2011). This naming of "immigrant youth from West African countries"—rather than "West African immigrants," including in our previous work (e.g., Knight & Watson, 2014)—shifts from a monolithic accounting of immigrant youth as homogeneous. In discussing literature in this review, we use terms used by authors when referring to immigrant youth in their work, for example, "sub-Saharan African immigrants" in Zong and Batalova (2014). We furthermore use terms used by authors in their work in referring to the geographic region of West Africa, for example, "Western Africa" in Zong and Batalova (2014). These shifts in naming call attention to how future research may refer to "immigrant youth from West African countries," and countries themselves, with greater nuance.

CONTEXTS OF MIGRATION

The "new African Diaspora," with "origins" in independence movements in African countries in the 1950s (Gordon, 1998, p. 84), emerged from increased migration to the United States over the past 60 years (Zong & Batalova, 2014). For example, the number of immigrants from African countries in the United States grew from 35,000 in 1960 to 130,000 by 1980 (McCabe, 2011). Between 1980 and 2013, the "sub-Saharan African immigrant population" (Zong & Batalova, 2014, para. 1) in the United States further expanded to 1.5 million. By 2013, "sub-Saharan African immigrants" comprised roughly 4% of the total U.S. immigrant population (Zong & Batalova, 2014). Importantly, since 1990, more Black immigrants arrived in the United States from African countries than Africans during the slave trade (Roberts, 2005). Moreover, Black immigrants from African countries are "among the fastest-growing immigrant populations in the United States" (Capps, McCabe, & Fix, 2011, p. 2). By 2020, Capps et al. (2011) note, "Africa will likely replace the Caribbean as the major source region for the U.S. Black immigrant population" (p. 3).

Tremendous growth of Black immigrants from African countries to the United States emerged in part with federal immigration policies such as the Hart-Celler Immigration Act of 1965, which abolished national quotas; made migration legal from Africa, Asia, Latin America, and the Caribbean; and increased educational opportunities in the United States (Balogun, 2011). From 2001 to 2010, more than 860,000 immigrants from African countries were granted lawful permanent residence (McCabe, 2011). In 2013, for example, "sub-Saharan African immigrants" coming to the United States obtained legal residency as immediate relatives of U.S. citizens (45%), through family sponsorship (10%), refugee and asylum programs (21%), employment (5%), or the Diversity Immigrant Visa Program (17%; Zong & Batalova, 2014), which requires immigrant populations to possess at least a high school degree, or 2 years of work experience in a job requiring 2 years of training (Capps et al., 2011). Immigrants from African countries reside throughout the United States in rural, suburban, and urban environments. Similar to many U.S.-born Black residents, Black immigrants from African countries are heavily concentrated in California, Florida, Illinois, New York, and Texas. Black immigrants from African countries and U.S.-born Black residents substantially overlap in Georgia, Maryland, Ohio, Pennsylvania, North Carolina, and Virginia (Capps et al., 2011; Zong & Batalova, 2014). Black immigrants from African countries also reside in Minnesota and Washington (Capps et al., 2011). The largest number of immigrants from African countries in the United States, more than 188,000, live in New York City (Wilson & Habecker, 2008), the majority of whom come from West Africa. However while immigrants from "sub-Saharan African" countries make up 0.8% of the New York City population, immigrants from "sub-Saharan African" countries comprise an even larger 2.6% of the Washington, D.C., metro area (Zong & Batalova, 2014).

Dei (1994) asserts, "All black people of African descent share a common experience, struggle, and origin" (p. 4), and furthermore "commonalities in African peoples' culture(s) [. . .] should be interrogated and investigated" (p. 7). Avoseh (2011) notes, "Sub-Saharan Africa" shares a "common bond of history and culture" (p. 34). Nearly three quarters of immigrants to the United States from West African countries, or 1.1 of 1.5 million, reported their race as "Black," and 70% either speak English as their primary language or are fluent in English (Capps et al., 2011). Yet, as Avoseh (2011) notes, "The enormous diversity of Africa makes it difficult to define anything in a universal 'African' sense" (p. 34). We understand immigrant youth in the United States from West African countries as heterogeneous and having vast ethnic, language, religious, and geographic diversity. Moreover, examining educational lives of immigrant youth from 54 countries comprising the continent of Africa is beyond the scope of this chapter. We purposefully focus on immigrants from West African countries, who comprise the largest population of "sub-Saharan African immigrants" to the United States, at 647,200, or 43% (Zong & Batalova, 2014).

The "sub-Saharan African immigrant" population in the United States (Zong & Batalova, 2014) is highly educated, with 38% attaining a bachelor's degree or higher—more than the 28% of the U.S. immigrant population, and 30% of "native-born" U.S. residents holding such degrees (Zong & Batalova, 2014, para. 9). The "new African Diaspora" (Gordon, 1998) is younger, more likely to be female (Kent, 2007), as well as speakers of multiple languages (Zong & Batalova, 2014). We consider how researchers, policymakers, and educators begin to address racialized and linguistic understandings of immigrants from West African countries who come from Black, multilingual-dominant, populated countries to White, monolingual, Christian-Judeo rural contexts, or middle-class Black communities in the United States (Clark, 2008). Moreover, immigrant population growth creates the need to better understand social processes of immigrant youth navigating identities and engaging civically to disrupt areas of inequality in the lives of immigrant youth.

A THEORETICAL FRAMEWORK FOR EXAMINING IMMIGRANT YOUTH FROM WEST AFRICAN COUNTRIES NAVIGATING IDENTITIES AND ENGAGING CIVICALLY

In considering social processes impeding immigrant youth from West African countries from accessing high-quality, rigorous, and equitable educational experiences across educational settings, we construct an interdisciplinary framework grounded in social science and education research. The framework provides an understanding of immigrant youth from West African countries navigating identities and engaging civically as practices of decolonizing knowledge (Dei, 2000)—such as "heritage practices" (Paris, 2012, 2015) and attending to Indigenous knowledges (Dei, 2000). We then engage a *Sankofan approach* in an analysis of social processes of navigating identities and engaging civically as disrupting areas of inequality affecting schooling experiences of immigrant youth from West African countries.

Practices of Decolonizing Knowledge: Using Heritage Practices and Attending to Indigenous Knowledges

Practices of decolonizing knowledge in educational lives of immigrant youth from West African countries in the United States involve moving beyond Eurocentric paradigms when examining how immigrant youth navigate identities and engage civically. By practices of decolonizing knowledge we refer, as Dei (2000) notes, to "seeing Africa beyond the boundaries created by colonial authorities and making the necessary internal and external linkages with local groups and Diasporic and other colonized peoples" (p. 118). Moreover, practices of decolonizing knowledge such as navigating identities and engaging civically build on and extend heritage practices of culturally and linguistically diverse youth.

By heritage practices, Paris and Alim (2014) note, for instance, research Paris engaged with Mexicana/o, Mexican American, and Pacific Islander youth at a high school and in a California community. Youth negotiated identities across "cultural practices" of African American Language and hip-hop, as well as "heritage practices" of Spanish or Samoan learned from community elders (p. 91). Paris and Alim (2014) note deficit perspectives in pedagogies in U.S. schools have historically required that youth of color experience a loss of "heritage practices and ways of knowing" (p. 90). The authors further argue, "Equity and access can best be achieved by centering pedagogies on the heritage and contemporary practices of students and communities of color" (p. 87). We ask how may researchers, policymakers, and educators view heritage practices of immigrant youth from West African countries, such as their linguistic assets, or immigrant communities' stance-taking toward learning as involving varied lifelong experiences, as social processes disrupting areas of inequalities. Paris (2012) furthermore cautions that pedagogies involving heritage practices must involve "considering the shifting and changing practices of students and their communities" (p. 94). In this way, Paris and Alim (2014) understand "heritage practices" and "community practices" as based in contemporary understandings of culture as dynamic, shifting, and encompassing both past-oriented heritage dimensions and present-oriented community dimensions. These dimensions in turn are not entirely distinct but take on different salience depending on how young people live race, ethnicity, language, and culture. (p. 90)

We furthermore consider how may researches, policymakers, and educators view immigrant youth from West African countries, navigating identities across varied contexts such as families, peers, and schooling, as enacting fluid, ongoing heritage practices as social processes across youth's past, present, and future experiences of teaching and learning.

Disrupting Inequalities as Shifting, Changing Local Knowledge

Considerations of "shifting and changing" (Paris, 2012, p. 94) heritage practices are further evoked in Dei's (2012) understandings of "local knowledge." Dei (2012) understands local knowledge in a case study of educational reforms across schools in Ghana as meanings held "by any group [. . .] who have lived in a particular place/location or space for a period of time and come to know by experiencing that social environment through time" (p. 111). For example, Avoseh (2013) discusses proverbs across Ogu and Yoruba cultures in southwest Nigeria as practices demonstrating the importance of spoken word in adult education. We consider how examining heritage practices as local knowledge, extending from ancestors and evolving across generations as practices of teaching and learning with immigrant youth from West African countries, asserts a stance-taking distinct from Eurocentric paradigms. In attending to local knowledges as heritage practices, researchers, policymakers, and educators in the lives of immigrant youth may, as Dei (2012) notes, "resist the everyday devaluation, denial, [and] negation of the creative, agency, resourcefulness and knowledge systems of African peoples" (p. 106).

Navigating Shifting Identities Across Understandings of Active Citizenship

Decolonizing knowledge across heritage practices and Indigenous knowledges further involves considering notions of "lifelong learning" in communities such as Yoruba culture in southwest Nigeria (Avoseh, 2001, p. 480). For example, Avoseh (2001) notes, lifelong learning extended across life spans, as families and communities took on participatory roles of teaching and learning across varied social and geographic contexts such as schools, homes, community institutions, and religious events. This inseparability of shifting notions of lifelong learning toward active citizenship is further extended in writings of Julius Nyerere, Tanzania's first president (Avoseh, 2000, 2001). As Stöger-Eising (2000) notes, Nyerere "conveys a strong sense of communal spirit, belonging together, and mutual responsibility" (p. 130). Moreover, Nyerere positioned possibilities of education as "strongly influenced by the past and serves to influence but not control the future" (Nyerere, 1985, as cited in Obiakor, 2004, p. 403).

Situating practices of decolonizing knowledge as using heritage practices and attending to Indigenous knowledges furthermore builds on Dei's (2002) understanding that a "profoundly challenging task in the academy is to facilitate the recognition and validation of the legitimacy of Indigenous knowledges as a pedagogic instructional communicative tool in the education processes of delivering education" (p. 8). We caution that attending to practices of decolonizing knowledge does not prescribe a single, "uniform" view of Indigenous knowledges (Antal & Easton, 2009, p. 602). Rather, situating decolonizing knowledge and heritage practices of immigrant youth from West African countries evokes a stance-taking Antal and Easton (2009) discuss in a comparative study examining possibilities for school-based civic education drawn from formal and informal educational settings and practices in Madagascar and West Africa. A heritage practice emerges as regional farmers' organizations discuss issues of importance until reaching a consensus, rather than rendering a decision through voting. Such a heritage practice extends ways in which, as, Avoseh (2000) notes, "dialogue [. . .] is a deep-rooted educational process that combines language, culture and other activities that give meaning to life" (p. 575). Antal and Easton (2009) situate such heritage practices as "building on the Indigenous [. . .] both drawing on existing cultural resources and adapting them to changing circumstances" (p. 603; see also Nnaemeka, 2004).

Toward a Sankofan Approach in Navigating Identities and Engaging Civically

"Sankofa" refers to the Adinkra pictorial image symbol in Akan culture in Ghana, of a bird looking back as simultaneously its body is positioned to move forward. Scholars note Sankofa has come to mean, "'Go back and fetch it,' 'return to your past,' and 'it is not taboo to go back and retrieve what you have forgotten or lost'" (Temple, 2010, p. 127). Haile Gerima's 1993 movie, titled *Sankofa*, introduced Sankofa to many U.S. audiences, portraying an African American model symbolically transported across present, past, and future, from Cape Coast Castle, in Ghana, to enslavement on a Louisiana plantation in the United States, then back to Ghana. Massaquoi (2004) asserts the film underscored "how we as Diasporic Africans harness our collective memory and learn from our collective experience" (p. 143). Uses of Sankofa, Temple (2010) notes, have since emerged in the United States as "Diasporan practice," for example, in the "naming of schools, bakeries, beauty products, businesses, [and] rites of passage programs" (pp. 128–129). Temple notes Black residents in the United States use Sankofa in such ways to evoke a "reversal of [. . .] ahistorical thinking" (p. 129) toward "deliberately and concisely cultivat[ing] and preserv[ing] African culture and philosophies" (p. 130).

Jorgensen (2001) complicates a notion of Sankofa as underscoring static pasts, noting that Kwame Nkrumah, Ghana's first president, "revived the old Akan symbol, Sankofa" to emphasize "the interrelatedness of past, present and future [. . .] rallying Ghanaians around the same symbols (p. 123). Jorgensen (2001) examined how students and teachers' negotiated cultural identities as students created TV and film productions at a professional film school in Accra, Ghana. Students and teachers continually evoked Sankofa across discussions, lectures, and cultural gatherings, complicating boundaries of past-present-future. Students understood Sankofa, as Jorgensen notes, as "traditional," yet "something with a continuity from the past [. . .], thus closely tied to a conscious or unconscious view of time as being split between past, present and future" (p. 139). In this way, with meanings "survived and adapted to the changing social and cultural changes" (p. 140), Sankofa across contexts of public discourses of TV and film narratives produced by Ghanaians underscored heritage practices as evolving.

As academic inquiry, Temple (2010) notes, understandings of Sankofa have "not yet benefited from systematic study" (p. 133). However scholars have used Sankofan approaches across education research literature (Tedla, 1995; M. J. Watson & Wiggan, 2016), health (Earl, 2010), and psychology; Hamilton Abegunde (2011), for example, examining urban violence in Chicago, notes Sankofa as a process "allows an individual to see his or her connections and responsibilities to a community, without limitations of space and time, and with a fuller grasp of history" (p. 21).

Tedla (1995) conceptualizes a "Sankofan education" across Akan and Yoruban culture, writings of W. E .B. DuBois and Marcus Garvey, and Malawian language; and further grounded in "indigenous African thought and education while it judiciously borrows ideas and technologies from other peoples of the world" (p. 209). Moreover, Tedla asserts the urgency of a Sankofan education at a time of dominant public discourses such as popular-media narratives, and "the uncritical and often unconscious absorption of the negative images projected about Africans through the media, music, books, and the education system" (p. 209). In health research, Earl (2010) conducts a "Sankofan socio-ethical" analysis of 10 years of the Tuskegee University National Center for Bioethics in Research and Health Care, considering the center's "past, present, and possible future" (p. 8). For example, Earl notes how historian Susan Reverby, in her 2009 book examining the syphilis study, "employs a research method that [. . .] values the voices of the victims (testifiers) as having as much right to be heard as those of the physicians who were in charge of the study" (p. 12). Reverby evokes in Sankofa the notion of looking back, in "affirming and releasing the voices of the Black poor, in recognizing their authentic power to bear witness to the truth" (p. 14).

Karenga (2005) furthermore notes Sankofa in Ancient Egyptian studies as a facet of a "cultural movement" and "project of continuous research of the past in search of paradigms of thought and practice useful in understanding and improving the present and enhancing the future" (p. 94). In this chapter, a Sankofan approach is apt to examine social processes of navigating identities and engaging civically as disrupting areas of inequality affecting the schooling experiences of immigrant youth from West African countries. We move purposefully from Eurocentric paradigms toward "ways of knowing grounded in making connections" (Flowers, 2003, p. 40) with past, present, and future changing heritage practices and knowledges of immigrant youth.

MODES OF INQUIRY

An established and increasing body of literature investigates experiences of teaching and learning of immigrant youth in the United States (S. Lee, 2001; Ríos-Rojas, 2011; Valenzuela, 2010). Moreover, research is beginning to appear on educational experiences of immigrant youth in the United States from African countries outside of West Africa, such as the Congo (Davila, 2015), Eretria (Stebleton, 2012), Ethiopia (Hersi, 2012; Mims, Mims, & Newland, 2009; Stebleton, 2007), Somalia (Basford, 2010; Bigelow, 2008; Dryden-Peterson, 2010; Njue & Retish, 2010; Roy & Roxas, 2011; Oropeza, Varghese, & Kanno, 2010; Watkinson & Hersi, 2014), and Uganda (Muwanguzi & Musambira, 2012). Research is also beginning to appear on immigrant youth from African countries across global contexts, including immigrant youth to Canada from Sierra Leone and Liberia (Usman, 2012); Ghana, Kenya, Nigeria, Liberia, Ethiopia, Rwanda, Somalia, and Sudan (Dlamini & Anucha, 2009); Togo, Madagascar, the Congo, Burundi, and Rwanda (Masinda, Jacquet, & Moore, 2014), and unspecified African countries (Chareka & Sears, 2006). Research is also focused on immigrant youth to France from countries in North Africa (Beaman, 2012) and to Australia from Ethiopia (Bitew & Ferguson, 2010; 2011) and Sudan (Hatoss, 2012). This literature is significant in identifying social processes of immigrant youth navigating experiences of schooling, constructing relationships, and engaging civically since the early 2000s. Moreover, scholars are increasingly examining strengths and assets in teaching and research with immigrant youth from West African countries, while noting challenges and possibilities with which youth grapple.

We focus purposely on immigrant youth from West African countries, as there is scant research involving social processes of navigating identities and engaging civically across heritage practices and Indigenous knowledges of immigrant youth, who comprise the largest population of "sub-Saharan African immigrants" (Zong & Batalova, 2014) to the United States. Moreover, examining social processes disrupts distinctive inequalities affecting educational experiences of immigrant youth, such as homogenizing notions of a monolithic West Africa and immigrant youth's West African countries, deficit understandings of identities and the heterogeneity of Black immigrant youth from West African countries living in the United States, and singular views of youth's civic engagement.

Data Sources

We conducted a selective review of research literature to examine education research on immigrant youth from West African countries in the United States. We refined our search to review articles published between 2000 and 2016, as nearly half of immigrants from African countries have come to the United States since 2000 (Capps et al., 2011). From 2000 to 2009, the number of "Black African immigrant[s]" in the United States increased 92%, compared to Black Caribbean immigrants growing only 19% (Capps et al., 2011). Also, in 2000, Arthur published *Invisible Sojourners: African Immigrant Diaspora in the United States*, a widely cited text across varied social science disciplines, highlighting ways immigrants in the United States from African countries navigate identities across contexts of families, communities, and work lives. We conducted a search of EBSCO (Education Full Text), ERIC, Scopus, Google Scholar, and JSTOR interdisciplinary electronic databases. We conducted searches of connected keywords including "African" and "immigrant" or "immigration" and "education" or "school" until common literature was found across databases. We focused attention on peer-reviewed, empirical articles with qualitative, quantitative, or mixed-methods research designs. The inclusion of conceptual articles reflects education research only recently beginning to yield empirical articles on educational experiences of immigrant youth from West African countries. We excluded literature focused on studies of immigrant youth across both multiple African countries and the Caribbean (Griffin, Cunningham, & George Mwangi, 2015). We excluded literature giving marginal attention to immigrant youth from West African countries in analysis of educational experiences of immigrant youth and/or youth of color. We excluded literature on immigrant youth from West African countries giving marginal emphasis to youth's educational experiences. We therefore reviewed articles meeting the following: published since 2000, focused on immigrant youth from West African countries, situated in preK–20 schooling contexts in the United States, and used qualitative, quantitative, or mixed-methods designs.

In examining immigrant youth from West African countries navigating identities, we drew on 26 articles to examine how immigrant youth and young adults from West Africa countries construct and negotiate complex, multilayered identities within and across varied social and educational contexts such as families, peers, and schools (Alidou, 2000; Awokoya, 2012; Balogun, 2011; Clark, 2008; Dlamini & Anucha, 2009; Harushimana & Awokoya, 2011; Imoagene, 2015; Knight, 2011, 2013; Knight & Watson, 2014; Kumi-Yeboah & Smith, 2016; Masinda et al., 2014; McIntosh Allen, Jackson, & Knight, 2012; Mensah & Williams, 2015; Njue & Retish, 2010; Ogundipe, 2011; Okpalaoka, 2011; Okpalaoka & Dillard, 2012; Park, 2013; Roubeni, De Haene, Keatley, Shah, & Rasmussen, 2015; Somé-Guiébré, 2016; Stebleton, 2012; Takyi, 2002; Thomas, 2012; Traoré, 2004, 2008). Articles primarily included research on first- and second-generation Nigerians, as Nigeria is the largest sender of immigrants from West African countries, followed by Ghana (Okpalaoka & Dillard, 2012; Zong & Batalova, 2014). In examining immigrant youth engaging civically, we draw on seven articles to construct understandings of the interplay of identities of immigrant youth from West African countries, focused on civic engagement across local knowledges, emerging communicative assets, and life-long experiences of teaching and learning (Clark, 2008; Jaffee, Watson, & Knight, 2014; Knight, 2011; Knight, Bangura, & Watson, 2012; Knight & Watson, 2014; Takougang, 2003; V. W. M. Watson, Knight, & Jaffee, 2014).

While the positioning of immigrant youth from West African countries as highly educated appears in research literature and popular-media narratives, immigrant youth in research literature grapple with navigating varied shifting identities

(Awokoya, 2012; Roubeni et al., 2015), and what it means to engage civically (Knight & Watson, 2014) at a time when education research on immigrant youth from West African countries is only recently beginning to address lived experiences and educational lives of immigrant youth.

Data Analysis

Karenga (2006) notes, Sankofa "is not simply the collection of data but also a critical analysis of meaning from an African-centered standpoint" (p. 413). This review therefore draws on a Sankofan approach, influenced by several orientations toward African consciousness (Temple, 2010), for example, in examining the legacy of cultural and linguistic heritage practices such as language use, and resistance with respect to Eurocentric worldviews of Africa, people of Africa, and immigrant youth from West African countries. We build on and extend understandings of education research examining what teaching and learning may be across experiences of immigrant youth past, present, and to come. A Sankofan approach affords opportunities to look back, consider the present, and engage the future within literature to disrupt polarizing public discourses and challenge inequitable teaching and learning opportunities for immigrant youth from West Africa.

We uploaded articles to Nvivo 10 for data analysis. Literature we reviewed included a range of methodological approaches, including autobiography, observation, census data, field notes, questionnaire, participant writing, interviews, focus group, and case study methodologies. The range of theoretical approaches included autobiographical and conversational (Alidou, 2000), multiple worlds (Awokoya, 2012), culturally relevant theory (McIntosh Allen et al., 2012), and sociocultural perspectives (Park, 2013). We engaged an iterative approach to analysis of research literature (Charmaz, 2006). We constructed in vivo codes. Focused coding and memo writing, in conversation with research questions, involved asking analytic and comparative questions, such as in what ways do immigrant youth from West African countries construct cultural, racial, and/or ethnic identities; how do youth embrace or resist varied identities; and how might varied identities extend views of civic engagement across experiences past, present, and future? We further developed categories, such as "experiencing lifelong learning across communities and families," "asserting linguistic assets," and "asserting racialized, ethnic identities across schooling experiences" (see the appendix). Analytic questions emphasized themes from research literature of navigating identities and engaging civically across educational lives of immigrant youth from West African countries.

Authors' Positionalities

Our varied experiences in teaching and learning extend our approaches and commitments to enacting research focused on immigrant youth from West African countries as a growing immigrant community rendered less visible in education research literature (Knight, Norton, Bentley, & Dixon, 2004; Milner, 2007). The first author identifies as Black; he is of African descent, grew up in the U.S. Northeast, and currently lives and works in a midsized Midwestern metro area. His extended family resides primarily in the U.S. Northeast, and metro Toronto, Ontario, Canada. He taught high school English in Brooklyn, New York, for 12 years, including teaching immigrant youth from Ghana and Nigeria. The second author is of African and European descent; she grew up in Pennsylvania in a small town. Her initial interest in immigrant youth and young adults from West African countries in New York City emerged through volunteering her research expertise in partnership with community members at the Sauti Yetu Center for African Women. The authors, while not immigrants, in more than 10 years working in research and teaching in New York City, a highly populated immigrant city, continue to seek to contribute to research on the schooling experiences of immigrant youth from West African countries.

FINDINGS

Constructing and Negotiating Identities Within and Across Social Contexts

I didn't have to think about being Black, being African when I was in New York 'cause I went home [from college] and I spoke Pular all the time. (Alimatu interview, McIntosh Allen et al., 2012, p. 7)

I read his [President Obama's] book, the first one, *Dreams of My Father* . . . We share a bicultural background . . . The fact that he had lived in Indonesia and the way that he talked 'bout it connected to the way that I experienced Nigeria at the age of six. . . . The way class and race and things function very differently, like I'm grateful that I didn't grow up here [the United States]. I lived from six to fifteen in a Black country. (Ade interview in Knight et al., 2012, p. 143)

Like Alimatu and Ade, the growing presence of immigrant youth and young adults from West Africa in the United States draws attention to complex and multilayered identities they are constructing and negotiating across different yet interrelated educational and social contexts such as families, peers, and schooling. In disrupting the inequalities that immigrants from West African countries face across educational contexts, we must first understand how negotiations of their complex and multilayered identities challenge and, in turn, disrupt dominant public discourses of immigrant youth in the United States and inequitable teaching and learning opportunities.

The notion of identity we explore in this review is based on "a multidimensional, dialectical concept, embodying complex processes" that is "not internal, or self-attributed, but also external or ascribed by others" (Mensah & Williams, 2015, p. 42; see also Vertovec, 2001). Depending on social and educational contexts and relationships within those contexts, some identities of immigrant youth from West African countries were more salient than others. Moreover, several questions emerged as we reviewed literature on roles contexts of families and K–16 schools play in construction and negotiation of identities of immigrant youth from West African countries, and their (in)equitable educational experiences. For example, how can a new interpretive framework trouble negative dominant discourses while seeking to develop new understandings of possible relationships between people of African countries, immigrants from West African countries, African Americans, and Black education (Clark, 2008; Howard, 2013; Ogundipe, 2011; Okpalaoka & Dillard, 2012; Traoré, 2008)? How do immigrant youth from West African countries construct their identities while living in close proximity to, and attending school with, African Americans (Awokoya, 2012)? Much of the discourse in educational literatures situates relationships between people of African countries, immigrant youth from African countries, and African Americans in the United States as full of tension and mistrust (Clark, 2008; Imoagene, 2015; Okpalaoka & Dillard, 2012). How do intersections of ethnicity, race, and social class contribute to different understandings of relationships between immigrant youth from West African countries and African Americans (Balogun, 2011)?

In considering Sankofa as an African philosophical approach, and questions emerging in literature, we examine how a more complex rendering of multiple and fluid identities disrupts deficit and simplistic notions of immigrant youth and young adults to portray a more complete understanding of immigrant youth and young adults from West African countries. Specifically, we examined messages taught and learned within families, school, and peer contexts to better understand constructions and negotiations of multiple identities of immigrant youth and young adults from West African countries, including racial, ethnic, and linguistic identities. We consider how immigrant youth and young adults construct, embrace, and question a national and ethnic identity and African American identities and enact multiple identities and fashion linguistic identities within varied contexts. We challenge polarizing views of immigrants; develop new understandings of heterogeneity within Black communities in the United States; and push back against dominant discourses or knowledges surrounding people of Africa, immigrants from African immigrant countries, and African Americans' educational experiences in U.S. schools (Knight, Roegman, & Edstrom, 2015; Traoré, 2008).

Embracing National and Ethnic Identities Through Family Ties

Family is one of the central contexts in which identities of immigrant youth and young adults from West African countries are constructed and negotiated in the United States. Within family contexts, questions about national, ethnic, and racial identity come to the fore. Past and current generations of immigrants from West African countries were both ethnically diverse and the racial majority in their home countries before migrating to the United States (Awokoya, 2012; Clark, 2008; Okpalaoka & Dillard, 2012). Thus, ties to an ethnic identity (e.g., Nigerian, Ghanian) were more prevalent and ties to a racialized identity prior to migrating to the United States were not realized in many of their home countries. Some African premigratory perceptions of African Americans center on stereotypes influenced by negative media depictions of African Americans (Traoré, 2008) as "violent, rude, and on welfare" (Okpalaoka & Dillard, 2012). Messages and expectations about maintaining an African and ethnic identity are taught and reinforced while messages about distancing oneself from African Americans are prevalent. However, more nuanced understandings of immigrant youth and young adults from African countries embracing national and ethnic identities emerged from the literature, especially in relation to their lived proximity to African Americans (Alidou, 2000; Balogun, 2011; Imoagene, 2015; Ogundipe, 2011).

Many African parents living in the United States were, and still are, extremely concerned about their children becoming Americanized, and sought to teach their children about their cultural heritage, language, and values. For example, in McIntosh Allen et al.'s (2012) study, 13 of 17 second- and 1.5-generation participants from eight countries in West Africa (Cameroon, Gambia, Ghana, Guinea, Liberia, Nigeria, Senegal, and Sierra Leone) who spoke English noted how uses of their Indigenous language enabled them to sustain connections to heritages of their West African countries. Speaking heritage languages connected them to their nationality and ethnicity and in many ways insulated them from feeling marginalized in other places.

Parents also tended to emphasize their ethnicity and nationality as one strategy used to de-emphasize their race and discrimination toward them. Many sought to distance themselves from African Americans in terms of racial hierarchy in the United States, and assimilation with African Americans involving downward mobility (Imoagene, 2015; Ogundipe 2011). Living in close proximity to African Americans also caused many parents to fear their children would adopt U.S. African American cultural values and mannerisms (Awokoya, 2012; Okpalaoka & Dillard, 2012). However, society within the United States does not always distinguish between the two groups as a result of racism and discrimination.

In particular, Awokoya's (2012) study of 12 1.5- and second-generation Nigerian college students within metropolitan Washington, D.C., revealed how their parents emphasized importance of cultural norms and traditions and expressed a desire for their children to view themselves as ethnically Yoruba or Igbo, Nigerian, or "at the very least African" (p. 265). Nigerian parents did not want their children to adopt behaviors they associated with African Americans and viewed as problematic as a result of the media or personal interactions, such as criminal behavior and a lack of academic achievement. These young adults also reflected on their parents not helping them negotiate their "Nigerianness" and Blackness simultaneously although they were experiencing their ethnic and racial identities together. Instead, emphasis from their parents was on either being Black—and as a Black person they were expected to work harder than their White and African American peers in order to be successful— or being Nigerian and upholding their Nigerian cultural values.

In addition to family playing a central role in the construction of a national and ethnic identity, a variety of factors emerged and merged in dynamic ways across the lifespan of 1.5- and second-generation immigrants, such that immigrant youth and young adults from West African countries viewed themselves as "African" (Clark, 2008). For example, Clark (2008) noted that second-generation immigrants who identified with national identities of West African countries were rooted in African countries such as Nigeria; they were members of African student organizations, they socialized with other Nigerians and West Africans, their family community involvement was in an African country, they tended to reject an African American identity, and they married people of African descent. Interestingly, Stebleton (2012) argued that most "African immigrants want to be identified as African" (p. 54).

Questioning an African and Ethnic Identity in Varied Peer Contexts

Within varied peer groups, immigrant youth from West African countries negotiate being too African, not Black enough, or not African enough. They have to prove their "Africanness," especially if they do not speak an African language and spoke English without an accent (Awokoya, 2012; Clark, 2008). Awokoya's (2012) study found that 1.5- and second-generation Nigerians were teased and ridiculed for being African because of negative views many of their peers had of them. As a consequence, they tried to downplay their heritage and assert a more Americanized identity. African American peers challenged Nigerian youth and young adults' notions of Blackness, and how, for example, Blackness was not simply a function of skin color but also about how to walk, talk, and interact with other African American peers. Immigrant youth from Nigeria who were most successful in middle and high school were able to "code switch" (p. 272) and use the language and social behaviors of their African American peers. However, co-ethnic Nigerians also challenged their Nigerian identities, and whether they were "African" enough if they had been born in the United States, spoke with an American accent, and had African American friends. Struggling to understand how they did not look African, or being subjected to be the authentic Nigerian, they found themselves questioning their ethnic authenticity. Surprisingly, only Park's (2013) study addressed these complex relationships. In the study, Tara, a young African women from Guinea, lived in an urban neighborhood with Mexican and Mexican American youth. Tara was bullied by several Mexican and Mexican American youth, which caused her to leave her local soccer club. Thus, in these studies on constructions and negotiations of identities within peer contexts, African Americans, co-ethnic Nigerians, and Mexican and Mexican American peers challenged immigrant youth from West African countries to negotiate their national and ethnic identities, and what constitutes an authentic African or Nigerian identity across educational and social contexts.

Resisting Imposed Depictions of an African and Ethnic Identity in Schools

Schooling contexts are contested terrain for many immigrant youth and young adults from West African countries as they construct and negotiate their complex, multilayered identities. In particular, the curriculum and teachers' pedagogical practices shaped perceptions immigrant youth and young adults from West Africa held of themselves and their interactions with African American students. They were challenged in constructing a positive national and racial identity, navigating negative depictions of "Africans" within K–12 schooling context, being "African ambassadors," and contending with the model Black minority myth. Their negotiations were mediated by colonizing knowledges of immigrant youth and young adults from West African countries and African Americans highlighting stereotypic constructions of both groups.

The knowledges embedded within the curriculum play a pivotal role in shaping identities of immigrant youth and young adults from West African countries. Unfortunately, curriculum continues to uphold colonizing knowledge and negative stereotypical images of Africans as primitive, diseased, poor, and coming from a "Dark Continent" (Traoré, 2008, p. 12; see also Harushimana & Awokoya, 2011; Okpalaoka, 2011). These stereotypes led many immigrant youth from West African countries to downplay their national and ethnic identities. These negative images also affected academic achievement and relationships with their African American peers. In Kumi-Yeboah and Smith's study (2016) of 60 first-generation Ghanaian youth and young adults, youth assert negative portrayals of Africans in the curriculum made them feel "their identities as students from a part of Africa were negated and they lost a sense of self" (p. 12). Meanwhile, their African American peers were negotiating their understandings of Africa, people of Africa, and immigrants from countries in Africa through this same colonizing framing and, in turn, may distance themselves from immigrant youth and negative depictions of immigrant youth's culture within the curriculum (Okpalaoka & Dillard, 2012). Similarly, Traoré's (2004) research with 15 newly arrived immigrants from African countries emphasized how a colonial curriculum led to "suppression and distortion of African culture, language and contributed to negative relationships with African American students" (p. 349).

However, tensions created between immigrant youth from West Africa and African American students are further heightened through teachers' pedagogical practices. For example, in Awokoya's (2012) study, teachers' pedagogical practices among 1.5- and second-generation Nigerians and their African American peers facilitated the notion of the model Black minority myth. Nigerian immigrant youth who were in honors classes had to negotiate their roles as African ambassadors and being the good Black student who represented the entire continent of Africa, while African American students were depicted in disparaging ways. Therefore, contradictory messages of the model Black minority and negative stereotypical curricular images affected both Nigerian students and African Americans in negative ways. Moreover, Imoagene's (2015) study of 75 second-generation Nigerian students found every participant experienced discrimination in ethnic slurs such as "African booty scratcher" (p. 180), leaving African students struggling with what it meant to have Black skin but be different from their Black peers. Tensions were further heightened between immigrant youth from West Africa and African Americans they perceived as not knowing much about the heritage of their West African home countries. Slurs were drawn from popular-media images of both groups and used against both groups, to further create boundaries between them.

These studies emphasize how youth become marginalized by and from their peers, and how misperceptions of both African cultures and African American culture are sustained. In particular, immigrant youth and young adults from West Africa countries negotiate negative curricular images of people from Africa, and teaching and learning experiences do not address who they are and their heritage practices such as Indigenous knowledges and cultural ways of knowing (Dei, 2002). Traoré's (2008) more recent research findings focus on how on a shared cultural heritage within the curriculum can serve as a mediator of "myths, misperceptions, or stereotypes" (p. 12) of people from Africa and African Americans, and contribute to more positive relationships between them.

Embracing and/or Resisting African American Identities Across Multiple Contexts

Much of the discourse in educational literature situates the relationship between people of Africa, immigrants to the United States from African countries, and African Americans in the United States as full of tension (Clark, 2008; Okpalaoka & Dillard, 2012). As noted in the previous section, this relationship is mediated by colonizing cultural knowledges and images of immigrant youth from West Africa and African Americans highlighting stereotypic constructions of both groups. This knowledge shapes perceptions of themselves and interactions with one another.

In the midst of this sociocultural and educational context, researchers examined how and why immigrant youth and young adults from West Africa embraced and resisted an African American identity. For example, Clark (2008) noted second-generation immigrant youth and young adults from West African countries who identified as African Americans lost their accents, adopted African American values, had family involvement in the African American community, and lived in more rural areas or small cities. Moreover, Awokoya (2012) argued although some immigrant youth and young adults from West Africa identified as African, they were constantly negotiating an African American identity ascribed to them by others in and outside of school contexts due to their phenotype and lack of an accent.

Immigrant youth and young adults from West Africa in McIntosh Allen et al.'s (2012) work created a hybrid notion of cultural identity and considered themselves both "African" and American. They expressed pride in how their home countries and the United States shaped their ideologies and identification after living in the United States for several years. Embracing both identities challenged the dichotomy defining cultural identities as in opposition to one another.

Enacting Multiple, Fluid Black Situated Identities

Immigrant youth and young adults from West Africa hold multiple Black identities simultaneously, and particular Black identities are more salient in some contexts versus others (Awokoya, 2012; Balogun, 2011; Knight, 2011). These identities reflect Sankofan practices stressing interrelatedness of past, present, and future. For example, Okpalaoka (2011) called attention to the fluid identities of immigrant girls from West Africa as they chose contexts in which to associate or disassociate from ascribed and debilitating stereotyped meanings of being African or African American by each group. For example, they identified as Ghanaian across Ghanaian settings and African American when associating with African American peers. Immigrant youth's fluid identities provide support for integrating varied contexts they will also find themselves in the future. Moreover, in Clark's (2008) study, second-generation immigrant youth from West Africa who navigated multiple identities were simultaneously raised in African communities, and listened to multiple languages in the home while also listening to Black Entertainment Television. They did not have an accent and were knowledgeable about both communities. For example, a U.S.-born college freshman of Nigerian parents living in Houston, Texas, and having a southern accent, identified as Nigerian American and African American.

Balogun (2011) challenged conventional notions that second-generation, middle-class Nigerians in the United States do not want to embrace a Black racial identity in order to separate from downwardly mobile African Americans. Rather, she emphasized how second-generation middle-class Nigerians identify and associate with middle-class African Americans in sharing a culture of upward mobility in college, thereby negotiating tensions between Black Nigerian and American identities. Balogun also offered insights into ways Nigerian students in predominantly White colleges aligned with other Black students on campus as they shared a context of racial discrimination, which in turn shaped how they embraced their racial identity, as in many cases they were perceived as African American. However, on historically Black campuses, they emphasized their ethnic Nigerian identity within the larger Black population. Their ethnic Nigerian identity was also strengthened through transnational ties while sojourning back to Nigeria for visits with family and charity work.

In a qualitative case study of Kwame, an immigrant youth from Ghana, Knight (2011) drew attention to the birthing of his dual citizenship as he negotiated his multiple identities as Ghanaian and American. Kwame shared the following:

My Ghanaian identity will never leave me. [. . .] It will always be with me and my kids when I have one someday, and being American is who I am now. I feel, because my understand the way I see the world [. . .] is Ghanaian but American made. (Knight, 2011, p. 1279)

Kwame's negotiations afford opportunities for educators to see how multiple identities and allegiances are forged rather than ascribing to notions that immigrant youth from West Africa must belong to one country or the other.

Fashioning Black Identities Through Language

Language use by immigrant youth and young adults from West Africa mediate connections to home countries and cultural identities as well as academic literacies in K–12 public schools. While educational issues regarding English language learners in the United States have received significant attention in the literature of academic achievement of immigrant children of Latino and Asian backgrounds, literature on heritage practices such as language use of immigrant children from West African countries is sparse.

Connecting to Cultural and Linguistic Identities

In McIntosh Allen et al.'s (2012) study of 18 immigrant youth and young adults from West Africa, participants all spoke English and used Indigenous languages such as Pular and Twi to sustain connections to home countries and negotiate their K–16 schooling experiences. They sought to "affirm, develop or negotiate their cultural identities and viewed their ability to speak their mother tongue as an asset worth maintaining" (p. 9). Jake, a Ghanaian participant, attributed his ability to speak Twi, albeit with an American accent, to his ability to sustain connections to his Ghanaian and West African identities. Clark (2008) also argued that immigrant youth from West Africa in her study who spoke English without an accent were simultaneously ascribed an African American identity while negating African identities. In so doing, they were troubling the privilege of speaking English without an accent and (in)visibility of Indigenous languages and knowledges. Okpalaoka and Dillard (2012) noted one female Nigerian expressed pride in her heritage and had an "advantage" over classmates because she spoke a language other than English. Interestingly, the role of an accent or lack thereof contributed to struggles over identity constructions. For example, second-generation immigrants from West Africa who identified with national and ethnic identities, or who were raised in small towns, resisted an ascribed African American identity as they did not speak English with an accent. These studies on language use offer compelling insights into intertwining heritage practices in supporting linguistic and cultural identities of immigrant youth from West Africa.

Promoting Academic Literacies

Park (2013) studied multilingual academic literacy practices of one adolescent female immigrant from Sierra Leone and Guinea. The young woman, Tara, spoke Krio, French, and English while living in Guinea. Park noted Tara's high academic achievement could be attributed to attendance at an English-dominant speaking school in Africa, and her high proficiency in English before coming to the United States, which allowed Tara to incorporate her learning experiences in Guinea and the United States. Using the dual frame of reference of Tara's heritage practices served as an entry point into varied literacy assignments in the United States. For example, she incorporated the value of memorization and reading comprehension as part of her integrated literacy practice. Tara's dual frame of references for learning academic literacy points to ways teachers can leverage students' heritage practices and Indigenous knowledges as frames of references they bring to school-based learning. Few studies focus on immigrant students from West Africa who arrive speaking multiple languages from their home countries, and ways their language and literacy practices are supported in K–12 classrooms (Somé-Guiébré, 2016). While Somé-Guiébré's (2016) study of two immigrant young girls from West Africa highlights uses of speaking French and Lingala in their fifth-grade classroom, English Language and content teachers were not equipped with knowledge of how to build on home languages as heritage practices to support academic literacies. More studies are needed that focus on linguistic assets and uses of assets of immigrant youth from West Africa in supporting cultural and linguistic identities, and ways multiple linguistic strengths can be supported and leveraged to support promotion of academic literacies in school.

Complicating Civic Engagement

Considerations of civic engagement, taking place as recent political debates in the United States, turn on contested notions of immigration, citizenship status, and what it may mean to be civically engaged. For example, as we write, comprehensive immigration reform resounds as a primary issue debated in the U.S. presidential election. As researchers expand understandings of what counts as civic engagement (Jensen, 2008; Kahne & Sporte, 2008; Westheimer & Kahne, 2004), varied cultural norms and citizenship statuses bring further complexities and prompt new understandings of civic engagement of immigrant youth across contexts local and global (Abu El-Haj, 2011). Specifically, we examine ways in which immigrant youth from West African countries complicate evolving heritage practices and local knowledges as enactments of civic engagement; and in their civic engagement demonstrate already-present active citizenship across contexts meaningful to youth.

Complicating Local Knowledges as Enacting Civic Engagement

For some immigrant youth from West African countries, civic participation underscores and extends a notion of active citizenship (Avoseh, 2001). Henry, highlighted in Clark's (2008) research, moved from Kenya to the New York City area at 9 years old. Henry was born to Kenyan parents, and identifies as "African" (p. 176). However, as Clark (2008) notes, Henry, at 17, participates civically in the African American community—as a "more active" participant than the "African community" (p. 176). For Henry, a tension emerges between his participation across African American and Kenyan communities, and his citizenship status. As Henry is not a U.S. citizen, he seeks not to "claim" (p. 176) an African American identity. Yet Henry notes community members position him as African American as he engages civically at the community level. Henry's civic participation underscores and extends a notion of active citizenship (Avoseh, 2001) across which members of a community take on roles as learners, notably outside of formal schooling contexts (C. Lee, 2009). In doing so, Henry engages actively in the African American community, different than his parents, who, while not active in the African American community, are "very active" in the Kenyan community in both Kenya and the United States (p. 176). However, Henry, in enrolling in a historically Black university in the United States, took "more of an interest in Africa" (p. 176), underscoring a notion of active citizenship as participating across both immigrant youth's West African countries, and African American lived experiences.

Immigrant youth from West African countries demonstrate a complexity of experiences as they enact civic stances important to their understandings and meaning making of affiliations, highlighting the urgency of local knowledges and complex identities toward civic engagement. Moreover, for immigrant youth, moving across new, formal, and informal schooling spaces ushers forward emerging local knowledges, complicating an interplay of past, present, and future experiences of teaching and learning (Dlamini & Anucha, 2009). For example, in Knight's (2011) work, the "global lifestyle and civic engagement" (p. 1275) of Kwame, a 23-year-old transnational immigrant youth, provide further insight into how immigrant youth from West African countries construct, navigate, and contest norms of citizenship. Moreover, Knight demonstrates how Kwame extends K–16 civic learning opportunities, using news technologies toward civic engagement. For example, the Internet provides Kwame opportunities to contribute civically and politically in local, national, and global areas through messaging, blogs, or news websites including BBC. Enactment of technologies galvanizes new forms of peer-to-peer interactions toward political action. In this way, Kwame further complicates local knowledges as he asserts new understandings as salient issues and questions pertaining to immigrant civic life within varied teaching and learning environments, and across local/global contexts.

Immigrant youth from West African countries further negotiate emerging civic identities as local knowledges facilitated across participatory new media technologies spanning global and local contexts on- and off-line. For example, V. W. M. Watson et al. (2014) note "social-civic" literacies as understandings and enactments of political literacy, and constructing civic identities for immigrant youth and young adults. Youth use social media as emergent opportunities binding notions of schools and community, and understandings of past, present, and teaching-and-learning to come, as youth across geographic boundaries of the United States and West African countries enact roles in an engaged global society, civically learning and participating toward human rights stances (Jaffee et al., 2014; Knight, 2011).

Demonstrating Already-Present Active Citizenship Across Contexts Meaningful to Youth

Across several studies, Knight and colleagues drew on interdisciplinary theoretical approaches to contest deficit views of civic life of immigrant youth from West African countries and highlight civic assets many immigrant youth bring to varied schooling experiences (Knight, 2011; Knight et al., 2012; Knight & Watson, 2014; V. W. M. Watson et al., 2014). The already-present civic assets of immigrant youth from West African countries challenge traditional notions of civic engagement prioritizing one-time activities, such as voting, which render immigrant youth who may not be permanent residents and cannot vote, and youth under age 18, as not engaged in civic action (Chareka & Sears, 2006; Knight & Watson, 2014). Moreover, immigrant youth from West African countries enact local knowledges toward civic engagement as participatory in different ways. For example, local knowledges take place against backdrops of lived experiences such as cultural and religious events, yet also across social, online communities as networks across the United States, Canada, or immigrant youth's West African countries (Chareka & Sears, 2006; V. W. M. Watson et al., 2014). Knight and Watson (2014), for instance, render visible a multitiered view of civic teaching, learning, and action of immigrant youth from West African countries, extending within and across past, present, and futures, and participatory communal contexts of families, identities, and schooling in the United States and Africa. In this way, immigrant youth from West African countries are constructing and reimagining an "action-oriented global worldview of cosmopolitan citizenship" (Jaffee et al., 2014, p. 1) across which to rethink civic engagement involving social justice issues in the United States and globally. Immigrant youth attending to but also building on and remaking local knowledge, identities, and attachments enact complex identities toward, in, and as a return to youth's communities in the United States, and West African countries.

IMPLICATIONS

This review of varied ways in which immigrant youth from West African countries construct and negotiate identities and engage civically across the "new African Diaspora" (Gordon, 1998) offers alternative ways of understanding the heterogeneity of Black youth and young adults within the United States. Moving beyond monolithic notions of Blackness, we built on and troubled existing research on constructions of identities of immigrant youth from West African countries, and how these constructions shape relationships youth form (or not) with youth across ethnic boundaries. First, different factors supporting varied processes of constructing identities points to understandings immigrant youth from West African countries identify along single dimensions such as through references to Africa, while others self-identify to their community within the Diaspora. Simultaneously, immigrant youth used multiple and intersecting self-identifications, such as Nigerian, Nigerian American, and African American, across different times and contexts. Second, varied ways of constructing identities draw attention to how youth negotiate identities across space and time in ways shaping processes of identification in the United States. For example, exploring heritage practices of language use and accents in contexts of cultural and educational practices suggests a central role in heritage practices and Indigenous knowledges shaping identities of immigrant youth from West African countries as people of Africa, African Americans, and immigrants to the United States from African countries. Youth were making choices about language use at home, in school, and with one another. Researchers and educators can, in turn, reconsider how the fluidity of Black identities and strengths-based understandings of immigrant youth and young adults from West African countries can be a starting point for further research and re-envisioning schooling practices. Third, multiple and fluid identities of immigrant youth and young adults speak to complex relationships within and among Black racial groups such as African Americans, with whom immigrant youth from West African countries live in close proximity.

Moreover, ways in which immigrant youth from West African countries enact civic engagement varies according to intersecting identities. For example, immigrant youth participate civically across their present, past, and futures as they engage geographic spaces of the United States, and their West African countries. Creating opportunities to support complex considerations of civic engagement of immigrant youth therefore involves attentiveness to multiple communities in which youth live and participate. For instance, broadened considerations of civic engagement reflect ways in which immigrant youth from West African countries enact emerging understandings of civic action across uses of social media.

DIRECTIONS TOWARD FUTURE RESEARCH

This chapter points to several areas where future research would be worthwhile to challenge inequitable processes of identifications, schooling outcomes, and civic understandings for immigrant youth from West African countries.

Examining Complex Identities in Research

The extent to which immigrant's identity constructions are continuously shaped and being reshaped living in the "new African Diaspora" (Gordon, 1998) needs to be examined as the population continues to grow across the United States. For example, research is needed on complex identities and meanings of Blackness for immigrant youth from varied countries in West Africa, such as Cape Verde (Sánchez Gibau, 2005; Saucier, 2015). Moreover, researchers may note immigrant youth's specific West African countries in future research, disrupting homogenizing notions of a monolithic West Africa, to more fully render visible heritage practices, ethnic, and language variations of a diverse continent of 54 countries (Kamya, 1997). It is also important to understand how varied identity constructions of immigrant youth from West African countries influence negative nationalist sentiments regarding immigrants and immigration.

Future research on Black immigrants from African countries should explore different national and ethnic origins of newer Black populations, and examine various factors shaping their identities. Several questions arising from the literature on families as an influential context for identity construction and negotiation of immigrant youth from West African countries, especially Nigerian contexts, point to a need for further research. For example, consideration may be given to roles reunification plays in family contexts, and how identity is thereby constructed and negotiated. Furthermore, future research may offer nuanced treatments of variation in identity across ethnic groups who share similar class backgrounds (Balogun, 2011), and how notions of identity affect educational and social relationships across immigrant youth, African Americans, and other ethnic groups with whom immigrant youth live in close proximity. Future research may furthermore study youth patterns of identity construction and negotiations, how immigrant youth self-identity, and how and why youth develop varied social relationships illuminating notions of belonging and marginalization.

"Talking Back" to Schooling as Envisioning Varied Research on Teaching and Learning

"Talking back" to schooling influences that perpetuate inaccurate stereotypes of diverse populations, shape negative identity constructions, and marginalize heritage practices and local, cultural knowledges requires challenging inequitable teaching and learning practices taking place within schools. For example, Joyce King (1992) argued for a "Diaspora literacy" taking into account Black people's multiple identities, and a "human consciousness to take back one's humanity from destructive views of "Blackness" (p. 319). Specifically, Busia (1989) describes "Diaspora literacy" as an "ability to read a variety of cultural signs of the lives of African children at home and in the 'new World'" (as cited in King, 1992, p. 318). With inclusion of such practices, distortions of and inequalities within and among such Black racial groups as people of Africa, immigrants from West African countries, and African Americans may be challenged and addressed. Moreover, racial and social dynamics accompanying immigrant youth from West African countries hold definite implications for their academic and social school experiences.

Research is furthermore needed with preservice teachers, and collaborators working with teachers, across professional development for teachers, staff, and community collaborators to challenge stereotypes in the curriculum and classrooms. Such further research may consider more nuanced understandings of multiple and varied experiences and perspectives of immigrant youth from West African countries across schooling contexts. Research is also needed in demonstrating roles of educators in fostering connections and learning, for example, across contexts where tensions exist between immigrant youth from West African countries and African American youth. Further research may consider teaching and learning at a time of mutual stereotyping of both groups in the curriculum. Additional research could explicitly address tensions in examining dominant public discourses such as popular-media narratives and images of Africans and African Americans (Traoré & Lukens, 2006) as integral aspects of schooling and postsecondary contexts.

While literature on immigrant youth speaks to emergent bilinguals and literacy practices (Garcia & Kleifgen, 2010), there is scant research involving multiple language use and literacies of immigrant youth of West African countries (Davila, 2015; Park, 2013) and how interplays of youth's linguistic identities, heritage practices, and local and cultural knowledges are supported in schools.

Extending Varied Research Approaches

In understanding how varied research design opens up new avenues of inquiry, there is a need for multiple types of research design, including participatory research methodologies, quantitative and mixed-methods research approaches, and longitudinal research studies, to examine experiences of immigrant youth from West African countries, and static notions of Black identities and civic teaching and learning. Moreover, while this review focused on immigrant youth from West African countries in the United States, as contexts of migration call attention to possibilities for a global citizenship education (Banks, 2004), further empirical studies are needed building on literature on immigrant youth from West African countries globally (e.g., Beaman, 2012; Bitew & Ferguson, 2010, 2011; Chareka & Sears, 2006; Dlamini & Anucha, 2009; Hatoss, 2012; Masinda et al., 2014; Usman, 2012).

Toward Research and Teaching With African Immigrant Youth as Civic Imaginaries

We enacted a Sankofan approach to analyze education research literature on social processes of navigating identities and engaging civically across immigrant youth's heritage practices and Indigenous knowledges. In disrupting areas of inequalities affecting educational experiences of immigrant youth, we ask how researchers, policymakers, and educators, as collaborators in educational lives of immigrant youth, may—as Nigerian poet Tanure Ojaide (2015) notes—"imbued with experience of the past [. . .] lead to the future by offering a vision of possibilities" (p. 50). A Sankofan approach points to possibilities of envisioning past, present, and future strengths as heritage practices and knowledges immigrant youth from West African countries bring to classrooms and communities. Moreover, at a time of polarizing popular-media narratives in dominant public discourses of immigrant youth from West African countries, a Sankofan approach asserts possibilities of youth enacting "civic imaginaries" (V. W. M. Watson & Marciano, 2015, p. 39) "across which 'discourses not only represent the world as it is (or rather as seen to be), they are also projective, imaginaries, representing possible worlds which are different from the actual world' (Fairclough, 2003, p. 124)" (V. W. M. Watson & Marciano, 2015, p. 39). Fairclough (2003) further notes discourses as

ways of representing aspects of the world— the processes, relations, and structures of the material world, the "mental world" of thoughts, feelings, beliefs and so forth, and the social world. [. . .] Discourses [are] tied in to projects to change the world in particular directions. (p. 124)

DeChaine (2009), writing in communication studies, draws on rhetoric of contemporary bordering practices on the U.S.–Mexico border to contextualize "struggles over the boundaries of citizenship" as both enabling and constraining a "civic imaginary" and reconsidering of geographical borders as "performative, sociocultural productions" (p. 45; see also DeJaeghere & McCleary, 2010). In envisioning immigrant youth from West African countries as enacting civic imaginaries, researchers, policymakers, and educators as collaborators in the lives of youth position immigrant youth as participants and contributors, simultaneously extending possibilities and meanings of negotiating identities and engaging civically in schools and communities in the United States, and youth's home countries, across experiences past, present, and to come. We ask how may further research with immigrant youth from West African countries build on and extend understandings of the multitude and heterogeneity of their educational experiences, given ways in which immigrant youth are viewed in polarizing ways in dominant public discourses such as popular-media narratives (Egbedi, 2016). Such work as envisioning civic imaginaries of immigrant youth in research and teaching is particularly needed today, in disrupting inequitable educational experiences of schooling of immigrant youth from West African countries, living and learning in the United States.

APPENDIX

Focused Coding

Asserting assets
Asserting civic identities
Asserting communal, familial roles
Asserting contexts
Asserting identities
Asserting identities based on socioeconomic status
Asserting identities, religious
Asserting immigrants as high achieving
Asserting linguistic assets
Asserting racialized, ethnic identities across schooling experiences
Challenges faced by African immigrant youth, varied
Challenging deficit labels based on generation status
Challenging deficit notions based on race, ethnicity
Challenging deficit notions based on religion
Challenging grouping of immigrant and African American youth
Challenging limiting notions of civic learning, actions
Challenging, navigating deficit labels
Experiencing lifelong learning across communities, families

Coding Categories

Asserting multiple assets across varied contexts
Challenging, navigating homogenizing notions of race, ethnicity
Enacting varied civic identities
Navigating varied identities across contexts

REFERENCES

Abu El-Haj, T. R. (2011). "The beauty of America": Nationalism, education, and the war on terror. *Harvard Educational Review, 80,* 242–274.

Alidou, H. (2000). Preparing teachers for the education of new immigrant students from Africa. *Action in Teacher Education, 22*(2A), 101–108.

Antal, C., & Easton, P. (2009). Indigenizing civic education in Africa: Experience in Madagascar and the Sahel. *International Journal of Educational Development, 29,* 599–611.

Arthur, J. A. (2000). *Invisible sojourners: African immigrant Diaspora in the United States.* Westport, CT: Praeger.

Avoseh, M. B. M. (2000). Adult education and participatory research in Africa: In defence of tradition. *Canadian Journal of Development Studies, 21,* 565–578.

Avoseh, M. B. M. (2001). Learning to be active citizens: Lessons of traditional Africa for life-long learning. *International Journal of Lifelong Learning, 20,* 479–486.

Avoseh, M. B. M. (2011). Informal community learning in traditional Africa. In S. Jackson (Ed.), *Innovations in lifelong learning: Critical perspectives on diversity, participation, and vocational learning* (pp. 34–48). New York, NY: Routledge.

Avoseh, M. B. M. (2013). Proverbs as theoretical frameworks for lifelong learning in indigenous African education. *Adult Education Quarterly, 63,* 236–250.

Awokoya, J. T. (2012). Identity constructions and negotiations among 1.5- and second-generation Nigerians: The impact of family, school, and peer contexts. *Harvard Educational Review, 82,* 255–281.

Balogun, O. M. (2011). No necessary tradeoff: Context, life course, and social networks in the identity formation of second-generation Nigerians in the U.S. *Ethnicities, 11,* 436–466.

Banks, J. A. (2004). Teaching for social justice, diversity, and citizenship in a global world. *The Educational Forum, 68,* 289–298.

Basford, L. (2010). From mainstream to East African charter: Cultural and religious experiences of Somali youth in US schools. *Journal of School Choice, 4,* 485–509.

Beaman, J. (2012). But madam, we are French also. *Context, 11*(3), 46–51.

Bigelow, M. (2008). Somali adolescents' negotiation of religious and racial bias in and out of school. *Theory Into Practice, 47*(1), 27–34.

Bitew, G., & Ferguson, P. (2010). Parental support for African immigrant students' schooling in Australia. *Journal of Comparative Family Studies, 41,* 149–165.

Bitew, G., & Ferguson, P. (2011). The Ethiopian adolescent and the effect of cultural difference on immigrant students' learning. *Diaspora, Indigenous, and Minority Education, 5*(1), 1–16.

Capps, R., McCabe, K., & Fix, M. (2011). *New streams: Black African migration to the United States.* Washington, DC: Migration Policy Institute.

Chareka, O., & Sears, A. (2006). Civic duty: Young people's conceptions of voting as a means of political participation. *Canadian Journal of Education, 29,* 521–540.

Charmaz, K. (2006). *Constructing grounded theory: A practical guide through qualitative analysis.* Thousand Oaks, CA: Sage.

Clark, M. K. (2008). Identity among first and second generation African immigrants in the United States. *African Identities, 6,* 169–181.

Cooper, H. (2015, December 10). Liberia's shunned "Ebola burners." *The New York Times,* p. A1.

Davila, L. T. (2015). Diaspora literacies: An explanation of what reading means to young African immigrant women. *Journal of Adolescent & Adult Literacy, 58,* 641–649.

DeChaine, D. R. (2009). Bordering the civic imaginary: Alienization, fence logic, and the minuteman civil defense corps. *Quarterly Journal of Speech, 95,* 43–65.

Dei, G. J. S. (1994). Afrocentricity: A cornerstone of pedagogy. *Anthropology & Education Quarterly, 25*(1), 3–28.

Dei, G. J. S. (2000). Rethinking the role of Indigenous knowledges in the academy. *International Journal of Inclusive Education, 4,* 111–132.

Dei, G. J. S. (2002). Learning culture, spirituality and local knowledge: Implications for African schooling. *International Review of Education, 48,* 335–360.

Dei, G. S. (2012). Indigenous anti-colonial knowledge as "heritage knowledge" for promoting Black/African education in diasporic contexts. *Decolonization: Indigeneity, Education & Society, 1,* 102–119.

DeJaeghere, J. G., & McCleary, K. S. (2010). The making of Mexican migrant youth civic identities: Transnational spaces and imaginaries. *Anthropology & Education Quarterly, 41*, 228–244.

Dlamini, S. N., & Anucha, U. (2009). Trans-nationalism, social identities, and African youth in the Canadian Diaspora. *Social Identities, 15*, 227–242.

Dryden-Peterson, S. (2010). Bridging home: Building relationships between immigrant and long-time resident youth. *Teachers College Record, 112*, 2320–2351.

Earl, R. R., Jr. (2010). Sanokfan socio-ethical reflections: The Tuskegee University National Bioethics Center's decade of operation, 1999-2009. *Journal of Health Care for the Poor and Underserved, 21*(3a), 6–20.

Egbedi, H. (2016, July 19). *African booty scratcher: This sitcom by a 24-year-old aims to portray a realistic image of African immigrants.* Retrieved from http://venturesafrica.com/features/african-booty-scratcher-this-comedy-sitcom-by-a-24-year-old-aims-to-portray-a-realistic-image-of-african-immigrants/

Fairclough, N. (2003). *Analyzing discourse.* London, England: Routledge.

Flowers, D. (2003). An Afrocentric view of adult learning theory. In L. M. Baumgartner, M. Lee, S. Birden, & D. Flowers (Eds.), *Adult learning theory: A primer*—Information Series No. 392 (pp. 35–42). Columbus: Center on Education and Training for Employment, College of Education, The Ohio State University.

Garcia, O., & Kleifgen, J. (2010). *Education emergent bilinguals.* New York, NY: Teachers College Press.

Gordon, A. (1998). The new diaspora: African immigration to the United States. *Journal of Third World Studies, 15*, 79–103.

Griffin, K. A., Cunningham, E. L., & George Mwangi, C. A. (2015). Defining diversity: Ethnic differences in Black students' perceptions of racial climate. *Journal of Diversity in Higher Education, 9*, 34–49.

Hamilton Abegunde, M. E. (2011). Sankofa in action: Creating a plan that works: Healing the causes of violence to stop the violence. *Black Diaspora Review, 2*(2), 13–26.

Harushimana, I., & Awokoya, J. (2011). African-born immigrants in U.S. schools: An intercultural perspective on schooling and diversity. *Journal of Praxis in Multicultural Education, 6*(1), 34–48.

Hatoss, A. (2012). Where are you from? Identity construction and experiences of 'othering' in the narratives of Sudanese refugee-background Australians. *Discourse & Society, 23*(1), 47–68.

Hersi, A. A. (2012). Transnational immigration and education: A case study of an Ethiopian immigrant high school student. *Creative Education, 3*(1), 149–154.

Howard, T. C. (2013). How does it feel to be a problem? Black male students, schools, and learning in enhancing the knowledge base to disrupt deficit frameworks. *Review of Research in Education, 37*, 54–86.

Imoagene, O. (2015). Broken bridges: An exchange of slurs between African Americans and second generation Nigerians and the impact on identity formation among the second generation. *Language Sciences, 52*, 176–186.

Jaffee, A. T., Watson, V. W. M., & Knight, M. G. (2014). Toward enacted cosmopolitan citizenship: New conceptualizations of African immigrants' civic learning and action in the United States. *Journal of Global Citizenship & Equity Education, 4*(1), 1–18.

Jensen, L. A. (2008). Immigrants' cultural identities as sources of civic engagement. *Applied Developmental Science, 12*, 74–83.

Jorgensen, A. M. (2001). Sankofa and modern authenticity in Ghanaian film and television. In M. E. Baaz, & M. Palmberg (Eds.), *Same and other: Negotiating African identity in cultural production* (pp. 119–142). Stockholm, Sweden: Nordiska Afrikainsitutet.

Kahne, J. E., & Sporte, S. E. (2008). Developing citizens: The impact of civic learning opportunities on students' commitment to civic participation. *American Educational Research Journal, 45,* 738–766.

Kamya, H. A. (1997). African immigrants in the United States: The challenge for research and practice. *Social Work, 42,* 154–165.

Karenga, M. (2005). Ancient Egyptian studies movement. In M. K. Asante, & A. Mazama (Eds.), *Encyclopedia of Black studies* (pp. 93–97). Thousand Oaks, CA: Sage.

Karenga, M. (2006). The field, function, and future of Africana studies: Critical reflections on its mission, meaning, and methodology. In M. K. Asante, & A. Karenga (Eds.), *Handbook of Black studies* (pp. 402–420). Thousand Oaks, CA: Sage.

Kent, M. M. (2007). *Immigration and America's Black population.* Washington, DC: Population Reference Bureau.

King, J. (1992). Diaspora literacy and consciousness in the struggle against miseducation in the Black community. *Journal of Negro Education, 61,* 317–340.

Knight, M. (2011). "It's already happening": Learning from civically engaged transnational immigrant youth. *Teachers College Record, 113,* 1275–1292.

Knight, M. (2013). Living the legacies and continuing the struggle: Immigration, preK-16 education, and transnationalism. *Texas Education Review, 1,* 225–233.

Knight, M., Bangura, R., & Watson, V. W. M. (2012). (Re)framing African immigrant women's civic leadership: A case study of the role of families, schooling, and transnationalism. *Global Studies Journal, 4,* 135–148.

Knight, M. G., Norton, N. E. L., Bentley, C. C., & Dixon, I. R. (2004). The power of Black and Latina/o counterstories: Urban families and college-going processes. *Anthropology & Education Quarterly, 35,* 99–120.

Knight, M. G., Roegman, R., & Edstrom, L. (2015). My American dream: The interplay between structure and agency in West African immigrants' educational experiences in the United States. *Education and Urban Society, 48,* 827–851.

Knight, M. G., & Watson, V. W. M. (2014). Toward participatory communal citizenship: Rendering visible the civic teaching, learning, and actions of African immigrant youth and young adults. *American Educational Research Journal, 51,* 539–566.

Kumi-Yeboah, A., & Smith, P. (2016). Cross-cultural educational experiences and academic achievement of Ghanaian immigrant youth in urban public schools. *Education and Urban Society.* Advance online publication. doi:10.1177/0013124516643764

Lacey-Bordeaux, E. (2014, October 28). Father says sons beaten at school while attackers called them "Ebola." Retrieved from http://www.cnn.com/2014/10/28/us/ebola—school-beatings/

Lee, C. (2009). From DuBois to Obama: The education of peoples of African descent in the United States in the 21st century. *Journal of Negro Education, 78,* 367–384.

Lee, S. (2001). More than "model minorities" or "delinquents": A look at Hmong American high school students." *Harvard Educational Review, 71,* 505–529.

Lee, W. (2016, June 30). Africa-born US residents embrace politics to bring about change. *Voice of America.* Retrieved from http://www.voanews.com/content/africa-born-united-states-residents-embrace-politics-bring-about-change/3399834.html

Masinda, M. T., Jacquet, M., & Moore, D. (2014). An integrated framework for immigrant children and youth's school integration: A focus on African Francophone students in British Columbia, Canada. *International Journal of Education, 6,* 90–107.

Massaquoi, N. (2004). An African child becomes a Black Canadian feminist: Oscillating identities in the Black Diaspora. *Canadian Woman Studies, 23,* 140–144.

McCabe, K. (2011, July 21). African immigrants in the United States. *Migration Information Source.* Retrieved from http://www.migrationpolicy.org/article/african-immigrants-united-states

McIntosh Allen, K., Jackson, I., & Knight, M. G. (2012). Complicating culturally relevant pedagogy: Unpacking West African immigrants' cultural identities. *International Journal of Multicultural Education, 14*(2), 1–28.

Mensah, J., & Williams, C. J. (2015). Seeing/being double: How African immigrants in Canada balance their ethno-racial and national identities. *African and Black Diaspora, 8*(1), 39–54.

Milner, H. R. (2007). Race, culture, and researcher positionality: Working through dangers seen, unseen, and unforeseen. *Educational Researcher, 36*, 388–400.

Mims, M. J., Mims, G. A., & Newland, L. A. (2009). Career counselling an African immigrant student in a USA school setting: Merging transition theory with a narrative approach. *South African Journal of Higher Education, 23*, 590–607.

Muwanguzi, S., & Musambira, G. W. (2012). Communication experiences of Ugandan immigrants during acculturation to the United States. *Journal of Intercultural Communication, 30*, 71–86.

Nnaemeka, O. (2004). Nego-feminism: Theorizing, practicing, and pruning Africa's way. *Signs: Journal of Culture and Women in Society, 29*, 357–385.

Njue, J., & Retish, P. (2010). Transitioning: Academic and social performance of African immigrant students in an American high school. *Urban Education, 45*, 347–370.

Obiakor, F. E. (2004). Building patriotic African leadership through African-centered education. *Journal of Black Studies, 34*, 402–420.

Obiakor, F. E., & Afolayan, M. O. (2007). African immigrant families in the United States: Surviving the sociocultural tide. *The Family Journal, 15*, 265–270.

Ogundipe, V. A., Jr. (2011). *The development of ethnic identity among African-American, African immigrant and Diasporic African immigrant university students.* Retrieved from http://scholarworks.gsu.edu/cgi/viewcontent.cgi?article=1027&context=sociology_theses

Ojaide, T. (2015). *Indigeneity, globalization, and African literature: Personally speaking.* New York, NY: Palgrave Macmillan.

Okpalaoka, C. (2011, April). *Troubling the "African" in African American: When old and new (im)migrations collide in our schools.* Paper presented at the American Educational Association Annual Meeting, New Orleans, LA.

Okpalaoka, C. L., & Dillard, C. B. (2012). (Im)migrations, relations, and identities of African peoples: Toward an endarkened transnational feminist praxis in education. *Educational Foundations, Winter-Spring 2012*, 121–142.

Oropeza, M. V., Varghese, M. M., & Kanno, Y. (2010). Linguistic minority students in higher education: Using, resisting, and negotiating multiple labels. *Equity & Excellence in Education, 43*, 216–231.

Paris, D. (2012). Culturally sustaining pedagogy: A needed change in stance, terminology, and practice. *Educational Researcher, 41*(3), 93–97.

Paris, D. (2015). The right to culturally sustaining language education for the new American mainstream: An introduction. *International Multilingual Research Journal, 9*, 221–226.

Paris, D., & Alim, H. S. (2014). What are we seeking to sustain through culturally sustaining pedagogy? A loving critique forward. *Harvard Educational Review, 84*, 85–100.

Park, J. Y. (2013). Becoming academically literate: A case study of an African immigrant youth. *Journal of Adolescent & Adult Literacy, 57*, 298–306.

Ríos-Rojas, A. (2011). Beyond delinquent citizenships: Immigrant youth's (re) visions of citizenship and belonging in a globalized world. *Harvard Educational Review, 81*, 64–95.

Roberts, S. (2005, February 21). More Africans enter U.S. than in days of slavery. *The New York Times.* Retrieved from http://www.nytimes.com/2005/02/21/nyregion/more-africans-enter-us-than-in-days-of-slavery.html?_r=0

Roubeni, S., De Haene, L., Keatley, E., Shah, N., & Rasmussen, A. (2015). "If we can't do it, our children will do it one day": A qualitative study of West African immigrant parents' losses and educational aspirations for their children. *American Educational Research Journal, 52,* 275–305.

Roy, L., & Roxas, K. (2011). Whose deficit is this anyhow? Exploring counter-stories of Somali Bantu refugees' experiences in "doing school." *Harvard Educational Review, 81,* 521–542.

Sánchez Gibau, G. (2005). Contested identities: Narratives of race and ethnicity in the Cape Verdean diaspora. *Identities: Global Studies in Culture and Power, 12,* 405–438.

Saucier, P. K. (2015). *Necessarily Black: Cape Verdean youth, hip-hop culture, and a critique of identity.* East Lansing: Michigan State University Press.

Somé-Guiébré, E. (2016). Mainstreaming English language learners: Does it promote or hinder literacy development? *English Language Teaching, 9,* 33–40.

Stebleton, M. J. (2007). Career counseling with African immigrant college students: Theoretical approaches and implications for practice. *Career Development Journal, 55,* 290–312.

Stebleton, M. J. (2012). The meaning of work for Black African immigrant adult college students. *Journal of Career Development, 39,* 50–75.

Stöger-Eising, V. (2000). "Ujamaa" revisited: Indigenous and European influences in Nyerere's social and political thought. *Africa: Journal of the International African Institute, 70,* 118–143.

Takougang, J. (2003). Contemporary African immigrants to the United States. *Irinkerindo: A Journal of African Migration, 2,* 1–15.

Takyi, B. K. (2002). The making of the second Diaspora: On the recent African immigrant community in the United States of America. *Western Journal of Black Studies, 26,* 32–43.

Tedla, E. (1995). *Sankofa: African thought and education.* New York, NY: Peter Lang.

Temple, C. N. (2010). The emergence of Sankofa practice in the United States: A modern history. *Journal of Black Studies, 41,* 127–150.

Thomas, K. J. A. (2012). Race and school enrollment among the children of African immigrants in the United States. *International Migration Review, 46,* 37–60.

Traoré, R. L. (2004). Colonialism continued: African students in an urban high school in America. *Journal of Black Studies, 34,* 348–369.

Traoré, R. (2008). Cultural connections: An alternative to conflict resolution. *Multicultural Education, 15*(4), 10–14.

Traoré, R., & Lukens, R. J. (2006). *This isn't the America I thought I'd find: African students in the urban U.S. high school.* Lanham, MD: University Press of America.

Usman, L. M. (2012). Communication disorders and the inclusion of newcomer African refugees in rural primary schools of British Columbia, Canada. *International Journal of Progressive Education, 8,* 102–121.

Valenzuela, A. (2010). *Subtractive schooling: US-Mexican youth and the politics of caring.* Albany: SUNY Press.

Vertovec, S. (2001). Transnationalism and identity. *Journal of Ethnic and Migration Studies, 27,* 573–582. doi:10.1080/13691830120090386

Watkinson, J. S., & Hersi, A. A. (2014). School counselors supporting African immigrant students' career development: A case study. *Career Development Quarterly, 62,* 44–55.

Watson, M. J., & Wiggan, G. (2016). Sankofa healing and restoration: A case study of African American excellence and achievement in an urban school. *Africology: The Journal of Pan African Studies, 9,* 113–140.

Watson, V. W. M., Knight, M. G., & Jaffee, A. T. (2014). Beyond #talking and #texting: African immigrant youth's social-civic literacies and negotiations of citizenship across participatory new media technologies. *Citizenship Teaching and Learning, 10*(1), 43–62.

Watson, V. W. M., & Marciano, J. E. (2015). Examining a social-participatory youth co-researcher methodology: A cross-case analysis extending possibilities of literacy and research. *Literacy, 49*, 37–44.

Westheimer, J., & Kahne, J. (2004). What kind of citizen? The politics of educating for democracy. *American Educational Research Journal, 41*, 237–269.

Wilson, J., & Habecker, S. (2008). The lure of the capital city: An anthro-geographical analysis of recent African immigration to Washington, DC. *Population, Space and Place, 14*, 433–448.

World Health Organization. (2014). *The outbreak of Ebola virus disease in Senegal is over.* Retrieved from http://www.who.int/mediacentre/news/ebola/17-october-2014/en/

Zong, J., & Batalova, J. (2014). Sub-Saharan African immigrants in the United States. *Migration Information Source.* Retrieved from http://www.migrationpolicy.org/article/sub-saharan-african-immigrants-united-states

Chapter 13

YPAR and Critical Epistemologies: Rethinking Education Research

Limarys Caraballo
Queens College of the City University of New York

Brian D. Lozenski
Macalester College

Jamila J. Lyiscott
Ernest Morrell
Teachers College, Columbia University

Knowledges from academic and professional research-based institutions have long been valued over the organic intellectualism of those who are most affected by educational and social inequities. In contrast, participatory action research (PAR) projects are collective investigations that rely on indigenous knowledge, combined with the desire to take individual and/or collective action. PAR with youth (YPAR) engages in rigorous research inquiries and represents a radical effort in education research to value the inquiry-based knowledge production of the youth who directly experience the educational contexts that scholars endeavor to understand. In this chapter, we outline the foundations of YPAR and examine the distinct epistemological, methodological, and pedagogical contributions of an interdisciplinary corpus of YPAR studies and scholarship. We outline the origins and disciplines of YPAR and make a case for its role in education research, discuss its contributions to the field and the tensions and possibilities of YPAR across disciplines, and close by proposing a YPAR critical-epistemological framework that centers youth and their communities, alongside practitioners, scholars, and researchers, as knowledge producers and change agents for social justice.

Knowledges from academic and professional research-based institutions have long been valued over the organic intellectualism of those who are most affected by educational and social inequities. Participatory research recognizes what Antonio

Review of Research in Education
March 2017, Vol. 41, pp. 311–336
DOI: 10.3102/0091732X16686948
© 2017 AERA. http://rre.aera.net

Gramsci described as "the intellectual and political power of 'organic intellectuals' from whom counter-hegemonic notions derive," which presents a "fundamental challenge to what . . . John Gaventa called 'official knowledge' as the sole legitimate claim to truth" (Fine, Torre, et al., 2004, p. 98). Unlike positivist and postpositivist epistemological traditions and research methods that rely on the objectivity and expertise of university-sanctioned researchers (Isenhart & Jurow, 2011; Noffke, 1997), participatory action research (PAR) projects are collective investigations that rely on local knowledge, combined with the desire to take individual and/or collective action (Fine, Torre, et al., 2004; McIntyre, 2000). PAR with youth (YPAR) engages in rigorous research inquiries and represents a radical effort in education research to take inquiry-based knowledge production out of the sole hands of academic institutions and include the youth who directly experience the educational contexts that scholars endeavor to understand. In this chapter, we outline the foundations of YPAR and examine the distinct epistemological, methodological, and pedagogical contributions of an interdisciplinary corpus of YPAR studies and scholarship. We outline the origins and disciplines of YPAR and make a case for its role in education research, discuss its contributions to the field and the tensions and possibilities of YPAR across disciplines, and close by proposing a YPAR critical-epistemological framework that centers youth and their communities, alongside practitioners, scholars, and researchers, as knowledge producers and change agents for social justice.

CONCEPTUAL FRAMEWORK AND METHODS

Fine (2008) asserts that "*PAR is not a method*"—it is a "radical *epistemological challenge* to the traditions of social science, most critically on the topic of where knowledge resides" (p. 215). Because researchers across generations, contexts, and roles must "*deliberate deeply* within and across differences, *seeking dissent* and *exploring competing interpretations* of the evidence" (p. 222), the interpretive nature of this work, and a reflection of its ontological and epistemological assumptions, has been nurtured by participatory methodologies that are critical, dialectical, and hermeneutical (Arthur, Waring, Coe, & Hedges, 2012, p. 16). The epistemological work of PAR encompasses quantitative and qualitative data collection methods ranging from "surveys, logistic regressions, ethnography, public opinion polls, life stories, testimonies, performance, focus groups, and varied other methods," yet its common purpose across disciplines and research designs is "to interrogate the conditions of oppression and surface leverage points for resistance and change" (Fine, 2008, p. 215). PAR "can be regarded as a methodology that argues in favor of the possibility, the significance, and the usefulness of involving research partners," yet it is not fundamentally distinct from other empirical social research procedures" and bears "numerous links" especially to critical qualitative methodologies and methods (Bergold & Thomas, 2012, p. 2; Bogdan & Biklen, 2007). Working against assumptions about neutrality, objectivity, and bias in qualitative inquiry (Roulston & Shelton, 2015), PAR is marked by efforts to validate and create spaces for the production of knowledge by and with those who are indigenous to their respective communities (Miskovic & Hoop, 2006).

PAR with youth,[1] or YPAR, is therefore a critical research methodology that carries specific epistemological commitments toward reframing who is "allowed" to conduct and disseminate education research with/about youth in actionable ways. Its origins in critical pedagogy inform its role as a pedagogical approach based on a conception of teaching and learning through collaborative and transformative inquiry. In the first study to document YPAR in education, grounded in the field of critical psychology, McIntyre (2000) argues for the power of "engaging in a process that positions youth as agents of inquiry and as 'experts' about their own lives" (p. 126). Embedded in contexts of poverty, violence, and inadequate educational resources, the youth researchers addressed these inequalities by drawing on epistemologies of resistance, learning and then using various methods to draw on community narratives, toward "co-creating student-initiated intervention or action programs that promote community well-being" (p. 129). Our review thus focuses on the ways in which YPAR has transformed research on educational inequality by understanding it from the perspectives of those most affected by inequitable educational conditions, as well as how marginalized youth have used YPAR to critique, redefine, and overcome the very asymmetries they face in their schools and communities. Yet we are also careful not to fetishize YPAR as a panacea for the vast inequities plaguing youth, in and outside of schools. We examine the inherent tensions in positioning youth as knowledge creators, understanding that these tensions are typically not the focus of the literature but are often subtly addressed within research narratives.

METHOD AND RESEARCH QUESTIONS

In April 2016, a Google Scholar search using the keywords "youth participatory action research" and "education" yielded just over 1,000 scholarly articles,[2] with emerging scholarship on participatory research with youth in fields such as sociology dating back to the 1990s (Kelly, 1993). When the results are restricted to those published after the McIntyre (2000) study, the number is reduced minimally to about 990 entries. Further refined from 2010 to the present, the results are again minimally reduced to 910 articles, indicating that the vast majority of entries have been published very recently—indeed, over 275 of these entries have been published since 2015. These numbers, while not meant to be definitive (nor exhaustive), demonstrate that YPAR, as examined in our review, has become increasingly prevalent within the last 10 to 15 years.

While space constraints prevent us from including all of these articles, we provide a framework for examining the various epistemological, methodological, and pedagogical traditions and disciplines of YPAR scholarship and research in education published since 2000. We analyze YPAR scholarship and empirical studies based on the following foundational questions that allow a broad analysis of empirical and theoretical YPAR studies:

Research Question 1: In what ways have inequality and its root causes contributed to the need for YPAR as a critical epistemology and research methodology?

Research Question 2: How has YPAR sought to address educational inequality and promote justice through its methodological and pedagogical foundations?

Research Question 3: How has YPAR scholarship drawn on and extended critical research in education and beyond?

Our interdisciplinary analysis documents how YPAR scholarship in recent decades has informed prevalent dilemmas in critical research in education, such as: the production of critical epistemologies (Fals-Borda & Rahman, 1991), issues of representation in qualitative inquiry (Denzin, 1994), activist research traditions that build on the critical meta-awareness of individuals and communities (Hale, 2008; Souto-Manning, 2014), and the contributions and tensions inherent in the process of decolonizing research (Paris & Winn, 2014; Smith, 1999; Tuck & Yang, 2012). Our analysis highlights the necessity of working across critical research, epistemological, and pedagogical frameworks and also describes what makes YPAR itself a unique and generative endeavor at the intersection of these disciplines.

YPAR IN THE CONTEXT OF EDUCATIONAL INEQUALITY

A deep history of social inequality and its root causes across disciplines have contributed to the need for YPAR as a methodology and educational epistemology. Within communities with the highest rates of violence, steeped in deep racial, economic, and class struggle, the earliest recorded YPAR studies were born (Cahill, 2007; Fine, Torre, et al., 2004; McIntyre, 2000). Led by youth ready to take research about themselves into their own hands, YPAR work emerged in response to discrimination, racism, poverty, underresourced schools, and the constant threat of violence felt by youth researchers and their communities. Other YPAR projects focused more explicitly on academic disparities, reflecting a disconnect between student ability and student achievement in standardized test scores, advanced placement exams, and college readiness (Morrell, 2004, 2008). Across broad fields of research, a long history of dehumanizing and colonizing methods, positioning affected communities as objects rather than subjects and authorities over the study of their lives, called for the critical and reflexive methodologies and epistemologies encompassed by YPAR (Fals-Borda & Rahman, 1991).

Tracing Critical Participatory Action Research With Youth

In its development as a research epistemology as well as a pedagogical project, PAR has been inspired by numerous intellectual and critical traditions (Cammarota & Fine, 2008; Mirra, Garcia, & Morrell, 2015). Critical PAR has antecedents in the work of John Collier and Kurt Lewin in action research (Bargal, 2006; Collier, 1945; Neilsen, 2006), who rejected the positivist assumption of objectivity in research. They suggested that researchers could take action upon and have an impact on the issues they were investigating, and not only "academic" researchers could conduct research on issues that have an impact on practice. Other scholars argue that origins of what has come to be called PAR can be found in the practices of indigenous communities of Africa, the Americas, and South Pacific before Western paradigms of thought were ever encountered (Mirra, Garcia, & Morrell, 2015; Nabudere, 2008; Smith, 1999). In the 20th century, PAR has been practiced on multiple continents, typically by communities who have experienced some form of colonization, and gained recognition as social science research in Latin America in the 1970s (Morrow & Torres, 1995). From its inception, PAR has articulated an explicit goal of social justice and societal transformation. PAR intentionally seeks to disrupt power structures, in an effort to transform the ways in which traditionally marginalized communities have been subjugated by Western conceptions of research (Fine, 2008; Smith, 1999; Zeichner & Noffke, 2001). Fals-Borda and Rahman (1991) articulate the transformational goals of PAR in their juxtaposition of researchers and participants:

[S]uch a relationship must be transformed into subject/subject rather than subject/object. Indeed, the destruction of the asymmetric binomial is the kernel of the concept of participation as understood in the present context (researcher/researched). (p. 5)

This idea of the transformational impact of intellectual work can also be seen in the history of PAR's ideological and educational partner—critical pedagogy.

Morrell (2006) traces the roots of PAR and YPAR as an educational project to Brazilian educator Paulo Freire, who "fundamentally believed that any meaningful social transformation would only occur in conjunction with everyday people" united in a "conscious effort to disrupt or call into question this paradigm of knowledge production" (pp. 6–7). PAR had its educational roots in the Freirian tradition of adult education in Australia, New Zealand, and South America (Freire, 1982; Smith, 1999; Stringer, 1996).

YPAR, or critical participatory action research (CPAR) with youth,[3] is a more recent pedagogical project that has developed out of the tradition of critical pedagogy (Cammarota & Fine, 2008; Rodriguez & Brown, 2009; Morrell, 2004). YPAR has the same transformational goals as PAR but recognizes youth as intellectual beings capable of engaging in the practice of critical investigation of community issues and the production of viable, usable knowledge. For Cammarota and Fine (2008), "YPAR teaches young people that conditions of injustice are produced, not natural; are designed to privilege and oppress; but are ultimately challengeable and thus changeable" (p. 2). Through its epistemological foundations, YPAR challenges who has the right to produce and disseminate knowledge by placing students at the center of knowledge production. As pedagogy, YPAR has helped place knowledge production at the center of engaged teaching. Perhaps the most powerful aspect of YPAR is that it creates the conditions for young people to step back from their world and see that what they might have taken for granted is something that can be transformed (Lozenski, Casey, & McManimon, 2013). By recognizing YPAR's intention to demystify and deconstruct power structures, then transform them in order to construct a new reality, critical agency is fostered in youth who participate in this type of learning through research.

Foundations and Disciplines of YPAR

According to Creswell (2013a), PAR belongs within the *transformative framework* in qualitative inquiry, where research should "contain an action agenda for reform that may change the lives of participants, the institutions in which they live and work, or even the researchers' lives" (p. 26). He organizes qualitative research according to the "five approaches that have now stood the test of time": narrative research, phenomenology, grounded theory, ethnography, and case study, stating that he has considered others, and "participatory action research, for example, could be a sixth approach" (p. 5). Within the transformative framework, Creswell (2013b) argues that many participatory action researchers, along with critical theorists and researchers who work with marginalized communities, are informed by a *transformative worldview* that has developed since the 1980s and 90s among "individuals who felt that the postpositivist assumptions imposed structural laws and theories that did not fit marginalized individuals in our society or issues of power and social justice, discrimination, and oppression that needed to be addressed" (p. 22).

Creswell's (2013b) definition of the transformative worldview reflects many of the elements taken up by YPAR scholars, many of whom trace the origins of their work to a various parallel and/or overlapping critical theories and movements. Mirra, Garcia, and Morrell (2015)

find it instructive to consider how some of these movements expanded the range of individuals and ideas that could *participate* in research—for example, feminism (women), postcolonialism (the colonized "other"), critical race studies (communities of color), postmodernism (historicity, discursiveness, and meta-analysis), and poststructuralism (instability of the structures that guide human thought and action). (p. 17)

Furthermore, the overlap among movements in YPAR underscores the need for an intersectional lens that transcends the implicit boundaries in critical movements to address inequities with youth.

As a transformative approach to research, YPAR is of particular importance in education, where Noguera (2009) underscores the significance of YPAR by arguing that in "most research into policy and school reform initiatives, particularly in education, youth are treated as the passive objects" whose "experiences, perceptions, and aspirations" are often overlooked by those who are responsible for identifying and "fixing" educational problems (p. 18). In the past two decades, YPAR projects have positioned youth as knowers, researchers, and agents of change in areas ranging from racial injustice (Torre, 2005), educational inequality and school reform (Fine, Roberts & Torre, 2004; Rubin & Jones, 2007), and students' critical literacy experiences (Mirra, Filipiak, Garcia, 2015; Morrell, 2008), to the transformative impact of YPAR in experiential curricular approaches (Schensul & Berg, 2004).

ADDRESSING INEQUALITY AND PROMOTING JUSTICE VIA YPAR PEDAGOGY AND METHODS

As a participatory methodology, YPAR is epistemologically primarily centered in who is involved in the conception, design, implementation, analysis, dissemination, and action-based impact of research, rather than a specific set of methods that are employed. YPAR uses a vast array of qualitative and quantitative approaches, complicating reviews of literature that span disciplines. YPAR can be found in educational studies, geography, ethnic studies, social work, health, psychology, sociology, and other disciplines seeking to draw from the critical knowledges and unique positionalities of youth to unearth and imagine new perspectives. Thus, YPAR tends to saturate areas where the voices of youth have not historically been privileged.

Although in the past decade YPAR has been increasingly recognized within the academy as a legitimate epistemological framework and a necessary innovation in how research is conceptualized, it is still often seen as marginal in many disciplines. Thus, researchers who document YPAR have contributed widely to discipline-specific journals as well as those with more justice- and action-oriented missions, who are often more open to nontraditional research paradigms. Additionally, research collectives have disseminated critical findings outside of academic journals through special reports (see Voices of Youth in Chicago Education, 2011), community-based publications (Tuck & Neofotistos, 2013), and online spaces (see the Public Science Project[4]). Rather than a reflection of the research itself, this speaks to the need for those with decision-making power in education research to develop more expansive notions of the epistemological and methodological variety needed in the field.[5] We were challenged to take these complexities into account as we collected and categorized articles for this review. While we used the foundational literature to help define the field, we did not presume to be the arbiters of what counts as YPAR. Using the basic criteria of youth-led inquiry that seeks to influence the lives of youth through action, we drew from literature in which authors identified their studies as YPAR or as drawing from YPAR. Additionally, we recognize that there are methodological, ethical, social, and political "failures" in YPAR that are not reflected in the literature to the extent that they exist. We do not speculate regarding the transformative outcomes of the studies reviewed beyond what was documented by the authors.

YPAR literature demonstrates varied methodological interpretations of this epistemological construct, such that grouping the studies across discipline did not capture the convergences and divergences within the research. For instance, studies that were topically similar employed disparate methods ranging from traditional surveys and semistructured interviews to arts- and photo-based data generation strategies. There are significant and tangible differences in how YPAR is conceived and practiced. In determining the distinctions within YPAR, we observed an emergent theme across the literature: The work often morphed from its original conception, or what we call entry points. The following sections outline four distinct, yet overlapping, entry points that help explain how youth researchers and adult coresearchers/facilitators may have arrived at, or initially conceptualized, YPAR.

Entry Points for YPAR

The first entry point is through *academic learning and literacies*. Understanding that all of the learning is inherently academic, we use this terminology to address the literature that explicitly focuses on the development of traditional educational capacities in youth through exploration in specific disciplines (e.g., sciences, literacy, social studies). This literature also includes critical service learning–based approaches to YPAR. The second entry point is through *cultural and critical epistemological* research. These studies explore how youth take up cultural knowledge and heritage as epistemological frameworks. Youth draw from, and at times merge, Indigenous, Asian, African, Latinx, Feminist, and Queer knowledge systems to inform their implementation of YPAR. Here, cultural knowledge development and self-actualization become foregrounded as potential outcomes for action-based research. The next entry point is through *youth development and leadership*. The literature documenting YPAR through this lens focuses on skill development, apprenticeship, mentoring, and ways of healing and building strength in youth, often in out-of-school community spaces. The final entry point is through *youth organizing and civic engagement*. These studies foreground the impact of youth research on specific issues of focus. While the majority of texts focus on a particular issue, these studies tend to highlight the issue itself as the locus of the research. Again, research that uses one of these specific entry points may diverge in some other direction, or one of the foci of a specific entry point may be transformed or overlap with another. These are not definitive or exclusive categories, yet they reflect pathways that have informed and shaped areas of research and action in the field. A common denominator for each of the entry points is the desire of youth and adult coresearchers to transform the status quo. Whether through the development of school-based literacies or radical community civic engagement, these research collectives seek to make change at a local level, tackling major issues such as shifting curricular content, ending the carceral state, exposing rape culture, resisting gentrification, or ending compulsory heteronormativity.

Academic Learning and Literacies

As the singular focus on high stakes standardized testing and the resulting narrowed curriculum in schools continues to yield no positive results toward educational equity (Hagopian, 2014), YPAR stands as the antithesis of these problematic frameworks. As Scorza, Mirra, and Morrell (2013) suggest,

schools should be looking at [YPAR-based] programs to understand how their activities demonstrate that students learn, develop academic competencies and produce college-level work. Further, we reason that it is because of the use of critical pedagogy that students have developed these academic capabilities and that high stakes testing does not adequately assess learning, skills or competencies. (p. 31)

Academic skill building as an entry point to YPAR addresses the structural inequity that limits access to the high-level thinking skills that postsecondary institutions look for in potential students. The foundational assumptions of YPAR run opposite to the dominant logics of deficit-based evaluation and remediation of marginalized youth.

Morrell's (2004) critical ethnographic research with youth pays close attention to the impact that the process of YPAR has on the identities of his students. He suggests that as youth begin to construct identities as critical researchers, they develop activist dispositions and seek to change their environment—whether it is their neighborhood, school, or the policies by which they are governed:

> Becoming critical researchers, for them, meant becoming more agentive in the world; acting upon the world instead of merely being acted upon, oppressed. It also meant the inability to separate research from social action; for the students, there was no authentic research that was not political and conducted for the purpose of changing the world. (p. 114)

Pedagogically, YPAR positions youth as critical inhabitants of their social world; however, it is still incumbent on educators to have a deep methodological understanding of how YPAR can be further bolstered through moments of crisis. Morrell (2004, 2006, 2008) has documented the academic development of youth researchers, particularly through the lens of critical literacy, demonstrating the capabilities of high school youth to perform at academic levels traditionally reserved for postsecondary scholarship. Kinloch's (2010) critical ethnography documents youth in Harlem as they use their rapidly gentrifying neighborhood as a unit of analysis to develop critical literacy skills such as writing across genres and public speaking. Kinloch explores how YPAR enabled the youth with whom she coresearched to enhance these academic literacies:

> As Khaleeq expanded his literacy narrative during the course of our work together, writing became not only an activity that he performed at school; it became an activity that allowed him to express difficult ideas and emotions in and about the community. (p. 47)

Similarly, Stovall and Delgado (2009) explicate how YPAR facilitated a sophisticated understanding of legal studies and the criminal justice system for youth in Chicago. Using an increase in drug arrests of students near their school to frame their research, the youth developed academic competencies to make meaning of their and their peers' experiences with the legal system. Rubin (2012) highlights the overlapping relationship between the development of academic proficiencies in social studies classrooms and youth civic engagement through YPAR, as discussed below.

Expanded academic literacies through YPAR are not limited to the social sciences and humanities. Yang (2009) documents how YPAR propelled youth in a California math class to produce sophisticated quantitative analyses connected to their lived experiences:

> [Youth researchers'] ability to confidently enter uncharted territory was made possible through the transference of previously developed skills . . . (1) new academic literacy in producing descriptive statistics, analyzing distributions, and comparing means; (2) new media literacy in SPSS (Statistical Package for the Social Sciences) . . . and (3) critical code fluency in interpreting statistics with respect to the social world. (p. 111)

These transferable academic literacies become apparent across science, technology, engineering, and mathematics (STEM) disciplines, yet there remains a dearth of STEM-focused YPAR studies, which may be due to the fact that qualitative fields have embraced YPAR in ways that the physical sciences have not. Perhaps due to the lack of opportunities to publish in academic journals, or maybe to make their work more accessible, and thus actionable, STEM researchers using YPAR have documented their work in online hubs such as University of California Berkeley's YPAR Hub.[6] Due to the inherently critical nature of YPAR, it has become more prevalent in the social sciences, staying true to its roots in liberatory struggles of oppressed communities.

Cultural/Critical Epistemologies

The documentary *Precious Knowledge* (Palso, 2011) illuminated the impact of ethnic studies on the academic and social development of youth, while also exposing the lengths those invested in the status quo of educational inequity are willing to go to block structural change. While the film did not focus on YPAR specifically, it showed glimpses of the interconnection between cultural knowledge, critical epistemologies, and youth inquiry. As an entry point into YPAR, cultural knowledge provides youth with a purpose that goes deeper than acquiring skills for college. It provides a framework through which heritage and identity can be reclaimed through youth studying themselves and the contexts of their environment (Cushing-Leubner & Lozenski, in press). Irizarry (2009) provides a theoretical framework for YPAR to play a central role in critical multicultural education: "Eschewing 'melting pot' models of assimilation, multicultural education proactively seeks to affirm cultural pluralism . . . . In addition to fostering collaboration among diverse individuals, much of the content explored within YPAR reflects a commitment to promoting cross-cultural understanding" (p. 197).

True to its roots in critical research and pedagogical traditions of Central and South America, the impetus for cultural and critical epistemologies as entry points to YPAR resides within Latinx/Chicanx Studies. Romero et al. (2008), Cammarota and Romero (2009), Ayala (2009), Cahill (2010), Duncan-Andrade (2007), Torre (2009), Sanchez (2009), and Mayorga (2014) all use some form of Latinx/Chicanx Studies to provide a theoretical framing for the action research in which the youth are engaged. Romero et al. (2008) and Cammarota and Romero (2009) focus on school-based courses that combine social studies, U.S. Government, and Chicanx Studies for the dual purpose of using critical cultural knowledge to inform how youth engage in political action to gain power. These cultural and linguistic frameworks permeated the youths' research from inception to dissemination.

Ayala (2009) and Torre (2009) extend these critical cultural epistemologies by building from Gloria Anzaldúa's feminist mestiza scholarship. Both studies provide important nuances and also critiques of positioning YPAR as an all-encompassing framework for educational justice. Ayala incorporates what she describes as "border-lands consciousness" to inform the YPAR through its notions of "house[ing] multi-plicity, hybridity, conflict and collaboration, within the bodies of women of color" (p. 72). As a critical epistemology, Ayala suggests that the focus on cultural knowledge fundamentally affects how YPAR is enacted. Torre uses Anzaldúa's theorization of *nos/otras*, which represents the implication of the colonizer and the colonized in each oth-ers' lives to frame her research with youth investigating the "opportunity gap" in New York City schools.

Indigenous scholars Tuck (2009) and Johnston-Goodstar (2013) reframe YPAR through Indigenous epistemologies in the fields of education and social work, respec-tively. Tuck explores how using the vantage points of sovereignty, contention, bal-ance, and relationship, which drew from her Indigeneity, allowed her to make alternative meaning of the complexities and limitations she saw in her work with youth researching the GED system in New York. Johnston-Goodstar highlights how Indigenous conceptions of YPAR can have transformative impacts on the field of social work. These cultural entry points illustrate how the purpose and conception of the research can greatly affect the process and outcomes of YPAR.

Youth Development and Leadership

Kirshner (2015) highlights the natural overlap of YPAR and youth develop-ment. He writes, "The effort to engage youth as researchers is consistent with youth development principles that emphasize opportunities for leadership and mattering" (p. 91). An often-overlooked aspect of YPAR is the social and emotional development that occurs through the process of research, providing youth with the capacity and hope to withstand and transform inequitable educational environ-ments. Youth development is enacted in various ways from social and emotional development to placing youth in positions of organizational leadership. For Galletta and jones (2010), creating opportunities for youth to question their educational environments was a primary goal. Their study illustrates some of the important outcomes, processes—and also challenges—of establishing collaborations between college students and middle schoolers across institutions. This coresearching/men-toring framework illuminates yet another duality in YPAR. Similarly, Cahill's (2007) study investigates the ethical commitments of youth researchers as they endeavored to take on inequitable legislation preventing access to higher education for undocumented youth. Positioning youth as researchers requires developing their ethical sensibility with regard to the historical and continuing problematic practices of researchers in communities. Similarly, Kirshner, Pozzoboni, and Jones (2011) explicate their work understanding bias with youth researchers. This study examines how bias manifests as both motivating and obfuscating ways for youth as they work with data that disconfirms previous predictions. Like Cahill's study, this meta-analysis of how YPAR affects youths' perceptions of the work they are doing speaks to the social and cognitive developmental aspects of the research.

Flicker, Maley, Ridgeley, and Skinner (2008) explore a digital YPAR methodology they call e-PAR where youth researchers across seven youth-serving organizations participated in a project investigating holistic health in young people, emphasizing how youth conceptualized the ways in which "self-esteem, self-efficacy, and civic engagement" influenced their perceptions of "better futures" leading to healthier life choices. Payne, Starks, and Gibson (2009) illuminate Black male youths' self-perceptions of "street life" as a response to inadequate educational conditions. They argue that "allowing the phenomenological perspectives of the boys to drive or guide the analysis is an approach that would inform interventions designed to reach them" (p. 48). Many of the studies focusing on youth development came to similar conclusions, suggesting that youth researchers with sophisticated understandings of their social world are well positioned to inform the developmental interventions targeted at them.

Youth Organizing and Civic Engagement

Understanding education as a contested space, structural discrimination and violence through the intersections of race, ethnicity, class, language, gender, and sexual/gender identity have continued to define the experiences of marginalized youth. From school closings, to language rights, to gendered bathrooms, youth have been at the forefront of many of these contentious issues. YPAR has provided a pathway for youth to gain useful organizing skills and provide pertinent data for issue-based campaigns to influence decision-makers. Written collaboratively with youth researchers, Tuck et al. (2008) epitomize youth organizing and civic engagement as entry points into YPAR. Outlining the development of their theoretical framing and research design, the authors share their praxes:

We would not be researchers without an inherent commitment to action toward the relief of social injustice, especially in education. We would not be researchers without an inherent commitment to participation, dissolving the traditional researcher–subject hierarchy. (p. 63)

While much of the literature focuses on the impacts of YPAR on youth researchers themselves, youth engaged in YPAR have also been able to effectively influence policy and practice on a local scale. Yonezawa and Jones (2009) document the direct impact of youth researchers' findings at multiple schools in San Diego: After a student coresearcher team's presentation, a principal reported, "The faculty identified three main areas of needed growth for their . . . accreditation visit in parallel to concerns the [team] raised regarding student apathy and how the school's structure and culture acts as a mediator" (p. 209). Youth in McIntyre's (2000) study created school-community cleanup projects and career exploration programs as a result of their research. These smaller scale impacts provide youth with a sense of their power to effect change while also demonstrating to educators that they may be underestimating the analytical capacity of their students. However, as Fox and Fine (2015) articulate, possibly the most powerful impact of YPAR is that it spreads seeds of change that inspire more action-based research:

> Most significantly, several research projects based out of the Public Science Project at the CUNY Graduate Center picked up where [Polling for Justice] (a YPAR project) left off, including two studies on policing and community safety: the Morris Justice Project and Researchers for Fair Policing; and a study looking at the school discipline experiences for high school students identifying as LGBTQ. (p. 56)

These rhizomatic characteristics of youth research were evident across the research as YPAR collectives again and again produced small-scale impacts that contributed to prolonged struggles that may produce larger scale impacts, over time.

YPAR Methods and Pedagogies

Situating YPAR only as an epistemological construct with various entry points to implementation paints a partial picture of the field. YPAR contains inherent pedagogical elements, as there is almost always an adult coresearcher/facilitator working alongside novice researchers. Using YPAR as a lens for teaching qualitative and quantitative research blurs boundaries between research and action, and research and teaching, and encourages a critical broadening of conventional conceptions of rigor, positionality, and pedagogy. It is through this duality of research and pedagogy that the transformative potential of YPAR to address educational inequity is realized. According to Freire (1982),

> instead of taking the people here as the object of my research, I must try, on the contrary, to have the people dialogically involved also as subjects, as researchers with me. . . This method of investigation . . . is at the same time a learning process . . . . Thus, in doing research, I am educating and being educated with the people. (p. 30)

The inherent fluidity between teaching, learning, and coresearching in YPAR emerged as another organizing theme in the literature. The interrelatedness of YPAR epistemology, methodology, and pedagogy is conducive to understanding the interpretive and recursive nature of qualitative research. According to Zaal and Terry (2013), "YPAR has significant epistemological effects on students: that is, an increased knowledge and awareness of what they can do and who they can be in the research process and in their communities" (p. 52). They claim, based on their research findings, that the cycles of YPAR allow youth "to engage in research, to act and educate others about their findings, and to receive feedback from teachers, their peers, and other audiences" (p. 52). Similarly, several studies highlighted how the pedagogical environment of the research informed the study. It is important to note that as students moved from novice to more experienced researchers, and took on increasing responsibilities as cofacilitators and creators of the space, the pedagogical environment was shaped by their choices and perspectives. As we attempted to understand the ways in which these pedagogies and environments affected the research, four aspects emerged from the literature that made certain studies distinct in how YPAR was practiced and the outcomes they were able to produce.

The first aspect was the *environment* in which the research was implemented. As a pedagogical practice, YPAR can be situated in school spaces as well as out of school in community centers or alternative educational environments. These environments influence the conception, purpose, time constraints, and resources available for YPAR. For instance, school-based research often focused on school-based issues (Galletta & jones, 2010; Livingstone, Celemencki, & Calixte, 2014; Rubin & Jones, 2007; Schultz, 2008), whereas out-of-school research often dealt with larger societal issues (Fine, Tuck, & Zeller-Berkman, 2008; Fox et al., 2010; Torre & Fine, 2008). The second aspect was the *configuration* of the participatory collective. By definition, YPAR is youth-driven, but the degree to which the collective was intergenerational played a role in how the research was conceptualized and implemented. Torre and Fine (2008) illuminate the impact of configurations as they theorize PAR collectives as "contact zones," where differently positioned youth and adults grapple with contested ideas.

Third, the pedagogical and research-based emphases often coalesced around *critical multiliteracies*, including digital literacies (Jocson, 2014; Kamler & Comber, 2005; Mayorga, 2014; Morrell, 2006). Drawing on the background knowledge and literate identities of youth, these studies highlight the value of critically engaging students around relevant interests and cultural ways of knowing. These studies also discuss shifts in teachers' perception of students once they reworked their literacy curriculum to include relevant technology, media, and popular culture (Kamler & Comber, 2005). As youth are challenged to create and disseminate knowledge, they often take up innovative and accessible modes through which to generate and analyze data, as well as disseminate their work and take action. These innovations manifest in the last aspect we explore, *performance as action*.

We found pedagogical and research-based engagement to revolve around performance as action throughout a subset of the literature (Fine, Roberts, & Torre, 2004; Cahill, 2010; Mirra, Filipiak, & Garcia, 2015). On a fundamental level, YPAR scholars have used art for outreach as a powerful medium to provoke public awareness and action. But the use of performance through theater, visual art, music, poetry, and spoken word also helps researchers to make sense of social issues through ways of knowing that they would not otherwise be able to articulate (Cahill, 2010; M. T. Winn & Ubiles, 2011). Acknowledging that the aims of social justice are not just about political change, these researchers foreground the value of psychic and emotional healing made necessary by social and educational injustices in their schools and communities (M. T. Winn & Ubiles, 2011). Regarding the arts as inherently critical, studies featuring performance as action assert performance as a critical medium for both healing and revelation, extending the research process in powerful ways.

YPAR AS EDUCATION RESEARCH: CONTRIBUTIONS, TENSIONS, AND POSSIBILITIES

Assuming that "only an empowered, engaged and literate citizenry can form the foundation of an equitable and inclusive society" (Morrell, 2006, p. 1), YPAR challenges education researchers to engage in a "conscious effort to disrupt or call into question" a mainstream "paradigm of knowledge production" (p. 7). In this section, we highlight major areas of education research to which YPAR scholarship offers long-standing contributions and implications. We end with a discussion of some of the tensions and challenges encountered by the researchers who engage in this work, as reflections on praxis that serve as a point of departure for future possibilities in the field.

Critical Qualitative Research

As a methodology centered on inquiries designed, conducted, reported, and acted on by those who are closest to the issue of interest, YPAR is especially significant for historically marginalized populations whose experiences, identities, and literacies are frequently overlooked in mainstream educational environments. Scholars argue that "the tradition of inquiry for advocacy is as old as the tradition of inquiry itself. This is important to keep in mind amid contemporary conversations about quality, validity, and rigor in social scientific research" (Morrell, 2006, p. 6). According to Fine (2008), "YPAR done well deepens the very social practices of objectivity, validity, and generalizability" (p. 222) because youth and adult researchers engage in difficult conversations about their assumptions, deepen validity and expertise via "intentional and sustained deliberative processes" (p. 224), reconsider the validity of constructs, and push their findings beyond understanding what is to imagining what could be.

In addition, since the postmodern turn, as qualitative researchers grapple with the complexities of representation and positionality in research (Denzin, 1994), particularly with marginalized populations, YPAR can disrupt the traditional induction of new generations of qualitative researchers. An emergent debate considers how to teach qualitative research critically, "as involving a set of transgressive practices that sustain and realize critical perspectives" (Hsiung, 2016, p. 60). Using YPAR as a lens for teaching qualitative research blurs boundaries between research and action and encourages a critical broadening of conventional conceptions of pedagogy, rigor, and positionality. In 11 years of work with the Council of Youth Research, Mirra, Garcia, and Morrell (2015) demonstrate that rigorous activist research is nurtured by researchers' personal commitments to justice:

Critical research opens up possibilities for new innovations that continue to honor the curiosity, hope, and potential of young people. This has been an exhilarating professional journey for us, but much more importantly, a deeply personal one as well. (p. xii)

In this sense, approaches such as Souto-Manning's (2014) critical narrative analysis, which challenges youth and adult researchers to "analyz[e] narratives in the lifeworld–the everyday stories individuals tell" as they deconstruct the discourses in them, nurtures a critical meta-awareness of the self in relation to society (p. 205). YPAR invites such critical approaches, contributing to the theory and practice of decolonizing inquiry and humanizing qualitative research (Paris & Winn, 2014).

Curriculum, Pedagogy, and Education Reform

YPAR has made significant contributions to critical research and reform in education in a wide variety of ways and in multiple educational contexts. However, one overarching element in all of these major contributions is the presence and participation of youth in education debates that have been historically waged between and among scholars, researchers, and practitioners with little to no input from students, particularly in the areas of school reform (Kelly, 1993; Noguera, 2007) and education policy (Bertrand & Ford, 2015), where YPAR has yielded actionable results.

Beyond the direct physical and intellectual participation of youth in education reform, YPAR has catalyzed rethinking and reframing of students' academic experiences and the identities that they construct in and beyond school, as well as conceptualizations of curriculum and pedagogy. Recent studies document the transformative impact of youth research in students' literacy experiences (Morrell, 2008) and college readiness (Knight & Marciano, 2013), as well as in experiential curricular approaches (Wright, 2015). Integrating YPAR in the curriculum incorporates student voice in academic contexts (Cook-Sather, 2009) leading to the rethinking of curriculum and pedagogy in ways that support the learning of minoritized students. Within a YPAR third space, youth construct and negotiate critical literacies and identities (Caraballo & Hill, 2014) as they complicate existing structures and hierarchies such as those connected to the role of "learner" and "educator" in academic and institutional contexts (Cook-Sather, 2009). Caraballo (2016) notes, "Participatory approaches can bear an integral role in the reconceptualization of curriculum as an assemblage of the many literacies, discourses, and interests, whether individual, cultural, or institutional, that are continuously negotiated in any academic discipline" (p. 20).

Gutiérrez (2008) argues that the sociocritical literacy concept of third space is also a "transformative space where the potential for an expanded form of learning and the development of new knowledge are heightened" (p. 152). The collective third space that YPAR offers youth is not adult-centered scaffolding, but a space where curriculum and pedagogy are "grounded in the historical and current particulars of students' everyday lives" toward becoming "conscious 'historical actors' (Espinoza, 2003) who invoke the past in order to remediate it so that it becomes a resource for current and future action" (Gutiérrez, 2008, p. 154). YPAR third spaces can foster skills and agency development in collaborations, sometimes carefully designed to undo much of what traditional schooling perpetuates (Paris & Winn, 2014).

Teacher Education

Beyond its impact in youths' experiences, teachers' participation in YPAR offers the opportunity to broaden their understanding of curriculum and pedagogy for historically marginalized populations, whose rich experiences, identities, and literacies are often excluded from traditional and standardized curricular and pedagogical approaches. Through this pedagogical framing, YPAR as a critical epistemology encompassing various teaching methods illuminates the merging of teaching and research as an interwoven practice. Research on the role of fieldwork in the preparation of preservice teachers to work in racially and socioeconomically diverse contexts suggests that justice-oriented and community-based field experiences can have a positive impact on preservice teachers' multicultural awareness and beliefs (Akiba, 2011; Brayko, 2013; Whipp, 2013). For example, Morrell and Collatos's (2002) research with high school youth and preservice teachers in Los Angeles demonstrated the potential for authentic communities of practice where preservice teachers and urban students can forge relationships as coparticipants (p. 68). Educators who have led YPAR projects during their teacher preparation and doctoral programs have contributed powerful scholarship that is grounded in their experiences with youth researchers in academic and community contexts (Morrell, Duenas, Garcia & Lopez, 2013).

YPAR can inform areas of study that seek to broaden conceptualizations of teaching and learning in teacher education, such as practitioner research (Cochran-Smith & Lytle, 2009), multicultural fieldwork experiences (Brayko, 2013; Whipp, 2013), and the interrelatedness of students' and teachers' experiences of curriculum, identities, and literacies (Caraballo, 2016; Luttrell & Parker, 2001). Building on these alternative critical approaches and previous research, YPAR can position teachers, students, and communities as agents of social change (Fine, Roberts, & Torre, 2004; Morrell, 2008) to disrupt inequality and dismantle hierarchies among cultural and experiential knowledge(s) and "official" or disciplinary knowledge(s).

Youth Studies

As the field of youth studies continues to ask critically reflexive questions about the practices, imaginings, and possibilities of studying youth (Lesko & Talburt, 2011), YPAR offers unique opportunities for an emic understanding of youth engagement, desires, frustrations, and abilities in contexts where their voices are usually underregarded. According to Morrell (2004),

although they are the population with the most at stake in schools, youth are rarely engaged in conversations about the conditions of schools or school reform. . . Simply put, youth do not often participate as researchers or experts in dialogues concerning the present and future of urban education. (p. 156)

In the face of this, Morrell's (2004) YPAR work apprenticed youth as critical researchers of popular culture, where educators undertook the interests of students (i.e., popular culture) as valid sites of interrogation replete with value.

In centering youth interests (Morrell, 2004; Kamler, & Comber, 2005), arming students with the tools for critical inquiry (Fine et al., 2008; Fox et al., 2010), and asking them to speak (Flicker et al., 2008; Livingstone et al., 2014), YPAR offers the field of youth studies cases where youth interests, perspectives, and identities are seriously engaged as assets to their learning and social transformation. For example, the YPAR work of Fox et al. (2010) led the collective toward a theory of method for youth engagement, where they assert the importance of recognizing the knowledge and expertise carried by youth, and that the privileging of this knowledge and expertise offers more varied outcomes of academic, social, psychological, and political well-being. They argue that youth and adults can engage in serious inquiry where "emphasizing youth leadership, in partnership with adults, frames youth themselves as assets and actors, contributing to growth and change in adults, institutions, systems, communities and society" (Fox et al., 2010, p. 634).

Tensions and Challenges of/in YPAR

While virtually all YPAR studies and analyses begin or end with the assertion that youth develop critically, intellectually, and socially as a result of their participation, the process is not unproblematic. YPAR scholarship raises important challenges and tensions that emerge as youth and adult researchers engaged in transformative work. While YPAR

is positioned as a new(er) hope for socially relevant, hierarchy-disrupting, counter-hegemonic research . . . there are splits that we all contend with in doing this work; splits . . . between its hope or promise, and its potential for social reproduction and co-optation. (Ayala, 2009, p. 67)

In their study of a multiyear YPAR project across peer mentoring programs in five California public schools, Ozer, Newlan, Douglas, and Hubbard (2013) studied tensions in program implementation. Although youth "manage[d] to experience meaningful power despite constraints," Ozer et al.'s codes for the data they collected serves as a summary of the kinds of challenges faced by YPAR coresearchers (p. 24). Examples of challenges include projects co-opted by mandates, lack of continuity, internal politics, practical barriers such as scheduling, conflicting values among facilitators, and administrators' lack of recognition for teachers' efforts in participatory work—examples of some typical challenges to YPAR in school settings.

The tensions and challenges raised by those who work with youth in afterschool or community spaces are also situated and contextual, and usually related to the complexity of adjusting to new roles and relationships with/in institutions and communities (Irizarry, 2009). For example, reflecting on their participation in two distinct YPAR projects, L. T. Winn and Winn (2016) grappled with the "complexities and tensions" of engaging in YPAR with youth who are usually confined to a curriculum with less opportunity for creativity and critical discussion:

Although we understood YPAR as a process of becoming engaged civic actors for young people, we did not expect to be so central to the projects for so long as we hoped that the work would, indeed, be "owned" by youth. (L. T. Winn & Winn, 2016, p. 128)

Many adult facilitators express similar concerns about the degree to which they should provide instruction, guidance, and framing, particularly in light of the usual constraints of time and resources that could shorten or restrict the scope of a YPAR inquiry (Galletta & jones, 2010).

Like L. T. Winn and Winn (2016), many facilitators experience tensions with respect to "when and where to enter, as well as exit" and perhaps also how to do so:

> In our efforts to decolonize research methods and practices, we lost sight of the fact that some youth might benefit from purposeful scaffolding such as "guided participation" in YPAR to get to the phase where youth take ownership of the process and, when relevant, the product(s). (p. 128)

Similarly, Caraballo and Lyiscott (2016) discuss the need to initiate youth into collaborative inquiry, "deschooling," in a sense, in order to create a more democratic context for critical participation. They also highlight the logistical constraints of their afterschool YPAR seminar, where facilitators needed to protect the urgency of the YPAR projects while negotiating schedule changes related to preparation for tests, service hours, and as others have noted, other conflicts with seminar meeting times (Schensul & Berg, 2004).

More powerful than the tensions themselves, however, is the legacy of praxis in YPAR. Scholars and their youth collaborators frequently demonstrate the capacity and desire to engage in critical reflection and work through relational struggles (Tuck et al., 2008). Scholars convey these "experiences with YPAR projects and a purposeful reflection of this work, hoping to build capacity for adult allies of youth" (L. T. Winn & Winn, 2016, p. 112).

History has taught us that such research practices and methods, framed as liberatory interventions with the power to support meaningful social and political change, often lose their radical capacity as they are co-opted or absorbed into the mainstream. This concern has been argued for the work of multiculturalism, action research, participatory research, culturally relevant pedagogy, and other frameworks offered as transformative until they were moved from the margins to the center (Casey, 2010). Given the cyclical nature of transformative/mainstream work, we push the critical-epistemological call of YPAR as a *stance* for future possibilities. That is, while the methodological tools of intervention will inevitably change with time and space, we assert the urgency of sustaining critical orientations in this work, even as new methods might one day emerge from the ashes of YPAR.

TOWARD CRITICAL EPISTEMOLOGIES IN TEACHING, RESEARCH, AND SOCIAL ACTION IN EDUCATION

YPAR, like PAR, represents "a new paradigm, a challenge to existing epistemologies, and, thereby, a competing (or complementary) entry into the political economy of knowledge production" (Noffke, 1997, p. 307). Through an analysis of how youth and their adult collaborators have conducted inquiries, created knowledge, and enacted change via performance, protest, lobbying, social media, and many other forms, our chapter documents the impact of YPAR on education research in almost two decades. Considering the role and impact of YPAR as epistemology, methodology, and pedagogy contributes to efforts that problematize orthodox research and teaching practices and asserts antihegemonic knowledges in education. Grounded in its catalytic nature, we propose that a YPAR critical-epistemological approach leads to the coconstruction of critical knowledges that can, in turn, reframe the question of what counts as knowledge and research, and what constitutes action, in education research and scholarship. Such a critical-epistemological framework must be grounded in the contexts of inequality in which it is to be employed, and developed in juxtaposition to the theoretical and methodological shifts of our time.

In their critical coconstructed autoethnography, DeMeulenaere and Cann (2013) frame their thinking about qualitative research according to three dimensions: *ideological*, or research that "attempts to challenge or disrupt ideology"; *material*, "the degree to which a project results in material change for participants"; and *scale*, how many people are affected by this work (p. 558). Their goal is not to measure research, "but rather to offer a heuristic for reflection" in response to critical theorists, critical pedagogues, and critical race theorists who have long called for an engagement in a praxis that incorporates activist work with ongoing reflection (p. 561). Similarly, we argue for YPAR frameworks that are centered in decolonizing research methodologies (Paris & Winn, 2014; Smith, 1999; Tuck & Yang, 2012) and activist research traditions that support youth's critical meta-awareness of the inequalities that shape their educational experiences (Souto-Manning, 2014).

In addition, a critical-epistemological framework challenges all who collaborate in YPAR inquiries to theorize about what counts as social action and agency in current contexts of inequality. In their YPAR work with high school youth, Mirra, Filipiak, and Garcia (2015) define agency as

the power [derived] from the pursuit of those questions that matter most to students. It is what fuels action. . . . It is contextually bound, always in negotiation, and mediated by the histories, social interactions, and cultures that young people's identities are entangled within"; they frame agency "as a capacity to imagine and act upon the world. (p. 53)

In a 2009 issue on YPAR in *New Directions for Youth Development*, guest editors Rodriguez and Brown also stress the importance of "oppressed peoples' interrogating and intervening into the conditions of their own oppression" (p. 1), where interrogation (research) and intervention (action) are inextricably connected, regardless of the extent of the action in question. Bigelow (2002) suggests that even small actions and victories can combat the despair connected to feeling overwhelmed by the enormity of many social issues.

Nonetheless, those of us engaged in YPAR wonder what "counts" as action, and scholars have attempted to codify action in the context of action research.[7] Coulter (2011) traces Arendt's retheorization of Aristotle's and Marx's depictions of human action, and suggests that "Arendtian action research instead aims at better understanding experience, creating consistency (however limited), generating knowledge and understanding (which will always be in some ways inadequate). Such research aims at helping people make better sense of their lives" (p. 203). As such, his Arendtian notion of action research encapsulates Freire's (1970) argument for praxis, which combines reflection and action: "If action is emphasized exclusively to the detriment of reflection, the word is converted into activism. The latter—action for action's sake—negates the true praxis and makes dialogue impossible" (p. 88). In the context of a critical-epistemological YPAR framework, the action implicit in youths' self-transformation and knowledge production bears promise for large-scale social transformation.

In order to disrupt inequality, education researchers must continue to explore alternative research (and action) paradigms that actively seek to redistribute methodological and analytical power to those who hold an intimate knowledge of the struggles of navigating systemic oppression. Without a legitimate consideration of what YPAR offers to the landscape of education research, we may continue to base our accounts of inequality on those with the most access, the most privilege, and the least to lose from the maintenance of the status quo.

NOTES

[1]The term *youth* often refers to an age range of 15 to 24 years, although the "definition of youth perhaps changes with circumstances, especially with the changes in demographic, financial, economic and socio-cultural settings" (United Nations' "Definition of Youth"; www.un.org/esa/socdev/documents/youth/fact-sheets/youth-definition.pdf). YPAR scholarship in education encompasses work with youth within a wider age range, inclusive of elementary school age through undergraduates in college.

[2]Excluding citations.

[3]We use YPAR and CPAR with youth interchangeably. CPAR is used in social science research and critical psychology to distinguish it from forms of PAR that do not center inequitable distributions of power.

[4]http://publicscienceproject.org/

[5]The recognition of participatory research as part of the research and scholarship agendas of tenure track faculty is of particular importance (Fine, 2008), as well as how such research is categorized and evaluated by tenure and promotion committees within and across institutions (Doberneck, Glass, & Schweitzer, 2010).

[6]http://yparhub.berkeley.edu/

[7]This debate takes place in various areas of YPAR research and scholarship; for example, while YPAR work is codeveloped and enacted with youth who often also feature as coauthors in YPAR scholarship, many of the articles that report on this work are still authored primarily by academics. As discussed above, it is our hope that the critical epistemological shifts that YPAR demands will continue to permeate academic structures and encourage more prevalent coauthorship with youth and community partners.

REFERENCES

Akiba, M. (2011). Identifying program characteristics for preparing pre-service teachers for diversity. *Teachers College Record, 113*, 658–697.

Arthur, J., Waring, M., Coe, R., & Hedges, L. V. (2012). *Research methods and methodologies in education*. Thousand Oaks, CA: SAGE.

Ayala, J. (2009). Split scenes, converging visions: The ethical terrains where PAR and border-lands scholarship meet. *The Urban Review, 41*, 66–84.

Bargal, D. (2006). Personal and intellectual influences leading to Lewin's paradigm of action research. *Action Research, 4*, 367–388.

Bergold, J., & Thomas, S. (2012). Participatory research methods: A methodological approach in motion. *Forum: Qualitative Social Research, 13*(1), 1–24.

Bertrand, M., & Ford, A. J. (2015). Planting the seeds: The influence of the council on education policy and practice. *Teachers College Record, 117*, 189–202.

Bigelow, B. (2002). Defeating despair. *Rethinking Schools, Spring*, 1–4.

Bogdan, R., & Biklen, S. (2007). *Qualitative research for education: An introduction to theory and practice* (5th ed.). Upper Saddle River, NJ: Prentice Hall.

Brayko, K. (2013). Community-based placements as contexts for disciplinary learning: A study of literacy teacher education outside of school. *Journal of Teacher Education, 64*, 47–59.

Cahill, C. (2007). Repositioning ethical commitments: Participatory action research as a relational praxis of social change. *ACME: An International E-Journal for Critical Geographies, 6*, 360–373.

Cahill, C. (2010). "Why do they hate us?" Reframing immigration through participatory action research. *Area, 42*, 152–161.

Cammarota, J., & Fine, M. (Eds.). (2008). *Revolutionizing education: Youth participatory action research in motion*. New York, NY: Routledge.

Cammarota, J., & Romero, A. (2009). A social justice epistemology and pedagogy for Latina/o students: Transforming public education with participatory action research. *New Directions for Youth Development, 2009*(123), 53–69.

Caraballo, L. (2016). Multiple identities and literacies in a figured world of achievement: Toward a framework for culturally sustaining curriculum and pedagogy. *Urban Education*. Advanced online publication. doi:10.1177/0042085915623344

Caraballo, L., & Hill, M. (2014). Curriculum-in-action: Cultivating literacy, community, and creativity in urban contexts. *English Leadership Quarterly, 37*, 5–11.

Caraballo, L., & Lyiscott, J. (2016). *Collaborative inquiry: Youth, social action, and critical qualitative research*. Manuscript submitted for publication.

Casey, Z. A. (2010). Remembering to be radical in teacher education: Defanged multicultural education. *Journal of Multiculturalism in Education, 6*(1), 1–19.

Cochran-Smith, M., & Lytle, S. (Eds.). (2009). *Inquiry as stance: Practitioner research for the next generation*. New York, NY: Teachers College Press.

Collier, J. (1945). United States Indian administration as a laboratory of ethnic relations. *Social Research, 12*, 265–303.

Cook-Sather, A. (2009). "I am not afraid to listen": Prospective teachers learning from students. *Theory Into Practice, 48*, 176–183.

Coulter, D. (2011). What counts as action in educational action research? *Educational Action Research, 10*, 189–206.

Creswell, J. (2013a). *Qualitative inquiry and design: Choosing among five approaches* (3rd ed.). Thousand Oaks, CA: SAGE.

Creswell, J. (2013b). *Research design: Qualitative, quantitative, and mixed methods approaches* (4th ed.). Thousand Oaks, CA: SAGE.

Cushing-Leubner, J., & Lozenski, B. D. (in press). "I'm in the ocean! I'm in the ocean!!" Standing with youth at the waters of heritage literacy. In K. Schmitz & N. Grant (Eds.), *Radical youth pedagogy: Flipping the culture of the classroom*. New York, NY: Peter Lang.

DeMeulenaere, E. J., & Cann, C. N. (2013). Activist educational research. *Qualitative Inquiry, 19*, 552–565.

Denzin, N. (1994). Evaluating qualitative research in the poststructural moment: The lessons James Joyce teaches us. *International Journal of Qualitative Studies in Education, 7,* 295–308.

Doberneck, D. M., Glass, C. R., & Schweitzer, J. (2010). From rhetoric to reality: A typology of publically engaged scholarship. *Journal of Higher Education Outreach and Engagement, 14*(4), 5–36.

Duncan-Andrade, J. M. (2007). Urban youth and the counter-narration of inequality. *Transforming Anthropology, 15*(1), 26–37.

Fals-Borda, O., & Rahman, M. A. (Eds.). (1991). *Action and knowledge: Breaking the monopoly with participatory action-research.* New York, NY: Apex Press.

Fine, M. (2008). An epilogue, of sorts. In J. Cammarota, & M. Fine (Eds.), *Revolutionizing education: Youth participatory action research in motion* (pp. 213–234). New York, NY: Routledge.

Fine, M., Roberts, R. A., & Torre, M. E. (2004). *Echoes of Brown: Youth documenting and performing the legacy of Brown V. Board of Education.* New York, NY: Teachers College Press.

Fine, M., Torre, M. E., Boudin, K., Bowen, I., Clark, J., Hylton, D., . . . Upegui, D. (2004). Participatory action research: From within and beyond prison bars. In L. Weis, & M. Fine (Eds.), *Working method: Research and social justice* (pp. 95–120). New York, NY: Routledge.

Fine, M., Tuck, E., & Zeller-Berkman, S. (2008). Do you believe in Geneva? Methods and ethics at the global local nexus. In N. Denzin, Y. Lincoln, & L. T. Smith (Eds.), *Handbook of critical and Indigenous methodologies* (Reprinted ed., pp. 157–180). Thousand Oaks, CA: SAGE.

Flicker, S., Maley, O., Ridgeley, A., & Skinner, H. (2008). e-PAR: Using technology and participatory action research to engage youth in health promotion. *Action Research, 6,* 285–303.

Fox, M., & Fine, M. (2015). Leadership in solidarity: Notions of leadership through critical participatory action research with young people and adults. *New Directions for Student Leadership, 2015,* 45–58.

Fox, M., Mediratta, K., Ruglis, J., Stoudt, B., Shah, S., & Fine, M. (2010). Critical youth engagement: Participatory action research and organizing. In L. Sherrod, J. Torney-Puta, & C. Flanagan (Eds.), *Handbook of research and policy on civic engagement with youth* (pp. 621–650). Hoboken, NJ: Wiley.

Freire, P. (1970). *Pedagogy of the oppressed.* New York, NY: Continuum International.

Freire, P. (1982). Creating alternative research methods. In B. Hall, A. Gillette, & R. Tandon (Eds.), *Creating knowledge: A monopoly? Participatory research in development* (pp. 29–37). New Delhi, India: Participatory Research Network.

Galletta, A., & jones, v. (2010). "Why are you doing this?" Questions on purpose, structure, and outcomes in participatory action research engaging youth and teacher candidates. *Educational Studies, 46,* 337–357.

Gutiérrez, K. D. (2008). Developing a sociocritical literacy in the third space. *Reading Research Quarterly, 43,* 148–164.

Hale, C. R. (Ed.). (2008). *Engaging contradictions: Theory, politics, and methods of activist scholarship.* Los Angeles: University of California Press.

Hagopian, J. (Ed.). (2014). *More than a score: The new uprising against high-stakes testing.* Chicago, IL: Haymarket Books.

Hsiung, P. C. (2016). Teaching qualitative research as transgressive practices: Introduction to the special issue. *Qualitative Inquiry, 22*(2), 59–71.

Irizarry, J. (2009). Reinvigorating multicultural education through youth participatory action research. *Multicultural Perspectives, 11,* 194–199.

Isenhart, M., & Jurow, A. S. (2011). Teaching qualitative research. In N. K. Denzin, & Y. K. Lincoln (Eds.), *The SAGE handbook of qualitative research* (pp. 699–714). Thousand Oaks, CA: SAGE.

Jocson, K. (2014). Critical media ethnography: Researching youth media. In D. Paris, & M. T. Winn (Eds.), *Humanizing research: Decolonizing qualitative inquiry with youth and communities* (p. 105–123). Thousand Oaks, CA: SAGE.

Johnston-Goodstar, K. (2013). Indigenous youth participatory action research: Re-visioning social justice for social work with indigenous youths. *Social Work, 58*, 314–320.

Kamler, B., & Comber, B. (2005). Designing turn-around pedagogies and contesting deficit assumptions. In B. Comber, & B. Kamler (Eds.), *Turn-around pedagogies: Literacy interventions for at-risk students* (pp. 1–13). Newtown, New South Wales, Australia: Primary English Teaching Association.

Kelly, D. M. (1993). Secondary power source: High school students as participatory researchers. *The American Sociologist, 24*, 8–26.

Kinloch, V. F. (2010). *Harlem on our minds: Place, race, and the literacies of urban youth.* New York, NY: Teachers College Press.

Kirshner, B. (2015). *Youth activism in an era of education inequality.* New York: New York University Press.

Kirshner, B., Pozzoboni, K., & Jones, H. (2011). Learning how to manage bias: A case study of youth participatory action research. *Applied Developmental Science, 15*, 140–155.

Knight, M. G., & Marciano, J. E. (2013). *College ready: Preparing Black and Latina/o youth for higher education, a culturally relevant approach.* New York, NY: Teacher College Press.

Lesko, N., & Talburt, S. (2011). *Youth studies: Keywords and movement.* New York, NY: Routledge.

Livingstone, A. M., Celemencki, J., & Calixte, M. (2014). Youth participatory action research and school improvement: The missing voices of black youth in Montreal. *Canadian Journal of Education, 37*(1), 283–307.

Lozenski, B. D., Casey, Z. A., & McManimon, S. K. (2013). Contesting production: Youth participatory action research in the struggle to produce knowledge. *Cultural Logic: Marxist Theory & Practice, 2013*, 80–95.

Luttrell, W., & Parker, C. (2001). High school students' literacy practices and identities, and the figured world of school. *Journal of Research in Reading, 24*, 235–247.

Mayorga, E. (2014). Toward digital, critical, participatory action research: Lessons from the #BarrioEdProj. *Journal of Interactive Technology and Pedagogy, June*. Retrieved from http://jitp.commons.gc.cuny.edu/toward-digital-critical-participatory-action-research/

McIntyre, A. (2000). Constructing meaning about violence, school, and community: Participatory action research with urban youth. *The Urban Review, 32*, 123–154.

Mirra, N., Filipiak, D., & Garcia, A. (2015). Revolutionizing inquiry in urban English classrooms: Pursuing voice and justice through youth participatory action research. *English Journal, 105*(2), 49–57.

Mirra, N., Garcia, A., & Morrell, N. (2015). *Doing youth participatory action research: Transforming inquiry with researchers, educators, and students.* New York, NY: Routledge.

Miskovic, M., & Hoop, K. (2006). Action research meets critical pedagogy theory, practice, and reflection. *Qualitative Inquiry, 12*, 269–291.

Morrell, E. (2004). *Becoming critical researchers: Literacy and empowerment of urban youth.* New York, NY: Peter Lang.

Morrell, E. (2006). Critical participatory action research and the literacy achievement of ethnic minority groups. In J. V. Hoffman, D. L. Schallert, C. M. Fairbanks, J. Worthy, & B. Maloda (Eds.), *55th Yearbook of the National Reading Conference* (pp. 1–18). Oak Creek, WI: National Reading Conference.

Morrell, E. (2008). Six summers of YPAR: Learning, action, and change in urban education. In J. Cammarota, & M. Fine (Eds.), *Revolutionizing education: Youth participatory action research in motion* (pp. 155–187). New York, NY: Routledge.

Morrell, E., & Collatos, A. (2002). Toward a critical teacher education: High school student sociologists as teacher educators. *Social Justice, 29*(4), 60–70.

Morrell, E., Duenas, R., Gárcia, V., & Lopez, J. (2013). *Critical media pedagogy: Teaching for achievement in city schools.* New York, NY: Teachers College Press.

Morrow, R. A., & Torres, C. A. (1995). *Social theory and education: A critique of theories of social and cultural reproduction.* Albany: State University of New York Press.

Nabudere, D. W. (2008). Research, activism, and knowledge production. In C. Hale (Ed.), *Engaging contradictions: Theory, politics, and methods of activist scholarship* (pp. 62–87). Los Angeles: University of California Press.

Neilsen, E. (2006). But let us not forget John Collier. *Action Research, 4,* 389–399.

Noffke, S. E. (1997). Professional, personal, and political dimensions of action research. *Review of Research in Education, 22,* 305–343.

Noguera, P. A. (2007). How listening to students can help schools to improve. *Theory Into Practice, 46,* 205–211.

Noguera, P. A. (2009). Foreword. *New Directions for Youth Development, 2009*(123), 15–18.

Ozer, E. J., Newlan, S., Douglas, L., & Hubbard, E. (2013). "Bounded" empowerment: Analyzing tensions in the practice of youth-led participatory research in urban public schools. *American Journal of Community Psychology, 52*(1–2), 13–26.

Palso, A. (Director). (2011). *Precious knowledge* [Motion picture]. United States: Dos Vatos Productions.

Paris, D., & Winn, M. T. (Eds.). (2014). *Humanizing research: Decolonizing qualitative inquiry with youth and communities.* Thousand Oaks, CA: SAGE Publications.

Payne, Y. A., Starks, B. C., & Gibson, L. R. (2009). Contextualizing black boys' use of a street identity in high school. *New Directions for Youth Development, 2009*(123), 35–51.

Rodríguez, L. F., & Brown, T. M. (2009). From voice to agency: Guiding principles for participatory action research with youth. *New Directions for Youth Development, 2009*(123), 19–34.

Romero, A., Cammarota, J., Dominguez, K., Valdez, L., Ramirez, G., & Hernandez, L. (2008). "The opportunity if not the right to see": The social justice education project. In J. Cammarota, & M. Fine (Eds.), *Revolutionizing education: Youth participatory action research in motion* (pp. 131–151). New York, NY: Routledge.

Roulston, K., & Shelton, S. A. (2015). Reconceptualizing bias in teaching qualitative research methods. *Qualitative Inquiry, 21,* 332–342.

Rubin, B. C. (2012). *Making citizens: Transforming civic learning for diverse social studies classrooms.* New York, NY: Routledge.

Rubin, B. C., & Jones, M. (2007). Student action research: Reaping the benefits for students and school leaders. *NASSP Bulletin, 91,* 363–378.

Sanchez, P. (2009). Chicana feminist strategies in a participatory action research project with transnational Latina youth. *New Directions for Youth Development, 2009*(123), 83–97.

Schensul, J., & Berg, M. (2004). Youth participatory action research: A transformative approach to service-learning. *Michigan Journal of Community Service Learning, 10*(3), 76–78.

Schultz, B. D. (2008). *Spectacular things happen along the way: Lessons from an urban classroom.* New York, NY: Teachers College Press.

Scorza, D. A., Mirra, N., & Morrell, E. (2013). It should just be education: Critical pedagogy normalized as academic excellence. *International Journal of Critical Pedagogy, 4*(2), 15–34.

Smith, L. (1999). *Decolonizing methodologies: Research and indigenous peoples.* New York, NY: Zed Books.

Souto-Manning, M. (2014). Critical narrative analysis: The interplay of critical discourse and narrative analyses. *International Journal of Qualitative Studies in Education, 27,* 159–180.

Stovall, D., & Delgado, N. (2009). "Knowing the ledge": Participatory action research as legal studies for urban high school youth. *New Directions for Youth Development, 2009*(123), 67–81.

Stringer, E. (1996). *Action research: A handbook for practitioners.* Thousand Oaks, CA: SAGE.

Torre, M. E. (2005). The alchemy of integrated spaces: Youth participation in research collectives of difference. In L. Weis, & M. Fine (Eds.), *Beyond silenced voices* (pp. 251–266). Albany: State University of New York Press. Retrieved from http://www.pbs.org/beyondbrown/resources/legacylinks.html

Torre, M. E. (2009). Participatory action research and critical race theory: Fueling spaces for nos-otras to research. *The Urban Review, 41,* 106–120

Torre, M., & Fine, M. (with Alexander, N., Billups, A. B., Blanding, Y., Geneno, E., Marboe, E., Salah, T., & Urdang, K.). (2008). Participatory action research in the contact zone. In J. Cammarota, & M. Fine (Eds.), *Revolutionizing education: Youth participatory action research in motion* (pp. 23–44). New York, NY: Routledge.

Tuck, E. (2009). Re-visioning action: Participatory action research and indigenous theories of change. *The Urban Review, 41,* 47–65.

Tuck, E., Allen, J., Bacha, M., Morales, A., Quinter, S., Thompson, J., & Tuck, M. (2008). PAR praxes for now and future change: The collective of researchers on educational disappointment and desire. In J. Cammarota, & M. Fine (Eds.), *Revolutionizing education: Youth participatory action research in motion* (pp. 49–83). New York, NY: Routledge.

Tuck, E., & Neofotistos, T. (Eds.). (2013). *Youth to youth guide to the GED(r)* [Electronic publication]. Retrieved from http://www.evetuck.com/y2yguideged/

Tuck, E., & Yang, K. W. (2012). Decolonization is not a metaphor. *Decolonization: Indigeneity, Education & Society, 1*(1), 1–40.

Voices of Youth in Chicago Education. (2011). *Failed policies, broken futures: The true cost of zero tolerance in Chicago.* Chicago, IL: Author.

Whipp, J. (2013). Developing socially just teachers: The interaction of experiences before, during, and after teacher preparation in beginning urban teachers. *Journal of Teacher Education, 64,* 454-467.

Winn, L. T., & Winn, M. T. (2016). "We want this to be owned by you": The promise and perils of youth participatory action research. In S. Greene, K. J. Burke, & M. K. McKenna (Eds.), *Youth voices, public spaces, and civic engagement* (pp. 111–130). New York: Routledge.

Winn, M. T., & Ubiles, J. R. (2011). Worthy witnessing: Collaborative research in urban classrooms. In A. Ball, & C. Tyson (Eds.), *Studying diversity in teacher education* (pp. 295–308). New York, NY: Rowman & Littlefield.

Wright, D. (2015). *Active learning: Social justice education and participatory action research.* New York, NY: Routledge.

Yang, K. W. (2009). Mathematics, critical literacy, and youth participatory action research. *New Directions for Youth Development, 2009*(123), 99–118.

Yonezawa, S., & Jones, M. (2009). Student voices: Generating reform from the inside out. *Theory Into Practice, 48,* 205–212.

Zaal, M., & Terry, J. (2013). Knowing what I can do and who I can be: Youth identify transformational benefits of participatory action research. *Journal of Ethnographic & Qualitative Research, 8,* 42–55.

Zeichner, K., & Noffke, S. (2001). Practitioner research. In V. Richardson (Ed.), *The handbook for research on teaching* (4th ed., pp. 298–330). Washington, DC: American Educational Research Association.

Chapter 14

Disrupting Educational Inequalities Through Youth Digital Activism

Amy Stornaiuolo
Ebony Elizabeth Thomas
University of Pennsylvania

This article reviews scholarship on youth and young adult activism in digital spaces, as young users of participatory media sites are engaging in political, civic, social, or cultural action and advocacy online to create social change. The authors argue that youth's digital activism serves as a central mechanism to disrupt inequality, and that education research should focus on these youth practices, particularly by young people from marginalized communities or identities, in order to provide important counter-narratives to predominant stories circulating about "at-risk" or disaffected youth. The article examines young people's use of online tools for organizing toward social change across three lines of inquiry— young people's cultural and political uses of participatory tools and spaces online, new forms of youth civic engagement and activism, and adult-supported programs and spaces facilitating youth activism. In centering the review on youth digital activism, the authors suggest that education researchers can learn from youth themselves about how to disrupt educational inequalities, resulting in a more humanizing stance for education research that takes into fuller account the human potential of all youth, beyond school walls.

I believe that the birth of social media catalyzed the fourth wave of feminism, allowing women from all over the world to connect, share ideas and empower each other . . . I feel fortunate to be alive during this time, and my goal is to contribute to the Internet revolution by sharing my knowledge on feminism, LGBTQIA+ [lesbian, gay, bisexual, transgender, queer, intersex, asexual] rights and everything political. Feminists of the past laid the groundwork for us today, and my goal is to pick up their torch.

—Sylva, 17 (Paoletta, 2015)

We open this review with Sylva's words to call attention to the ways young people are using digital tools and online spaces to document inequalities, address

Review of Research in Education
March 2017, Vol. 41, pp. 337–357
DOI: 10.3102/0091732X16687973
© 2017 AERA. http://rre.aera.net

injustice, and take social action, building on the groundwork of previous generations of activists even as they seek to extend and transform those efforts. While contemporary scholarship on youth media, hip-hop literacies, and community-based activism has extensively documented the breadth of contemporary adolescents' literate lives (e.g., Fisher, 2003; Lam, 2009; Moje, 2004; Morrell, 2008), adolescents are all too often positioned in education research, policy, and popular discourse as unformed, at risk, or apathetic (see Lesko, 2012). Perhaps unsurprising in the current zeitgeist, these deficitizing discourses are particularly prevalent in characterizing the lives and literacies of teens of color, LGBTQIA youth, and other young people from marginalized groups (Gadsden, Davis, & Artiles, 2009; O'Connor, Hill, & Robinson, 2009; Vasudevan & Campano, 2009). Young people today, however, are using participatory media sites like Twitter, Instagram, and Tumblr to engage in advocacy and social activism that often goes unheralded, invisible until it is viewed as disruptive of schooling or society.

From #BlackLivesMatter to #LoveWins, young people are using digital media in myriad ways to connect with each other, promote social change, and counternarrate the world from their perspective. Rather than allowing adults to dominate narratives on issues facing adolescents—including gentrification, mass incarceration, neoliberal educational reform, and socioeconomic precarity in an age of global capitalism (Kinloch, 2010; Lipman, 2004, 2013; Winn, 2010)—young people today, particularly those from marginalized groups, are using social media, online fandom, and other kinds of digital affinity groups to *restory* the popular imagination by shaping it into their own image (Thomas & Stornaiuolo, 2016). In this chapter, we undertake a review of the literature on youth and young adult activism in digital spaces, examining how these activist practices are forms of counternarration. Defining youth digital activism as adolescent and young adult online practices that involve political, civic, social, or cultural action oriented toward social change or transformation, we argue that such activist practices can serve as a central mechanism to disrupt inequality.

Furthermore, we suggest that education research should focus on activist practices by youth from marginalized communities or identities to provide important counternarratives to discourses circulating about "at risk" or disaffected adolescents. Such a focus begins from the premise that it is vital to understand and learn from what youth are *doing* (how they are accessing and using these digital tools and spaces to document their experiences of injustice) and the *impact* and *consequences* of those practices (Brock, Kvasny, & Hales, 2010). An emphasis on how youth are disrupting inequalities through their social actions resists predominant perspectives about digital divides that begin from what is missing—whether from a lack of resources, practices, or opportunities. Without romanticizing youth digital activities or holding them up as transformative in and of themselves, we seek to emphasize and amplify youth efforts to be heard and to affect change in order to disrupt deficit discourses; we see such efforts as central to a humanizing stance for education research (Paris & Winn, 2013), one in which researchers focus on the full development of the person and not just adolescents' schooled lives (Del Carmen Salazar, 2013).

After describing our framework for examining youth digital advocacy and activism, we organize our discussion into three main sections examining young people's use of online tools for organizing toward social change. First, we review studies that examine the spaces and tools youth are using to document inequalities and take social action, including fan and hashtag activism. Next, we review studies documenting youth civic engagement and activism and consider the changing definitions of civicness. In the final section, we concentrate on educational programs and adult-mediated online spaces dedicated to youth social activism. We conclude by framing youth's digital activism as a form of restorying (Thomas & Stornaiuolo, 2016), in which young people's counternarrative work is seen as a central mechanism for disrupting normative and deficitizing frameworks.

Framework for Examining Youth Digital Advocacy and Activism

Keeping our goal of honoring the voices and experiences of young people in mind, we embrace a critical, sociocultural approach to researching youth digital activism, arguing that all young people have a wealth of resources and experiences they bring to bear in their engagement with the world (Blackburn, 2002, 2007; Garcia, Mirra, Morrell, Martinez, & Scorza, 2015; Lam & Rosario-Ramos, 2009; Morrell, 2008). We believe education research should operate from this asset-based stance, examining inequities from the perspectives of people who experience them while actively resisting normative epistemologies that further marginalize the multiple ways people develop knowledge of the world (Paris, 2012). With these theoretical commitments in place, we deliberately excluded scholarship that invokes discourses of the digital divide (DiMaggio, Hargittai, Celeste, & Shafer, 2004; Warschauer & Matuchniak, 2010). While such work provides one lens through which to examine inequities in digital access and opportunity, we are taking a different stance—one that foregrounds youth epistemologies and experiences. As Brock et al. (2010) argued, research on the digital divide often begins from the premise that something is missing, which normalizes Western, heteronormative, masculinized, White, middle-class, able-bodied, and adult ways of engaging with digital technologies. To resist such framing, we sought scholarship that rooted inquiry in youth perspectives and that actively positioned youth as agents of change.

To that end, we approached this review with a wide lens, reading broadly in literacy studies, media studies, fan studies, anthropology, cultural movement studies, critical youth studies, sociology, peace and conflict studies, and related fields to get a general sense of how different constituencies define and characterize *youth digital activism*. From this initial reading and discussion, we developed three questions to guide our review:

- In what ways are youth addressing issues of injustice in schooling and society through their use of digital tools and practices online?
- How are youth using digital media to facilitate their activist participation and engagement online?

- What can education researchers, practitioners, and policymakers learn from youth engagement in participatory cultures for the purposes of social change?

We began searching academic databases (JSTOR, ERIC, Web of Science, Google Scholar, EBSCO) for peer-reviewed journal articles using combinations of search terms related to digital youth activism (e.g., adolescents, digital, online, network, media, critical, social activism, civic activism, civic engagement, civic action, social action, education, literacy). Due to the evolving nature of online media, we limited our searches to the past 20 years. With a pool of potential articles, we narrowed the search to empirical work (defined as scholarship engaged in systematic inquiry, with clear description of methods of data collection and analysis) focused primarily on youth (defined as people aged 12 to 25 years). We further refined the search to studies that took a youth-centered approach (defined as the close examination of youth experiences and inclusion of youth voices and perspectives). We then hand-searched references from key articles to identify additional articles and books, though only entire books that fit these criteria (e.g., youth-centered perspectives, empirical, focused primarily on online activism) and not individual chapters.

With an initial pool of 78 articles and books fitting this profile, we narrowed it to 43 on closer review. One of the central challenges was the ephemeral nature of youth activism online; as a new field, for example, scholars across multiple fields defined *activism* and *youth* in different ways, with a number of relevant articles never using those exact terms (e.g., examining political engagement or protest) or focusing directly on young people (e.g., including multiage populations in their studies). A number of articles focused less on the online aspects of youth activism and more on digital tools young people used (e.g., computers to make activist-oriented films). Other relevant, youth-centered articles purported to be empirical in nature but did not include sustained attention to or systematic inquiry into young people's activities. Therefore, while we sought to be as comprehensive as possible, we acknowledge that our efforts may not have captured all of the salient scholarship in this emerging area of study. Our questions guided the subsequent content analysis, which distilled into three categories: (a) youth social activism (including fan and hashtag activism), (b) youth digital civic engagement (including its participatory dimensions), and (c) youth participation in educational spaces oriented toward social change (including adult-facilitated programs). These three categories, mapped onto the three questions guiding the review, provided the blueprint for the sections below.

YOUTH, FAN CULTURE, AND DIGITAL ACTIVISM

In this section, we review scholarship that traces how young people participate in self-expressive, issue-oriented, and interest-driven activist practices online, spotlighting work that highlights youth voices, agency, and initiative taking. We first review research that links the cultural and political, exploring how young people engage as fans to connect their interests and identities. We examine the ways that cultural, social, and political dimensions of online practice involve new forms of representation and counternarration, as young people tell their stories, share their experiences, and bear witness to one another as well as to the world around them. In the subsequent section, we review studies that highlight the generative power of collective action through social media, foregrounding scholarship that explores how such collective efforts open new spaces to influence public life. We conclude by discussing the ways these endeavors demand that previously disenfranchised and marginalized voices are heard in and across communities, powerfully demonstrated in hashtag campaigns like #BlackLivesMatter, #BringBackOurGirls, #1000BlackGirlBooks, and #LoveWins, which in turn expand local and global audiences for social activism.

The Cultural as Political: Fan Activism and Online Representations

Whether discussing a TV show's recent plot developments in an online forum, writing and sharing a fictional story inspired by a gaming franchise, or protesting the casting of a favorite movie, young people participate in contemporary culture in myriad ways. While critics may dismiss these participatory activities as frivolous, solipsistic, or diversionary, scholars are beginning to view these cultural practices as relevant to civic and political life, nested within a web of participatory culture where new forms of activism are possible (e.g., Earl & Kimport, 2009; Jenkins, 2012; Vie, 2014). Such new forms of activism can include cultural activities in which consumers actively resist, offer alternate representations, appropriate and remix cultural forms, and draw attention to these intersections of the cultural and political. Earl and Kimport (2009) have studied the ways young people are adopting tactics of political protests—namely, petitions, letter-writing efforts, boycotts, and e-mail campaigns— to address cultural concerns and record grievances. These strategies for holding institutions accountable offer a means of actively negotiating power, illustrating how popular culture infuses our everyday lives and provides a generative avenue for taking activist positions.

A prevalent form of cultural activism involves fanwork, which allows fans to participate in fictional worlds by writing fan fiction, engaging in cosplay, or making fan videos, for example. Such fanwork can take the form of fan activism, especially when marginalized groups wield it to speak back to canons. Jenkins's (2012, 2013) work on fan activism positions audiences as active rather than passive consumers of media content. Jenkins (2012) defines *fan activism* as

forms of civic engagement and political participation that emerge from within fan culture itself, often in response to the shared interests of fans, often conducted through the infrastructure of existing fan practices and relationships, and often framed through metaphors drawn from popular and participatory culture. (Section 1.8)

Fan activism shares a number of features with other forms of activism, such as resisting censorship, pushing back against misrepresentations, or contesting commercial interests by mobilizing through multiple media channels and outlets.

Fan activism can also lead to explicit participation in more traditional forms of social action. Indeed, Jenkins (2012) has argued that "fandom may represent a particularly powerful training ground for future activists and community organizers" (Section 2.6). Kligler-Vilenchik, Mcveigh-Schultz, Weitbrecht, and Tokuhama (2012) studied fan activism as a powerful mode of mobilization for young people because it combines shared media experiences, a sense of community, and a desire to help. One example of fan activism analyzed by both Kligler-Vilenchik et al. (2012) and Jenkins (2012) is the Harry Potter Alliance (HPA), an activist organization inspired by the fictional world of the J. K. Rowling novels that has mobilized more than 100,000 young fans in campaigns to address literacy and human rights issues. Like other fan communities, HPA has raised money for specific causes (e.g., sending planes with medical supplies to Haiti after the earthquake) but also works toward structural changes that link the magic of Rowling's stories with change in the real world—as the website notes, "We know fantasy is not only an escape from our world, but an invitation to go deeper into it" (HPA, n.d.). In flexibly responding to issues as they arise and capture the interest of members, HPA engages in an activist model that founder Andrew Slack calls "cultural acupuncture"—as the organization identifies "key cultural pressure points" that can direct action toward real world problems (Jenkins, 2012, Section 4.7). By recognizing the power of art to influence hearts, minds, and emotions, fan activism embraces young people who are engaged culturally, offering models and supportive structures for deploying those skills and energies to other civic and political ends.

Artistic expression in fan activism can take the form of counternarratives of resistance (Duncan-Andrade, 2007), particularly for young people who are misrepresented, marginalized, or erased from mainstream media. One example of these online fan counternarratives we have recently explored is racebending (Thomas & Stornaiuolo, 2016), which Pollock (2004) and Moll (2004) both observed as a phenomenon in schools where youth choose to emphasize certain racial features and characteristics in order to fit in. Online, however, the concept of racebending emerged as a campaign from the *Avatar: The Last Airbender* fan community. Aghast at the casting discrimination in the film adaptation of *Airbender*, fan activists began a grassroots organization to call attention to the ways Hollywood studios and casting directors change the race or ethnicity of characters to discriminate against people of color (Racebending.com, n.d.). Racebending has subsequently emerged as powerful fan advocacy for diverse literary and media landscapes through the use of fanwork to change the race of a character (Thomas & Stornaiuolo, 2016). Youth engage in other kinds of bending practices on Tumblr and other social media sites, including genderbending and queerbending (Jenkins, Shresthova, Gamber-Thompson, & Kligler-Vilenchik, 2016). While genderbending has a long history that predates the digital age (Abate, 2008), queerbending is activist fanwork created by and for queer fans for political ends, in contrast to slash fanfiction and fanart, which is often created by cisgender girls and young women (Persaud, 2016; Tosenberger, 2008). Although such activist responses by audiences and interpreters certainly precede the digital world, fanbent images and stories now circulate to wider audiences—and broader effects—via the tools of social media.

Whether "bending" the race, gender, or sexual identity of characters they find (Thomas & Stornaiuolo, 2016), engaging in "lifestreaming" to gain voice and visibility online (Wargo, 2015), or taking "selfies" to circulate self-representations (Brager, 2015), young people are now writing themselves into the media that have excluded them. For example, when 11-year-old Marley Dias did not see herself in the books she was reading, she took matters into her own hands by creating the online campaign #1000BlackGirlBooks. While also inspiring other young people, Dias drew attention to the broader issue of representation in children's literature, which according to the Cooperative Book Center, only 180 titles out of 3,500 books published in 2014 featured African or African American characters (Flood, 2016). Similarly, Wargo (2015) described how participants in his study created complex identity texts to write themselves into media that has silenced or ignored them. One of his participants, Jake, a gender-queer-trans-youth in transition, produced and curated social media texts that blended his affinities, fan identities, and documentary practices to assert his identity online in visible and consequential ways. Increasingly, youth and young adults are using social media to position themselves and their experiences at the center of the culture, often through a variety of artistic and expressive practices.

Collective Action Through Social Media

One of the most powerful dimensions of social media for youth activists is its collective nature, as young people no longer need traditional gatekeepers (teachers, librarians, community organizers) to build or share knowledge, find other like-minded people, or plan and coordinate actions. Instead of relying on the well-trodden pathways of the past, contemporary young people form new coalitions and connections based on shared interests, using social media as a form of collective activism (Velasquez & LaRose, 2015). As an information hub that allows for exchange of information and provides multiple channels for feedback and peer interaction, social media facilitates the generation and sharing of information that may not be distributed or available on mainstream news outlets. For example, people can use social media and geolocational tools to address sexual harassment and report sexual assaults (Damodar, 2012) or engage in protest behavior across online and offline spheres (Carney, 2016). Examining social media use and youth protest behavior in Chile, Valenzuela, Arriagada, and Scherman (2012) found that these social media sites allowed people to develop personal and group identities as they built relationships with one another and gained insight into others' perspectives.

Whether joining privately on apps like Snapchat or WhatsApp, posting videos or images on Instagram or YouTube, or reaching out to and mobilizing local and global audiences via Tumblr or Twitter, young people are using established and emerging platforms to come together in multiple ways, for multiple purposes. Vie (2014) described how many young people changed their profile picture in 2013 to the modified logo of the Human Rights Campaign or rainbow flag to signal affiliation with marriage equality. While some might argue that changing one's picture online represents a shallow form of activism (sometimes derisively called slacktivism), Vie (2014) argued that such massive group identification can signal rapid visual support for a cause, combating microaggressions and spurring some people to further action.

Yet just as these new platforms and spaces open up the possibilities of new forms of participation, scholars like Love and Bradley (2014) have pointed out the "messiness of new media as a cultural and resistant space" (p. 259) as these sites open young people to bullying, abuse, explicit racism, sexism, homophobia, xenophobia, ableism, and surveillance. In particular, Love and Bradley (2014) argued that tracing the online calls for racial justice that emerged in response to Trayvon Martin's death in 2012 revealed how the "signifying of cyber and literal violence against Black bodies demands new discourse and critical frameworks to reflect how Blacks' self-definition and calls to action are treated within new social media" (p. 259). Bonilla and Rosa (2015) suggested that despite the need for caution, these social media platforms have emerged as powerful sites for documenting state-sanctioned violence and mainstream media portrayals of marginalized communities and racialized bodies because young people now carry the tools with them to engage in those documentary practices, disseminating those experiences to others, and finding solidarity with others similarly facing forms of oppression and marginalization.

One of the most prevalent and widely recognized ways young people are engaging in collective forms of activism online is through the use of hashtags, which are a kind of indexing system that emerged on Twitter to allow quick retrieval of information. Some of this hashtag activism (Williams, 2015) is action-based, like the #BringBackOurGirls campaign to recover over 200 kidnapped Nigerian schoolgirls, while others are targeted toward shifting traditional media to examine global systems of power (Brager, 2015). A number of scholars have begun to investigate how Twitter can function as a space for constructing counternarratives and reimagining group identities by using hashtags not only to find information but to link to other ideas and conversations and to participate in real time (Bonilla & Rosa, 2015). More recently, after the landmark 2015 Supreme Court decision upholding marriage equality, *Obergefell v. Hodges*, the hashtag #LoveWins trended, but was preceded by digital activism and education that circulated among LGBTQIA youth, many of whom used the Internet to learn and teach others about identity (Fox & Ralston, 2016; Killham & Chandler, 2016).

One of the most relevant and powerful examples of collective organizing online involves the cultural power of Black Twitter (Brock, 2012), characterized by Black users of the social media platform. Perhaps the most salient activist function of Black Twitter is the #BlackLivesMatter movement, founded by Patrisse Cullors, Opal Tometi, and Alicia Garza after the shooting death of Trayvon Martin by his neighbor George Zimmerman (Ransby, 2015). As a decentralized but coordinated movement that has called attention to "racialized policing, the vulnerability of black bodies, and the problematic ways in which blackness is perceived as a constant threat" (Bonilla & Rosa, 2015, p. 8), the #BlackLivesMatter movement was motivated and driven forward by young people talking about and taking pictures of themselves in hoodies or putting their hands in the air to signal solidarity with Trayvon Martin and Michael

Brown, unarmed young Black men killed by police (Carney, 2016). These efforts to produce collective representations that challenge the ways Black bodies are misrepresented by mainstream media offer new means for addressing educational inequality, and have inspired other groups to be engaged in similar hashtag activism for their own purposes (see Bosch, 2016).

DIGITAL CIVIC ENGAGEMENT: YOUTH AS CIVIC ACTORS ONLINE

As youth leverage new tools and networks to participate in collective action on political, social, and community issues of concern, one strand of scholarship on youth digital activism examines young people's civic activities online. Growing out of research into youth civic engagement (e.g., Buckingham, 2000; Ginwright, Noguera, & Cammarota, 2006; Kirshner, 2015; Rogers, Mediratta, & Shah, 2012), recent work examining young people's digital civic activism is challenging traditional understandings of *civicness* by foregrounding youth perspectives and definitions. We begin this section by reviewing research that theorizes civicness through close examination of young people's perspectives, activities, and identities as they are lived and practiced in various cultural and social contexts. We spotlight scholarship that actively resists characterizations of youth—particularly youth from marginalized positions—as apathetic, uninterested, or unwilling to participate in civic or political life. Such deficit framing of young people often uses normative frameworks and metrics that do not adequately capture shifting cultural practices and alternate ways of knowing and being. We then locate these shifting definitions of civicness in what scholars have characterized as a participatory turn in contemporary life (Jenkins, Clinton, Purushotma, Robison, & Weigel, 2006), surveying research on participatory civics and politics that repositions young people as political and civic actors who produce and share content that connects their passions, interests, and identities to influence public discourse.

Shifting Definitions of Civicness

Examples abound of young people participating in civic and political life through digital means: mobilizing on social media for Obama's 2008 campaign, organizing protests in Egypt via Twitter, or circulating online petitions to defeat the Stop Online Piracy Act. In one study of "Egypt's young cyber citizens" using new technologies for social change, Herrera (2012) traced examples of peer-to-peer online mobilizing, like the ways youth built solidarity across diverse constituencies in the antitorture campaign "We Are All Khaled Said" (p. 348). Despite a number of youth participating in more traditional forms of civic engagement—voting, contacting political representatives, volunteering, protesting—discourses of youth civic disengagement are prevalent, often framed as a gap in young people's knowledge, opportunity, or empowerment (Coleman, 2008; Kahne & Middaugh, 2008; Levinson, 2010), particularly for young people of color (Jensen, 2010; Levine, 2009). In addition to conceptualizing "young people as the root causes of their own problems" (Ginwright & James, 2002, p. 29), however, this paradigm of youth disengagement misses new forms of civic participation that are not rooted in the same system of beliefs about citizenship or revealed on traditional metrics (Bennett, Wells, & Freelon, 2011; Cohen & Kahne, 2012; Zuckerman, 2014). We suggest that foregrounding youth perspectives and attending to youth's online practices can help alert scholars to the "changing repertoires of civic practice" (Bennett et al., 2011, p. 838) that push back against normative understandings of citizenship and political involvement.

New patterns of digital activism like changing one's profile picture in solidarity with a cause, signing and circulating online petitions, and boycotting/buycotting online (Fournier, 2013; Pew Research Center for the People and the Press, 2010) require that scholars closely examine young people's beliefs and practices across various spheres, including their public expressions, community organizing, awareness building, and lifestyle politics. These actions involve loose affiliations with peer networks that crowdsource information and maximize self-expression, and they take on even more importance in societies where such expression is curtailed, regulated, or excluded. In Singapore, for example, Zhang (2013) examined how young people eschewed the traditional label of activist, which was historically rooted in oppositional party politics and civil disobedience, and instead engaged in various online activities oriented to social change (e.g., advocating public causes on Facebook, becoming "bloggervists"). A number of studies have similarly examined the role of context and culture in youth's civic and political activities, as young people redefined the nature and scope of what counts as activism through the creative use of new tools and networks (e.g., de Vreese, 2007; Lin, Cheong, Kim, & Jung, 2010; Östman, 2012; Xenos, Vromen, & Loader, 2014). These efforts to highlight youth perspectives and beliefs, challenge so-called neutral definitions, and take into account cultural and contextual factors and identities demonstrate how researchers can push back on deficit framing by centering the experiences of young people and working toward shifting public opinion and raising awareness of these forms of activism.

Youth engaged in self-expressive practices are not just expanding the definition of what counts as civic engagement or carving new political pathways that circumvent more traditional routes to public action—they are also resisting the very idea of citizenship that lies at the heart of most definitions of *civicness* (Buckingham, 2000). In a transnational era characterized by voluntary and involuntary movements of people across national boundaries, especially in conditions of precarity and under threat of violence, it becomes both more challenging and more pressing to trace these evolving understandings of citizenship and the role it plays in civic and political engagement. Examining these contingent dimensions of civic engagement, Beltrán (2015) studied undocumented young people calling themselves DREAMers, young people who support the DREAM (Development, Relief, and Education for Alien Minors) Act (bipartisan federal legislation under consideration since 2001 that would provide a pathway to citizenship for children who grew up in the United States). In her study, these young DREAMers used social media to engage in "strategies of visibility" (p. 80) that both redefined the terms of the debate over immigration and humanized undocumented young people (cf. Patel & Sanchez Ares, 2014).

Some DREAMers employed new tools and networks to "come out" by openly and publicly declaring their undocumented status, using strategies from the LGBTQIA community, to "queer the movement" (Beltrán, 2015, p. 81). By posting and circulating first-person accounts, DREAMers used the collective and public nature of these online postings to challenge criminalizing logic and highlight the politics of immigration. Georgina Perez, one young DREAMer, shared her name and story to resist the neoliberal framing of immigration:

We've done the petitions, we've done the flyering, the lobbying, the protests, the rallies, and instead of our voices being heard, we're just not seeing any change. We're seeing that our communities are being criminalized; we're seeing racist legislation; we're seeing family separation. And that's why today I'm coming out as undocumented and unafraid. I will no longer stand and wait for someone to come and save me. (Beltrán, 2015, p. 91)

Perez and her DREAMer colleagues resisted more normative forms of civic engagement by engaging in acts of civil disobedience to frame the issue as an emergency, offering their own first-person testimony despite its incriminating nature. As Beltrán (2015) argued, this "queering" of immigration activism by DREAMers highlights the fraught and complex nature of democratic membership—and draws attention to the changing social, historical, and cultural dimensions of civic practice, the need for humanizing practices that shift the terms of debate, and the responsibilities of institutions toward individuals and groups who have experienced systemic oppressions.

Participatory Dimensions of Civic Practice

As the previous sections demonstrated so clearly, young people's participation in civic and political life now is driven by their passions and interests (not just a sense of duty or obligation to the polity) as well as by their peer networks (rather than established coalitions or traditional gatekeepers). As Ito, Soep, Kligler-Vilenchik, Shresthova, and Zimmerman (2015) described in their framework of "connected civics," young people are often driven to act on issues of public concern when those issues are connected to their deeply felt interests, affinities, and identities. In their qualitative meta-analysis of research from MacArthur-funded studies, the authors focused on youth-driven activities to identify mechanisms that facilitate consequential connections across youth interests, agency, and civic opportunities. They identified different capacities youth develop in affinity settings—such as telling stories, mobilizing publics, and managing publicity (see Soep, 2014)—that can be mobilized to broader effect.

While some may dismiss forms of "thin" civic engagement like changing a profile picture or circulating a video online as inconsequential, Zuckerman (2014) has argued that this kind of mobilization of youth's interests and identities needs to be understood on a continuum that includes "thicker" forms of civic and political engagement (e.g., leading a protest, organizing a funding drive). Today's pathways to civic and political life are now often paved through popular culture and peer networks, as young people engage in new forms of organizing and coalition building across online and offline communities oriented to social interaction and entertainment, oftentimes only tangentially connected to more conventional civic and political realms (Bennett, 2008).

In an era in which (a) people are networked together in multiple configurations, (b) digital tools for production and circulation of artifacts are widely available, and (c) young people have grown accustomed to sharing ideas and perspectives with a wide array of friends and strangers online, young people now expect their contributions to matter and institutions to be responsive to issues they discuss and debate in the public sphere (Kahne, Middaugh, & Allen, 2015). The Youth and Participatory Politics group has conducted a number of studies of youth's civic and political engagement, developing the framework of "participatory politics" to describe the "interactive, peer-based acts through which individuals and groups seek to exert both voice and influence on issues of public concern" (Cohen & Kahne, 2012, p. vi). In a large scale, nationally representative study of youth aged 15 to 25 years, Cohen and Kahne (2012) found a strong association between nonpolitical, interest-driven activity and participatory politics, suggesting that those interest-driven practices serve as a foundation for civic engagement by providing relevant knowledge, skills, and networks.

The concept of *voice* has emerged as a central one in theorizing participatory forms of civic engagement, as young people exercise their voices by creating and circulating meaningful content (Kahne et al., 2015; Kirshner & Middaugh, 2015). As the personal form of expression that identifies one as unique, voice is often seen as the link between more general media participation and civically engaged participation as people write themselves into public narratives: "Moving from a private to a public voice can help students turn their self-expression into a form of public participation" (Rheingold, 2008, p. 101). Zuckerman (2014) argued that this creative expression of voice can be "an important path to civic engagement" because it builds affinities and identification with broader causes, allowing young people to see their impact on an issue. A number of scholars investigating how queer youth "write [themselves] into the world" as a form of social action (Blackburn, 2002, p. 323) have focused on how young people can use their voices to resist homophobia and heterosexism and express multiple subject positions (e.g., Blackburn, 2007, 2014; Driver, 2007). Gray (2009), for example, examined how rural youth represented their LGBTQIA identities online in coming-out narratives, highlighting the importance of online collective spaces of engagement for "the transformative power of self-identification to organize politics, culture, and intimacy" (p. 1182). In her ethnographic scholarship, Gray (2009) centered the voices of her participants, focusing on stories such as Brandon's, who struggled with how to publicly represent himself as a gay African American young man. He asked himself "What kind of civil rights leader would I be?" if he were to ignore the political struggles of groups to which he belonged, and he found ways to reconcile those identity conflicts by participating online. These forms of participation online, engaging in self-expression to "authenticate queerness" (p. 1182) through first-person narratives, are ways of engaging in the politics of representation that have come to characterize new forms of civic activism.

EDUCATIONAL OPPORTUNITIES FOR YOUTH DIGITAL ACTIVISM

Whereas the previous sections foregrounded young people's self-sponsored activism in online spaces, this section concentrates on the role that educational programs, community organizations, and adult-mediated spaces play in supporting youth social activism online. The past two decades have demonstrated the growth and educative potential of youth organizing programs, voluntary groups focused on social change that are often led by young adults and composed of middle and high school youth of color (Ginwright & Cammarota, 2007; Kirshner, 2007, 2008; Rogers et al., 2012); similarly, youth media programs with critical, transformative pedagogies have proven to be powerful and effective in supporting young people to document inequities in their lives (Duncan-Andrade, 2007; Poyntz, 2006; Zimmerman, 2007). We are particularly interested in how these educational programs are extending and expanding their work by using new tools to engage in collective action and link to others. Some studies suggest that the biggest shift for these organizations involved broadening the span and scope of their mobilization efforts (e.g., McDonald, Geigel, & Pinguel, 2011). For example, Conner and Slattery (2014) found in their study of the Philadelphia Student Union, one of the oldest contemporary youth organizing groups, that when the youth-led organization incorporated new media activities like podcasts and blogs into its activist repertoire, those activities synergistically expanded the reach of the organization's core mission. Youth worked toward promoting educational equity across more venues and amplified the core message using these new tools.

Educational programs that support youth online activism across multiple spheres often do so by providing access to a variety of resources and scaffolds to critical activist engagement, such as intergenerational networks, apprenticeship models, community alliances, and historical framing about social change across local and global contexts. One example of the potential of community organizations in supporting online youth activism is Asthana's (2015) study of Palestinian youth media narratives across community and online contexts. He focused on one community organization in the Western Bank, Ibdaa, offering opportunities for refugee youth to create digital films as well as connect to other Palestinian refugee groups online. On Ibdaa Facebook pages, young people shared images and videos documenting the material realities of persistent violence of the Israeli occupation; these images and video were accompanied by commentary and critique that illustrated the shared pain and persistent resoluteness (*sumud*) of the Palestinian youth and highlighted the affective and embodied dimensions of their lives. These online practices of solidarity moved away from victimization narratives embedded in humanitarian discourses, instead focusing on youth agency in their capacity to rework narratives of trauma into acts of resistance and resilience.

One of the most powerful resources educational organizations offer is the mentoring and apprenticeship structures that support young people in exploring new forms of activism. Garcia et al. (2015) describe one such program, the Council of Youth Research, which honored what students of color brought with them but also provided important scaffolding for "critical digital civic literacy," a pedagogy of academic literacies, critical literacies, digital literacies, and civic practice (p. 165). One Council of Youth Research participant, Graciela, illustrated the importance of young people documenting, sharing, and mobilizing around their counterstories when she shared her response to a deficitizing film at an academic conference: "We are not a community based on dropouts, gangs, and violence but a community based on revolutions that have helped desegregate our schools and better the education for my fellow compañeros" (Garcia et al., p. 152). Graciela's words foregrounded the centrality of the youth's work and their power to act as agents of change in their own lives and communities.

We offer two cautions that arose when examining youth digital organizing in educational spaces. One caveat offered by Fleetwood (2005) revolves around organizations that may be tempted to use youth's stories for other purposes (e.g., as a marketing tool) or that flatten or essentialize youth narratives. She cautioned youth media arts organizations to be mindful of how they might use video to "document an authentic urban experience from the position of racialized youth"—a search for a racialized version of authenticity, or "realness," that draws on broader, essentializing cultural narratives (p. 156). These broader discourses, echoed in popular media and advertising, position racialized youth as outside of normative White society and responsible for their own marginalization—"while also serving as the vehicle of consumption of a particular racialized youthful identity through its association with a range of commodities" (p. 156). A second caveat emerged from Shiller's (2013) study of two Bronx-based community organizations. In foregrounding the importance of adult and young adult mentors as community resources, this study serves as a caution for organizations and education researchers to recognize the agency youth already possess and not slip into assuming adults are "giving them [youth] agency" (p. 88) in becoming change makers.

Haddix, Everson, and Hodge (2015) offer an important counterstory to such essentializing uses of new media tools in their study of the Writing Our Lives community program, oriented to supporting the activist, civically engaged writing lives of urban youth. In their article, the authors—one youth participant, one teacher, and one scholar—think together about how this program's efforts to support youth in writing about the inequities they experience offered a pathway for the youth author to bridge multiple spheres of her life. Coauthor Josanique Everson wrote about her experiences using social media and other digital tools to organize a youth rally in response to the barrage of killings of unarmed Black people in the United States. She said, in part, "Oh, our school didn't really talk about it [the killing of Mike Brown and the Ferguson protests]. . . . And that's what really made me mad" (Haddix et al., p. 263). After discussing the ways that the program and its participants facilitated, supported, and amplified Josanique's efforts, the authors concluded: "Josanique's resolve toward inquiry, discovery, and action is an exemplar of the ways that many young people are grabbing their pens, their phones, and their keyboards and changing the world. The youth will lead the revolution" (Haddix et al., p. 265). By foregrounding youth voices and involving youth in leadership positions, educational programs and organizations like Writing Our Lives keep the spotlight on the work youth are engaged in, adopting the digital tools youth are already adept in using to extend their reach and expand their missions.

CONCLUSION: RESTORYING TOWARD A RENEWED DIGITAL ACTIVIST IMAGINATION

We have examined youth digital activism across several loci in order to call for education research that "build[s] critical hope and a bank of counter-narratives" to counteract dominant deficitizing discourses about young people more generally and youth of color specifically (Duncan-Andrade, 2007, p. 27). A humanizing stance for education research not only centers youth perspectives and actions but also attempts to take into better account the full human potential of all youth. When we look to online spaces of youth engagement and the kinds of socially attuned practices they engage in across the myriad spaces of their daily lives, we can learn from youth themselves about how to disrupt educational inequalities and broaden the focus on youth literacy practices beyond school walls.

We frame the rise in youth digital activism as one form of *restorying* (Thomas & Stornaiuolo, 2016), which understands young people's counternarrative work to be a central mechanism for disrupting normative and deficitizing frameworks. In an era of struggle and contestation over narrative and meaning, young people today are, in the words of literacy scholar Vivian Vasquez (2014), "reading and writing the self into existence," using digital participatory cultures to restory schooling and society by making it into their own image. Restorying describes the complex ways that contemporary young people narrate the word and the world, analyze their lived experiences, and then synthesize and recontextualize a multiplicity of stories in order to form new narratives. Education researchers can foreground restorying efforts as one means of disrupting inequalities in their own work, by paying close attention to the ways we represent youth and pushing back on mainstream and normative frameworks that often position young people as "at risk" (Vasudevan & Campano, 2009).

Issues of representation—how we represent others and how people represent themselves—are at the heart of youth digital activism. In the recent past, young people had few opportunities to represent themselves on a wide scale, instead relying on mass media and established institutions (e.g., education, publishing, mass media) to craft the stories that dominated our understandings of each other and ourselves. People who were marginalized and minoritized needed to adhere to dominant notions of civic participation—notions that were influenced by White, able-bodied, cisgender, and middle-class or wealthy men. Today, however, there are new possibilities for restorying those representations. *Hamilton*, the revolutionary Broadway musical by Lin-Manuel Miranda is a case in point. A staged adaptation of Ron Chernow's (2005) biography of Alexander Hamilton, Miranda chose to use nontraditional casting for the play. The only visibly White actor in the original Broadway cast with a speaking role was Jonathan Groff, who played a comical yet ominous King George III. The rest of the characters, including Alexander Hamilton, Aaron Burr, George Washington,

Thomas Jefferson, and the Schuyler sisters, were all magnificently played by actors of color. While the historical accuracy of the musical has been rightly questioned by scholars (e.g., Monteiro, 2016), the overwhelmingly positive reception of *Hamilton* from young people studying U.S. history provides hope that change is coming faster than even Miranda might have imagined.

It is significant that much of this reception has been facilitated through social media. Although most youth and young adults cannot afford to attend the Broadway show, a libretto on Genius.com, as well as lively hashtags from #Hamiltunes to #Hamiltrash, have encouraged discourse about the Founding Fathers as not distant and lofty Great Men of History who invented the world as we know it, but as everyday people who had many of the same concerns as people living in contemporary United States. Positioning Hamilton himself as an immigrant from the Caribbean is a way of, in the words of Eliza from the musical, writing the self "back in the narrative" (Miranda, 2015) and controlling who tells one's story. Indeed, the rising generation is moving toward a kind of collective restorying—which Nigerian author Chinua Achebe once suggested was a "balance of stories" (Bacon, 2000)—to begin to address the myriad gaps in our world. If a Founding Father like Alexander Hamilton can be reimagined through the eyes of a young Puerto Rican American, the possibilities and promise of youth restorying the world around them through media are immeasurable. In our current landscape of persistent inequality, the efforts of marginalized people to author themselves in order to be heard, seen, and noticed—to assert that their lives *matter*—has the potential to contribute not only to a new activist imagination but also to the making of a new world.

REFERENCES

Abate, M. A. (2008). *Tomboys: A literary and cultural history*. Philadelphia: Temple University Press.

Asthana, S. (2015). Youth, self, other: A study of Ibdaa's digital media practices in the West Bank, Palestine. *International Journal of Cultural Studies*. Advance online publication. doi:10.1177/1367877915600546

Bacon, K. (2000, August 2). An African voice. *The Atlantic*. Retrieved from http://www.theatlantic.com/magazine/archive/2000/08/an-african-voice/306020/

Beltrán, C. (2015). "Undocumented, unafraid, unapologetic": DREAM activists, immigrant politics, and the queering of democracy. In D. Allen & J. S. Light (Eds.), *From voice to influence: Understanding citizenship in a digital age* (pp. 80–104). Chicago, IL: University of Chicago Press.

Bennett, W. L. (2008). Changing citizenship in the digital age. In W. L. Bennett (Ed.), *Civic life online: Learning how digital media can engage youth* (pp. 1–24). Cambridge: MIT Press.

Bennett, W. L., Wells, C., & Freelon, D. (2011). Communicating civic engagement: Contrasting models of citizenship in the youth web sphere. *Journal of Communication, 61*, 835–856. doi:10.1111/j.1460-2466.2011.01588.x

Blackburn, M. V. (2002). Disrupting the (hetero)normative: Exploring literacy performances and identity work with queer youth. *Journal of Adolescent & Adult Literacy, 46*, 312–324.

Blackburn, M. V. (2007). The experiencing, negotiation, breaking, and remaking of gender rules and regulations by queer youth. *Journal of Gay & Lesbian Issues in Education, 4*(2), 33–54. doi:10.1300/J367v04n02

Blackburn, M. V. (2014). (Re)Writing one's self as an activist across schools and sexual and gender identities: An investigation of the limits of LGBT-inclusive and queering discourses. *Journal of Language & Literacy Education*, 10(1), 1–13.

Bonilla, Y., & Rosa, J. (2015). #Ferguson: Digital protest, hashtag ethnography, and the racial politics of social media in the United States. *American Ethnologist*, 42, 4–17. doi:10.1111/amet.12112

Bosch, T. (2016, July). Twitter activism and youth in South Africa: The case of #RhodesMustFall. *Information, Communication & Society*, 4462, 1–12. doi:10.1080/1369118X.2016.1162829

Brager, J. (2015). The selfie and the other: Consuming viral tragedy and social media (after) lives. *International Journal of Communication*, 9, 1660–1671.

Brock, A. (2012). From the blackhand side: Twitter as a cultural conversation. *Journal of Broadcasting & Electronic Media*, 56, 529–549.

Brock, A., Kvasny, L., & Hales, K. (2010). Cultural appropriations of technical capital: Black women, weblogs, and the digital divide. *Information, Communication & Society*, 13, 1040–1059. doi:10.1080/1369118X.2010.498897

Buckingham, D. (2000). *The making of citizens: Young people, news and politics*. London, England: Routledge.

Chernow, R. (2005). *Alexander Hamilton*. New York, NY: Penguin.

Cohen, C., & Kahne, J. (2012). *Participatory politics: New media and youth political action*. Chicago, IL: MacArthur Research Network on Youth and Participatory Politics. Retrieved from http://ypp.dmlcentral.net/sites/default/files/publications/Participatory_Politics_Report.pdf

Coleman, S. (2008). Doing IT for themselves: Management versus autonomy in youth e-citizenship. In W. L. Bennett (Ed.), *Civic life online: Learning how digital media can engage youth* (pp. 189–206). Cambridge: MIT Press.

Conner, J., & Slattery, A. (2014). New media and the power of youth organizing: Minding the gaps. *Equity & Excellence in Education*, 47(1), 14–30. doi:10.1080/10665684.2014.866868

Carney, N. (2016). All lives matter, but so does race: Black Lives Matter and the evolving role of social media. *Humanity & Society*, 40(2), 1–20. doi:10.1177/0160597616643868

Damodar, A. (2012). The rise of "great potential": Youth activism against gender-based violence. *Harvard International Review*, 34(2), 44–52.

de Vreese, C. H. (2007). Digital renaissance: Young consumer and citizen? *Annals of the American Academy of Political and Social Science*, 611, 207–216. doi:10.1177/0002716206298521

Del Carmen Salazar, M. (2013). A humanizing pedagogy: Reinventing the principles and practice of education as a journey toward liberation. *Review of Research in Education*, 37, 121–148. doi:10.3102/0091732X12464032

DiMaggio, P., Hargittai, E., Celeste, C., & Shafer, S. (2004). From unequal access to differentiated use: A literature review and agenda for research on digital inequality. In K. Neckerman (Ed.), *Social inequality* (pp. 355–400). New York, NY: Russell Sage Foundation.

Driver, S. (2007). *Queer girls and popular culture: Reading, resisting, and creating media*. New York, NY: Peter Lang.

Duncan-Andrade, J. M. R. (2007). Urban youth and the counter-narration of inequality. *Transforming Anthropology*, 15(1), 26–37.

Earl, J., & Kimport, K. (2009). Movement societies and digital protest: Fan activism and other nonpolitical protest online. *Sociological Theory*, 27, 220–243. doi:10.1111/j.1467-9558.2009.01346.x

Fisher, M. (2003). Open mics and open minds: Spoken word poetry in African diaspora participatory literacy communities. *Harvard Educational Review*, 73, 362–389.

Fleetwood, N. (2005). Authenticating practices: Producing realness, performing youth. In S. Maira & E. Soep (Eds.), *Youthscapes: The popular, the national, the global* (pp. 155–172). Philadelphia: University of Pennsylvania Press.

Flood, A. (2016, February 16). Girl's drive to find 1,000 "black girl books" hits target with outpouring of donations. *The Guardian*. Retrieved from http://www.theguardian.com/books/2016/feb/09/marley-dias-1000-black-girl-books-hits-target-with-outpouring-of-donations

Fournier, R. (2013, August 26). The outsiders: How can millennials change Washington if they hate it? *The Atlantic*. Retrieved from http://www.theatlantic.com/politics/archive/2013/08/the-outsiders-howcan-millennials-change-washington-if-they-hate-it/278920/

Fox, J., & Ralston, R. (2016). Queer identity online: Informal learning and teaching experiences of LGBTQ individuals on social media. *Computers in Human Behavior, 65*, 635–642. doi:10.1016/j.chb.2016.06.009

Gadsden, V. L., Davis, J. E., & Artiles, A. J. (2009). Introduction: Risk, equity, and schooling. *Review of Research in Education, 33*, vii–xi.

Garcia, A., Mirra, N., Morrell, E., Martinez, A., & Scorza, D. (2015). The Council of Youth Research: Critical literacy and civic agency in the digital age. *Reading & Writing Quarterly, 31*, 151–167. doi:10.1080/10573569.2014.962203

Ginwright, S., & Cammarota, J. (2007). Youth activism in the urban community: Learning critical civic praxis within community organizations. *International Journal of Qualitative Studies in Education, 20*, 693–710. doi:10.1080/09518390701630833

Ginwright, S., & James, T. (2002). From assets to agents of change: Social justice, organizing, and youth development. *New Directions for Youth Development, 96*, 26–46.

Ginwright, S., Noguera, P., & Cammarota, J. (2006). *Beyond resistance! Youth activism and community change*. New York, NY: Routledge.

Gray, M. L. (2009). Negotiating identities/queering desires: Coming out online and the remediation of the coming-out story. *Journal of Computer-Mediated Communication, 14*, 1162–1189. doi:10.1111/j.1083-6101.2009.01485.x

Haddix, M., Everson, J., & Hodge, R. Y. (2015). "Y'all always told me to stand up for what I believe in": 21st-Century youth writers, activism, and civic engagement. *Journal of Adolescent & Adult Literacy, 59*, 261–265. doi:10.1002/jaal.474

Harry Potter Alliance. (n.d.). *What we do*. Retrieved from http://www.thehpalliance.org/what_we_do

Herrera, L. (2012). Youth and citizenship in the digital age: A view from Egypt. *Harvard Educational Review, 82*, 333–353. doi:10.4324/9780203747575

Ito, M., Soep, E., Kligler-Vilenchik, N., Shresthova, S., & Zimmerman, A. (2015). Learning connected civics: Narratives, practices, infrastructures. *Curriculum Inquiry, 45*, 10–29. doi:10.1080/03626784.2014.995063

Jenkins, H. (2012). "Cultural acupuncture": Fan activism and the Harry Potter alliance. *Transformative Works and Cultures, 10*, 1–29. doi:10.3983/twc.2012.0305.J

Jenkins, H. (2013). *Textual poachers: Television fans and participatory culture* (Rev. ed.). New York, NY: Routledge.

Jenkins, H., Clinton, K., Purushotma, R., Robison, A. J., & Weigel, M. (2006). *Confronting the challenge of participatory culture: Media education for the 21st century*. Chicago, IL: John D. and Catherine T. MacArthur Foundation. Retrieved from http://www.macfound.org/press/publications/white-paper-confronting-the-challenges-of-participatory-culture-media-education-for-the-21st-century-by-henry-jenkins/

Jenkins, H., Shresthova, S., Gamber-Thompson, L., & Kligler-Vilenchik, N. (2016). 17 Superpowers to the people! How young activists are tapping the civic imagination. In E. Gordon & P. Mihailidis (Eds.), *Civic media: Technology, design, practice* (pp. 295–320). Cambridge: MIT Press.

Jensen, L. A. (2010). Immigrant youth in the United States: Coming of age among diverse civic cultures. In L. R. Sherrod, J. Torney-Purta, & C. A. Flanagan (Eds.), *Handbook of research on civic engagement in youth* (pp. 425–443). Hoboken, NJ: Wiley.

Kahne, J., & Middaugh, E. (2008). Democracy for some: The civic opportunity gap in high school. In J. Youniss & P. Levine (Eds.), *Forging citizens: Policies for youth civic engagement* (pp. 29–57). Nashville, TN: Vanderbilt University Press.

Kahne, J., Middaugh, E., & Allen, D. (2015). Youth, media, and the rise of participatory politics. In D. Allen & J. S. Light (Eds.), *From voice to influence: Understanding citizenship in a digital age* (pp. 35–59). Chicago, IL: University of Chicago Press.

Killham, J. E., & Chandler, P. (2016). From Tweets to telegrams: Using social media to promote historical thinking. *Social Education, 80*, 118–122.

Kinloch, V. (2010). *Harlem on our minds: Place, race, and the literacies of urban youth.* New York, NY: Teachers College Press.

Kirshner, B. (2007). Introduction: Youth activism as a context for learning and development. *American Behavioral Scientist, 51*, 367–379.

Kirshner, B. (2008). Guided participation in three youth activism organizations: Facilitation, apprenticeship, and joint work. *Journal of the Learning Sciences, 17*, 60–101.

Kirshner, B. (2015). *Youth activism in an era of education inequality.* New York: New York University Press.

Kirshner, B., & Middaugh, E. (2015). *#Youthaction: Becoming political in the digital age.* Charlotte, NC: Information Age.

Kligler-Vilenchik, N., Mcveigh-Schultz, J., Weitbrecht, C., & Tokuhama, C. (2012). Experiencing fan activism: Understanding the power of fan activist organizations through members' narratives. *Transformative Works and Cultures, 20*, 1–26. doi:10.3983/twc.2012.0322.J

Lam, W. S. E. (2009). Multiliteracies on instant messaging in negotiating local, translocal, and transnational affiliations: A case of an adolescent immigrant. *Reading Research Quarterly, 44*, 377–397. doi:10.1598/rrq.44.4.5

Lam, W. S. E., & Rosario-Ramos, E. (2009). Multilingual literacies in transnational digitally mediated contexts: An exploratory study of immigrant teens in the United States. *Language and Education, 23*, 171–190.

Lesko, N. (2012). *Act your age! A cultural construction of adolescence* (2nd ed.). New York, NY: Routledge.

Levine, P. (2009). The civic opportunity gap. *Educational Leadership, 66*(8), 20–25.

Levinson, M. (2010). The civic empowerment gap. In L. Sherrod, J. Torney-Purta, & C. Flanagan (Eds.), *Handbook of research on civic engagement in youth* (pp. 316–346). Hoboken, NJ: Wiley.

Lin, W. Y., Cheong, P. H., Kim, Y.-C., & Jung, J.-Y. (2010). Becoming citizens: Youths' civic uses of new media in five digital cities in East Asia. *Journal of Adolescent Research, 25*, 839–857. doi:10.1177/0743558410371125

Lipman, P. (2004). *High stakes education: Inequality, globalization, and urban school reform.* London, England: Psychology Press.

Lipman, P. (2013). *The new political economy of urban education: Neoliberalism, race, and the right to the city.* New York, NY: Taylor & Francis.

Love, B., & Bradley, R. (2014). Teaching Trayvon: Teaching about racism through public pedagogy, hip hop, black trauma, and social media. In J. L. Martin (Ed.), *Racial battle fatigue: Insights from the front lines of social justice advocacy* (pp. 255–268). Santa Barbara, CA: Praeger.

McDonald, C. A., Geigel, J., & Pinguel, F. (2011). The role of new media in youth organizing for educational justice. *Voices in Urban Education, 30*, 41–48.

Miranda, L-M. (2015). Who lives, who dies, who tells your story [Original Broadway Cast of *Hamilton.*] In *Hamilton: An American musical—Original Broadway cast recording.* New York, NY: Atlantic.

Moje, E. B. (2004). Powerful spaces: Tracing the out-of-school literacy spaces of Latino/a youth. In K. Leander & M. Sheehy (Eds.), *Spatializing literacy research and practice* (pp. 15–38). New York, NY: Peter Lang.

Moll, L. C. (2004). Rethinking resistance. *Anthropology & Education Quarterly, 35*, 126–131.

Monteiro, L. D. (2016). Review essay: Race-conscious casting and the erasure of the black past in Lin-Manuel Miranda's *Hamilton. The Public Historian, 38*(1), 89–98.

Morrell, E. (2008). *Critical literacy and urban youth: Pedagogies of access, dissent, and liberation.* New York, NY: Routledge.

O'Connor, C., Hill, L. D., & Robinson, S. R. (2009). Who's at risk in school and what's race got to do with it? *Review of Research in Education, 33*, 1–34.

Östman, J. (2012). Information, expression, participation: How involvement in user-generated content relates to democratic engagement among young people. *New Media & Society, 14*, 1004–1021. doi:10.1177/1461444812438212

Paoletta, R. (2015, 5 September). 8 Inspiring teens who are using social media to change the world. *MTV News.* Retrieved from http://www.mtv.com/news/2270448/teen-social-media-activists/

Paris, D. (2012). Culturally sustaining pedagogy: A needed change in stance, terminology, and practice. *Educational Researcher, 41*, 93–97.

Paris, D., & Winn, M. (Eds.). (2013). *Humanizing research: Decolonizing qualitative inquiry with youth and communities.* Thousand Oaks, CA: Sage.

Patel, L., & Sanchez Ares, R. (2014). Framing youth resistance: The politics of coming out undocumented. In E. Tuck & K. W. Yang (Eds.), *Youth resistance and theories of change* (pp. 139–152). New York, NY: Routledge.

Persaud, C. (2016, July 5, 6:59–7:01 p.m.). "So I think a useful way of differentiating the two, is that queerbending is also more about imagining a better way to be for queer characters I think (canon or not) in a fictional world whereas slash fiction to me seems to be more often than not written by/for cishet people. queerbending = by/for queer people" [Twitter post]. Retrieved from https://twitter.com/audrelordte/status/750464186136813569

Pew Research Center for the People and the Press. (2010). *Millenials: Confident. Connected. Open to change.* Retrieved from http://www.pewsocialtrends.org/files/2010/10/millennials-confident-connected-open-to-change.pdf

Pollock, M. (2004). Race bending: "Mixed" youth practicing strategic racialization in California. *Anthropology & Education Quarterly, 35*, 30–52.

Poyntz, S. R. (2006). Independent media, youth agency, and the promise of media education. *Canadian Journal of Education, 29*, 154–175. doi:10.2307/20054151

Racebending.com. (n.d.). What is "racebending"? Retrieved from http://www.racebending.com/v4/about/what-is-racebending/

Ransby, B. (2015). The class politics of Black Lives Matter. *Dissent, 62*(4), 31–34.

Rheingold, H. (2008). Using participatory media and public voice to encourage civic engagement. In W. L. Bennett (Ed.), *Civic life online: Learning how digital media can engage youth* (pp. 97–118). Cambridge: MIT Press.

Rogers, J., Mediratta, K., & Shah, S. (2012). Building power, learning democracy: Youth organizing as a site of civic development. *Review of Research in Education, 36*, 43–66. doi:10.3102/0091732X11422328

Shiller, J. T. (2013). Preparing for democracy: How community-based organizations build civic engagement among urban youth. *Urban Education, 48*, 69–91. doi:10.1177/0042085912436761

Soep, E. (2014). *Participatory politics: Next-generation tactics to remake the public sphere.* Cambridge: MIT Press.

Thomas, E. E., & Stornaiuolo, A. (2016). Restorying the self: Bending toward textual justice. *Harvard Educational Review, 6*, 313–338.

Tosenberger, C. (2008). Homosexuality at the online Hogwarts: Harry Potter slash fanfiction. *Children's Literature, 36,* 185–207.

Valenzuela, S., Arriagada, A., & Scherman, A. (2012). The social media basis of youth protest behavior: The case of Chile. *Journal of Communication, 62,* 299–314. doi:10.1111/j.1460-2466.2012.01635.x

Vasquez, V. M. (2014, March). *Critical ethnography and pedagogy: Bridging the audit trail with technology.* Keynote address presented at the 35th Annual Ethnography in Education Forum, University of Pennsylvania, Philadelphia.

Vasudevan, L., & Campano, G. (2009). The social production of adolescent risk and the promise of adolescent literacies. *Review of Research in Education, 33,* 310–353. doi:10.3102/0091732X08330003

Velasquez, A., & LaRose, R. (2015). Youth collective activism through social media: The role of collective efficacy. *New Media & Society, 17,* 899–918. doi:10.1177/1461444813518391

Vie, S. (2014). In defense of "slacktivism": The human rights campaign Facebook logo as digital activism. *First Monday, 19*(4), 1–14. doi:10.5210/fm.v19i4.4961

Wargo, J. M. (2015). "Every selfie tells a story . . .": LGBTQ youth lifestreams and new media narratives as connective identity texts. *New Media & Society.* Advance online publication. doi:10.1177/1461444815612447

Warschauer, M., & Matuchniak, T. (2010). New technology and digital worlds: Analyzing evidence of equity in access, use, and outcomes. *Review of Research in Education, 34,* 179–225. doi:10.3102/0091732X09349791

Williams, S. (2015). Digital defense: Black feminists resist violence with hashtag activism. *Feminist Media Studies, 15,* 341–344. doi:10.1080/14680777.2015.1008744

Winn, M. T. (2010). "Our side of the story": Moving incarcerated youth voices from margins to center. *Race Ethnicity and Education, 13,* 313–325.

Xenos, M., Vromen, A., & Loader, B. D. (2014). The great equalizer? Patterns of social media use and youth political engagement in three advanced democracies. *Information, Communication & Society, 17,* 151–167. doi:10.1080/1369118X.2013.871318

Zimmerman, K. (2007). Making space, making change: Models for youth-led social change organizations. *Children, Youth and Environments, 17,* 298–314.

Zhang, W. (2013). Redefining youth activism through digital technology in Singapore. *International Communication Gazette, 75,* 253–270. doi:10.1177/1748048512472858

Zuckerman, E. (2014). New media, new civics? *Policy & Internet, 6,* 151–168. doi:10.1002/1944-2866.POI360

Chapter 15

Fostering Sociopolitical Consciousness With Minoritized Youth: Insights From Community-Based Arts Programs

Bic Ngo
Cynthia Lewis
Betsy Maloney Leaf
University of Minnesota

In this chapter, we review the literature on community-based arts programs serving minoritized youth to identify the conditions and practices for fostering sociopolitical consciousness. Community-based arts programs have the capacity to promote teaching and learning practices in ways that engage youth in the use of academic skills to pursue inquiry, cultural critique, and social action. In this review, we pay particular attention to literary arts, theatre arts, and digital media arts to identify three dimensions of sociopolitical consciousness: identification, mobilization, and cosmopolitanism. By advancing the principle of sociopolitical consciousness within the theory and practice of critical and cultural relevant pedagogies, our review provides ways toward mitigating social and educational disparities.

Against the backdrop of school as a site that often marginalizes and underserves minoritized students, out-of-school educational settings may provide youth with opportunities to combat "humiliating public representations of their race, ethnicity, class, gender and sexuality" by engaging youth in projects that deconstruct deficit representations and invent new identities and possibilities (Fine, Weis, Centrie, & Roberts, 2000, p. 132). These programs often are run by adults who deeply understand the social context of the community (Ginwright, 2005) and offer "opportunities for young people to learn [that] derive primarily from an ethos that actively considers them to be resources for themselves, their peers, families and communities" (Heath, 1998, p. 2).

In this chapter, we review the literature on community-based arts programs serving minoritized youth to identify the conditions and practices for fostering

Review of Research in Education
March 2017, Vol. 41, pp. 358–380
DOI: 10.3102/0091732X17690122
© 2017 AERA. http://rre.aera.net

sociopolitical consciousness. Our focus on the arts takes seriously the notion that "education is simultaneously an act of knowing, a political act, and an artistic event" (Freire, 1985b, p. 17). Community-based arts programs have the capacity to promote teaching and learning practices that engage youth in the use of academic skills to pursue inquiry, cultural critique, and social action (Barron, Gomez, Pinkard, & Martin, 2014; Scharber, Isaacson, Pyscher, & Lewis, 2015; Sefton-Green, 2013). Simultaneously, arts programs call particular attention to the multimodal possibilities of arts for reflection and expression that allow for "the living of lyrical moments, moments at which human beings (freed to feel, to know, and to imagine) suddenly understand their own lives in relation to all that surrounds" (Greene, 2001, p. 7).

Our examination of community-based arts settings is grounded in the belief that "we need to attend to the broader learning ecologies that students access and develop, and find ways to make these more diverse, generative, and interconnected" (Barron, Walter, Martin, & Schatz, 2010, p. 188). It aims to inform both community-based and K–12 educational practices, fuel potential collaborations, and enable educators to better support minoritized youth. Significantly, by advancing the principle of sociopolitical consciousness within the theory and practice of critical and cultural relevant pedagogies, our review provides ways toward their aspirations for "liberatory," "transformative," or "empowering" education (Giroux & Simon, 1989; Shor, 1992).

FRAMING THE REVIEW
Sociopolitical Consciousness

Researchers concerned with addressing educational disparities revealed incorporating the experiences, interests, and cultures of minoritized students into curriculum and instruction enhances academic engagement and achievement (e.g., Gay, 2000; Ladson-Billings, 1995; Moll & Gonzalez, 2004; Paris, 2012). Theories of critical, culturally relevant, and culturally sustaining pedagogies specifically emphasize the role of education in disrupting inequality through the development of sociopolitical consciousness in students, which allows them to recognize and act on the historical and sociopolitical contexts under-girding their current experiences and struggles (Freire, 1970/2005; Ladson-Billings, 1995). From this perspective, the goal of teaching and learning is one of "unveiling . . . the reality and thereby coming to know it critically" (Freire, 1970/1996, p. 51) and making possible "political self-recovery" (hooks, 1990, p. 345) as students are able to see and imagine themselves differently, and take action against oppression.

More specifically, Freire (1970/2005) suggested critical consciousness or "conscientization" requires individuals to

develop their power to perceive critically *the way they* exist in the world *with which* and *in which* they find themselves; they come to see the world not as a static reality, but as a reality in the process, in transformation. (p. 83)

Fostering *conscientization* requires educators to start with the student's "present, existential, concrete situation" posed as a problem that can challenge them to respond "not just at the intellectual level, but at the level of action" (Freire, 1970/2005, pp. 95–96). Engaging students in the material conditions of their lives might include working with students to identify poorly used space in their community and designing and presenting alternative urban plans to the city council (Ladson-Billings, 1995; see also, Shor, 1992; Souto-Manning, 2010). Such a critical pedagogy is

a deliberate attempt to influence how and what knowledge and identities are produced within and among particular sets of social relations. It can be understood as a practice through which people are incited to acquire a particular "moral character." As both a political and practical activity, it attempts to influence the occurrence and qualities of experiences. (Giroux & Simon, 1989, p. 239)

Since youth often already possess knowledge of social inequality, educators who nurture sociopolitical consciousness do so by drawing on students' empirical knowledge of lived oppression and structuring opportunities for them to systematically "use the various skills they learn to better understand and critique their social position and context" rather than forcing a political agenda in the classroom (Ladson-Billings, 2006, p. 37).

While school districts and teachers may endorse culturally relevant pedagogy, teachers are often constrained by curricular standards that address "cultural sensitivity," or "culturally relevant strategies" to increase proficiency on standardized tests rather than having the autonomy to develop sociopolitical consciousness as an integrated pedagogical approach to academic engagement and achievement (Young, 2010, p. 253). Furthermore, educators within school contexts have struggled to nurture social critique and social action in teaching and learning practices. Writing about the struggles preservice and in-service teachers have with fostering sociopolitical consciousness, Ladson-Billings (2006) observed that teachers often have not experienced and thus do not understand the sociopolitical issues (e.g., unemployment, healthcare, housing) that impinge on the lives of minoritized young people. Our review addresses these gaps by explicating the features of fostering sociopolitical conscious central to critical pedagogy and culturally relevant pedagogy.

Notes on the Review

In this chapter, we use "minoritized" rather than "minority" or "youth of color" to emphasize the (ongoing) process of marginalization based on race, ethnicity, class, gender, sexual orientation, language, religion, and dis/ability, among other dimensions of difference that are socially constructed in specific societal contexts. We focus on recent studies (published since 2000) of arts programs that were administered by community-based organizations such as arts organizations, social service organizations, museums, libraries, and community centers. Although research exists on exemplary arts-based, social justice programs that are part of school (e.g., Cahnmann-Taylor & Souto-Manning, 2010) or span school and community contexts (e.g., Kinloch, 2010; Morrell, 2004), we seek to spotlight the contributions of research in community-based settings. And while we understand that community-based arts programs are not inherently "safe" spaces or empowering settings (and indeed may perpetuate inequality), we focus on the practices of programs that have the potential to innovate critical and culturally relevant pedagogies to disrupt the educational disparities faced by minoritized youth.

Our review of the research pays particular attention to three areas of the arts: literary arts (e.g., spoken word poetry, creative writing), theatre arts, and digital media arts (e.g., digital storytelling). We highlight a select number of studies in order to elucidate programmatic content and practices that may provide more specific insight for promoting sociopolitical consciousness and addressing educational disparities. Studies we include in this chapter afford minoritized youth opportunities to grapple with complex issues in their lives, such as domestic violence, gang membership, incarceration, sexuality, and citizenship, among others. Due to minimal information about the role of staff, our analysis primarily centers on the activities youth engaged in within the arts programs.

In order to provide nuance to the pedagogical practices of arts programs, our comprehensive review of published scholarship identifies three dimensions of sociopolitical consciousness: identification, mobilization, and cosmopolitanism. The process for identifying these dimensions involved four stages. First, we drew on the literature to explicate our understanding of sociopolitical consciousness and its multiple dimensions. Second, we each took one arts genre and collected studies pertaining to our respective genre. We then analyzed the studies for contributions to fostering sociopolitical consciousness, paying attention to specific dimensions of sociopolitical consciousness of the arts activities. Fourth, we came together and discussed the various dimensions from our respective genres, highlighting the major patterns, which allowed us to identify the three dominant dimensions. We especially discussed overlaps between identification and mobilization and agreed that identification focuses more on "naming" to promote awareness and understanding or express personal experiences, while mobilization also includes action toward internal or external change. Cosmopolitanism focuses on exploring belonging across difference. Last, we reviewed the literature again, analyzing practices that illustrate each of the three dimensions of fostering sociopolitical consciousness.

While we understand that aspects of the three dimensions of identification, mobilization, and cosmopolitanism may overlap, in this review we isolate each dimension in order to tease out specificity that may provide educators, policymakers, and community members with better insight to mitigate the challenges of fostering sociopolitical consciousness. We begin each of the following three sections with a synopsis of our theoretical lens for each dimension. We close the chapter with a discussion that includes suggestions for future research.

IDENTIFICATION: NAMING TO EXPRESS AND UNDERSTAND

Freire (1985a) argued that education that fosters sociopolitical consciousness "involves a constant clarification of what remains hidden within us while we move about in [a] world" that is continuously shaped by broader social, political and historical forces (pp. 106–107). The identification of the forces that shape the material conditions of human experience requires individuals to "name the world":

Human existence cannot be Silent, nor can it be nourished by false words, but only by true words, with which men and women transform the world. To exist, humanly, is to *name* the world, to change it. Once named, the world in its turn reappears to the namers as a problem and requires of them a new *naming*. Human beings are not built in silence, but in word, in work, in action-reflection. (Freire, 1970/2005, p. 88)

Speaking from one's own circumstance is the foundation for identifying collective injustices, constructing a critique of inequality, and developing agency to advance social change. Community-based arts programs have the capacity to animate creative and imaginative capacities in ways that magnify opportunities for minoritized youth to individually and collectively name the world.

Against the backdrop of school's environment of surveillance and heavily standardized curriculum (Alim, 2011), research on community-based settings has shown the ways in which out-of-school writing contextualizes and acknowledges the potency of the lived experiences of minoritized youth (Jocson, 2006; Mahiri & Sablo, 1996). For example, Weinstein and West's (2012) study of youth spoken word programs across the United States and the United Kingdom and multiple spoken word poetry festivals noted that teen youth drew on the potency of both words and body language to name injustices and construct counternarratives. Active and dialogic audience participation gave performers support and helped them imagine possible selves. The interactive nature of spoken word events between artist and audience generated tangible encouragement, where performers are able to receive immediate feedback from the audience. While the authors acknowledged the importance of active audience participation, they cautioned such contexts can also be detrimental because they create an element of spectacle and contribute to "a star system" (p. 232).

Other studies illustrated the ways in which spoken word programs provided young poets a means to author their existence *against* larger social structures defining youth but *within* local communities of slam poets committed to one another and democratic change. For example, Jocson (2006) analyzed the relationship between spoken word and adolescent construction of self in Youth Speaks (San Francisco), highlighting the construction of hybrid identity encompassing "poet, performer, and mentor" (p. 250). Their identities as artists were informed by a "kind of mentorship" (p. 250) between peers and staff who contributed to a "better understanding of [one's] place in the world" (p. 250). Creating *against* and *within* afforded youth slam poets the opportunity to not just respond to society's construction of youth identity but also reclaim their identity as commendable and worth listening to.

Rivera (2013) also pointed to dimensions of *against/within* by explaining that "spoken word poetry is not merely an art form that aims to represent one's lived experience, but it is a medium of producing self offstage" (p. 114). Producing self was the core from which youth poets working at Urban Word NYC made sense of their lives. In particular, spoken word poetry was *parrhesia* or "truth-telling that comes at great risk to the speaker" (p. 119) because the youth performers are expected to "'be what you're talking about,' and that both the speaker and the utterance must be 'authentic'" (p. 120). Spoken word poetry was a "gateway to actually be within the world" through writing about personally relevant topics such as racism and other aspects of their actual experiences (p. 122). While Rivera acknowledged authenticity as constructed identity, we suggest research should further consider how arts programs offer ways for youth to construct identity as multiple and shifting.

In a different way, the concept of "producing self" was integral to the dramaturgical process of composing and producing a play in community-based theatre. Such programs created avenues for youth to explore identities and experiences through storytelling, and in the process author and narrate lives (Halverson, 2005, 2010; Hammock, 2011; Winn, 2010, 2011; Winn & Jackson, 2011). Halverson's (2005) analysis of the stories LGBTQQ (lesbian, gay, bisexual, transgender, queer, and questioning) youth wrote in About Face Youth Theatre explicated the multiple dimensions of identity that youth examined as part of the dramaturgical process. Against the backdrop of (negative) labeling by others, writing stories was a means for youth to delve into their self-perception and call themselves something. Youth used "I am" statements to make literal descriptors of identity (e.g., "I am a girlie girl"; p. 77) as well as metaphorical descriptors of identity (e.g., "I am constantly evolving . . . I am becoming-evolving-changing"; p. 77). More than descriptive statements, the writing of stories was a means for youth to express views of people's perceptions and treatment of them (see also Winn, 2010; Winn & Jackson, 2011). The exploration of the ways in which they see themselves and others see them presented points of comparison for youth to re-present themselves.

Identification work in theatre programs also promoted awareness that provided youth with labels for understanding their experiences. Hammock's (2011) research with The Wellness Players, a community educational youth theatre troupe, found that youth who participated in a play to prevent dating violence learned to recognize themselves as survivors of violence. As youth acquired knowledge about intimate partner violence through work on the play (e.g., discussions, videos), they gained better conception of relationship violence in their past and present lives. For example, one female participant was able to see similarities between the behaviors of her boyfriend and those illustrated in a video on the warning signs of dating violence. She was able to identify relationship violence with her partner that enabled her to leave him a few months later when his behaviors evolved into physical violence. Another youth was able to name experiences of molestation and "realize that that was the title for what had happened" to her (p. 372). Participation in the theatre program allowed youth to learn about domestic violence, while acting in the play made the experience "more real" (p. 373). The embodiment of a character in the play facilitated emotional and physical linkages between stage and life that confirmed for the youth the reality of their experiences.

In addition to facilitating internal reflection and awareness, community-based theatre was a forum for minoritized young people to engage with perpetrators of injustices against them. Sonn, Quayle, Belanji, and Baker (2015) showed that the On the Radar Playback Theatre project was specifically designed to enable dialogue between minoritized youth and police. Youth discussed their marginalized status in the community, media misrepresentation, and experiences of racialization and criminalization by local police within structured workshops. The stories youth shared during the workshops formed the foundation of a live playback performance that include members of the local police in the audience. Youth re-presented their experiences and were able to "speak back" (p. 250) to dominant society through the telling and performing of stories. The public performance was a medium for youth to express an alternative story to cultural stereotypes in a tangible, embodied way that was difficult for the local police to ignore.

However, storytelling by youth did not necessarily always reach critical awareness of damaging representations. Edell (2013) showed from over 13 years of work with viBe Theatre Experience, a performing arts education organization that engaged minoritized teenage girls in the writing and performing of "personal and truthful collaborative theater pieces" (p. 52), that girls often wrote stories that repeat and perpetuate detrimental stereotypes. Their writing about sex, for example, often reiterated a cultural narrative about girls and sex that emphasized the unwilling loss of virginity due to succumbing to peer pressure (all her friends were doing it), being taken advantage by a boy, and then crying and regretting the experience afterward. Despite different real-life experiences, girls sought to reproduce this narrative, because it is a "safe" story to tell, a story that is also expected of them. Such a narrative excluded "stories of girls' desire, girls' agency, and girls' pleasure" as well as emotions such as excitement, curiosity, and joy that are also a part of first-time experiences with sexual intercourse (p. 54). Despite the opportunity to "name" their experiences, the familiar story line about girls and sex embedded in the young women's stories did not challenge dominant representations but preserved and propagated insidious stereotypes of dominant boys and submissive girls (Tolman, 2012).

While the process of exploring stories and representations in theatre programs took place across intensive weeks or months, the scholarship on digital media arts programs showed that drop-in community sites also served as spaces for minoritized young people to name and reimagine identities (Peppler & Kafai, 2007; Barron et al., 2014; Sefton-Green, 2013). London, Pastor, Servon, Rosner, and Wallace (2010) found in a study of youth in five drop-in community technology programs in Boston, California, New York City, and Seattle that the programs bolstered the social capital of the participants and "democratized who speaks and from what vantage point" (p. 215). For example, an indigenous youth noted the importance of sharing knowledge about indigenous identities that she felt were absent from dominant discourse. The authors found that the emphasis on producing knowledge through digital stories was central to creating an interest in college for this particular young woman, who reported that through the experience she had the ability to communicate her life stories and their meanings in ways that could influence others. Other projects provided youth openings to share and critique their stories by creating materials that could name and challenge the way others view, such as through public service announcements and social documentaries that focused on police brutality, women's activism, and youth violence.

Whether drop-in or intensive, youth programs focused on digital storytelling offered minoritized youth generative opportunities to explore their various and sometimes conflicting identities, using the digital arts to create an "agentive self" (Hull & Katz, 2006). Moreover, digital storytelling decenters logocentric forms of storytelling and privileges visual and oral forms in ways that promoted intergenerational communication in communities with strong oral traditions (Iseke & Moore, 2011). For example, Salazar's (2010) study, a partnership between a nonprofit media arts organization (Information and Cultural Exchange organization) and researchers at the University of Western Sydney, revealed that a project designed to provide African and Cambodian migrant youth with media-making skills to document their histories resulted in digital stories that circulated and reverberated into the larger community. Youth were engaged in larger public discourses about migration through telling stories of forced histories of migration, challenges of resettlement, and adjustments to the new urban landscape, which allowed them to name their experiences and promote understanding among Anglos and other community members. Youth were divided into two groups: one group of recent refugees from African countries and the other a group of second-generation Cambodian youth. The article did not examine this decision to divide the groups but assumed that each group will have a distinct culturally relevant focus. Indeed, within each community, the stories cultivated intergenerational dialogue and healing related to fears of cultural loss in the face of social and cultural change and the need for youth to talk back to these fears. Whether or not some of the issues addressed in each group could resonate across the assumed cultural boundaries was not explored, but the critical conversations within each group spoke to intersectional identities related to gender and generation.

Studies in this section on identification revealed that the lives of minoritized youth provided abundant "funds of knowledge" (Moll & Gonzalez, 2004) to examine and name the world. As a "generative theme" the individual experiences of young people "contain the possibility of unfolding into again as many themes" (Freire, 1970/2005, p. 102, endnote). Spoken word, theatre, and digital media arts were means for minoritized youth to unveil their realities in ways that allowed them to animate past and current struggles and critically respond to larger societal depictions of their identities with counternarratives that contributed to community awareness.

MOBILIZATION: ENGAGING IN SOCIAL TRANSFORMATION

Education that fosters sociopolitical consciousness is more than an intellectual pursuit of understanding but necessarily involves action to challenge dominant culture's power to domesticate and suppress human consciousness, and change existing conditions of oppression (Freire, 1970/2005). Sociopolitical consciousness is a constant process that involves "praxis" or "reflection and action upon the world in order to transform it" (Freire, 1970/2005, p. 51). This dialectical practice is reflected in recognizing the work of community-based arts programs as a "community narrative" that simultaneously "[disrupts] the existing social text and [leaves] more room for dialogue" (Thomas & Rappaport, 1996, p. 330). However, many youth generally disdain politics as usual but hunger for a "range of nonmainstream forms of civil involvement that can become mobilized" (Youniss et al., 2002, p. 128). This section illuminates the ways minoritized youth within community-based arts programs mobilized to transform discourse into collective action (Kwon, 2008) that opened up "nonmainstream" opportunities for "youth [to] define, negotiate, and struggle for their identities in oppressive environments" (Ginwright & Cammarota, 2002, p. 83).

The research on literary arts underscored the role of community-based spoken word programs in leveraging artistic practice as vehicles for social change (Fields,

Snapp, Russell, Licona, & Tilley, 2014; Weinstein & West, 2012; Flores-Gonzalez, Rodriguez, & Rodriguez-Muniz, 2006). Minoritized youth in spoken word communities created and civically engaged through the performance of their writing. In many studies, the creative process was also the springboard for mobilization, where youth performers engaged in community dialogue during performances or used the artwork itself as a catalyst for discussion. For example, Fields et al. (2014) investigated young people's use of poetry in the Tucson Youth Poetry Slam to learn about and respond to legislation restricting access to resources devoted to reproductive health or sexuality, particularly for adolescent youth. Youth used slam poetry to advocate for their rights, community action, and policies and practices that reflect the complexity of their lived experiences. According to the authors, youth "used poetry as an expression of social action and change" (p. 310) that enabled them to counter policies and practices that influence their lives (p. 320).

Similarly, youth poets at Multicultural Alliance and Teen Justice in California employed spoken word as an extension of hip-hop culture to inform their "social justice organizing" (Clay, 2006, p. 112; see also Flores-Gonzalez et al., 2006). Clay (2006) demonstrated that by arranging public events, youth were able to use the organization's performances as a "strategy" (p. 112) for revealing power structures. At slam events the youth performed poems, rapped, and sang about the issues affecting the material conditions of their lives, including experiencing gang violence in their communities and being pulled over by police. They conceptualized spoken word as a way to develop collective identity with audience members through various activities during their performances, including call and response, conversations, and petition drives to address school suspensions, gang violence, and intraracial conflict.

Like spoken word, playwriting within community-based theatre programs afforded young people with the opportunity to name their experiences as well as rewrite, recast, and respond to representations (Halverson, 2005; Wernick, Kulick & Woodford, 2014; Winn, 2011, 2012; Winn & Jackson, 2011). Winn and Jackson (2011) found in their work with incarcerated African American girls in the *Girl Time* theatre program that youth use writing as a means to "re-introduce themselves to the world" (p. 616). The re-writing of life scripts was facilitated by a prompt to "say something that they may have never had the opportunity to say" (p. 617) that enabled youth to "feel very powerful," construct stories out of negative experiences with judgmental people and "naysayers" and re-cast their identities as worthy individuals (p. 616). The performance of stories was a means for the youth to grapple with people and experiences in their past and reconcile their circumstances of incarceration (see also Palidofsky & Stolbach, 2012). Young women came to terms with the difficult realities of life and moved forward in life through the "healing dialog" of the script (Winn & Jackson, 2011, p. 617).

Whereas Winn and Jackson (2011) showed theatre affords youth with a medium for the healing of selves (see also Palidofsky & Stolbach, 2012), Halverson's (2005) study of About Face Youth Theatre's work with LGBTQQ youth found theatre was a site for trying on multiple "possible selves." The dramaturgical process engaged youth in writing personal stories, adapting the stories into a play, and then performing the stories of other youth's lives. As the young people portrayed the stories of program members, they tried on different identities in their various roles in the play, including those of other youth and supporting characters (e.g., teacher, mother). Youth who thought they did not have anything in common with one another discovered different facets of themselves in ways that were "liberating" because they were able to let go of rigid ideas about their identities through telling others' stories (Halverson, 2005, p. 86). In contrast, youth who saw their stories beyond themselves found the activity to be an opportunity for "giving up" or "letting go" (p. 86) of past experiences and move forward.

Moreover, the youth theatre research stressed the potential of the ensemble facet of theatre for the mobilization of young people in collective struggle (Winn, 2010; Winn & Jackson, 2011; Wernick et al., 2014). Wernick et al. (2014) found that the storytelling process of Gayrilla Theatre to disseminate findings from a participatory action research study on the local high school climate for LGBTQQ youth dismantled the isolation experienced by minoritized LGBTQQ youth. Theatre games such as role-playing real-life experiences and fictional scenarios and improvisational skits facilitated discussions for youth to understand their own experiences and see connections with those of others (Souto-Manning, 2011). The youth then worked collaboratively with an adult advisor to develop a script comprising stories collected from the theatre games, climate survey findings, and their policy recommendations for change. Preparation for performances involved one required rehearsal where youth read from scripts so that youth with various theatre and memorization skills and time availability could participate in performances. Gayrilla Theatre performers then read from scripts during performances in local high schools that were sites of the research project. Storytelling transformed what youth felt from an individual problem into a shared experience of community connected by the effects of marginalization. The collective telling of their stories to peers and adult decision makers in a structured performance was a means for LGBTQQ youth to systematically collect, analyze, and disseminate "difficult knowledge" (Britzman, 1998) and contribute to social transformation.

Mobilization in arts can occur during the creative process or when the artistic product is used to communicate within or between communities about social issues and conditions. For example, Sandoval and Latorre's (2008) study of the César Chávez Digital Mural Lab's work with Chicanx and Latinx youth underscored that art is a form of action, and the public art youth take up as part of the program is transformative of self and world (Chappell, 2009). Youth brought their knowledge of digital culture to the lab and pushed adult staff and other youth in new directions as "artistic equals" (Sandoval & Latorre, 2008, p. 84). Digital tools (e.g., Photoshop) were used to create art focusing on collaboratively identified topics such as immigration, urban gentrification, and displacement, among other topics of concern to youth and families. Once completed, the artwork was disseminated through websites, video, and other digital formats.

The "Shoulder to Shoulder" project was an exemplar of the potential of the lab's "digital artivism" (i.e., art activism) through structured collaborative creation. The project brought together 125 racially and ethnically diverse 14-year-olds from segregated neighborhoods of Los Angeles "to create a space of healing" through an opportunity to work with and interact with youth from different neighborhoods (Sandoval & Latorre, 2008, p. 97). For multiple sessions, youth were paired with partners from a different social or cultural background than their own, and engaged in conversations about differences across race, gender, and class that revealed their own roles in systems that construct and maintain difference. The youth digitally created banners representing their conversations and took to the streets with the vinyl-printed placards to share their messages about the complexities of diversity and intersectionality with the broader community. Whereas sociopolitical consciousness in many of the programs highlighted in the research we reviewed developed around specific raced and gendered identities, sociopolitical consciousness in this program drew on coalitional work across markers of identity. This work highlights the need for considerations of sociopolitical consciousness to study the intersectional identities of youth, who are often mobile and connected across a broader range of communities than their elders.

In addition to collaboration between youth, Chávez and Soep's (2005) study of Youth Radio illuminated youth-adult collaboration in social change projects. Grounded in "a pedagogy of collegiality" characterized by "shared collective responsibility" (p. 418) between youth and adults, the program positioned youth as social agents who pitched ideas and made production decisions informed by collegial relationships with adults. This work challenges the notion of "giving voice" to youth, endorsed by some other programs in this review, and problematic for its paternalistic stance toward minoritized youth who are viewed as lacking the agency to speak their truths. Four features of collegial pedagogy disrupted this idea and, instead, promoted a productive interdependence among youth and adults: (1) joint framing, (2) youth-led inquiry, (3) mediated intervention, and (4) distributed accountability. These features grappled with the balance between "sufficient mentorship and excessive intervention" (p. 424) and contribute to mobilizing youth capacity for activism that is informed, includes multiple perspectives, and recognizes vulnerable subjects.

Goldman, Booker, and McDermott (2008) highlighted the importance of a dialogic relationship between youth and adults for youth development as media producer-activists at Global Action Project. They showed the importance of understanding digital technologies as intertwined with social and cultural technologies that shape interaction, adult/youth collaboration, and modes of dissemination. For example, in the first video production cycle, the youth decided to focus on "adultism" (when adults have power over young people and dismiss their concerns and choices). Despite richly textured preproduction discussions about the various roles adults played in their lives, the youth's actual video production included little involvement by adults, which resulted in a thinly developed video. For the next video, adult staff encouraged youth to focus on a community issue of concern to them. The adults developed a curriculum to scaffold the preproduction and production process, which resulted in a more complex and perspectival video on leaving high school before graduation. Adult facilitators thus enabled youth to produce a stronger, more articulate video from which youth were able to enact their perspectives as media producer-activists. The authors acknowledge that adult facilitation can become heavy-handed in a critical social justice curriculum, but they pointed out that adults and youth in the program negotiated leadership and power dynamics over time. While this research focused on youth-adult interaction, more research is needed that analyzes the dynamics of youth-youth interaction.

Mobilization within the arts programs involves youth and adults "moving from complaints to action" (Kwon, 2008), which includes processes of internal transformation (e.g., healing, imagining possibilities) as well as external action and engagement, or what Ginwright and Cammarota (2002) refer to as "social justice youth development." The focus on internal processes such as Ginwright's (2010) notion of "radical healing" significantly shifts from critical pedagogy's emphasis on structural transformation to developing the capacity of youth to create the neighborhoods in which they wish to inhabit (p. 78). Furthermore, our explication of the above studies suggests the importance of maximizing collaborative opportunities to address existing concerns in the lives of minoritized young people. Artistic practice as civic engagement cultivated collaborative relationships among youth and between youth and program staff and engaged the broader community in awareness and change efforts. Such generative collaboration developed when the curriculum and interactional norms worked together to mobilize the capacity for critical and compassionate action.

COSMOPOLITANISM: EXPLORING BELONGING AND DIFFERENCE

Cosmopolitanism's utopian goal of reciprocal communication among global citizens in a fragmented world (Appiah, 2003) has been critiqued as overly optimistic (Hansen, 2008), but it remains alluring. Its powerful promise has traction in the context of community organizations, which typically aspire for a "better," more equitable world while also recognizing the forces that work against such a vision (Hull & Stornaiuolo, 2014; Wahlström, 2012). Mobility is often named as a positive outgrowth of global citizenship, but the mobility of affluent individuals negatively affects poor individuals through confinement (and containment) to particular neighborhoods, communities, schools, and countries that the affluent choose not to inhabit (Bauman, 2007). As we move toward disrupting the global/local binary, we understand being cosmopolitan to mean being (trans)local citizens who experience "[s]imultaneous situatedness across different locales" and temporal spaces (Brickell & Datta, 2011, p. 4). We highlight below youth programs that recognize the complex landscape that translocal youth must navigate.

From a cosmopolitan perspective, dialogic interactions between global and local communities are imperative to understanding lived experiences. Whereas cosmopolitan theory often forefronts cross-community conversation, interactions between self and society, especially using creative capacities, can also exemplify cosmopolitanism. Gregory's (2013) research with Young Identity and Urban Word NYC, two youth slam and spoken word organizations that interfaced online, illustrated a cosmopolitan tendency to create shared culture at the threshold of "a larger world, a broader horizon of human doings" (Hansen, 2014, p. 8). For instance, a group performance developed by members of the two geographically distant organizations relied exclusively on digital technologies (e.g., Skype) to meet, create, rehearse and present their group poems. Youth leveraged digital resources in both organizations to create new work together despite not being in the same physical space. The youth came to recognize the "reality of other people and their modes of dwelling" as they gave rise to "questions about ourselves" (Hansen, 2014, p. 11). Social media sites and online technology became transformative tools used to communicate, connect, and ultimately create transglobally.

As youth regenerate writerly identities (Bickerstaff, 2012), organize spoken word contexts to address social inequalities, and civically engage with their communities, they have the potential to connect cross-culturally through unscripted communication and "creativity-in-response-to-change" (Hansen, 2014, p. 5). Some studies revealed that youth slam poets took up civic engagement at the nexus of policy regulation, institutional practice, and artistic craft. For example, when youth in the Tucson Youth Poetry Slam worked to counter harmful and repressive legislation regulating access to reproductive health resources (Fields et al., 2014), they did so in aesthetic dimensions that created "relations with self, other, and the world" (Hansen, 2014, p. 7). When they used their poetry to challenge restrictive legislation, performed their work in public spaces, and engaged peers through conversations and petitions (Fields et al., 2014), the civic engagement was not only with their spoken word community but also with those in spaces where they attended school, where they lived, and where they worked.

Likewise, Flores-Gonzalez et al. (2006) illustrated that Batey Urbano was a space for Puerto Rican/Latino youth to cultivate cultural competency and political awareness through poetry writing and slams. As participants in the program, they first identified inequalities and then actively worked to overcome those inequalities by raising awareness of the issues through public performances. Indeed, "in the process of listening to or performing hip-hop . . . many youth [began] to understand how this form of expression and these activities are connected to a history of struggle" (Flores-Gonzalez et al., 2006, p. 186). The art of hip-hop as activism linked the struggles of youth against oppression to those of others in global communities, and provided a means for them to develop "a social and/or global awareness" (p. 177) as they considered difference, belonging, and positionality in the world.

Engaging young people in interactions that require them to (re)consider identity, difference, and belonging was a characteristic of cosmopolitanism in theatre programs (e.g., Pruitt, 2015; Sonn et al., 2015; Vasudevan, 2014) For example, Sonn et al.'s (2015) study of The Chronicles oral history theatre project explicated the use of storytelling and performance in fostering identity, community and belonging among Australian youth. The first stage of the project engaged youth in the exploration of the cultural histories and experiences of their families through interviews with parents, which the youth then retold through performances. In the second stage, participants and parents travelled from Melbourne to the Aboriginal community of Beagle Bay in Northwestern Australia, where the youth collected oral histories about Aboriginal cosmology or dreamtime stories and stories about precolonial periods. Similar to the first stage, the stories were then transformed by the youth into a theatre performance for the Beagle Bay community. While the first stage promoted self-reflection, the second stage nurtured understanding of relationships between self and other and constructed new narratives about identity, belonging, and interconnections between Aboriginal people and themselves. The embodied interaction and the embodiment of history in performance promoted deeper awareness and empathy than merely studying history in school. One Vietnamese Australian youth observed,

"I done the history of it, I've studied history, Australian history, you know, stolen generation, you know, the reconciliation, their riots . . . . But this is the first time I've ever sat down and really understand what their, that history really meant to them." (Sonn et al., 2015, pp. 252–253)

While the authors focused on program youth and staff's "encounter with Aboriginal Australia" (Sonn et al., 2015, p. 252), we are left with questions about how the organization mitigated the challenges of cultural tourism prevalent in travels to communities of the Other. Future research should be attentive to the contradictory ways cosmopolitan explorations of difference may reinscribe Othering and inequality.

Understanding and sharing life experiences through improvisation were at the center of Vasudevan's (2014) work with the Theatre Initiative. Vasudevan found that "belonging was expressed through various forms of participation and functioned as a signifier of various forms of citizenship" (p. 54). She suggested that directed improvisation is a cosmopolitan approach to pedagogy, due to the ways in which it puts into conversation differing perspectives of youth. Facilitators first invited youth to reenact challenging moments from their life experiences. The participants played out the conflict in ways that often follow an obvious resolution. Next, the facilitators introduced conditions to direct another improvisation, enabling youth to probe, consider, and understand other potential outcomes to common scenarios. Directed improvisations thus facilitated "cosmopolitan conversations" (Wahlström, 2012) in the form of an embodied dialogic interaction.

Hull, Stornaiuolo, and Sahni (2010) demonstrated that youth involved in a digital media program called "Kidnet" in one of India's poorest states, engaged girls in critical conversations that questioned local realities (e.g., child labor) as constituted through the political economy of globalization. These realities were then communicated to others through a Web-based hub for adolescents in Norway, the United States, South African, and India to share digital artifacts about their lives, experiences, and interests. The multimodal design of the girls' messages served as a vehicle for communicating a self to others whose lives were previously imagined but not encountered. Two kinds of cosmopolitanism were prevalent. First, the girls represented their commonalities and differences through "everyday cosmopolitan-ism," (p. 360), which included photos, blog entries, and greetings as ways to con-nect around common interests and demonstrate audience awareness and a desire for response across cultures. Second, the girls communicated "intercultural trig-gers" (p. 361), which animated cross-cultural activity and cosmopolitan under-standings. For example, one girl's digital story told the story of her social world—including the effects of poverty, hard labor at home and work, and lack of parental support—with a hopeful narration that led to critical conversations.

As youth met through digital media, they sometimes collided at complex and challenging points of contact or "contact zones" (Pratt, 1991). Hull and Stornaiuolo (2014) drew on Silverstone's (2007) concept of "proper distance" (Hull & Stornaiuolo, 2014, p. 19) to analyze youth learning to build capacity for respectful understanding across differences without making assumptions about the lives of others. For exam-ple, New York City youth involved in Arts Collective crafted a video about the com-plexity of violence and gang life to connect with a video they had seen about domestic violence in the lives of the girls in India. The girls surmised the New York youth were wrong to submit to gang membership and thought they should follow the girls' col-lective action to combat domestic violence in their community. The New York youth felt misunderstood, and thought their struggle had been judged harshly by their audi-ence—the girls in India. This tension illustrated for the authors the difficulty of maintaining a proper distance that allows for hospitable dialogue without making assumptions across difference. In response, one of the New York youth created a video that expressed the struggle of communicating across vast differences. He adopted a "reciprocal stance" that placed the two peer groups in conversation with one another, reflexive about their own experiences and open to dialogue. Young peo-ple involved in the project learned to navigate spaces of belonging, exclusion, and understanding, as well as judgment.

Research on digital media production among youth from continuing histories of colonization especially foregrounded the significance of interactions within contact zones. The studies challenged notions of "civic engagement" (Kahne, Middaugh, & Allen, 2014) and "participatory politics" (Soep, 2014; as they are positively charac-terized in some of the studies in this chapter), for the supposition that youth inher-ently have citizenship and are welcomed to engage in democracy. Desai (2015) upended such assumptions in a study of Youth Against the Settlements' work with Palestinian youth, who had no citizenship and suffered discrimination and violence in the occupied territories. Desai drew on Willis's (1990) concept of symbolic cre-ativity to argue that the work of the youth to document injustice in their lives and neighborhoods (i.e., leveraging video rather than violence to "shoot back" at the occupiers and flip "the dominant script of the 'violent' and 'backwards' Palestinian" (Desai, 2015, p. 119)). These videos were used as court evidence in cases prosecuting violent attacks. Since Palestinian actions are rarely contextualized as a response to violence and discrimination, their video work was a kind of public pedagogy to raise sociopolitical consciousness among Palestinian and Israeli youth.

El-Haj (2009) also challenged the notion of civic identity in a study of a documentary video project at Al-Bustan, an Arab American arts organization that engaged Arab American youth in digital media social activism in ways that called into question cohesive notions of civic identity in light of their transnational experiences. The youth created a video that articulated a postnational citizenship defined as "one in which political and human rights are not limited by belonging to nation-states" (p. 2). As the video invited viewers into a changing democratic landscape, it depicted a world in which human rights were honored within and across borders. This work emphasized the power of visual and narrative stories to create "community without closure" (Couldry, 2004, p. 17). Such communities are not easily regulated but instead are contact zones where digital media art can inspire a sense of belonging, even as it recognizes difference.

Community-based arts programs allow youth to explore and share their experiences of "simultaneous situatedness" across space/time as it manifests discursively, materially, and in the social imaginary. Brickell and Datta (2011) understood this "simultaneous situatedness" to be a given in the lives of translocal youth, including indigenous youth, refugee and immigrant youth, youth without citizenship, youth who live in homeless shelters, and African American and Chicanx youth whose histories of migration are central to their present lives. The research in this section troubles the notion of "giving voice" or fostering empathy among youth across glocal (global/local) contexts. Rather, the studies show arts programs create conditions for youth to figuratively write the (multimodal) scripts of their lives in more of their intersectional complexity and draw on the legacies of their communities. Adult mentorship is important in this process as youth—who are always already cosmopolitan citizens—must determine how to communicate the intricacies of their lives, and challenge rigid and harmful citizenship discourses.

TOWARD INVENTION AND REINVENTION IN FOSTERING SOCIOPOLITICAL CONSCIOUSNESS

Literary, theatre, and digital media arts programs foster sociopolitical consciousness through supporting youth to name in order to re-present and share their identities, mobilize for social transformation, and navigate belonging and difference as translocal or cosmopolitan youth. Notably, the development of sociopolitical consciousness in the research we reviewed was *entwined with the process of creating something with materials and people* and structured to include various publics. Literary arts, including spoken word, promote sociopolitical consciousness by locating artistic practice within a framework of civic engagement and community building (Cahnmann, 2003). The potential of theatre for transforming educational disparities is in the way it is designed "to set a process in motion, to stimulate transformative creativity, [and] to change spectators into protagonists" (Boal, 1992, p. 245). The video-making and digital storytelling of digital media arts programs foreground the visual and aural in ways that speak to intergenerational communities.

All of the art forms highlighted in this review draw on multiple modes in addition to language to support embodied dialogic interaction and collective action. Spoken word, theatre, and digital media creation are all publicly oriented arts with collaboration embedded into the preproduction, production, and/or dissemination phases. Even as the art forms hold affordances that result in explorations of identity, mobilization of collective action, and transcultural communication, the programs intentionally integrated mentorship and collegial cooperation (youth-youth and youth-adult), cultivated intergenerational audiences, constructed trust, reimagined curriculum, created structures for collaboration, and attended to social organization as well as cultural norms for interaction.

As we spotlight community arts programs that promote sociopolitical consciousness, Edell (2013) cautions that "[s]ometimes the very space that seems to be a gift, a positive site for empowerment and resistance, can ignite into destruction as [youth] speak their truths about trauma, challenges, and survival" (p. 53). Sharing "real" stories that involve delving into sensitive content and traumatic experiences of discrimination, abuse, and symbolic, physical, or sexual violence is difficult, and needs further exploration into the intricacies and layers of complexity involved in the teaching and learning practices. For example, pedagogy and research needs to consider the ways in which artistic storytelling in work with minoritized youth may unintentionally surface repressed trauma (Hammock, 2011) or subconsciously repeat, re-embody, and perpetuate oppression (Edell, 2013). Dominant story lines colonize our imaginations (hooks, 1991), and their repetition reinforces and serves the interests of those who are most powerful—White, cis-gendered males. Minoritized youth (like all of us) need support and community to "unveil" (Freire, 1970/2005) reified story lines and to invent new ones.

Our analysis suggests research needs to examine the difficulty of constructing supposedly "safe" spaces for minoritized young people to share experiences of oppression. We need to deconstruct and explicate notions of safety within collaborative learning contexts, public performances, and dialogic interactions (Edell, 2013). Although our review has illuminated significant insight from community-based youth arts programs for fostering sociopolitical consciousness, they are not inherently free from conflicts within and across difference or from the persistent, recuperative tendencies of domination. Within the collective space of (re)storying youth experiences, we need a better understanding of how youth and adults are navigating contact zones of difference. What are the roles of staff in the programs? How do dimensions of difference such as class, race, ethnicity, and gender and their intersections (among others) enhance or complicate the pedagogical process? How do programs engage in a praxis that interrogates the contradictions of "empowerment" efforts (Ellsworth, 1989)? As educators, when we ask youth to tell their stories, take action, and engage with communities, how are we prepared to respond to the potential emotional and physical impact on the youth?

Significantly, our review brings attention to cosmopolitanism as a dimension of sociopolitical consciousness. Cosmopolitanism relates directly to the communication flows that result from technologies that have transformed all contemporary art forms, constructing communication flows across space/time scales and new identities and forms of citizenship (Appadurai, 1996; Santos, 2006). It is worth repeating that these changes often serve the interests of those whose citizenship and mobility are not constrained. Leander, Phillips, and Taylor (2010) argued that "problems of equity can be framed as problems of immobility rather than mobility" (pp. 381–382). However, Blasco and Hansen (2006) reaffirmed the importance of "place-specific collectives" (p. 472):

> The tension experienced by social movements between the need for global communication in order to mobilize, and for resonance among place-specific collectivities. New media such as the Internet provide an important means for improving global communication and developing cosmopolitanism, but they do not automatically prompt collective identities to emerge across borders. (p. 472)

This tension between the relative affordances of global and local communities is important in light of the conception of translocal youth as having loyalties and histories in multiple locations and communities (Brickell & Datta, 2011), while remaining situated within local and global power structures that seldom fail to register their bodies as raced, classed, and gendered (Smith, 2011).

We argue for a reimagining of "community" and "collective" in ways that are less bounded by physical structures and geographic location and more oriented to broader networks that youth often seek when their local communities are dismissive, resistant, or violent. Despite the expanding online networks for LGBTQQ youth (Driver, 2006) and transnational youth (McGinnis, Goodstein-Stolzenberg, & Saliani, 2007), we lack research on how these networked spaces work to promote sociopolitical consciousness. This points to the need for researchers to work in the in-between space that recognizes the "resonance among place-specific collectives" and the affordances and opportunities of mobile and constantly shifting collectives. Our review also revealed the need for researchers to further study the practices that promote opportunities for youth to learn how to navigate inclusion/exclusion and empathy/judgement. There also remains a need to illuminate the ways in which the trust and reciprocal relationships that characterize cosmopolitanism are achieved rather than inherent in community-based programs (Campano, Ghiso, & Welch, 2015).

Minoritized young people are those most often identified as deficient or disengaged in institutions. Yet it is these youth—fully aware of social injustice and how it has affected their lived realities—who are most compelled to examine the sociopolitical implications of dominant discourses and engage in social change efforts. Arts organizations that successfully engage young people in this work create conditions that enable them to name injustice, mobilize for action, and embody cosmopolitanism. Despite the persistent, domesticating capacity of oppression to submerge consciousness and reproduce systemic inequalities, our review reveals the counterhegemonic promise of youth cultural productions for disrupting social and cultural inequalities (Freire, 1970/2005; Paris & Alim, 2014). This potential lies in the praxis of community-based youth arts programs that underscores creation, "invention, and re-invention, through the restless, impatient, continuing, hopeful inquiry human beings pursue in the world, with the world, and with each other" (Freire, 1970/2005, p. 72).

REFERENCES

Alim, H. (2011). Global ill-literacies: Hip hop cultures, youth identities, and the politics of literacy. *Review of Research in Education, 35*(1), 120–146. doi:10.3102/0091732X10383208

Appadurai, A. (1996). *Modernity at large: Cultural dimensions of globalization.* Minneapolis: University of Minnesota Press.

Appiah, K. A. (2006). *Cosmopolitanism: Ethics in a world of strangers.* New York, NY: Norton.

Barron, B., Gomez, K., Pinkard, N., & Martin, C. K. (2014). *The digital youth network: Cultivating digital media citizenship in urban communities.* Cambridge: MIT Press.

Barron, B., Walter, S. E., Martin, C. K., & Schatz, C. (2010). Predictors of creative computing participation and profiles of experience in two Silicon Valley middle schools. *Computers & Education, 54,* 178–189. doi:10.1016/j.compedu.2009.07.017

Bauman, Z. (2007). *Liquid time: Living in an age of uncertainty.* Cambridge, England: Polity Press.

Bickerstaff, S. (2012). I am the rock goddess of lyrics: Writerly identities of adolescents returning to school. *Journal of Adolescent & Adult Literacy, 56,* 56–66. doi:10.1002/JAAL.00102

Blasco, M., & Hansen, H. K. (2006). Cosmopolitan aspirations: New media, citizenship education and youth in Latin America. *Citizenship Studies, 10,* 469–488. doi:10.1080/13621020600857890

Boal, A. (1992). *Games for actors and non-actors* (A. Jackson, Trans.). London, England: Routledge.

Brickell, K., & Datta, A. (Eds.). (2011). *Translocal geographies: Spaces, places and connections.* Farnham, England: Ashgate.

Britzman, D. P. (1998). *Lost subjects, contested objects: Toward a psychoanalytic inquiry of learning.* Albany: State University of New York Press.

Cahnmann, M. (2003). The craft, practice, and possibility of poetry in educational research. *Educational Researcher, 32*(3), 29–36. doi:10.3102/0013189X032003029

Cahnmann-Taylor, M., & Souto-Manning, M. (2010). *Teachers act up! Creating multicultural learning communities through theatre.* New York, NY: Teachers College Press.

Campano, G., Ghiso, M. P., & Welch, B. (2015). Ethical and professional norms in community-based research. *Harvard Educational Review, 85,* 29–49. doi:10.17763/haer.85.1.a34748522021115m

Chappell, S. (2009). Young people talk back: Community arts as a public pedagogy of social justice. In J. Sandlin, B. Schulz, & J. Burdick (Eds.), *Handbook of public pedagogy: Education and learning beyond schooling* (pp. 318–326). New York, NY: Routledge.

Chávez, V., & Soep, E. (2005). Youth radio and the pedagogy of collegiality. *Harvard Educational Review, 75,* 409–488. doi:10.17763/haer.75.4.827u365446030386

Clay, A. (2006). All I need is one "mic": Mobilizing youth for social change in the post-civil rights era. *Social Justice, 33,* 105–121.

Couldry, N. (2004). In the place of common culture, what? *Review of Education, Pedagogy & Cultural Studies, 26*(1), 3–21.

Desai, C. (2015). Shooting back in the occupied territories: An anti-colonial participatory politics. *Curriculum Inquiry, 45,* 109–128. doi:10.1080/03626784.2014.995062

Driver, S. (2006). Virtually queer youth communities of girls and birls: Cultural spaces of identity work and desiring exchanges. In R. Willett (Ed.), *Digital generations* (pp. 229–246). Mahwah, NJ: Lawrence Erlbaum.

Edell, D. (2013). "Say it how it is": Urban teenage girls challenge and perpetuate stereotypes through writing and performing theatre. *Youth Theatre Journal, 27*, 51–62. doi:10.1080/08929092.2012.722903

El-Haj, T. R. A. (2009). Imagining postnationalism: Arts, citizenship education, and Arab American Youth. *Anthropology & Education Quarterly, 40*, 1–19. doi:10.1111/j.1548-1492.2009.01025.x

Ellsworth, E. (1989). Why doesn't this feel empowering? Working through the repressive myths of critical pedagogy. *Harvard Educational Review, 59*, 297–325. doi:10.17763/haer.59.3.058342114k266250

Fields, A., Snapp, S., Russell, S., Licona, A., & Tilley, E. (2014). Youth voices and knowledge: Slam poetry speaks to social policy. *Sexuality Research & Social Policy, 11*, 310–321. doi:10.1007/s13178-014-0154-9

Fine, M., Weis, L., Centrie, C., & Roberts, R. (2000). Educating beyond the borders of schooling. *Anthropology & Education Quarterly, 31*, 131–151. doi:10.1525/aeq.2000.31.2.131

Flores-Gonzalez, N., Roderiguez, M., & Roderiguez-Muniz, M. (2006). From hip-hop to humanization: Batey Urbano as a space for Latino youth culture and community. In P. Noguera, J. Cammarota, & S. Ginwright (Eds.), *Beyond resistance! Youth activism and community change* (pp. 175–196). New York, NY: Routledge.

Freire, P. (1985a). *The politics of education*. South Hadley, MA: Bergin & Garvey.

Freire, P. (1985b). Reading the world and reading the word: An interview with Paulo Freire. *Language Arts, 62*(1), 15–21.

Freire, P. (2005). *Pedagogy of the oppressed*. New York, NY: Continuum. (Original work published 1970)

Gay, G. (2000). *Culturally responsive teaching: Theory, research and practice*. New York, NY: Teachers College Press.

Ginwright, S. A. (2005). On urban ground: Understanding African-American intergenerational partnerships in urban communities. *American Journal of Community Psychology, 33*, 101–110. doi:10.1002/jcop.20045

Ginwright, S. A. (2010). Peace out to revolution! Activism among African American youth: An argument for radical healing. *Young, 18*, 77–96. doi:10.1177/110330880901800106

Ginwright, S., & Cammarota, J. (2002). New terrain in youth development: The promise of a social justice approach. *Social Justice, 29*(4), 82–95.

Giroux, H., & Simon, R. (1989). Popular culture and critical pedagogy: Everyday life as a basis for curriculum knowledge. In H. Giroux, & P. McLaren (Eds.), *Critical pedagogy, the state, and cultural struggle* (pp. 236–252). Albany: State University of New York Press.

Goldman, S., Booker, A., & McDermott, M. (2008). Mixing the digital, social, and cultural: Learning, identity, and agency in youth participation. In D. Buckingham (Ed.), *Youth, identity, and digital media* (pp. 185–206). Cambridge: MIT Press.

Greene, M. (2001). *Variations on a blue guitar*. New York, NY: Teachers College Press.

Gregory, H. (2013). Youth take the lead: Digital poetry and the next generation. *English in Education, 47*, 118–133. doi:10.1111/eie.12011

Halverson, E. R. (2005). InsideOut: Facilitating gay youth identity development through a performance-based youth organization. *Identity, 5*, 67–90. doi:10.1207/s1532706xid0501_5

Halverson, E. R. (2010). The dramaturgical process as a mechanism for identity development of LGBTQ youth and its relationship to detypification. *Journal of Adolescent Research, 25*, 635–668. doi:10.1177/0743558409357237

Hammock, A. C. (2011). Identity construction through theatrical community practice. *Qualitative Social Work, 10*, 364–380. doi:10.1177/1473325011408481

Hansen, D. (2008). Education viewed through a cosmopolitan prism. *Philosophy of Education, 2008*, 206–214.

Hansen, D. (2014) Cosmopolitanism and cultural creativity: New modes of educational practice in globalizing times. *Curriculum Inquiry, 44*, 1–14. doi:10.1111/curi.12039

Heath, S. B. (1998). Living the arts through language plus learning: A report on community–based youth organizations. *Americans for the Arts Monograph, 2*(7), 1–19.

hooks, b. (1990). *Yearning: Race, gender, and cultural politics.* Boston, MA: South End Press.

hooks, b. (1991). Narratives of struggle. In P. Mariani (Ed.), *Critical fictions: The politics of imaginative writing* (pp. 53–61). Seattle, WA: Bay.

Hull, G. A., & Katz, M. L. (2006). Crafting an agentive self: Case studies of digital storytelling. *Research in the Teaching of English, 41*, 43–81.

Hull, G. A., & Stornaiuolo, A. (2014). Cosmopolitan literacies, social networks, and "proper distance": Striving to understand in a global world. *Curriculum Inquiry, 44*, 15–44. doi:10.1111/curi.12035

Hull, G. A., Stornaiuolo, A., & Sahni, U. (2010). Cultural citizenship and cosmopolitan practice: Global youth communicate online. *English Education, 42*, 331–367.

Iseke, J., & Moore, S. (2011). Community-based indigenous digital filmmaking with elders and youth. *American Indian Culture and Research Journal, 35*(4), 10–37.

Jocson, K. (2006). "Bob Dylan and hip hop:" Intersecting literacy practices in youth poetry communities. *Written Communication, 23*, 231–259. doi:10.1177/0741088306288154

Kahne, J., Middaugh, E., & Allen, D. (2014). *Youth, new media, and the rise of participatory politics* (Youth & Participatory Politics Research Network Working Paper No. 1). Retrieved from http://ypp.dmlcentral.net/sites/default/files/publications/YPP_WorkinPapers_Paper01.pdf

Kinloch, V. (2010). *Harlem on our minds: Place, race, and the literacies of urban youth.* New York, NY: Teachers College Press.

Kwon, S. A. (2008). Moving from complaints to action: Oppositional consciousness and collective action in a political community. *Anthropology & Education Quarterly, 39*, 59–76. doi:10.1111/j.1548-1492.2008.00005.x

Ladson-Billings, G. (1995). Toward a theory of culturally relevant pedagogy. *American Educational Research Journal, 32*, 465–491. doi:10.3102/00028312032003465

Ladson-Billings, G. (2006). Yes, but how do we do it? Practicing culturally relevant pedagogy. In. J. Landsman & C. Lewis (Eds.), *White teachers/diverse classrooms* (pp. 29–42). Sterling, VA: Stylus.

Leander, K. M., Phillips, N. C., & Taylor, K. H. (2010). The changing social spaces of learning: Mapping new mobilities. *Review of Research in Education, 34*, 329–394. doi:10.3102/0091732X09358129

London, R. A., Pastor, M. Jr., Servon, L. J., Rosner, R., & Wallace, A. (2010). The role of community technology centers in promoting youth development. *Youth & Society, 42*, 199–228. doi:10.1177/0044118X09351278

Mahiri, J., & Sablo, S. (1996). Writing for their lives: The non-school literacy of California's urban African American youth. *Journal of Negro Education, 65*, 164–180. doi:10.2307/2967311

McGinnis, T., Goodstein-Stolzenberg, A., & Saliani, E. C. (2007). "indnpride": Online spaces of transnational youth as sites of creative and sophisticated literacy and identity work. *Linguistics and Education, 18*, 283–304. doi:10.1016/j.linged.2007.07.006

Moll, L., & Gonzalez, N. (2004). Engaging life: A funds of knowledge approach to multicultural education. In J. Banks, & C. Banks (Eds.), *Handbook of research on multicultural education* (pp. 699–715). San Francisco, CA: Jossey-Bass.

Morrell, E. (2004). *Becoming critical researchers: Literacy and empowerment for urban youth.* New York, NY: Peter Lang.

Palidofsky, M., & Stolbach, B. C. (2012). Dramatic healing: The evolution of a trauma-informed musical theatre program for incarcerated girls. *Journal of Child & Adolescent Trauma, 5*, 239–256. doi:10.1080/19361521.2012.697102

Paris, D. (2012). Culturally sustaining pedagogy: A needed change in stance, terminology, and practice. *Educational Researcher, 41*(3), 93–97. doi:10.3102/0013189X12441244

Paris, D., & Alim, H. S. (2014). What are we seeking to sustain through culturally sustaining pedagogy? A loving critique forward. *Harvard Educational Review, 84*, 85–100.

Peppler, K. A., & Kafai, Y. B. (2007). From SuperGoo to Scratch: exploring creative digital media production in informal learning. *Learning, Media and Technology, 32*, 149–166. doi:10.17763/haer.84.1.982l873k2ht16m77

Pratt, M. L. (1991). Arts of the contact zone. *Profession, 91*, 33–40.

Pruitt, L. J. (2015). Multiculturalism at play: Young people and citizenship in Australia. *Journal of Youth Studies, 19*(2), 1–17. doi:10.1080/13676261.2015.1059926

Rivera, T. (2013). You have to be what you're talking about: Youth poets, amateur counter-conduct and parrhesiastic value in the amateur youth poetry slam. *Performance Research, 18*, 114–123. doi:10.1080/13528165.2013.807175

Salazar, F. J. (2010). Digital stories and emerging citizens' media practices by migrant youth in Western Sydney. *3CMedia, August*(6), 54–70.

Sandoval, C., & Latorre, G. (2008). Chicana/o artivism: Judy Baca's digital work with youth of color. In A. Everett (Ed.), *Learning race and ethnicity: Youth and digital media* (pp. 81–108). Cambridge: MIT Press

Santos, B. (2006). Globalizations. *Theory, Culture & Society, 23*, 393–399.

Scharber, C., Isaacson, K., Pyscher, T., & Lewis, C. (2015). Teens, tech, and learning: Pathways for all. In L. Miller, D. Becker, & K. Becker (Eds.), *Technology for transformation: Perspectives of hope in the digital age* (pp. 195–235). Charlotte, NC: Information Age.

Sefton-Green, J. (2013). *Learning at not-school: A review of study, theory, and advocacy in non-formal settings*. Cambridge: MIT Press.

Shor, I. (1992). *Empowering education: Critical teaching for social change*. Chicago, IL: University of Chicago Press.

Silverstone, R. (2007). *Media and morality: On the rise of the mediapolis*. Cambridge, England: Polity.

Smith, M. P. (2011). Translocality: A critical reflection. In K. Brickell & A. Datta (Eds.), *Translocal geographies: Spaces, places, connections* (pp. 181–198). Surrey, England: Ashgate.

Soep, E. (2014). *Participatory politics: Next-generation tactics to remake public spheres*. Cambridge: MIT Press.

Sonn, C. C., Quayle, A. F., Belanji, B., & Baker, A. M. (2015). Responding to racialization through arts practice: The case of participatory theatre. *Journal of Community Psychology, 43*, 244–259. doi:10.1002/jcop.21676

Souto-Manning, M. (2010). *Freire, teaching, and learning: Culture circles across contexts*. New York, NY: Peter Lang.

Souto-Manning, M. (2011). Playing with power and privilege: Theatre games in teacher education. *Teaching and Teacher Education, 27*, 997–1007. doi:10.1016/j.tate.2011.04.005

Thomas, R., & Rappaport, J. (1996) Art as community narrative: A resource for social change. In B. Lykes, A. Banuazizi, R. Liem, & M. Morris (Eds.), *Myths about the powerless: Contesting social inequalities* (pp. 317–336). Philadelphia, PA: Temple University Press.

Tolman, D. L. (2012). Female adolescents, sexual empowerment and desire: A missing discourse of gender inequity. *Sex Roles, 66*, 746–757. doi:10.1007/s11199-012-0122-x

Vasudevan, L. M. (2014). Multimodal cosmopolitanism: Cultivating belonging in everyday moments with youth. *Curriculum Inquiry, 44*, 45–67. doi:10.1111/curi.12040

Wahlström, N. (2012, April). *Educational cosmopolitanism: Making meaning through reflective conversations*. Paper presented at the annual meeting of the American Educational Research Association, Vancouver, British Columbia, Canada.

Weinstein, S., & West, A. (2012). Call and responsibility: Critical questions for youth spoken word poetry. *Harvard Educational Review, 82*, 282–302.

Wernick, L. J., Kulick, A., & Woodford, M. R. (2014). How theatre within a transformative organizing framework cultivates individual and collective empowerment among

LGBTQQ youth. *Journal of Community Psychology, 42,* 838–853. doi:10.1002/jcop.21656

Willis, P. (1990). *Common culture: Symbolic work at play in the everyday cultures of the young.* Buckingham, England: Open University Press.

Winn, M. T. (2010). "Betwixt and between": Literacy, liminality, and the celling of Black girls. *Race, Ethnicity and Education, 13,* 425–447.

Winn, M. T. (2011). *Girl time: Literacy, justice, and the school-to-prison pipeline (Teaching for social justice).* New York, NY: Teachers College Press.

Winn, M. T. (2012). The politics of desire and possibility in urban playwriting: (Re) reading and (re) writing the script. *Pedagogies, 7,* 317–332. doi:10.1080/1554480X.2012.715737

Winn, M. T., & Jackson, C. A. (2011). Toward a performance of possibilities: Resisting gendered (in) justice. *International Journal of Qualitative Studies in Education, 24,* 615–620. doi:10.1080/09518398.2011.600261

Young, E. (2010). Challenges to conceptualizing and actualizing culturally relevant pedagogy: How viable is the theory in classroom practice? *Journal of Teacher Education, 61,* 248–260. doi:10.1177/0022487109359775

Youniss, J., Bales, S., Christmas-Best, V., Diversi, M., McLaughlin, M., & Silbereisen, R. (2002). Youth civic engagement in the twenty-first century. *Journal of Research on Adolescence, 12,* 121–148. doi:10.1111/1532-7795.00027

Chapter 16

Toward a New Understanding of Community-Based Education: The Role of Community-Based Educational Spaces in Disrupting Inequality for Minoritized Youth

Bianca J. Baldridge
Nathan Beck
Juan Carlos Medina
Marlo A. Reeves
University of Wisconsin-Madison

Community-based educational spaces (CBES; afterschool programs, community-based youth organizations, etc.) have a long history of interrupting patterns of educational inequity and continue to do so under the current educational policy climate. The current climate of education, marked by neoliberal education restructuring, has left community-based educational spaces vulnerable in many of the same ways as public schools. Considering the current political moment of deep insecurity within public education, this review of research illuminates the role community-based educational spaces have played in resisting forms of educational inequality and their role in the lives of minoritized youth. With a review of seminal education research on community-based spaces, we intend to capture the ways these diverse out-of-school spaces inform the educational experiences, political identity development, and organizing and activist lives of minoritized youth. Further, this piece contends that reimagining education beyond the borders of the school is a form of resistance, as community-based leaders, youth workers, and youth themselves negotiate the dialectical nature of community-based educational spaces within a capitalist and racialized neoliberal state.

Community-based educational spaces (CBES; e.g., afterschool programs, community-based youth organizations, etc.) have a long history of interrupting patterns of educational inequity and continue to do so under the current educational policy climate. Today's education system is marked by neoliberal education

Review of Research in Education
March 2017, Vol. 41, pp. 381–402
DOI: 10.3102/0091732X16688622
© 2017 AERA. http://rre.aera.net

restructuring (Lipman, 2011a) leaving CBES vulnerable like their public school counterparts. In this way, community-based organizations are often held to many of the same standardized measures of success and the critical dimensions of their work are compromised (Baldridge, 2014). Considering the current political moment of deep insecurity within public education, a crisis of education privatization, anti-Black racism, and displacement and marginalization of communities of color, this review of research illuminates the role CBES have played in the lives of minoritized youth. With a review of seminal education research on community-based spaces, we intend to capture the ways these diverse out-of-school spaces inform the educational experiences, political identity development, and organizing and activist lives of minoritized youth.

This chapter recognizes the important ways in which community-based spaces interrupt and disrupt inequality within schools and communities, while fostering spaces for youth of color to build, connect, and thrive. While we celebrate the pedagogical practices and possibilities within CBES and intend to show how they are necessary to include in broader education discourse, we also highlight their precarity and forced reliance on the state, foundations, and other agencies for financial support, which subsequently enforces narratives that may not be aligned with the organization's purpose or methods for engaging youth. As such, the purpose of this review is to situate CBES within a broader history of radical education within minoritized communities, which disrupts educational inequality and challenges dominant discourses stemming from schools and other state institutions. While we illuminate community-based spaces as sites of pedagogical possibility and radical care, we also suggest that acts of disruption to various forms of inequality, and structural and symbolic violence against youth of color are threatened by neoliberal educational policy. Although CBES are and should be regarded as critical spaces for minoritized youth, as a result of this neoliberal turn in education policy (Dumas, 2016; Spence, 2015), they are implicated in the reproduction of inequality due to their precarious relationship with the political economy that creates tension with funders that are deeply tied to neoliberal ideals and deficit racialized ideologies (Gilmore, 2007; Kwon, 2013). This reality situates community-based educational programs in a contradictory space where they are beholden to neoliberal logics of academic success by the state and also act as liberatory spaces for minoritized youth.

Method of Inquiry and Guiding Questions

As researchers and former and current practitioners of youth work within CBES, we welcomed the challenge of this special issue to go beyond restating well-established problems in order to illuminate the ways in which research has catalyzed forms of resistance against educational inequality within out-of-school spaces. In this chapter, we assert that neoliberal education reforms are often overlooked in the ways they affect afterschool community-based spaces. Broader educational problems including the neoliberal turn in policy and practice threatens the pedagogical work of CBES. While understanding problems are imperative, we seek to highlight the ways in which community-based spaces have disrupted educational inequality. As such, this chapter is guided by the following questions: How have CBES historically and contemporarily reimagined education to include social, cultural, and political development while also fostering academic achievement? In what ways is the pedagogical work of community-based spaces contradictory and transformative within highly neoliberal and racialized contexts? Given the multiple dimensions of community-based youth work including academic, cultural, social, and political development, what are the themes and findings generated from studies on CBES that push back on deficit oriented thinking about minoritized youth and underscore their methods of disruption and resistance?

To begin our review, we first situate CBES within the current political and educational landscape marked by neoliberal restructuring and reforms. We review three linked bodies of literature centering the pedagogical work of community-based youth spaces. First, we highlight the ways in which minoritized youth that have been pushed out, humiliated, and harmed within traditional school spaces as well as how their value as whole beings are nurtured within community-based spaces through strong relationships with adult allies and youth workers. Second, we examine literature on community-based youth programs that demonstrate how they are spaces that center youth voice and connect youth with supportive adult allies and youth workers. Additionally, we capture the ways in which these spaces reimagine education beyond academic achievement to include social, cultural, and political development that ultimately results in social action and resistance among youth. Finally, we explore critically important literature addressing the ways that young people's political identity building are then connected to the ways that they resist and organize for educational and community reform through community-based organizations. In conclusion, we make a case for moving community-based educational youth work from the periphery of educational discourse to the center. We make this case with caution as we urge education researchers, policymakers, and educators to acknowledge, challenge, and disrupt the neoliberal discourse of educational innovation and reform that poses a significant threat to the flexibility, heterogeneity, and resistance located within CBES. The areas of literature we explore are important as they each display the variation, diversity, and depth of the pedagogical work of CBES.

THE NEOLIBERAL POLITICAL ECONOMY OF COMMUNITY-BASED EDUCATIONAL SPACES

Community-centered programs for minoritized youth of color, both formal and informal, have been essential to marginalized communities. In addition, groups of color in the United States have long formed physical spaces to educate and protect young people from racial hostility as well as and to affirm their culture and identity (McKenzie, 2008). Community-based spaces serving racially and economically marginalized youth have been instrumental in fostering academic achievement, building social capital, fostering social awareness, and facilitating organizing for social change in schools and neighborhoods (Akom, 2006; Ginwright, 2007; Ginwright & James, 2002; Kirshner, 2015; Kwon, 2013). Often referred to as afterschool programs or community-based youth organizations, the term *community-based educational spaces* can signal a broader capacity for pedagogical practices employed within such settings

(Baldridge, in press). By decentering schools, CBES exemplify the capacity of these programs to complement and supplement student learning or growth (Baldridge, in press). The heterogeneity of community-based spaces makes them unique and flexible to address the contextual needs of the youth and communities they serve. However, the flexibility that many organizations have enjoyed is jeopardized by larger politics of education and neoliberal discourse changing the nature of education and learning, particularly for low-income communities of color. Here, we want to be clear that while research on community-based organizations has shown how instrumental they are in creating spaces for youth to disrupt various forms of inequality within their schools and neighborhoods (Ginwright, 2007; Kirshner, 2015; Warren, Mira, & Nikundiwe, 2008), to challenge discourses of deficiency about youth of color (Baldridge, 2014; Kwon, 2013), and to offer spaces of redemption and healing (Ginwright, 2010; Hill, 2009), they are also implicated in the reproduction of inequality. As Heath and McLaughlin's (1994) early work on connecting community afterschool programs to schools suggests, there is a dialectic relationship between school and community spaces. Although they are separate spaces (politically and geographically), the content, structure, and programming of these spaces can both resist and replicate repressive academic trends.

Scholarship on community-based youth organizations stretches across many disciplines. Within education research, a large body of work has examined the role of community-based afterschool programs or community-based organizations that foster academic development, academic tutoring, and support for youth (Durlak & Weissberg, 2007; Kataoka & Vandell, 2013; Posner & Vandell, 1994; Woodland, 2008). Early research in this area acknowledged the impact of community-based programming and school-based partnerships for the optimal academic development for students (Heath & McLaughlin, 1994; McLaughlin, 2000). In the public imagination, CBES are important in providing youth with additional academic support while engaging them in a wide range of activities such as social, emotional, cultural and political support. Yet given the critical role community-based spaces occupy in youth's educational experiences, they are greatly influenced by the current broader social and political context surrounding education. As U.S. education becomes increasingly characterized by neoliberal agendas like privatizing education, mass production of privately run charter schools, the promotion of assessment driven measures, and racialized and classed governmentality through education policy (Apple, 2006; Dumas, 2016; Lipman, 2011a), the philosophies and pedagogical practices of CBES are compromised. This political context is central to the construction and possibilities of community-based spaces as well as the educational experiences and outcomes for minoritized youth.

Community-based educational spaces are informed by neoliberal education reforms and ideologies about race, gender, class, and power (Baldridge, 2014; Kwon, 2013). Yet the deep pedagogical work of CBES is often peripheral to mainstream educational discourse. Given this reality, understanding how CBES reimagine education requires a firm grounding in the context that CBES operate within and the sites from which youth imagine their futures. As scholars like Noguera and Cannella (2006) suggest, "Society has disinvested itself of association with and responsibility to a generation of youth . . . our institutions have effectively disowned their children" (p. 346). While this predicament places CBES in a critical position to support schools the needs of vulnerable populations (Baldridge, Hill, & Davis, 2011), they often achieve this by mirroring coursework that students are taking in high school (Anderson & Larson, 2009). Unfortunately, as school curricula continue to be narrowed, young people explore other spaces for relevant and culturally responsive educational opportunities (Dimitriadis, 2009). Too often, those spaces to which they turn reproduce similar harms enacted by schools that students resist in myriad ways (Quinn, 2012; Tuck & Yang, 2011). Due to the neoliberal funding climate, this is a difficult, but imperative trend to resist (Baldridge, 2014; Kwon, 2013; Quinn, 2012), as the neoliberal approach to schooling has deemed Black, Brown, and poor bodies as disposable (Giroux, 2003, 2009).

Herein lies the tension that CBES navigate, as they are situated within a political economy wherein they simultaneously reproduce and interrupt inequality. CBES are situated in a dialectical space, responding to the ravages of neoliberalism on youth and schools while also being structured and influenced by neoliberalism. For example, CBES may resist deficit views of students and disrupt the inequalities students experience within them; however, they may reproduce the same outcomes by preparing students for entry-level work or by measuring students against the same limited and deficit-based standards of schools. CBES rooted in critical pedagogy often have the intention to teach minoritized youth to "read the world" around them (Freire, 1979/2000; Freire & Macedo, 1987), and as a result disrupt inequality. However, if students are prepared to thrive in the world without a larger political analysis, CBES end up reproducing neoliberal effects (e.g., deficit views of youth as low skilled labor). As such, this provides a complicated foundation from which to reimagine education. In particular, when dominant and deficit-oriented discourse surrounding youth and community-based spaces often blames young people as the cause of their own problems (Ginwright & James, 2002; Scott, Deschenes, Hopkins, Newman, & McLaughlin, 2006). While CBES are separate from the state apparatus, because of their situation in the political economy, they are deeply affected by shifting public policy trends and discourses (Gilmore, 2007). Due to their heterogeneity, CBES are impossible to essentialize and, while the literature demonstrates that they are not immune to the "preoccupation with discipline and academic standards among low-income children" (Halpern, 2002, p. 204), they are situated with more possibility and flexibility and less rigid hierarchies and bureaucracies to operate in liberatory ways underneath the surveillance of neoliberal testing regimes (Baldridge, 2014). To that end, honoring the complexity and contradiction of these spaces, we will focus on literature that documents how CBES disrupt educational inequality— and with an eye toward replication—attempt to unearth the Web of practices that these spaces deploy to interrupt inequality. While not without risks and contradictions, we believe that there is capacity for a different approach within CBES, one in which there lies deep pedagogical work, "learning through life" (Winn, 2011, p. x), and respect for the humanity and knowledge young people bring with them to all of the educational spaces they occupy.

CENTERING AND HUMANIZING YOUTH WITHIN COMMUNITY-BASED SPACES

Youth experiences within schools and CBES vary. Yet research findings can either display community-based sites that treat youth as individuals with worth, value, and humanity (Baldridge, 2014; Jones & Deutsch, 2013; Paris & Winn, 2013) or as sites where youth are framed in deficit ways and viewed as being in need of saving, controlling, and directing (Baldridge, 2014; Kwon, 2013; Lesko, 1996; Zhang & Byrd, 2006). With research that documents practices that view youth as valuable, a consistent theme emerges once youth voices are centralized—one in which youth describe how they came to be involved in community-based spaces by sharing their perception of the harm and distrust they experienced in traditional school spaces and within society at large (Heath & McLaughlin, 1994; O'Donoghue, 2006). According to Schmidt (2011), a space becomes a place once it has been imbued with meaning through a complex intersection of self-identification, need, and perception. With this in mind, the following section centers youth voices and demonstrates the dialectical relationship between schools and community-based spaces in the minds of youth. Considering the narrowing of school curriculum described earlier, negative interactions with nonfamilial adults and peers, and feeling unwelcomed or pushed out, the following section highlights minoritized youths' awareness of the inequalities and lowered expectations they experience in schools and the subsequent meaning given to school spaces. By contrast, unless CBES replicate school practices, these spaces are perceived by youth to be fairly positive across the literature.

Young people always have a critique of their educational experiences, and if given the opportunity, they have a lot to say about the state of education. Such was the case in early research on community-based afterschool programs and traditional school spaces. Heath and McLaughlin's (1994) study found multiple students who explained their involvement in community-based afterschool programs, as one student put it, stemming from "negative, negative, negative" experiences within schools (p. 280). Furthermore, youth in this study reinforced the idea that adults within schools do not understand the circumstances of students' lived experiences, "They just don't listen to us; they just kick us out or fail us" (p. 290), and, fail to challenge students in neither developmentally nor culturally appropriate ways. This neglect was confirmed in Baldridge et al.'s (2011) study with Black male youth who had been pushed out of traditional school spaces.

In an effort to understand the potential of CBES to reimagine traditionally marginalized youth, in particular, underperforming students and those who have been pushed out, Baldridge et al. (2011) centered youth voices and found they often framed their participation in CBES by contrasting their experience in these spaces with negative experiences in schools. In their study, youth were disillusioned with the education they had received pointing to a perceived lack of understanding of their circumstance, lack of challenges, and lack of support or respect in schools as causes for their departure. Coupled with their experience, these perceptions led them to feel vulnerable and view schools as an obstacle to their success, with a participant stating, "I mean, you don't learn nothing. You learn nothing. I mean you pass if you show up to class . . . there's no real point in going" (Baldridge et al., 2011, p. 128). Echoing these findings in their study of social and identity development, Jones and Deutsch (2013) highlight youth who felt vulnerable at school, "–you know [people in the club] don't judge you as much as people at school" (p. 32), while simultaneously experiencing developmentally inappropriate practices indicating a lack of trust and respect. As one youth indicated, "I mean, at school, you've got to ask to go to the bathroom and stuff" (p. 31).

Across these studies youth point to many of the same experiences that leave them feeling as if school were an obstacle they must overcome as opposed to a place for growth. As such, they summarize their experiences in negative terms, describe feeling unwanted or disposable, and pushed away from school, leading many traditionally marginalized youths to drop out. As we have seen, much of this is accomplished through higher rates of punishment (Crenshaw, 2016; Downey & Pribesh, 2004; Gregory, Skiba, & Noguera, 2010; Nicholson-Crotty, Birchmeier, & Valentine, 2009; Wun, 2014); lower teacher expectations and support leading predictably to poor performance (Blanchett, Klingner, & Harry, 2009; Heath & McLaughlin, 1994); and a lack of trust in youth (Bulanda, McCrea, 2012; Jones & Deutsch, 2013). Thus, when given the opportunity, marginalized youth tend to explain their involvement in CBES by highlighting the institutional, interpersonal, and pedagogical practices that shape their perception of traditional academic spaces as negative sites.

Contrary to examples provided by youth above, community-based spaces offer youth experiences that foster positive perceptions of place (Brice-Heath & McLaughlin, 1994; Bulanda & McCrea, 2012; Deutsch & Hirsch, 2002; Green & Gooden, 2014; Schmidt, 2011), meet their developmental needs (Jones & Deutsch, 2013; Lerner, Dowling, & Anderson, 2003; Mahoney, Lord, & Carryl, 2005), and provide youth with the support needed to feel welcomed, accepted, challenged, and engaged (O'Donoghue, 2006; Riggs, Bohnert, Guzman, & Davidson, 2010). For instance, in the same study that provided insight on youth disillusionment with traditional educational settings, Baldridge et al. (2011) found that youth responded to opportunities and skills that prepared them for their transition into adulthood. In line with their finding, students in the study seemed to respond to the increased level of program and curricular flexibility offered by community-based spaces, as they raved about instructors' ability to relate to students; "They, they sit down with you, they want to know about your personal life and everything. They just, they were cool" (p. 130).

Similarly, in Jones and Deutsch's (2013) study, youth shared their appreciation having a stronger connection with adults in the community organization. According to one participant, "I like the fact that you get to talk to them and hear about the everyday things they go through and you go through the same times and your [*sic*] not alone" (p. 32). Authentic relationship building with adults and increased trust and responsibility were appreciated by youth, even those who stopped participating or those who have not participated in community-based programming. For instance, in a survey of youth who are not involved with CBES, Terzian, Giesen, and Mbwana (2009) reinforced the aforementioned statements when they found that youth not involved would attend CBES programs if they were staffed by people who would treat them with respect. Additionally, Terzian et al. (2009) found youth respond to program and curricular flexibility that allows a CBES to offer a variety of programming and activities, provide opportunities to learn practical skills, and make programming culturally relevant and useful to students lived experiences (i.e., addressing family issues or reading and responding to issues they encounter on a daily basis).

Adult Allies and Authentic Relationship Building

Community-based educational spaces serve as a resource to connect young people with each other, their community, and adult allies. These connections form a critical social capital (Ginwright, 2007) that young people can call on to access other forms of capital as they seek to interrupt inequality in their communities. To interrupt educational inequality and envision alternatives, "inspiration and imagination are critical to radical thought" (Jones de Almeida, 2007, p. 189), and community-based programs provide space for young people to imagine beyond the borders of neoliberalism, standards-based assessment, and zero tolerance policies. Through this imagining, young people are able to construct alternative visions of society and social relationships. Fine, Weis, Centrie, and Roberts (2000) suggest, "These spaces are . . . a crack, a fissure, a fleeting or sustained set of commitments. Individual dreams, collective work, and critical thoughts are smuggled in and reimagined" (p. 132). In this way, CBES can provide young people with more stable, productive, and reciprocal relationships with peers, teachers, and other adult allies. Community-based spaces provide the structured strategic space for youth and adults to reimagine and cocreate alternatives to suggest how communities should address social issues like education violence and health care (Burrowes, Cousins, Rojas, & Ude, 2007). By doing the work of creating alternatives to neoliberal approaches to redress inequality, youth are able to heal, create, and resist within community-based spaces.

Research has also shown that CBES interrupt educational inequality by creating spaces for young people and supportive adults to work together. Literature has shown the positive effects of adult relationships with youth (Bulanda & McCrea, 2012; Ginwright, 2010; O'Donoghue, 2006; Riggs et al., 2010), and CBES are positioned to nurture these intergenerational relationships in more culturally and personally relevant ways (Woodland, Martin, Hill, & Worrell, 2009). In these spaces, adults seek to go beyond safe and supportive relationships by creating intergenerational ties that cultivate high expectations and opportunities to engage in social change within their communities (Ginwright, 2007) and opportunities for youth to belong (Eccles & Gootman, 2002). In CBES, relationships with adults are repositioned in ways that uplift youth and disrupt inequality by forging an appreciation of shared struggle between youth and adults (Ginwright, 2007) and employing an "ethos of care to acknowledge that for the community to flourish, individuals must recognize their interconnected relationships to one another" (Jackson, Sealey-Ruiz, & Watson, 2014, p. 399). According to Ginwright (2010), these adult–youth relationships "are not simply about trust, dependence, and mutual expectations. Rather, they are political acts that encourage youth to heal from trauma" (p. 56). With schools as a site of suffering (Dumas, 2014) for many youth of color where deficit discourses render them disposable and create a chasm between them and the state/state workers/teachers, these opportunities for meaningful relationships are indispensable to interrupting educational inequality.

While relationships with adults are not exclusive to community-based spaces, their less bureaucratic and hierarchical positioning (Baldridge, in press; O'Donoghue, 2006) and structure allow for more culturally relevant (Ladson-Billings, 1995), culturally sustaining (Paris, 2012), and equalized relationships between youth and adults (Ginwright, 2007; Woodland et al., 2009). In a society in which minoritized youth have been increasingly labeled as disposable, threatening, and objects for control (O'Donoghue, 2006), authentic caring relationships (Valenzuela, 1999) are essential to overcome the predominant deficit discourse and produce the equalized terrain to interrupt educational inequality.

REDEFINING EDUCATION: IDENTITY, CULTURE, AND POLITICAL DEVELOPMENT

Traditional school settings educate increasingly across and within the domain of privatized and politicized standardized testing regimes (Fabricant & Fine, 2013; Giroux, 2008; Lipman, 2011a, 2011b). The hyperfocus on academic achievement ignores critically important social, emotional, and economic disparities facing youth (Anderson & Larson, 2009; Baldridge, 2014). CBES are uniquely situated with the flexibility to educate within and beyond the cognitive domain. Because of these opportunities, Douglas and Peck (2013) found that community-based sites are important for learning, socialization, and support—and often have a more substantial impact on the lives of youth. The educational impact of CBES lies in their capacity to connect political, social, and cultural education with the dominant academic standards of school. This connection allows students to bridge their lived reality and identity development with the academic standards deemed important and has been shown to increase typical measures of student success.

Moje et al. (2004) found that CBES can center a broader discourse of education, while not ignoring the traditional academic standards of school and their connections to economic imperatives. Moje et al. (2004) found that CBES can foster strong racial and ethnic identities and encourage learning and community activism. In school settings where minoritized youth experience a diminishing self-concept, are "stripped of humanity as they are ignored by the curriculum, instruction, and culture of schooling" (Jackson et al., 2014, p. 408), it is critical that youth of color and other marginalized youth have a "socio-political space where dialogue can occur beyond the confines of [traditionally white spaces]" (Douglas & Peck, 2013, p. 77). Community-based spaces, thus, serve as sites to connect and interrogate academic learning with a broader sociopolitical and cultural stance.

In this same vein, Woodland (2008) observed that cultural rites of passage programs have led to successful social and academic outcomes for young Black males. These programs use culture-based approaches to supplement and support the transition of Black youth to adulthood (Woodland, 2008). While even rites of passage programs acknowledge academic outcomes, traditional academics overshadow the more paramount goal of connecting education to the perils of navigating space as Black men. Without ignoring the traditional academic gains and impacts of CBES, Baldridge's (2014) scholarship demonstrates a more paramount deficit for Black and marginalized youth in a neoliberal state and locates the problem more squarely within traditional schooling practices and larger systems of power and structures of inequality. As such, learning or education in the broadest sense is often at odds with school-based academic achievement (Patel, 2016). Yet many community-based spaces are savvy and able to reimagine education beyond school walls to include sociopolitical and cultural development, while also including and honoring the knowledge youth bring to schools that are vital to their survival. By attending to the core domains of education in holistic ways, community-based spaces reimagine education and make space for students' experiences and culture while practically acknowledging the academic and economic imperatives of learning traditional standards.

Expanding Educational Possibilities

Across the landscape of community-based programming for minoritized youth, they have flexibility, often not found in traditional school spaces, to address education in more holistic ways that focus on developmental skills that promote intellectual growth, as well as social and emotional growth (Eccles & Gootman, 2002). A central characteristic of community-based spaces that work with youth is the flexibility they have had, historically and today, in regards to their programmatic and curricular offerings (Halpern, 2002). Halpern (2002) reminds us that community-based organizations have been around for over 100 years and have operated, for the most part, as institutions separate from and different than traditional schools. Furthermore, he believes that CBES have differentiated themselves from traditional education settings by offering services directly tied to community interests, concerns, and/or needs. As a result, effective community-based spaces have been marked by variation in organizational focus and program offerings as they respond to the different community contexts in which they find themselves. Additionally, as Hirsch (2011) notes, "These programs often had humble beginnings in church basements, storefronts, and settlement houses" (p. 66), indicating their separate existence, and often privately funded origins (Zhang & Byrd, 2006). As Zhang and Byrd argue, "Early after-school programs were primarily regional and local operations, which attempted to function without federal subsidy. Much of the funding for after-school efforts came from miscellaneous sources" (p. 3). Given their origins as privately funded institutions separate from schools, CBES could focus their programs directly toward the interests of the community rather than being constrained by the academic standards that limit school practice. Thus, the history of CBES alone, as separate, responsive, privately funded organizations, help educators understand the flexibility in programs that CBES as a field, have possessed.

Since 1994, when the first federally funded grants for community-based organizations, the 21st Century Community Learning Center grants (Hirsch, 2011; Zhang & Byrd, 2006), were approved, major socioeconomic developments have compounded to limit the flexibility of CBES programming and curricular offerings. For instance, current neoliberal ideals have shaped education policy, leading to changes in the political context in which CBES operate (Baldridge, 2014; Kwon, 2013). Said policies normalize privatization and standardization and perpetuate the deskilling of teachers, and lead schools to become increasingly inflexible (Apple, 2006; Giroux, 2003). More important, these central ideas (e.g., privatization, standardization, deskilling) are tied to the federal grants that have been made available for community-based youth spaces. Organizations that receive federal funds are asked to demonstrate "effectiveness" via improved academic and standardized test scores making academic preparation an increasingly larger focus of programmatic offerings (Baldridge, 2014). Furthermore, as Baldridge (2014), and various other scholars have noted (Apple, 2006; Dumas, 2016; Lipman, 2011a), privatization of education in the form of charter schools has constrained the practices of schools, affected communities, and place CBES into direct competition with them over funding. As a result of these multiple influences (e.g., funding, standards, competition), CBES are at risk of becoming increasingly inflexible as they are asked to focus on academics, align with schools, and demonstrate effectiveness via increased student performance. However, as Hirsch (2011) and other scholars of community-based afterschool programs have found, programmatic flexibility within CBES have been associated with improved academic performance as well as psychosocial growth, which furthers the point that reimagining education beyond grades and test scores actually improves academic achievement.

Although times are changing and CBES are pressured to shift their focus to academics in response, programmatic and curricular flexibility should still be a priority. Programs that accommodate the lived experiences students face are in a better position to capture student interest through relevant highly engaging programs; foster strong youth-adult partnerships; help disrupt inequalities by supporting student success and civic engagement; and promote healthy social identity development. In order to achieve these outcomes, institutional as well as programmatic and curricular flexibility is necessary. Flexibility can allow organizations to incorporate youth voice (O'Donoghue, 2006), be responsive to their interests, concerns, and unique lived experiences by offering programs aligned with their needs (Riggs et al., 2010); and utilize pedagogical practices that foster community through structured interactions (Bulanda & McCrea, 2012; Jones & Deutsch, 2013; Lerner et al., 2003).

RESISTANCE AND ORGANIZING WITHIN COMMUNITY-BASED EDUCATIONAL SPACES

Theories of resistance have informed educational theory, research, and practice in myriad ways. Some scholars have suggested that both traditional and radical views of education have been caught in a "theoretical straitjacket" that either neglects the importance of individual agency and resistance or ignores structural barriers (Giroux, 1997). Despite the social forces that make schooling unequal for marginalized youth, parents, teachers, and youth themselves are not complacent. Instead, it is widely accepted that educators, youth, and community members resist the imposition of dominant culture and ideology in multiple ways (Aronowitz & Giroux, 1985; Fine et al., 2000; Kirshner, 2015; Kwon, 2008; Nygreen, Sanchez, & Kwon, 2006; Tuck & Yang, 2011). While we suggest that CBES exist and operate within a contradictory space, we understand that mechanisms of social and cultural reproduction are always met with various forms of opposition or resistance. Even though much literature on CBES capture how young people are engaged in forms of organizing or acts of resistance against unfair policies within their schools and neighborhoods, it is important to note here that resistance itself can be contradictory and hold contradictory aims (Leonardo, 2009).

Considering that hegemonic discourses and the actions that follow can also be called "resistance," it is imperative to understand that not all forms of resistance are progressive and lead to the liberation of marginalized groups (Leonardo, 2009). For example, as Apple (2009) has argued, the Right's neoliberal economic and educational agendas can be a form of resistance even as it has catastrophic impacts on the state of public education. We hold that CBES have the potential to be sites of resistance in two important ways. First, CBES can disrupt conventional forms of learning to broaden or reimagine education beyond academic achievement to include cultural, social, and political development. This is an ideological shift that actors within community-based spaces must hold to move past conventional methods of teaching and learning, as well as what constitutes education. Second, this ideological shift must be met with intentional acts—through pedagogical practices in the type of programming CBES provide for young people—despite the control and power the state or foundations may have (Baldridge, 2014). Last, as we highlight below, many CBES have been sites where young people foster critical consciousness and acquire tools to act on and create social and political change within their school and community contexts. We contend that reimagining education beyond the borders of the school is a form of resistance, as community-based leaders, youth workers, and youth themselves negotiate the dialectical nature of CBES within a capitalist and racialized neoliberal state.

In the neoliberal era of education policy, youth are typically constructed as threats rather than allies, (Hosang, 2006), but some CBES are repositioning young people as key actors in the struggle to interrupt inequality. As Hosang (2006) notes, the organizing found within CBES is heterogeneous and not without risk, but by linking personal and neighborhood-based challenges that youth encounter with broader structural inequalities, organizing efforts and campaigns focused on policy reforms can contribute to long-term change. Youth activism wins small victories that focus on ameliorating conditions, by contesting and disrupting deficit racialized discourses about youth and their communities. This interruption and challenge to deficit discourses drives the transformations they are able to create. Therefore, this is where CBES have the political flexibility to make connections where school and other state institutions cannot.

Many CBES provide structured experiences through which young people and community-based educators can process the challenging and contradictory social and political forces that inform their lives while also allowing them space to create opportunities for organizing and resistance (Hosang, 2006). Herein, the political location of CBES is emphasized. State institutions have neither the political flexibility nor the will to organize against their own vested interests. This does not mean that governmentality, as a form of power and control over human action, ideas, and social and cultural practices (Dumas, 2016; Foucault, 1980; Kwon, 2013; Rhee, 2013), does not pose a risk for CBES. Because community-based spaces are situated, as Gilmore (2007) suggests, "in the shadow of the shadow state," they are both vulnerable and beholden to the state and also positioned to subvert state power. Governmentality narrows and limits the narratives ascribed to minoritized youth and community-based spaces as sites of containment and control (Kwon, 2013; Spence, 2015). CBES and the actors within them can be situated to interrupt inequality and subvert neoliberal governmentality by developing critical consciousness and enacting a politicized critical pedagogy aimed at reform and resistance "that is rooted in a deliberate critique of one's circumstances" (Noguera & Cannella, 2006, p. 335). By nurturing youth–adult partnerships to help reimagine possibilities as well as forging common struggle among young people, youth are resisting, organizing, and positioning each other, their adult allies, and CBES as resources in the struggle for transformative change against overt and subtle forms of control.

When community-based youth workers help young people make sense of how political and social problems shape their lives, schools, and communities (Ginwright, 2007), they are able to work toward a more just world, while also developing their own level of critical consciousness and liberation. Community-based organizations help advance consciousness by advancing intergenerational ties, challenging negative racial and ethnic concepts of self among minoritized youth, and moving toward social change (Ginwright, 2007). When thinking about the pedagogical approaches to these goals, Kirshner (2015) expands on the need to move away from positive youth development as the basis for interactions between youth and adults in community-based organizations. Positive youth development as pedagogy and curriculum tends to ignore the sociopolitical development of young people (Ginwright & James, 2002). However, through relationship building, encouraging critical consciousness and emphasizing political efficacy for community change, CBES can offer youth opportunities to learn more about organizing and resistance when compared with standard classroom curriculum (Shiller, 2013).

Community organizations that engage youth in organizing and resistance aim to improve community institutions, such as schools, youth programs, and police departments, by mobilizing networks of youth and forming intergenerational ties with adult allies and policymakers (Kirshner & Ginwright, 2012). As young people become more familiar with the processes for organizing, programming efforts shift from adult-led to a collaborative, adult–student environment aiming to teach students the benefits of cooperating across groups (Zeldin, Christens, & Powers, 2012). Similarly, as Rogers, Morrell, and Enyedy (2007) found, the community of practice approach is predicated on teaching from a joint adult–student learning model emphasizing the learning–acting cycle in which students are perpetually engaged within. Students learn social theory and investigation techniques from the instructors who allow them to take on roles as change agents. The community of practice approach teaches community organizing as a dual action, in turn, giving both students and adults the opportunity to engage in more authentic learning (Rogers et al., 2007).

In order to create a pedagogical space for youth, community-based youth programs provide opportunities for youth and youth workers to become public intellectuals through innovative forms of civic participation, increasing students' agency and increasing their involvement and engagement (Mirra, Morrell, Cain, Scorza, & Ford, 2013). Participation starts with indirect forms of community engagement in which students discuss the community and cultural issues most important to the group while learning the intricacies of the political process (Shiller, 2013). Ginwright and Cammarota (2007) assert that community organizations provide opportunities for youth to link their growing ideologies through interactions with their peers, parents, and teachers and youth workers. The authors conceptualize "critical civic praxis" (p. 693), or the processes used by community organizations to engage youth in civic participation and raise their critical consciousness. By describing the critical civic praxis methods employed by two community-based organizations in California, Ginwright and Cammarota (2007) describe how youth workers built a foundation based on collective identity and promoted community action as that identity was solidified.

Analyzing one's ecological context is essential when considering the impact of sociopolitical interpretations, and subsequently, how young people understand and engage in social action (Kirshner & Ginwright, 2012). As students' cultural identities form alongside their agency to learn, their ability to own and change their community increases. Nygreen, Kwon, and Sanchez (2006) explain how adults serving as allies in youth activism for community change should consider the social and political identities of youth when thinking about partnerships and relationship building. Grounding their work in their own experiences engaging with environments that align with their racial background, these scholars assert that to connect with youth and begin collaborative relationships, identity gaps are bridged between youth and adults.

In community-based spaces, youth have organized for education reform through myriad strategies (Checkoway & Richards-Schuster, 2006; Shah & Mediratta, 2008; Warren et al., 2008). Whether they construct an academic environment that welcomes traditionally marginalized students, push for large-scale changes in standardized testing practices, or address issues of sexual harassment in schools for students of all genders, youth experience self-efficacy as part of their education. Conner and Zaino (2014) claim that youth organizing for educational reform has a significant impact on reform efforts. These scholars identify a number of strategies in relationship building, organizing tactics, and self-representation employed by organizations when moving toward decision making on reform efforts. Yet organizing for education reform is no easy feat. Urban school reform fails because of the lack of an organized political constituency in schools (Warren, 2011). Criticism around community organizing is sometimes based on its inability to show quantifiable results. Although groups may feel more empowered and attached to school, because the improvements are not solely centered on test preparation, scores tend to suffer (Warren, 2011). Warren et al. (2008) also add that prior research on youth organizing in community-based organizations tended to favor only other forms of community change, rather than local school reform. Other institutionalized educational reformers often trump community-based organizations working alongside youth toward education reform—especially when their rhetoric for change does not match acceptable branding, messages, and tactics. Furthermore, an obvious risk noted in Shah and Mediratta's (2008) work is the disapproval of youth organizing efforts by school actors. However, Shah and Mediratta also assert that engagement in youth organizing may spark long-term structural and ideological changes in both adults and youth in regard to their relationships. Youth organizing for education policy change conducted alongside their adult partners helps other adult allies acknowledge youth as "critical stakeholders" in reform (Shah & Mediratta, 2008, p. 57). Warren et al. (2008) asserts that when motivated by their self-interests and partnered with adults, youth in community-based organizations feel more empowered and are more apt to organize for school change.

The results of intentional engagement of youth voice and power are critical for educational change, particularly within community-based organizations. Stovall (2006) describes how community organizations in Chicago intentionally engaged youth to construct a local community high school. Highlighting the high-stakes nature of the high school's development, youth exceeded simple recommendations in their roles as decision makers in the process. According to Stovall (2006), youth roles included planning protest tactics, working collaboratively with teachers in the creation of ideal curriculum and facilitating disciplinary decisions. Aligning with Checkoway and Richards-Schuster's (2006) work, both pieces assert that youth in community-based organizations should participate in educational reform because their ample amount of relevant input makes them a necessary source of information and ideas. Similarly, in Cabrera's (2013) important work on a community-based organization's youth-led ethnic studies program in Tucson, he details how student organizers were critical in creating a community space for analysis, reflection, and organizing when their efforts to reform their schools were unrecognized.

Considering the threat neoliberalism poses to community-based youth work, Kwon's (2013) conception of affirmative governmentality details the contentious relationship between community-based organizations, youth organizing, and the neoliberal state. Describing it as "the efforts to turn young people into functioning citizens-subjects" (p. 128), affirmative governmentality views youth organizing as an "exercise of personal empowerment [and] human development skills" (p. 128), rather than an active, valid voice in decision making within the state. The neoliberal state, as Kwon (2013) describes, values nonprofits like CBES as long as they fit into the neoliberal agenda. This agenda, based on political individuality and the transference of social services to the private sector, institutionalizes community-based organizations through philanthropic, and many times, state-connected funding sources. Youth organizing, thus, can operate within contradictory frameworks. Many programs are expected to invigorate the desire to be politically active in youth; however, the possibilities for change can be limited by the connected, dependent relationship between the neoliberal state and community-based organizations. Even still, the pedagogical work of engaging minoritized youth in critical consciousness and political development, identifying social, political, and educational problems to then act on them through community-based spaces is a necessary process. Although the barriers to this work are growing within an ever-increasing hyperneoliberal educational context, the resistance and organizing developed by youth in CBES is precisely the kind of disruption needed to preserve the flexibility and dynamic experiences youth have within community-based spaces.

CONCLUSION: A NOTE OF CAUTION

As many schools serve as sites of suffering for Black and other minoritized youth (Dumas, 2014), CBES have long offered respite, healing, and tools that help strengthen academic performance, and cultivate strong social, cultural, and political identities. The literature reviewed in this chapter speaks to the myriad ways CBES function in the lives of young people. The heterogeneity and flexibility of these spaces allow for a broader imagining of education. Schools are not, nor have they ever been, the sole places of learning for youth. Community-based spaces within marginalized communities of color, in particular, have been intentional about educating beyond the borders of the school due to racial stratification and structural inequality.

Education scholars conducting research on community-based spaces must continue to examine beyond academic achievement to include the social, emotional, and political dimensions of community-based youth work that ultimately inform the academic lives of young people. Education scholars must also recognize that the threat to public education as result of neoliberal logics of reform and academic success also shapes and reshapes the construction and pedagogical practices of community-based spaces. More important, the heterogeneity and flexibility lauded by youth participants and adult allies/youth workers detailed throughout literature on these spaces are greatly compromised by the neoliberal turn in educational policy. Education policymakers and funders looking to support CBES must understand that narrow neoliberal measures of academic achievement (via test scores, grade point averages, etc.)

are short sided and neglects the social, cultural, and political lives of young people. And, it ultimately ignores their humanity.

CBES are politically, theoretically, and methodologically rich settings to study. As the research highlighted in this chapter suggests, these spaces can complement, supplement, and challenge what young people learn in schools. The opportunities within community-based spaces to disrupt and dislodge hegemonic narratives and practices, while also affirming and acknowledging the voice and humanity of young people is imperative. Yet danger lurks closely as neoliberal reforms in public education and funding narrows the work of community-based spaces. Moreover, the dialectical space community-based programs exist within must also be explored by education researchers. Their tensions, contradictions, and victories are critical to explore in order to theorize these spaces more fully and capture the myriad ways in which their pedagogical strengths matter to educational policy.

Given the current state of public education, community-based spaces continue to be recognized as critical settings for minoritized youth in disenfranchised contexts. Although the diverse pedagogical practices and philosophies of youth and education within these spaces must be illuminated within education research, we caution researchers, educators, and policymakers to grasp the broader implications of neoliberal reforms and remain cognizant of the political, economic, and social context community-based spaces exist within. As places of immense pedagogical strength and possibility, CBES have interrupted patterns of inequality and continue to do so even under the current political climate.

Community-based educational spaces have been instrumental at shifting the discourse by challenging dominant deficit narratives stemming from schools about minoritized youth, because of their flexibility and fewer political constraints that traditional schools and classroom teachers experience. Yet youth-work within CBES is particularly vulnerable in the current political educational context that poses major threats to their flexibility and capacity for broad pedagogical possibility that humanizes youth by engaging their full lives. Our hope is that CBES will continue to exist with as much heterogeneity as the context they operate within demands. As education researchers, community-based educators, and activists continue to challenge, disrupt, and shed light on the impact of neoliberal education restructuring—CBES must be included in education discourse and the threats to their work must be taken seriously.

REFERENCES

Akom, A. A. (2006). The racial dimensions of social capital: Toward a new understanding of youth empowerment and community organizing in America's urban core. In S. Ginwright, P. Noguera, & J. Cammarota (Eds.), *Beyond resistance: Youth activism and community change* (pp. 81–92). New York, NY: Routledge.

Anderson, N., & Larson, C. (2009). "Sinking, like quicksand": Expanding educational opportunity for young men of color. *Educational Administration Quarterly, 45,* 71–114.

Apple, M. (2006). Understanding and interrupting neoliberalism and neconservatism in education. *Pedagogies: An International Journal, 1*(1), 21–26.

Apple, M. (2009). A response to Zeus Leonardo's "Critical empiricism: Reading data with social theory." *Educational Researcher, 39,* 160–161.

Aronowitz, S., & Giroux, H. (1985). *Education under siege.* South Hadley, MA: Bergin & Garvey.

Baldridge, B. (2014). Relocating the deficit: Reimagining Black youth in neoliberal times. *American Educational Research Journal, 51,* 440–472.

Baldridge, B. (in press). On educational advocacy and cultural work: Situating community-based youth work[ers] in broader educational discourse. *Teachers College Record.*

Baldridge, B., Hill, M., & Davis, J. (2011). New possibilities: (Re)engaging Black male youth within community-based educational spaces. *Race Ethnicity and Education, 14,* 121–136.

Blanchett, W. J., Klingner, J. K., & Harry, B. (2009). The intersection of race, culture, language, and disability: Implications for urban education. *Urban Education, 44,* 389–409.

Brice-Heath, S., & McLaughlin, M. (1994). The best of both worlds: Connecting schools and communities youth organizations for all day-all year learning. *Educational Administration Quarterly, 30,* 278–300.

Bulanda, J., & McCrea, K. (2012). The promise of an accumulation of care: Disadvantaged African-American youths' perspectives about what makes an after school program meaningful. *Child and Adolescent Social Work Journal, 30,* 95–118.

Burrowes, N., Cousins, M., Rojas, P., & Ude, I. (2007). On our own terms: Ten years of radical community building with Sista II Sista. In INCITE! Women of Color Against Violence (Ed.), *The revolution will not be funded: Beyond the non-profit industrial complex* (pp. 227–234). Cambridge, MA: South End Press.

Cabrera, N. (2013). "If there is no struggle, there is no progress": Transformative youth activism and the school of ethnic studies. *Urban Review, 45*(1), 7–22.

Checkoway, B., & Richards-Schuster, K. (2006). Youth participation for educational reform in low-income communities of color. In S. Ginwright, P. Noguera, & J. Cammarota (Eds.), *Beyond resistance: Youth activism and community change* (pp. 319–332). New York, NY: Routledge.

Conner, J., & Zaino, K. (2014). Orchestrating effective change: How youth organizing influences education policy. *American Journal of Education, 120,* 173–203.

Crenshaw, K. (2016). *Black girls matter: Pushed out, overpoliced, and underprotected.* New York, NY: African American Policy Forum, Center for Intersectionality and Social Policy Studies.

Deutsch, N., & Hirsch, B. (2002). A place to call home: Youth organizations in the lives of inner city adolescents. In T. Brinthaupt, & R. Lipka (Eds.), *Understanding early adolescent self and identity: Applications and interventions* (pp. 293–320). Albany: State University of New York Press.

Dimitriadis, G. (2009). *Performing identity, performing culture: Hip hop as text, pedagogy, and lived practice.* New York, NY: Peter Lang.

Douglas, T., & Peck, C. (2013). Education by any means necessary: Peoples of African descent and community-based pedagogical spaces. *Educational Studies, 49,* 67–91.

Downey, D., & Pribesh, S. (2004). When race matters: Teachers' evaluations of students' classroom behavior. *Sociology of Education, 77,* 267–282.

Dumas, M. (2014). "Losing an arm": Schooling as a site of black suffering. *Race Ethnicity and Education, 17*(1), 1–29.

Dumas, M. (2016). My brother as "problem": Neoliberal governmentality and interventions for Black men and boys. *Educational Policy, 30,* 94–113.

Durlak, J. A., & Weissberg, R. P. (2007). *The impact of after-school programs that promote personal and social skills* (1st ed.). Retrieved from http://www.uwex.edu/ces/4h/afterschool/partnerships/documents/ASP-Full.pdf

Eccles, J., & Gootman, J. (2002). *Community programs to promote youth development.* Washington, DC: National Academies Press.

Fabricant, M., & Fine, M. (2013). *The changing politics of education: Privatization and the dispossessed lives left behind.* Boulder, CO: Paradigm.

Fine, M., Weis, L., Centrie, C., & Roberts, R. (2000). Educating beyond the borders of schooling. *Anthropology & Education Quarterly, 31,* 131–151.

Foucault, M. (1980). *Power/knowledge.* Brighton, England: Harvester.

Freire, P. (2000). *Pedagogy of the oppressed.* New York, NY: Continuum. (Original work published 1979)

Freire, P., & Macedo, D. (1987). *Reading the word and the world.* Westport, CT: Bergin & Garvey.

Gilmore, R. (2007). In the shadow of the shadow state. In INCITE! Women of Color Against Violence (Ed.), *The revolution will not be funded: Beyond the non-profit industrial complex* (pp. 41–52). Cambridge, MA: South End Press.

Ginwright, S. (2007). Black youth activism and the role of critical social capital in black community organizations. *American Behavioral Scientist, 51,* 403–418.

Ginwright, S. (2010). *Black youth rising: Activism and radical healing in urban America.* New York, NY: Teachers College Press.

Ginwright, S., & Cammarota, J. (2007) Youth activism in the urban community: Learning critical civic praxis within community organizations. *International Journal of Qualitative Studies, 20,* 693–710.

Ginwright, S., & James, T. (2002, Winter). From assets to agents of change: Social justice, organizing, and youth development. *New Directions for Youth Development, 96,* 27–46.

Giroux, H. (2003). Racial injustice and disposable youth in the age of zero tolerance. *International Journal of Qualitative Studies in Education, 16,* 553–565.

Giroux, H. (2008). Education and the crisis of youth: Schooling and the promise of democracy. *Educational Forum, 73*(1), 8–18.

Giroux, H. (2009). *Youth a suspect society: Democracy or disposability?* New York, NY: Palgrave MacMillan.

Giroux, H. A. (1997). *Pedagogy and the politics of hope: Theory, culture, and schooling.* Boulder, CO: Westview Press.

Green, T., & Gooden, M. (2014). Transforming out-of-school challenges into opportunities: Community schools reform in the urban Midwest. *Urban Education, 49,* 930–954.

Gregory, A., Skiba, R., & Noguera, P. (2010). The achievement gap and the discipline gap: Two sides of the same coin. *Educational Researcher, 39,* 59–68.

Halpern, R. (2002). A different kind of child development institution: The history of after-school programs for low-income children. *Teachers College Record, 104,* 178–211.

Heath, S., & McLaughlin, M. (1994). The best of both worlds connecting schools and community youth organizations for all-day, all-year learning. *Educational Administration Quarterly, 30,* 278–300.

Hill, M. L. (2009). *Beats, rhymes, and classroom life: Hip-Hop pedagogy and the politics of identity.* New York, NY: Teachers College Press.

Hirsch, B. (2011). Learning and development in after-school programs: Educators need to learn how best to work with after-school programs and use their contributions to young people. *Kappan, 92*(5), 66–69.

Hosang, D. (2006). Beyond policy: Ideology, race and the reimagining of youth. In S. Ginwright, P. Noguera, & J. Cammarota (Eds.), *Beyond resistance! Youth activism and community change* (pp. 3–19). New York, NY: Routledge.

Jackson, I., Sealey-Ruiz, Y., & Watson, W. (2014). Reciprocal love: Mentoring Black and Latino males through an ethos of care. *Urban Education, 49*, 394–417.

Jones, J., & Deutsch, N. (2013). Social and identity development in an after-school program. *Journal of Early Adolescence, 33*(1), 17–43.

Jones de Almeida, A. (2007). Radical social change: Searching for a new foundation. In INCITE! Women of Color Against Violence (Ed.), *The revolution will not be funded: Beyond the non-profit industrial complex* (pp. 185–196). Cambridge, MA: South End Press.

Kataoka, S., & Vandell, D. (2013). Quality of afterschool activities and relative change in adolescent functioning over two years. *Applied Developmental Science, 17*(3), 123–134.

Kirshner, B. (2015). *Youth activism in an era of education inequality.* New York: New York University Press.

Kirshner, B., & Ginwright, S. (2012). Youth organizing as a developmental context for African American and Latino adolescents. *Child Development Perspectives, 6*, 288–294.

Kwon, S. (2008). Moving from complaints to action: Oppositional consciousness and collective action in a political economy. *Anthropology & Education Quarterly, 39*, 59–76.

Kwon, S. (2013). *Uncivil youth: Race, activism, and affirmative government mentality.* Durham, NC: Duke University Press.

Ladson-Billings, G. (1995). Toward a theory of culturally relevant pedagogy. *American Educational Research Journal, 32*, 465–491.

Leonardo, Z. (2009). Critical empiricism: Reading data with social theory. *Educational Researcher, 39*, 155–160.

Lerner, R. M., Dowling, E., & Anderson, P. (2003). Positive youth development: Thriving as the basis of personhood and civil society. *Applied Developmental Science, 7*, 172–180.

Lesko, N. (1996). Denaturalizing adolescence: The politics of contemporary representations. *Youth & Society, 28*, 139–161.

Lipman, P. (2011a). Neoliberal education restructuring: Dangers and opportunities of the present crisis. *Monthly Review, 63*(3). Retrieved from http://monthlyreview.org/2011/07/01/neoliberal-education-restructuring/

Lipman, P. (2011b). *The new political economy of urban education: Neoliberalism, race, and the right to the city.* New York, NY: Routledge.

Mahoney, J., Lord, H., & Carryl, E. (2005). An ecological analysis of after-school program participation and the development of academic performance and motivational attributes for disadvantaged children. *Child Development, 76*, 811–825.

McKenzie, B. (2008). Reconsidering the effects of bonding social capital: A closer look at Black civil society institutions in America. *Political Behavior, 30*, 25–45.

McLaughlin, M. W. (2000). *Community counts: How youth organizations matter for youth development.* Retrieved from http://eric.ed.gov/?id=ED442900

Mirra, N., Morrell, E. D., Cain, E., Scorza, D., & Ford, A. (2013). Educating for a critical democracy: Civic participation reimagined in the council of youth research. *Democracy & Education, 21*(1), 3.

Moje, E., Ciechanowski, K., Kramer, K., Ellis, L., Carrillo, R., & Collazo, T. (2004). Working toward third space in content area literacy: An examination of everyday funds of knowledge and discourse. *Reading Research Quarterly, 39*(1), 38–70.

Nicholson-Crotty, S., Birchmeier, Z., & Valentine, D. (2009). Exploring the impact of school discipline on racial disproportion in the juvenile justice system. *Social Science Quarterly, 90*, 1003–1018.

Noguera, P., & Cannella, C. (2006). Youth agency, resistance, and civic activism: The public commitment to social justice. In S. Ginwright, P. Noguera, & J. S. Cammarota (Eds.),

Beyond resistance! Youth activism and community change (pp. 333–347). New York, NY: Routledge.

Nygreen, K., Kwon, S. A., & Sanchez, P. (2006). Urban youth building community: Social change and participatory research in schools, homes and community-based organizations. In B. N. Checkoway, & L. M. Gutierrez (Eds.), *Youth participation and community change* (pp. 107–123). New York, NY: Haworth Press.

O'Donoghue, J. (2006). "Taking their own power": Urban youth, community-based youth organizations, and public efficacy. In S. Ginwright, P. Noguera, & J. Cammarota (Eds.), *Beyond resistance! Youth activism and community change* (pp. 3–19). New York, NY: Routledge.

Paris, D. (2012). Culturally sustaining pedagogy a needed change in stance, terminology, and practice. *Educational Researcher, 41*, 93–97.

Paris, D., & Winn, M. T. (2013). *Humanizing research: Decolonizing qualitative inquiry with youth and communities.* Thousand Oaks, CA: Sage.

Patel, L. (2016). Pedagogies of resistance and survivance: Learning as marronage. *Equity and Excellence in Education, 49*(4), 397–401.

Posner, J. K., & Vandell, D. L. (1994). Low-income children's after-school care: Are there beneficial effects of after-school programs? *Child Development, 65*, 440–456.

Quinn, J. (2012). Advancing youth work: Opportunities and challenges. In D. Fusco (Ed.), *Advancing youth work: Current trends, critical questions* (pp. 207–215). New York, NY: Routledge.

Rhee, J. (2013). The neoliberal racial project: The tiger mother and governmentality. *Educational Theory, 63*, 561–580.

Riggs, N. R., Bohnert, A. M., Guzman, M. D., & Davidson, D. (2010). Examining the potential of community-based after-school programs for Latino youth. *America Journal of Community Psychology, 45*, 417–429.

Rogers, J., Morrell, E., & Enyedy, N. (2007). Studying the struggle: Contexts for learning and identity development for urban youth. *American Behavioral Scientist, 51*, 419–443.

Schmidt, S. J. (2011). Theorizing place: Students' navigation of place outside the classroom. *Journal of Curriculum Theorizing, 27*(1), 20–35.

Scott, W., Deschenes, S., Hopkins, K., Newman, A., & McLaughlin, M. (2006). Advocacy organizations and the field of youth services: Ongoing efforts to restructure a field. *Nonprofit and Voluntary Sector Quarterly, 35*, 691–714.

Shah, S., & Mediratta, K. (2008). Negotiating reform: Young people's leadership in the educational arena. *New Directions for Youth Development, 2008*(117), 43–59.

Shiller, J. T. (2013). Preparing for democracy: How community-based organizations build civic engagement among urban youth. *Urban Education, 48*, 69–91.

Spence, L. (2015). *Knocking the hustle: Against the neoliberal turn in black politics.* New York, NY: Punctum Books

Stovall, D. (2006). From hunger strike to high school: Youth development, social justice, and school formation. In S. Ginwright, P. Noguera, & J. Cammarota (Eds.), *Beyond resistance: Youth activism and community change: New democratic possibilities for policy and practice for America's youth* (pp. 97–110). Oxford, England: Routledge.

Terzian, M., Giesen, L., & Mbwana, K. (2009). *Why teens are not involved in out-of-school time programs: The youth perspective.* Retrieved from http://www.childtrends.org/wp-content/uploads/2013/04/6.pdf

Tuck, E., & Yang, K. W. (2011). Youth resistance revisited: New theories of youth negotiations of educational injustices. *International Journal of Qualitative Studies in Education, 24*, 521–530.

Valenzuela, A. (1999). *Subtractive schooling: U.S.-Mexican youth and the politics of caring.* Albany: State University of New York Press.

Warren, M. (2011). Building a political constituency for urban school reform. *Urban Education, 46*, 484–512.

Warren, M., Mira, M., & Nikundiwe, T. (2008, Spring). Youth organizing: From youth development to school reform. *New Directions in Youth Development, 117,* 27–42.

Winn, M. (2011). *Girl time: Literacy, justice, and the school-to-prison pipeline.* New York, NY: Teachers College Press.

Woodland, M. (2008). Whatcha doin' after school? A review of the literature on the influence of afterschool programs on young Black males. *Urban Education, 43*, 537–560.

Woodland, M., Martin, J., Hill, R., & Worrell, F. (2009). The most blessed room in the city: The influence of a youth development program on three young black males. *Journal of Negro Education, 78*, 233–245.

Wun, C. (2014). Unaccounted foundations: Black girls, anti-black racism, and punishment in schools. *Critical Sociology, 42*, 737–750.

Zeldin, S., Christens, B., & Powers, J. (2012). The psychology and practice of youth-adult partnership: Bridging generations for youth development and community change. *American Journal of Community Psychology, 51*, 385–397.

Zhang, J. J., & Byrd, C. E. (2006). Successful after-school programs: The 21st century community learning centers. *Journal of Physical Education, Recreation & Dance, 77*(8), 3–12.

Chapter 17

Combating Inequalities in Two-Way Language Immersion Programs: Toward Critical Consciousness in Bilingual Education Spaces

Claudia G. Cervantes-Soon
University of Texas at Austin

Lisa Dorner
University of Missouri-Columbia

Deborah Palmer
University of Colorado Boulder

Dan Heiman
University of Texas at Austin

Rebecca Schwerdtfeger
Jinmyung Choi
University of Missouri-Columbia

This chapter reviews critical areas of research on issues of equity/equality in the highly proclaimed and exponentially growing model of bilingual education: two-way immersion (TWI). There is increasing evidence that TWI programs are not living up to their ideal to provide equal access to educational opportunity for transnational emergent bilingual students. Through a synthesis of research from related fields, we will offer guidelines for program design that attend to equality and a framework for future research to push the field of bilingual education toward creating more equitable and integrated multilingual learning spaces. Specifically, this review leads to a proposal for adding a fourth goal for TWI programs: to develop "critical consciousness" through using critical pedagogies and humanizing research.

Review of Research in Education
March 2017, Vol. 41, pp. 403–427
DOI: 10.3102/0091732X17690120
© 2017 AERA. http://rre.aera.net

This chapter critically examines issues of inequality in the highly proclaimed and exponentially growing model of bilingual education: two-way immersion (TWI). Despite the "rich promise" (Lindholm-Leary, 2005b) and "astounding effectiveness" (Collier & Thomas, 2004) of TWI programs to develop high academic achievement and bilingualism for integrated, culturally and linguistically diverse youth through content instruction in two languages, there is increasing concern that many TWI programs are not providing equal educational opportunities for transnational bilinguals, or "English Learners," from immigrant families (Boyle, August, Tabaku, Cole, & Simpson-Baird, 2015; Christian, 2016)—the focal students for whom bilingual education was originally developed in the United States (Flores, 2016; Grinberg & Saavedra, 2000). This analysis of research demonstrates that TWI's stated goals may be necessary but insufficient and unrealized, particularly for transnational emergent bilinguals whose journey to become biliterate, achieve academically, enact agency, and develop powerful academic/cultural identities may not be supported to the same degree as their White, English-speaking peers in TWI.

After a description of our methods and definition of TWI goals and history in the United States, this chapter examines how inequalities are manifested in three areas: (1) the larger sociopolitical context, including economic and ideological forces, state and school policies, and community participation; (2) TWI teachers' orientations, preparation, and backgrounds; and (3) TWI classroom contexts, including pedagogy, language trends, and students' identities and relations. Next, we summarize TWI-related discourses from a range of fields, in order to identify competing interests and orientations that permeate TWI education and, sometimes, compound issues of inequality. Finally, we offer recommendations for research and program design, to ensure that TWI programs *equally and equitably* fulfill their promise, meeting not only the stated goals of high academic achievement and bilingualism for all but also the original "race radical" goals of bilingual education for transnational bilinguals (Flores, 2016). Specifically, this analysis leads to a proposal for adding a fourth goal for TWI programs: to develop "critical consciousness" through using critical pedagogies and humanizing research.

METHOD AND TERMINOLOGY

The following research questions guided our analysis:

Research Question 1: What manifestations of inequalities/inequities have been documented in research on TWI?
Research Question 2: What are the prevalent discourses and frameworks in the study and promotion of TWI?

These questions led us to conduct two separate but simultaneous literature searches and respective analyses. Ultimately, our goal was to discern how research has recognized, explained, addressed, or ignored inequities/inequalities in TWI in order to imagine new directions.

Search 1: Analysis of Inequalities in TWI

The first question sought to examine manifestations of inequalities/inequities demonstrated in studies of TWI. Following an interpretive approach to research synthesis that incorporated elements of metaethnography (Noblit & Hare, 1988), we first searched for relevant papers using terms such as "two-way immersion," "dual language," "dual immersion," and "bilingual immersion." From this literature, which was not limited by any date range and informed by Valdés's (1997) seminal cautionary note, we selected studies that revealed that students or communities from minoritized groups were experiencing marginalization or were not benefiting equally from programs as much as White English speakers/communities. While prior reviews on TWI education are widely cited and offer important insights (e.g., Howard, Sugarman, & Christian, 2003; Lindholm-Leary, 2005a; Parkes & Ruth, 2009), our selection of scholarship purposefully sought to identify empirical studies and conceptual papers that captured inequalities in TWI contexts that may go unrecognized when concentrating on conventional measures of success. This approach was necessary given that scholarly accounts of TWI's benefits—rather than research that critically analyzes limitations—have been the cornerstone of TWI program proliferation.

Notably, while not excluding quantitative studies, most of the empirical work from this search used qualitative approaches. An examination of 80 papers and six books yielded five potential areas of inequality that served as initial thematic codes for analysis: (1) student access and experiences; (2) classroom pedagogy, curriculum, and linguistic choices; (3) teachers' preparation, background, and orientations; (4) parents and community engagement; and (5) district- and state-level policies, economic contexts, and politics. We created a database with these categories where we classified meaningful units of data, including key metaphors, themes, or concepts from each study as well as descriptors for the type of paper/book, methodology, insights for equitable practices, and our own questions. After this initial coding, we reorganized and refined codes by looking for relationships and overlapping themes or concepts, examining contradictions, and building general interpretations. This led to our final identification of the three areas of inequality and respective subcategories presented in the analysis that follows.

Search 2: Cross-Disciplinary Discourse Analysis

Our second search specifically sought to identify prominent discourses framing TWI across disciplines: anthropology of language, bilingual education, foreign language/world education, immersion education, international multilingual education, teaching English to speakers of other languages, and child development. We selected one leading journal from each area, identified by its impact factor/number of citations and reputation, and conducted a search using the same terms previously noted. Recognizing that disciplines are not static and discourses evolve over time, we limited the article selection in this search to the most recent perspectives framing the expansion of TWI in the past decade (2005–present). This was not an exhaustive search but rather a purposeful one, to gain insight into common, current discursive trends defining TWI. We conducted an inductive, interpretative analysis similar to the process described above, coding 141 studies for their definitions of TWI/dual-language education, purpose of research, purpose of TWI/language education, and discourse on TWI/language students. Secondary analyses noted particularities within and across the disciplines.

Several papers went through a dual analysis as they were captured in both searches. Finally, while our analysis is based on an examination of all selected scholarship, due to space we limit our discussion to the studies that best reflected or illustrated the themes that emerged in the analysis.

Notes on Terminology

Because the literature on TWI uses various terms, defining our terminology is necessary. First, although "dual language" and "dual-language immersion" are commonly used, we prefer TWI because it specifies the integration of two languages (as in the case of all "dual-language" programs) *and* students from two different language backgrounds. Meanwhile, DL programs can encompass "one-way immersion" programs designed primarily for one language group, often the "dominant" one (e.g., English; Tedick & Wesely, 2015).

Second, in line with this volume, we usually use the term *inequality* but interchange this at times with *inequity*. We conceptualize inequalities in a way that includes a call to fairness, much like equity, with both concepts "advocating for *equality* and giving people who have been historically excluded, segregated, and discriminated against, what they need and deserve" by fully acknowledging their unequal histories (Horsford, 2015, p. 23).

Third, recognizing that labels problematically categorize individuals and deny their rich experiences and identities (Kibler & Valdés, 2016), we prefer using terms that highlight either people's strengths/diversity or the power structures that frame their lives. For example, when writing about children from immigrant families in TWI programs, we refer to them as "transnational" or "emergent" bilinguals rather than "English Learners;" these terms indicate that they have traversed cultures, have one or more foreign-born parents, and speak language(s) other than, or in addition to, English at home. We use the term *minoritized*, to indicate racial, ethnic, or linguistic groups that may be labeled *minority* by whitestream society (Urrieta, 2010) but who are by no means "minor."

DEFINING TWI EDUCATION AND GOALS

"Bilingual education" in the United States has strong historical roots in immigrant, traditionally marginalized communities (Flores, 2016). In conjunction with larger Civil Rights movements in the 1960s, the Bilingual Education Act was created explicitly to serve the needs of children who came to school speaking languages other than English, highlighting language rights and providing additional funding for schools with such students (de Jong, 2002). Over time, legal and political actions—including the reauthorization of the federal Elementary and Secondary Education Act No Child Left Behind (2002) and several state initiatives—dismantled the Bilingual Education Act's original focus on bilingualism. Such moves increased funding and support for "English-only" and "English immersion" and enhanced English monolingualism and assimilationist ideologies (Flores, 2016).

Notwithstanding and almost simultaneously, a trend in language education with new constituencies was forming. With rapid economic globalization at the turn of the century, geopolitical events like 9/11, and research demonstrating the benefits of bilingualism, proficiency in languages other than English emerged as an important goal "for all." Mainstream English-dominant families developed interest in language immersion education, which provided content-based instruction in English and another language (Dorner, 2011a). Consequently, advocates of bilingual education—those seeking to use home languages in the schooling of transnational children—as well as foreign/world language educators found hope in language immersion models.

These developments led to widespread expansion of TWI, often described in binary terms: TWI models in the United States provide academic instruction in English and an additional language (most commonly Spanish) to an integrated group of students from those two language groups. Core goals for TWI students—who may be dominant in either "target" language or already have some bilingual/multilingual capacities—include high academic achievement and linguistic fluency in the standardized registers of both languages, as well as cross-cultural or multicultural competence (Christian, 2016; de Jong, 2016). A handful of TWI programs started in the 1960s to 1980s, but scholars now estimate well over 1,000 (Wilson, 2011) across the country, including in areas with less recent history of bilingual education, for example, the District of Columbia (de Jong, 2016), North Carolina (Cervantes-Soon, 2014), and Utah (Valdez, Delavan, & Freire, 2014).

Importantly, TWI frames bilingual education as enrichment—rather than remediation—and uses students' home languages as resources (Ruiz, 1984). TWI has admirably moved bilingual education beyond the aim of English monolingualism. TWI students' academic achievement/growth (Lindholm-Leary, 2005a; Thomas & Collier, 2002) and metacognitive and metalinguistic development (Bialystok, Peets, & Moreno, 2014) are noteworthy. However, highlighting only such "rich promise" (Lindholm-Leary, 2005b) and "astounding" effects (Collier & Thomas, 2004) ignores the hegemonic forces and inequalities that continue to shape bilingual education and the experiences of transnational youth in this country (Flores, 2016).

AREAS OF INEQUALITY IN TWI

The following review demonstrates that as TWI initiatives expand, the interests of language-minoritized students may be overtaken by the interests of English speakers. Guadalupe Valdés (1997) described this risk in her seminal "cautionary note," and more recently, scholars have written about the potential neoliberal assault

(Cervantes-Soon, 2014; Petrovic, 2005) and reconfiguration of bilingual education by "hegemonic Whiteness" (Flores, 2016). That is, TWI programs often commodify and marginalize emergent bilingual speakers' and their communities' linguistic resources, which can lead to inequalities for transnational youth that are too often obscured by programs' laudable goals of integration, bilingualism, biliteracy, and multicultural competence for all. This review presents the documented inequalities in TWI at three different levels: the larger sociopolitical, teacher-focused, and classroom/student contexts.

Inequalities in TWI's Sociopolitical Context

In this section we review research documenting how borders of race, class, and social status and a neoliberal logic frame the sociopolitical context of TWI. We highlight how such borders and frameworks have resulted in inequalities in TWI implementation.

The Borders of Race and Class: Interest Convergence and Symbolic Integration in TWI

The theory of interest convergence (Bell, 1980) posits that policy changes for racial integration and equity will occur only insofar as the interests of dominant and minoritized groups converge, specifically, when White citizens perceive that such policies will benefit them. TWI, in fact, emerged when the goals of bilingualism for transnational students and those of White, wealthier, and English-speaking students appeared to converge, at a time when political hostility threatened bilingual education for minoritized children (Varghese & Park, 2010) and economic decline endangered foreign language programs for English speakers (Osborn, 2006). However, becoming bilingual means different things for each constituency, and inequalities have emerged as the interests of the dominant group took precedence in many contexts.

Research in California and the Midwest has made evident inequalities of access stemming from contexts characterized by interest convergence. In one California study, enrollment and admission policies, which existed at a TWI "strand" (one classroom/grade) within an elementary school, favored White English-speaking families; despite comprising 30% of the school population, African Americans made up only 5% of enrollment (Palmer, 2010). In the Midwestern case, mostly White English-speaking families dominated the public debate about the development of a TWI program (Dorner, 2011a). Ultimately, the district placed program strands across each of the district's elementary schools, which reflected whitestream desires, rather than those of the transnational, Spanish-speaking, and bilingual families who preferred expanding TWI at schools that had traditionally served immigrant communities.

Research has also explored the privileging of dominant group interests in the framing and support of TWI from administrative (M. M. López, 2013; Paciotto & Delany-Barmann, 2011; Peña, 1998) and parent (Muro, 2016; Pearson, Wolgemuth, & Colomer, 2015) perspectives. In the Midwestern case described above, opportunities to learn about the new TWI program were more easily accessed by White, English-speaking families; the district made few efforts to recruit and explain the program to Spanish-speaking families (Dorner, 2011b). In another context, Pimentel, Diaz Soto, Pimentel, and Urrieta (2008) documented the use of screening tests in order to manage long waitlists of English speakers, while placing language-minoritized students in the program by default. Such policies of selecting high-scoring English speakers created academic disparities along the borders of race and class among TWI students.

Interest convergence is also evident in TWI's distinction as "enrichment" for White/English-speaking families. In a Texas TWI program, the idea of enrichment aligned with the interests of mainly native English-speaking students, while Spanish-speaking parents resisted this label; one described the program instead as being about her family's Mexican *raíces* (roots), central to her child's personal and academic identity (López, 2013). In a rural Midwestern town experiencing a recent influx of Spanish-speaking immigrant students, a new TWI program was initially rejected by White English-speaking parents, until it was framed in enrichment terms, as "beneficial for future job opportunities" (Paciotto & Delany-Barmann, 2011, p. 234). Interest convergence also materialized in one Colorado district that implemented TWI to "save" a segregated school with steadily increasing low-income Spanish-speaking students and decreasing standardized test scores (Pearson et al., 2015). White parents, opting into TWI for language enrichment, delighted in being "part of a school community that benefits Latina/o students" (p. 18). The presence of White families was a major factor in framing the school as a "beacon of hope," as opposed to a "school in decline" (p. 17).

Researchers also found that in TWI, as in other contexts, integration alone does not necessarily lead to equity. Muro (2016), for example, described TWI parents from dominant and language-minoritized groups in a rapidly gentrifying community as engaging in "symbolic integration," the "polite, surface-level, interactions that are enjoyable, voluntary, and additive" (p. 2), while covert prejudice and racial stratification remained entrenched. Together, these studies demonstrate that the interest convergence inherent in TWI may result in advancing the goals of the dominant group, while benefits for minoritized students may be rendered only as a by-product of such efforts.

The Neoliberal Logic: Issues of Accountability and Commodification

Neoliberal discourses in education, such as an imperative to prioritize economic markets/exchanges in all interactions (Cervantes-Soon, 2014), have fostered a punitive and largely monolingual accountability system that undermines schools' abilities to meet TWI's bilingual and biliteracy goals. For example, the demands of standardized testing contributed to one TWI program's decision to abandon its biliteracy goals for several months in order to prepare students for tests only in students' stronger language (Palmer, Henderson, Wall, Zúñiga, & Berthelsen, 2015). This decision was especially damaging to language-minoritized students. Despite their bilingualism, they experienced primarily monolingual instruction in whichever language a practice test determined was currently "stronger" (for most students, in fact, English), rather than drawing on their full linguistic repertoire and continuing to develop their bilingualism. Meanwhile, Peña (1998) documented a TWI program that aimed for transformational change as the school worked with immigrant parents' desires "to preserve and protect their values and ways of knowing;" however, this aim was undermined, as parents felt like "material objects" in a system focused on outcomes and evidence (pp. 254–255). These technical attributes and goals, as framed by administrators, deterred generative opportunities with minoritized parents and were more in line with neoliberal norms of efficiency and individualism. Across programs, state accountability and promotion requirements have often emphasized and considered only English-medium tests (Freeman, 2000; McCollum, 1999; Warhol & Mayer, 2012).

Finally, mounting research has documented the commodification of language skills and erasure of transitional/emergent bilinguals' experiences in TWI policies and discourse. A critical discourse analysis of five newspapers' framing of TWI in Utah uncovered how a global human capital framework, which focused on commerce and future employment, overshadowed an equity/heritage framework on language maintenance and community (Valdez et al., 2014). Similarly, the Spanish language was commodified in a California school, as native English-speaking parents talked about it as a "useful tool" for their children to communicate with "workers" (Muro, 2016). Opportunity for their children to learn from "live specimens" (Petrovic, 2005, p. 406) while practicing their Spanish was positioned by the dominant group as an added bonus that *should* be commodified in striving to increase one's human capital. In this process, "white bilingualism is interpreted as an achievement to be acknowledged, and Latino bilingualism one to be anticipated" (Muro, 2016, p. 11). These studies have revealed the reconfiguration of TWI through hegemonic Whiteness (Flores, 2016).

Inequalities Related to Teachers' Backgrounds, Orientations, and Preparation

As "policymakers" in the classroom, teachers are crucial agents with the most power to directly influence students' relationships, experiences, and learning (Menken & García, 2010). Our review reinforces a growing understanding that teachers' linguistic backgrounds, training, ideologies, and orientations influence TWI classroom dynamics, often resulting in an exacerbation of inequalities between student groups in the classroom.

On the one hand, TWI programs often rely on monolingual English-speaking teachers for English-medium instruction (Amrein & Peña, 2000), as well as filling positions as librarians, coaches, substitute teachers, counselors, "specials" teachers (art, PE) and leaders of extracurricular activities (Fitts, 2006). This leads to linguistic imbalance across a student's school day and, in turn, to inequalities in communication norms and language status: English is the only nonnegotiable language. Furthermore, while bilingual teachers can allow students access to their entire linguistic repertoire, monolingual English teachers can only build on English skills (Amrein & Peña, 2000). With training that focuses on mainstream students, teachers often lack the preparation to support language-minoritized students' access to the English curriculum (Fitts, 2006). This dynamic opens up greater opportunities for the centering of English-dominant children. For example, Palmer (2009) reported that while the bilingual TWI teacher worked to balance students' status and power, monolingual English-speaking teachers tended to allow White English-dominant children to interrupt, delay lessons, and dominate learning processes.

However, recruiting bilingual teachers is a challenge, particularly in contexts lacking bilingual teacher certification. Only 25 states and DC have bilingual education certificates, and only seven states require TWI teachers to have such certification (Boyle et al., 2015). Even as more states develop credentials, there remain questions about who is considered bilingual. Guerrero (1997) argued that in the case of Spanish, most locally grown bilingual teachers themselves experienced a "subtractive schooling" (Valenzuela, 1999), significantly hindering the development of their academic Spanish skills. Five TWI principals in Ramos, Dwyer, and Pérez-Prado's (2013) study indicated that their teachers' command of Spanish was adequate for informal conversations but not for teaching academic content in upper elementary grades; they also lacked the cultural knowledge to apply in their lessons. Korean parents in Lee and Jeong's study (2013) similarly complained that their bilingual Korean teachers' proficiency levels were appropriate to teach English speakers but not Korean-dominant children.

In response, some TWI programs recruit teachers from Latin America, Spain and other places, particularly in regions of the country where bilingual teachers are scarce (Cervantes-Soon, 2014). These international teachers might be deemed more authentic, cosmopolitan, and proficient speakers of the minority language. However, they may be underprepared to work with children from different class, race, and ethnic backgrounds, with little understanding about the United States' complex race relations and challenges (Valdés, 2002). Moreover, as highly educated, elite bilinguals, they might not identify with students from marginalized groups (de Mejía, 2002; Smith, 2001). This emphasis on prestige may privilege rigid ideologies of linguistic purism and elite cosmopolitanism that devalues language-minoritized students' everyday language practices, experiences, identities, and knowledges (Martínez, Hikida, & Durán, 2015). Moreover, as Flores and Rosa (2015) posit, racialized subjects' standardized language practices are perpetually constructed and perceived as deficient regardless of how closely they follow "standardized" norms precisely because these norms are determined by the White English-speaking subjects (Martín-Beltrán, 2010). Thus, students and teachers from marginalized groups are often viewed as insufficiently bilingual and biliterate.

Importantly, we should consider how teachers' ideologies and orientations shape program implementation and their views and treatment of students (Martínez et al., 2015; Menken & García, 2010). For example, while teachers in one study endorsed a color-blind orientation toward social differences, some used language as a proxy for race, articulating students' linguistic differences as an obstacle for learning (Juárez & McKay, 2008). In another study, teachers believed Latino children were raised to be quiet and submissive, an assumption that naturalized English speakers' dominance in classroom discourse (Cervantes-Soon & Turner, 2017).

Guerrero (1997) noted that many bilingual teachers face tension as their own instructional practices collide with the effects of assimilationist language ideologies that they experienced growing up. For example, Puerto Rican teachers in Freeman's (2000) study at a Philadelphia middle school used code-switching practices in the classroom that implicitly sanctioned students' local language practices, yet they also expressed fears that Spanish instruction might be detrimental for their Puerto Rican students. Similarly, Korean teachers in California were uncertain about the meaning of Korean American biculturalism (Lee & Jeong, 2013).

In conclusion, TWI teachers experience wide-ranging challenges given their linguistic backgrounds, training, and ideologies, as well as the realities they face in maintaining classrooms in minoritized languages (Amrein & Peña, 2000; Lee & Jeong, 2013). To combat inequalities, TWI teachers should possess the necessary pedagogical skills, be bilingual, and have critical understandings of what it means to serve students within TWI's inherent diversity and complexity (Palmer & Martínez, 2013).

Inequalities in TWI Classrooms

TWI classrooms are *figured worlds* where people are positioned in relation to each other through culturally constituted activities (Holland, Lachicotte, Skinner, & Cain, 1998). Specifically, encounters between students from minoritized and dominant groups—mediated by pedagogical practices and larger ideologies—frame students' sense of self and agency. The research reviewed in this section demonstrates how curriculum, instruction, and classroom discourse/identities in TWI often privilege English-dominant students (Fitts, 2009).

The Hegemony of English in the Classroom

A widely recognized challenge in TWI is to battle the hegemony of English and the devaluing of the program's other language, the home language of transnational bilingual students (Martínez et al., 2015). Many TWI programs do not offer sufficient instruction in the minority language (Torres-Guzmán, Kleyn, Morales-Rodríguez, & Han, 2005), even though the goal is to do so at least 50% of the time (Tedick & Wesely, 2015). Research has found that as students move up grade levels, English content instruction and use increase substantially, resulting in negligible amounts of instruction in the non-English language at the secondary level (Bearse & de Jong, 2008; Freeman, 2000).

While English speakers tend to naturally favor English, the hegemony of English is often also embedded in minoritized families' and students' beliefs about which language counts for their access to opportunities and status (Dorner, 2010; Freeman, 2000; Lee &

Jeong, 2013; Lucero, 2015; McCollum, 1999). Therefore, even when teachers encourage and use the minoritized language during instruction, English tends to prevail when students interact independently (DeNicolo, 2010; DePalma, 2010; Potowski, 2004).

In the case of Spanish, de Jong and Howard (2009) posit that diminishing its role results in unequal learning opportunities with potentially harmful consequences for Latino students. Students who prefer to use Spanish or are Spanish monolingual may become socially marginalized (McCollum, 1999). A number of studies have noted how the overuse of English in TWI contexts gives English speakers an academic advantage (Amrein & Peña, 2000; Muro, 2016; Palmer, 2008, 2009), increasing their ability to dominate classroom discourse and develop confidence (Palmer, 2008, 2009), particularly as they move up in grades. Meanwhile, minoritized students' opportunities to build on their linguistic repertoires, and particularly oral abilities, in content-area classes decline (Bearse & de Jong, 2008).

Valdés (1997) reminded us that the acquisition of English is expected for language-minoritized children, while learning a new language tends to be enthusiastically celebrated for English-dominant White students (McCollum, 1999; Muro, 2016). Therefore, while Latino students in TWI may experience heritage language loss as they grow older, White English-speaking children maintain their linguistic privilege, all while adding just enough bilingualism to distinguish themselves as gifted or competitive for college and the job market (Bearse & de Jong, 2008; L. M. López & Tápanes, 2011; Muro, 2016).

Language, Pedagogy, and Power

While TWI programs attempt to balance the status of two languages, these attempts have not consistently produced more equality. Language separation is perhaps the most widely used approach to protect the minority language for a determined amount of instructional time, by segmenting the school day or week or by assigning specific teachers or classrooms to individual languages (Howard & Sugarman, 2006). However, teachers might find this separation artificial and difficult to enact (Lee & Jeong, 2013; Palmer, Martínez, Mateus, & Henderson, 2014). Strict practices of language separation may also promote monoglossic views of bilingualism and language purism (García, 2014; M. M. López & Fránquiz, 2009; Martínez et al., 2015; McCollum, 1999) resulting in the restriction and stigmatization of "nonstandard" and everyday language practices and bicultural identities, such as those of bilingual Latino (García, 2014) and African American students (Valdés, 2002).

McCollum's (1999) study, for example, described the Spanish language arts class of a TWI secondary program as the battleground for political confrontations about the value of a "vernacular" versus a "high" academic variety of Spanish. Here, the teacher's overcorrection of students' Spanish pushed them into more English use. At the same time, the English teacher stigmatized students' developing English skills by also focusing on error correction. In this way, "many of the Mexican-background students in this study were in a regrettable double bind, in which both their Spanish and their English were devalued" (McCollum, 1999, p. 123). Latino/a students did not understand the criticism of their everyday language practices, while their peers were being praised for simple production of Spanish vocabulary words.

Language separation policies may not deter students from reverting to English. In one study, many English-dominant students switched frequently into English when they did not know a word in Spanish and openly corrected Spanish-dominant classmates' developing English (Palmer, 2008). In contrast, Spanish speakers rarely switched to Spanish during English-focused interactions and did not tend to correct their peers' Spanish. Thus, the enforcement of language separation may actually increase English speakers' opportunities to assert their power, as the "Spanish-only" times are more often disrupted by English use and the support that English-dominant students demand (Palmer et al., 2014).

A strategy used in some TWI classrooms to counter students' preference for English is the initiation-response-evaluation model (teachers leading question-and–known answer sessions; Cazden, 2001). Unfortunately, while initiation-response-evaluation gives teachers more control over discourse dynamics and language of instruction, this practice can still privilege English-dominant students as it tends to align with middle-class, Euro-American parent–child discourse styles (Fitts, 2006; Martín-Beltrán, 2010). It also positions students to compete for the floor, disadvantaging students from marginalized groups. Therefore, current language separation approaches appear inadequate, even when they aim to resist the hegemony of English.

A more child-centered pedagogical practice in TWI is language brokering: the practice of interpreting, translating, and mediating across cultural and linguistic differences that leads to a range of literacies for transnational bilinguals who broker for their immigrant families and communities (Orellana, Reynolds, Dorner, & Meza, 2003). In TWI contexts, language brokering might facilitate comprehension, participation, mutual peer support, and renegotiation of academic identities (Coyoca & Lee, 2009; Lee, Hill-Bonnet, & Raley, 2011). However, like other circumstances in TWI classrooms, brokering is subtly shaped by asymmetrical power relations. Lee et al. (2011) found that language brokering publicly positioned the student receiving the services negatively. While sometimes this power was renegotiated, language-minoritized students' attempts to position themselves as brokers were hindered by the lower status of their language and stigmatized position as "English learners." Meanwhile, students perceived as proficient English speakers were more often positioned as brokers and thus "able" students (Coyoca & Lee, 2009). The potential of bilingual status and brokering to create elite groups in the classroom also became evident when students with stronger bilingual and biliterate skills were not equally accessible for brokering services; they preferred to associate with English monolinguals or students of similar bilingual proficiency, rather than Spanish monolingual peers (Amrein & Peña, 2000).

On another note, brokers might become overburdened. In Palmer et al. (2014), Spanish-dominant bilinguals were regularly required to translate for struggling English speakers in Spanish-medium instruction, a service that was rarely reciprocated during

English instruction. In this case, the unequal distribution of services placed Spanish-dominant bilinguals in a subservient position catering to English speakers. An imbalanced dynamic was also evident in DeNicolo (2010), who highlighted how Spanish-dominant bilingual students not only supported English-speaking peers' learning of Spanish but also advocated for their marginalized monolingual Spanish-dominant peers. This "language warrior" role revealed problem solving, mediating skills, and advocacy, but such attributes are rarely recognized by academic assessments (p. 234).

That students from the dominant group often outperform their peers on standardized tests and control classroom discourse may be a reflection of cultural capital (Fitts, 2009), mainstream norms (de Jong & Howard, 2009), and dominant perspectives on literacies (Rubinstein-Ávila, 2003). Wiese (2004) demonstrated how dominant views of literacy as limited to academic reading and writing established instructional priorities in a TWI classroom, ultimately leading to unequal access to biliteracy instruction. Fears that English speakers would not succeed in TWI if they did not read and write in Spanish compelled the teacher to focus literacy instruction on English-dominant students. Meanwhile, African American children received little access to Spanish literacy instruction because of educators' concern about their English literacy, and Latino children believed to have strong Spanish literacy skills received the least instructional priority.

TWI Classrooms as the Crossroads of Difference

Integrating diverse students in the same classroom is one of TWI's greatest challenges. The often unacknowledged diversity *within* TWI programs' "two" linguistic groups—that is, TWI students include African American multilinguals, simultaneous bilinguals, and asylees escaping persecution—further complicates the academic and social dynamics in the classroom. Tensions emerge related to legacies of colonization, imperialism, and assimilation, as power dynamics and sociopolitical histories shape students' and teachers' interactions. For example, Freeman's (2000) study of a TWI program serving mainly Puerto Rican students noted their resistance to Spanish due to the stigma associated with it. Smith (2001) documented the influence of "elite bilinguals"—those from more privileged social class and educational backgrounds in their country of origin—in the decision making and curriculum of a TWI program near the U.S.–Mexico border. Amrein and Peña (2000) found that elite bilinguals preferred to associate with English-speaking monolingual peers, such that "success in school came more readily for those willing to understate, separate from or deny their Mexican culture" (Peña, 1998, p. 13). Furthermore, research has yet to explore how children from undocumented families might experience TWI when their lives are restricted in ways rarely experienced by White, English-speaking peers.

There is also a common assumption that English-speaking children in TWI always come from the dominant White group. Valdés (2002) critiqued the lack of consideration of African Americans in TWI, particularly those who are speakers of a variety of Englishes. Considering the historical exclusion of African Americans and other minoritized groups from foreign language education (Hubbard, 1980) and deficit ideas about their everyday language practices, there is a danger of positioning Black students from working-class backgrounds as incapable of learning a second language unless they attain oral and reading/writing proficiency in standardized English first (Kubota, Austin, & Saito-Abbott, 2003), as Wiese (2004) revealed.

The socioeconomic, racial, and ethnic disparities and wide range of cultural identities between and within ethnic/linguistic groups have important implications for social relations in TWI classrooms, often leading to segregation along linguistic, racial, ethnic, and class lines (Amrein & Peña, 2000; Feinauer & Whiting, 2014; Fitts, 2006; Hernández, 2015; Muro, 2016). Despite teachers' deliberate efforts to integrate language groups, separation still occurred during instructional and informal interactions as soon as students had some degree of choice about peer associations (Feinauer & Whiting, 2014).

Considering the often-overlooked goal of TWI to foster cross-cultural relations and competencies (Feinauer & Howard, 2014), diverse TWI classrooms could help disrupt power asymmetries. However, the whitestream curriculum as well as hegemony of English and exclusive focus on standardized languages may undo such efforts, reproducing dominant discourses and social hierarchies. In Palmer's (2008) study, despite the teacher's deliberate attempts to balance the distribution of power and build agentic academic identities among marginalized students through alternative discourses, the durability of the identities ascribed by the dominant discourses and larger social structures tended to prevail. In sum, given the tendency to center students from the dominant group and promote whitestream curriculum, there is still work to be done in TWI.

TWI-RELATED DISCOURSES ACROSS THE DISCIPLINES

Pulling from our second search across disciplines, this section now presents salient discourses that inform TWI practice and research and structure its inequalities: specifically, discourses of globalization, neoliberalism, accountability, and monolingualism. The conclusion then argues that we can combat such discourses and inequalities by adding a fourth goal to TWI: the development of critical consciousness.

The Rationale for TWI: Discourses of Globalization and Neoliberalism

The rationale for TWI programs often starts with a declaration that increased transnational flows and global commerce mean that students need bilingualism for instrumental reasons: to compete for future jobs and be "globally competitive students in the 21st century" (Rhodes, 2014, p. 116). While many scholars, parents, and children have also mentioned "integrative" reasons for bilingualism and bilingual education—to build identities and multicultural competencies—such notes are usually placed alongside, or secondary to, the instrumental focus (Boyle et al., 2015; Dorner, 2015; Tedick & Wesely, 2015).

This privileging of an instrumental rationale flows from globalization and neoliberal discourses (Cervantes-Soon, 2014). In turn, such rationales position diverse TWI students quite differently. Global migrants or transnational bilinguals, who are moving across borders to the United States, are viewed as needing a new language (English) in order to survive, whereas middle-class English-dominant youth are positioned to become "cosmopolitan" as they prepare to join global businesses (Collins, 2012; Kibler & Valdés, 2016; Morales & Razfar, 2016). Most poignantly, these discourses neglect the knowledges and experiences that transnational youth already have, positioning them as empty vessels rather than as individuals with rich linguistic repertoires and unique literacies rooted in the navigation of at least two cultures (Skerrett, 2012). They also depoliticize and ignore the original goals of bilingual education (Flores, 2016).

TWI Students as Outcomes: Discourses of Accountability

While many studies reviewed earlier used critical and ethnographic approaches to understand the experiences and perspectives of youth in TWI programs, the larger discourses around education and policymaking still view students primarily as *outcomes*. Due to accountability pressures, educators and policymakers must study and report students' performances on academic assessments. While such research importantly has found that TWI students typically outperform their peers over time (e.g., Lindholm-Leary & Hernández, 2011), outcome-based studies often use imperfect categorizations and the monolingual English speaker as the standard against whom bilingual learners are measured. For example, in child development, studies almost exclusively examine students' growth and achievement (e.g., Han, 2012). Meanwhile, across the fields of language education, researchers compare groups, using such classifications as *English/Spanish speakers, language majority/minority groups*, or *L1/L2* (first and second language), even while noting that such terms do not reflect the complexity of individuals' sociolinguistic realities (Cook, 2002; de Jong, 2016; Hopewell & Escamilla, 2014). In comparing groups using cross-sectional models, they also often neglect selection bias (Steele, Slater, Li, Zamarro, & Miller, 2013). Large-scale funding agencies have encouraged these foci, as they push researchers to categorize children for the purpose of experimental designs that aim to prove causality (Kibler & Valdés, 2016).

Outcome-oriented, problem-focused questions and categorizations are inevitable in education research. However, we assert that these frames fail to account for the knowledge that children actually have, the ways they experience the world, and the ways in which policies, curriculum, instruction, and schools could change. In turn, we still need more research on the everyday interactions that occur in dynamic bilingual contexts (Martín-Beltrán, 2010), so we could better describe students as "users" of languages or active transnational learners, rather than merely "outcomes." Such perspectives better highlight youths' complex, negotiated movements (Skerrett, 2012) and the micro-level foundations of political structures that they encounter.

Languages in TWI: Discourses of Monolingualism and Standardization

Related discourses about bilingualism as two separate monolingual systems and a focus on a "monoglot" society also undergird the inequalities found in TWI programs (Gort, 2015; Morales & Razfar, 2016). That is, monolingualism has long been the ideological "standard" in the United States, situated within the history of the nation state (Flores & García, 2013). In turn, discourses of monolingualism have defined how individuals imagine, define, and design educational programs toward bilingualism as the development of two separate and standardized monolingual systems. Such discourses have likely shaped the strict separation of instructional languages in TWI and the study of distinct language development in particular categories of students (e.g., L1 vs. L2).

The notion of "bilingual hegemonic Whiteness" (Flores, 2016, p. 2) brings attention to the historically racialized processes embedded in institutionalized forms of "additive" bilingual education like TWI. Insisting that students become bilingual only in standardized forms of English and another language reinforces hegemonic Whiteness—or the commonsense ideal of the White subject in opposition to racialized others—and continues to construct students from low-status minoritized groups in deficit terms by marginalizing their everyday bilingual practices. Despite current conceptions of plurilingualism that reframe humanity's linguistic experiences as dynamic, situated, and ever-changing (García & Sylvan, 2011; Hornberger & Link, 2012; May, 2013), our institutions and policies are still shaped in mostly White, monolingual, standardized terms (Kibler, Valdés, & Walqui, 2014). We must interrogate these discourses to confront the inequalities found in TWI education.

ADDRESSING INEQUALITIES THROUGH CRITICAL CONSCIOUSNESS

In line with the goals of this volume, we now propose a way forward to confront the persistent inequalities in TWI. Building on scholarship that draws from critical pedagogies and theories, we conceptualize a fourth goal: to develop critical consciousness, in addition to TWI's oft-stated goals of bilingualism and biliteracy, high academic achievement, and multicultural competence. Critical consciousness can be developed through expanding politically oriented curriculum and instruction that originate in the very knowledges and ways that students from marginalized communities experience language. In turn, as will be discussed below, humanizing research projects that explicitly interrogate TWI's sociopolitical and historical circumstances can support such pedagogies.

The Fourth Pillar for TWI: Critical Consciousness

To define critical consciousness as a foundational pillar of TWI, we turn to critical pedagogies (Bartolomé, 2004; Darder, 2015; P. Freire, 1970; Ladson-Billings & Tate IV, 1995), border pedagogies (Cervantes-Soon & Carrillo, 2016; Giroux, 1988), and critical bilingual/language studies (Crump, 2014; McCarty, Collins, & Hopson,

2011). Critical consciousness involves the process of overcoming pervasive myths through an understanding of the role of power in the formation of oppressive conditions (P. Freire, 2007). TWI teachers, students, and parents can take part and take action only to the extent that they problematize the history, culture, and societal configurations that brought them together. TWI children, parents, teachers, and school leaders must work toward critical consciousness in order for the programs' integrated groups to result in cross-cultural understanding and greater equality; each stakeholder must interrogate his or her own position, privilege, and power. By reframing TWI spaces as problem-posing (P. Freire, 2007), we can raise critical consciousness around the discourses, macro-level inequalities, and power relations that shape TWI practice, pedagogy, and policies.

We use the word "position" purposefully here, as it draws attention to interactive relationships in which TWI participants are positioned relative to others; it goes beyond the self and one's current moment in time. As Reyes and Vallone (2007) argued, TWI's third goal—to develop positive cross-cultural attitudes—originally foregrounded one's understanding of *others*, thus neglecting an examination of TWI's potential to shape one's *self* and cultural identities. They argued convincingly that there are intimate links between language and identity, which TWI programs must address (though they do not usually do so). Subsequently, Feinauer and Howard (2014) agreed that this area is undertheorized but concluded that "self" was actually included in the third goal, as multi/cross-cultural competencies *begin* with understanding one's identity within diverse TWI classrooms. Crump (2014) then argued for the recognition that identities are not unidimensional; they are "imposed, assumed, and negotiated" (p. 209). Although the categories reviewed earlier (e.g., English/Spanish speakers, L1/L2) are certainly imperfect, they do discursively exist, and so we must question them, in order to break them down (Souto-Manning, 2010). However, there is a danger of understanding identity as a depoliticized process, an "unproblematic affirmation of student experience" (Giroux, 1988). TWI students from different language/cultural backgrounds are "invited to because bilingual," so TWI programs could be "considered transformational. However, whether or not power relations are ever formally explored is up to the pedagogical stance of the particular teacher and the particular school" (Reyes & Vallone, 2007, p. 8).

Therefore, we propose the use of border pedagogies (Giroux, 1988) to bring together interrogations of the self (identity, agency) and others (culture, society, structures), *to examine one's position, how it is "read" and how it relates to power* in the word and the world by encouraging each individual to locate her or his identity within particular histories of power, colonization, imperialism, and difference. Simultaneously, such work will challenge the limits of individual perspectives and develop abilities to act against oppression. Furthermore, border pedagogies push us to uncover the voices and knowledges of the subaltern by decentering hegemonic Whiteness and individualist notions of success and instead centering the experiences, languages, and worldviews generated by those in the margins (Cervantes-Soon & Carrillo, 2016). In short, TWI students, parents, and educators must study the effects of power relations in language education in order to transform pedagogical stances, positions, and curricula. The next two sections explore how we can bring critical consciousness to TWI programs and research, first with a focus on children and then with adult stakeholders.

Children's Translanguaging and Knowledges

Child-centered studies are central to inform critical consciousness, particularly ones that consider children's lives in the present moment, the shaping of identities, and the subaltern knowledges in TWI classrooms. Scholars across many fields are increasingly employing concepts like translanguaging, which highlight dynamic bilingualism and language as a social practice/activity (Gort, 2015). A blend of languaging—language as something people *do*, the constant adaptation of meaning and use of varied linguistic resources in social interactions—and *transculturación*, translanguaging "is a product of border thinking, of knowledge that is autochthonous and conceived from a bilingual, not monolingual, position" (García & Sylvan, 2011, p. 389). It is the communicative norm of multilingual speech communities; it includes children's and teachers' full range of linguistic repertoires and the "complex discursive practices" that they use "to 'make sense' of, and communicate in, multilingual classrooms" (García & Sylvan, 2011, p. 389).

Translanguaging as a lens and developing critical language awareness with students (Alim, 2005; Fairclough, 2001; Martínez, 2013) will reshape TWI's focus on what children *do* with language, rather than how teachers must develop a particular "standard" *of* language *for* students (Crump, 2014). First, studies with children will help educators recognize that language is an active, dynamic tool; translanguaging is the creative language play, complex negotiations, and brokering that occur in plurilingual settings (Dorner & Layton, 2014; Gort & Sembiante, 2015; Martín-Beltrán, 2010; Zentella, 1997). Second, because languaging processes are not void of power relations, infusing a border pedagogy within translanguaging practices may help reframe and reimagine TWI spaces through fostering critical consciousness. This type of pedagogy may involve implementing Freirean "culture circles" with young students (Souto-Manning, 2010), making space for students' fears and embracing their complexities (Osorio, 2015), working to understand the relationship between language and power and redefining terms like *Spanglish* with students (Martínez, 2013), and developing multilingual learning spaces by following children's leads in love and play (Orellana, 2016).

In summary, translanguaging is part of a transformative (Gort, 2015) and critical border pedagogy (Cervantes-Soon & Carrillo, 2016) that decenters Anglo-centric knowledge. Working with children and documenting their translanguaging, educators will have deeper knowledge of their students and their multilayered linguistic, racial, and ethnic backgrounds. In turn, together they can recognize and rework the artificial separation of languages and sociopolitical contexts in TWI classrooms. Educators will better understand how "official" discourses work alongside subaltern ones, which can actually better support the development of academic discourses for TWI students (Gort & Sembiante, 2015).

Humanizing Research With All Stakeholders

Humanizing research—where children, parents, teachers, and researchers work alongside each other—is likewise crucial to dismantle TWI inequalities. Humanizing studies build "relationships of care and dignity and dialogic consciousness-raising for both researchers and participants" (Paris & Winn, 2014, p. xvi). Such work requires recognizing how traditional research and approaches to TWI programs can be "dehumanizing," that is, as they imagine students as outcomes or critique teachers for their own lack of language. Researchers and practitioners alike must be critical of their work, rethink previous writing and assumptions, analyze their own linguistic/political histories, and engage with a range of TWI stakeholders in collective ongoing critical reflection; in turn, they can develop new curricula and work toward social justice goals (Bartolomé, 2004; Palmer, 2010).

Already, a few TWI studies have employed humanizing methodologies, highlighting the potential of the proposed pillar of critical consciousness. For example, framed as a critical collaborative action research project, a researcher-teacher and eight TWI teachers charted their transformations and challenges, as they worked to employ culturally relevant pedagogies (J. Freire, 2014). Hadi-Tabassum (2006) worked with a fifth-grade class to document TWI students' and teachers' efforts to grapple with discourses of race, class and gender inequities as they learned language and content together. Heiman (2017) has collaborated with parents and a fifth-grade critical educator in a rapidly gentrifying TWI community, documenting critical responses to issues of power/class.

These approaches may also promote the development of new curricula. Our review suggests that the conditions of TWI call us to consider the pitfalls of simply teaching mainstream curriculum in two languages. Teaching for critical consciousness and human connection requires that whitestream curriculum is decentered for all students. Future research alongside children and families could develop new content, based on communities' rich linguistic repertoires and transcultural/*transfronterizo* (border crossing) experiences (de la Piedra & Araujo, 2012; Mateus, 2016; Zapata & Laman, 2016). This work would promote an understanding of the histories of colonization, imperialism, forced migration, racism, and neoliberalism, which are reflected in our language practices. Such curricula, which need to move beyond literacy/language arts and into all the content areas, have the potential to combat utilitarian and disembodied purposes for language learning.

CONCLUSION

This chapter is a call to researchers and practitioners to critically attend to the documented inequalities and recall the original "race radical" goal of bilingual education (Flores, 2016). Making the development of critical consciousness TWI's fourth pillar draws strong attention to the power dimensions, hegemony of English and standardized languages, and subalternization of minoritized communities in bilingual education; it offers a decolonizing and humanizing framework for the future. We must work more critically to analyze these integrated bilingual spaces by recognizing the political power structures and ideologies that discursively shape the interactions (or lack thereof) in TWI. While some TWI programs may state equity goals or take critical stances, we are hopeful that explicitly naming critical consciousness as the fourth pillar will inspire and encourage all TWI communities to integrate counterhegemonic discourses into their policymaking, teacher preparation, classroom contexts, and pedagogies.

REFERENCES

Alim, H. S. (2005). Critical language awareness in the United States: Revisiting issues and revising pedagogies in a resegregated society. *Educational Researcher, 34,* 24–31.

Amrein, A., & Peña, R. A. (2000). Asymmetry in dual language practice: Assessing imbalance in a program promoting equality. *Education Policy Analysis Archives, 8,* 8.

Bartolomé, L. I. (2004). Critical pedagogy and teacher education: Radicalizing prospective teachers. *Teacher Education Quarterly, 31,* 97–122.

Bearse, C., & de Jong, E. J. (2008). Cultural and linguistic investment: Adolescents in a secondary two-way immersion program. *Equity & Excellence in Education, 41,* 325–340.

Bell, D. (1980). Brown v. Board of Education and the interest convergence principle. *Harvard Law Review, 93,* 518–533.

Bialystok, E., Peets, K. F., & Moreno, S. (2014). Producing bilinguals through immersion education: Development of metalinguistic awareness. *Applied Psycholinguistics, 35,* 177–191.

Boyle, A., August, D., Tabaku, L., Cole, S., & Simpson-Baird, A. (2015). *Dual language education programs: Current state policies and practices.* Washington, DC: American Institutes for Research.

Cazden, C. B. (2001). *Classroom discourse: The language of teaching and learning.* Portsmouth, NH: Heinemann.

Cervantes-Soon, C. G. (2014). A critical look at dual language immersion in the New Latin@ diaspora. *Bilingual Research Journal, 37,* 64–82.

Cervantes-Soon, C. G., & Carrillo, J. F. (2016). Toward a pedagogy of border thinking: Building on Latin@ students' subaltern knowledge. *The High School Journal, 99,* 282-301.

Cervantes-Soon, C. G., & Turner, A. M. (2017). Countering silence and reconstructing identities in a Spanish/English two-way immersion program: Latina mothers' pedagogies in El Nuevo Sur. In X. Rong, & J. Hilburn (Eds.), *Immigration and education in North Carolina: The challenges and responses in a new gateway state.* Boston, MA: Sense.

Christian, D. (2016). Dual language education: Current research perspectives. *International Multilingual Research Journal, 10,* 1–5.

Collier, V. P., & Thomas, W. P. (2004). The astounding effectiveness of dual language education for all. *NABE Journal of Research and Practice, 2,* 1–20.

Collins, J. (2012). Migration, sociolinguistic scale, and educational reproduction. *Anthropology & Education Quarterly, 43,* 192–213.

Cook, V. (2002). *Portraits of the L2 user.* Clevedon, England: Multilingual Matters.

Coyoca, A. M., & Lee, J. S. (2009). A typology of language-brokering events in dual-language immersion classrooms. *Bilingual Research Journal, 32,* 260–279.

Crump, A. (2014). Introducing LangCrit: Critical language and race theory. *Critical Inquiry in Language Studies, 11,* 207–224.

Darder, A. (2015). *Culture and power in the classroom: Educational foundations for the schooling of bicultural students.* New York, NY: Routledge.

de Jong, E. J. (2002). Effective bilingual education: From theory to academic achievement in a two-way bilingual program. *Bilingual Research Journal, 26,* 1–20.

de Jong, E. J. (2016). Two-way immersion for the next generation: Models, policies, and principles. *International Multilingual Research Journal, 10,* 6–16.

de Jong, E. J., & Howard, E. (2009). Integration in two-way immersion education: Equalising linguistic benefits for all students. *International Journal of Bilingual Education and Bilingualism, 12*, 81–99.

de la Piedra, M. T., & Araujo, B. (2012). Transfronterizo literacies and content in a dual language classroom. *International Journal of Bilingual Education and Bilingualism, 15*, 705–721.

de Mejía, A.-M. (2002). *Power, prestige, and bilingualism: International perspectives on elite bilingual education.* Clevedon, England: Multilingual Matters.

DeNicolo, C. P. (2010). What language counts in literature discussion? Exploring linguistic mediation in an English language arts classroom. *Bilingual Research Journal, 33*, 220–240.

DePalma, R. (2010). *Language use in the two-way classroom: Lessons from a Spanish-English bilingual kindergarten.* Clevedon, England: Multilingual Matters.

Dorner, L. M. (2010). English and Spanish "para un futuro"—or just English? Immigrant family perspectives on two-way immersion. *International Journal of Bilingual Education and Bilingualism, 13*, 303–323 doi:10.1080/13670050903229851

Dorner, L. M. (2011a). Contested communities in a debate over dual language education: The import of "public" values on public policies. *Educational Policy, 25*, 577–613.

Dorner, L. M. (2011b). US immigrants and two-way immersion policies: The mismatch between district designs and family experiences. In T. W. Fortune, D. Christian, & D. J. Tedick (Eds.), *Immersion education: Practices, policies, possibilities* (pp. 231–250). Clevedon, England: Multilingual Matters.

Dorner, L. M. (2015). From global jobs to safe spaces: The diverse discourses that sell multilingual schooling in the U.S. *Current Issues in Language Planning, 16*, 114–131.

Dorner, L. M., & Layton, A. (2014). "¿Cómo se dice?" Children's multilingual discourses (or interacting, representing, and being) in a first-grade Spanish immersion classroom. *Linguistics and Education, 25*, 24–39.

Fairclough, N. L. (2001). *Language and power.* London, England: Longman.

Feinauer, E., & Howard, E. (2014). Attending to the third goal: Cross-cultural competence and identity development in two-way immersion programs. *Journal of Immersion and Content-Based Language Education, 2*, 257–272.

Feinauer, E., & Whiting, E. F. (2014). Home language and literacy practices of parents at one Spanish-English two-way immersion charter school. *Bilingual Research Journal, 37*, 142–163.

Fitts, S. (2006). Reconstructing the status quo: Linguistic interaction in a dual-language school. *Bilingual Research Journal, 30*, 337–365.

Fitts, S. (2009). Exploring third space in a dual-language setting: Opportunities and challenges. *Journal of Latinos and Education, 8*(2), 87–104.

Flores, N. (2016). A tale of two visions: Hegemonic whiteness and bilingual education. *Educational Policy, 30*, 13–38.

Flores, N., & García, O. (2013). Linguistic third spaces in education: Teachers' translanguaging across the bilingual continuum. In D. Little, C. Leung, & P. V. Avermaet (Eds.), *Managing diversity in education: Languages, policies, pedagogies* (pp. 243–256). Bristol, England: Multilingual Matters.

Flores, N., & Rosa, J. (2015). Undoing appropriateness: Raciolinguistic ideologies and language diversity in education. *Harvard Educational Review, 85*, 149–171.

Freeman, R. D. (2000). Contextual challenges to dual-language education: A case study of a developing middle school program. *Anthropology & Education Quarterly, 31*, 202–229.

Freire, J. (2014). *Teachers' beliefs and practices of culturally relevant pedagogy in a two-way Spanish-English dual language immersion program* (Unpublished doctoral dissertation). University of Utah, Salt Lake City.

Freire, P. (1970). *Pedagogy of the oppressed.* New York, NY: Herder & Herder.

Freire, P. (2007). *Education for critical consciousness.* New York, NY: Continuum.

García, O. (2014). US Spanish and education global and local intersections. *Review of Research in Education, 38*(1), 58–80.

García, O., & Sylvan, C. E. (2011). Pedagogies and practices in multilingual classrooms: Singularities in pluralities. *Modern Language Journal, 95*, 385–400.

Giroux, H. A. (1988). Border pedagogy in the age of postmodernism. *Journal of Education, 170*, 162–181.

Gort, M. (2015). Transforming literacy learning and teaching through translanguaging and other typical practices associated with "doing being bilingual." *International Multilingual Research Journal, 9*, 1–6.

Gort, M., & Sembiante, S. F. (2015). Navigating hybridized language learning spaces through translanguaging pedagogy: Dual language preschool teachers' languaging practices in support of emergent bilingual children's performance of academic discourse. *International Multilingual Research Journal, 9*, 7–25.

Grinberg, J., & Saavedra, R. (2000). The constitution of bilingual/ESL education as a disciplinary practice: Genealogical explorations. *Review of Educational Research, 70*, 419–441.

Guerrero, M. D. (1997). Spanish academic language proficiency: The case of bilingual education teachers in the US. *Bilingual Research Journal, 21*, 65–84.

Hadi-Tabassum, S. (2006). *Language, space and power: A critical look at bilingual education.* Clevedon, England: Multilingual Matters.

Han, W. J. (2012). Bilingualism and academic achievement. *Child Development, 83*, 300–321.

Heiman, D. (2017). *Two-way immersion, gentrification, and critical pedagogy: Teaching against the neoliberal logic* (Unpublished doctoral dissertation). University of Texas at Austin, Austin, TX.

Hernández, A. M. (2015). Language status in two-way bilingual immersion: The dynamics between English and Spanish in peer interaction. *Journal of Immersion and Content-Based Language Education, 3*, 102–126.

Holland, D., Lachicotte, W. J., Skinner, D., & Cain, C. (1998). *Identity and agency in cultural worlds.* Cambridge, MA: Harvard University Press.

Hopewell, S., & Escamilla, K. (2014). Struggling reader or emerging biliterate student? Reevaluating the criteria for labeling emerging bilingual students as low achieving. *Journal of Literacy Research, 46*, 68–89.

Hornberger, N. H., & Link, H. (2012). Translanguaging and transnational literacies in multilingual classrooms: A biliteracy lens. *International Journal of Bilingual Education and Bilingualism, 15*, 261–278. doi:10.1080/13670050.2012.658016

Horsford, S. D. (2015). Magnet school mom. In G. Theoharis, & S. Dotger (Eds.), *On the high wire: Education professors walk between work and parenting* (pp. 17–24). Charlotte, NC: Information Age.

Howard, E. R., & Sugarman, J. (2006). *Realizing the vision of two-way immersion: Fostering effective programs and classrooms.* Crystal Lake, IL: Delta Publishing.

Howard, E. R., Sugarman, J., & Christian, D. (2003). *Trends in two-way immersion education: A review of the research.* Baltimore, MD: Center for Research on the Education of Students Placed at Risk.

Hubbard, L. J. (1980). The minority student in foreign languages. *Modern Language Journal, 64*, 75–80.

Juárez, B. G., & McKay, D. O. (2008). The politics of race in two languages: An empirical qualitative study. *Race, Ethnicity and Education, 11*, 231–249.

Kibler, A. K., & Valdés, G. (2016). Conceptualizing language learners: Socioinstitutional mechanisms and their consequences. *Modern Language Journal, 100*(Suppl. 1), 96–116.

Kibler, A. K., Valdés, G., & Walqui, A. (2014). What does standards-based educational reform mean for English language learner populations in primary and secondary schools? *TESOL Quarterly, 48*, 433–453.

Kubota, R., Austin, T., & Saito-Abbott, Y. (2003). Diversity and inclusion of sociopolitical issues in foreign language classrooms: An exploratory survey. *Foreign Language Annals, 36*, 12–24.

Ladson-Billings, G., & Tate IV, W. F. (1995). Toward a critical race theory of education. *Teachers College Record, 97*, 47–68.

Lee, J. S., Hill-Bonnet, L., & Raley, J. (2011). Examining the effects of language brokering on student identities and learning opportunities in dual immersion classrooms. *Journal of Language, Identity, and Education, 10*(5), 306–326.

Lee, J. S., & Jeong, E. (2013). Korean-English dual language immersion: Perspectives of students, parents, and teachers. *Language, Culture and Curriculum, 26*, 89–107.

Lindholm-Leary, K. J. (2005a). *Review of research and best practices on effective features of dual language education programs*. Washington, DC: Center for Applied Linguistics.

Lindholm-Leary, K. J. (2005b). The rich promise of two-way immersion. *Educational Leadership, 62*(4), 56–59.

Lindholm-Leary, K. J., & Hernández, A. M. (2011). Achievement and language proficiency of Latino students in dual language programmes: Native English speakers, fluent English/previous ELLs, and current ELLs. *Journal of Multilingual & Multicultural Development, 32*, 531–545.

López, L. M., & Tápanes. (2011). Latino children attending a two-way immersion program in the United States: A comparative case analysis. *Bilingual Research Journal, 34*(2), 142–160.

López, M. M. (2013). Mothers choose: Reasons for enrolling their children in a two-way immersion program. *Bilingual Research Journal, 36*, 208–227.

López, M. M., & Fránquiz, M. E. (2009). "We teach reading this way because it is the model we've adopted": Asymmetries in language and literacy policies in a Two-Way Immersion programme. *Research Papers in Education, 24*, 175–200.

Lucero, A. (2015). Cross-linguistic lexical, grammatical, and discourse performance on oral narrative retells among young Spanish speakers. *Child Development, 86*, 1419–1433.

Martín-Beltrán, M. (2010). The two-way language bridge: Co-constructing bilingual language learning opportunities. *Modern Language Journal, 94*, 254–277.

Martínez, R. A. (2013). Reading the world in Spanglish: Hybrid language practices and ideological contestation in a sixth-grade English language arts classroom. *Linguistics and Education, 24*, 276–288.

Martínez, R. A., Hikida, M., & Durán, L. (2015). Unpacking ideologies of linguistic purism: How dual language teachers make sense of everyday translanguaging. *International Multilingual Research Journal, 9*, 26–42.

Mateus, S. (2016). *"She was born speaking English and Spanish!" Co-constructing identities and exploring children's bilingual language practices in a two-way immersion program in central Texas* (Unpublished doctoral dissertation). Austin: University of Texas at Austin.

May, S. (2013). *The multilingual turn: Implications for SLA, TESOL, and bilingual education*. New York, NY: Routledge.

McCarty, T. L., Collins, J., & Hopson, R. K. (2011). Dell Hymes and the new language policy studies: Update from an underdeveloped country. *Anthropology & Education Quarterly, 42*, 335–363.

McCollum, P. (1999). Learning to value English: Cultural capital in a two-way bilingual program. *Bilingual Research Journal, 23*, 113–134.

Menken, K., & García, O. (Eds.). (2010). *Negotiating language policies in schools: Educators as policy makers*. New York, NY: Routledge.

Morales, P. Z., & Razfar, A. (2016). Advancing integration through bilingualism for all. In E. Frankenberg, L. M. Garces, & M. Hopkins (Eds.), *School integration matters: Research-based strategies to advance equity* (pp. 135–144). New York, NY: Teachers College Press.

Muro, J. A. (2016). "Oil and water"? Latino-white relations and symbolic integration in a changing California. *Sociology of Race & Ethnicity, 2*. Advance online publication.

Noblit, G. W., & Hare, R. D. (1988). *Meta-ethnography: Synthesizing qualitative studies.* Newbury Park, CA: Sage.

Orellana, M. F. (2016). *Immigrant children in transcultural spaces: Language, learning, and love.* New York: NY: Routledge.

Orellana, M. F., Reynolds, J. F., Dorner, L. M., & Meza, M. (2003). In other words: Translating or "para-phrasing" as a family literacy practice in immigrant households. *Reading Research Quarterly, 38*(1), 12–34.

Osborn, T. (2006). *Teaching world languages for social justice: A sourcebook of principles and practices.* Mahwah, NJ: Lawrence Erlbaum.

Osorio, S. L. (2015). ¿Qué es deportar?" Teaching from students' lives. *Rethinking Schools, 30*(1). Retrieved from http://www.rethinkingschools.org/archive/30_01/30-1_osorio.shtml

Paciotto, C., & Delany-Barmann, G. (2011). Planning micro-level language education reform in new diaspora sites: Two-way immersion education in the rural Midwest. *Language Policy, 10,* 221–243.

Palmer, D. (2008). Building and destroying students' "academic identities:" The power of discourse in a two-way immersion classroom. *International Journal of Qualitative Studies in Education, 21*(6), 1–24.

Palmer, D. (2009). Middle-class English speakers in a two-way immersion bilingual classroom: "Everybody should be listening to Jonathan right now . . ." *TESOL Quarterly, 43,* 177–202.

Palmer, D. (2010). Race, power, and equity in a multiethnic urban elementary school with a dual-language "strand" program. *Anthropology & Education Quarterly, 41,* 94–114.

Palmer, D., Henderson, K., Wall, D., Zúñiga, C. E., & Berthelsen, S. (2015). Team teaching among mixed messages: Implementing two-way dual language bilingual education at third grade in Texas. *Language Policy, 15,* 393–413.

Palmer, D., & Martínez, R. A. (2013). Teacher agency in bilingual spaces: A fresh look at preparing teachers to educate Latina/o bilingual children. *Review of Research in Education, 37,* 269–297.

Palmer, D., Martínez, R. A., Mateus, S. G., & Henderson, K. (2014). Reframing the debate on language separation: Toward a vision for translanguaging pedagogies in the dual language classroom. *Modern Language Journal, 98,* 757–772.

Paris, D., & Winn, M. (Eds.). (2014). *Humanizing research: Decolonizing qualitative inquiry with youth and communities.* Thousand Oaks, CA: Sage.

Parkes, J., & Ruth, T. (2009). *Urgent research questions and issues in dual language education.* Retrieved from http://www.dlenm.org/images/Documents/Research_Report.pdf

Pearson, T., Wolgemuth, J. R., & Colomer, S. E. (2015). Spiral of decline or "beacon of hope:" Stories of school choice in a dual language school. *Education Policy Analysis Archives, 23.* Retrieved from http://epaa.asu.edu/ojs/article/view/1524/1559

Peña, R. A. (1998). A case study of parental involvement in a conversion from transitional to dual language instruction. *Bilingual Research Journal, 22,* 237–259.

Petrovic, J. E. (2005). The conservative restoration and neoliberal defenses of bilingual education. *Language Policy, 4,* 395–416.

Pimentel, C., Diaz Soto, L., Pimentel, O., & Urrieta, L. (2008). The dual language dualism: ¿Quiénes ganan? *Texas Association for Bilingual Education Journal, 10,* 200–223.

Potowski, K. (2004). Student Spanish use and investment in a dual immersion classroom: Implications for second language acquisition and heritage language maintenance. *Modern Language Journal, 88,* 75–101.

Ramos, F., Dwyer, E., & Pérez-Prado, A. (2013). Improving the preparation of teachers wishing to work in two-way bilingual education programs: Listening to the practitioners. In *Proceedings of the BilngLatAm 2004 First International Symposium about Bilingualism and Bilingual Education in Latin America* (pp. 257–267). Retrieved from http://digital commons.fiu.edu/cgi/viewcontent.cgi?article=1045&context=sferc

Reyes, S. A., & Vallone, T. L. (2007). Toward an expanded understanding of two-way bilingual immersion education: Constructing identity through a critical, additive bilingual/ bicultural pedagogy. *Multicultural Perspectives, 9*(3), 3–11.

Rhodes, N. (2014). Elementary school foreign language teaching: Lessons learned over three decades (1980-2010). *Foreign Language Annals, 47*, 115–133.

Rubinstein-Ávila, E. (2003). Negotiating power and redefining literacy expertise: Buddy Reading in a dual-immersion programme. *Journal of Research in Reading, 26*, 83–97.

Ruiz, R. (1984). Orientations in language planning. *NABE Journal, 7*, 15–34.

Skerrett, A. (2012). Languages and literacies in translocation: Experiences and perspectives of a transnational youth. *Journal of Literacy Research, 44*, 364–395.

Smith, P. H. (2001). Immersion in two languages and funds of linguistic knowledge; La inmersion en dos idiomas y los fondos de conocimiento linguistico. *Estudios de Linguistica Aplicada, 19*(34), 37–50.

Souto-Manning, M. (2010). *Freire, teaching, and learning: Culture circles across contexts*. New York, NY: Peter Lang.

Steele, J. L., Slater, R., Li, J., Zamarro, G., & Miller, T. (2013, September). *The effect of dual-language immersion on student achievement in math, science, and English language arts*. Paper presented at the Society for Research on Educational Effectiveness conference, Washington, DC.

Tedick, D. J., & Wesely, P. M. (2015). A review of research on content-based foreign/second language education in US K-12 contexts. *Language, Culture and Curriculum, 28*, 25–40.

Thomas, W. P., & Collier, V. P. (2002). *A national study of school effectiveness for language minority students' long-term academic achievement*. Washington, DC: Center for Research on Education, Diversity & Excellence.

Torres-Guzmán, M. E., Kleyn, T., Morales-Rodríguez, S., & Han, A. (2005). Self-designated dual-language programs: Is there a gap between labeling and implementation? *Bilingual Research Journal, 29*, 453–474.

Urrieta, L. (2010). *Working from within: Chicana and Chicano activist educators in whitestream schools*. Tucson: University of Arizona Press.

Valdés, G. (1997). Dual-language immersion programs: A cautionary note concerning the education of language-minority students. *Harvard Educational Review, 67*, 391–429.

Valdés, G. (2002). Enlarging the pie: Another look at bilingualism and schooling in the US. *International Journal of the Sociology of Language, 155*(156), 187–195.

Valdez, V. E., Delavan, G., & Freire, J. A. (2014). The marketing of dual language education policy in Utah print media. *Educational Policy*. Advance online publication.

Valenzuela, A. (1999). *Subtractive schooling: U.S.-Mexican youth and the politics of caring*. Albany: State University of New York Press.

Varghese, M. M., & Park, C. (2010). Going global: Can dual-language programs save bilingual education? *Journal of Latinos and Education, 9*, 72–80.

Warhol, L., & Mayer, A. (2012). Misinterpreting school reform: The dissolution of a dual-immersion bilingual program in an Urban New England elementary school. *Bilingual Research Journal, 35*, 145–163.

Wiese, A.-M. (2004). Bilingualism and biliteracy for all? Unpacking two-way immersion at second grade. *Language and Education, 18*(1), 69–92.

Wilson, D. M. (2011). Dual language programs on the rise. *Harvard Education Letter, 27*(2). Retrieved from http://hepg.org/hel-home/issues/27_2/helarticle/dual-language-programs-on-the-rise

Zapata, A., & Laman, T. T. (2016). "I write to show how beautiful my languages are:" Translingual writing instruction in English-dominant classrooms. *Language Arts, 93*, 366–378.

Zentella, A. C. (1997). *Growing up bilingual: Puerto Rican children in New York*. Oxford, England: Blackwell.

Chapter 18

Intersection of Language, Class, Ethnicity, and Policy: Toward Disrupting Inequality for English Language Learners

Oscar Jiménez-Castellanos
Eugene García
Arizona State University

This chapter proposes a conceptual framework that merges intersectionality and policy analysis as an analytical tool to understand the nuanced, multilayered, compounded educational inequality encountered specifically by low-income, Latino Spanish-speaking students in Arizona K–12 public schools as a function of intersecting educational policies. In addition, it provides a conceptual framework that counters and provides an alternative to the Arizona model that strives toward interrupting inequality. The conceptual framework is grounded in culture, language, and learning that provides a pathway to interrupt inequality by acknowledging the intersectional social constructs of an English language learner (ELL).

English language learners (ELLs), students learning English as a second language, represent a significant and growing segment of students attending K–12 public schools in the United States. Currently, ELLs represent about 4.9 million students, 9.8% of the total student population with states in the southwest representing some of the densest populations of ELLs by total percentage share of ELLs among K–12 students (California, 24.5%; Texas, 15.2%; Colorado, 13.3%; Nevada 17.4%; Ruiz-Soto, Hooker, & Batalova, 2015). Providing a comprehensive program of instruction leading toward greater equal educational opportunities for ELLs requires effective resource allocations and instructional programs that meet the needs of this diverse group of students to build on the cultural and language skills embedded within this group (García, 2005; Jiménez-Castellanos, 2010). This task is complicated by the within-group diversity of ELLs due to family background, countries of origin, language spoken primarily within the home and daily interaction, parent education, familiarity with compulsory education, and formal schooling (Menken, Kleyn, &

Review of Research in Education
March 2017, Vol. 41, pp. 428–452
DOI: 10.3102/0091732X16688623

Chae, 2007). Of prominence are the majority native-born ELL students that represent this group (National Education Association, 2008) since this refutes the notion that most ELLs are immigrants, in particular, undocumented immigrants. In U.S. compulsory schools, native-born ELLs represent 85% of PreK to 5th-grade students and 62% of 6th- to 12th-grade students overall (Zong & Batalova, 2015). Regrettably, this diverse group of students also experience higher rates of poverty, higher mobility rates, and they are more likely to attend segregated, underfunded, and unsafe schools, compared with their non-ELL counterparts, drawing the attention of education researchers, policymakers, and practitioners (Haas & Huang, 2010; Kim & García, 2014; Soto, 2011).

In recent decades, significant federal and state ELL policies have attempted to address this student population incorporating stricter targeted educational programing along with funding, standards, language and academic assessments, and related accountability domains directly influencing ELLs' educational experiences (Conger, 2012; Gándara, Moran, & García, 2004; Powers, 2014). Education policy and their related practices have been central to the education of ELLs in the United States at the federal (e.g., Elementary and Secondary School Act [ESEA]; No Child Left Behind [NCLB]; Every Student Succeeds Act), state, and local levels and have received critical attention from federal and state courts (Gamoran, 2008). Federal policies affecting ELLs come directly out of the Civil Rights era and the War on Poverty that were priorities of the Johnson administration, primarily the Bilingual Education Act or Title VII of ESEA, with many individual states following suit and developing their own policies to serve ELLs. These historical origins of ELL policy are important when examining the narrow focus of the policies that develop around access to English language instruction, grade-level content, and the shifts in federal education policy toward systemic changes in standards (Cohen, 1995; Smith & O'Day, 1991). Almost five decades have passed since a Nation at Risk (Gardner, 1983) triggered a series of events that led to the "Standards-Based Reform" movement, which continues today.

The standards and reform movement would find its base in the early 1990s when President Bill Clinton signed into law Goals 2000: The Educate America Act of 1994 establishing state standards. Soon after ESEA, at that time named the Improving America's Schools Act of 1994 followed suit by authorizing programs around the newly created core education standards (Rasco, 1994; Riley, 1994). Largely education is localized at the state level and states began developing their own content of instruction that evolved the popular discourse away from accountability for spending toward accountability for demonstrated results. A new millennium ushered in another strong set of policies as the NCLB of 2001 added stricter accountability provisions for students attaining standards and for reducing gaps between subgroups of students, including ELLs (Fuhrman & Elmore, 2004; NCLB, 2002). Title I of the bill accomplished its goal of making schools, local districts, and states accountable for the performance of ELLs, with corrective actions required of systems failing to do so (Fuhrman & Elmore, 2004; NCLB, 2002; Rudo, 2001). The newly authorized Every Student Succeeds Act continues to employ accountability standards with regard to

ELLs, but places the major responsibility for identification, assessment, program characteristics, and accountability on individual state processes, procedures, and metrics. The federal law remains heavy on accountability but does not provide requirements for states to develop and implement systems of support to ensure improved academic achievement for ELLs.

The language of instruction issue has been the most intensely debated aspect of education policy and practice for ELLs in K–12 for decades and is often politically charged (Gándara & Hopkins, 2010). These policies and practices have ranged from identifying the non-English language of ELLs as a problem/barrier or as a resource to equal educational opportunity (Ruiz, 1995). Using Ruiz's (1995) framework, policies address language as either a "problem" to be corrected in order to provide equal opportunity or as a "right" to access English (i.e., bilingual education). Scarcely distributed among the language of policy are statements that refer to bilingualism as an asset, even in the nonbinding "Whereas . . ." portions of the legislation or in court rulings that might reflect Ruiz's perspective of language as a resource. In general, educators and researchers agree that to succeed in U.S. schools and participate in civic life in the United States, all children need to develop strong English proficiency and literacy skills. The debate focuses on attention on how to best support the acquisition of English and whether it should come at the expense of continued attention to the development and maintenance of the child's home language (L1). Questions about the ongoing role of L1 development as English skills deepen, the social and cultural costs of losing proficiency of the home language, the role of education programs in systematically supporting L1 language development, and community values that may promote English-only approaches have not been resolved. Furthermore, there are still many practical questions around the "best" methods to promote English language development while continuing to support multiple home languages in English-dominant settings. For the U.S. population of ELLs, there is a strong body of evidence indicating that they can attain proficiency in more than one language at early ages without difficulty (e.g., Baker, Keller-Wolff, & Wolf-Wendel, 2000; Genesee, 2006) and that instructional arrangements and strategies targeting these children specifically can produce positive developmental and learning outcomes (Calderon & Minaya-Rowe, 2010; Genesee, Lindholm-Leary, Saunders & Christian, 2006; Wright, 2015). Yet there exist misunderstandings and stereotypes about the population and its subgroups due to the monolingual and/or English as a second language frame of reference used to judge ELL achievement, the complexity of second language acquisition, and the processes by which development and learning occur for children acquiring two or more languages. A monolingual reference may ignore how linguistic properties between language systems, and related processing, influence one another in the diverse social and learning environments in which these children live (García & García, 2012). Moreover an English as a second language frame of reference pits the student's native language against Second Language (L2) acquisition in a manner that simplifies the teaching/learning equation: teach/learn English as a second language, with language as the focus, not overall learning goals (Valdés, 2001). Educators are well aware of their obligations to serve the complex needs of these students, which require resources and solutions that are not always readily available. What becomes clear is that consideration of instructional practices in programs for ELLs and what policy at the school level is often dictated by politics and policy as much as determined by research and pedagogy. This chapter focuses on Arizona since this state has been the center of high-profile legislation, litigation, and federal oversight that has fueled controversy with regard to how it has approached educating ELLs far more draconian, experimental, and consequential than any other state in the United States. The most prevalent Arizona ELL litigation began in 1992 when a group of Nogales parents sued the State of Arizona for inadequate ELL funding in K–12 public schools. *Flores v. Arizona* (2000) would eventually rise to the level of the U.S. Supreme Court in 2009 as *Horne v. Arizona*, yet many of the issues raised such as adequate funding and effective instructional programming in the original 1992 lawsuit remain largely unresolved in 2016. This chapter will use the *Flores* case (1992–2016) to exemplify the inequality created for ELLs in K–12 public schools through intersecting discriminatory educational policies implemented through the *Flores* case affecting ELLs. We examine the interaction of these policies in hindering educational opportunity for ELLs, which are salient, urgent, and ongoing since ELLs remain largely severely underserved. To date, Arizona stands out as the clear outlier with regard to its extreme treatment of ELLs—a go it alone state—this makes it an ideal case study to inform other states that may be considering the Arizona model. For example, it has chosen not to collaborate with the 33 state consortiums known as World-class Instructional Design and Assessment in addressing the education of these students. Many of its close neighbors Utah, Nevada, Colorado, and New Mexico are members of World-class Instructional Design and Assessment. Moreover, Arizona legislators have consciously chosen to ignore the extensive body of empirical research on how to best serve ELLs and enact policies that are driven more by political anti-Latino and anti-immigrant sentiment (Arias & Faltis, 2012). Nevertheless, the case of Arizona and its policies related to ELLs is instructive with many lessons learned that have salient implications to the research community and policy makers.

There has been a substantial and important body of scholarly work conducted related to the *Flores* case related to instructional programming and segregation (Arias & Faltis, 2012; Gándara & Hopkins, 2010; García, Lawton, & Diniz de Figueiredo, 2011; Powers, 2014). We build on the previous body of research and, we believe, offer a few timely and significant scholarly contributions. First, we apply intersectionality as an analytic framework to better understand and explain the inequality encountered by ELLs. The *Flores case* has been primarily examined through a theoretical perspective through the conceptual lenses of language and segregation policy (e.g., Powers, 2014), hegemony (Rios-Aguilar & Gándara, 2012), Latin@ critical race theory (e.g., Jiménez-Silva, Gomez, & Cisneros, 2014), and racist nativism (e.g., Jiménez-Castellanos et al., 2014). Each theoretical lens additively scrutinized and attempted to explore the lived experience of ELLs primarily through one or two social constructs (i.e., race, language). In this chapter, we propose a working conceptual framework that merges intersectionality and policy analysis as an analytical tool to understand the nuanced, multilayered, compounded educational inequality encountered specifically by low-income, Latino Spanish-speaking students in Arizona K–12 public schools as a function of intersecting educational policies.

Second, we attempt to provide a holistic and comprehensive framing through the subcontext of *Flores*, and its iterations, as a case study. Most of the previous research related to the *Flores* case examines the policy and/or instructional context focusing on one specific policy (i.e., segregation, home language survey, teacher preparation), we move away by examining the multifaceted aspect of this seminal litigation. Currently, there exist two edited books (Arias & Faltis, 2012; Gándara & Hopkins, 2010) published on this topic and a couple of reports (Jiménez-Castellanos, Combs, Martinez, & Gomez, 2014; Mahoney, MacSwan, & Thompson, 2005) that have provided valuable timelines and analysis of the litigative and legislative events. As a whole the *Flores* literature implicitly suggests the changes that have occurred are to the detriment of ELLs educational potentiality, and have minimized the opportunities present for ELLs. Yet, we further argue that only through a holistic examination of these overlapping discriminatory policies can we truly comprehend the multifaceted nature of the policy impact experienced by ELLs. Third, we provide a conceptual framework that counters and provides an alternative to the Arizona model that strives toward interrupting inequality. The conceptual framework is grounded in culture, language, and learning that we believe provides a pathway to interrupt inequality by acknowledging the intersectional social constructs of an ELL.

The remainder of the chapter is organized into four primary sections. The first section lays out the intersectionality framework, the second section contains the *Flores* case study, the third section posits a conceptual framework grounded in culture, language, and learning to interrupt inequity for ELLs, and the final section offers a discussion and conclusion section.

INTERSECTIONALITY AND POLICY: UNDERSTANDING CUMULATIVE INEQUALITY

Crenshaw (1989) is often credited as the progenitor of intersectionality as a concept deeply rooted in Black feminism to understand the juxtaposition of feminist and race landscapes. Her theories on racial discrimination, sexism, and oppression highlighted the overt discrimination felt by African American women navigating the landscape as female and non-Caucasian. In the past 25 years, scholars from a variety of disciplines have incorporated intersectionality to understand how varying existences affect an individual. McCall (2005) asserts that intersectionality "is the relationship among multiple dimensions and modalities of social relations and subject formations and is itself a central category of analysis" (p. 1771). In essence the intersectionality is the study of overlapping social identities (e.g., gender, race, class, ability, sexual orientation) and the related structures that create systems of oppression. Artiles (2013) summarize intersectional analysis as a method for "documenting the convergence of multiple forms of oppression in people's lives as shaped by distinct markers of difference," which often occurs on multiple, and often simultaneous, levels (p. 336).

For example, Crenshaw (1989) explains the multiple and/or simultaneous forms of discrimination experienced specifically as a Black woman:

I am suggesting that Black women can experience discrimination in ways that are both similar to and different from those experienced by white women and Black men. Black women sometimes experience discrimination in ways similar to white women's experiences; some-times they share very similar experiences with Black men. Yet often they experience double-discrimination-the combined effects of practices which discriminate on the basis of race, and on the basis of sex. And sometimes, they experience discrimination as Black women-not the sum of race and sex discrimination, but as Black women. (p. 149)

This work lead McCall (2005) to develop both an intercategorical and intracategorical approach to intersectionality. The intercategorical approach (also referred to as the *categorical approach*) begins at the inception of inequality within relationships that exists among already constituted social groups and centralizes these challenges as the point of analysis, the intercategorical then explicates these relationships, requiring provisional use of categories. This approach is more pragmatic in terms of the defining categories, acknowledging them as segments of social reality requiring at least temporary accommodations. McCall (2005, p. 1777) posits intracategorical relationships are more nuanced and uncompromising accepting labels than intercategorical approach in any form claiming "the use of categories suspect because they have no foundation in reality: language (in the broader social or discursive sense) creates categorical reality rather than the other way around."

Furthermore, McCall (2005) asserts that the

deconstruction of master categories is understood as part and parcel of the deconstruction of inequality itself. That is, since symbolic violence and material inequalities are rooted in relationships that are defined by race, class, sexuality, and gender, the project of deconstructing the normative assumptions of these categories contributes to the possibility of positive social change. (p. 1777)

Intersectionality theory proposes examining one's existence as a whole with subsets of each element or trait of a person as inextricably linked with each other to fully understand one's identity. Crenshaw (1991) asserts,

The problem with identity politics is not that it fails to transcend difference, as some critics charge, but rather the opposite—that it frequently conflates or ignores intra-group differences. . . . Moreover, ignoring difference within groups contributes to tension among group. (p. 1242)

While the theoretical deconstruction of intersectionality continues to expand, Hankivsky and Cormier (2011) remind us that the knowledge gap between the theoretical construct of intersectionality and its practical application are of major concern. In other words, it is much harder to implement policies or practices that embrace nuanced intersectionality than to theorize or conceptualize about them creating a real challenge in application.

Intersectionality, Policy, and Inequality

The scope of policy and all of the competing relationships in the policy-crafting process lend itself to the examination through intersectionality due to its inherent orientation toward fostering social change that is grounded in social justice and equity. Varcoe, Pauly, and Laliberté (2011) assert the research community must begin to understand the policy-varied values underpinning the policy-crafting process and its intersection with the policy influence particularly focused on the sociohistorical and structural conditions shaping the ways in which groups participate and influence social life.

It should be noted that many critical scholars have long engaged the issue of policy, power, and individual social constructs such as race or class or have suggested implications of intersectionality in policy development. For example, Collins (2000) explicitly connects power and hegemony, and their influence on institutions and policy. Collins asserts that the

structural and disciplinary domains of power operate through system wide social policies managed primarily by bureaucracies. In contrast, the hegemonic domain of power aims to justify practices in these domains of power. By manipulating ideology and culture, the hegemonic domain acts as a link between social institutions (structural domain), their organizational practices (disciplinary domain), and the level of everyday social interaction (interpersonal domain). (p. 284)

Moreover, Collins developed a matrix of domination framework that links the social identity categories and juxtaposes privileged and targeted social groups and the corresponding "ism" associated with discrimination and oppression. In doing so, she simultaneously links and distinguishes between two concepts where intersectionality refers to particular forms of intersecting oppressions (e.g., race and gender, or of sexuality and nation). Collins (2003) goes on to state,

Intersectional paradigms then remind us that oppression cannot be reduced to one fundamental type, and that oppressions work together in producing injustice. In contrast, the matrix of domination refers to how these intersecting oppressions are actually organized. Regardless of the particular intersections involved, structural, disciplinary, hegemonic, and interpersonal domains of power reappear across quite different forms of oppression. (p. 18)

Embedded in Collins's matrix of domination are the issues related to hegemony and structural inequality that have direct impact on policy design and analysis for (in) equality.

Although initiated in the United States, the most recent innovation melds intersectionality and public policy research. There has been a concerted effort by Canadian and European academics to conduct scholarship that combines both theory and application in this arena. This may be due to their long history of proactively dealing with complex diversity issues within their populations and their government's willingness to acknowledge and engage not only existing issues of diversity but more explicitly intersectionality. This openness is not common in the United States submitting to assimilation as the normative expectations of behavior and performance for immigrants and expats. Siim (2013) reminds us that

it [intersectionality] does not address only one single dimension of diversity but examines multiple and intersecting categories of differences, often having its focus on multiple and complex inequalities and the problem usually perceived to be inequalities, not differences. The aim of the intersectionality approach is to conceptualize differences and to address multiple inequalities, intersecting categories of difference and overlapping identities [and inequalities]. (p. 13)

Ultimately, utilizing intersectionality in policy analysis explicitly exposes inequality in policy design and implementation and their impact. As Artiles (2013, p. 337) articulates, "An implication of this analytic perspective includes policy responses that are sensitive [or not] to the convergence of multiple forms of oppression."

Moreover, Hankivsky and Cormier (2011) assert that intersectionality based policy analysis

has the capacity to (1) identify the underlying (sometimes complex) sources of inequality; (2) be citizen focused, taking into account the whole person and not just a single aspect of identity or experience; (3) maintain the distinctions between the origins of inequality between "strands" but provide an integrated method of working that will enable resources to be targeted toward reducing the greatest inequalities; and finally (4) enhance the forms of democratic participation that recognize the equal worth and dignity of all "strands." (p. 225)

The influence of the structure and its ability to assert domination often fails to embrace the complexities of these varying intersections so that struggle as a matter unto itself is consistently categorized as a singular issue and not a challenge of several aggressions (Crenshaw, 1989).

There is significant literature that uses intersectionality in education research to explain students' lived experiences; in particular, the teaching and learning process. Less common are studies that directly and explicitly merge intersectionality and education policy. Hankivsky and Cormier (2011) begin to theorize how intersectionality could serve education policy reform and go beyond school-based solutions to improve the achievement, challenging the status quo to link outcomes with the lived context of an individual and its effect on employment, health, and even food scarcity. The author's main premise in this context is that to fully understand the lives of those affected by policy requires some form of participation and inclusion in order to highlight the barriers that exist which policy should address. This turns the participatory scale from top-down, to bottom-up caring for not only the stakeholder opinion, but delivery of center stakeholder solution. This multistrand approach prioritizes identification of and effective responses multiple structures of oppression that shape all aspects of education.

Intersectionality and English Language Learners

There is limited literature that deeply examines intersectionality with an analytical focus on ELLs. Often ELLs are relegated to the status of "a student that is learning English" yet intersectionality makes explicit that although language is a unique and important characteristic we must not forget the multiple dimensions and lived experiences of this group of students. This focus seems to be warranted not only in the Southwestern United States but globally as well.

Figure 1 demonstrates the aspects of ELL students and their lived realities juxtaposing among each other to create a central individual.

FIGURE 1
Mosaic Incorporating the Multiple Lived Realities of an
English Language Learner

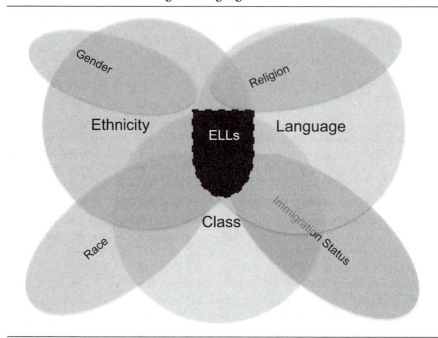

Note. ELL = English language learner.

Siim (2013) suggests European scholars acknowledge the new horizon in research are these intersections of migration creating conflict between citizens' and noncitizens' willingness to acknowledge and accommodate cultural and religious diversity of new migrant groups.

A few prominent studies that have been conducted on intersectionality scholarship have primarily analyzed the intersection of disability and language (Artiles, 2011, 2013; Artiles et al., 2005). Most academics and policymakers tend to emphasize the linguistic dimension of ELLs. Again, while language is an important social construct that uniquely distinguishes ELLs from other students, we must be wary not to frame it as the only salient dimension. ELLs have the same dimensions that other students have such as gender, religion, and sexual orientation, among others. Another distinctive dimension for some ELLs is immigration status in particular if they are refugees and if they are undocumented—though it is worthwhile reiterating that the majority of ELLs are U.S.-born contrary to many people's beliefs that ELLs are primarily recent immigrants.

It is crucial to be aware of the intragroup complexity and diversity of ELLs while effectively engaging the contextual diversity of this group within the Southwestern states including Arizona. In Arizona, ELLs are predominantly a marginalized, low-income, Spanish-speaking community of Mexican origin born in the United States.

This is not to suggest that ELLs in Arizona form a homogenous and static group: Intersectionality allows us to untangle and legitimize the singularity of each social construct while recognizing the cumulative impact of discrimination. In schooling, segregation is one of the most disturbing effects of discrimination, both across schools and within schools. Orfield and Lee (2005) highlight a triple segregation referring to schools as isolated by race, class, and language through majority–minority enrolment. Although mostly framed as a Latino issue, the primary driver for triple segregation is language not race or class since without the social construct of language, it would be deemed double segregation by race and class. In practice, in the Southwest there are many schools that have high poverty, high Latino and high ELL populations (Heilig & Holme, 2013). Finally, Gándara and Orfield (2012a) note the triple segregation of Arizona's English learners by ethnicity, language, and poverty, which cumulatively effects students negatively. Overall, the policy of Arizona that has created linguistic segregation at the classroom level intensifies all the negative impacts of school segregation. For this reason, it is important to organize instruction design in ways that mitigate the multiple forms of segregation experienced by students within this subgroup.

FLORES V. ARIZONA

The purpose of this section is to provide a holistic and comprehensive framing of education policies targeting ELLs, specifically low-income Mexican American Spanish-speaking students through the subcontext of *Flores*, and its iterations, as a case study. Due to space and the focus of this chapter, we will not provide a chronology of all events that have occurred related to the Flores case since the original lawsuit was filed in 1992. We recommend reading Jiménez-Castellanos et al. (2013) for a more thorough chronology. More specifically, we will use intersectionality as an analytical tool to understand the nuanced, multilayered, cumulative educational inequality encountered by ELLs in the Arizona compulsory K–12 public school system as a function of multiple and overlapping educational policy.

Figure 2 outlines the plethora of decisions that have culminated in low ELL achievement.

We believe that some of the most important factors to understanding the inequality experienced by ELLs in Arizona are "politics, politics, and politics." Therefore, it is important to situate this case within a sociohistorical and sociopolitical context since much of what happens in education policy, and particularly in Arizona was, and is, predicated and heavily influenced by politics.

Arizona Demographics and Anti-Immigrant Sentiment

Arizona, a Southwestern border state with Mexico, has a long and rich yet troubled history with that country given that prior to 1848 it was Mexican land (Acuña, 1998; Weber, 2003). Thus, the relationship between Arizona and Mexican Americans is complex and full of tension manifested over time. Currently, there are approximately

FIGURE 2
Policy Dimensions Affecting ELL Student Academic Growth in Arizona

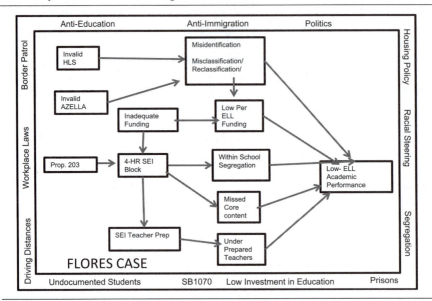

Note. ELL = English language learner; SEI = structured English immersion.

6.3 million residents in Arizona, 30% identifying as Latino. Of this population, over-whelmingly 38% subsist under poverty and of Latinos in education, 60% qualify for Free and/or Reduced-price Lunch Program (FRLP), 6% to 15% of which are ELLs (Kena et al., 2016). This demographic shift is not only an Arizona phenomenon but nationally Latinos are the fastest growing majority–minority group. Thus, Arizona and many Southwestern states are seen as operating in a White/Brown paradigm simi-larly to other southwestern states and similar to the White/Black paradigm in many southern states (Alemán & Alemán, 2010).

Historically there have always been waves of anti-immigrant sentiment in the United States usually in time of war and/or economic uncertainty (Mayda, 2006; Perea, 1997). However, the current demographic shifts have, at least to some degree, reignited a new wave of anti-immigrant sentiment politics due to fear that Caucasian, Anglo-Protestant, culture and the English language is increasingly the minority within its borders (Goldstein & Peters, 2014). Anti-immigrant sentiment intensified during the period of the Great Recession from 2008 to 2013 due to significant unem-ployment and housing foreclosure, even though the economic crisis disproportion-ately negatively affected working class Latinos. Anti-immigrant sentiment during this time intersected with other social constructs such as ethnicity, language, class, and immigrant status (i.e., SB1070).

Politics and Power (Re)frame *Flores* Case

The attorneys for the *Flores* class had a tough political decision to make regarding the initial litigation filing. If they filed with the more democrat friendly U.S. District Court, they risked an unfavorable decision due to the 1973 U.S. Supreme Court *Rodriguez v. San Antonio* decision. This case ultimately ruled education was a state and not federal matter with regard to funding. On the other hand, if they filed the complaint with the less friendly State of Arizona Court, they risked proceeding in front of the Arizona Governor (a Republican at the time) elected justices, albeit knowing that in several states when standing before state justices, final determinations were often favorable for the plaintiffs. Ultimately, they decided to file the case with the U.S. District Court avoiding the Republican Governor's appointed judges. No significant changes occurred several years following the primary filing, 1992 to 1999; however, Arizona was on the cusp of a fundamental shift in ELL politics by 2000.

In January 2000, the U.S. District Court ruled in favor of the plaintiffs noting that inadequate state funding resulted in program deficiencies for ELLs. The court found the state's ELL appropriation was "arbitrary and capricious." Furthermore, as Jiménez-Castellanos et al. (2013) stated in August 2000, the then Superintendent of Public Instruction, Lisa Graham Keegan, entered into a consent decree with the plaintiffs that resolved the lawsuit's allegations. The 2000 *Flores v. Arizona* consent decree mandate focused on ensuring ELLs learned English through English Language Development but also stipulated that content subject matter should be comprehensible and appropriate using acceptable strategies for teaching ELL students. Furthermore, the consent decree specifically referenced bilingual education as an acceptable instructional program model for instruction. This decision came on the heels of the anti-bilingual education proposition, Prop. 203, known as "English for the Children."

During this same period, Arizona's residential and cultural landscape looked much different with 65% Caucasian making up the majority of the state, while Latinos made up only 25% of the total population. Arizona voters passed Proposition 203 changing the language policy of the state to a restrictive language model mandating ELLs be taught in English only, requiring an intensive 1–year Sheltered English Immersion program of instruction, that forced schools to comply with a mandate which viewed the native language, Spanish, of Mexican ELL students, as a negative trait instead of a resource (Ruiz, 1995). Moreover, local school and district flexibility and choice regarding the type of program model(s) offered to ELLs was eliminated and Sheltered English Immersion was the required instructional method for ELLs in school districts and charter schools across the state. Previously Arizona schools were allowed to select from a variety of acceptable program models, including English as a second language and transitional bilingual programs or dual language education, to develop English proficiency and academic achievement for their English learners. The irony of Proposition 203 is that it reduced choice and local control, two principles that Arizona Republicans usually staunchly support but not when it came to educating "Latino immigrant" children.

Cumulative Impact of Discriminatory Educational Policies

Over the next decade and a half, English-only language policy helped frame various bills passed by the Arizona legislature designed to address ELL instructional needs and funding. The evidence suggests that, in the wake of Flores, Proposition 203 set in motion a series of legislative attempts that ultimately had a detrimental effect on educational opportunities for ELLs in Arizona, magnifying instead of eliminating inequality for these students.

Specifically on the funding policy domain, the State of Arizona performed two cost studies (2001, 2004) to estimate the cost of an "adequate" education for ELLs in an attempt to respond to the consent decree. Cost studies typically establish a base cost determining a minimum amount of money needed to educate the general population of students to meet specified outcomes (i.e., performance on state standardized tests), and denote the additional costs needed to educate special populations of students, such as ELLs (Jiménez-Castellanos & Topper, 2012). Both studies suggested that more funding was necessary to adequately educate ELLs but were deemed invalid and ultimately not accepted by the legislature. Without using any empirical evidence the legislature then passed HB 2010 in late 2001 increasing the ELL weight from .06 to .115. The plaintiffs challenged this increase and the courts again ruled in favor of the plaintiffs calling the weighted funding level increase "arbitrary and capricious" and inadequate (Jiménez-Castellanos et al., 2013). In the eyes of Arizona legislators, the funding increase they passed was an appropriate attempt at resolution toward appropriated adequate funding, but had no clear instructional model that would support ELLs' learning needs. After several years of inaction, the Arizona Legislature passed HB1064 in 2006, which among other things created a Task Force charged with designing a research-based English instruction program that included at least 4 hours per day of English development (Arizona Revised Statute §§ 15-756.01). Informed and guided by Proposition 203, the bill required that the Task Force limit the available models of language acquisition to only those that helped develop English proficiency in 1 year. The ultimate recommendation of the Task Force was a form of structured English immersion (SEI) resulting in segregation of students for 4 of the estimated 6.5 hours per day of instruction, and limited access to compressive curriculum (Gándara & Orfield, 2012b). HB1064 and the resulting Task Force recommendation have received widespread criticism from within Arizona and across the nation. The bill itself has been strongly criticized by the scholarly and educational community for its emphasis on the most "cost-efficient" method of English instruction, rather than the most effective (Gándara & Orfield, 2010). Many academic studies argue that English proficiency can take language learners between 4 and 5 years to achieve, making HB1064's expectation of proficiency in 1 year seem largely unrealistic (Gándara & Orfield, 2010). A survey by Rios-Aguilar, González-Canche, and Moll (2010a) of 880 English language teachers in Arizona found that a large majority of teachers, 78%, believed it would take 3 or more years for ELLs to achieve English proficiency. The most opposed feature of the Task Force's ultimate recommendation has been its segregation of ELLs from their peers. In fact, Arizona State University researchers Jiménez-Castellanos et al. (2013) conclude that, in the final *Flores v. Arizona* hearings, plaintiffs argued that the SEI block not only failed to constitute appropriate funding for ELLs but also created a "segregation of ELLs from their English-speaking peers" constituting a "withholding of content [that] violated the students' civil rights" (p. 9).

The Arizona Office of the Auditor General issued a report in 2011 discussing the implementation and effectiveness of the Task Force recommendation. Their primary two conclusions were that, by 2010, "almost two-thirds of schools had not fully implemented" the mandated SEI models and, though proficiency rates had increased since SEI-adoption, the impact of the recent changes could not be reliably known. To externally gauge the efficacy and impact of the new SEI instruction, as well as to understand the implications and rhetoric surrounding Arizona ELL policy, the UCLA Civil Rights Project conducted an extensive series of Arizona education studies in 2010 called the "Arizona Education Equity Project." Many of the studies already cited within this chapter are from that series. Most papers in the series present pessimistic findings about the state's ELL practices. García et al. (2011) concluded Arizona was by proxy stimulating larger achievement gaps, due in part to its restrictive language policy. In related research on the Arizona policy context, Arizona teachers strongly believe in their ELL students' ability to succeed. In fact 85% of teachers voiced their opinions that separation from English-speaking peers would harm ELL's learning and English development (Rios-Aguilar, González-Canche, & Moll, 2010b). Lillie, Markos, Arias, and Wiley (2012) would add to this context highlighting the potential divide that would occur with regard to limited curriculum access, and felt the Arizona SEI model would stigmatize this group of students.

Jiménez-Castellanos et al. (2013, p. 3) conclude that "the empirical evidence supports the argument that funding and instructional practices implemented post *Flores v. Arizona* continues to be inadequate as it does not appear to be improving the academic attainment for Arizona's ELLs." Arizona's "English-only" instruction policy, initiated through Proposition 203 in 2000, is a detriment to teaching as well, ultimately limiting the available ELL strategies available for front line teachers to support L2 acquisition. Hopkins (2012) denotes the availability of English as a second language and the subsequent teacher endorsements to that regard as something that has affective positive change in the learning, and teaching, of an ELL student.

In mid-2009, the Supreme Court ruled 5–4 in favor of Arizona remanding the case to a U.S. district court for further consideration of possible violations to the Equal Educational Opportunities Act. Currently, several English language instruction paradigms could be affected by the district court's future decisions, such as the segregation of non-English speakers and sequential instruction (i.e., students learning English and core academic contents; Rios-Aguilar & Gándara, 2012).

The New America Foundation published a comprehensive examination of language education policy across the United States, with a focus of reclassification standards. Williams (2014) remarks on the wide variability of reclassification policies across states, a chaos that "translates into widespread confusion about how [ELLs] experience public education" (p. 2). If reclassification policies are arbitrary and not supported by empirical research, as voiced by Williams, and the original English language instruction is flawed, ELLs could face enormous obstacles under English-only regular classroom instruction. Federal Civil Rights evaluations, and its definition of these student populations, and the assessments utilized to reclassify students, were found to be discriminatory and in need of corrective action. In the Flores case, courts have determined that the required implementation of the Arizona instructional model for ELLs is in need of assessment for positive outcomes. Overwhelmingly, academic research has indicated that Arizona has flawed, if not unjust English Language Learning policies. The above research is comprehensive in its analysis of how current ELLs are addressed and supported in Arizona.

TOWARD A CULTURE, LANGUAGE, AND LEARNING CONCEPTUAL FRAMEWORK

Current research in the United States lacks attention to federal, state, and program policies that are part of the sociopolitical and historical contexts (segregation, immigration-related social policies are examples) affecting ELLs' experiences in educational settings. Arizona, in particular, has exhibited a great deal of inequality in both policy and practice with regard to its large and ever present marginalized, low-income, Latino, Spanish-speaking ELL student community. This context provides an opportunity to examine the state of educational policy through research literature that attempts to interrupt inequality. Currently, the theoretical and research contributions that add a layer of nuance to understanding students in poverty who are developing two languages simultaneously have been limited to the context of language and special needs populations (Hammer et al., 2014). Research focused on differences between ELL and non-ELL populations have neglected the aspect of heterogeneity *within* the ELL population, and, very few studies offered longitudinal evidence related to ELL educational trajectories across various developmental domains (language, cognitive and social–emotional domains). The bulk of this scholarship, not surprisingly, foregrounds attention to linguistic factors, while other developmental and contextual influences (family, community, society) too often tend to be considered only as secondary variables of interest (García, Castro, & Markos, 2015). Recent research conducted by the Center for Early Care and Educational Research–Dual Language Learners (2011a, 2011b) reveal key limitations in the existing body of literature (García & Náñez, 2011). This research points to critical familial, community and related societal factors that influence the overall development and learning of ELLs, including the development of language and academic repertoires, Education policy, much like the scholarship related to ELLs, has not attended to this complexity of the ELL student experience (García et al., 2015; García & García, 2012; Moll, 2002).

In light of the backlog juxtaposing ELL policy and practice, we propose a conceptual framework that recognizes culture, language, and learning in general as interdependent and situated within cultural practices and specific institutions to better inform educational policy and related practices and research. Furthermore, it incorporates the principles of intersectionality theory and attends to the intersecting linguistic and cultural needs of this diverse demographic. This conceptual perspective defines culture as located in the minds of people and in their everyday practices, and views culture as patterned, dynamic, historically grounded, and instrumental (Rogoff, 2003)—it is the beliefs, values, and practices through which we live every aspect of our lives. This means culture affords and constrains human behavior, including language and is itself a transmitter of culture. It also signifies language and learning are cultural phenomena constituted by the intersections within the individual and the interpersonal and institutional spaces they occupy (García et al., 2015). There is a recognition that the individual actively engages and develops culture in everyday activities within ecological niches in which the individual, and their language plays a fundamental role. Understanding these intersecting dialectal tensions between the individual and the environment is important to understanding ELL educational development within a full compulsory curriculum.

By that token, ELLs are active participants in the environments influencing their linguistic development and in turn influence that same environment. Just as individuals use their linguistic skills and capacities in the contexts of interpersonal processes, this framework recognizes that individuals participate in social practices that are consistently imbedded within institutional milieus (e.g., families, communities, schools). These institutional layers constitute by rules and expectations, roles that can be invisible to observers if these multifaceted layers are not accounted for. This is an important departure from ELL language development frameworks, transcending the exclusive analytic focus on individual language and learning of a second language, toward a rounded notion that intertwines language within the context of institutional paradigms and subtextual policies, which oppress the mosaic of subgroups making up the individual.

Implications of Culture, Language, and Learning Framework

This conceptual framework encourages recognition of a complexity featuring both within and across formal education settings to fully understand the cultural, language development, and learning of ELLs. It is critical to recognize the intersecting elements that influence family, community, and societal contexts draw on each other and the lived experiences of the individual to create their learned epistemology. This framework is not intended as a theoretical entity, instead allowing for varied theoretical interpretations, while enumerating a constellation of elements that must be addressed within those entities and their importance to policy construction and implementation. Without attention to these interrelated elements of the ELL experience, optimizing the development and learning of this significant demographic in the United States cannot be fully understood, and institutionally imbedded interventions to foster learning will fall critically short of their learning and equity goals. Thus equity issues related to achievement gaps will continue to be revisited for ELLs, continually focusing on language difference issues in a vacuum with limited attention highlighting all of the requisite spaces these students occupy. A more useful response calls for moving forward within this framework at every level of policy and related practice moving beyond focusing only on the linguistic bits and pieces of ELLs as insufficient.

The future organization of our educational policy that act to influence teaching and learning environments for ELLs must consider the sociocultural-specific contexts that are reflective of the ELL students and the family including history, context, activities, and cultural underpinnings, and the lived experiences of these students (e.g., Ortega, 2013, 2014). An important corollary of this framework implies also that there is a need to move beyond a monolingual perspective and examine the unique linguistic and cognitive consequences of dual language learning and use (Castro, García, & Markos, 2013). Moreover, given the knowledge base regarding the effects of social circumstances in which children and families are immersed and the relationship to development and learning outcomes, selective attention for ELLs that would explore a "vulnerability/asset" analysis of social circumstances as a focus is promising. In each variable regarding social circumstances (including sociopolitical context, immigration and integration, and issues of discrimination/racism/oppression), an assessment can be made regarding the "vulnerability" as well as the "asset" ingredients of these circumstances. This funds of knowledge approach can address important implications and important social circumstance of ELLs in early care, education, and broader social and community environments (González, Moll, & Amanti, 2005; Moll, 2002).

This emerging body of research attempting to understand the early care and formal educational circumstances that are important for advancing the growth and development of ELLs is emerging (Espinosa, 2012; García & García, 2012). The research highlights an array of methods, including teacher observation, parent evaluations, self-evaluation where appropriate, among others, as are necessary to reliably and validly assess ELLs development for different purposes, including screening, progress monitoring, and instructional planning (Snow & Van Hemel, 2008). Additionally, we recognize that specific enhancements to foundational curriculum and instruction that must be driven by informed policy will lead to improved academic and developmental competencies for ELLs. Currently, there exists knowledge about when and how to best introduce English as a language in schooling, specific strategies that can be implemented in English-dominant classrooms, and how to implement and monitor progress in more than one language but have limited awareness of the intersections that exist by nature of culture, religion, immigration, race, gender, socioeconomic status, sexual orientation, and policy on the existing challenges of ELL educational development (August, Shanahan, & Escamilla, 2009). Specifically researchers have linked both cognitive/language aspects of development as well as those that build on important socioemotional/cultural strengths, but have omitted the implications of policy on this development (Bialystok, 2009).

FIGURE 3
Implications of the Conceptual Framework

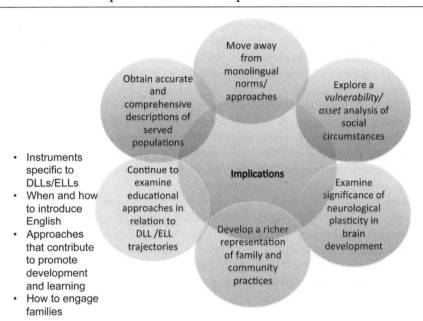

- Instruments specific to DLLs/ELLs
- When and how to introduce English
- Approaches that contribute to promote development and learning
- How to engage families

In addition, the research community has engaged families that are not proficient in English, the home language development and home English language acquisition necessary to support their students, the role of parents in the early care and education of ELLs, and family's deep knowledge of their child, their culture, their language, and their customs. This discussion of Arizona policy directly addresses these important knowledge domains within the conceptual framework introduced and allows policy and full cultural contextual awareness to juxtapose against the fine-grained definitions of students in the educational setting and moves beyond the general acknowledgement of "a child from a non-English-speaking home." This potentially could provide an accurate and comprehensive description of the samples of learners we are studying or those to whom we are providing services including information with respect to, the age of acquisition of each language, the extent and nature of exposure to each language, and key family, community, and educational characteristics (see Figure 3).

In summary, the framework and implications offered here builds on the significant previous contributions regarding issue of development and learning and ELLs (August & Hakuta, 1997). The Culture, Language, and Learning framework proposed is founded on a sociocultural and sociohistorical perspective (Rogoff, 2003). As such, it emphasizes that an individual's development and learning cannot be understood isolated from the social, cultural, and historical contexts in which it occurs. We acknowledge and build on this conceptual framework as an archetype for guiding our above review and discussion of the knowledge base and the implications for practice, policy, and research, believing it is helpful for determining factors that need to be taken into consideration when designing, conducting, and interpreting findings from new policies, practice, and research specifically addressing issue of inequality for ELLs. Future policy and practice, and research related to these issues, must consider the following attributes:

- The development and learning of multiple languages in ELLs are critically important in understanding the development, learning, and well-being of ELLs.
- The acquisition of two languages in children and students has no inherent negative social, linguistic, cognitive, or educational consequences and, to the contrary, may generate advantages in a variety of social, linguistic, cognitive, and academic domains.
- Understanding development and learning of ELLs require understanding the array of activities that are practiced by children in and outside of formal educational institutions and the learning opportunities in families, communities, and societies in which they reside.
- Educational policies at all levels in the United States play a particularly important role in shaping the formal educational experience of ELLs as has been discussed in depth for Arizona.

CONCLUSION

This chapter examines the extreme level of inequality that exists in Arizona for ELLs; in particular low-income Latino Spanish-speaking students through the use of intersectionality as an analytical tool to illuminate the complex, intersecting social constructs define an ELL and how these identities are oppressed by both the litigative and policy processes limiting both the potentiality of this subdomain of students and the opportunities presented to them educationally, stunting their social and economic well-being, and creating inequality (Gándara & Orfield, 2012a). The Arizona approach is informed by anti-immigrant nativist conservative politics, a multieducational policy, leading to practice, absent of a strong theoretical and empirical research base is necessary in order to understand the cross sectional demands placed on this diverse group (Powers & Williams, 2013). This is becoming a far too common theme in Arizona education, traditional conservative education reform efforts chose to discriminate against children rather than support them toward greatness, with the largest causes coming in the form of grossly underfunding schools. These types of policies have thus limited the actuality of achievement for the ELL subpopulation, burying their potential achievement in bad policy and gross miscalculations of culture (Mahoney et al., 2005; Rolstad, Mahoney, & Glass, 2005). We hope this chapter makes it clear to any other state considering adopting the Arizona model to look toward the research literature instead of the short-run efficiency these types of policies create.

The research community must also begin to bolster this area of research further developing and sustaining this much needed area, which juxtaposes the cultural components of ELLs against policies that chose to stifle cultural strengths and are often viewed as normative weaknesses (Good, Masewicz, & Vogel, 2010). It is critical that future research examining the development of ELLs be conducted with reference to the specific sociocultural and learning contexts that reflect the history, circumstances, activities, and culture of ELL children and their families (Andrade, 2015). Now is the time for a valid and thorough understanding of the development of ELLs requiring an interpretation of results with reference to the sociocultural contexts in which development occurs. To this effect, we emphasize the following implications for research that reflect our understandings of ELL competencies and the social, community, family, and education contexts surrounding ELLs.

First, there is a need for a more fine-grained definition of children and students in any study, moving beyond the general "child from a non-English-speaking home," or "a bilingual child," or "an ELL child" (Flynn & Hill, 2005). It is imperative that researchers provide accurate and comprehensive descriptions of the samples of learners they are studying, including information with respect to, for example, the age of acquisition of each language, the extent and nature of exposure to each language (in and out of educational venues), and key family, community, and educational characteristics (Echevarria & Graves, 2007; Gersten & Baker, 2000). Without adequate descriptions of the learners who participate in specific studies, it is impossible to determine the generalizability of research findings, and consumers of research on ELLs, including educators and policymakers, risk inappropriate overgeneralizing findings. Given the knowledge base regarding the effects of social circumstances in which children and families are immersed and the relationship to development and learning outcomes, a research agenda that uses a vulnerability/asset analysis of social circumstances is needed. With respect to each variable regarding social circumstances (including sociopolitical context, immigration and integration, and issues of discrimination/racism/oppression), assessment can be made regarding the vulnerability as well as the asset ingredients of these circumstances. For instance, are their laws in a state that allows adaption of instruction/standards/credentials related to ELLs (an asset) versus highly restrictive requirements that do not address the ELL circumstances (a vulnerability)? Such vulnerability/asset analyses should reflect each important social circumstance, including, but not limited, to socioeconomic status, level of parent education, and parent's level of English proficiency (Gutierrez & García, 1989).

Further research is needed inside of ELL communities that examine the mechanisms by which neighborhoods and communities provide opportunities for ELLs to participate in everyday activities in those settings (August et al., 2009). Most research on community and neighborhood affects focus on demographic characteristics of these learners (e.g., census data) and their potential associations with developmental outcomes. Little is known about how different features of actual community life serve as mechanisms that affect children's participation in those activities and subsequently promote their developmental competencies (Norton & Toohey, 2001). Needed now is a research catalogue that bridges these demographic and structural influences rather than focusing on parents' and families' subjective appraisals of their communities and experiences living in them. This could potentially illuminate the role of community-based mechanisms in the development of ELLs. Finally as is the case for all children, the family serves as the most salient and enduring context in which ELLs learn and develop. Understanding demographic influences is an initial step in understanding the portraiture of an ELL family but is not enough to uncover the rich processes that both characterize and distinguish the context of this group (Peirce, 1995; Valdés, 2001). Processes related to culture-specific parenting goals, practices, beliefs, home language, and literacy related to bilingualism are key aspects of the family that are unique to ELLs. Future research should explore these family needs to move toward a richer appreciation of such family processes helping better understand how ELL families behave privately, and how they live within and interact with their respective sociopolitical, community, and other salient contexts. This information is pivotal for improving our knowledge of how ELLs acquire skills across all developmental competencies.

REFERENCES

Acuña, R. (1998). *Occupied America: The Latino/a condition: A critical reader.* New York: New York University Press.

Alemán, E. Jr., & Alemán, S. M. (2010). Do Latin@ interests always have to "converge" with White interests? (Re) claiming racial realism and interest-convergence in critical race theory praxis. *Race Ethnicity and Education, 13*(1), 1–21.

Andrade, B. M. (2015). *The parental involvement of non-English speaking Latino parents in secondary education* (Unpublished master's thesis). California State University, Monterey Bay.

Arias, M. B., & Faltis, C. (Eds.). (2012). *Implementing educational language policy in Arizona: Legal, historical and current practices in SEI.* Bristol, England: Multilingual Matters.

Artiles, A. J. (2011). Toward an interdisciplinary understanding of educational equity and difference the case of the racialization of ability. *Educational Researcher, 40,* 431–445.

Artiles, A. J. (2013). Untangling the racialization of disabilities. *Du Bois Review, 10,* 329–347.

Artiles, A. J., Rueda, R., Salazar, J. J., & Higareda, I. (2005). Within-group diversity in minority disproportionate representation: English language learners in urban school districts. *Exceptional Children, 71,* 283–300.

August, D., & Hakuta, K. (Eds.). (1997). *Improving schooling for language-minority children: A research agenda.* Washington, DC: National Academies Press.

August, D., Shanahan, T., & Escamilla, K. (2009). English language learners: Developing literacy in second-language learners—Report of the National Literacy Panel on Language-Minority Children and Youth. *Journal of Literacy Research, 41,* 432–452.

Baker, B. D., Keller-Wolff, C., & Wolf-Wendel, L. (2000). Two steps forward, one step back: Race/ethnicity and student achievement in education policy research. *Educational Policy, 14,* 511–529.

Bialystok, E. (2009). Bilingualism: The good, the bad, and the indifferent. *Bilingualism, 12*(1), 3–11.

Calderon, M. E., & Minaya-Rowe, L. (2010). *Preventing long-term ELs: Transforming schools to meet core standards.* Thousand Oaks, CA: Corwin Press.

Castro, D. C., García, E. E., & Markos, A. M. (2013). *Dual language learners: Research informing policy.* Chapel Hill: Center for Early Care and Education in the Frank Porter Graham Child Development Institute at the University of North Carolina.

Center for Early Care and Education Research–Dual Language Learners. (2011a). *Language and literacy development in dual language learners: A critical review of the research*. Chapel Hill: Center for Early Care and Education in the Frank Porter Graham Child Development Institute at the University of North Carolina.

Center for Early Care and Education Research–Dual Language Learners. (2011b). *Policy and practice issues related to serving dual language learners*. Chapel Hill: Center for Early Care and Education in the Frank Porter Graham Child Development Institute at the University of North Carolina.

Cohen, N. H. (1995). *Ada as a second language*. Columbus, OH: McGraw-Hill Higher Education.

Collins, P. H. (2000). *Black feminist thought*. New York, NY: Routledge.

Collins, P. H. (2003). Some group matters: Intersectionality, situated standpoints, and black feminist thought. In T. L. Lott, & J. P. Pittman (Eds.), *A companion to African-American philosophy* (pp. 205–229). Hoboken, NJ: Wiley-Blackwell.

Conger, D. (2012). *Immigrant peers and academic performance in high school*. Retrieved from https://aefpweb.org/sites/default/files/webform/Conger_ImmigrantPeers_AEFP2012.pdf

Crenshaw, K. (1989). Demarginalizing the intersection of race and sex: A black feminist critique of antidiscrimination doctrine, feminist theory and antiracist politics. *University of Chicago Legal Forum, 8*, 139–167.

Crenshaw, K. (1991). Mapping the margins: Intersectionality, identity politics, and violence against women of color. *Stanford Law Review, 43*, 1241–1299.

Echevarria, J., & Graves, A. W. (2007). *Sheltered content instruction: Teaching English language learners with diverse abilities*. Los Angeles, CA: Allyn & Bacon.

Espinosa, L. (2012). Assessment of young English-language learners. In *The encyclopedia of applied linguistics*. Advance online publication. doi:10.1002/9781405198431.wbeal0057

Flynn, K., & Hill, J. (2005). *English language learners: A growing population*. Denver, CO: Mid-Continent Research for Education and Learning.

Fuhrman, S., & Elmore, R. F. (Eds.). (2004). *Redesigning accountability systems for education*. Philadelphia: University of Pennsylvania Press. Retrieved from http://files.eric.ed.gov/fulltext/ED498338.pdf

Gamoran, A. (2008). Persisting social class inequality in US education. In L. Weiss (Eds.), *The way class works: Readings on school, family, and the economy* (pp. 169–179). New York, NY: Routledge.

Gándara, P., & Hopkins, M. (2010). *Forbidden language: English learners and restrictive language policies*. New York, NY: Teachers College Press.

Gándara, P., Moran, R., & García, E. (2004). Legacy of Brown: Lau and language policy in the United States. *Review of Research in Education, 28*(1), 27–46.

Gándara, P., & Orfield, G. (2010). *A return to the "Mexican room": The segregation of Arizona's English learners*. Los Angeles, CA: Civil Rights Project/Proyecto Derechos Civiles. Retrieved from http://files.eric.ed.gov/fulltext/ED511322.pdf

Gándara, P., & Orfield, G. (2012a). Segregating Arizona's English learners: A return to the "Mexican room." *Teachers College Record, 114*(9), 1–27.

Gándara, P., & Orfield, G. (2012b). Why Arizona matters: The historical, legal, and political contexts of Arizona's instructional policies and US linguistic hegemony. *Language Policy, 11*(1), 7–19.

García, E. E. (2005). *Teaching and learning in two languages: Bilingualism & schooling in the United States*. New York, NY: Teachers College Press.

García, E. E., Castro, D., & Markos, A. (2015). *Helping dual language learners succeed: A research-based agenda for action*. Minneapolis, MN: McKnight Foundation.

García, E. E., & García, E. H. (2012). *Understanding the language development and early education of Hispanic children*. New York, NY: Teachers College Press.

García, E. E., Lawton, K., & Diniz de Figueiredo, E. H. (2011). *The education of English language learners in Arizona: A legacy of persisting achievement gaps in a restrictive language policy climate.* Los Angeles, CA: Civil Rights Project/Proyecto Derechos Civiles.

García, E. E., & Náñez, Sr., J. E. (2011). *Bilingualism and cognition: Informing research, pedagogy, and policy.* Washington, DC: American Psychological Association.

Gardner, D. P. (1983). *A nation at risk.* Washington, DC: National Commission on Excellence in Education, U.S. Department of Education.

Genesee, F. (2006). *Educating English language learners: A synthesis of research evidence.* Cambridge, English: Cambridge University Press.

Genesee, F., Lindholm-Leary, K., Saunders, W. M., & Christian, D. (2006). Conclusions and future directions. In F. Genesee (Ed.), *Educating English learners: A synthesis of research evidence* (pp. 223–234). Cambridge, England: Cambridge University Press.

Gersten, R., & Baker, S. (2000). What we know about effective instructional practices for English-language learners. *Exceptional Children, 66,* 454–470.

Goldstein, J. L., & Peters, M. E. (2014). Nativism or economic threat: Attitudes toward immigrants during the great recession. *International Interactions, 40,* 376–401.

González, N., Moll, L., & Amanti, C. (2005). *Funds of knowledge: Theorizing practices in households, communities, and classrooms.* New York, NY: Routledge.

Good, M. E., Masewicz, S., & Vogel, L. (2010). Latino English language learners: Bridging achievement and cultural gaps between schools and families. *Journal of Latinos and Education, 9,* 321–339.

Gutierrez, K. D., & García, E. E. (1989). Academic literacy in linguistic minority children: The connections between language, cognition and culture. *Early Child Development and Care, 51,* 109–126.

Haas, E., & Huang, M. (2010). *Where do English language learner students go to school? Student distribution by language proficiency in Arizona* (REL Technical Brief, REL 2010–No. 015). Washington, DC: U.S. Department of Education. Retrieved from http://ies.ed.gov/ncee/edlabs

Hammer, C. S., Hoff, E., Uchikoshi, Y., Gillanders, C., Castro, D. C., & Sandilos, L. E. (2014). The language and literacy development of young dual language learners: A critical review. *Early Childhood Research Quarterly, 29,* 715–733.

Hankivsky, O. (2011). *Health inequities in Canada: Intersectional frameworks and practices.* Vancouver, British Columbia, Canada: University of British Columbia Press.

Hankivsky, O., & Cormier, R. (2011). Intersectionality and public policy: Some lessons from existing models. *Political Research Quarterly, 64,* 217–229.

Heilig, J. V., & Holme, J. J. (2013). Nearly 50 years post-Jim Crow: Persisting and expansive school segregation for African American, Latina/o, and ELL students in Texas. *Education and Urban Society, 45,* 609–632.

Hopkins, M. (2012). Arizona's teacher policies and their relationship with English learner instructional practice. *Language Policy, 11*(1), 81–99.

Jiménez-Castellanos, O. (2010). Relationship between educational resources and school achievement: A mixed method intra-district analysis. *Urban Review, 42,* 351–371.

Jiménez-Castellanos, O., Cisneros, J., & Gómez, L. (2013). Applying racist nativism theory to K-12 education policy in Arizona, 2000–2010. *Aztlan, 38,* 175–190.

Jiménez-Castellanos, O., Combs, M. C., Martinez, D., & Gomez, L. (2014). *English language learners: What's at stake for Arizona?* Tempe: Morrison Institute for Public Policy at Arizona State University.

Jiménez-Castellanos, O., & Topper, A. M. (2012). The cost of providing an adequate education to English language learners: A review of the literature. *Review of Educational Research, 82,* 179–232.

Jiménez-Silva, M., Gomez, L., & Cisneros, J. (2014). Examining Arizona's policy response post Flores v. Arizona in educating K–12 English language learners. *Journal of Latinos and Education, 13,* 181–195.

Kena, G., Hussar, W., McFarland, J., de Brey, C., Musu-Gillette, L., Wang, X., . . . Dunlop Velez, E. (2016). *The condition of education 2016* (NCES 2016-144). Washington, DC: National Center for Education Statistics. Retrieved from http://nces.ed.gov/pubsearch

Kim, W. G., & García, S. B. (2014). Long-term English language learners' perceptions of their language and academic learning experiences. *Remedial and Special Education, 35,* 300–312.

Lillie, K. E., Markos, A., Arias, M. B., & Wiley, T. G. (2012). Separate and not equal: The implementation of structured English immersion in Arizona's classrooms. *Teachers College Record, 114*(9), 1–33.

Mahoney, K., MacSwan, J., & Thompson, M. (2005). The condition of English language learners in Arizona: 2004. In D. García, & A. Molnar (Eds.), *The condition of PreK-12 education in Arizona, 2005* (pp. 1–24). Tempe: Education Policy Research Laboratory, Arizona State University.

Mayda, A. M. (2006). Who is against immigration? A cross-country investigation of individual attitudes toward immigrants. *Review of Economics and Statistics, 88,* 510–530.

McCall, L. (2005). The complexity of intersectionality. *Signs, 30,* 1771–1800.

Menken, K., Kleyn, T., & Chae, N. (2007). *Meeting the needs of long-term English language learners in high school.* New York, NY: Research Institute for the Study of Language in an Urban Society.

Moll, L. (2002). The concept of educational sovereignty. *University of Pennsylvania Graduate School of Education Perspectives on Urban Education, 1*(2), 1–11.

National Education Association. (2008). *English language learners face unique challenges.* Washington, DC: Author. Retrieved from www.nea.org/assets/docs/mf_PB05_ELL.pdf

No Child Left Behind Act of 2001, Pub. L. No. 107-110, § 115, Stat. 1425 (2002).

Norton, B., & Toohey, K. (2001). Changing perspectives on good language learners. *TESOL Quarterly, 35,* 307–322.

Ontario Human Rights Commission. (2001). *An intersectional approach to discrimination: Addressing multiple grounds in human rights claims.* Toronto, Ontario, Canada: Author.

Orfield, G., & Lee, C. (2005). *Why segregation matters: Poverty and educational inequality.* Los Angeles, CA: Civil Rights Project/Proyecto Derechos Civiles.

Ortega, L. (2013). SLA for the 21st century: Disciplinary progress, transdisciplinary relevance, and the bi/multilingual turn. *Language Learning, 63*(1), 1–24. doi:10.1111/j.1467-9922.2012.00735.x/full

Ortega, L. (2014). Ways forward for a bi/multilingual turn in SLA. In S. May (Ed.), *The multilingual turn: Implications for SLA, TESOL and bilingual education* (pp. 32–53). New York, NY: Routledge.

Peirce, B. N. (1995). Social identity, investment, and language learning. *TESOL Quarterly, 29,* 9–31.

Perea, J. F. (1997). The Black/White binary paradigm of race: The "normal science" of American racial thought. *California Law Review, 85,* 1213–1258.

Powers, J. M. (2014). From segregation to school finance the legal context for language rights in the United States. *Review of Research in Education, 38,* 81–105.

Powers, J. M., & Williams, T. R. (2013). State of outrage: Immigrant-related legislation and education in Arizona. *Association of Mexican American Educators Journal, 6*(2), 13–21.

Rasco, C. H. (1994). *Schools as neighborhood service centers: Summary of the talking points of Carol H. Rasco, Assistant to the President for Domestic Policy.* Washington, DC: Domestic Policy Council.

Riley, R. W. (1994). Improving America's schools act and elementary and secondary education reform. *Journal of Law & Education, 24,* 513–566.

Rios-Aguilar, C., & Gándara, P. (2012). Horne v. Flores and the future of language policy. *Teachers College Record, 114*(9), 1–13.

Rios-Aguilar, C., González-Canche, M., & Moll, L. C. (2010a). *A study of Arizona's teachers of English language learners.* Los Angeles, CA: Civil Rights Project/Proyecto Derechos Civiles.

Rios-Aguilar, C., González-Canche, M., & Moll, L. C. (2010b). *Implementing structured English immersion in Arizona: Benefits, costs, challenges, and opportunities.* Los Angeles, CA: Civil Rights Project/Proyecto Derechos Civiles.

Rogoff, B. (2003). *The cultural nature of human development.* Oxford, England: Oxford University Press.

Rolstad, K., Mahoney, K., & Glass, G. V. (2005). The big picture: A meta-analysis of program effectiveness research on English language learners. *Educational Policy, 19*, 572–594.

Rudo, Z. H. (2001). Corrective action in low-performing schools and school districts. *Education Policy Analysis Archives, 13*(48). Retrieved from http://epaa.asu.edu/ojs/article/view/153

Ruiz, N. T. (1995). The Social Construction of Ability and Disability II. Optimal and at-risk lessons in a bilingual special education classroom. *Journal of Learning Disabilities, 28*, 491–502.

Ruiz-Soto, A. G., Hooker, S., & Batalova, J. (2015). *Top languages spoken by English language learners nationally and by state.* Washington, DC: Migration Policy Institute.

Siim, B. (2013). Intersections of gender and diversity: A European perspective. In B. Siim (Eds.), *Negotiating gender and diversity in an emergent European public sphere.* Basingstoke, England: Palgrave Macmillan.

Smith, M. S., & O'Day, J. (1991). Educational equality: 1966 and now. In D. A. Verstegen, & J. G. Ward (Eds.), *Spheres of justice in education* (pp. 53–100). New York, NY: Harper Collins.

Snow, C. E., & Van Hemel, S. B. (Eds.). (2008). *Early childhood Assessment: Why, what, and how.* Washington, DC: National Academies Press.

Soto, M. (2011). *The effects of teaching the academic language of language arts to secondary long-term English learners* (Unpublished dissertation). University of Texas Rio Grande Valley, Brownsville, TX.

U.S. National Education Goals Panel. (1995). *The national education goals report: Executive summary: Improving education through family-school-community partnerships.* Washington, DC: Author.

Valdés, G. (2001). *Learning and not learning English: Latino students in American schools* (Multicultural Education Series). New York, NY: Teachers College Press.

Varcoe, C., Pauly, B., & Laliberté, S. (2011). *Intersectionality, justice and influencing policy. Health inequities in Canada: Intersectional frameworks and practices.* Vancouver, British Columbia, Canada: University of British Columbia Press.

Weber, D. J. (2003). *Foreigners in their native land: Historical roots of the Mexican Americans.* Albuquerque: University of New Mexico Press.

Williams, C. (2014). *Chaos for dual language learners: An examination of state policies for exiting children from language services in the pre-K-3rd grades.* Washington, DC: New America Foundation.

Wright, W. E. (2015). *Foundations for teaching English language learners: Research, theory, and practice.* Philadelphia, PA: Caslon.

Zong, J., & Batalova, J. (2015). *Indian immigrants in the United States.* Washington, DC: Migration Policy Institute.

Chapter 19

Classroom Conversations in the Study of Race and the Disruption of Social and Educational Inequalities: A Review of Research

AYANNA F. BROWN
Elmhurst College

DAVID BLOOME
The Ohio State University

JEROME E. MORRIS
University of Missouri-St. Louis

STEPHANIE POWER-CARTER
Indiana University, Bloomington

ARLETTE I. WILLIS
University of Illinois at Urbana-Champaign

This review of research examines classroom conversations about race with a theoretical framing oriented to understanding how such conversations may disrupt social and educational inequalities. The review covers research on how classroom conversations on race contribute to students' and educators' understandings of a racialized society, their construction of and reflection on relationships among students, as well as to their learning of academic content knowledge. The review considers research across grades P–12, as well as conversations in teacher education, with a specific focus on the U.S. context. Limiting the review to the U.S. context is done not to obfuscate conceptions of race and inequalities globally, but to elucidate how race becomes manifested in unique ways in the United States—often positioning African Americans and Blackness as the "fundamental other." The review offers a social, historical, and political discussion that contextualizes how classroom conversations, and their omission, are not conversations only relegated to the classroom, but are part of a larger dialogue within the broader society.

It is not really a "Negro revolution" that is upsetting the country. What is upsetting the country is a sense of its own identity. If, for example, one managed to change the curriculum in all the schools so that

Review of Research in Education
March 2017, Vol. 41, pp. 453–476
DOI: 10.3102/0091732X16687522
© 2017 AERA. http://rre.aera.net

Negroes learned more about themselves and their real contributions to this culture, you would be liberating not only Negroes, you'd be liberating White people who know nothing about their own history. And the reason is that if you are compelled to lie about one aspect of anybody's history, you must lie about it all. If you have to lie about my real role here, if you have to pretend that I hoed all that cotton just because I loved you, then you have done something to yourself. You are mad.

—Baldwin (1963/2008, p. 17)

Race is not a biological category but a social construction that is given meaning and significance in specific historical, political, and social contexts (Appiah, 1989; Omi & Winant, 1994) with long-term and enduring effects on people, communities, and even research. Language plays a crucial role in the social construction of race. As people interact with each other, the language they use in how they respond to one another reflects and refracts (cf. Volosinov, 1929/1973) extant conceptions of race and race relations. Language also signals meaning explicitly through the denotational meanings of words and implicitly through indexicals (implicit references to social, cultural, and historical contexts), language choice (e.g., register, language variation, key), and other subtle but powerful ways that often lay just below consciousness (Gumperz, 1986). Thus, the social construction of race through people's use of language occurs both when it is an explicit topic of conversation and when it is not. We also recognize the problematic nature of the word "race" because despite the present acceptance that [it] is a social construction, the term was used for political gain and economic advantaging that traverses the Black–White binary (Lewis, 2003).

Given the social, historical, and political contexts of race in the United States, an argument can be made that race is ubiquitous in conversations within and across social institutions, including classrooms. One of the reasons for specific attention to classroom conversations and race is the unfulfilled promise placed in public education in the United States for promoting equality, equity, social mobility, and a democratic society (cf. Kluger, 1985; Spring, 1991). Yet, it also must be recognized that historical analysis questions whether U.S. law and legal processes and educational policies and practices ever intended to devote an equitable opportunity for educating and liberating all of its citizens because of race (cf. Ladson-Billings, 2004). A key question to ask, therefore, is, "How might classroom conversations on race disrupt the inequalities that students suffer both within the classroom and outside it, both in their present and in their future?"

Despite the importance of the question above, there has been relatively little research in P–12 classrooms on classroom conversations, race, and the disruption of inequality (although there has been a plethora of research on race in classroom education, per se). Some researchers have suggested that teachers and students in the United States rarely explicitly discuss or confront issues of race in their classrooms or curricular discussions (Pollock, 2004; Schultz, Buck, & Niesz, 2000) and when they do, as noted by Bolgatz (2006) it is usually "within carefully controlled boundaries of scope and sequence . . . neatly package and limit the treatment of race into confined arenas" (p. 260). Why are there so few discussions of race in classrooms given the ubiquitous presence of race in all aspects of life in the United States? Is the absence of discussions of race in classrooms a form of silencing, thereby, maintaining the illusions Baldwin (1963/2008) referred to in the quotation at the beginning of this chapter? How might conversations on race in schools disrupt the inequalities manifest in and through education policies, structures, and practices?

We have organized this review to, first, address the question how has (and how might) classroom conversations on race be researched? Thus, we offer a social, historical, and political discussion that contextualizes how classroom conversations, and their omission, are not conversations only relegated to the classroom, but are part of a larger dialogue within the broader society. We then discuss the logic-of-inquiry used in research on classroom conversations on race to understand the nature of the knowledge such studies yield. The two sections following—(a) the nature of classroom conversations on race and teacher education and (b) classroom conversations on race—address a second question: What is known about how classroom conversations on race might disrupt inequalities?

Methodologically, several considerations have guided our approach. First, given the historic nature of *Brown v. Board of Education* in 1954, we have chosen to use this court case as a starting point to begin examining evidences of how researchers pursued inquiry into the pedagogical relationships between teachers and discussions of race in classroom settings. Another important consideration has been to examine studies where there were classroom conversations being presented by ways of audio recordings, video recordings, and forms of conversational analysis, as this approach aligns directly with our premise for the review. We have used several research databases such as ERIC, EBSCO, and Google Scholar. Our search terminologies included (a) conversations of race in classrooms, (b) race talk in classrooms, and (c) discussions of race. Using 1954 to 2016 as the time frame, the first publication that engaged in discussions of race in a university classroom settings was found in 1992 (Tatum, 1992). As discussed later, we believe there is tremendous opportunity to examine "race talk" in schools that analyzes both structures and contexts, but also to consider how are students and teachers engaging in conversations about race to develop their knowledge about the world in which we live and the critiques necessary to disrupt the inequalities within it.

SOCIOHISTORICAL AND POLITICAL CONTEXTS OF CLASSROOM CONVERSATIONS ON RACE

Heuristically, classroom conversations on race take place within both local and macro contexts. Here, we discuss the broader sociohistorical and political contexts acknowledging that particular local contexts may mediate how these broader contexts frame classroom conversations on race (Lewis, 2003).

During the first century of the United States, the educational climate for enslaved African people and colonized indigenous people of North America was oriented to

(a) deny schooling for Black people (Anderson, 1988) and (b) "civilize" Native American people through forced assimilation including language, Christianization, militarized social practices, and industrial training for servitude. Essentially, the purpose of schooling was to "kill the Indian [to] save the man" (Adams, 1995). During the 19th century, national identity politics dominated by scientific racism appropriated Christianity to justify and defend racial hierarchy (Goldberg, 2009). With the end of chattel slavery by 1865, the concept of race framed as a White/Black dichotomy provided European Americans with a new way to identify and to distinguish themselves from the formerly enslaved (Guèye, 2006). This new identification also privileged and normalized White experiences and knowledge, while marginalizing and "othering" those who were not White. Together, the *Three-Fifths Compromise* of the U.S. *Constitution*, the emergence of Jim Crow laws after Reconstruction, and the *Plessy v. Ferguson* decision of 1896 that established the doctrine of "separate but equal" codified a hierarchical relationship (Bell, 1992) and further concretized the role of race in shaping U.S. society. Part of what this historical context produced was a contested definition of personhood for people of African heritage in the United States. As sociolinguists have shown, whenever people use language they are always communicating who they are in relation to each other (Blommaert, 2015) and part of that is their personhood.

The passage of the historic 1954 Supreme Court decision in the United States, *Brown v. Board of Education*, legally inscribed *equality* as the federal law in public education and engendered a sense of renewed hope for millions of Black and Brown people that the "color line" might be removed. However, as Ladson-Billings (2004) reminds us, the Brown decision was in part a forced choice because of the political context of both the growing number of cases against segregation and silence from the federal government on its beliefs about education and civil rights. Then, it was hoped, children and educators from all backgrounds would truly experience democracy and have numerous opportunities to learn and talk across races (Allen, 2004). However, the passage of *Brown II* and its "all deliberate speed" requirement gave Whites who resisted *Brown* the opportunity to delay and deflect its implementation (Ogletree, 2004) thereby making White students become the primary beneficiaries of the education system (Bell, 1992; Morris, 2003). This active resistance to public school desegregation reified the racial hierarchy and the culture of racism. If *Brown v. Board of Education* had been equitably implemented, ideally, it would have created opportunities for interracial dialogue among students and educators. However, the resistance of White people to Brown resulted in the dismantling of public school desegregation (Boger & Orfield, 2005) and the displacement, demotion, and dismissal of Black teachers (Etheridge, 1979; Haney, 1978) from greater participation in such dialogues (Foster, 1998). Part of the challenge with regard to classroom conversations on race is that if the teaching profession is primarily composed of middle-class White women, their experiences and culture are privileged. It raises the question of who can engage and/or facilitate conversations on race and in which classrooms can such conversations occur. An argument can be made that a paucity of such conversation has further disenfranchised non-Whites in our educational system and schools remain primarily segregated and resegregated (Donnor & Dixson, 2013).

Before *Brown* and afterward, public schools actively and passively perpetuated constructions of race through curriculum and pedagogy that relegated the culture and experiences of various racial groups to the margins (DuBois, 1903/1994; Hartlep, 2013; Ladson-Billings, 2000; Woodson, 1933). In so doing, school leaders contributed to the promulgation of Whiteness (the taken-for-granted and hegemonic privileging of White people, their cultural capital, their history, their languages, etc.). Part of what makes Whiteness pernicious is that it is mostly unnamed and invisible and thus becomes the context for interpretation and action as if it were the only conceivable framework. Attempts to employ a different knowledge base, set of experiences, way of talking, and using language, all have the potential of marginalizing the person and labeling him or her as irrational.

Recently, there have been multiple key events in the United States that have made discussions of race more visible in mainstream and social media. Here, we only name a few. Perhaps most notably, the presidential candidacy of Barack Obama in 2007 promulgated dialogues about race and racial identity on national and international levels (Walters, 2007; Wise, 2009). Obama's candidacy for president unleashed articulated and visual representations of racism. Ironically, these representations of race were juxtaposed with a positivistic sociopolitical analysis of postracialism in which the latter seemed to neutralize discussions of race (Morris & Woodruff, 2015).

In 1998, White assailants, used a pickup truck, dragging James Byrd, an African American man, three miles in Jasper, Texas, resulting in his death. What is notable about this case is that in 2008, Oprah Winfrey began a nationally broadcast conversation about the case and whether things had changed in Jasper 10 years after the event. A claim can be made that the conversation initiated by Winfrey was landmark because she broadcasted a discussion of race to a racially diverse public (Jensen, 2003). Tragically, other African Americans have since been killed because they were Black, including deaths by police officers. Whether the murders received media attention or not, the events have sparked an effort led primarily by Black women to name the policing of Black lives as a life and death under siege (Black Lives Matter, 2016). Public media forums like Twitter, Facebook, Instagram, and Snapchat enable cross-racial public discussions of race, unsanctioned and unregulated, sparking national and international protests and awakening national consciousness on race. It was within this context that the Black Lives Matters movement began. (The counterresponse to the Black Lives Matter movement, All Lives Matter, disregards the caste-like status and unprotected lives of Black people).

Part of the recent broader context also includes the passage of laws. In 2011, Alabama passed laws requiring police officers and school officials to arrest and report, respectively, any person who could not provide legal documentation of their citizenship status (Southern Poverty Law Center, 2016). Arizona also passed laws that attacked ethnic studies curricula in high schools and claimed that such curricula were anti-American and unpatriotic and that discussions of race in schools are dangerous and generated unhappiness among minority students (Horne, 2007).

In 2010, Andrew Breitbart, a White conservative journalist, manipulated a video presentation of Shirley Sherrod, the U.S. Department of Agriculture administrator, and accused her of being a racist because of her reflective storytelling at a National Association for the Advancement of Colored People banquet. She told of her own evolutionary understanding of racism as she worked to help a White farming family retain their farm. Sherrod's narrative became a target for *reverse* racism in a *new postracial era* (Stolberg, Dewan, & Stelter, 2010). For the purposes of this review, part of what remains remarkable about Sherrod's situation is that although her storytelling was about hope and healing, she was punished for talking about race.

Shirley Sherrod's case, the laws against ethnic studies, and the pushback against Black Lives Matter reveal the difficulty for people of color to tell their stories, to have ownership of them, and to have their stories heard. Each of these events above and others reflect a national context of vacillation of racial discourse; defining the U.S. society as racialized yet devoid of accountability to question and transform cultural practices that promulgate racial inequalities. It is within these contexts that classroom conversations on race occur; and thus it is important that both the study of such conversations and reviews of research on those conversations need to account for these contexts. It is perhaps ironic that while there is vigorous and pervasive discussion of race in the popular culture, the mainstream media, and on social media, such discussions are rare as are education research studies.

THE LOGICS-OF-INQUIRY OF RESEARCH ON CLASSROOM CONVERSATIONS ON RACE

Researchers deploy diverse theoretical frameworks, methodologies, and research designs to define and make sense of classroom conversations on race (hereafter, logic-of-inquiry). Explicitly and implicitly, the logic-of-inquiry of a study defines what counts as knowledge, how knowledge can be constructed, how learning, personhood, and inequities are defined both socially and educationally, and how the study of classroom conversations on race are contextualized. The logic-of-inquiry of a study is not neutral with regard to epistemology, ontology, and ideology.

In the studies we review, many established an a priori theoretical footing with predetermined characteristics of what counted as a "good" classroom conversation on race. Although the theoretical footing varies across studies—including critical race theory, Whiteness studies, critical discourse analysis, critical ethnography, and critical theory more generally—the syntax of the logic-of-inquiry is similar (and is illustrated in Figure 1).

Since the theoretical footing predetermines what characteristics are used as criteria for examining and evaluating a classroom conversation on race, the logic-of-inquiry in such studies can be called "top-down." For example, in Rogers and Mosley's (2006) study of a second-grade classroom, the researchers (which included the classroom teacher) construct three primary categories: noticing race, enacting White privilege, and disrupting White privilege. They look for patterns across guided reading lessons in which the three primary categories are evident. Their analysis provides examples of each of the three categories and also showed what they call "hybrid discourses of

FIGURE 1
Top Down Logic-of-Inquiry

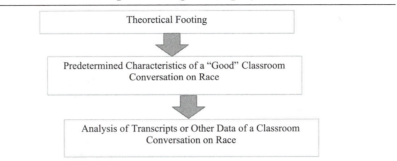

Theoretical Footing

Predetermined Characteristics of a "Good" Classroom
Conversation on Race

Analysis of Transcripts or Other Data of a Classroom
Conversation on Race

FIGURE 2
An A Priori Theoretical Syntax

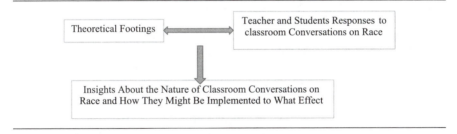

Theoretical Footings

Teacher and Students Responses to
classroom Conversations on Race

Insights About the Nature of Classroom Conversations on
Race and How They Might Be Implemented to What Effect

Whiteness enacted and Whiteness disrupted, sometimes within the same book and within the same day" (Rogers & Mosley, 2006, p. 473).

The strength of a top-down logic-of-inquiry is defining its epistemology and ideology through the theoretical framing it employs. Its weakness is lacking the mechanisms for describing those aspects of classroom conversations on race that do not neatly fit within the chosen theoretical framing, emic perspectives, situated meaning, and the retheorizing of extant theoretical frames.

One variation of the top-down logic-of-inquiry we describe above focuses on how students and teachers experience and respond to classroom conversations on race (see Figure 2).

Methodologically, studies employing such a logic-of-inquiry often involve interviews and conversations with teachers and students. For example, Quay (2014) interviews professors who were attendees at a conference focused on addressing racial issues in higher education and who regularly orchestrate conversations in their classrooms on race. The interviews focus on what strategies they use to engage their students in what the professors view as productive conversations on race. Quay uses thematic analysis of the collected data to identify findings about the form of the class (e.g., lecture vs. discussion), the content of the course (the readings used), the place

FIGURE 3
Grounded Theoretical Constructs Logic-of-Inquiry

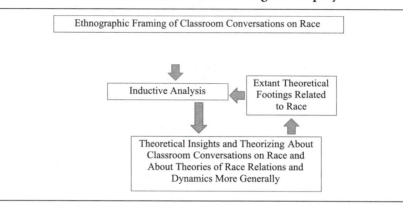

of student and professor reflection, debriefing with students, and other activities (e.g., service learning). While this resembles the top-down logic-of-inquiry discussed earlier, it conceptualizes students' reflections and responses as mediating how an a priori theoretical frame might drive the conduct of a classroom conversation on race. In brief, who the students are, their experiences, and the agency they take in reflecting on the conversations all need to be considered.

Research that employs an inductive perspective while informed by various theoretical footings, emphasizes a dialectical relationship between extant theories and the theoretical constructs derived from the inductive analysis of the conversations themselves. As such, it emphasizes the generation of grounded theoretical constructs regarding how classroom conversations on race might disrupt inequalities (see Figure 3).

Carter's (2007) research on silence is an example of this perspective. Using ethnographic perspectives, participant observation, and interviews with students that foregrounded their classroom experiences and their interpretations of what was happening in their classrooms, Carter reconceptualizes "silence." It is an active, agentive strategy the African American young women used in their predominately White high school literature class to establish solidarity among themselves, and to contest explicit and implicit racialized nature of their educational experience. Essential to this logic-of-inquiry is respect for the situated perspectives, voices, and insights of students and teachers as they experience instructional conversations on race. The logic-of-inquiry here affords the generation of new concepts and the reconceptualization of extant concepts, providing new ways of naming, describing, and interpreting what is happening in particular conversations about race in classrooms. Thomas (2015) illustrates this variation of logic-of-inquiry (see Figure 4).

Thomas (2015) asks three questions: (a) What are the teachers' linguistic strategies and tactics for handling race talk dilemmas that arise during the teaching of literature? (b) What challenges do teachers confront while attempting to navigate these

FIGURE 4
Situated Perspective Logic-of-Inquiry

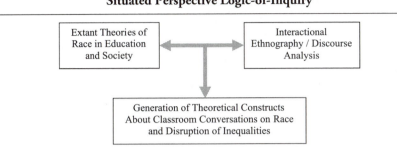

dilemmas? (c) How do they attempt to resolve the challenges? Using an interactional ethnographic approach that foregrounds attention to the use of language, Thomas provides descriptions of what happens in the conversations of two veteran English language arts teachers, one African American and one White. Thomas's interpretation of the data is informed by multiple theoretical perspectives including Black feminist theory, interactional sociolinguistics, discourse analysis, critical sociology of education, systemic functional linguistics, and critical race theory. These multiple perspectives foreground the complexity of engaging in conversations about race. Although the ways the teachers use language differs, both show adeptness and insight into how they orchestrate conversations about race matters. Both teachers value student perspectives and encourage responses while guiding students toward a shared ethical position. Nonetheless, in both classrooms, there is silence and evasion. The logic-of-inquiry Thomas employs allowed her to foreground complexity and ambiguity in the orchestration of the classroom conversations.

Chapman (2007) raises questions about the logic-of-inquiry underlying research on African American students in general that is pertinent to research on classroom conversations on race. She argues for foregrounding the inherent "messy, contradictory nature of human experiences and behaviors . . . [and] conflicting actions to present an overall picture of determination and agency" (p. 160). The issues Chapman raises can be interpreted as a concern for how personhood is implicitly defined through the logic-of-inquiry of a study. She cautions about the reification of people's lives as a consequence of the methodology employed and the need for researchers to be reflective about the consequences of their logic-of-inquiry.

Earlier, we noted that research on classroom conversations on race needs to be situated within sociohistorical and political contexts. One of the ways that research indexes sociohistorical and political contexts is through reflection on the epistemological and ontological nature of the study. Milner (2006) argues that "research ought to do more than merely tell us something or give us some information; it should be used to empower researchers and research participants to actually do something to improve circumstances and situations." (pp. 367–368). Building on the theorizing of Dillard (2006), Milner further argues for attending to spirituality in research involving the experiences and lives of African Americans. Milner focuses attention on the language of research and proposes an agenda pertinent to research on classroom conversations on race.

Dillard's ideas to rename, to recategorize and to reconceptualize how we use and construct language is, on some levels, liberating and can be connected to hooks's (1994) discussion of healing that takes place when dominant views and ideologies are critically examined, particularly among people of color who have been mistreated through educational research. Shahjahan (2005) declared that a goal of researchers should be "to heal . . . and to work towards equity and social justice for human beings and all creation" (p. 690). (Milner, 2006, pp. 369–370)

What is at issue in the calls by Chapman, Milner, Dillard, and others, is the importance for researchers to reflect on and interrogate the logic-of-inquiry in their studies, how it pushes back against Whiteness, acknowledges the ubiquity of race and racism in education and in the institution of research, defines personhood, and engages in the project of what Winn (2013) calls restorative education.

We would be remiss if we did not illuminate that within the logic-of-inquiry, there is also the researcher foregrounding their own racial identity as observer and in several cases, participant-observer. We find across the studies, the researcher provides a context for personhood noting that one's own racial identity is relevant to the field (Brown, 2013). In some cases, but not conclusively, the racial identities of the participants are emphasized beyond the demographic description in the methodology. This is most prevalent in research that situates racial theory(ies) as a framework for the study. Perhaps, the examination of discussions of race in school settings also includes the ways identity influences the theoretical footing.

THE LANGUAGING OF CLASSROOM CONVERSATIONS ON RACE

In this section, we frame the languaging of classroom conversations on race in three heuristic categories: (a) curricular, (b) discursive, and (c) and disruptive. By curricular, we mean the ways in which teachers explicitly plan for conversations through the instructional choices they make (e.g., what texts to use, what concepts to consider, what academic tasks to engage). Discursive, unlike curricular, relates to the uses of language that emerge during the conversations. Disruptive involves the use of critical moves (e.g., questioning, problematizing, use of counternarratives) away from dominant ideologies and coded language that works to maintain the status quo. Disruptive does not necessarily seek to create closure to complex ideas but may leave issues unresolved and open for more discussion. Disruptive also includes silence and the ways students and teachers utilize discourses to build community or to protect themselves.

The review of languaging classroom conversations on race here considers research across Grades P–12 (in the next section, we consider conversations on race in teacher education classes). While conversations on race outside of the classroom—in families, peer groups, and communities—influence racialization and conversations in the classroom (Lewis, 2003), we do not consider them here because of space limitations.

The review is limited to studies conducted in the United States because of its particular historical context including the enslavement of people of African heritage and the dismissal of the humanity and experiences of African, Native, Latina/os, and Asian Americans, while positioning African Americans as the "fundamental other" (Waters, 1999; West, 1993).

Discussions of Race as Curricular

Bloome, Power Carter, Morton Christian, Otto, and Shuart-Faris (2005) examine uses of language in a working-class community middle school, where an African American early career teacher invites seventh-grade students into discussions of race through the selection of literature as well as the questioning processes. The students discuss a poem that has features of African American language (AAL). The teacher initiates the classroom lesson in relatively traditional approach, using a teacher initiation, student response, and teacher evaluation participation structure. The discussion of race begins as the students consider the voice and perspective of the speaker in the poem. The teacher asks "Who is the speaker?" and "How do you know?" as a means to encourage the students to reflect on the relationship of language, identity, and race. As the instructional conversation continues, the topic shifts from claims and warrants about the meaning of the poem to what constitutes AAL speech patterns, to student narratives about their encounters with language variation, language attitudes, and race, to exploration of language, race, power, and notions of self in their own lives. The research suggests that it is not the surface-level participation structure itself that matters but rather incorporation of the students in problematizing taken-for-granted notions of race and language, the opportunity for them to share narratives of their own experience with race and language, and the use of knowledge and insight from the sociolinguistics of language variation to reflect on their own lives.

Where the teacher in the Bloome et al. (2005) study explicitly focuses on students' attention on the use of AAL in a poem, in classrooms studied by Rex (2006), the students' use of AAL brought race into classroom conversations. Using both ethnographic and discourse-analytic methods, Rex looks at how the teachers and students react to the use of AAL language. Mostly the responses either marginalize the students or discredits the intended social moves. Rex characterizes the students uses of AAL as cultural practices that the students brought into the classroom and raises questions about the degree to which classrooms can be inclusive if students' use of AAL (see Vetter, 2013, for a similar study of response to the use of AAL).

Dixson and Bloome (2007) provide another study regarding race and the use of AAL. The African American middle school language arts teacher of a predominantly African American classroom conducts a literature lesson and switches the register of the classroom talk to a conversational style that had some resemblances to the call and responses and sermonizing practices of Black churches. In so doing, she pulls the students into a series of narratives they tell about themselves that reinforce their social identities as academically oriented. Taken together, the Rex and Dixson and Bloome studies show how uses of and responses to AAL can either distance students from academic social identities or promote and include them in academic social identities.

Hollingsworth (2009) presents a case study of a fifth-grade teacher's exploration of race as an orchestrated attempt to protect herself from being perceived as racist. The teacher creates a multicultural unit to engage social issues with her students. However, in order to avoid possible discomforts with contemporary issues, the teacher structures text choice with historical frames of inequality including stereotypical positionings of victimization and heroism without contextualization or alternative framings. Discussions of race within this curricular frame function as a means to silence students' alternative frames of reference (cf. Fine, 1987). The students were not asked to and consequently, do not insert their own experiences into their readings about race and racism effectively foreclosing them from making connections and engaging in more transformative ways for thinking about race in everyday life.

As noted earlier, Carter (2007) makes a distinction among silence, silencing, and silenced. Silence and silencing are complex processes that are not necessarily mutually exclusive of each other. While silencing can be thought of as a process that contradicts evidence, ideologies, and experiences (Fine, 1987). Silence also can been thought of as one's response to silencing (Carter, 2007). Silenced can be thought of as submission to hegemonic processes, a response to silencing and/or a void or absence of voice. The distinctions among silence, silencing, and silenced provide a way to make visible students' sub rosa uptake on how race is formulated in classroom conversations on race where it may not be safe to publically contest those conceptions of race.

Bolgatz (2006, 2007) examines discussions of race at both the elementary and high school grades. At the elementary level, Bolgatz (2006) reports a study in a fifth-grade classroom in which the teacher chooses to study the Revolutionary War, a subject that might easily be packaged in romanticized notions of freedom and democracy centering Whiteness. However, the teacher presents the Revolutionary War through the experience of enslaved people and the fears of Southern Whites. While the teacher asks targeted comprehension questions to guide the reading process, students make "sophisticated connections," questioning the meaning of enslaved people carrying weapons to fight. Bolgatz's analysis focuses on how questioning and discussion build multidirectional lenses for discussion, for example, the students seek to juxtapose Southern Whites controlling Blacks' access to guns with colonists' desire for freedom from Britain. The researcher notes the complex interpretations the students construct through reading and, importantly during class time, the exchange of information and collaborative dialogue. Disruption functions to construct new opportunities for students to engage in conversations, in this case, that are initiated by the students, "going beyond factual understanding to make connections between ideas and events" (Bolgatz, 2006, p. 263).

At the secondary level, Bolgatz (2005) explores how structures and materials support student engagement, focusing on strategies and techniques employed by two teachers coteaching an interdisciplinary U.S. history and language arts class. Bolgatz

(2005) notes that the class structure utilizes a conversational approach that "freed students to interact" (p. 34). Significant in the study was the teachers' use of questioning to aggravate complacency rather than creating "neat" conclusions.

In the studies by Bolgatz, Bloome et al. and Hollingsworth (2009), race is made a curricular topic by how the teachers orchestrate classroom conversations. In each case, the instructional conversation provides opportunities for students to interrogate and problematize taken-for-granted concepts, to share narratives of their own experiences with race matters, and to connect those conversations with reflection on matters outside the classroom.

Discussions of Race as Discursive

In the previous section, the teachers deliberately selected instructional topics to disrupt hegemonic conceptions of race. In this section, we review studies that examine how uses of intertextuality, counternarratives, and critical discourse analysis destabilize dominant ideologies of race and their accompanying inequalities as well as studies reporting how the use of language stabilize dominant ideologies.

A study by Anagnostopoulos, Everett, and Carey (2013) concerns the reading of Harper Lee's *To Kill a Mockingbird* (1960), a canonical literary text used in a large number of high schools, often taught with a focus on morality and character development related to heroism and ethics. Anagnostopoulos et al. (2013), however, focus on the uses of language in class discussions that reveal White students' dysconciousness of race in a ninth-grade classroom. The authors argue that their findings reflect the discourse of the "new racism," a strategy of forgetting. We find this study of particular interest because it suggests that without discussions of race, students are invited to forget and then blame those victimized and minoritized by race for undermining racial harmony by remembering. In contrast to the White students, the Black students use language in ways that engage personhood in the literary text as well as in their present identities. As the classroom conversation evolves, it is not the literary text that is key but rather the students' uses of intertextuality in juxtaposiong race as represented in literature to race in contemporary political, familial, and communicative situations.

Pixley and VanDerPloeg (2000) present a case study of an online writing exchange between White private school students in Connecticut and African American, Puerto Rican, and Dominican public school students in New York, where the researchers were the classroom teachers, both of whom were White women. One of the explicit purposes of the online writing exchange was to build relationships across states and communities, deconstructing race, and stereotypes. In a writing exchange, one of the White students from the Connecticut school used discourses of fear and victimization in his writing to express why White people are afraid of Black people. As a result of receiving this writing, the students in the New York classroom engaged in discussions of racialization, historical framings of racism, and racialized privilege and constructed counternarratives. The discursive turns in the class dialogue elevated the discussion of race from the immediate context, the Connecticut letter, to a greater discussion about accountability and discomfort. Although the outcomes of such classroom conversations are complex, the White teachers (of minoritized students) report that "Today my students and I bury ourselves in silence. We wrap and wrap the silence around us, thick and White as cotton. Silence is safer than language. Silence allows us to ignore what we do not wish to see" (Pixley & VanDerPloeg, 2000, p. 284). That is, even in cases where students and teachers productively engage in classroom conversations constructing counternarratives and contesting White privilege, the affective nature of those conversations may be such that silence is preferred.

Similarly, Schaffer and Skinner (2009) report a 2-year ethnographic study among fourth-grade students that shows the difficulties of overcoming "colorblind" ideologies in classroom conversations on race and students' use of language to constrain efforts to have such conversations. The study describes the school as a "model elementary school," rich with programs and curriculum that explore diversity. The teachers in the study employ lessons that explore inequality, difference, and include students studying and sharing their cultural identities. However, racial boundaries enact forms of resistance to discussing race were equally present. This resistance manifests itself in social events, unregulated by teacher control or school curriculum (e.g., recess, lunch, break time). Discussions of race among students worked to "reclaim racial stereotypes and slurs" and evoked students' self-proclamations of being "cultural experts" among peers. The study reports that the White students adopted "colorblind" stances and placed judgments on discussions of race as "rude" and "inappropriate" (p. 282). One White student explains the racial tension at the schools as "Not a lot. Just some . . . It's mostly the black people who start those conversations. Like I don't really know why, but they do" (p. 283). Uses of coded language as pseudonyms for race function to serve as insults as well as bravado for the students. Unresolved discourses like "acting White" or "acting Black" remain active alongside pop culture terms like *bling bling* or "Eminem wannabe" to establish racial group memberships.

Discussions of Race as Disruptive

Brown (2010) reports a yearlong ethnographic study examining an African American history course of 14 African American students taught by an African American teacher. Revealing one of the ways in which race is implicated in classroom conversations were a series of lessons in which the students are asked rap songs about "Black History." Brown describes the lesson as culturally misaligned with the students' membership in hip-hop culture and their understanding of authentic voice, defined in hip-hop with bravado and resistance to the status quo. That is, while the teacher believes the lesson indexes cultural alignment, the students viewed the task as asking them to be inauthentic and superficial. Throughout the week of in-class writing, students used nonverbal cues, silence, and attempts to conference with the teacher to express their disapproval of the Black History rap assignment. As Collins (1990) writes,

Oppressed groups are frequently placed in the situation of being listened to only if we frame our ideas in the language that is familiar to and comfortable for a dominant group. This requirement often changes the meanings of our ideas and works to elevate the ideas of the dominant group. (p. xiii)

The impasse fueled by resistance, opposition, and silence is broken by one student's request, "Can I just write a paper?" The analysis of the classroom interactions over several days leading to this one request reveal that despite the course and teacher's commitment to discussions of race and racism, the context for writing was framed in terms of the teacher's representation of Black history and culture, eschewing the students' experiences outside the classroom. Students' initiation of topics like violence in their community, drugs, and the government's role in crime are viewed as inappropriate. The student's request to write a paper, an approved product to display academic knowledge, reflects an unwillingness to employ hip-hop language and culture, an urban Black cultural art form, to produce an academic rendering. In brief, while the students' willingness to engage in academic work functions respectfully, they are not willing to erase Black culture, language, and their experiences with race to write what the teacher calls "raps," discursively reconstitute as "poems." Part of what is suggested here is that the languaging of classroom conversations on race that disrupt inequalities does not ipso facto mean bringing conversational styles from outside the classroom into the classroom. Any language practice exists and is authentically meaningful within a field (cf. Bourdieu, 1977). In this case, pulling the language practice out of its field made it, and those engaged, inauthentic—threatening their racial and cultural identities both in and outside of the classroom.

Copenhaver-Johnson (2000) explores the omnipresence of Whiteness in the imaginations of students in a K–2 classroom. In brief, the students' responses to children's literature reflects the predominance of Whiteness, even in their imaginary characters. As students engage in reading many different genres, the students elucidate racial meanings for texts. Students openly discuss the unfairness of "White-only" drinking fountains reported in one of the books they read. But the findings are complex as later students express the idea that the angels in heaven as Black and White but sit on segregated clouds. The African American children are able to discuss and name race in ways that demonstrate a level of understanding, unlike their White peers.

Sassi and Thomas (2008) focus on the role of the teacher in classroom conversation on race with particular focus on privilege and race in a ninth-grade classroom. Although there is student diversity, there is also student self-segregation. While segregation practices among students in school are not unusual (Tatum, 1997), students' awareness of their privileged positions within these segregation patterns belie their expressed idealism about equality. The ongoing racial tensions in the class appear agitated by reading texts that decentralize Whiteness and profile the voices of historically oppressed communities, which created social interaction patterns that encouraged the teacher to dig more deeply into those texts. Nonetheless, despite the teacher's efforts, several White male students assert the benefits of slavery for African Americans. While many teachers might consider strategies for "moving on" or working toward a more harmonious classroom community, this teacher takes another position toward discussions of race, disrupting the need to resolve the tensions with silence. What Sassi and Thomas (2008) demonstrate is that disruption to "colormuting" in classroom conversations on race is not easy, are often complex, and do not necessarily entail closure or completeness.

CLASSROOM DISCUSSIONS OF RACE IN PRESERVICE TEACHER EDUCATION CLASSROOMS

If teachers and students are to engage in classroom conversations on race in ways that disrupt inequalities, teacher education would seem to be a promising location for promoting doing so. The assumption is that teacher education can provide opportunities for teachers to learn how to orchestrate classroom conversations on race that disrupt inequalities in their particular classrooms. Given teacher education's rich history of engaging issues of diversity as well as racial issues, and the large corpus of studies on preparing preservice teachers for multicultural/multiethnic, underserved, minoritized, and racial diversity, one might expect an equally robust set of research studies; this is not the case.

A review of the extant literature from 1950 to 2016 yields few research articles on university/college classroom discussions of race. Overwhelmingly, those studies focus on White preservice teachers, while there is limited research that investigates discussions of race among minoritized preservice teachers (e.g., Haddix, 2010; Irizarry, 2011).

In many ways, preservice teacher education classrooms are similar to P–12 classrooms: a large number of students and one teacher, a curriculum prescribed mostly by government agencies, and an evaluation scheme based on acquisition of predetermined learning. What is different is that preservice teachers are predominately English-dominant, middle-class, and White. In addition, what they learn is mediated by their experiences in their internship experiences in schools (which can offer a different orientation to race than their teacher education classes). Furthermore, preservice teacher educators have chosen both their field and their educational institution and can be viewed as consumers who, if they are unhappy, take their "business" elsewhere. Similarities and differences notwithstanding, there is little reason to believe that preservice teachers have had substantive conversations in classrooms on race prior to entering their teacher education programs, especially given the research on how rare such discussions are in P–12 education.

Much of the research on classroom conversations on race in preservice teacher education classrooms references Tatum's (1992, 1994, 1997, 2000) scholarship on classroom conversations on race in university classrooms in general. Tatum's scholarship is a narrative of her experiences teaching a course on the psychology of racism and is also based on her students' writings and sidebar conversations. Tatum (1992) offers university instructors four guidelines:

1. The creation of a safe classroom atmosphere by establishing clear guidelines for discussion
2. The creation of opportunities for self-generated knowledge
3. The provision of an appropriate developmental model that students can use as a framework for understanding their own process
4. The exploration of strategies to empower students as change agents

Although Tatum's research is not specific to teacher education, in the studies we reviewed on classroom conversations on race in teacher education, the findings replicate Tatum's findings.

Consider McIntyre's (1997) oft-cited study that draws on theories of antiracism, Freireian pedagogy, and multiculturalism. In her participatory action research study, the participants are 13 English-dominant, female, upper-middle to middle-class White, undergraduate preservice teachers. Her goal was to

examine what it means to have a White identity, (2) discover ways of making meaning about Whiteness and thinking critically about race and racism, and (3) recognize how our White racial identity and the system of Whiteness are implicated in the formulation of educational practices, thereby fostering the development of individual transformation, collective transformation, or both. (p. 21)

The participants are coresearchers as they also explored the interview data transcripts and did audit and member checks. McIntyre (1997) collects data on eight group sessions that she held with preservice teachers to deconstruct Whiteness. The purposes of the group sessions were (a) to engage the participants in dialectical consciousness-raising experiences around issues of White racial identity and Whiteness; (b) to provide an opportunity for participants to locate themselves within the larger educational arena as White female student teachers, thinking critically about educational practice in relation to their own identities and White teachers; and (c) to make explicit the need for examining Whiteness and how as White teachers, they can be committed to a process of teaching and learning that is antiracist and transformative in nature. McIntyre (1997) reveals a range of responses from her participants regarding their evolving understanding of Whiteness "Whites as living a fairy tale, White power and privilege, We're good, they're bad, and don't blame us, Good Whites versus Bad Whites, White skin color as a negative connotation" (pp. 80–116). The researcher and the participants are often conflicted about their beliefs and understanding of Whiteness (identity and racism) in U.S. society. McIntyre (1997) collapses these general ideas into three broad categories: White Talk, Constructions of Whiteness, and Teacher Image. Among her key findings is a definition of *White Talk* as "talking uncritically with/to other Whites, all the while resisting critique and massaging each other's racist attitudes, beliefs, and actions" (pp. 45–46). Furthermore, McIntyre (1997) characterizes White Talk as "derailing the conversation, evading questions, dismissing counterarguments, withdrawing from the discussion, remaining silent, interrupting speakers and topics, and colluding with each other in creating a 'culture of niceness' that made it very difficult to 'read the White world'" (p. 46).

Marx and Pennington's (2003) cross-case study is methodologically more typical of research on classroom conversations on race in preservice teacher education. They use qualitative ethnographic techniques (field notes, interviews, observations) to craft individual case studies of White preservice teachers addressing race, racism, and Whiteness. The purpose of the study was "to bring up the topic of Whiteness with three White preservice teachers completing their field experience semester in the community where I taught for 13 years" (p. 96). Using a narrative format, Pennington reports that White preservice teachers appeared eager to talk about antiracism, race, and racism; however, they were less comfortable confronting their Whiteness and White hegemony.

Similar findings come from studies by Trainor (2005), Haviland (2008), and Seidl (2007). In conversations on race, White preservice teachers tend to avoid and distance themselves from uncomfortable topics about race, White privilege, and Whiteness. Relatedly, Case and Hemmings' (2005) study examines the importance of creating a safe space for White preservice teachers to engage conversations on race and the disruption of inequalities. Beyond the four studies referenced in this paragraph, we often found that researchers' discussions of the role of emotions during conversations/discussions about racial issues tended to supersede the actual data presented about classroom discussions of antiracism, race, and racism. The extant research is flush with articulations of English-dominant, female, upper-middle-class, White preservice teachers' emotional states, but limited articulation of the actual classroom discussions of race.

In many of the studies we have reviewed, the inequalities that were intended to be disrupted through classroom conversations on race in preservice teacher education classrooms were not articulated. However, in the few they are clearly expressed. Tatum (1992), for example, links classroom conversations on race to racial identity development (both for White and African American students), the improvement of interracial dialogue and interaction, the creation of a safe classroom atmosphere, and empowering students as change agents. Examples of studies that include the experiences and feelings of minoritized preservice teachers are rare and have been conducted by scholars of color. Following Tatum's article about race among undergraduates, Willis and Meacham (1996), African American scholars, describe a shift in classroom climate and discourse among multiracial preservice teachers around discussions of race. They refer to the shift as a breakpoint (i.e., an identifiable point where public discussions and responses about race evolve from being distant and cautiously polite to personal and less cautious). The authors share excerpts from responses by minoritized preservice teachers who publically give voice to their ethnic/racial roots and contrast these statements with the responses by White preservice teachers who express discomfort with identifying as White and acknowledging their Whiteness. Willis and Meacham report White students' expressing feelings of anger, denial, guilt, and resentment prior to the breakpoint.

Several researchers of classroom conversations on race in preservice teacher education (Haviland, 2008; Marx & Pennington, 2003; McIntyre, 1997; Mosley & Rogers, 2011) articulate the complexity of the research process, as English-dominant, White, middle-class females that conducting studies among Whites, especially people whose life experiences are most like their own, complicates the research process. They experience the difficulty of being an insider, while simultaneously submitting that philosophically, they also are positioned as outsiders given their antiracist, critical pedagogical, and White studies stances. Such reflections are reminiscent of calls by Cochran-Smith et al. (2015) for teacher educators to examine their own experiences, perspectives, histories and practices with regard to diversity.

Looking across the studies on classroom conversations on race in preservice teacher educational classrooms, there are a series of common findings:

1. The researchers' and participants' discussions of race rarely include the voices of minoritized students.
2. The majority of students in these preservice teacher education classrooms appear to lack experiences among people of color, they have lived and been educated in predominately White environments all their lives.
3. The discussions that occur, mediated by the English-dominant, female, upper- to middle-class White researchers and/or instructors, recenter and reprivilege Whiteness, although stated goals are to address anti-racism, racism, and race.
4. In most studies, university classroom discussions emerge in response to assigned readings or in response to field placements.
5. There is a focus on the emotional burden of reconciling Whiteness for participants, in some cases the emotional burden overwhelms discussions of antiracism, race, and racism; thus, the deconstruction of antiracism, race, and racism is incomplete, with the foci on the emotional state of the White preservice teachers, White hegemony is recentered, reprivileged, and reempowered.
6. Conclusions generally (a) describe the difficulties experienced by the researchers in addressing issues of race, racism, Whiteness, White supremacy among their students and (b) reference the students' emotional state and lack of language to discuss race in general, but specifically Whiteness.

Taken together the studies can be viewed as calling for improved theory building, teaching strategies, and restructuring curriculum for holding classroom conversations on race in preservice teacher education.

FINAL COMMENTS

Classroom conversations on race are rare in P–12 classrooms, and only a small number of them are empirical studies. We argue that researchers (and educators) need to acknowledge that classroom conversations occur within sociohistorical and political contexts. We describe the diverse logics-of-inquiry found in these studies, noting that some studies are framed top-down by a theory or theories, while others are framed by a dialectical relationship between extant theories and the inductive construction of grounded theoretical constructs.

Within these empirical studies, we note that although carefully selected, curricular content may facilitate classroom conversations on race that deepen academic curriculum, facilitate the development of positive social identities for students, and disrupt inequalities; however, how teachers and students use language are critical to what is accomplished during and through classroom conversations on race. Research suggests the importance of teachers problematizing taken-for-granted interpretive frameworks derived from dominant racial ideologies and the importance of having students make connections between the discussions of race at a distance (e.g., in a literary text or of a historical event) and with their own lives close-up. Research also showed the importance of narratives of students' experiences as counternarratives to dominant racial narratives.

However, we also noted research also shows the course of classroom conversations on race do not always lead to the disruption of inequalities or closure or eschewing dominant racial ideologies (including the centrality Whiteness, colorblindness/colormutedness, and racial hierarchies), while some students may contest the imposition of Whiteness others will contest attempts to disrupt it. Last, although preservice teacher education would seem like a promising site to lay the foundations for promoting well-orchestrated and meaningful classroom conversations on race, research shows that it is a complex site with all of the difficulties for having such conversations as P–12 classrooms.

What is the work to be done? First, the corpus of studies is small; many more studies are needed and in particular studies are needed that provide detailed, discourse analysis of the conversations themselves (perhaps through conversational analysis, interactional sociolinguistic analysis, linguistic ethnography, or microethnographic discourse analysis, etc.) informed by social and critical theories of race (e.g., Brown, 2008; Dixson & Bloome, 2007; Carter, 2007). Second, education researchers should intentionally work to expand research to include classroom discussions of race that address all racial groups in the United States. Third, and as noted earlier, whereas teachers' own racial identities were implicated in the nature of and the extent to which they engaged in classrooms conversations on race, researchers' and teacher educators' identities must be included as an integral component of theorizing about classroom conversations on race. Several studies in this review illustrate this point. Beyond the need for empirical studies is the need for theorizing how classroom conversations on race reciprocally influence conversations on race in other settings. Further theorizing is needed on how classroom conversations on race leading to disruptions of inequality might be conceived at multiple levels including local, situated contexts and broader social, institutional, and societal contexts.

REFERENCES

Adams, D. W. (1995). *Education for extinction: American Indians and the boarding school experience, 1875–1928.* Lawrence: University Press of Kansas.

Allen, D. (2004). *Talking to strangers: Anxieties of citizenship since Brown v. Board of Education.* Chicago, IL: University of Chicago Press.

Anagnostopoulos, D., Everett, S., & Carey, C. (2013). "Of course we're supposed to move on, but then you still got people who are not over those historical wounds": Cultural memory and US youth's race talk. *Discourse & Society, 24,* 163–185.

Anderson, J. (1988). *The education of Blacks in the south, 1860–1935.* Chapel Hill: University of North Carolina Press.

Appiah, K. A. (1989). The conservation of race. *Black American Literature Forum, 23*(1), 37–60.

Baldwin, J. (2008). A talk to teachers. *Yearbook of the National Society for the Study of Education, 107*(2), 15–20. (Original work published 1963)

Bell, D. A. (1992). *Faces at the bottom of the well: The permanence of racism.* New York, NY: Basic Books.

Black Lives Matter. (2016, May 18). *The creation of a movement.* Retrieved from http://black-livesmatter.com/herstory/

Blommaert, J. (2015). Chronotopes, scales, and complexity in the study of language in society. *Annual Review of Anthropology, 44,* 105–116.

Bloome, D., Power Cater, S., Morton Christian, B., Otto, S., & Shuart-Faris, N. (2005). *Discourse analysis and the study of classroom language and literacy events: A microethnographic perspective.* Mahwah, NJ: Erlbaum.

Boger, C., & Orfield, G. (Eds.). (2005). *School resegregation: Must the South turn back?* Chapel Hill: University of North Carolina Press.

Bolgatz, J. (2005). Teachers initiating conversations about race and racism in a high school class. *Multicultural Perspectives, 7*(3), 28–35.

Bolgatz, J. (2006). Revolutionary talk: Elementary teacher and students discuss race in a social studies class. *Social Studies, 96,* 259–264.

Bolgatz, J. (2007). More than Rosa Parks: Critical multicultural social studies in a fourth-grade class. *Transformations, 18*(1), 39–51.

Bourdieu, P. (1977). *Outline of a theory of practice.* Cambridge, England: Cambridge University Press.

Brown, A. F. (2008). *Constructing "race" through talk: A micro-ethnographic investigation of discussions of "race" among African American secondary students* (Doctoral dissertation). Available from Vanderbilt University, Nashville, TN.

Brown, A. F. (2010). "Just because I am Black and male doesn't mean I am a rapper!" Sociocultural dilemmas in using "rap" music as an educational tool in classrooms. In D. Alridge, J. Stewart, & V. P. Franklin (Eds.), *Message in the music: Hip hop history and pedagogy* (pp. 281–300). Washington, DC: ASALH Press.

Brown, A. F. (2013). We will understand it better by and by: Sojourning to racial literacy. In L. William-White, D. Muccular, G. Muccular, & A. F. Brown (Eds.), *Critical consciousness in curricular research: Evidence from the field* (pp. 146–160). New York, NY: Peter Lang.

Carter, S. P. (2007). "Reading all that White crazy stuff": Black young women unpacking Whiteness in a high school British literature classroom. *Journal of Classroom Interaction, 41*(2), 42–54.

Case, K. A., & Hemmings, A. (2005). Distancing strategies: White women preservice teachers and antiracist curriculum. *Urban Education, 40,* 606–626.

Chapman, T. (2007). Interrogating classroom relationships and events: Using portraiture and critical race theory in education research. *Educational Researcher, 36*(3), 156–162.

Cochran-Smith, M., Villegas, A. M., Abrams, L., Chavez-Moreno, L., Mills, T., & Stern, R. (2015). Critiquing teacher preparation research: An overview of the field, Part II. *Journal of Teacher Education, 66,* 109–121.

Collins, P. (1990). *Black feminist thought: Knowledge, consciousness, and the politics of empowerment*. Cambridge, MA: Unwin Hyman.

Copenhaver-Johnson, J. F. (2000). Silence in the classroom: Learning to talk about issues of race. *Dragon Lode, 18*(2), 8–16.

Dillard, C. B. (2006). When the music changes, so should the dance: Cultural and spiritual considerations in paradigm 'proliferation'. *International Journal of Qualitative Studies in Education, 19*, 59–76.

Dixson, A., & Bloome, D. (2007). Jazz, critical race theories, and the discourse analysis of literacy events in classrooms. In C. Clark, & M. Blackburn (Eds.), *New directions in literacy research for political action and social change* (pp. 29–52). New York, NY: Peter Lang.

Donnor, J. K., & Dixson, A. (2013). *The resegregation of schools: Education and race in the twenty-first century*. New York, NY: Routledge.

DuBois, W. E. B. (1994). *The souls of Black folk*. New York, NY: Dover. (Original work published 1903)

Etheridge, S. B. (1979). Impact of the 1954 *Brown vs. Topeka Board of Education* decision in Black educators. *Negro Educational Review, 30*, 217–232.

Fine, M. (1987). Silencing in public schools. *Language Arts, 64*, 157–174.

Foster, M. (1998). *Black teachers on teaching*. New York, NY: New Press.

Goldberg, D. M. (2009). *The curse of ham: Race and slavery in early Judaism, Christianity, and Islam*. Princeton, NJ: Princeton University Press.

Guèye, K. (2006). *Mapping the Liminal Identities of Mulattas in African, African American, and Caribbean Literatures* (Unpublished doctoral dissertation). University Park: Pennsylvania State University.

Gumperz, J. (1986). *Discourse strategies*. New York, NY: Cambridge University Press.

Haddix, M. (2010). No longer on the margins: Researching the hybrid literate identities of Black and Latina preservice teachers. *Teaching of English, 45*, 97–123.

Haney, J. E. (1978). The effect of the Brown decision on Black educators. *Journal of Negro Education, 47*, 88–95.

Hartlep, N. D. (2013). The "not so silent" minority: Scientific racism and the need for epistemological and pedagogical experience in curriculum. In L. William-White, D. Muccular, G. Muccular, & A. F. Brown (Eds.), *Critical consciousness in curricular research: Evidence from the field* (pp. 60–76). New York, NY: Peter Lang.

Haviland, V. S. (2008). "Things get glossed over": Rearticulating the silencing power of Whiteness in Education. *Journal of Teacher Education, 59*, 40–54.

Hollingsworth, L. (2009). Complicated conversations: Exploring race and ideology in an elementary classroom. *Urban Education, 44*, 30–58.

hooks, b. (1994). *Teaching to transgress: Education as the practice of Freedom*. New York, NY: Routledge.

Horne, T. (2007). *An open letter to the citizens of Tucson*. Retrieved from http://nau.edu/uploadedfiles/academic/cal/philosophy/forms/an%20open%20letter%20to%20citizens%20of%20tucson.pdf

Irizarry, J. G. (2011). En la lucha: The struggles and triumphs of Latino/a preservice teachers. *Teachers College Record, 113*, 2804–2835.

Jensen, E. (2003, January 21). PBS "jasper" opens a dialogue about race. *Los Angeles Times*. Retrieved from http://articles.latimes.com/2003/jan/21/entertainment/et-jensen21

Kluger, R. (1985). *Simple justice: A history of Brown vs. Board of Education and Black America's struggle for equality*. New York, NY: Alfred A. Knopf.

Ladson-Billings, G. (2000). Fighting for our lives: Preparing teachers to teach African American students. *Journal of Teacher Education, 51*, 206–214.

Ladson-Billings, G. (2004). Landing on the wrong note: The price we paid for Brown. *Educational Researcher, 33*(7), 3–13.

Lewis, A. (2003). *Race in the schoolyard: Negotiating the color line in classrooms and communities.* New Brunswick, NJ: Rutgers University Press.

Marx, S., & Pennington, J. (2003). Pedagogies of critical race theory: Experimentations with White preservice teachers. *International Journal of Qualitative Studies in Education, 16,* 91–110.

McIntyre, A. (1997). *Making meaning of whiteness: Exploring racial identity with white teachers.* Albany: State University of New York.

Milner, H. R. (2006). Culture, race and spirit: A reflective model for the study of African Americans. *International Journal of Qualitative Studies in Education, 19,* 367–385.

Morris, J. E. (2003). Race, ethnicity and culture: Cultural expectations and student learning. In J. Guthrie (Ed.), *Encyclopedia of education* (2nd ed., pp. 1961–1966). New York, NY: Macmillan Reference.

Morris, J. E., & Woodruff, S. E. (2015). Adolescents' perception of opportunities in the U.S. south: Postracial mirage or reality in the new Black Mecca? *Peabody Journal of Education, 90,* 404–425.

Mosley, M., & Rogers, R. (2011). Inhabiting the "tragic gap": Preservice teachers practicing racial literacy. *Teaching Education, 22,* 303–324.

Ogletree, C. J. (2004). *All deliberate speed: Reflections on the first half-century of Brown v. Board of Education.* New York, NY: New Press.

Omi, M., & Winant, H. (1994). *Racial formation in the United States: From the 1960s to the 1990s.* New York, NY: Routledge.

Pixley, M. F., & VanDerPloeg, L. S. (2000). Learning to see: White. *English Education, 32,* 278–289.

Pollock, M. (2004). *Colormute: Race talk dilemmas in an American school.* Princeton, NJ: Princeton University Press.

Quay, S. J. (2014). Facilitating dialogues about racial realities. *Teachers College Record, 116,* 2–42.

Rex, L. (2006). Acting "cool" and "appropriate": Toward a framework for considering literacy classroom interactions when race is a factor. *Journal of Literacy Research, 38,* 275–325.

Rogers, R., & Mosley, M. (2006). Racial literacy in a second-grade classroom: Critical race theory, Whiteness studies, and literacy research. *Reading Research Quarterly, 41,* 462–495.

Sassi, K., & Thomas, E. E. (2008). Walking the talk: Examining privilege and race in a ninth-grade classroom. *English Journal, 97*(6), 25–31.

Schaffer, R., & Skinner, D. G. (2009). Performing race in four culturally diverse fourth grade classrooms: Silence, race talk, and the negotiation of social boundaries. *Anthropology & Education Quarterly, 40,* 277–296.

Schultz, K., Buck, P., & Niesz, T. (2000). Democratizing conversation: Racialized talk in a post-desegregated middle school. *American Educational Research Journal, 37,* 33–65.

Seidl, B. (2007). Working with communities to explore and personalize cultural relevant pedagogies: Push, double images, and raced talk. *Journal of Teacher Education, 63,* 168–183.

Shahjahan, R. A. (2005). Spirituality in the academy: Reclaiming from the margins and evoking a transformative way of knowing the world. *International Journal of Qualitative Studies in Education, 18,* 685–711.

Southern Poverty Law Center. (2016, May 18). *Hica, et al. v Robert Bentley, Luther Strange, et al.* Retrieved from https://www.splcenter.org/seeking-justice/case-docket/hica-et-al-v-robert-bentley-luther-strange-et-al

Spring, J. (1991) *American education.* New York, NY: Longman.

Stolberg, S. G., Dewan, S., & Stelter, B. (2010, July 21). With apology, fired official is offered a new job. *The New York Times.* Retrieved from http://www.nytimes.com/2010/07/22/us/politics/22sherrod.html

Tatum, B. (1992). Talking about race, learning about racism: The application of racial identity development theory in the classroom. *Harvard Educational Review, 62*(1), 1–25.

Tatum, B. (1994). Teaching White students about racism: The search for White allies and the restoration of hope. *Teachers College Record, 95,* 462–476.

Tatum, B, (1997). *"Why are all the black kids sitting together in the cafeteria" and other conversations on race.* New York, NY: Basic Books.

Tatum, B. D. (2000). Defining racism: "Can we talk?" In M. Adams, W. J. Blumenfeld, R. Castaneda, H. W. Hackman, M. L. Peters, & X. Zuniga (Eds.), *Readings for diversity and social justice* (pp. 65–67). New York, NY: Routledge Press.

Thomas, E. E. (2015). "We always talk about race": Navigating race talk dilemmas in the teaching of literature. *Research in the Teaching of English, 50,* 154–175.

Trainor, J. S. (2005). "My ancestors didn't own slaves": Understanding white talk about race. *Research in the Teaching of English, 40,* 140–167.

Vetter, A. (2013). "You need some laugh bones!" Leveraging AAL in a high school English classroom. *Journal of Literacy Research, 45,* 173–206.

Volosinov, V. (1973). *Marxism and the philosophy of language* (L. Matejka & I. Titunik, Trans.). Cambridge, MA: Harvard University Press. (Original work published 1929)

Walters, R. (2007). Barack Obama and the politics of blackness. *Journal of Black Studies, 38,* 7–29.

Waters, M. C. (1999). *West Indian immigrant dreams and American realities.* New York, NY: Russell Sage Foundation.

West, C. (1993). *Race matters.* Boston, MA: Beach.

Willis, A. I., & Meacham, S. J. (1996). Break point: The challenges of teaching multicultural education courses. *Journal of the Assembly for Expanded Perspectives on Learning, 2*(1), 8.

Winn, M. T. (2013). Toward a restorative English education. *Research in the Teaching of English, 48,* 126–135.

Wise, T. (2009). *Between Barack and a hard place: Racism and White denial in the age of Obama.* San Francisco, CA: City Lights Books.

Woodson, C. (1933). *The miseducation of the Negro.* Washington, DC: Associated Publishers.

Chapter 20

Leveraging Students' Communicative Repertoires as a Tool for Equitable Learning

Danny C. Martinez
University of California, Davis

P. Zitlali Morales
University of Illinois at Chicago

Ursula S. Aldana
University of San Francisco

Leveraging is often described as the process of using the home and community languages of children and youth as a tool to access the "academic" or "standard" varieties of languages valued in schools. In this vein, researchers have called on practitioners to leverage the stigmatized language practices of children and youth in schools for their academic development. In this review, we interrogate the notion of leveraging commonly used by language and literacy scholars. We consider what gets leveraged, whose practices get leveraged, when leveraging occurs, and whether or not leveraging leads to robust and transformative learning experiences that sustain the cultural and linguistic practices of children and youth in our schools, particularly for students of color. We review scholarship steeped in Vygotskian-inspired research on learning, culturally relevant and culturally sustaining pedagogies, and bilingual education research that forefront the notion that the language practices of children and youth are useful for mediating learning and development. We conclude with a discussion of classroom discourse analysis methods that we believe can provide documentation of transformative learning experiences that uncovers and examines the linguistic resources of students in our twenty-first-century classrooms, and to gain a common language around notions of leveraging in the field.

English as taught in city schools does not always reflect the Englishes city students travel with. Their urban English landscape is enriched by a procession of many voices that march in various directions in, around, and through the monuments of the city. In them are the spoken souls of the crowded, colored earth, the distinguishable dialects and silences that creep loudly but defiantly down the city block and into the linguistic mainstream.

—Kirkland (2010, p. 293)

Review of Research in Education
March 2017, Vol. 41, pp. 477–499
DOI: 10.3102/0091732X17691741
© 2017 AERA. http://rre.aera.net

Youth enter schools and bring with them a range of linguistic resources that *could* be used in the service of learning. For many youth, however, their linguistic resources or ways of communicating in their homes and communities do not align with ways of communicating privileged in schools. This is particularly true for minoritized and racialized children and youth of color whose linguistic flexibility often indexes for educators a host of deficit categorizations (Flores & Rosa, 2015). Kirkland's (2010) imagery above illustrates for us how "city schools" do not reflect the rich languages that youth bring with them, from their homes and communities. He centralizes the "many voices" that make up the communicative repertoires of city youth that "defiantly" make their way into the linguistic mainstream, despite schools that wish to wash these "Englishes" away. Minoritized and racialized children and youth often experience their ways of speaking as "marked" by educators and in society as well. Yet, despite efforts to rid youth of their languages, they will persist, and likely make their way into the "linguistic mainstream," without due credit.

Researchers inspired by the ethnography of communication tradition (Gumperz & Hymes, 1972) point to differences between languages expected in schools and those spoken at home (Au, 1980; Heath, 1983; Philips, 1983). For example Au (1980) and Philips (1983) documented different ways children used language to participate in conversations across the two settings, noting the closer home practices (language or ways of using language) match with school expectations, the better students generally perform. Some of this work has been thoroughly reviewed elsewhere (see Hull & Schultz, 2001; Orellana, Martinez, Lee, & Montaño, 2012) and includes Kathryn Au's (1980) significant study examining young students in Hawaii and Susan Philips's (1983) important research focusing on the Warm Springs Indians of Central Oregon. These were groundbreaking studies at the time, using discourse analytic tools applied in diverse settings to demonstrate the cultural incongruence between how students had been socialized to communicate in their home communities and the differing expectations at school.

Heath's (1983) classic research examined how adults and children communicate in three communities within the Piedmont Carolinas: Trackton, Roadville, and Maintown. She found that communication styles for each respective community were closely tied to individuals' socialization within a cultural community. The ways children were socialized to language in Trackton, an all-Black working-class community, and Roadville, an all-White working-class community, were examined in contrast to the "mainstream" practices of Black and White children and adults from Maintown who held positions of power economically, educationally, and politically. Practices across three communities differed in how children were ultimately prepared to navigate expected language norms of academic, and eventually work life. In their homes, Maintown children were already engaged in language practices reflecting patterns used in school contexts, preparing them for the language usage and questioning patterns they would encounter in schools. White Maintown children experienced home and school as linked, and their parents engaged children in activities they believed added to their academic knowledge. Many children from Trackton and

Roadville, in contrast, experienced a discontinuity between the two environments and experienced greater school failure than the children of Maintown, despite Heath's finding that the "ways with words" of children from all three communities were sophisticated, yet different from each other.

Au (1980), Heath (1983), and Philips (1983) each made clear that children from "nonmainstream" communities they studied had communicative repertoires that mediated their participation within home and community contexts, yet the discontinuities experienced by these children in school were enough for educational inequities to occur, in various forms. In a similar tradition, other scholars have provided foundational understandings about the language practices of Black children in out of school contexts in Philadelphia (Goodwin, 1990), the code-switching practices of Puerto Rican bilinguals in New York (Zentella, 1997), and the experiences of Mexican mothers and their children in the Arizona borderlands (González, 2001), to name a few. As education researchers interested in the project of equitable schooling, we challenge narratives that mark and stigmatize students' languages as deficient. The actions of educators to demean, belittle, or cast aside any language simply for sounding "different" reduce opportunities for learning in classrooms (Cole, 1998). It is our belief that education researchers interested in language should both address and work toward normalizing the multilingual and multidialectical communicative repertoires of students in our increasingly diverse schooling contexts. Of priority should be to identify how teachers can capitalize on the communicative repertoires of students in ways that mediate their learning and development, what many scholars call "leveraging."

In this review, we interrogate the notion of leveraging commonly used by language and literacy scholars in education. In many empirical studies, there are calls by researchers (including us) asking practitioners to leverage underused, less recognized, and too often stigmatized linguistic practices of children and youth in schools. In reviewing notions of leveraging discussed in relevant language and literacy research in K–12 settings, we explore various approaches to leveraging. We examine *what* gets leveraged, *whose* practices get leveraged, *when* leveraging occurs, and whether or not leveraging may lead to robust and transformative learning experiences that sustain the cultural and linguistic practices of children and youth in our schools, particularly students of color historically deemed as inferior.

We argue for the use of leveraging through a review of scholarship steeped in Vygotskian-inspired research on learning, followed by more recent scholarship that argues for culturally relevant (Ladson-Billings, 1995, 2014) and culturally sustaining pedagogies (Paris, 2012; Paris & Alim, 2014). These traditions already begin from the assumption that the language and literacy practices of children and youth developed outside of schools, in their homes and varying community contexts, are useful tools for mediating their learning and development in school. Next, we examine the scholarship of researchers who discuss leveraging specifically within classrooms. This will be followed by a review of classroom discourse analysis methodologies that we believe can be used by teachers, in addition to researchers, as a powerful tool to uncover and examine the linguistic resources of students in our 21st-century classrooms.

COMMUNICATIVE REPERTOIRES IN MULTILINGUAL
SOCIETIES/CLASSROOMS

Prior to entering any discussion about leveraging, it is important to explore how the communicative tools of individuals have been theorized within sociocultural language scholarship, particularly in our use of the term *communicative repertoire*. In revisiting Gumperz's (1964) notion of linguistic repertoire, Betsy Rymes (2010a, 2014) coined the term *communicative repertoire* to capture how individuals use language and literacy, and other semiotic means of communication including gestures, body language, and dress to function effectively in multiple communities. Gumperz's (1964) notion of verbal repertoire was developed in the context of multilingualism in India where switching languages functioned similarly to style switching in monolingual communities, to communicate different meanings in different social situations. Gumperz defined verbal repertoire as "the totality of linguistic forms regularly employed in the course of socially significant interaction" (p. 137). For Gumperz, sociocultural context was a significant feature to any communicative interaction. Therefore he argued that the idea of verbal repertoires encompassed more than the term *language* could adequately describe within a multilingual society.

Rymes's (2010a, 2014) notion of communicative repertoire explores how a focus only on the "linguistic" might ignore other dynamic means of communication that individuals draw on to communicate meaning, their identities, and their affiliations with varied cultural communities and groups. Attention to the communicative repertoires of students can garner generative tools for teachers in the task of leveraging students' underexplored and untapped communicative practices in classrooms. In our own work, we have strived to expand what counts as language while working toward expanding the communicative repertoires of students (Martinez & Montaño, 2016) and teachers (Zentella, 1997). Exploring the notion of communicative repertoires highlights the various linguistic tools individuals have available to navigate the multiple communities to which they belong. The previous scholars mentioned, among others, are integral to our understanding that all languages are grammatical and rule governed. With this in mind, we move on to explore how previously mentioned research provides a framework for naming which communicative repertoires should be built on, or leveraged, in our classrooms.

METHOD FOR ORGANIZING REVIEW

In reviewing articles, we sought to cultivate a base of literature where scholars explicitly used the term *leveraging* or *leverage* to describe the purposeful use of children's or youths' communicative repertoires for a classroom-related outcome including the development of a new language-related skill. We did not include parameters for specific years because we were eager to note the first use of the term, and we wanted to cast a wide enough net, initially. Overall we sought research that noted (1) which researchers were influential in highlighting the communicative repertoires of racialized and minoritized groups, (2) which researchers used the term *leveraging* for the purpose of building on the communicative strengths for learning in classrooms, and more broadly (3) work that aligns with the perspective of taking seriously the language skills that students from racialized and minoritized groups possess and use regularly, while acknowledging the need to expand their communicative repertoires.

We began with a search on Education Resource Information Center of peer-reviewed articles with the terms "leverage," "leveraging," and "language." From a total of 33 results, only 9 articles related to leveraging the communicative repertoires of a specific community for academic purposes (see Table 1). Only five articles had the word or a version of the word "leverage" in the title, and others used the term *leveraging* to discuss notions of "drawing on," "using," "cultivating," or "recruiting" the communicative repertoires of a racialized or minoritized community. We note that Michaels (2005) appears to be the first scholar to use the term *leveraging* in the way that we focus on it within this review, as a way to draw on the linguistic skills and strengths of nondominant and racialized youth who do not come to school proficient in mainstream academic English (MAE).

Finally, we trace the work of language and literacy scholars who come from the tradition of viewing the linguistic differences of racialized and minoritized youth as valid and valuable, with the perspective of desiring these differences be maintained rather than stamped out for the sake of closer alignment to MAE. Broadly, these areas of work include the following: funds of knowledge, bilingual education theory, cultural modeling, and culturally relevant and sustaining pedagogies.

CONCEPTUALIZATIONS OF LEVERAGING

As previously stated, Sarah Michaels was the first scholar in our review to mention leveraging for the purposes of recruiting the communicative strengths of working-class children. In her commentary on research reported by Miller, Cho, and Bracey (2005), Michaels (2005) asks in her title, "[Can] working-class storytelling be leveraged in school?" Michaels calls on researchers and practitioners to consider the affordances of building on practices readily available to communities often treated as lacking in language abilities. Michaels makes this argument building on Miller et al. (2005), who found that working-class children from South Baltimore and Chicago, who are commonly treated as "nonverbal" or "inadequately verbal," engaged in sophisticated storytelling practices. Taking cues from the Miller et al. article, Michaels (2005) argues that we must "take seriously the linguistic and sociocultural strengths of members of nondominant communities in the hope that demonstrations of these strengths could influence schools and the reception and progress of non-mainstream children within them" (p. 137).

While Miller et al. (2005) showcase working-class family storytelling, Michaels (2005) asks larger questions about the validity of these stories for school learning. She continues,

We can note the fact that teachers like the rest of us are seeing through the eyes of their own dominant genres and find it hard on the fly to see the logic and cogency in ways with words or slants on experience

TABLE 1

Search Results for "Leveraging" Communicative Repertoires of Schooling Tasks

Citation	Term Used	Examples
Gutiérrez, Bien, Selland, and Pierce (2011)	*Leverage, leveraged, leveraging*	"In this article, we discuss the importance of leveraging DLLs' [dual language learners] linguistic repertoires towards the development of emergent academic language and writing practices, while promoting their identities as imaginative and productive meaning-makers, that is, learning language and using language to learn (Wells, 1986)." (p. 235)
Hopewell (2011)	*Leveraging, leverage*	"The teacher must engage students in dialogs and learning activities that explicitly leverage cross-language connections to lighten students' learning burdens." (p. 606)
Jiménez et al. (2015)	*Leverage, leveraging*	"We now present one approach that incorporates the recommended teacher practices, dispositions, and types of knowledge needed for leveraging English learners' linguistic strengths in instruction. When used as part of an instructional activity, translating has the potential to improve the English reading comprehension of ELs." (p. 409)
Lee (2006)	*Leveraging*	"This article explicates the Cultural Modeling Framework for designing robust learning environments that leverage everyday knowledge of culturally diverse students to support subject-matter specific learning." (p. 305)
Martínez (2010)	*Leveraging, leverage*	"We can then help them [students] apply the skills embedded in their use of Spanglish to relevant academic literacy tasks and contexts. Leveraging the skills embedded in students' use of Spanglish could thus radically transform how students view the relationship between everyday and academic knowledge, and thereby have a transformative impact on their academic literacy learning." (p. 146)
Michaels (2005)	*Leveraged*	"Can the intellectual affordances of working-class storytelling be leveraged in school?" (p. 136, from title)
Orellana and Reynolds (2008)	*Leveraged, leveraging*	"The goal of leveraging is neither to simply celebrate students' everyday linguistic virtuosity nor to transfer those skills in a direct way to schools tasks but rather to expand students' abilities to work with the various tools in their linguistic toolkits—the full range of practices that they use in both home and school contexts. Leveraging may simultaneously cultivate hybrid abilities that merge different elements from students' repertoires of practice as these elements are displayed across contexts, tasks, and relationships." (p. 50)

(continued)

TABLE 1 (CONTINUED)

Citation	Term Used	Examples
Pacheco (2012)	*Leverage, leveraged, leveraging*	"To resolve these emerging and evolving double binds, social actors engaged in productive learning as they transformed and created new artifacts and instruments. Thus, in making explicit connections to curriculum and schooling, I emphasize that leveraging the cultural resources generated in/through everyday resistance requires a significant recognition of Latina/o students' problem-solving inclinations and solution-driven actions and activities." (p. 129)
Vetter (2013)	*Leverage, leveraged, leveraging*	"I chose the verb **leverage**, a word traditionally used in the financial world that means 'to use for maximum advantage,' to explore how Gina attempted to use students' language as a tool to gain respectful members of a literacy classroom ("Leverage," 2012)." (p. 7)

that diverge from their own… We, as a community, have got to go beyond claims and documentation of difference (even differences on their own terms) and show specifically how these differences can be recruited, in school, as strengths. (p. 137)

Michaels (2005) highlights tensions faced by educators when asked to see beyond the "eyes of their own dominant genres." She, however, offers an important perspective for going "beyond" simply noting differences, asking researchers and practitioners to consider ways to recruit differences "as strengths" in schools. Michaels's call is not a radical one; however, she makes clear that decades have passed since similar calls were made, and practitioners and researchers still experience difficulties accepting and enacting teaching that recruits the neglected strengths of children and youth for learning. We now urge education researchers to take Michaels's initial question, can "Working-class storytelling be leveraged in school?" and extend it to other well-researched communities and practices: *Can signifying in the Black community be leveraged in school? Can immigrant children's language brokering skills be leveraged in school? Can code-switching be leveraged in school?* In other words, researchers now need to investigate what gets leveraged in schools, how, and when.

LEVERAGING: WHAT GETS LEVERAGED, WHO GETS TO LEVERAGE, AND WHEN?

Within education research, various pedagogical approaches recruit the practices of "nonmainstream" children and youth as a resource for learning in schools, particularly when the communicative repertoires of a specific group are noncongruent to those expected in "mainstream" or "traditional" classrooms. In this section, we highlight scholars that document the cultural and communicative repertoires of practices in which their respective participants engaged, such as the rhetorical features of young Black Language speakers (Lee, 2006), immigrant youth language brokering (Orellana & Reynolds, 2008), and the Spanglish practices of Latina/o youth (Martínez, 2010). These researchers map practices observed through long-term ethnographic methods, onto discipline-specific modes of reasoning and demonstrate how to leverage students' communicative repertoires for academic purposes.

The "cultural modeling" (Lee, 1995) approach demonstrates how teachers can adopt language and literacy practices that links students' tacit knowledge (cultural models) outside of school with academic curriculum. Lee's (2006) cultural modeling study in a Chicago high school serving predominantly African American youth demonstrates how the teachers' use of African American English Vernacular "rhetorical and performance features" (p. 318) facilitated the students' participation in a speech community. Lee emphasizes, "During the modeling phase, the goal of instructional discourse is to make public students' tacit knowledge of how to tackle these problems, and to provide them with a meta-language with which to describe their reasoning" (p. 310). In these classroom moments, students experience being holders of knowledge and disrupt the normalized student–teacher learning hierarchy. This recognition of students' tacit knowledge and naming is particularly momentous for students of color who are often marginalized in classroom settings. Students also developed their reasoning skills with everyday texts and applied these to literary texts. Lee (2006) suggests,

> The teacher's role is to help students recognize the similarities between what they did to interpret the cultural data sets and what, in the case of these literature classrooms, students would do to interpret canonical literary texts that also involved major attention to symbolism. (p. 310)

In this manner, students' tacit knowledge was leveraged to facilitate their learning and development.

Orellana (2009) draws from her own decades-long ethnographic research in Los Angeles and Chicago with children of immigrants who served as interpreters and translators, or language brokers, for adults in their homes and communities. Orellana and Reynolds (2008) drew on Lee's (2007) cultural modeling framework seeking to leverage the language brokering skills of children for academic tasks, specifically paraphrasing in the literacy classroom. They explain that leveraging required purposeful attempts to take parts of a linguistic practice with which students were already familiar, "that can be examined with students while also drawing their attention to how these practices connect with disciplinary constructs and ways of thinking" (p. 50). Orellana and Reynolds argue that the language brokering in which these youth engage out of school mapped directly onto the literacy task of paraphrasing. That is, to restate a text "in one's own words" is similar to the translating and interpreting practices engaged in as language brokers (p. 54). They add specifically about leveraging,

> The goal of leveraging is neither simply to celebrate students' everyday linguistic virtuosity nor to transfer those skills in a direct way to school tasks but rather to expand students' abilities to work with the various tools in their linguistic toolkits—the full range of practices that they use in *both* home and school contexts. Leveraging may simultaneously cultivate hybrid abilities that merge different elements from students' repertoires of practice as these elements are displayed across contexts, tasks, and relationships. (p. 50)

Leveraging, for Orellana and Reynolds (2008), cultivated a learning environment where youths' home and community communicative repertoires were useful within the classroom context, and beyond. The goal was not to rid the home practice, or deem it as less valuable; rather it was to make clear the usefulness of a practice that is often ignored and left untapped by educators.

Martínez (2010) provides a similar approach to leveraging in his ethnographic research on Latina/o middle school youths' code-switching practices, or Spanglish, in a middle school classroom to explore potential leverages for academic purposes. He found that these youth were engaging in creative and nuanced code-switching practices that mapped onto practices encouraged by the California standards for English language arts at the time, such as the need to communicate "subtle shades of meaning" across words. Martínez (2010) argues that his purpose, similar to others researching "nondominant" language practices, should not be simply to celebrate what these students are already doing well through their everyday use of *Spanglish*.

We certainly need to *begin* by acknowledging the skill and intelligence embedded and displayed in their use of *Spanglish*. However, if we only recognize and celebrate students' everyday language practices without providing them access to *dominant* language and literacy practices, then we do them a fundamental disservice. (p. 140)

For Martínez (2010) the goal of leveraging must be to provide children and youth of color with classroom communities where their language practices are represented. However, he argues that this is not productive unless we are also providing students with access to dominant language practices. This call is central to many scholars who take on an additive approach to language and literacy research.

LITERACY AND LANGUAGE RESEARCH WITH AN ADDITIVE PERSPECTIVE: BILINGUAL EDUCATION AND LANGUAGE EDUCATION

Bilingual and language education research have long featured similar ideas to leveraging when theorizing linguistic transfer. Research on bilingual education programs demonstrates how effective pedagogy uses students' first language, with a language as resource approach (Ruiz, 1995), in order to transfer known information to the second language, resulting in academic and social benefits (Morales & Aldana, 2010). However, some attempts by bilingual researchers and practitioners tended to dichotomize or falsely separate two languages within and across linguistic communities, leading to critiques of privileging idealized notions of standard languages. That is, views of successful bilingualism included idealized notions of a speaker who used "standard" varieties of two language without mixing these language together. This approach limited and made "vernacular" and hybrid language practices invisible in some contexts (García, 2009), or highly marked in others (Urciuoli, 1996; Zentella, 1997). Therefore, questions regarding whose communicative repertoires to leverage and for what purposes are important to consider. In the bilingual classroom setting, are the home languages of children and youth who are emerging bilinguals being leveraged, and if so, how? Are teachers creating hierarchies in languages when leveraging the home language only to access the dominant language? How might the practice of leveraging create pedagogical practices where communicative repertoires are being expanded while simultaneously sustaining the communicative repertoires of children and youth?

Hornberger and Link (2012) present ethnographic case studies of two educational contexts where teachers draw on the linguistic resources of students, yet vary in the ways they promote standard language. In one setting, teachers allowed youth to use their home languages in class; however, the school, and teachers continued to adopt an English-only approach to instruction, which hindered biliteracy development and essentially diminished students' access to developing Spanish skills. In contrast, the second setting points to the importance of translanguaging (García & Wei, 2014) as necessary for bilingual students' development. At this educational site, teachers focused on "the fluid, multilingual, oral, contextualized practices at the local level, because they are essential for learners' development" (Hornberger & Link, 2012, p. 245) and were better able to engage students in learning tasks given that students of multiple languages and dialects were able to speak freely. The researchers emphasize,

Translanguaging practices in the classroom have the potential to explicitly valorize all points along the continua of biliterate context, media, content, and development. They offer the possibility for teachers and learners to access academic content through the communicative repertoires they bring to the classroom while simultaneously acquiring new ones. (Hornberger & Link, 2012, p. 245)

For immigrant and emerging bilingual students, sociolinguistic research must expand beyond a first language and second language model of learning to include a more dynamic language model of learning that legitimizes the communicative repertoires students bring from home and the translanguaging skills they employ when faced with a learning task. Gutiérrez, Morales, and Martinez (2009) call attention to increasing transnational migration, resulting in a range of linguistic practices, reflecting "the ways that the local and the global are always implicated in the everyday linguistic practices of nondominant students, thus challenging narrow and essentialized notions of students' linguistic repertoires" (pp. 215–216).

CULTURALLY RELEVANT AND SUSTAINING PEDAGOGIES

For youth of color in particular, their schooling experiences rarely capture their tacit cultural knowledge nor recognize their linguistic dexterity. Culturally relevant teaching highlights how teachers can leverage the cultural and linguistic practices of students but also points to how choosing to leverage students' culture requires a pedagogical approach that aims to see, understand, and love the whole child. In her study of highly effective teachers of African American students, Gloria Ladson-Billings (1995) used culturally relevant theory to emphasize that teachers need to center on student experiences and local context as a resource for instruction. She proposed a culturally relevant theory of education as a way to bridge culture and teaching and provide educators a pedagogical approach that could capture the social and cultural context of African American, Latino, and Native American students' lives while also providing an explanation for minority students' academic success. The study defined the characteristics of culturally relevant teachers as "an ability to develop students academically, a willingness to nurture and support cultural competence, and the development of a sociopolitical or critical consciousness" (Ladson-Billings, 1995, p. 483). More important, this body of research challenged educators to do more than tolerate students' language and culture in the classroom but also acknowledge it, embrace it, and teach with it (Gay, 2009; Ladson-Billings, 1995). These studies of culturally relevant teaching serve to decenter the White, middle-class child, and position children of color at the center when we ask teachers to leverage the language and culture of students.

Over time, culturally relevant teaching has evolved, taking up various names such as culturally "sensitive," "centered," "congruent," "reflective," "mediated," "contextualized," "synchronized," and "responsive," as various researchers engaged in questions about "why it is important to make classroom instruction more consistent with the cultural orientations of ethnically diverse students" (Gay, 2009, p. 31). In this tradition, Camangian's (2015) research presents a humanizing pedagogy that emphasizes the experiences of youth of color as academic strengths rather than cultural deficits. Camangian demonstrates pedagogical strategies that leverage student voice and communicative expressions about experience, making authentic student voice a standard resource available in the classroom. He privileges student dialogue or "real talk" that moves students beyond academic interpretations of social theory to rich and sometimes intense conversations about how these theories apply to experiences in their community. His research highlights how teachers can employ the principles of culturally relevant teaching in tandem with critical literacy and critical pedagogy to center on the social and material realities of students of color, youth culture, and critical thinking. This work is an important reminder of the need for research to move beyond the theoretical notions behind culturally relevant teaching towards understanding what it looks like in the classroom, particularly in leveraging youth experiences via their communicative repertoires.

Culturally relevant teaching initially provided the framework to bridge teaching and culture together for educators focused on the education of children of color. In the over 20 years since culturally relevant teaching was first conceived, our country has become increasingly multiracial and multilingual, and teachers might find it difficult to leverage the culture of students given highly fluid and dynamic sets of practices (Paris & Alim, 2014). In increasingly diversifying contexts, the culturally relevant framework may not provide the tools "to support the linguistic and cultural dexterity and plurality (Paris, 2009, 2011) necessary for success and access in our demographically changing U.S. and global schools and communities" (Paris, 2012,

p. 95). In light of these tensions, Paris (2012) offers the term *culturally sustaining pedagogy* and explains,

The term culturally sustaining requires that our pedagogies be more than responsive of or relevant to the cultural experiences and practices of young people—it requires that they support young people in sustaining the cultural and linguistic competence of their communities while simultaneously offering access to dominant cultural competence. (p. 95)

Moving toward a culturally sustaining pedagogy requires that children and youth maintain their position at the center of instruction and honors the fluidity of youth culture (Paris & Alim, 2014), while asking teachers to affirm the multiple identities and cultures of students in order to fully engage them in their learning. As teachers engage students as subjects in their own learning process, students are better positioned to participate in critical thinking as teachers leverage aspects of their multilayered identities.

Rather than focus singularly on one racial or ethnic group, their work [culturally sustaining pedagogies] pushes us to consider the global identities that are emerging in the arts, literature, music, athletics, and film. It also points to the shifts of identity that now move us toward a hybridity, fluidity, and complexity never before considered in schools and classrooms. (Ladson-Billings, 2014, p. 82)

A culturally sustaining pedagogy responds to the diversity of classrooms and the fluidity of youth culture, and in turn, future research will need to respond and provide studies that not only demonstrate how language and culture can be leveraged in the classroom but also sustain the language and culture of students. We believe classroom discourse analysis can provide the theoretical and methodological tools to document and provide practical evidence of leveraging to support a transformative, culturally and linguistically sustaining pedagogy.

DISCOURSE, DISCOURSE ANALYSIS, AND CLASSROOM DISCOURSE ANALYSIS

In taking up the practice of leveraging for this review, we were aware that researchers benefitted from a range of methods to complete their empirical work. Scholars discussed at the opening of our chapter drew heavily on traditions from the ethnography of communication (Gumperz & Hymes, 1972) that called for ethnographic and linguistic methods to analyze the everyday communicative repertoires of various communities for comparative purposes, and for capturing language in use within its respective sociocultural context. Other work reviewed drew on sociocultural perspectives on language and literacy that weave traditions from linguistic anthropology, sociolinguistics, literacy, psychology, and sociology while relying on Vygotskian perspectives on learning and development. We want to now look toward classroom discourse analysis as one method we argue provides a powerful framework to explore and examine the everyday communicative repertoires that are deployed within classroom interactions. Through attention to the communicative repertoires of children, youth, and teachers in classrooms, we can explore and document what leveraging looks like, how it is practiced, and for what purposes in the quest to provide equitable and sustaining learning environments for children and youth. We look to classroom discourse analysis as a tool for researchers and practitioners to document, review, and interrogate the communicative repertoires of children and youth in classrooms.

In her book designed for practitioners, Rymes (2009) argues that classroom discourse analysis is useful for the following reasons:

1. Insights gained from classroom discourses analysis have enhanced mutual understanding between teachers and students.
2. By analyzing classroom discourse themselves, teachers have been able to understand local differences in classroom talk—going beyond stereotypes or other cultural generalizations.
3. When teachers analyze discourse in their own classrooms, academic achievement improves.
4. The process of doing classroom discourse analysis can foster an intrinsic and lifelong love for the practice of teaching and its general life-affirming potential. (p. 1)

Relationships established between students and teacher, teacher learning and understanding of local ways of communicating, improved academic achievement by students, and lifelong love for teaching are powerful reasons for engaging in and supporting classroom discourse analysis research. We believe classroom discourse analysis also has the potential to create data sets for researchers and practitioners to garner a better understanding of what leveraging looks like in practice.

According to Cazden and Beck (2003), "discourse" traditionally meant "any stretch of spoken or written language longer than a single sentence" (p. 166). However, researchers have since made clear how sociocultural factors mediate the discourses individuals deploy in order to perform socially, culturally, and sometimes politically acceptable ways of communicating (Gee, 2005). A seemingly general definition of discourse is *language in use* (Cazden, 2001; Gee, 2005; Rymes, 2009). This definition highlights the sociocultural dimensions of language in that we need more information about the context in which language is being used to make sense of discourse. Rymes (2009) positions her understanding of discourse in contrast with linguists who argue, "A defining feature of language is its ability to be *de*contextualized" (p. 6). Per Rymes's example, if a student told us, "I saw a tree," it is because of the ability of language to be decontextualized that we know what a "tree" is without needing to see a tree. Rymes argues that *discourse* as language in use offers researchers the ability to consider analytically, the "capacity of language to do infinitely different things when being used in different kinds of situations" (p. 7). To know *why* a student is uttering, "I saw a tree," we would need more information. "Understanding what an utterance like 'I saw a tree' means involves understanding how that student was *using* the word *tree* in context and her purpose for telling you she saw one" (p. 6). It is therefore accepted that the sociocultural context in which a communicative interaction takes place mediates our understanding of utterances.

Given this, classroom discourse analysis takes the classroom as its context. Classrooms however are not bounded spaces; they are influenced by outside discourses, rules for participating, and power dynamics that privilege certain participants over others. Cazden (2001) powerfully demonstrated how classroom discourse analysis had the power to shed light on children's ways of participating in classroom routines that silenced some children while privileging others. Like previous scholars mentioned, Cazden was highly influential in demonstrating what might occur in classrooms when the communicative repertoires of children from "nonmainstream" backgrounds were not leveraged for learning. In the first edition of *Classroom Discourse: The Language of Teaching and Learning,* Cazden argued, "The task for both teachers and researchers is to make the usually transparent medium of classroom discourse the object of focal attention" (Cazden, 2001, p. 4). This was a clear argument for discourse analysis in classrooms since researchers and teachers could take the opportunity to review classroom discourse through the replaying of audio or video recordings with the goal of improving instruction.

Rymes (2010a) argues that in addition to teachers developing discourse analytical skills, students can also benefit from becoming aware of their own communicative repertoire, a statement also evoked by Cazden (2001). She points out that students benefit from learning the repertoires of school success, and perhaps just as importantly, teachers learn that students' home and community repertoires are just as valuable for learning.

When students' native communicative repertoires are recognized, they begin to see themselves as academically capable (i.e., capable of expanding their repertoire) . . . for schools to be successful, they do not necessarily need new curriculum or radical restructuring, but a change in culture and attitude—a change that recognizes that with teaching comes a commitment to build knowledge *of* our students as much as to build knowledge *in* our students. (Rymes, 2010a, p. 538–539)

These reflective habits developed in teachers and students are not only critical in our increasingly linguistically and ethnically diverse classrooms, but they allow students to "shuttle between communities, and not to think of only joining *a* community" (Canagarajah, 2007, p. 238, quoted in Rymes, 2010a, p. 544). We argue that this direction is where teacher education programs must go, building on the present skills and lived experiences of students in our classrooms rather than primarily supporting students' developing mainstream linguistic practices.

LEVERAGING DYNAMIC CLASSROOM COMMUNICATIVE REPERTOIRES

In the opening to the previous section, we argued that classroom discourse analysis research has the potential to provide data sets for researchers and practitioners to gain an understanding of leveraging in classroom interactions. In the following section we provide an example of a data set from our own research (Martinez, 2016) to highlight the everyday linguistic dexterity of racialized and minoritized youth in an urban high school. We make use of this transcript to offer a sense of the possibilities of leveraging as we move forward in our thinking about diverse communicative repertoires that children and youth bring with them to schools, and how teachers might better draw on these resources. As an illustrative example of the communicative repertoires heard in urban U.S. high schools, we provide the following transcript from a 10th-grade English language arts class in a Southern California community. Here, Ms. Luz,[1] a Latina teacher, is in the midst of an activity about Shakespeare's *Julius Caesar* with a group of Black and Latin@ youth. In this 22-second interaction, we catch a glimpse of the city "Englishes" that Kirkland (2010) refers to in the opening of this chapter, in addition to city "Spanishes" and other hybrid languages, gestures, and semiotic tools that characterize these youths' communicative repertoires. Youth were seated in pods of three desks facing the front of the classroom where Ms. Luz facilitated a class activity while standing in front of an overhead projector. She asked her students a series of known-answer questions about several characters from the play, specifically whether or not characters were "pro-" or "anti-" Caesar. After skipping Portia because she proved to be "tricky," Ms. Luz returned to this character, whose role in the assassination of Julius Caesar garnered debate among students. The following interaction began as Ms. Luz took the discussion "back to Portia."

TRANSCRIPT 1.0: "BACK TO PORTIA"

1	Ms. Luz:	Now let's go back to Portia. ((to class))
2		Portia's tricky. [Okay?
3	Troy:	[Where she- where she from ((to Ms. Luz))
4	Lorenzo:	*Con permiso.* ((to Ms. Luz)) (Excuse me)
5		Can you push it up [miss?
6	Ms. Luz:	[she's Brutus' **wife?** ((to Troy))
7	Troy:	She a **pro**
8	Lorenzo:	(2.0 sec) pa'**rri**ba:: ((to Ms. Luz)) (up)
9	Dave:	Yeah but she was- she was
10	Troy:	She don't even know whas up
11	Lorenzo:	[Hey miss:: ((to Ms. Luz))
12	Ms. Luz:	[She doesn't know what's going on
13		but [she's worried about her father right? ((to class))
14	Troy:	[((stands up blocking Lorenzo's view))
15	Lorenzo:	[Stu::pid **move** yo' bald head ma::n ((to Troy))
16	Ms. Luz:	So [**maybe** she would be neutral?
17	Lorenzo:	[Ms. Luz. (1.0 sec)
18		move yo (xxx xxx) man:: ((to Troy))
19	Student:	Yeah:
20	Ms. Luz:	Yeah. Okay.
21		Or-so we would just need to add another character
22	Lorenzo:	((stands up at his seat))(1.5) pick it up miss Luz
23		**I can't see::**
24	Ms. Luz:	hold on ((adjusts image projection))

Excerpted from Martinez (2016a, p. 67)

In this interaction, Lorenzo, Troy, and Dave made contributions to the official classroom space (Gutiérrez, Rymes, & Larson, 1995). What becomes clear in this transcript is the range of languages deployed by Lorenzo and Troy in particular. Lorenzo displayed his linguistic flexibility as he shifted from addressing Ms. Luz and Troy throughout the interaction, quickly adapting his utterances to each interlocutor. In Lines 4 and 5, Lorenzo code-switches from English to Spanish while speaking to Ms. Luz, "Con permiso (excuse me), can you pick it up miss?" Lorenzo shifted into what he and his peers identified as "hood" or "ghetto" talk when he addressed Troy in Line 15, "Stu::pid **move** yo' bald head ma::n" since Troy's head blocked Lorenzo's view of the image being displayed. Some might find Lorenzo's utterances here indicative of language crossing (Rampton, 1995) or sharing (Paris, 2011) since he is a Latino male uttering a language traditionally belonging to Blacks. Finally Lorenzo shifted his communication style when becoming frustrated by Ms. Luz who did not meet his request to move the projection up when he stood up at his desk in Line 22 uttering, "Pick it up miss Luz. **I can't see::**" moving away from his previous formal code.

Given this short 22-second interaction, Lorenzo flexibly shifts his communication style, providing an example of his extensive communicative repertoire. We also witness Troy engaging in a literary conversation with Ms. Luz and Dave while deploying utterances inflected with features of Black Language. For example, in Line 3 and 7, Troy invokes the use of a zero copula, "Where Θ she. Where Θ she from?" and "She Θ a pro" rather than "mainstream" varieties of English which might translate into "Where is she from" and "She is a pro." Additionally, Troy utters in Line 10, "She don't even know whas up" invoking the use of the third-person singular "s" rather than the MAE "doesn't." Invoking Kirkland (2010), we note that Lorenzo and Troy shift between their "city" Englishes, and for Lorenzo, his city Spanishes, not bound by traditional rules or ideologies of languages that demarcate where a language starts, ends, or begins again.

Neither Lorenzo nor Troy "checked their languages" at the classroom door to perform an imagined "standard" or "academic" English that many treat as a prerequisite for learning in U.S. classrooms (Fránquiz & de la Luz Reyes, 1998). In moving away from imagined monoglot standard ideologies of language (Silverstein, 1996), Lorenzo and Troy's linguistic flexibility would be treated as a normative feature of living in urban contexts, particularly a space where Black and Latina/o youth have socialized one another and expanded each other's communicative repertoires (Martinez, 2016a). Additionally, it is no longer necessary to continue the research trope that compares the languages of racialized and minoritized communities to middle-class monolingual communities (Baquedano-López, Solís, & Kattan, 2005; Flores & Rosa, 2015; Paris & Alim, 2014). A move away from the aforementioned conditions allows for a reimagination of the classroom interaction above. When we consider Lorenzo's and Troy's interactions, would Ms. Luz respond to Lorenzo (if she had actually heard him) in Spanish or Spanglish perhaps? In our reimagined classroom, Troy's contribution in Line 10, "She don't even know whas up," would not have been marked as it was by Ms. Luz's utterance, "She doesn't know what is going on" in Lines 12 and 13. We would hope to imagine a classroom where Troy's communicative repertoire would be leveraged to facilitate his meaning-making about Portia's role in Caesar's assassination in ways that would foster debate without *any* attention being placed on his linguistic features.

In actuality, Lorenzo and Troy do not treat their practices as remarkable in their classroom or larger community. In the larger study, Black and Latina/o youth described their communicative repertoires as filled with the necessary tools required for interacting across school, home, and community contexts, with some youth reporting their desire to learn "good" or "better" English or to learn how to "speak right." Yet this larger study and others highlighted in this chapter make the case that racialized and minoritized children and youth are linguistically flexible, evidence of a sophisticated and untapped resource for learning. While these practices were normative for these youth, they were also aware that teachers evaluated their utterances as flawed and potentially indicative of their lack of motivation to learn, particularly when heard in official classroom spaces.

In addition to showcasing the communicative repertoires of these youth, we interrogate the idea of "leveraging." Given the dynamic communicative repertoires that exist in our increasingly diverse classrooms, we note here that Ms. Luz did not leverage the communicative repertoires of her students. While Lorenzo addressed her in a range of Spanishes and Englishes, Ms. Luz responded to him only in English: "Hold on" in Line 24. This may be understandable given that perhaps Ms. Luz did not hear Lorenzo. However, despite bilingual abilities, Ms. Luz did not use her bilingualism to interact with her students. Additionally, her interaction with Troy confirmed her strict adherence to a standard English-only ideology that mediated her instruction. While Troy deploys utterances that feature copula absences ("She~Ø~a~pro" rather than "She is a pro") and omission of third-person singular ("She don't even know wassup" rather than She doesn't know what's up/happening), Ms. Luz provided corrective feedback to Troy. Therefore, while *leveraging* has the potential to facilitate the expansion of students' communicative repertoires, teachers might find corrective and repair practices as the most useful feature of facilitating the learning of a new task, such as a language and/or literacy competency (Razfar, 2005; Martinez, 2016a), this despite inconclusive findings on repair practices (Russell, 2009).

This short interaction provides a data set to the field, with a call for scholars to reimagine the potential for leveraging in language research. Powerful leveraging practices would shift any attempt to devalue the communicative repertoires of *any* student in our classrooms. Powerful leveraging practices would not only treat the communicative repertoires of racialized and minoritized youth as a strength but also raise the prestige of these languages through curricular and pedagogical practices. Transformative leveraging practices would begin with normalizing speakers like Lorenzo and Troy who were using their languages to communicate meaning and make meaning.

IMPLICATIONS AND CONCLUSIONS: CENTERING CHILDREN AND YOUTHS' COMMUNICATIVE REPERTOIRES

We bring this chapter to an end by considering the contributions of language and literacy scholars of color who shifted the ways in which researchers treated the communicative repertoires of children and youth in schools. Many of these scholars entered their research sites reflecting on their own positionalities, not taking for granted how they occupied spaces where they might be considered "native" ethnographers or researchers (Mangual Figueroa, 2014; Martinez, 2016b; Winn & Ubiles, 2011). These scholars have made clear to the field that we cannot make assumptions about our roles in contexts where we reflect one or more of the cultural groups represented, and that any scholar must enter these spaces working toward humanizing the research experiences for the participants (Paris & Winn, 2014). Souto-Manning (2014) reminds us that we must move away from ethnocentric research that does not centralize children or youth, and their own needs. Mangual Figueroa (2014) also challenges us to consider not only how we enter our research sites but also how we exit, since we leave our research sites after building relationships that our participants may also value beyond our research. These perspectives are important to consider as researchers move toward documenting the various communicative skills with which children and youth today participate.

In Heath's (1983) classic work, her central thesis is that families in the communities of Trackton and Roadville had rich, complex, and useful language practices that reflected norms and values of members of their respective communities, but these practices have varying degrees of difference from the language practices expected by "mainstreamers" in school and business. It may be obvious to most researchers today who study the language practices of nondominant communities that speakers have rich, complex, and useful language practices. However, there is still much distance between what researchers have demonstrated and language ideologies circulating in society today, perhaps best exemplified by the debate around the supposed word gap between toddlers of White, middle-class families and toddlers from more economically underresourced, and nondominant communities (Avineri et al., 2015; González, 2015). Heath contextualized her study as being relevant and necessary for the communities at that specific time and within their particular political context, with the possibility of wider reaching impact for children who come to school with language practices that are not considered mainstream. With more language researchers studying their own communities and language practices that are familiar and normal, what is contextually mainstream is in constant flux, even if teachers remain largely White, middle class, and English monolingual.

An argument made by many scholars who study and conduct research with and alongside communities of color is that we must decenter whiteness in our work. That is, we must no longer support a narrative that treats the (imagined) practices of White middle-class communities as unmarked, normalizing them and viewing their practices as the unexamined targets of instruction for children and youth of color. Recently, Paris and Alim (2014) argued,

We must move away from the pervasiveness of pedagogies that are too closely aligned with linguistic, literate, and cultural hegemony and toward developing a pedagogical agenda that does not concern itself with the seemingly panoptic 'White gaze' (Morrison, 1998) that permeates educational research and practice with and for students of color, their teachers, and their schools. (p. 86)

They continue, "For too long, scholarship on 'access' and 'equity' has centered implicitly or explicitly around the question of how to get working-class students of color to speak and write more like middle-class White ones" (p. 86). Here they point to a crucial need expressed by many scholars who contend that children and youth of color have sophisticated and creative language and literacy practices already, yet some researchers continue to treat the practices of an idealized White middle-class community as the norm. Gutiérrez (2006) calls on scholars to question notions of *White innocence* that may permeate our research by the use of theoretical frameworks and methodologies that "preserves racial subordination and the differential benefits for the *innocent* who retains her own dominant position vis-à-vis the 'objects' of study. From this perspective, we are all implicated in some way in maintaining *white innocence*" (p. 226). It is our hope that a renewed and purposeful interest in leveraging can facilitate conversations, alongside those around culturally sustaining pedagogies, where we work toward disrupting business as usual practices in our schools and redirecting the White gaze that education research has been preoccupied with for too long (Paris & Alim, 2014).

An argument that aligns with notions of White innocence and the need to humanize the learning experiences of children and youth comes from the view that simply providing access to dominant language and literacy codes will guarantee access to dominant institutions of power. For example, Martínez (2010) warns that access to dominant practices does not guarantee upward mobility or economic advancement as often promised by scholars, teachers, policymakers, and parents (Morrell, 2008). This perspective highlights power structures intricately related to language, and how leveraging practices might benefit from pedagogies of language awareness (Alim, 2004; Baker-Bell, 2013). However, educational reform efforts continue to laud approaches to learning that make false promises of upward mobility without taking into consideration institutionalized and educational disparities that limit access for students of color.

In the future work of language and literacy scholars, it would be beneficial to consider how we move away from treating adults, (teachers, educators, more expert others) as the only individuals capable of leveraging a practice for their students. Sociocultural learning scholars remind us that learning is a bidirectional process. Too often this process view adults as the more knowledgeable participant that is capable of leveraging learning (Eksner & Orellana, 2012). We can imagine many instances when a child or youth leverages an adult's cultural and/or linguistic practices for the purposes of learning. Our future research must also move in that direction, to document *how* students in our classrooms become the experts who can successfully leverage for adult learning.

As narratives of increasing diversity in schools continue, so does the normalizing of mainstream American English as the lingua franca of our learning environments, despite reports that linguistic diversity is on the rise. In U.S. schools today, we are witnessing an increase in school segregation patterns resulting in multiple communities of Black and Latina/o youth in hypersegregated schools with one another more than any other racialized group (Orfield & Frankenberg, 2014). In these spaces, educators will encounter students who use a range of languages to communicate meaning across their daily lives, bringing in sophisticated, yet highly marked and stigmatized language practices. More than likely, these will not align with what schools have come to privilege. However, as Paris and Alim (2014) point out, as our society becomes more multiracial and multilingual, the "culture of power" (Delpit, 1988) shifts as well.

In this review, we have highlighted the transformative work of scholars who have neither settled on normalizing White "ways with words" nor set as a goal the leveraging of communicative repertoires strictly to acquire or to become socialized into dominant communicative repertoires privileged in schools. Rather, these scholars have contributed to an ongoing conversation that seeks to amplify narratives that position racialized and minoritized children and youth as producers of knowledge mediated by diverse, flexible, and robust communicative repertoires. We believe that classroom discourse analytic methods can provide insightful and educative data that can work to leverage for researchers and practitioners a much more complex and dynamic understanding of how to understand classroom life, at the discourse level, and ways to leverage for transformative learning that works to sustain and raise the prestige of stigmatized communicative repertoires.

NOTE

[1]All names of individuals or places are pseudonyms.

REFERENCES

Alim, H. S. (2004). *You know my steez: An ethnographic and sociolinguistic study of style shifting in a black American speech community.* Durham, NC: Duke University Press.

Au, K. H. (1980). Participation structures in a reading lesson with Hawaiian children: Analysis of a culturally appropriate instructional event. *Anthropology & Education Quarterly, 11,* 91–115.

Avineri, N., Johnson, E., Brice Heath, S., McCarty, T. L., Ochs, E., Kremer-Sadlik, T., . . . Paris, D. (2015). Invited forum: Bridging the "language gap." *Journal of Linguistic Anthropology, 25,* 66–86.

Baker-Bell, A. (2013). I never really knew the history behind African American Language: Critical language pedagogy in an advanced placement English language arts class. *Equity and Excellence in Education, 46,* 355–370.

Baquedano-López, P., Solís, J. L., & Kattan, S. (2005). Adaptation: The language of classroom learning. *Linguistics and Education, 16*(1), 1–26.

Camangian, P. (2015). Teach like lives depend on it: Agitate, arouse, and inspire. *Urban Education, 50,* 424–453.

Cazden, C. B. (2001). *Classroom discourse: The language of teaching and learning* (2nd ed.). Portsmouth, NH: Heinemann.

Cazden, C. B., & Beck, S. W. (2003). Classroom discourse. In A. C. Graesser, M. A. Gernsbacher, & S. R. Goldman (Eds.), *Handbook of discourse processes* (pp. 165–197). Mahwah, NJ: Erlbaum.

Cole, M. (1998). Can cultural psychology help us think about diversity? *Mind, Culture, and Activity, 5*, 291–304.

Delpit, L. (1988). The silenced dialogue: Power and pedagogy in educating other people's children. *Harvard Educational Review, 58*, 280–299.

Eksner, J. H., & Orellana, M. F. (2012). Shifting in the zone: Latina/o child language brokers and the co-construction of knowledge. *Ethos, 40*, 196–220.

Flores, N., & Rosa, J. (2015). Undoing appropriateness: Raciolinguistic ideologies and language diversity in education. *Harvard Educational Review, 85*, 149–171.

Fránquiz, M. E., & de la Luz Reyes. (1998). Creating inclusive learning communities through English language arts: From chanclas to canicas. *Language Arts, 75*, 211–220.

García, O. (2009). *Bilingual education in the 21st century: A global perspective.* Malden, MA: Wiley-Blackwell Publishers.

García, O., & Wei, L. (2014). *Translanguaging: Language, bilingualism and education.* New York, NY: Palgrave Macmillan.

Gay, G. (2009). *Culturally responsive teaching: Theory, research and practice* (2nd ed.). New York, NY: Teachers College Press.

Gee, J. P. (2005). *An introduction to discourse analysis: Theory and method* (2nd ed.). New York, NY: Routledge.

González, N. (2001). *I am my language: Discourses of women & children in the borderlands.* Tucson: University of Arizona Press.

González, N. (2015, December). *Imagining literacy equity: Theorizing flows of community practices.* Keynote presented at the annual meeting of the Literacy Research Association, Carlsbad, CA.

Goodwin, M. H. (1990). *He-said-she-said: Talk as social organization among black children.* Bloomington: Indiana University Press.

Gumperz, J. (1964). Linguistic and social interaction in two communities. *American Anthropologist, 66*, 137–153.

Gumperz, J. J., & Hymes, D. (1972). *Directions in sociolinguistics: The ethnography of communication.* New York, NY: Holt, Rinehart & Winston.

Gutiérrez, K. D. (2006). White innocence: A framework and methodology for rethinking educational discourse and inquiry. *International Journal of Learning, 12*, 223–230.

Gutiérrez, K. D., Bien, A. C., Selland, M. K., & Pierce, D. (2011). Polylingual and polycultural learning ecologies: Mediating emergent academic literacies for dual language learners. *Journal of Early Childhood Literacy, 11*, 232–261.

Gutiérrez, K. D., Morales, P. Z., & Martinez, D. C. (2009). Re-mediating literacy: Culture, difference, and learning for students from non-dominant communities. *Review of Research in Education, 33*, 212–245.

Gutiérrez, K. D., Rymes, B., & Larson, J. (1995). Script, counterscript, and underlife in the classroom: James Brown versus Brown v. Board of Education. *Harvard Educational Review, 65*, 445–471.

Heath, S. B. (1983). *Ways with words: Language, life, and work in communities and classrooms.* New York, NY: Cambridge University Press.

Hopewell, S. (2011). Leveraging bilingualism to accelerate English reading comprehension. *International Journal of Bilingual Education and Bilingualism, 14*, 603–620.

Hornberger, N., & Link, H. (2012). Translanguaging in today's classrooms: A biliteracy lens. *Theory Into Practice, 51*, 239–247.

Hull, G., & Schultz, K. (2001). Literacy and learning out of school: A review of theory and research. *Review of Educational Research, 71*, 575–611.

Hymes, D. (1964). Toward ethnographies of communication. *American Anthropologist, 66*(6), 1–34.

Jiménez, R. T., David, S., Pacheco, M., Risko, V. J., Pray, L., Fagan, K., & Gonzales, M. (2015). Supporting teachers of English language learners by leveraging students' linguistic strengths. *The Reading Teacher, 68*, 406–412.

Kirkland, D. E. (2010). English(es) in urban contexts: Politics, pluralism, and possibilities. *English Education, 42*, 293–306.

Ladson-Billings, G. (1995). Toward a theory of culturally relevant pedagogy. *American Educational Research Journal, 32*, 465–491.

Ladson-Billings, G. (2014). Culturally relevant pedagogy 2.0: A.k.a. the remix. *Harvard Educational Review, 84*, 74–84.

Lee, C. D. (1995). A culturally based cognitive apprenticeship: Teaching African American high school students skills in literacy interpretation. *Reading Research Quarterly, 30*, 608–630.

Lee, C. D. (2006). "Every good-bye ain't gone": Analyzing the cultural underpinnings of classroom talk. *International Journal of Qualitative Studies in Education, 19*, 305–327.

Lee, C. D. (2007). *Culture, literacy, & learning: Taking bloom in the midst of the whirlwind.* New York: Teachers College Press.

Mangual Figueroa, A. (2014). La carta de responsabilidad: The problem of departure. In D. Paris, & M. T. Winn (Eds.), *Humanizing research: Decolonizing qualitative inquiry with youth and communities* (pp. 129–146). Thousand Oaks, CA: SAGE.

Martinez, D. C. (2016a). Emerging critical meta-awareness among Black and Latina/o youth during corrective feedback practices in urban English Language Arts classrooms. *Urban Education.* doi:10.1177/0042085915623345

Martinez, D. C. (2016b). "This ain't the projects": A researcher's reflections on the local appropriateness of our research tools. *Anthropology and Education Quarterly, 47*, 59–77.

Martinez, D. C., & Montaño, E. (2016). Toward expanding what counts as language for Latina and Latino youth in an urban middle school classrooms. *Literacy Research: Theory, Method, and Practice, 65*. Advance online publication.

Martínez, R. A. (2010). Spanglish as literacy tool: Toward an understanding of the potential role of Spanish-English code-switching in the development of academic literacy. *Research in the Teaching of English, 45*(2), 124–149.

Michaels, S. (2005). Can the intellectual affordances of working-class storytelling be leveraged in school? *Human Development, 48*, 136–145.

Miller, P. J., Cho, G. E., & Bracey, J. R. (2005).Working-class children's experience through the prism of personal storytelling. *Human Development, 48*, 115–135.

Morales, P. Z., & Aldana, U. S. (2010). Learning in two languages: Programs with political promise. In P. Gandara, & M. Hopkins (Eds.), *Forbidden Language: English learners and restrictive language policies* (pp. 159–174). New York, NY: Teachers College Press.

Morrell, E. (2008). *Critical literacy and urban youth: Pedagogies of access, dissent, and liberation.* New York, NY: Routledge.

Morrison, T. (1998, March). *Toni Morrison refuses to privilege white people in her novels!* [From an interview on Charlie Rose]. Public Broadcasting Service. Retrieved from http://www.youtube.com/watch?v=F4vIGvKpT1c

Orellana, M. F. (2009). *Translating childhoods: Immigrant youth, language, and culture.* New Brunswick, NJ: Rutgers University Press.

Orellana, M. F., Martínez, D. C., Lee, C. H., & Montaño, E. (2012). Language as a tool in diverse forms of learning. *Linguistics and Education, 23*, 373–387.

Orellana, M. F., & Reynolds, J. F. (2008). Cultural modeling: Leveraging bilingual skills for school paraphrasing tasks. *Reading Research Quarterly, 43*, 48–65.

Orfield, G., & Frankenberg, E. (2014). *Brown at 60: Great progress, a long retreat and an uncertain future.* Los Angeles, CA: The Civil Rights Project/Proyecto Derechos Civiles Retrieved from https://www.civilrightsproject.ucla.edu/research/k-12-education/integration-and-diversity/brown-at-60-great-progress-a-long-retreat-and-an-uncertain-future

Pacheco, M. (2012). Learning in/through everyday resistance: A cultural-historical perspective on community resources and curriculum. *Educational Researcher, 41,* 121–132.

Paris, D. (2009). "They're in my culture, they speak the same way": African American Language in multiethnic high schools. *Harvard Educational Review, 79,* 428–447.

Paris, D. (2011). *Language across difference: Ethnicity, communication, and youth identities in changing urban schools.* Cambridge, England: Cambridge University Press.

Paris, D. (2012). Culturally sustaining pedagogy: A needed change in stance, terminology, and practice. *Educational Researcher, 41,* 93–97.

Paris, D., & Alim, H. S. (2014). What are we seeking to sustain through culturally sustaining pedagogy? A loving critique forward. *Harvard Educational Review, 84,* 85–100.

Paris, D., & Winn, M. T. (Eds.). (2014). *Humanizing research: Decolonizing qualitative inquiry with youth and communities.* Thousand Oaks, CA: SAGE.

Philips, S. U. (1983). *The invisible culture: Communication in classroom and community on the Warm Springs Indian Reservation.* Prospect Heights, IL: Waveland Press.

Rampton, B. (1995). *Crossing: Language, and ethnicity among adolescents.* New York and London: Longman.

Razfar, A. (2005). Language ideologies in practice: Repair and classroom discourse. *Linguistics and Education, 16,* 404–424.

Ruiz, R. (1995). Language planning considerations in indigenous communities. *Bilingual Research Journal, 19,* 71–81.

Russell, V. (2009). Corrective feedback, over a decade of research since Lyster and Ranta (1997): Where do we stand today? *Electronic Journal of Foreign Language Teaching, 6,* 21–31.

Rymes, B. (2009). *Classroom discourse analysis: A tool for critical reflection.* Cresskill, NJ: Hampton Press.

Rymes, B. (2010a). Classroom discourse analysis: A focus on communicative repertoires. In N. Hornberger, & S. McKay (Eds.), *Sociolinguistics and language education* (pp. 528–548). London, England: Multilingual Matters.

Rymes, B. (2010b). Communicative repertoires and English language learners. In M. Shatz, & L. C. Wilkinson (Eds.), *The education of English language learners: Research to practice* (pp. 177–197). New York, NY: Guilford Press.

Rymes, B. (2014). *Communicating beyond language: Everyday encounters with diversity.* New York, NY: Routledge.

Silverstein, M. (1996). Monoglot "standard" in America: Standardization and metaphors of linguistic hegemony. In D. Brenneis, & R. Macaulay (Eds.), *The matrix of language: Contemporary linguistic anthropology* (pp. 284–306). Boulder, CO: Westview.

Souto-Manning, M. (2014). Critical for whom? Theoretical and methodological dilemmas in critical approaches to language research. In D. Paris, & M. Winn (Eds.), *Humanizing research: Decolonizing qualitative inquiry with youth and communities* (pp. 201–222). Thousand Oaks, CA: SAGE.

Urciuoli, B. (1996). *Exposing prejudice: Puerto Rican experiences of language, race, and class.* Boulder, CO: Westview Press.

Vetter, A. (2013). "You need some laugh bones!" Leveraging AAL in a high school English classroom. *Journal of Literacy Research, 45,* 173–206.

Winn, M. T., & Ubiles, J. R. (2011). Worthy witnessing: Collaborative research in urban classrooms. In A. F. Ball, & C. A. Tyson (Eds.), *Studying diversity in teacher education* (pp. 293–306). Lanham, MD: Rowman & Littlefield.

Zentella, A. C. (1997). *Growing up bilingual: Puerto Rican children in New York.* Malden, MA: Blackwell.

Chapter 21

Reimagining Critical Care and Problematizing Sense of School Belonging as a Response to Inequality for Immigrants and Children of Immigrants

CHRISTINA PASSOS DENICOLO
MIN YU
CHRISTOPHER B. CROWLEY
SUSAN L. GABEL
Wayne State University

This chapter examines the factors that contribute to a sense of school belonging for immigrant and immigrant-origin youth. Through a review of the education research on critical care, the authors propose a framework informed by cariño conscientizado— *critically conscious and authentic care—as central to reconceptualizing notions of school belonging. Research studies on teacher–student and peer relationships, student agency, and organizing are reviewed to identify how they function to disrupt structural factors that maintain educational inequities. Belonging as a concept is problematized through a re-envisioning of curriculum, pedagogy, and school–community relationships as a means to reduce inequality for immigrant and immigrant-origin youth and children.*

Inequality of educational experiences for immigrant youth and children of immigrants continues to be shaped by educational policies, programs, and practices that devalue students' knowledge and position them at the margins. This marginalization occurs largely due to prevailing ideologies of cultural deficit, the superiority of English, and meritocracy, the notion that one's success is determined solely by one's effort (Bartolomé, 2008b; Darder, Baltodano, & Torres, 2003; N. Flores & Rosa, 2015; Freire, 1970). Educational reform movements that center on accountability have contributed to the narrowing of perceptions of knowledge within schools (Zacher Pandya, 2011). The emphasis on standardization and high-stakes measurement of learning creates conceptions of learning that fail to acknowledge the linguistic complexity of

Review of Research in Education
March 2017, Vol. 41, pp. 500–530
DOI: 10.3102/0091732X17690498

bilingual language practices and the language-brokering skills that many immigrant-origin youth possess (Orellana, 2001). In this review, we argue that a lens informed by critical authentic care enables education researchers and practitioners to identify ideologies and structural barriers that maintain unequal access to education for immigrant-origin youth (Patel, 2013) and deter the enactment of culturally sustaining environments (Paris, 2012; Paris & Alim, 2014). We highlight studies that show the factors that enable students to build on the cultural and linguistic knowledge that they possess and construct a sense of belonging in schools.

Over the past several decades, there has been a growing body of research that has explored what it means for students to have a sense of school belonging and how that contributes to well-being (Kia-Keating & Ellis, 2007) and engagement with academic content in ways that produce positive outcomes for students (R. González & Padilla, 1997). Studies on a sense of school belonging have drawn primarily on quantitative methods to examine belonging as an internal process and identify its relationship to academic motivation (Goodenow & Grady, 1993) and self-efficacy (Bandura, 2000; Lewis et al., 2012). Few studies have explored the significance of school belonging for immigrant and immigrant-origin youth and children (Kia-Keating & Ellis, 2007). We build on these findings and define a sense of school belonging as both an individual feeling of being a valued member of a learning community and as a relational construct (Drolet & Arcand, 2013). Levitt and Schiller (2004) working from a social field perspective differentiate between ways of being and ways of belonging. Ways of being denote the interactions individuals have with others and participation within institutions that may or may not reflect their identities. Ways of belonging are reflected in the involvement with others and in activities within institutions in ways that communicate or contribute to a shared identity (Levitt & Schiller, 2004). We see school-based relationships and student agentive engagement within the school community as mechanisms that provide pathways for belonging in schools.

Given the persistence of inequities in educational access that position immigrant and immigrant-origin youth as outsiders and nonmembers, in this review we examine education research to understand the complexity of school belonging for this population and the significance it holds for learning and identity development. Studies have identified how the racialization and marginalization that Latinx[1] youth experience contributes to feelings of not belonging within U.S. society (Flores-González, Aranda, & Vaquera, 2014). For immigrant youth who are undocumented and migrate as young children, feeling a sense of connection or belonging in school settings is tenuous (R. G. Gonzales, Heredia, & Negrón-Gonzales, 2015) as belonging is inherently linked to citizenship (Abu El-Haj & Bonet, 2011) and those without citizenship in the United States are positioned as not belonging (Negrón-Gonzales, 2014).

We seek to understand from the existing research what a sense of school belonging means for reducing school inequality for immigrant youth and children of immigrants. The primary questions guiding this review are the following: What are the mediating factors that support a sense of school belonging for immigrant-origin youth? What is the relationship between critical care and school belonging? In what ways can the mechanisms associated with school belonging reduce educational inequality for immigrant-origin children and youth? Drawing on a theoretical framework of critical pedagogy we answer these questions by first providing a review of studies that examine critical care and school belonging. We then explore research on the mechanisms that promote belonging: participation, agency, and engagement of students from historically marginalized groups. Next we review research that explicates the politics of belonging through practices and policies that bring students and communities to the center of curriculum and pedagogy. We apply the findings and insights from the review of empirical studies to the educational experiences of immigrant and immigrant-origin children and youth.

As our main goal is to reimagine and reconceptualize the concepts of critical care and school belonging as a means of disrupting inequality for immigrant youth, we center our review on studies that address the structural conditions of schooling that undermine students' lived notions of belonging. We recognize the importance of considering the uniqueness of each immigrant group, the multiple identities that youth possess such as gender, dis/ability, sexual orientation, as well as contexts that bring together students from various backgrounds; however, it is beyond the scope of this chapter to review the extant literature on specific immigrant groups or the intersectionality of immigrant youth identities.

In this chapter, we argue that what we define as *cariño concientizado*—a pedagogy of critically conscious and authentic care is essential for reconceptualizing what it means to belong in school. In developing this term, we draw on the research on *cariño* (Prieto & Villenas, 2012; Rolón-Dow, 2005; Valdés, 1996; Valenzuela, 1999) and Freire's (1970) notion of critical consciousness to stress the critical and humanizing perspective necessary to disrupt hegemonic and racist policies and identify the mechanisms that promote school belonging for immigrant-origin youth and children. Care in school-based relationships must be reimagined to challenge discriminatory practices that maintain inequality in U.S. schools. This entails recentering the focus of studies on the processes through which students, teachers, families, communities, and other stakeholders are engaged in struggles to redefine and redevelop the means by which they might belong in schools.

As part of our discussion, we develop a reconceptualization of belonging through a review of studies that examine the concept of critical care and *cariño*. We highlight the important role of agency and social capital in conceptualizing belonging as a means of countering the policies and practices that perpetuate inequality for immigrant youth. Moreover, we want to challenge and extend existing research, which has traditionally been rooted in notions of psychological well-being as it relates to both defining and measuring students' feelings of belonging.

Our interest in understanding immigrant students' sense of school belonging is grounded in the importance of furthering education research focused on challenging longstanding inequalities. In framing our review and discussion in this way, we are seeking to disrupt inequalities by advocating for a paradigm shift in education research as it pertains to the school curriculum and pedagogy, school–community relationships, and opportunities for children and youth from bilingual, bicultural, and immigrant communities.

IMMIGRANT YOUTH IN U.S. SCHOOLS

For many immigrant youth and children of immigrants, experiencing a sense of school belonging may play an essential role in their academic and linguistic perseverance (Souto-Manning, 2013). Immigrant-origin youth vary in their prior educational experiences (Portés & Rumbaut, 2014), proficiency in English, and adaptation to U.S. cultural norms. They also vary in terms of the degree of stress experienced as a result of the political context, separation from family, forced relocation, or trauma (Kia-Keating & Ellis, 2007; Patel, 2013). Feeling a connection or sense of membership to others within the school community may provide support for processing, managing, and making sense of their experiences, academic learning, and the devaluation of their knowledge and abilities.

Immigrant youth and children of immigrants and their parents may experience gaps in communication and relationships due to differences in language proficiency and the pressure to adapt to U.S. customs that youth experience (Rumbaut, 2005). Families may experience a shift in roles, whereas children function as "experts" (Suárez-Orozco, Marks, & Abo-Zena, 2015) for their parents due to the development of language skills that enable them to translate for family members (Martinez, McClure, & Eddy, 2009; Orellana, 2001; Prieto & Villenas, 2012), and act as cultural brokers (Suárez-Orozco & Suárez-Orozco, 2001), due to their experiences navigating school and their communities. Some children and youth may feel a sense of pride in being an interpreter or cultural mediator for their adult family members; however, the skill level involved in language brokering may not be recognized within schools (Orellana, 2001).

While all youth experience the challenge of understanding themselves in new ways as they approach adolescence, this process is confounded for immigrant-origin youth who are forced to navigate multiple sets of expectations while developing their identities (R. G. Gonzales et al., 2015). In addition to expectations from their families, they may also adhere to religious principles and cultural practices that counter gender norms in the United States (Sarroub, 2001). Students entering middle and high schools face the added challenge of limited time before graduation to acquire the English language skills and content knowledge necessary to prepare them for college or the workforce. Educational programs that provide sustained instruction in students' primary language have been proven to be effective for English language acquisition for emergent bilinguals (Rolstad, Mahoney, & Glass, 2005; Umansky & Reardon, 2014); however, due to restrictive language policies, the majority of immigrant-origin students will not have access to programs (García, 2014; Menken & Solorza, 2014) designed to meet their linguistic and cultural strengths and needs (Hopkins, Lowenhaupt, & Sweet, 2015; Nieto, 1998). In addition to a lack of instructional support in their home languages, their linguistic knowledge is likely to be positioned as a barrier to academic achievement.

Studies have identified differences between immigrant students and children of immigrants. Newcomer youth demonstrate a higher level of motivation to engage in school (Kao & Tienda, 2005; Suárez-Orozco, Pimentel, & Martin, 2009; Valenzuela, 1999) and connect with teachers (Peguero, Shekarkhar, Popp, & Koo, 2015). These areas of school motivation have been found to weaken or diminish after the second generation (Peguero & Bondy, 2011; Portés & Rumbaut, 2014), contributing to a decrease in academic attainment or success (Portés & Rumbaut, 2001; Suárez-Orozco & Suárez-Orozco, 1995; Valenzuela, 1999). Although Suárez-Orozco, Suárez-Orozco, and Todorova (2008) found that over time some newcomer students' academic success improved, these differences across generations highlight the dehumanizing nature of schools that most likely contributes to decreases in motivation for second-generation students (Valenzuela, 1999).

The educational experiences and feelings of belonging of undocumented youth and children are inevitably rooted in the barriers to full participation in society that they encounter and the consistent contradiction of being immersed in ideologies of meritocracy and the American Dream in their schooling while being denied rights due to their citizenship (Negrón-Gonzales, 2014). Undocumented youth in mixed-status families experience additional layers of complexity regarding who belongs and are forced to navigate the responsibilities and emotions that go along with that (R. G. Gonzales et al., 2015). Many undocumented immigrants, youth, and their families live in a constant state of anxiety and stress stemming from the fear of being identified as undocumented due to the stigma it carries and risk posed by immigration raids.

Since the passing of *Plyler v. Doe* (1982), undocumented children and youth were granted the legal right to schooling in the United States, but this access to school was not a guarantee of equity or social mobility (R. G. Gonzales et al., 2015) and did not spare students from marginalization. Being tracked in overpopulated schools with limited resources created exclusionary contexts for undocumented students and blocked their access to curriculum and mentorship (R. G. Gonzales et al., 2015). R. G. Gonzales et al. (2015) found that students who gained entry to Advanced Placement or gifted classes experienced a sense of belonging and support, but for undocumented students who did not have the opportunity to develop positive relationships through courses such as these, school was an additional burden where they experienced a lack belonging.

The Development Relief and Education for Alien Minors (DREAM) Act, a bill presented to congress in 2001 was designed to provide undocumented youth with access to citizenship if they met specific criteria (Beltrán, 2014). The bill addressed some of the barriers undocumented youth encounter through provisions for voting rights, in-state tuition, and financial aid eligibility (S. Flores, 2010; R. G. Gonzales et al., 2015). It was designed as a potential pathway to citizenship for children who demonstrated academic success and traits aligned with being "good" and "worthy" through academic success and service to the community (Beltrán, 2014).

While the bipartisan bill has not passed, over the past two decades, immigrant rights efforts have developed into an organized movement (Flores-González &

Gutiérrez, 2010). Undocumented youth have contributed extensively to the DREAMer movement and due to their efforts, 10 states had in-state tuition laws by 2006, significantly increasing the number of undocumented higher education students in those states (S. Flores, 2010). While it is beyond the scope of this article to discuss the organizational strategies that gave life to the movement, it is important to note that youth enacted their agency (Negrón-Gonzales, 2014) as a way to "re-articulate their exclusion as inclusion" (p. 265). DREAMers, many of whom had previously taken great care to never reveal their undocumented status, spoke out to the media and in congress, to fight for fair pathways to citizenship. Negrón-Gonzales (2014) found through her study of undocumented youth activists in California that while the youth were consistently forced to navigate their exclusion from full participation in society, their agency and courage serve as testimonies to their potential and the potential that lies within marginalized and contradictory spaces (for a discussion on participation of lesbian, gay, bisexual, transgender, and queer youth, see Terriquez, 2015).

Social and Political Context

The criminalization of immigration adds to the complexity of the immigrant youth experience noted above. Regardless of the vast diversity among the immigrant population, the exclusionary focus of immigration policies and rhetoric extends to all marginalized groups (Pallares, 2014). Although studies have clearly indicated that immigrants are less likely to engage in criminal behavior, policies and rhetoric surrounding immigration position immigrants as criminals, particularly those who are undocumented (Ewing, Martínez, & Rumbaut, 2015),

The current political climate that has a presidential candidate calling for a ban on Muslims entering the United States and the construction of a wall to prevent immigration from Mexico, among other equally offensive and divisive statements, affects schools (Justice & Stanley, 2016). This anti-immigrant and xenophobic rhetoric is not new (Olsen & Dowell, 1989; Suárez-Orozco et al., 2008); however, it continues to marginalize undocumented (Flores-González et al., 2014) and immigrant-origin youth (Nieto, 1998) as well as U.S. born minoritized students. In a recent nonrandomized survey of 500 teachers across the United States, conducted by the Southern Poverty Law Center, teachers reported an increase in the use of hate language by students and a decrease in their capacity to respond to student anxieties (Costello, 2016). The survey results indicated that immigrant and U.S.-born students across racial and cultural groups expressed fear of future deportation under a Trump administration and despair due to their peers' support for the discriminatory stances displayed in the presidential campaign and media (Costello, 2016).

This political context contributes to the stigmatization, and exclusion experienced by immigrant youth, particularly those who are undocumented or in mixed status families. R. G. Gonzales, Suárez-Orozco, and Dedios-Sanguineti (2013) write, "Developing a sense of belongingness, of meaning, and purpose—all processes that are prone to disruption in the coming of age undocumented—require particular attention and nurture" (p. 1191). In the following section, we discuss the ways that school policies and practices deter belonging. We then review studies on care to identify how critical authentic care can provide the attention and nurturing necessary to create inclusive school contexts that manifest belonging.

THE RELATIONSHIP BETWEEN INEQUALITY AND LACK OF SCHOOL BELONGING

We draw from critical theories of education to examine the ways that schooling as an institution creates and maintains inequality for immigrant and immigrant-origin youth and children as well as students from historically marginalized communities. Freire (1998) posits that for education to be liberatory, the ideologies that shape instructional policies and practices must be identified and understood in relation to hegemony and maintenance of the status quo. Thus, the political nature of education must be kept at the forefront through *conscientização*—the development of a critical awareness regarding one's reality in relation to power in society, which, in turn, enables praxis (Freire, 1970). Through *conscientização* and praxis teachers and learners actively counter dehumanizing practices and reposition lived experience to the center of school-based learning.

In examining the politics of school belonging for immigrant-origin youth, we build on Goodenow and Grady's (1993) definition of belonging as "the extent to which [a student] feels personally accepted, respected, included and supported by others" (p. 61) in school contexts. Belonging is understood as a basic need (Maslow, 1970), feeling, and experience that is based on relationships with others; however, we acknowledge that a sense of belonging may not manifest in similar ways across contexts and cultures. Critical theories enable us to reconceptualize belonging through the concept of *cariño conscientizado* or critical and authentic care. Pedagogy rooted in critical care requires political and ideological clarity (Bartolomé, 2008b) and takes into account the situated nature of the expression and interpretation of caring behaviors. In the following section, these concepts are examined through studies of humanizing pedagogies that honor students' wholeness, acknowledge the intersectionalities they embody, and recenter students' lives in teaching and learning.

The relationship between school inequality and the lack of school belonging for students from historically marginalized groups has long been established (Antrop-González, 2006; Nieto, 1998; Valencia, 2002; Valenzuela, 1999). Throughout U.S. history, schools have been structured to systematically destroy students' connections to their home cultures, languages, and familial funds of knowledge as a means of domination and control (Del Valle, 2003). The erasure of students' languages and cultures was essential to the goal of assimilation through schooling through the 19th and much of the 20th century (Del Valle, 2003; Deyhle & Swisher, 1997; Moll & Ruiz, 2002; San Miguel, 2004; G. J. Sánchez, 2002; Valencia, 2002; Valencia & Solorzano, 1997). Wiley (2014) notes that while there have been periods in U.S.

history where bilingualism was supported, it was under the guise of assimilation for immigrants from Europe and subordination for American Indians. The intolerance of languages and language varieties other than Standard English became part of the U.S. national identity after World War I (Gándara & Hopkins, 2010; Wiley, 2014). As Ferguson, Heath, and Hwang (1981) describe, "Whenever speakers of varieties of English or other languages have been viewed as politically, socially, or economically threatening, their language has become a focus for arguments in favor of both restrictions of their use and imposition of Standard English" (p. 10). Underlying this intolerance are monoglossic language ideologies that situate monolingualism as the standard within society (García, 2009).

Ideologies surrounding the superiority of English, cultural deficits and assimilation (Bartolomé, 2008b; Deyhle & Swisher, 1997; Giroux, 1983) are reflected in specific aspects of schooling such as policies regarding language use (García, 2009), tracking (Valenzuela, 1999), Eurocentric curriculum, and low expectations for student learning (Antrop-González, 2006) on the part of teachers and administrators. Schooling continues to be organized in a way that normalizes dominant ideologies such as meritocracy (Patel, 2013) and colorblind perceptions that place responsibility for academic achievement on students and their families (Bonilla-Silva, 2006; Valenzuela, 1999).

Students' lack of school belonging is rooted in structural policies and practices that privilege Eurocentric values and norms while devaluing the cultural wealth (Yosso, 2005) and knowledge students' possess. School districts, in urban and culturally diverse contexts, as well rural new growth communities (Lichter, 2012) often lack teachers who reflect the cultures and languages of students (Quiñones, 2016; Valenzuela, 1999) and who are trained to meet students' linguistic learning needs (Faltis, 2013; Téllez & Varghese, 2013). For school districts experiencing shifts in student populations, program implementation may be negatively affected by lack of time dedicated to disrupting underlying ideologies (DeNicolo, 2016). For example, immigrant youth attending schools with bilingual programs may benefit from instruction in their home language; however, if their teachers hold deficit perceptions regarding their knowledge and abilities, students and parents will not feel a part of the school. According to N. Flores and Rosa (2015), raciolinguistic ideologies position the linguistic knowledge of bilinguals as deficient and lacking. The authors state, ". . . from a raciolinguistic perspective, heritage language learners' linguistic practices are devalued not because they fail to meet a particular linguistic standard but because they are spoken by racialized bodies and thus heard as illegitimate by the white listening subject" (p. 161). Lack of school belonging thus refers to the collective force of hegemonic ideologies, strategic actions, and unconscious perceptions and biases (Sabry & Bruna, 2007; Winn & Bezidah, 2012), that consistently devalue students' histories, languages, and cultural knowledge (Nieto, 1998; Rolón-Dow, 2005), negatively affecting their developing identities (Isik-Erkan, 2015; Urrieta, Kolano, Jo, 2015; Valencia, 2002), their belief in themselves as learners, and their academic potential.

EXAMINING BELONGING THROUGH TEACHER–STUDENT AND PEER RELATIONSHIPS

To understand factors that contribute to a sense of school belonging for immigrant-origin youth and children, we look to the research on care theory and caring as it relates to students placed at the margins through school policies and practices. Central to notions of belonging to a community within school is the sense that one is seen, heard, and valued as evidenced through the actions, relationships, and experiences of connectedness with others. Similar to "belonging," which is a term that encompasses a range of behaviors, scholars have cautioned that there is not a commonly shared or universal understanding of "caring" (Antrop-González & DeJesus, 2006; Cooper, 2009; McKamey, 2011; Valenzuela, 1999). In the paragraphs that follow, we discuss studies that have extended and built on Noddings's (1984) conceptualization of caring and connections between theories of care and belonging in education.

For Noddings (1984), schools and schooling should be centered on caring, thus establishing a learning environment created on a foundation of regard and respect. Noddings (1992/2005) stressed the difference between aesthetic caring, the attention to the aspects of teaching that are perceived as objective such as instructional goals, and authentic caring. Authentic caring is rooted in relationships that attend to the individual and their needs. This does not occur by happenstance but through seeing oneself as "one-caring" (Noddings, 2013, p. 5), committed to engaging in teaching and learning with students and knowing them as unique individuals with interests and agency. Noddings (2013) expressed that schools should enact an ethic of care through meaningful dialogue between teachers and students, opportunities for students to engage in caring for and with others, and confirmation of students' potential as learners.

Valenzuela's (1999) pivotal text *Subtractive Schooling* expanded on previous studies of care theory through her in-depth exploration of how care or a lack thereof shaped the educational experiences of Mexican and Mexican American high school students. The study illustrated how teachers and students utilized distinct interpretations of care to make sense of one another's behaviors and actions. The teachers' perceptions of their students' lack of care was based on external behaviors and rooted in deficit ideologies. Caring, for the students, was rooted in the concept of *educación*, which Valenzuela (1999) defined as, "the family's role of inculcating in children a sense of moral, social, and personal responsibility and serves as the foundation for all other learning" (p. 23). While the Mexican immigrant youth and U.S.-born students in Valenzuela's study had distinct experiences regarding the ways they were perceived by school staff, their perceptions of their teachers' sense of commitment to their learning and disinterest in helping them were based on *educación*, which prioritizes a person's well-being, use of good manners (Valdés, 1996), and what it means to be *bien educado*. Valenzuela noted that school staff, on the other hand, engaged in behaviors associated with aesthetic caring, prioritizing details within the learning environment, instead of authentic caring which was more aligned with *educación*.

Valenzuela found that immigrant youth drew on the strength of their identities as Mexicans alongside a deep appreciation for the opportunity to go to school. Due to this, their teachers viewed them as being more concerned about school than their Mexican American counterparts. Valenzuela cautioned however that the hopeful attitude and humility of the Mexican youth also contributed to a degree of invisibility. For all immigrant and children of immigrants to be fully seen in school, Valenzuela (1999) posited that authentic caring was needed. From an authentic caring stance, teachers take an active role to know their students, understand their resources, and engage in critical dialogue on topics that shape their experiences such as racism. This would allow for a repositioning of students' repertoires of knowledge to the center of teaching and learning and recognition of the structural policies that racialize and marginalize students.

Critical Care

Rolón-Dow's (2005) ethnographic study of nine Puerto Rican girls across their seventh- and eighth-grade years examined the ways that caring was understood and experienced by students and teachers. Complicating notions of caring through a critical race theory (CRT) and Latino critical race theory (LatCrit) lens, Rolón-Dow's study highlighted how history, power, and colonialism were key to understanding school-based relationships and perspectives on caring

Rolón-Dow's (2005) findings indicated ways that teachers' perceptions of students and the community where the school was located influenced their interpretations of the educational value families held for school. School staff viewed students' behavior as evidence of their parents' lack of care for education. The physical condition of the school communicated to students a lack of care for their well-being on the part of school staff. There were instances where teachers' perceptions were grounded in an understanding of the contexts of students' lives outside of school and Rolón-Dow found that when this occurred both aesthetic and authentic forms of caring were present. She noted however that while there were teachers that provided students with temporary refuge from the structural racism they encountered, this was not sufficient to counter the pervasiveness of the deficit perspectives that permeated their experiences in school. This study illustrates the situated nature of care and the need for school staff to examine the underlying ideologies that inform their perceptions of students and families.

Antrop-González and DeJesus (2006) use the term "soft caring" (p. 411) to refer to caring that is rooted in colorblind and deficit ideologies. Building on the work of difference scholars, Valenzuela (1999) and Thompson (1998) in particular, the authors advocate for a theory of "critical care" (p. 413), complicating colorblind theories (Thompson, 1998) on caring through social and cultural capital. Critical care in the schools that were part of their study was identified as value for students' cultural, linguistic community knowledge, and skills that enabled students' to access their multiple identities in school. Through the use of decolonizing methodology, Antrop-González and DeJesus found that authentic caring countered the marginalization students had experienced in previous schools and involved truly seeing students as agentive contributors to their education. Students experienced critical care through *personalismo* (Santiago-Rivera, Arredondo, & Gallardo-Cooper, 2002), a collection of behaviors that resembled the closeness within immediate and extended families and established a sense of community that enabled them to function like a family. The scholars used the term "hard caring" (2006, p. 413) to refer to the high expectations and accessibility of the staff. Due to the staff's awareness and understanding of the community, they identified ways to support students, such as staying in the building after school and ensuring that students had a way home. Teachers viewed all aspects of their students' development as their responsibility and this was evident to students and their families.

Beauboeuf-Lafontant's (2002) conceptualization of womanist caring is rooted in an understanding of the "cultural, historical, and political positionality of African American women, a group that has experienced slavery, segregation, sexism, and classism for most of its history in the United States" (p. 72). Drawing on Patricia Hill Collins's (1991) work, womanist epistemology recognizes the pervasiveness of hegemony and views collectivity as essential to social justice. From this humanizing perspective, womanist epistemology is concerned with freedom for all. Beauboeuf-Lafontant applies this to understanding womanist caring in education. Womanist caring educators embody maternal roles through a sense of investment and urgency and deep commitment to the academic learning and socioemotional well-being of their students (Beauboeuf-Lafontant, 2002). This form of caring is a by-product of othermothering (Collins, 1991; Dixson, 2003; Foster, 1993)—the identification of kinship with students and engagement with their learning connected to the greater good of the community. Womanist care is also an enactment of political consciousness (Beauboeuf-Lafontant, 2002): Womanist teachers view teaching as a social and political commitment to fight for equity and equality for African Americans through attention and care for each child (Cooper, 2009). This commitment is rooted in an "ethic of risk" (Beauboeuf-Lafontant, 2002, p. 83), a spiritual sensibility that is grounded in realism about the fact that social injustices exist and that work toward social justice is ongoing, challenging, and driven by hope. Cooper (2009) found that womanist care in schools is also evident in the caring practices of African American mothers. Similar to the ways that womanist teachers embody a critical understanding of the political nature of school and racism, Cooper's study identified the ways the mothers engaged in othermothering, supporting one another for the good of the community. The mothers in Cooper's study challenged the deficit perceptions held by school staff regarding their lack of care for their children's education. The mothers' authentic caring was rooted in their identities and lived experiences and informed by their experiences with racism and dedication to advocate for their children.

Cariño

Prieto and Villenas (2012) define *cariño* as "authentic notions of caring" (p. 423) and view this form of caring as intricately connected to critical awareness and advocacy. For Prieto and Villenas, this type of praxis embodies a holistic view of students situated within social and historical contexts. Through examining their own *testimonios*, Prieto and Villenas (2012) identified "pedagogies of *nepantla* rooted in *cariño*" (p. 426). *Cariño* was central to their pedagogy as it enabled them to view their teacher education students from a humanizing perspective that positioned students' biases as a reflection of hegemony. Prieto and Villenas (2012) viewed their students "not as individual racists, sexists, or nativists, but as cultural beings who are tapping into vast epistemological systems that support hierarchies of dominance" (p. 426). This highlights the ideological and political awareness that is central to *cariño*.

Similar to Rolón-Dow (2005) and Beauboeuf-Lafontant (2002), Bartolomé's (2008a) study illustrated that political awareness regarding equity and ideology are an essential aspect of what she calls authentic *cariño*. The preschool teachers in her study were committed to respecting their students and creating contexts where the knowledge they learned from home was honored and accessed for learning, such as the use of students' home language, Spanish. *Cariño* was expressed to students through Spanish, because the teachers recognized the language learning and academic benefits of students' developing and maintaining their home language. The teachers in Bartolomé's study stressed the need for monolingual educators to find ways to show their emergent bilingual students that they were important. They felt that through authentic care or *cariño* non-Latina/o English-speaking teachers could communicate respect to their Spanish-speaking students.

Freire (1998) referred to the words of poet Tiago de Melo, "armed love" (p. 40), to describe the courageous love that is required of teachers, rooted in advocacy and reflected in the persistence with which a teacher strives to know and teach their students. Teaching from a position of armed love is centered on humanity, involves the risk to speak out against inequities, and is expressed through dialogue. Valenzuela's (1999) account of Mr. Sosa, the band director who spent hours each evening preparing food for his students, exemplifies this type of love. Through learning about his students' lives, he realized a need they had and was able to fulfil his goal to connect with them. Authentic caring may require more than what can be done during school hours and can be taxing for teachers (Antrop-González, 2006). For this reason, *cariño* must be linked with a political consciousness that addresses caring at the school level through collaboration with students, families, and community members. Due to the history of schooling and structural racism, collective approaches to authentic care are necessary to disrupt inequities in policies and reconceptualize school belonging.

We draw on the studies above to reimagine critical care as a web of relationships and humanizing practices that make visible students' strengths to disrupt oppressive policies and promote a sense of belonging. This is important for all youth but is essential for undocumented students as R. G. Gonzales et al. (2015) describe based on their study,

The degree to which they felt included in school shaped the ways they understood and responded to their place in society. Indeed, this is not unique to undocumented students. But given the barriers they face to higher education (exclusion from financial aid, low-income families) and to the broader polity, they require integration into their schools at the level at which they can form trusting relationships with teachers and have access to resources that can help them navigate a truncated everyday life. (p. 328)

Informed by the Freireian (1998) concepts of armed love and *conscientização* (Freire, 1970), we argue that critical authentic care or *cariño conscientizado*—functions as a lens to identify the mechanisms for school belonging. We created the term *cariño conscientizado* joining the Spanish word *cariño* with *conscientização* in Portuguese to represent the scholarship on *cariño* and *conscientização* and to convey the critical awareness necessary to disrupt and challenge educational inequality. In the following section, we examine the ways that peer relationships and student agency function as mechanisms for the development of a sense of school belonging.

Peer Relationships and Student Psychosocial Well-Being

Furthering research on school belonging involves recognizing that while a positive network of friends and peers plays a role in assuring feelings of appreciation (Drolet & Arcand, 2013; Faircloth & Hamm, 2005) and access to classroom acceptance (Long, Bell, & Brown, 2004), this does not provide adequate shielding from the inequalities immigrant-origin youth and children encounter in schools. There is a crucial need for research that interrogates the structural conditions of schooling that undermine students' genuine notions of belonging. We argue for a deepened under-standing of the ways in which emergent bilinguals and immigrant-origin youth experience a sense of belonging in school as a means of informing policies and programs to counter the structural barriers that marginalize them.

Some of the research on belonging has been rooted in psychology-based approaches that focus on defining and measuring a sense of school belonging through peer rela-tionships as they relate to students' feelings of well-being. For example, Selman, Levitt, and Schultz (1997) reported that students' peers offered important emotional supports that enhanced the development of psychosocial competencies in young chil-dren and early adolescence. Part of this beneficial emotional support that students received served to buffer feelings of loneliness and embarrassment, while also bolster-ing self-confidence and self-efficacy. Peers were frequently cited as providing impor-tant emotional sustenance during challenging times that supported the development of psychological and social well-being (Suárez-Orozco et al., 2009), as well as accep-tance within a classroom community (S. Brown & Souto-Manning, 2007; Dyson, 1993).

Peer interactions affect students' sense of acceptance (Long et al., 2004), by pro-viding and offering tangible forms of support and guidance. Peers can moderate the effects of school-related violence and provide support and relief from anxiety (Gibson, Gándara, & Koyama, 2004). That said, while peers may contribute to students' feel-ings of belonging in a classroom or school, peer interactions and friendship cannot be the sole mechanisms for belonging and inclusion. Since immigrant youth often attend highly segregated, low-resourced schools (Orfield, 1998), they may have limited access to networks of support, for learning the steps necessary to pursue higher education (Suárez-Orozco et al., 2009). Social support from peer relationships has also been recognized as connected to aspects of schooling associated with achievement.

Peer Support and Student Achievement

In addition to the role that peers play in cultivating an emotional sense of belonging and acceptance, studies show that peers provide tangible help with homework assignments, language translation, and orientation within a new school setting (Gibson, Bejínez, Flidalgo, & Rolón, 2004). For newly arrived immigrant students, the companionship of conational friends has been found to function as a resource for information on navigating school culture and norms (Suárez-Orozco et al., 2009).

Furthermore, peers have the ability to support academic engagement in concrete ways by clarifying readings or lectures and helping one another complete homework assignments—as Stanton-Salazar (2004) notes, this process of exchanging information not only has an immediate impact on the day-to-day aspects of navigating schooling but it also affects their longer term success such as exchanging information about Scholastic Aptitude Tests, helpful tutors, volunteer positions, and other college pathway knowledge. Moreover, by valuing certain academic outcomes and by modeling specific academic behaviors, peers establish the "norms" of academic engagement (Ogbu & Simons, 1998; Steinberg, Brown, & Dornbusch, 1996).

Agency, Social Capital, and Organization

The body of research that examines peer relationships through a conceptual lens drawing on psychosocial well-being provides worthwhile insights; however, more research is needed to understand school belonging aimed at disrupting inequalities. To encourage further research and analyses along these lines, we address studies that incorporate critical discussions of the ways that agency, social capital, and organizing for change influence peer relationships and school belonging.

Zine's (2000, 2008) work highlights the significance of Muslim Student Associations for Muslim youth in Canadian schools. The student associations functioned as a space for students to acquire strategies for navigating the daily experiences of marginalization in school. This echoes research suggesting that organizations for Muslim youth support processes for positive identity formation and the negotiation of pressures stemming from being a religious minority within a secular society (Gilliat, 1997). Islamic student organizations provide Muslim students with a crucially important system of support, while at the same time offering notions of familiarity through the sponsorship of events and gatherings in accordance with Islamic conventions. As Zine (2000) notes, Muslim Student Associations provide social and religious support beneficial to Islamic subcultures within schools, while also serving the critically important function of both directly and indirectly challenging structural and institutional obstacles.

Traditionally, theories of resistance in education tend to focus on issues surrounding class and/or race (Dolby, Dimitriadis, & Willis, 2004) as a catalyst for solidifying student dissent and transforming it into collective action. Studies examining student organizations, youth participatory action research (YPAR) projects, and community-based extracurricular activities (Antrop-González, Vélez, & Garrett, 2008; Cammarota, 2016; Ginwright, Noguera, & Cammarota, 2006) demonstrate that student organizations and activities structure forms of resistance around racial/ethnic and religious identification as a site for both political and social action, as well as educational critique. It is through the formation of these grassroots student organizations that students from bi/multilingual, bi/multicultural, and immigrant communities are able to form bases for challenging Eurocentrism in public schooling. Moreover, the mobilization of strategies for formalized resistance involved developing foundations for collective political action and advocacy, empowering students to engage in struggles over the right to belong in schools.

Though formalized resistance, students can also directly challenge curriculum content and textbooks that present biased information such as an overtly hostile and intolerant perspective of Islam (Zine, 2008). Future research needs to take into consideration the importance of challenging structural conditions and institutionalized forms of discrimination in schools. Students' psychological and social well-being is important, but for inroads to be made toward systematically addressing inequalities, more research is needed on the extent to which an increase in student sense of school belonging might be a secondary outcome associated with addressing root causes of oppression.

DISRUPTING INEQUALITY THROUGH UNDERSTANDING THE POLITICS OF SCHOOL BELONGING

In this section, we seek to build on the research and arguments Abu El-Haj (2015) has put forth as it relates to the politics of belonging for Muslim transnational communities. This requires an understanding of students' sense of belonging in school as something that is deeply political (Castles & Davidson, 2000; Levinson, 2005; Maira, 2009; Ríos-Rojas, 2011, 2014; P. Sánchez, 2007; Yuval-Davis, 2011). Such understandings of school belonging involve "not only constructions of boundaries but also the inclusion or exclusion of particular people, social categories, and groupings within these boundaries by those who have power to do this" (Yuval-Davis, as cited in Abu El-Haj, 2015, p. 5).

Collective involvement is central to the politics of belonging and differs from psychosocial constructions of belonging rooted in notions of well-being. Abu El-Haj (2015) emphasizes that being part of a collectivity, especially a collectivity based on nationality, "is never given, but instead is actively constructed through political projects" (p. 5). Consequently, it is critical to move beyond "analyses that focus on questions of achievement, acculturation, and assimilation" (Abu El-Haj & Bonet, 2011, p. 51), when discussing the education of immigrant-origin children and youth.

Schools are one of the primary institutions where immigrant-origin youth learn to develop a sense of belonging at a societal level (Abu El-Haj & Bonet, 2011). The dominant discourses of assimilation and integration, as Levinson (2005) states, "presuppose certain 'desirable' social characteristics, the prerequisites of political participation, which may or may not be deemed educable" (p. 334). These characteristics entail the misrecognition of culture and identity and function through acts of marginalization. Problematizing traditional conceptualizations of student sense of school belonging is aimed at challenging longstanding inequities. Therefore, our goal in this work is to expand such a framework of understanding and advocate for a paradigm shift in education research to explore the need for "robust accounts of the role that schools play in shaping the parameters of social membership and political participation" (Abu El-Haj & Bonet, 2011, p. 32). Additional inroads toward advocating for a politics of belonging framed in this manner can occur through the school curriculum and pedagogy, school-community partnerships, and critically conscious teachers of children and youth from immigrant communities.

DISRUPTING INEQUALITY THROUGH CURRICULUM AND PEDAGOGY

We believe it is important to foreground our discussion in this section with a very brief mention of how we conceptualize our understanding of the curriculum. In one sense, the curriculum entails the process of sanctioning and transmitting official knowledge through the prescribed use of textbooks and curriculum materials (Apple, 2014). It is along these lines that the processes of sorting, selecting, organizing, and framing knowledge should be recognized as inherently ideological (Apple, 2004). And as such, the question of the curriculum has to do less with what knowledge and much more with whose knowledge is privileged. This conceptualization of the curriculum should also be recognized as encompassing both the official and hidden curriculum. Thus, curriculum refers to the content that is covered in a particular course or lesson as well as the instructional practices that are utilized to engage students with content and the decision making that places students in the course. Yosso (2002) stresses the need to view curriculum as encompassing the processes that shape instruction that are not made explicit such as the content selection, student placement, and rules of engagement. Looking at curriculum through a lens of *cariño conscientizado* means that we view curriculum as a process of environmental design that privileges and promotes ideologies surrounding belonging and inclusion. For example, items such as the posters with breakdowns of student performance on standardized tests or participation in extracurricular events are also part of the school curriculum. These types of displays send powerful messages to students about how they are (or are not) valued, in what ways they belong in school, how the institution of schooling positions them as both people and learners, and the kind of education they are viewed as deserving. For immigrant-origin youth, particularly those who are undocumented, curriculum more often communicates how they are not members of society and do not belong.

Despite greater attention in recent years to issues of power and identity in curriculum associated with analyses of race, culture, gender, and sexuality, more work needs to be done in this area so that immigrants, children of immigrants, and emergent bilingual students have greater opportunities to experience a sense of belonging in the schools they attend. A. L. Brown and Au (2014) draw from the theories of cultural memory and CRT to contextualize how the histories of race and curriculum are portrayed—noting that "the voices and curricular histories of communities of color in the United States are largely left out of the selective tradition associated with the narrative of the field's foundations" (p. 358). Another aspect of this work entails advancing conceptions of multiculturalism insofar as efforts are undertaken which focus on the critique of both the inequities of the status quo and liberal ideology that fails to advance the cause of justice for people of color (Dixson & Rousseau, 2005). Crucially, it is worth noting that Ladson-Billings and Tate's (1995) critique of multiculturalism, needs to be recognized as an effort to mobilize action as opposed to a dismissal of the need for more inclusive schooling.

Re-envisioning the curriculum—through a focus on bolstering students' sense of belonging in school—involves linkages to instructional practices grounded in culturally relevant pedagogies (K. D. Brown, Brown, & Rothrock, 2015; Ladson-Billings, 1995, 2009, 2014), culturally sustaining pedagogies (Paris & Alim, 2014), ethnic studies curriculum (Dee & Penner, 2016; Halagao, 2010; Sleeter, 2011; Vasquez, 2005), and a recognition of teachers as cultural workers (Freire, 1998; Knoester & Yu, 2015). Ladson-Billings (2014) discusses her work with the hip-hop and spoken word program First Wave as an example of how culturally sustaining pedagogy (Paris, 2012) allows for a fluid understanding of culture, and teaching practices that explicitly engage questions of equity and justice. Through this work, scholars and educators situate

culturally relevant pedagogy as the place where the "beat drops" and then layer the multiple ways that this notion of pedagogy shifts, changes, adapts, recycles, and recreates instructional spaces to ensure that consistently marginalized students are repositioned into a place of normativity—that is, that they become subjects in the instructional process, not mere objects. (Ladson-Billings, 2014, p. 76)

Again, this requires that teachers and educators use culturally relevant pedagogies in linguistically and culturally appropriate ways (Nieto, 2010; Roy & Roxas, 2011), counter forms of discrimination in schools while simultaneously advocating for students (Niyozov & Pluim, 2009; Rahman, 2013), work collaboratively through informal networks and inquiry groups (Abu El-Haj, 2003), actively confront forms of marginalization through culturally responsive teaching (Gay, 2010; Sleeter, 2012), and advocate for the values present in well-planned and well-taught ethnic studies curriculum (Sleeter, 2011).

It is with these points related to culturally relevant pedagogy in mind that we want to turn our discussion to conceptualizations of the curriculum that are explicitly connected to CRT. This work is not simply a matter of adding supplemental material to the existing curriculum, although doing so might be a valuable first step for some, but rather it is about reframing the curriculum around forms of resistance. For example, Yosso (2002) discusses the idea of a critical race curriculum as an approach to understanding curricular structures, processes, and discourses, informed by CRT—highlighting five tenets: the centrality and intersectionality of race and racism, the challenge to dominant ideology, the commitment to social justice, the value of experiential knowledge, and interdisciplinary perspectives.

While the process of establishing shifts in the curriculum is one piece of a structural project related to content and pedagogy, another part of this has to deal with epistemologies. S. M. Gonzales's (2015) work in this area uses personal narrative to examine the role of *las abuelitas*, or grandmothers, as educators in Mexican, Mexican American, and Chicana/o culture—paying careful attention to how grandmothers used *abuelita* epistemologies to counteract the subtractive schooling processes in the United States, in order to resist the assimilative pressures, and thus positively affect student adjustment and success. San Pedro (2015) also explores the notion of epistemological shifts within the curriculum by examining a Native American literature classroom composed of a multitribal and multicultural urban student body, where students in this course engage in whole-class discussions focusing on contemporary and historical issues concerning Native American tribes and communities. Often these conversations focus on issues of oppression, colonization, and the unjust treatment of people of color. Significantly, the study challenges traditional ways silence has been interpreted as a deficiency within standard schooling, moving toward a view of silence as engaging, rich in identity construction, and filled with agency.

To truly belong in school, the experiences of immigrant-origin youth and children need to be placed at the center of the curriculum (Cammarota, 2011; Campano, Ghiso, & Welch, 2016; Chan, Phillion, & He, 2015; Li, 2006). Souto-Manning (2013) uses critical narrative analysis to look at how institutional discourses of school success in the United States shape the ways in which emergent bilingual and multilingual students of color come to make sense of their schooling experiences. She explores the ways in which young bilingual and multilingual students construct their own identities through narratives both within and across settings and highlights the need to create spaces in which language (mis)alignments are acknowledged, repositioned at the center of the curriculum, and positively reframed. DeNicolo, González, Morales, and Romani (2015) attempt to counter deficit notions of Latinx students, families, and communities by illuminating the powerful ways that students utilize various forms of community cultural wealth (Yosso, 2005)—this entails challenging directly the racist assumptions about Spanish being of lesser value than English and Latinx students being less academically capable than their White, monolingual English-speaking counterparts.

Cammarota and Romero's (2011) work discusses participatory action research (PAR) and YPAR as forms of curriculum for Latina/o high school students and how it assisted in facilitating greater investment in both their participation in social settings and their awareness of how to engage in forms of personal and social transformation. PAR and YPAR informs the pedagogical and epistemological aspects of the Social Justice Education Project curriculum, which serves the cultural, social, and intellectual needs of Latina/o students and allows them to "engage in Freire's conception of culture and undertake a praxis that leads to a transformation of self and community" (Cammarota, 2011, pp. 840–841). One of the key takeaways from this work is the emphasis placed on providing multiple paths for connecting academic learning to the ways students use their cultural and linguistic knowledge outside of school and the potential for this to bolster students' sense of school belonging and address larger issues of inequality.

THE CULTURAL POLITICS OF BELONGING: REIMAGINING SCHOOL–COMMUNITY RELATIONSHIPS

In numerous regards, schools are considered the key institution through which children and youth from bilingual, multilingual, and immigrant communities come to understand and define their sense of belonging. School is also a site through which the cultural politics of power and hegemony play out in daily practice. Research examining the academic engagement and achievement of children and youth from these communities often use culture as an analytic lens to "explain differences in educational experiences, opportunities, and outcomes of ethnic and racial minority students" (Ngo, 2013, p. 959). At the same time that this work is being done, it is essential to be cautious about the fact that students, families, and communities can be problematically defined in terms of cultural deficits. Viewing ethnic and racial identities as subtractive is detrimental to the goals of supporting students' academic success (Warikoo & Carter, 2009). Conceptualizing ethnicities, cultures, and identities as assets that are essential to students' potential, orient students toward the goals of upward academic achievement. However, one of the substantial challenges to this involves countering the types of entrenched structural biases, forms of discriminations, and systematic mechanisms of oppression that continue to persist and that reflect the social, historical, and political context (Abu El-Haj & Bonet, 2011).

Having noted this, given the focus of this chapter, it is not possible to engage fully in extensive debates about the nuances and complexities surrounding notions of cultural politics. Instead, we are framing this review of research around both promoting and furthering a research agenda that is focused on challenging inequalities. As such, we have chosen to highlight a few studies in order to investigate how some are working to challenge the deficit constructions of children, families, and communities through the disruption of discriminatory practices in schools—specifically in terms of reimagining education in ways that establish more sustainable and responsive relationships between schools and communities.

A beginning point for challenging deficit notions of students, families, and communities entails embracing a critical care approach where diversity is an asset as opposed to an obstacle (Ayers, 2001) and that promotes drawing on local funds of knowledge (N. González, Moll, & Amanti, 2005). It is often the case that the cultural knowledge, skills, and abilities of individuals from socially marginalized communities often goes unrecognized and unacknowledged. Yosso (2005) identifies various forms of cultural wealth present in communities—aspirational, navigational, social, linguistic, familial and resistant capital—and how they have the potential to be nurtured and utilized in schools in powerful ways stressing,

They are not conceptualized for the purpose of finding new ways to co-opt or exploit the strengths of Communities of Color. Instead, community cultural wealth involves a commitment to conduct research, teach and develop schools that serve a larger purpose of struggling toward social and racial justice. (p. 82)

Another aspect related to school–community relationships insofar as the cultural politics of belonging has to deal with directly addressing policies for religious expression. Collet (2010) advocates for an understanding of schools as "sites of refuge"— meaning that schools are places where immigrants and refugee students should be able to express religious identities and religious expressions in the absence of discrimination or persecution. He argues for greater inclusion through the recognition of minority religions, given that they may involve group, and not only individualized expression. Thus, students should not only have equal opportunities to engage in silent prayer but also the right to observe religious holidays and participate in symbolic religious expressions (Noddings, 2005), such as the wearing of *hijab* by Muslim girls and the *kirpan* for Sikh boys. It is important to point out, in anticipation of potential resistance, that the acceptance of students' cultures and religious beliefs is not the same as the endorsement of a particular religion by a public school.

To strengthen school–community relationships, it is important that stakeholders maintain a proactive and cooperative model for collaboration (Sabry & Bruna, 2007). As such, education for immigrant-origin students can take the form of a multifaceted interplay between students' homes, community resources, school programs, and classroom practice to enrich the curricular experience for students (Schlein & Chan, 2010). Similarly, Abu El-Haj (2009) highlights some ways in which an Arab American community arts organization served as an important site for promoting youth civic participation and social activism—again, calling attention to the importance of communities as resources for educators. And as another example, Antrop-González (2006) notes how a small school, through its curriculum, was able to privilege the linguistic, cultural, and sociopolitical realities of its communities as a "sanctuary" for the students. This work echoes our earlier discussions in this chapter regarding student–teacher relationships, notions of critical care, in addition to the importance of affirming and incorporating students' racial, cultural, and ethnic identities into the discourses of schooling.

Returning to our earlier point about directly confronting and challenging deficit constructions of certain children, families, and communities, Long, Souto-Manning, and Vasquez (2016) note that if such work is not undertaken, marginalized and oppressed groups are going to continue to experience forms of discrimination through inculcated cycles of systemic and structural inequity (Winn & Behizadeh, 2012). The perpetuation of ongoing inequalities is evident in the processes through which children of color, emergent bilinguals, and those living in poverty are labeled as deficient in any number of ways. Such labels more often than not follow students throughout their time in school—not only affecting students' sense of worth or belonging but also becoming a self-fulfilling prophecy with regard to students' immediate and long-term academic success.

It is here that a focus on the cultural politics of belonging through a strengthening of school–community relationships has the potential to interrupt inequitable practices. As we discussed earlier, culturally relevant and sustaining pedagogies serve an important role in the enactment of the curriculum as it pertains to promoting students' success and achievement (Gay, 2010; Ladson-Billings, 1995; Paris, 2012). It is important to have school leaders who challenge the deficit views of children and families in order to "make the commitment to work with teachers to examine attitude, assumptions, practices, and policies [and] move beyond *talking* about educating every child to *taking action* for positive and transformative change" (Long et al., 2016, p. 18).

Stronger collaborations between and among local community grassroots organizations, school districts, university researchers, and the city municipalities to develop authentic curriculum projects, has the potential to facilitate change *beyond* immediate notions of classroom or school-based notions of belonging. As Valenzuela, Zamora, and Rubio (2015) document, a grassroots community revitalization curriculum project not only works to both value the cultural wealth of "participating students, parents, teachers, and local arts institutions" (p. 47) but also assists in the transformation of researchers and community leaders. Another example of how schools are taking an active role in responding to resources within local communities is occurring in New Zealand. Berryman, Glynn, Woller, and Reweti (2010) describe educational transformation to better reflect a Māori worldview through the use of culturally responsive pedagogies that seek to ensure Māori values are recognized and legitimized. Again, through the cooperative interplay between schools and communities, cultural consciousness can be supported in ways that foster a greater sense of school belonging. Ngo (2013) calls attention to forms of consciousness as a lens for analyzing immigrant education that highlights the deployment of culture as social critique and political strategy.

Supporting sense of school belonging for immigrant entails much more than their individual feelings of involvement or inclusion. Supporting students' sense of belonging in ways that challenge and disrupt inequalities is very much about *cariño conscientizado*—critical and authentic care that enables school staff to tackle structural racism directly, through multifaceted approaches to see, learn, collaborate with and engage immigrant communities as democratic partners in supporting the education of all students.

CONCLUDING THOUGHTS

Cariño conscientizado—a pedagogy of critical and authentic care, reconceptualizes what it means to belong in school for immigrant and immigrant-origin youth and children through the identification of mechanisms that promote school belonging. Relationships, curriculum, and pedagogical practices that engage immigrant students and their families as valued partners play central roles in disrupting inequality and creating opportunities for students to experience a sense of belonging in school. In working toward active and direct means for disrupting inequalities—particularly as it relates to forms of oppression and alienation experienced by immigrant and immigrant-origin youth and children—perhaps one of the most important areas where inroads toward addressing these problems might be made has to do with the education and preparation of teachers. To make genuine and authentic inroads toward supporting student sense of belonging, teacher education needs to recenter its focus on preparing teachers to work across languages, citizenship status, and immigration experiences in ways that not only create opportunities for teacher candidates to reflect and identify the prevalent myths they hold about immigrant communities but also require them to actively confront and struggle against them (Fránquiz, Salazar, & DeNicolo, 2011). The University of Arizona serves as one example of how colleges of education are responding to this need. The Department of Teaching, Learning & Sociocultural Studies developed a position statement expressing their commitment to hold themselves accountable to maintain an awareness regarding power, marginalization and equity, among many other factors that contribute to inequality at an individual and collective level. The Racial Literacy Roundtables at Teachers College (Sealy-Ruiz, 2013) are another example of current practices in teacher education that aim to disrupt inequality through critical awareness. The roundtables bring together community members, high school students, professors, and graduate students to engage in critical discussions on race, equity, and schooling.

Additional recommendations for this type of work entail greater partnerships between local communities and colleges of education. For example, as we discussed above, both PAR and YPAR offer possible means by which to provide rich opportunities for students to practice, engage, and/or develop authentic notions of personal, civic, and community/social activism. Furthermore, such endeavors also have potential to provide teacher candidates with worthwhile opportunities for reflection on the ways that school policies, programs, and practices marginalize and racialize immigrant youth in order to become critically conscious regarding their own identities, cultures, biases, and privilege (Valenzuela, 2016) and how these shape their instructional practices. Beginning this process during a teacher education program supports the development of dispositions in teacher candidates that will enable the enactment of *cariño conscientizado*—critical authentic care for immigrant and immigrant-origin students and their families (Bartolomé, 2008a; Freire, 1998; Mercado, 2016).

Teacher education is not simply training (Crowley & Apple, 2009). Teachers need to be recognized as generators of knowledge responsive to the diverse student populations they serve (Ladson-Billings, 1999; Goodwin, 2002; Goodwin et al., 2014) and advocates that position immigrant, refugee, and undocumented students as knowledge producers. While it should go without saying, such work involves active participation in struggles toward achieving justice for all students (Kumashiro, 2015; Zeichner, 2009), particularly within teacher education.

In order to foster schools as sites that are truly dedicated to notions of belonging and inclusion, education research must take up the challenge inherent in a lens informed by *cariño conscientizado*. There cannot be belonging within schools if the structural inequities that shape the education of immigrant-origin youth in the United States are not identified and dismantled. Exposing the ideologies that position immigrant-origin youth at the margins would make visible the policies and practices that devalue students' linguistic abilities (N. Flores & Rosa, 2015; Patel, 2013) and uphold the myth of meritocracy (Freire, 1970). Through this level of consciousness, we can disrupt the discourses that maintain illusions of inclusion for immigrant-origin youth and contribute to a broadening of the conceptions of learning. Problematizing belonging pushes the field of education research to demonstrate the possibilities that exist for school belonging that are rooted in the meaningful, agentive, and transformative participation of immigrant and immigrant-origin children, youth, and families.

NOTES

Min Yu and Christopher B. Crowley contributed equally to this work.

[1]We use the nonbinary and inclusive term *Latinx* to refer to Latinas/os; however, when referring to specific studies, we maintain the terminology used by the authors.

REFERENCES

Abu El-Haj, T. R. (2003). Constructing ideas about equity from the standpoint of the particular: Exploring the work of one urban teacher network. *Teachers College Record, 105,* 817–845.

Abu El-Haj, T. R. (2009). Imagining postnationalism: Arts, citizenship education and Arab American youth. *Anthropology & Education Quarterly, 40*(1), 1–19.

Abu El-Haj, T. R. (2015). *Unsettled belonging: Educating Palestinian American youth after 9/11.* Chicago, IL: University of Chicago Press.

Abu El-Haj, T. R., & Bonet, S. W. (2011). Education, citizenship, and the politics of belonging youth from Muslim transnational communities and the "war on terror." *Review of Research in Education, 35,* 29–59.

Antrop-González, R. (2006). Toward the *school as sanctuary* concept in multicultural urban education: Implications for small high school reform. *Curriculum Inquiry, 36,* 273–301.

Antrop-González, R., & De Jesús, A. (2006). Toward a theory of critical care in urban small school reform: Examining structures and pedagogies of caring in two Latino community-based schools. *International Journal of Qualitative Studies in Education, 19,* 409–433.

Antrop-González, R., Vélez, W., & Garrett, T. (2008). Examining familial-based academic success factors in urban high school students: The case of Puerto Rican female high achievers. *Marriage & Family Review, 43,* 140–163.

Apple, M. W. (2004). *Ideology and curriculum* (3rd ed.). New York, NY: Routledge.

Apple, M. W. (2014). *Official knowledge: Democratic education in a conservative age* (3rd ed.). New York, NY: Routledge.

Ayers, W. (2001). *To teach: The journey of a teacher* (2nd ed.). New York, NY: Teachers College Press.

Bandura, A. (2000). Self-efficacy: The foundation of agency. In W. J. Perrig & A. Grob (Eds.), *Control of human behavior, mental processes, and consciousness: Essays in honor of the 60th birthday of August Flammer* (pp. 17–33). Mahwah, NJ: Erlbaum.

Bartolomé, L. I. (2008a). Authentic cariño and respect in minority education: The political and ideological dimensions of love. *International Journal of Critical Pedagogy, 1*(1), 1–17.

Bartolomé, L. I. (2008b). *Ideologies in education: Unmasking the trap of teacher neutrality.* New York, NY: Peter Lang.

Beauboeuf-Lafontant, T. (2002). A womanist experience of caring: Understanding the pedagogy of exemplary Black women teachers. *Urban Review, 34,* 71–86.

Beltrán, C. (2014). No papers, no fear. DREAM activism, new social media, and the queering of immigrant rights. In A. Dávila & Y. M. Rivero (Eds.), *Contemporary Latina/o media: Production, circulation, politics* (pp. 245–266). New York: New York University Press.

Berryman, M., Glynn, T., Woller, P., & Reweti, M. (2010). Māori language policy and practice in New Zealand schools: Community challenges and community solutions. In K. Menken & O. Garcia (Eds.), *Negotiating language policies in classrooms: Educators as policymakers* (pp. 145–161). New York, NY: Routledge.

Bonilla-Silva, E. (2006). *Racism without racists: Color-blind racism and the persistence of racial inequality in the United States* (2nd ed.). Lanham, MD: Rowman & Littlefield.

Brown, A. L., & Au, W. (2014). Race, memory, and master narratives: A critical essay on US curriculum history. *Curriculum Inquiry, 44,* 358–389.

Brown, K. D., Brown, A. L., & Rothrock, R. (2015). Culturally relevant pedagogy. In M. F. He, B. Schultz, & W. Schubert (Eds.), *The SAGE guide to curriculum in education* (pp. 207–214). Thousand Oaks, CA: SAGE.

Brown, S., & Souto-Manning, M. (2007). "Culture is the way they live here": Young Latin@s and parents navigate linguistic and cultural borderlands in US schools. *Journal of Latinos and Education, 7*(1), 25–42.

Cammarota, J. (2011). From hopelessness to hope: Social justice pedagogy in urban education and youth development. *Urban Education, 46,* 828–844.

Cammarota, J. (2016). Social Justice Education Project (SJEP): A case example of PAR in a high school classroom. In A. Valenzuela (Ed.), *Growing critically conscious teachers: A social justice curriculum for educators of Latino/a youth* (pp. 90–104). New York, NY: Teachers College Press.

Cammarota, J., & Romero, A. (2011). Participatory action research for high school students: Transforming policy, practice, and the personal with social justice education. *Educational Policy, 25,* 488–506.

Campano, G., Ghiso, M. P., & Welch, B. J. (2016). *Partnering with immigrant communities: Action through literacy.* New York, NY: Teachers College Press.

Castles, S., & Davidson, A. (2000). *Citizenship and migration: Globalization and the politics of belonging.* New York, NY: Routledge.

Chan, E., Phillion, J., & He, M. F. (2015). Immigrant students' experience as curriculum. In M. F. He, B. Schultz, & W. Schubert (Eds.), *The SAGE guide to curriculum in education* (pp. 249–258). Thousand Oaks, CA: SAGE.

Collet, B. A. (2010). Sites of refuge: Refugees, religiosity, and public schools in the United States. *Educational Policy, 24,* 189–215.

Collins, P. (1991). *Black feminist thought: Knowledge, consciousness, and the politics of empowerment.* New York, NY: Routledge.

Cooper, C. W. (2009). Parent involvement, African American mothers, and the politics of educational care. *Equity & Excellence in Education, 42,* 379–394. doi:10.1080/10665680903228389

Costello, M. B. (2016). *The Trump effect. The impact of the presidential campaign on our nation's schools.* Retrieved from https://www.splcenter.org/sites/default/files/splc_the_trump_effect.pdf

Crowley, C. B., & Apple, M. W. (2009). Critical democracy in teacher education. *Teacher Education and Practice, 22,* 450–453.

Darder, A., Baltodano, M., & Torres, R.D. (2003). *The critical pedagogy reader.* New York, NY: Routledge.

Dee, T., & Penner, E. (2016). *The casual effects of cultural relevance: Evidence from an ethnic studies curriculum* (CEPA Working Paper No. 16-01). Retrieved http://cepa.stanford.edu/sites/default/files/wp16-01-v201601.pdf

Del Valle, S. (2003). *Language rights and the law in the United States: Finding our voices.* Clevedon, England: Multilingual Matters.

DeNicolo, C. P. (2016). "School within a school": Examining implementation barriers in a Spanish/English transitional bilingual education program. *Bilingual Research Journal, 39,* 91–106.

DeNicolo, C. P., González, M., Morales, S., & Romani, L. (2015). Teaching through testimonio: Accessing community cultural wealth in school. *Journal of Latinos and Education, 14,* 228–243.

Deyhle, D., & Swisher, K. (1997). Research in American Indian and Alaskan native education: From assimilation to self-determination. *Review of Research in Education, 22,* 113–194.

Dixson, A. D. (2003). "Let's do this!" Black women teachers' politics and pedagogy. *Urban Education, 38,* 217–235. doi:10.1177/0042085902250482.

Dixson, A. D., & Rousseau, C. K. (2005). And we are still not saved: Critical race theory in education ten years later. *Race Ethnicity and Education, 8*(1), 7–27.

Dolby, N., Dimitriadis, G., & Willis, P. E. (2004). *Learning to labor in new times.* New York, NY: RoutledgeFalmer.

Drolet, M., & Arcand, I. (2013). Positive development, sense of belonging, and support of peers among early adolescents: Perspectives of different actors. *International Education Studies, 6*(4), 29–38.

Dyson, A. (1993). *Social worlds of children learning to write in an urban primary school.* New York, NY: Teachers College Press.

Ewing, W. A., Martínez, D. E., & Rumbaut, R. G. (2015). *The criminalization of immigration in the United States.* Retrieved from https://www.americanimmigrationcouncil.org/research/criminalization-immigration-united-states

Faircloth, B. S., & Hamm, J. V. (2005). Sense of belonging among high school students representing 4 ethnic groups. *Journal of Youth and Adolescence, 34,* 293–309.

Faltis, C. (2013). Language, language development and teaching English to emergent bilingual users: Challenging the common knowledge theory in teacher education and K-12 school settings. *Association of Mexican-American Educators, 7*(2), 18–29.

Ferguson, C. A., Heath, S. B., & Hwang, D. (1981). *Language in the USA.* New York, NY: Cambridge University Press.

Flores, N., & Rosa, J. (2015). Undoing appropriateness: Raciolinguistic ideologies and language diversity in education. *Harvard Educational Review, 85,* 149–171.

Flores, S. (2010). State dream acts: The effect of in-state resident tuition policies and undocumented Latino students. *Review of Higher Education, 33,* 239–283.

Flores-González, N., Aranda, E., & Vaquera, E. (2014). "Doing race": Latino youth's identities and the politics of racial exclusion. *American Behavioral Scientist, 51,* 1834–1851.

Flores-González, N., & Gutiérrez, E. R. (2010). Taking the public square. The national struggle for immigrant rights. In A. Pallares & N. Flores-González (Eds.), *¡Marcha!: Latino Chicago and the immigrant rights movement* (pp. 3–36). Urbana: University of Illinois Press.

Foster, M. (1993). Othermothers: Exploring the educational philosophy of black American women teachers. In M. Arnot & K. Weiler (Eds.), *Feminism and social justice in education: International perspectives* (pp. 101–123). Washington, DC: Falmer Press.

Fránquiz, M. E., Salazar, M. D. C., & DeNicolo, C. P. (2011). Challenging majoritarian tales: Portraits of bilingual teachers deconstructing deficit views of bilingual learners. *Bilingual Research Journal, 34*, 279–300.

Freire, P. (1970). *Pedagogy of the oppressed.* New York, NY: Herder & Herder.

Freire, P. (1998). *Teachers as cultural workers: Letters to those who dare to teach.* Boulder, CO: Westview Press.

Gándara, P., & Hopkins, M. (2010). *Forbidden language: English learners and restrictive language policies.* New York, NY: Teachers College Press.

García, O. (2009). *Bilingual education in the 21st century: A global perspective.* Hoboken, NJ: Wiley.

García, O. (2014). Spanish and education: Global and local intersections. *Review of Research in Education, 38*, 58–80.

Gay, G. (2010). *Culturally responsive teaching: Theory, research, and practice.* New York, NY: Teachers College Press.

Gibson, M. A., Bejínez, L. F., Flidalgo, N., & Rolón, C. (2004). Belonging and school participation: Lessons from a migrant student club. In M. A. Gibson, P. Gándara, & J. P. Koyama (Eds.), *School connections: U.S. Mexican youth, peers, and school achievement* (pp. 129–149). New York, NY: Teachers College Press.

Gibson, M. A., Gándara, P., & Koyama, J. P. (2004). *School connections: U.S. Mexican youth, peers, and school achievement.* New York, NY: Teachers College Press.

Gilliat, S. (1997). Muslim youth organizations in Britain: A descriptive analysis. *American Journal of Islamic Social Sciences, 14*, 99–111.

Ginwright, S. A., Noguera, P., & Cammarota, J. (Eds.). (2006). *Beyond resistance! Youth activism and community change: New democratic possibilities for practice and policy for America's youth.* New York, NY: Routledge.

Giroux, H. (1983). *Critical theory and educational practice.* Geelong, Victoria, Australia: Deakin University Press.

Gonzales, R. G., Heredia, L. L., & Negrón-Gonzales, G. (2015). Untangling Plyler's legacy: Undocumented students, schools, and citizenship. *Harvard Educational Review, 85*, 318–341.

Gonzales, R. G., Suárez-Orozco, C., & Dedios-Sanguineti, M. C. (2013). No place to belong: Contextualizing concepts of mental health among undocumented immigrant youth in the United States. *American Behavioral Scientist, 57*, 1174–1199.

González, R., & Padilla, A. M. (1997). The academic resilience of Mexican American high school students. *Hispanic Journal of Behavioral Sciences, 19*, 301–317.

González, N., Moll, L. C., & Amanti, C. (2005). *Funds of knowledge: Theorizing practices in households, communities, and classrooms.* New York, NY: Routledge.

Gonzales, S. M. (2015). *Abuelita* epistemologies: Counteracting subtractive schools in American Education. *Journal of Latinos and Education, 14*(1), 40–54.

Goodenow, C., & Grady, K. E. (1993). The relationship of school belonging and friends' values to academic motivation among urban adolescent students. *Journal of Experimental Education, 62*, 60–71.

Goodwin, A. L. (2002). Teacher preparation and the education of immigrant children. *Education and Urban Society, 34*, 156–172.

Goodwin, A. L., Smith, L., Souto-Manning, M., Cheruvu, R., Tan, M. Y., Reed, R., & Taveras, L. (2014). What should teacher educators know and be able to do? Perspectives from practicing teacher educators. *Journal of Teacher Education, 65*, 284–302.

Halagao, P. E. (2010). Liberating Filipino Americans through decolonizing curriculum. *Race Ethnicity and Education, 13*, 495–512.

Hopkins, M., Lowenhaupt, R., & Sweet, T. M. (2015). Organizing English learner instruction in new immigrant destinations district infrastructure and subject-specific school practice. *American Educational Research Journal, 52*, 408–439.

Isik-Erkan, Z. (2015). Being Muslim and American: Turkish-American children negotiating their religious identities in school settings. *Race, Ethnicity and Education, 18*, 225-–250.

Justice, B., & Stanley, J. (2016). Teaching in the time of Trump. *Social Education, 80*, 36–41.

Kao, G., & Tienda, M. (2005). Optimism and achievement: The educational performance of immigrant youth. *Social Science Quarterly, 76*, 1–19.

Kia-Keating, M., & Ellis, B. H. (2007). Belonging and connection to school in resettlement: Young refugees, school belonging, and psychosocial adjustment. *Clinical Child Psychology and Psychiatry, 12*, 29–43.

Knoester, M., & Yu, M. (2015). Teachers as cultural workers. In M. F. He, B. D. Schultz, & W. H. Schubert (Eds.), *The SAGE guide to curriculum in education* (pp. 190–197.) Thousand Oaks, CA: SAGE.

Kumashiro, K. K. (2015). *Against common sense: Teaching and learning toward social justice* (3rd ed.). New York, NY: Routledge.

Ladson-Billings, G. (1995). Toward a theory of culturally relevant pedagogy. *American Educational Research Journal, 32*, 465–491.

Ladson-Billings, G. (2009). *The dreamkeepers: Successful teachers of African American children* (2nd ed.). San Francisco, CA: Wiley.

Ladson-Billings, G. (2014). Culturally relevant pedagogy 2.0: Aka the remix. *Harvard Educational Review, 84*, 74–84.

Ladson-Billings, G., & Tate, W. F. (1995). Toward a critical race theory of education. *Teachers College Record, 97*, 47–68.

Ladson-Billings, G. J. (1999). Preparing teachers for diverse student populations: A critical race theory perspective. *Review of Research in Education, 24*, 211–247.

Levinson, B. A. U. (2005). Citizenship, identity, democracy: Engaging the political in the anthropology of education. *Anthropology & Education Quarterly, 36*, 329–340.

Levitt, P., & Schiller, N. G. (2004). Conceptualizing simultaneity: A transnational social field perspective on society. *International Migration Review, 38*, 1002–1039.

Lewis, J. L., Ream, R. K., Bocian, K. M., Cardullo, R. A., Hammond, K. A., & Fast, L. A. (2012). Con cariño: Teacher caring, math, self-efficacy, and math achievement among Hispanic English learners. *Teachers College Record, 114*, 1–42.

Li, G. (2006). *Culturally contested pedagogy: Battles of literacy and schooling between mainstream teachers and Asian immigrant parents.* Albany: State University of New York Press.

Lichter, D.T. (2012). Immigration and the new racial diversity in rural America. *Rural Sociology, 77*, 3–35.

Long, S., Bell, D., & Brown, J. (2004). Making place for peer interaction: Mexican American kindergarteners learning language and literacy. In E. Gregory, S. Long, & D. Volk (Eds.), *Many pathways to literacy: Young children learning with siblings, grandparents, peers and communities* (pp. 93–104). New York, NY: RoutledgeFalmer.

Long, S., Souto-Manning, M., & Vasquez, V. M. (Eds.). (2016). *Courageous leadership in early childhood education: Taking a stand for social justice.* New York, NY: Teachers College Press.

Maira, S. M. (2009). *Missing: Youth, citizenship, and empire after 9/11.* Durham, NC: Duke University Press.

Martinez, C. R., Jr., McClure, H. H., & Eddy, J. M. (2009). Language brokering contexts and behavioral and emotional adjustment among Latino parents and adolescents. *Journal of Early Adolescence, 29*, 71–98.

Maslow, A. (1970). *Motivation and personality.* New York, NY: Harper & Row.

McKamey, C. (2011). Restorying "caring" in education: Students' narratives of caring for and about. *Narrative Works, 1*, 78–94.

Menken, K., & Solorza, C. (2014). No child left bilingual accountability and the elimination of bilingual education programs in New York City schools. *Educational Policy, 28*, 96–125.

Mercado, C. (2016). Teacher capacities for Latino and Latina youth. In A. Valenzuela (Ed.), *Growing critically conscious teachers: A social justice curriculum for educators of Latino/a youth* (pp. 24–38). New York, NY: Teachers College Press.

Moll, L. C., & Ruiz, R. (2002). The schooling of Latino children. In M. M. Suárez-Orozco & M. M. Páez (Eds.), *Latinos: Remaking America* (pp. 362–388). Los Angeles: University of California Press.

Negrón-Gonzales, G. (2014). Undocumented, unafraid and unapologetic: Re-articulatory practices and migrant youth "illegality." *Latino Studies, 12*, 259–278.

Ngo, B. (2013). Culture consciousness among Hmong immigrant leaders beyond the dichotomy of cultural essentialism and cultural hybridity. *American Educational Research Journal, 50*, 958–990.

Nieto, S. (1998). Fact and fiction: Stories of Puerto Ricans in U.S. schools. *Harvard Educational Review, 68*, 133–163.

Nieto, S. (2010). *Language, culture, and teaching: Critical perspectives* (2nd ed.). New York, NY: Routledge.

Niyozov, S., & Pluim, G. (2009). Teacher's perspectives on the education of Muslim students: A missing voice in Muslim education research. *Curriculum Inquiry, 39*, 637–677.

Noddings, N. (1984). *Caring, a feminine approach to ethics & moral education.* Berkeley: University of California Press.

Noddings, N. (2005). *The challenge to care in schools.* New York, NY: Teachers College Press. (Original work published 1992)

Noddings, N. (2013). *Caring: A relational approach to ethics & moral education* (2nd ed.). Berkeley: University of California Press.

Ogbu, J. U., & Simons, H. D. (1998). Voluntary and involuntary minorities: A cultural-ecological theory of school performance with some implications for education. *Anthropology & Education Quarterly, 29*, 155–188.

Olsen, L., & Dowell, C. (1989). *Bridges: Promising programs for the education of immigrant children.* San Francisco: California Tomorrow.

Orellana, M. F. (2001). The work kids do: Mexican and Central American Immigrant Children's contributions to households and schools in California. *Harvard Educational Review, 71*, 366–389.

Orfield, G. (1998). The education of Mexican immigrant children: A commentary. In M. M. Suárez-Orozco (Ed.), *Crossings: Mexican immigration in interdisciplinary perspective* (pp. 276–280). Cambridge, MA: David Rockefeller Center for Latin American Studies/Harvard University Press.

Pallares, A. (2014). *Latinidad: Transnational cultures in the United States: Family activism: Immigrant struggles and the politics of noncitizenship.* New Brunswick, NJ: Rutgers University Press.

Paris, D. (2012). Culturally sustaining pedagogy: A needed change in stance, terminology, and practice. *Educational Researcher, 41*(3), 93–97.

Paris, D., & Alim, H. S. (2014). What are we seeking to sustain through culturally sustaining pedagogy? A loving critique forward. *Harvard Educational Review, 84*(1), 85–100.

Patel, L. (2013). *Youth held at the border of education and the politics of inclusion*. New York, NY: Teachers College Press.

Peguero, A. A., & Bondy, J. M. (2011). Immigration and students' relationship with teachers. *Education and Urban Society, 43*, 165–183.

Peguero, A. A., Shekarkhar, Z., Popp, A. M., & Koo, D. J. (2015). Punishing the children of immigrants: Race, ethnicity, generational status, student misbehavior, and school discipline. *Journal of Immigrant & Refugee Studies, 13*, 200–220.

Plyler v. Doe, 457 U.S. 202 (1982).

Portés, A., & Rumbaut, R.G. (2014). *Immigrant America: A portrait* (4th ed.). Berkeley: University of California Press.

Prieto, L., & Villenas, S. A. (2012). Pedagogies from *Nepantla: Testimonio*, Chicana/Latina feminisms and teacher education classrooms. *Equity & Excellence in Education, 35*, 411–429.

Quiñones, S. (2016). "I get to give back to the community that put me where I am": Examining the experiences and perspectives of Puerto Rican teachers in Western New York. *Urban Education*. Advance online publication. doi:10.1177/0042085915623336

Rahman, K. (2013). Belonging and learning to belong in school: The implications of the hidden curriculum for indigenous students. *Discourse: Studies in the Cultural Politics of Education, 34*, 660–672.

Ríos-Rojas, A. (2011). Beyond delinquent citizenships: Immigrant youth's (re)visions of citizenship and belonging in a globalized world. *Harvard Educational Review, 81*, 64–95.

Ríos-Rojas, A. (2014). Managing and disciplining diversity: The politics of conditional belonging in a Catalonian Institute. *Anthropology & Education Quarterly, 45*, 2–21.

Rolón-Dow, R. (2005). Critical care: A color(full) analysis of care narratives in the schooling experiences of Puerto Rican girls. *American Educational Research Journal, 42*, 77–111.

Rolstad, K., Mahoney, K., & Glass, G. (2005). The big picture: A meta-analysis of program effectiveness research on English language learners. *Educational Policy, 19*, 572–594.

Roy, L. A., & Roxas, K. C. (2011). Whose deficit is this anyhow? Exploring counter-stories of Somali Bantu refugees' experiences in "doing school." *Harvard Educational Review, 81*, 521–542.

Rumbaut, R. G. (2005). Sites of belonging: Acculturation, discrimination, and ethnic identify among children of immigrants. In T. S. Weiner (Ed.), *Discovering successful pathways in children's development: Mixed methods in the study of childhood and family life* (pp. 111–164). Chicago, IL: University of Chicago Press.

Sabry, N. S., & Bruna, K. R. (2007). Learning from the experiences of Muslim students in American schools: Towards a proactive model of school-community cooperation. *Multicultural Perspectives, 9*, 44–50.

San Miguel, G. (2004). *Contested policy: The rise and fall of federal bilingual education in the United States, 1960–2001*. Denton, TX: University of North Texas Press.

San Pedro, T. (2015). Silence as weapons: Transformative praxis among Native American students in the urban Southwest. *Equity & Excellence in Education, 48*, 511–528.

Sánchez, G. J. (2002). "Y tú, ¿qué?" (Y2K): Latino history in the new millennium. In M. M. Suárez-Orozco & M. M Páez (Eds.), *Latinos remaking America* (pp. 45–58). Los Angeles: University of California Press.

Sánchez, P. (2007). Urban immigrant students: How transnationalism shapes their world learning. *Urban Review, 39*, 489–517.

Santiago-Rivera, A. L., Arredondo, P., & Gallardo-Cooper, M. (2002). *Counseling Latinos and la familia: A practical guide*. Thousand Oaks, CA: SAGE.

Sarroub, L. K. (2001). The sojourner experience of Yemeni American high school students: An ethnographic portrait. *Harvard Educational Review, 71*, 390–415.

Schlein, C., & Chan, E. (2010). Supporting Muslim students in secular public schools. *Diaspora, Indigenous, and Minority Education, 4*, 253–267.

Sealy-Ruiz, Y. (2013). Using urban youth culture to activate the racial literacies of Black and Latino Male high school students. In A. Cohan & A. Honigsfeld (Eds.), *Breaking the mold of education: Innovative and successful practices for student engagement, empowerment, and motivation* (pp. 3–11). Lanham, MD: Rowman & Littlefield.

Selman, R. L., Levitt, M. Z., & Schultz, L. H. (1997). The friendship framework: Tools for the assessment of psychosocial development. In R. L. Selman, M. Z. Levitt, & L. H. Schultz (Eds.), *Fostering friendship: Pair therapy for treatment and prevention* (pp. 31–52). New York, NY: Walter de Gruyter.

Sleeter, C. E. (2011). *The academic and social value of ethnic studies: A research review.* Retrieved from http://www.nea.org/assets/docs/NBI-2010-3-value-of-ethnic-studies.pdf

Sleeter, C. E. (2012). Confronting the marginalization of culturally responsive pedagogy. *Urban Education, 47*, 562–584.

Souto-Manning, M. (2013). Competence as linguistic alignment: Linguistic diversities, affinity groups, and the politics of educational success. *Linguistics and Education, 24*, 305–315.

Stanton-Salazar, R. D. (2004). Social capital among working-class minority students. In M. A. Gibson, P. Gándara, & J. P. Koyama (Eds.), *School connections. U.S. Mexican youth, peers, and school achievement* (pp. 18–38). New York, NY: Teachers College Press.

Steinberg, L., Brown, B. B., & Dornbusch, S. M. (1996). *Beyond the classroom.* New York, NY: Simon & Schuster.

Suárez-Orozco, C., Marks, A. K., & Abo-Zena, M. M. (2015). Introduction: Unique and shared experiences of immigrant-origin children and youth. In C. Suárez-Orozco, M. M. Abo-Zena, & A. K. Marks (Eds.), *Transitions: The development of children of immigrants* (pp. 1–26). New York: New York University Press.

Suárez-Orozco, C., Pimentel, A., & Martin, M. (2009). The significance of relationships: Academic engagement and achievement among newcomer immigrant youth. *Teachers College Record, 111*, 712–749.

Suárez-Orozco, C., & Suárez-Orozco, M. (1995). *Transformations: Immigration, family life, and achievement motivation among Latino adolescents.* Stanford CA: Stanford University Press.

Suárez-Orozco, C., & Suárez-Orozco, M. (2001). *Children of immigration.* Cambridge, MA: Harvard University Press.

Suárez-Orozco, C., Suárez-Orozco, M., & Todorova, I. (2008). *Learning a new land: Immigrant students in American society.* Cambridge, MA: Harvard University Press.

Téllez, K., & Varghese, M. (2013). Teachers as intellectuals and advocates: Professional development for bilingual education teachers. *Theory Into Practice, 52*, 128–135.

Terriquez, V. (2015). Intersectional mobilization, social movement spillover, and queer youth leadership in the immigrant rights movement. *Social Problems, 62*, 343–362.

Thompson, A. (1998). Not the color purple: Black feminist lessons for educational caring. *Harvard Educational Review, 68*, 522–554.

Umansky, I. M., & Reardon, S. F. (2014). Reclassification patterns among Latino English learner students in a bilingual, dual immersion, and English immersion classrooms. *American Educational Research Journal, 51*, 879–912.

Urrieta, L., Jr., Kolano, L., & Jo, J. (2015). Learning from the *testimonio* of a "successful" undocumented Latino student in North Carolina. In E. Hamann, S. Wortham, & E. Murrillo, Jr. (Eds.), *Revisiting education in the new Latino diaspora* (pp. 49–70). Charlotte, NC: Information Age.

Valdés, G. (1996). *Con respeto: Bridging the distances between culturally diverse families and schools.* New York, NY: Teachers College Press.

Valencia, R. R. (2002). *Chicano school failure and success: Past, present, and future* (2nd ed.). New York, NY: RoutledgeFalmer.

Valencia, R. R., & Solorzano, D. G. (1997). Contemporary deficit thinking. In R. R. Valencia (Ed.), *The evolution of deficit thinking: Educational thought and practice* (pp. 160–210). New York, NY: RoutledgeFalmer.

Valenzuela, A. (1999) *Subtractive schooling: U.S. Mexican youth and the politics of caring.* Albany: State University of New York Press.

Valenzuela, A. (Ed.). (2016). *Growing critically conscious teachers: A social justice curriculum for educators of Latino/a Youth.* New York, NY: Teachers College Press.

Valenzuela, A., Zamora, E., & Rubio, B. (2015). Academia Cuauhtli and the eagle: "Danza Mexica" and the epistemology of the circle. *Voices in Urban Education, 41,* 46–56.

Vasquez, J. M. (2005). Ethnic identity and Chicano literature: How ethnicity affects reading and reading affects ethnic consciousness. *Ethnic and Racial Studies, 28,* 903–924.

Warikoo, N., & Carter, P. (2009). Cultural explanations for racial and ethnic stratification in academic achievement: A call for a new and improved theory. *Review of Educational Research, 79,* 366–394.

Wiley, T. G. (2014). Diversity, super-diversity, and monolingual language ideology in the United States: Tolerance or intolerance? *Review of Research in Education, 38,* 1–33.

Winn, M. T., & Behizadeh, N. (2012). Right to be literate: Literacy, education, and the school-to-prison pipeline. *Review of Research in Education, 35,* 147–173.

Yosso, T. J. (2002). Toward a critical race curriculum. *Equity & Excellence in Education, 35,* 93–107.

Yosso, T. J. (2005). Whose culture has capital? A critical race theory discussion of community cultural wealth. *Race Ethnicity and Education, 8,* 69–91.

Yuval-Davis, N. (2011). *The politics of belonging: Intersectional contestations.* London, England: SAGE.

Zacher Pandya, J. (2011). *Overtested: How high stakes accountability fails English language learners.* New York, NY: Teachers College Press

Zeichner, K. M. (2009). *Teacher education and the struggle for social justice.* New York, NY: Routledge.

Zine, J. (2000). Redefining resistance: Towards an Islamic subculture in schools. *Race, Ethnicity, and Education, 3,* 293–316.

Zine, J. (2008). *Canadian Islamic schools: Unraveling the politics of faith, gender, knowledge, and identity.* Toronto, Ontario, Canada: University of Toronto Press.

About the Editors

Mariana Souto-Manning is associate professor of early childhood education and director of the doctoral program in curriculum and teaching at Teachers College, Columbia University. From a critical perspective, she examines in/equities and in/justices in early childhood teaching and teacher education, focusing on issues pertaining to language and literacy practices in pluralistic settings. In her research, she critically considers theoretical and methodological issues and dilemmas of doing research *with* communities of color. She has published six books, including the 2016 winner of the American Educational Studies Association Critics' Choice Award, *Reading, Writing, and Talk: Inclusive Teaching Strategies for Diverse Learners, K-2* (with Jessica Martell). Her work can also be found in journals such as *Linguistics and Education, International Journal of Qualitative Studies in Education, Research in the Teaching of English*, and *Teachers College Record*. She is the recipient of a number of research awards, including the 2011 American Educational Research Association Division K Innovations in Research on Diversity in Teacher Education Award.

Maisha T. Winn (formerly Maisha T. Fisher) is the Chancellor's Leadership Professor in the School of Education at the University of California, Davis, where she also codirects the Transformative Justice in Education Center. Her work examines the intersections of language, literacy, and youth justice. She has published numerous articles and books including *Writing in Rhythm: Spoken Word Poetry in Urban Classrooms*; *Black Literate Lives: Historical and Contemporary Perspectives*; *Girl Time: Literacy, Justice and the School-to-Prison Pipeline*; and *Humanizing Research: Decolonizing Qualitative Research Methods* (coedited with Django Paris). She was awarded the William T. Grant Distinguished Fellowship for her work examining restorative justice in educational contexts and is an American Educational Research Association Fellow.

Review of Research in Education
March 2017, Vol. 41, pp. 531
DOI: 10.3102/0091732X17694329
© 2017 AERA. http://rre.aera.net

About the Contributors

Ursula S. Aldana is an assistant professor of education at the University of San Francisco. She examines K–12 school culture with regard to issues of equity and access for racially/ethnically and linguistically diverse students. Her research highlights the voices of historically marginalized students, including immigrant and low-income students in various contexts such as Catholic schools and secondary bilingual education programs.

Bianca J. Baldridge is an assistant professor in the Department of Educational Policy Studies at the University of Wisconsin-Madison. Her research interests include the social and political context of community-based educational spaces, race, youth, and educational policy. Her research has appeared in publications such as the *American Educational Research Journal, Race, Ethnicity, and Education,* and *Contemporary Sociology.* Her experiences as an educator within community-based youth programs informs her research in profound ways.

Nathan Beck holds an MS in educational leadership and policy analysis from the University of Wisconsin-Madison and has directed nationally awarded programs with and for young people. He is interested in educational equity; racial, economic, and environmental justice; and imagining alternatives.

David Bloome is EHE Distinguished Professor at the Ohio State University, College of Education and Human Ecology, Department of Teaching and Learning. His research explores how people use language for constructing learning, social relationships, knowledge, communities, social institutions, and shared histories and futures.

Denise Boston is a doctoral student at the University of Illinois at Chicago. Her research interests focus on the ways Black women and girls experience mathematics socialization and identity development.

Ayanna F. Brown is an associate professor at Elmhurst College, Department of Education. Her research explores discussions of race in classroom settings and curricular issues in teacher preparation in such discussions. She is the coeditor and author in *Critical Consciousness in Curricular Research: Evidence From the Field* (2013) and past chair of the National Council of Teachers of English Assembly for Research (2013–2014).

Review of Research in Education
March 2017, Vol. 41, pp. 532–542
DOI: 10.3102/0091732X17697294
© 2017 AERA. http://rre.aera.net

Limarys Caraballo is an assistant professor of English education in the Department of Secondary Education at Queens College of the City University of New York and a senior research fellow at the Institute for Urban and Minority Education, Teachers College, Columbia University. Her scholarship focuses on the multiple identities and literacies of students of color, participatory action research with youth, and social justice–orientated teacher education.

Claudia G. Cervantes-Soon, PhD, is an assistant professor of bilingual/bicultural education at the University of Texas at Austin. A former bilingual and dual language educator in U.S. public schools, her interests focus on the fostering of voice, empowered identities, and transformative biliteracy among students from marginalized communities and in dual language/bilingual education. Her research draws on critical pedagogies, Chicana feminist frameworks, and ethnographic methods, with special attention to the borderlands and contexts highly affected by neoliberalism.

Jinmyung Choi is a doctoral student in the Department of Educational Leadership and Policy Analysis at the University of Missouri-Columbia. Her research focuses on bilingual education and educational policies for immigrant students and English language learners.

Krista Cortes is a doctoral student in the Graduate School of Education at the University of California, Berkeley. Her work is located at the nexus of education, linguistic anthropology, and African Diaspora studies and is focused on the experiences of Afrolatino/a students who, straddling the line between both "colors," are often silenced and rendered invisible by restrictive understandings of race and ethnicity within schools.

Arturo Cortez is a doctoral candidate in the Graduate School of Education at the University of California, Berkeley. His research explores teacher development and the role of policy, while drawing on sociocultural conceptions of learning. He previously taught for several years in the Bay Area and New York City. He is a practicing actor.

Christopher B. Crowley is an assistant professor of teacher education at Wayne State University. His primary area of research is in the field of curriculum studies and focuses on issues of privatization in teacher education. His research critically examines how various stakeholders, including nonprofit organizations, philanthropic foundations, the for-profit sector, and others, are becoming increasingly involved in multiple aspects of teacher education. His research has appeared in journals such as *Teacher Education & Practice*, *Teachers College Record*, and *Schools: Studies in Education*, as well as in several edited volumes.

Christina Passos DeNicolo is an assistant professor of bilingual and bicultural education in the College of Education at Wayne State University. Her research examines the ways sociopolitical contexts shape the implementation of bilingual education programs and the instructional practices and pedagogical tools that facilitate the use of students' cultural and linguistic knowledge as resources for learning in language arts classrooms. Her work has appeared in journals such as the *Journal of Latinos and Education, The Urban Review, Bilingual Research Journal,* and *Language Arts.*

Daniela DiGiacomo is a postdoctoral fellow at University of California, Riverside. As a community- and design-based researcher, her work investigates how to design for more equitable teaching and learning relationships between adults and young people across various lines of difference.

Lisa Dorner, PhD, is an associate professor in the Department of Educational Leadership and Policy Analysis and a fellow of the Cambio Center at the University of Missouri-Columbia. Her research centers on language policy and planning, educational policy implementation, and immigrant childhoods. Most recently, she cofounded the Missouri Dual Language Network to connect educators and families with critical resources for dual language learning and policy development (www .modlan.org). Her publications related to dual language education may be found in the *American Educational Research Journal, Current Issues in Language Planning, Educational Policy,* and *International Journal of Bilingual Education and Bilingualism.*

Beatrice S. Fennimore has focused over 25 years of university teaching, activism, and scholarship on areas related to child advocacy, social policy, public school equity, social justice, and multicultural/anti-bias education. A professor at Indiana University of Pennsylvania, her recent publications include *Standing Up for Something Every Day: Ethics and Justice in Early Childhood Classrooms* (Teachers College Press) and *Say That the River Turns: Social Justice Intentions in Progressive Public School Classrooms* (Bank Street Occasional Paper Series). She is currently cochairing Section 4 of American Educational Research Association Division K: Multicultural, Inclusive, & Social Justice Frameworks for Teaching and Teacher Education in PK-16+ Settings.

Edward Fergus is an assistant professor in educational leadership and policy at New York University. His work focuses on varying dynamics within the social context of schools, including racial/ethnic identity, school climate and culture, bias-based beliefs among practitioners, and cross-cultural interactions between youth and adults.

Susan L. Gabel is a professor of teacher education at Wayne State University. Her research focuses on disability studies in education, and she teaches courses on inclusive education. She has published in journals such as *The Journal of Diversity in Higher Education, Journal of Medical Humanities, Equity & Excellence in Education,* and *Disability & Society.* She has coedited several books, including *Disability & the Politics of Education* and *Vital Questions Facing Disability Studies in Education.*

Antero Garcia is an assistant professor in the Graduate School of Education at Stanford University. His teaching and research focus on developing critical literacies and civic identity through the use of participatory media and game play in formal learning environments.

Eugene García, PhD, is presently professor emeritus at Arizona State University. He has published extensively in the area of language teaching and bilingual development, authoring and/or coauthoring over 200 articles and book chapters along with 14 books and monographs.

Maisie L. Gholson is an assistant professor of mathematics education at the School of Education at the University of Michigan. Using Black feminist theories, her research focuses on the role of Black girls' relationships and social networks in their mathematics learning and identity development.

Anne Gregory, PhD, is an associate professor at the Graduate School of Applied and Professional Psychology at Rutgers University. Her research has focused on the persistent trend that African American adolescents are issued school suspension and expulsion at higher rates than adolescents from other groups. Through program development and evaluation, she aims to improve educational settings for students from diverse racial and ethnic backgrounds.

Kris D. Gutiérrez is Carol Liu Professor in the Graduate School of Education and Faculty Affiliate, Institute for the Study of Societal Issues, Race, Diversity, and Educational Policy Cluster, Haas Institute for a Fair and Inclusive Society, at the University of California, Berkeley. Her research examines learning and culture in designed environments and hybrid and syncretic approaches to learning, with attention to youth from nondominant communities. She served as American Educational Research Association president from 2010 to 2011.

Meseret Hailu is a PhD student in the Higher Education Department at the Morgridge College of Education, University of Denver. In her research, she focuses on the experiences of women in undergraduate STEM programs.

Dan Heiman is a doctoral candidate and teacher educator in the Department of Curriculum and Instruction at the University of Texas at Austin. His research focuses on equity, social justice, and critical pedagogy in two-way immersion contexts. Prior to joining his doctoral program, he was a bilingual teacher in El Paso, Texas, and teacher of English as a foreign language at the University of Veracruz, Mexico.

Jennifer Higgs is an assistant professor of digital technology and educational change at the University of California, Davis. Her research, which focuses on digital tool use that supports learning and teaching, adolescent literacies, and pre- and in-service teacher education, employs mixed methods and is informed and inspired by her experiences as an English teacher in Virginia and Illinois public high schools.

Oscar Jiménez-Castellanos, PhD, is an associate professor in education policy and evaluation in Mary Lou Fulton Teachers College at Arizona State University and a 2016–2017 visiting scholar at University of California, Berkeley, Graduate School of Education, with a courtesy affiliation with Policy Analysis for California Education at Stanford University. He has published extensively in the area of K–12 education finance, policy, and parent engagement and its impact on opportunity, equity, and outcomes in low-income ethnically and linguistically diverse communities.

Patrick Johnson is a doctoral candidate at the University of California, Berkeley, in the Social and Cultural Studies program in the Graduate School of Education. His research interests include critical media literacy, television, remix theory, and Black cultural politics. His research situates past Black television as a pedagogical resource that shapes Black collective memory and from which Black young adults learn about race and gender.

Nicole M. Joseph is an assistant professor of mathematics and science education in the Department of Teaching and Learning at Vanderbilt University. She is a 2014–2015 National Academy of Education/Spencer Postdoctoral Fellow, and her research interests include mathematics education and equity, access, retention, and achievement of African Americans; experiences of Black women and girls in mathematics and mathematics education; the role of race, class, and gender in mathematics identity development; and the history of mathematics education of African Americans (1837–1957).

Michelle G. Knight-Manuel is the associate dean and a professor in the Department of Curriculum and Teaching at Teachers College, Columbia University. Her research focuses on (urban) teacher education, college readiness and access, and immigrant youth civic engagement. She has published in journals such as the *American Educational Research Journal; Teachers College Record; Race, Ethnicity and Education*; and the *Journal of Educational Policy*. She is the coauthor (with Joanne Marciano) of *College Ready: Preparing Black and Latina/o Youth for Higher Education: A Culturally Relevant Approach*. She has also been involved for several years in a university-community-based organization research partnership with the Sauti Yetu Center for Women and Girls to support the literacy practices of African immigrant girls.

Rita Kohli is an assistant professor in the Education, Society, and Culture program in the Graduate School of Education at the University of California, Riverside. She also serves as codirector of the Institute for Teachers of Color Committed to Racial Justice and on the editorial board of the international journal *Race, Ethnicity and Education*. With almost 20 years of experience in urban public schools as a teacher, teacher educator, and researcher, her scholarship is focused on understanding, challenging and transforming the racializing structures of K–12 schooling.

Betsy Maloney Leaf, PhD, MFA, teaches in the Arts in Education program in the Department of Curriculum and Instruction at the University of Minnesota. She examines the intersection between arts education, culturally relevant pedagogy, and educational policy. Her work has been published in the *Journal of Dance Education*, the *Journal of Southeast Asian American Education & Advancement*, and *Arts Education Policy Review*.

Carol D. Lee is the Edwina S. Tarry Professor of Education and Social Policy at Northwestern University. Her research focuses on cultural and ecological supports for learning, with a specific focus on discipline-specific literacy learning. She served as AERA President from 2009 to 2010.

Cynthia Lewis is professor and chair of curriculum and instruction at the University of Minnesota, where she holds the Emma M. Birkmaier Professorship in Educational Leadership. Her current research examines the role of emotion in urban classrooms focused on critical media analysis and production. She has published widely on the intersection of social identities and literacy practices in and out of school and is coeditor of the Routlege book series *Expanding Literacies in Education*.

José Ramón Lizárraga is a doctoral candidate at the Graduate School of Education, University of California, Berkeley. His research interests include issues of language, culture, creativity, and ingenuity in today's digitized and interconnected world, especially for nondominant populations. Before attending Berkeley, José was an educator, literacy tutor, and administrator in the San Francisco Bay Area for more than 10 years. He is also a practicing visual artist and musician.

Brian D. Lozenski is an assistant professor of urban and multicultural education in the Educational Studies Department at Macalester College. His research interests combine youth participatory action research and African knowledge systems. As a community-engaged scholar he works in close partnership with a family literacy center called the Network for the Development of Children of African Descent.

Jamila J. Lyiscott is a postdoctoral fellow at Teachers College, Columbia University, and a recently named Cultivating New Voices fellow by NCTE Research Foundation. Her work focuses on the intersections of race, literacies, and social justice education. She is a teacher educator and codirector of Cyphers for Justice, a program apprenticing youth and educators as critical social researchers through hip-hop, spoken word, and digital literacy.

Danny C. Martinez is an assistant professor of language, literacy, and culture in the School of Education at the University of California, Davis. His research examines the language and literacy practices of Black and Latinx youth in urban secondary literacy classrooms. He is also interested in teacher learning as it relates to leveraging the communicative repertoires of youth in schools. Much of his research is informed by his own teaching in secondary schools in San Francisco and Los Angeles.

Juan Carlos Medina is a doctoral candidate in the Department of Educational Policy Studies at the University of Wisconsin-Madison. His research interests include the history of Chicanx/Latinx education, racialization, the intersection of language and race, and community-based spaces.

Kavitha Mediratta is the founding executive director of the Atlantic Fellows for Racial Equity. Based at Columbia University, the Atlantic Fellows for Racial Equity was launched by the Atlantic Philanthropies in 2016 to build diverse, multiracial leadership to dismantle anti-Black racism and advance equity and inclusion in the United States and South Africa. Previously, she was chief strategy advisor for Equity Initiatives and Human Capital Development at the Atlantic Philanthropies, a global foundation dedicated to opportunity and fairness for all people.

Elizabeth Mendoza is a postdoctoral fellow at the University of California, Santa Cruz. She is engaged in the design and research of learning ecologies that intersect participatory action research, sociocultural theories of learning, and equity and healing toward transformative ends.

Nicole Mirra is an assistant professor of English education at the University of Texas at El Paso. Her teaching and research focuses on the intersections of critical literacy and youth civic engagement across multiple contexts, including urban secondary English classrooms, grassroots community organizations, and digital learning communities.

P. Zitlali Morales is an assistant professor of curriculum and instruction in the College of Education, and affiliated faculty of the Latin American and Latino Studies program, at the University of Illinois at Chicago. She examines the language practices of Latin@ youth and linguistic interactions of students and teachers in bilingual classrooms. She is co–principal investigator of a National Science Foundation–funded project studying the digital literacy practices and transnational ties of immigrant youth.

Ernest Morrell is the Macy Professor of English Education and director of the Institute for Urban and Minority Education at Teachers College, Columbia University. He is also an elected fellow of AERA, a past president of the National Council of Teachers of English, and an appointed member of the International Literacy Association's Literacy Research Panel.

Jerome E. Morris is the E. Desmond Lee Endowed Professor of Urban Education (in conjunction with St. Louis Public Schools) and a research fellow with the Public Policy Research Center at the University of Missouri-St. Louis. His research studies in urban and suburban centers provide empirically grounded models for understanding race and education in post-*Brown* America. In addition to authoring *Troubling the Waters: Fulfilling the Promise of Quality Public Schooling for Black Children* (Teachers College Press, 2009), he has published in leading research journals such as the *American Educational Research Journal, Educational Researcher, Teachers College Record, Anthropology & Education Quarterly*, and *Urban Education*, as well as practitioner journals such as *Kappan*.

Arturo Nevárez is a doctoral student in the Education, Society, and Culture program in the Graduate School of Education at the University of California, Riverside. His research interests center on the racialized experiences of K–12 Latinx students and students of color, K–12 ethnic studies, critical and racial literacies, critical approaches to pedagogy and curriculum, campus racial climate in schools, and neoliberal multiculturalism in education. He is a former high school English teacher and a proud son of immigrant parents from México.

Bic Ngo, PhD, is the Rodney S. Wallace Professor for the Advancement of Teaching and Learning in the Department of Curriculum and Instruction at the University of Minnesota. She examines "culture" and "difference" in the education of immigrant students, and the implications for theorizing immigrant identity, culturally relevant pedagogy, and antioppressive education. Her publications include *Unresolved Identities: Discourse, Ambivalence and Urban Immigrant Students*, and articles in journals such as *American Education Research Journal, Review of Educational Research*, and *Educational Studies*.

Deborah Palmer, PhD, is an associate professor of bilingual education in the program in Educational Equity and Cultural Diversity in the School of Education at the University of Colorado Boulder. A former two-way dual language bilingual teacher in California, she conducts qualitative research using ethnography and discourse analysis in linguistically diverse settings. Her interests include bilingual education policy and politics; critical additive bilingual education; teacher preparation for linguistically/culturally diverse teaching contexts; language, power, and identity; and bilingual teacher leadership.

Michelle Salazar Pérez is an associate professor of early childhood education at New Mexico State University. She uses critical qualitative methodologies and Black feminist thought to examine dominant constructions of childhood/s, particularly how they influence public policy and subjugate the lived experiences of marginalized people/s and communities. She is co-editor of the books *Critical Examinations of Quality in Childhood Education and Care: Regulation, Disqualification, and Erasure* (Peter Lang) and *Critical Qualitative Inquiry: Foundations and Futures* (Routledge). Her work has been published in the journals *Equity & Excellence in Education, Journal of Early Childhood Teacher Education, Global Studies of Childhood*, and *Qualitative Inquiry*.

Marcos Pizarro is a professor in Mexican American studies at San José State University, is the faculty-in-residence for Chicanx-Latinx Student Success, and is the co-coordinator of Adelante, a multifaceted project that offers support to students and the university to enhance Latinx student engagement and academic success. He coordinates MAESTR@S, a social justice organization that develops and implements a transformative education model with Latinx communities, and works with schools on the development and implementation of Latinx Studies curricula to enhance Latinx student engagement. He is also the co-coordinator of the Institute for Teachers of Color Committed to Racial Justice.

Stephanie Power-Carter is an associate professor in the Literacy, Culture, and Language Education Department at Indiana University, Bloomington. Her research interests include African American education, discourse analysis, research on Whiteness, Black feminist theory, community literacy, cultural identity, and discourse analysis. She teaches secondary English education courses and is also engaged in several community-based initiatives for youth.

Marlo A. Reeves is a PhD student in educational policy studies at the University of Wisconsin-Madison. Her work explores youth resistance and activism in community-based educational spaces.

Cinthya M. Saavedra is an associate professor of bilingual/ESL education in the Department of Bilingual and Literacy Studies at the University of Texas Rio Grande Valley. Her research centers Chicana/Latina feminist epistemology in the investigation of emergent bilingual, immigrant, and borderland experiences in education. In addition, her scholarship addresses critical research methodologies such as *testimonios, pláticas,* and critical reflexivity. Her work is published in *Equity & Excellence in Education, International Journal of Qualitative Studies in Education, Language Arts,* and *TESOL Quarterly.* She has coedited special issues in the *Journal of Latino-Latin American Studies* on Chicana/Latina pedagogies and methodologies and in the journal *Global Studies of Childhoods* on centering global south onto-epistemologies in childhood studies.

Rebecca Schwerdtfeger is a third-year doctoral student in the Department of Learning, Teaching & Curriculum-Literacy at the University of Missouri-Columbia. She has 15 years of experience teaching Spanish, as a secondary building administrator, and as a district world language coordinator. Her research interests involve language, literacy, and identity development, primarily in dual language contexts.

Russell J. Skiba, PhD, is a professor in the School Psychology program at Indiana University and director of the Equity Project. His research has focused on school violence, school safety, and disproportionality in school discipline and special education.

Anna Stetsenko is a professor in the PhD programs in psychology and in urban education at the Graduate Center of the City University of New York (CUNY). She came to CUNY with years of experience in a number of leading research centers and universities across Europe. Drawing on interdisciplinary advances in psychology, philosophy, biology, sociocultural theory, and critical pedagogy, her recent publications focus on Transformative Activist Stance to understand processes at the intersection of human development and education with a focus on agency, equality, and social change.

Amy Stornaiuolo is an assistant professor in the Literacy, Culture, and International Education Division of the University of Pennsylvania's Graduate School of Education. Her research focuses on adolescents' digital literacies and new media composing, and her forthcoming coedited book is the *Handbook of Writing, Literacies, and Education in Digital Cultures* (Routledge, 2017).

Ebony Elizabeth Thomas is an assistant professor in the Literacy, Culture, and International Education Division at the University of Pennsylvania's Graduate School of Education. A former Detroit Public Schools teacher, her program of research is most keenly focused on children's and adolescent literature, the teaching of African American literature, and the role of race in English language arts classroom discourse and interaction. Her forthcoming book is *The Dark Fantastic: Race and the Imagination in Youth Literature, Media, and Culture* (New York University Press, 2018).

Kathleen A. King Thorius is an associate professor of special and urban education in Indiana University's School of Education, is the executive director and principal investigator of the Midwest and Plains Equity Assistance Center, and has been awarded over $14 million for research and technical assistance work on equity in disability, race, and language education policy and practice. She is on the board of the *Journal of Special Education*, and her work has been featured in interdisciplinary and special education publications such as *Harvard Educational Review, Exceptional Children*, and *The Handbook of Urban Education*. She is coeditor of *Ability, Equity, and Culture: Sustaining Urban Inclusive Education Reform* (Teachers College Press).

Joanne Tien is a doctoral candidate in the Graduate School of Education at the University of California, Berkeley. Her research examines competing notions of "liberatory" pedagogy within social justice education and curriculum theory. Prior to graduate school, she taught as an elementary school teacher.

Sepehr Vakil is an assistant professor of STEM education and associate director of Equity & Inclusion in the Center for STEM Education at the University of Texas at Austin. His research interests center primarily on the cultural and political dimensions of STEM education, with a disciplinary focus in computer science and engineering. Working in partnerships with communities and educators, he draws on design-based and participatory research methodologies to explore new transformative possibilities for STEM teaching and learning.

Catherine Kramarczuk Voulgarides received her doctorate from New York University in sociology of education. Her scholarship and professional training focus on understanding how educational policies relate to equity and equality in education. Her research examines the contextual factors that contribute to educational inequities and how educational practitioners, district, and school leaders use disability law—the Individuals With Disabilities Education Act—to address disproportionality in special education. She has a book contract with Teachers College Press on the subject and served as co–principal investigator on a William T. Grant Foundation project on disproportionality.

Vaughn W. M. Watson is an assistant professor in the Department of Teacher Education at Michigan State University. His research focuses on the interplay of literacy and identities in the lived experiences of Black youth, youth of color, and immigrant youth. His research examines social and cultural contexts of youth's practices within and beyond school, including contexts of English education, civic learning and action, and qualitative participatory research methodologies. He has published research findings in journals including *American Educational Research Journal*, the

International Journal of Qualitative Studies in Education, Urban Education, and *Literacy*. He taught high school English for 12 years in New York City.

Charles E. Wilkes is a doctoral candidate, Ford Fellow, and National Science Foundation Graduate Research Fellowship Program STEM Education Fellow at the School of Education at the University of Michigan. His research focuses on the intersection of teacher knowledge, teacher practice, and student experiences in a way that contributes to the understanding of mathematical instruction that is both equitable and empowering, particularly for historically marginalized children.

Arlette I. Willis is a professor at the University of Illinois at Urbana-Champaign, in the Department of Curriculum and Instruction. She is a Fulbright Scholar (2014), past president of the Literacy Research Association (2014–2015), and past president of the National Conference on Research in Language and Literacy (2008–2009). Her scholarship includes reenvisioning histories of African American literacies, examining the direction of preservice English teacher education, and applying critical theories to literacy policy and research.

Min Yu is an assistant professor in the Teacher Education Division in the College of Education at Wayne State University. Her work situates within the fields of curriculum studies and comparative and international education. Her main research focuses on how changing social, political, and economic conditions affect schools serving migrant and immigrant families and communities. Her work appears in the journals *Teachers College Record; Diaspora, Indigenous, and Minority Education*; and *Educational Action Research* and as chapters in various edited volumes. She is the author of the book *The Politics, Practices, and Possibilities of Migrant Children Schools in Contemporary China* (Palgrave Macmillan, 2016).